The Mounted Squad

An Illustrated History of
The Toronto Mounted Police
1886–2000

The Mounted Squad

An Illustrated History of
The Toronto Mounted Police
1886–2000

Bill Wardle

TO JUDY.
I HOPE THAT YOU ENJOY MY
HISTORY OF THE TORONTO POLICE
MANTOS ON IT.
Bill Wardle

Fitzhenry & Whiteside

The Mounted Squad : An Illustrated History of The Toronto Mounted Police 1886–2000
Copyright © 2002 Bill Wardle

Fitzhenry & Whiteside Limited
195 Allstate Parkway
Markham, Ontario L3R 4T8

In the United States:
121 Harvard Avenue, Suite 2
Allston, Massachusetts 02134

www.fitzhenry.ca   godwit@fitzhenry.ca

Fitzhenry & Whiteside acknowledges with thanks the Canada Council for the Arts, the Government of Canada through its Book Publishing Industry Development Program, and the Ontario Arts Council for their support of our publishing program.

National Library of Canada Cataloguing in Publication Data

Wardle, Bill
    The mounted squad : an illustrated history of the Toronto Mounted Police,
    1886-2000

Includes bibliographical references and index.

ISBN 1-55041-631-6

1. Toronto Mounted Police--History. 2. Mounted police—Ontario—Toronto—History.
3. Police horses—Ontario—Toronto—History. I. Title.

HV8160.T6W37 2002   363.1'09713'541   C2002-903133-5

Cover/book design by Karen Petherick, Markham, Ontario
Cover photograph by Derrick Speirs
Back cover photograph City of Toronto Archives,
    Globe and Mail collection 17701
Printed and bound in Canada

This book is dedicated to
the horses and officers of the Toronto Police Mounted Unit.

Contents

The Honourable Lincoln M. Alexander
Photograph, Marjorie Harding.

Foreword

I am very pleased to be asked to contribute this foreword to a history of the Toronto Police Mounted Unit.

During my term as Ontario's Lieutenant-Governor, I attended many special events. The occasions I remember most fondly are those where the Toronto Mounted transported me in the Government landau, and provided a full ceremonial escort. The spectacle of the finely turned out officers and their gleaming mounts exemplifies the tradition that is inherent to the office of the Queen's Representative. I always took the opportunity to speak with the officers who accompanied me, and developed a warm rapport with many of those individuals.

I was always impressed with the spirit and dedication to duty demonstrated by the Mounted officers. I remember in particular the Halton Regional Police 25th Anniversary Tattoo, to which I was invited as the Guest of Honour. The Toronto Mounted was scheduled to escort me, when organizers informed me that the Mounted would possibly not make the engagement due to a serious policing commitment. I was already seated in my vehicle when Sgt Bill Wardle, author of this book and the Officer in charge of the Mounted Drill Team, rode up beside me to announce that the unit was on hand and in position for the escort, just moments before the opening ceremonies commenced.

After a full day of crowd control duty, the officers of the Mounted were ready to provide a wonderful demonstration of ceremony and skill for the assembled spectators. Such enthusiasm and commitment are at the heart of the Mounted, and are what made our relationship a consistent pleasure.

While in office, I had the great honour of being appointed an Honourary Chief of Police for Metropolitan Toronto. I have always been proud of my association with this fine organization, and the men, women and noble animals who serve their community with integrity, compassion, and respect.

I can think of no finer tribute to my relationship with the Toronto Police than to have a highly skilled police mount named in my honour. The officers of the Mounted Unit selected the name "Lincoln" from among many submissions, and this handsome mount patrols the city under saddle today.

This book presents the foundation of a proud past, and will provide future officers the opportunity to use this knowledge to build a strong future for the Toronto Mounted Unit and the community in which it serves.

I feel that this comprehensive history will be a tremendous resource for all readers. It provides insight into many aspects of Toronto's social, political, and policing history, and is a fitting testament to the generations of officers and horses who serve and protect our ever-changing city.

The Honourable Lincoln M. Alexander

"General"
Photograph, Carol Robbins.

Acknowledgements

Compiling this history was an enormous project. It would not have been possible without the help of the many archivists, librarians, photographers and others who assisted me in my research. As well, I would like to give special recognition to some of the people whose help and support was crucial to making this project a success.

Special recognition should go to Constable Roy Butler who was the first to begin documenting the history of the Mounted Unit during our 100th Anniversary in 1986. It was Roy's work that initially interested me in learning more about the mounted unit.

I began the research for this book at the Toronto Police Museum. Former police historian Staff Superintendent Jack Webster and former Police Museum curator Sharon MacDonald allowed me unlimited access to the museum archives. My close relationship with the museum has continued with the current staff members Gabi Voigt and Norina D'Agostini.

The following officers assisted me by taking photographs or reproducing photographs for the book. Constable Les Bluestien of the South Simcoe Police, Sgt Lorna Kozmik and Constable Derrick Speirs of the Toronto Police. I would like to thank Constable Moreen Smith for spending many hours scanning and cataloguing photographs for both this book and the police service Web Site.

There were three privately compiled works in the Toronto Police Museum that were invaluable in helping me understand the development and history of the Toronto Police Service. The unselfish donation of this work made the writing of this history so much easier. These authors were Greg Marquis (P.H.D. Thesis), Jan K. Leibaers (Major Research paper) and Basil Jackson, who wrote an unpublished History of the Toronto Police.

I would like to acknowledge the extraordinary efforts of Karen Petherick of Intuitive Design. Not only did she provide the design for the book but she also managed the complex process that is involved in a project of this magnitude.

At my last minute request, my friend Bill White provided the artwork for the book. Many hours were spent developing the sketches that help to enliven this history. I was fortunate to have my first draft viewed by Toronto Historian Mike Filey, who encouraged me to complete the work and who also provided me with many old newspaper stories on the Mounted Squad.

Finally I would like to give special thanks to the following people who offered their support and encouragement through the duration of this project. My parents, Norman and Dorothy Wardle, Constable Jim Davis, Linda Davis, the late Jim MacDonald, Dorothy Keith, Patty Baughan, Gail Kondo, Sergeant Jim Patterson and especially Hilary Wollis.

Introduction

THE TORONTO POLICE SERVICE HAS MAINTAINED ITS FULL-TIME MOUNTED UNIT SINCE 1886. DESPITE THE ADVANCES IN TECHNOLOGY AND THE MECHANIZATION OF SOCIETY, THE POLICE STILL PRESERVE A UNIT MORE REFLECTIVE OF THE 19TH CENTURY THAN THE 21ST.

The Royal Salute at the Queen's Plate, June 25, 2000. PC Montgomery, PC Bowen, PC Mamak, Sgt Wardle, PC Bradford, PC Gilbert, PC Penney. Photograph, Michael Burns Photography.

There are sentimental reasons to cling to the past, and valuable gains to be made by maintaining the traditions of any organization. In police work, however, sentimentality never makes it past the budget meeting. Traditions change and police are compelled to accept these changes, evolving with the community they serve. The Toronto Police have kept their horses for one practical reason. Horses remain the most effective means of crowd control management.

The Toronto Police created its Mounted Unit to manage crowds in 1886; the Unit was maintained though the next century because it could keep public order. Decreased and increased in size in response to society's dissatisfaction and protest, the unit survived being disbanded during the recession of the early 1990s because no practical alternative could be found to equal the role of the unit's horses in successful crowd control.

One recurring theme running through this history is the continual series of calls to downsize or eliminate the Toronto Police Mounted Unit. I hope that this documentary will demonstrate the value of the police horse to a city our size. Maintenance of public order in Toronto would have been much different, and probably much more violent, had the police eliminated its mounted unit. The people the horses face in the course of crowd management duty today are becoming more organized and more violent. The demand and need for mounted police work increases every year.

Mounted officers also provide many valuable services to the community; these secondary law enforcement and public relations functions can be just as important. Unfortunately these secondary functions are not always recognized as cost effective. We hope the stories in this history will provide ample evidence of how valuable the Toronto Police Mounted Unit is to the city's public environment.

Members of the Mounted Unit have much of which to be proud. The events, people and horses described in these pages will help to preserve the pride and traditions of those that went before. The officers and horses of the Toronto Mounted Unit have proved time and time again that they are second to none.

The Little Things That Count

The following article appeared in the *Toronto Star*, Friday June 25, 1982. It provides a rare personal view of a young boy's childhood experiences with the officers of the Toronto Mounted Police. The special individual bonds that have formed between members of the Mounted Unit and the people they serve are much more important than any of the events detailed in this history.

One of the constant themes I have tried to portray throughout this chronicle is the special quality of those people who served with the Mounted Unit—not an easy task because most of these stories are rarely published or even talked about in any more than a personal forum. As you read this book, think of the author of this article, and the thousands of other people whose lives have been touched by their association with the officers of the Toronto Mounted Police. This is truly the force's greatest accomplishment.

I Was Too Short To Be One of My Boyhood Heroes

When Simon Wickens was a boy, he wanted to be one of Metro's mounted policemen. He never achieved his boyhood ambition and had to settle instead for being a news editor at the Toronto Star. *Now, as the argument rages over proposed cutbacks in their numbers, Wickens recalls his fond childhood memories of Metro's "Mounties."*

My mother had, at various times, dreams of me becoming either a naval officer or a detective—for whatever reasons better not gone into.

Although I knew better than to argue with maternal wisdom, since at that point she was still bigger than I, [still] I had plans of my own. And the only reason I ended up following neither of my chosen careers is heredity.

I inherited enough size from my father to be just too big to be a jockey, and too much of the midget from my mother to become a policeman on the Metro Mounted Unit.

It was when I was 11 and saw my first mounted cop, swaying along the curb lane down Yonge Street, that I decided that was what I wanted to do for a living.

I couldn't think of anything better than being paid to ride a horse all day and, when I got to know some of them, it became obvious that many of the men in the unit thought the same way.

Their basic duty was to patrol parks, acting as a buffer between kids and Slinger's "beautiful young men," and, while they weren't adverse to handing out the odd parking ticket, most of them were in the unit because they wanted to ride and meet people.

Not The Norm

It wasn't that they didn't take their jobs seriously, so much as men who volunteer in a mechanised world to work with horses aren't the norm.

One, a Lothario in blue, was a part-time opera singer and, eventually after a few years in uniform, became a full-time actor. Another raised fox hounds in his spare time and another, after finishing a degree, and planning to teach, ended up as the official historian of the R.C.M.P.

Then, as now, the man assigned to make a disciplined corps out of the most unlikely candidates was Staff Inspector Edwin Johnson.

And, now I've mentioned him, I might as well make a few confessions that would have given him a heart attack back in the days when he was a sergeant running a unit less than half of its present size. Since more than 20 years have elapsed, and many of the miscreants have moved out of his jurisdiction, it's probably safe to tell the truth.

Although it was against all the rules and regulations, my earliest riding, other than a few jogs around on a pony, was done on police horses in the ravine of Balfour Park, just below St. Clair Avenue, where most of the beautiful young men were rather dirty and old.

Reprinted with permission, *Toronto Star* Syndicate

"Eating Policemen's lunches and trying on their riding boots."
Picture, William White, Toronto, 2001.

I don't mean a policeman walked the horse a few steps while I sat in the saddle, but that a good half dozen policemen who will go unnamed, providing no one was around, let me take their mounts and ride them around the ravine bottom.

Not only did I ride Daisy, Marie, Major, Joe and Royal (my favourite), but more than once I took a jaunt on Johnson's own horse, Duke, a massive palomino with an uneven disposition. In size and colour he stood out from the other bay and black horses, but he was the biggest horse in the unit and the only one large enough to carry Johnson.

And, many was the evening I spent, unknown to Johnson (I think), in the police stables just off Davenport Road, feeding and grooming, playing checkers, eating policemen's lunches and trying on their riding boots to see if I'd grown into them. Since I now take a size 6 1/2, I presume none of the boots ever fit.

Took A Chance

Sometimes I now wonder whether senior police officers ever went looking for mounted policemen during lunch hour and were unable to find them. If so, it may have been because they were at our house, horses tethered in the backyard while they dropped in for a coffee. Or they might have been in the parks department office near the Rosehill Reservoir, while I practiced my riding, screened by the building and the bushes.

Why those policemen of 20 years ago took the chances they did with their jobs to keep me happy, I'll never know, unless it was because I was a skinny, little freckled kid with huge stick out ears, with a vague resemblance to Alfred E. Neuman, of Mad Magazine. But I'm awfully glad they did.

And, more important than letting me ride, or fool around in the stables, was the time they'd spend talking and listening to me, hour after hour, time that a mother raising eight children and a father working to support them just didn't have.

The friendships I made with some of those men lasted right through my teens and, although I got into as much, maybe more, trouble as most downtown Toronto kids, without them I would have got into a lot more.

Maybe, now that I think about it, Staff Inspector Johnson wouldn't or shouldn't have torn a strip off his men, because what they did for me is probably the most vital part of a policeman's job, but in massive, modern, mechanised Metro, it is sadly a next-to-impossible thing to do.

Forebears

The Origins of the Mounted Police

The use of horses in law enforcement is nothing new. Since it was first domesticated, the horse has been used to preserve social order. Beginning long ago, mounted soldiers have maintained domestic harmony by protecting those who commanded them and insuring that the rules they imposed were obeyed.

In wartime, the military horse has struck fear into the hearts of both soldiers and civilians. In peacetime, the military horse has performed important duties on the home front. The British cavalry was one of the tools used by the ruling class to maintain the status quo.

The officer corps of the military was recruited from society's elite. Up until the 1860s, promotion within the military was based on the purchase of commissions, rather than ability. This practice ensured that the army would always be commanded by those who had the most to lose should the government be overthrown. Insofar as the cavalry was the elite of the military, only the very rich could afford to be officers in this branch of the service.

It was the calvary officers who entrenched the service role of the military horse to those in power. In Great Britain, the cavalry would help free the country of the revolutionary and republican ideals that were sweeping through Europe and America.

A Bow Street Runner, c. 1820. Picture, William White, Toronto, 2001.

Enlisted men of the cavalry came from a much lower economic rung of society. They lived in a world of harsh discipline, often spending many years in the outposts of the Empire, isolated from the general population. The average citizen, in addition to having little social contact with these men, also viewed them as brutes. The structure of Britain's military produced an army trained to fight a foreign enemy in the field of battle, or a perceived enemy at home. Troopers would obey their orders to the letter, even when commanded to attack their own people.

The industrial revolution of the late 18th and early 19th centuries led to a population shift from the countryside to the cities. The developing urban centres, with their dense populations, caused new problems for those wishing to maintain public order. The cavalry was brought in to break up crowds, suppress riots and crush any revolutionary zeal which their leaders detected.

One of the most famous incidents was the Peterloo Massacre, on August 16, 1819. Some 60,000 to 100,000 reformists held a meeting in Manchester, England.

The British government responded by sending in 1,100 cavalry, 1,200 infantry and a troop of horse artillery.

The cavalry charged the unarmed crowd, driving the people helter-skelter on top of one another. Many reformists were trampled by the horses or cut down by cavalry sabres. The violence of the Peterloo Massacre shows the extreme measures those in power were willing to take in order to control crowds and repress ideals contrary to their own—as well as the blind obedience mounted troopers gave to orders from their officers.

There were reforms, however, and as the 19th century progressed, maintenance of social order began to pass from the military to newly created civilian police forces.

The first attempt at forming an organised police force in Great Britain was made by two liberally-minded brothers named Fielding, during the mid-18th century. In 1745, Henry Fielding assumed the office of Chief Bow Street Magistrate. He was one of the first people to look seriously at criminology, and the nation's penal policy. When Henry died in 1754, his office was taken over by his brother John.

With the financial support of government grants, the brothers hired men to pursue criminals and to gather and distribute criminal intelligence. Grants supported the employment of four pursuers and two mounted horse patrols—known as the Bow Street Runners. These men were probably the world's first civilian mounted police officers.

In 1763, Fielding obtained funding for eight mounted horse patrols to establish a nightly guard on roads leading into London. The grant was withdrawn the very next year, and the horse patrols were discontinued. It would be 40 years before London highways would again be patrolled by Mounted Police officers.[1]

In 1805, Sir Richard Ford became Chief Magistrate of Bow Street. He took vigorous steps to end the crime in and around London. Ford received permission to revive the mounted horse patrols to guard the main roads into London. He recruited sixty men, most of whom were cavalry veterans, for the renewed Mounted Police Unit. These men, a highly motivated and elite troop, gained international fame as the "Bow Street Runners." Their "Bow Street Patrol" greeting reassured those travellers who dared to use the dangerous highways surrounding the great city.

The Bow Street Mounted Patrol was the first uniformed police force in Britain. Its men wore blue coats with yellow metal buttons, a scarlet waistcoat, blue trousers, Wellington boots and a black hat. They soon earned the nickname "Robin Redbreast" because of their scarlet waistcoats.

Bow Street mounted men were very successful in suppressing criminal elements in the streets. Eventually the force would take on assignments all over England and abroad. In 1821, one hundred more men were hired to form the Unmounted Horse Patrol. This unit was established to train men for promotion to the Mounted Patrol, and to provide regular foot patrols in London.

On July 19, 1829 the Metropolitan Police Act became law and the first large municipal police force was formed. This new police force consisted of 3,000 officers, and was given jurisdiction over the area previously protected by the Bow Street Runners. The Bow Street Mounted Patrol continued until 1836, when it was absorbed into the Metropolitan Police as the Mounted Branch.

The Metropolitan Police became the prototype model for the establishment of civilian police forces all over the English-speaking world. The influence of the British Cavalry, and of England's Metropolitan Police can be seen in the Toronto Police Mounted Unit to this day.

Members of an early British police patrol, c. 1840. Photograph, Metropolitan Police Mounted Branch Museum, London, England.

The Toronto Police Department 1834-1956

Major Frank Draper Chief Constable of the Toronto Police Department, 1876. Photograph, Toronto Police Museum.

In 1834 the Village of York was incorporated as the City of Toronto. Although the largest urban area in Upper Canada, its population was only 9,254 citizens. The Toronto Police Force was established the same year, based on the principles enshrined by the British Parliament in their Metropolitan Police Act of 1829. Toronto's original force consisted of five full-time officers with fourteen reserve or special officers. Uniforms, based on those worn by the London Bobbie, were not issued until 1837.[1]

Captain Sam Sherwood was appointed Chief Constable in 1852 and immediately began to reorganize the police force giving the oath of allegiance to the dozen new men who were sworn in as police constables. These officers were all veterans of the Royal Irish Constabulary and had served the public from the police barracks at Phoenix Park, Dublin, Ireland. For the next seventy-five years, the influence of the Royal Irish Constabulary would make a major impact on the history of both Toronto and her police.

Toronto experienced a rapid growth in population with the introduction of railroads. The small police force proved unable to cope with the problems associated with urbanization, and numerous complaints were made to the provincial legislature to the effect that local politicians were interfering with the police force.

To distance the police from local control, a new Provincial Law was passed in 1858 that established a police commission for Toronto. New commission members set out to reorganize the police force based on the practices of the Boston Massachusetts Police and the Royal Irish Constabulary.

In 1874, Major Frank C. Draper, formerly of the Queen's Own Rifles, was appointed Chief Constable and almost immediately requested the Police Commission to permit him to form a mounted squad. These men and horses were needed for special occasions including crowd control, "when it is always found that a few mounted men are absolutely indispensable."[2]

In his 1875 annual report, Chief Draper complained about the difficulties he was having in providing patrols to outlying areas. Under the heading "Mounted Force" he made the following recommendation:

I would again most respectfully, but strenuously, recommend to the attention and careful consideration of the Board the great necessity existing for the organization of a Mounted Police for the outskirts. Such a force could be provided stabling at the different fire halls in the city, and would be of immense advantage to the residents in the suburbs, while its usefulness would again be apparent for escort duty during the passage of processions through the streets, and the recapture of prisoners who may occasionally effect their escape from Goal or the Central Prison.[3]

In 1881, the Police Commission approved the purchase of seven sets of used saddlery. The saddles were ordered from the firm of Lugsdin and Barnett. Chief Draper was pleased with the equipment and the officers assigned to part time mounted duty. He wrote, "They (the sets of saddlery) have proven very satisfactory, and when in use present a neat and soldier like appearance. They are stored, neatly, at No. 2 Station and carefully inspected from time to time." No. 2 police station was located on Agnes Street (now Dundas Street) at Bay Street.[4]

This was not a full-time mounted unit. The horses were rented from local livery stables when needed and fitted with the police equipment. There is no record of how officers were selected or how often they rode. Finding competent riders was not a problem as many members of the force had previous military service with both the regular and volunteer cavalry regiments. The creation of a full-time unit came one step closer in 1885 with the purchase of eight "new" saddles.

A mounted officer on patrol, c. 1886. Note the bobbed tail and mane on the horse. The officer is wearing the summer issue white helmet. Photograph, Strathy Smith Collection. SC 128-1-1284. City of Toronto Archives.

The mounted officer is wearing dark blue spring, fall, winter helmet, c.1886. Photograph, Toronto Police Museum.

The 1886 Toronto Street Railway Strike

The Toronto Street Railway Strike was the first documented event in the city where police on horses were used to control violent crowds. It was this strike in particular which prompted the Toronto Police Commission to maintain and expand the two-month-old Mounted Squad.

Street Railway employees worked fourteen hours a day, six days a week, with Sundays off. The company felt this was very fair, especially as comparable American cities made their employees work 16 hours a day, seven days a week. Nevertheless, in March 1886, 800 Toronto Street Railway Company employees moved to join the Knights of Labour Trade Union. These men were promptly fired and locked out by the company. Replacement workers were hired. The situation was explosive.

In response, the Toronto Police Force assigned eight officers to mounted duty. The men were split into two groups, one each to cover the two main streetcar barns in the city. The first four officers were placed under the command of Inspector Seymour; the second group was commanded by PC Watson.

Strikers and their sympathizers established pickets to prevent "scabs" from moving the streetcars out of the barns, although a number of cars managed to escape on the first day of the strike. One car was commandeered, ultimately to be rescued by a squad of police. As the strike wore on, tempers rose. On Friday, March 12 at about 9:00 a.m., a large crowd gathered in front of the streetcar stables at George and Front Street. Twelve foot police officers were dispatched to the scene, and ordered to form a line in front of the sidewalk.

The first car attempted to leave the barn, but was blocked. Police managed to get it moving without violent incident, but the car was only able to proceed a short distance before it was again blocked at Yonge Street. The police gave up, had the car unhitched and the horses returned to the stable. The developing crowd was becoming unruly. Detective Cuddy decided it was time to make an example of someone, and arrested one of the protesters for throwing a brick at the abandoned car. The man resisted, and was assisted in his efforts by a number of bystanders. Several policeman came to Cuddy's assistance when he attempted to transport his prisoner to the police station, and at that point, the officers were set upon by the crowd.

The *Globe* newspaper ran the following report:

The mob grew larger and more audacious and had not seven MOUNTED POLICEMEN under the command of Inspector Seymour, ridden up at this moment, the man would have been freed. The mounted men charged right into the crowd on the streets and sidewalk. People scattered to escape being trampled down, some running into hallways, jumping on fences, or clinging to the bars on shop windows. The police were successful in heading off the crowd and keeping it below King Street while the prisoner was conducted without difficulty to the station.

At 9:30 another car was started up George, along King, and up Yonge Street. It was escorted by several mounted police and a great force of police on foot, with batons drawn. It was followed by an immense mob hooting and yelling, and making a variety of demonstration against the authorities. But in this instance the police were determined not to be beaten, and skillfully manipulating their forces, the crowd was driven back and kept clear away from the track at all points. The police used their BATONS FREELY and not a few of the aggressive members of the mob went home with sore heads.[1]

Following this confrontation, Toronto's streetcars finally began to run freely, with three foot constables assigned to each vehicle. But the police were exhausted. They had been working constantly since the early morning hours—some officers were rumoured not to have had time to change their clothes since Monday, four days earlier.

By 12:30 p.m. a large crowd of drivers, conductors, and supporters had gathered at the Arcade on Yonge Street. Yonge Street itself was totally blocked, and the crowd spilled over onto Temperance and Adelaide Streets. A streetcar approached, escorted by mounted and foot police. The police charged the crowd in order to clear passage, and as the *Globe* reports:

Batons were vigorously used right and left, and the mounted policemen rode into the crowd. Their object of course was to clear the street. After the cars were escorted as far as Queen Street, where the opposition to their progress was fewer and less important, the policemen returned. Mounted policemen, and those on foot, formed a line across the street, and in this way the greater portion of the crowd was forced nearly to Bay, Toronto and Victoria streets. As the policemen returned to Yonge Street to charge the remainder of the crowd, those in the side streets pressed back towards Yonge Street. The duty of the policemen was a trying one, but they kept their temper pretty well, although there were MANY COMPLAINTS FROM CITIZENS who, while quietly, and as they thought safely, watching the scene from the sidewalk or the Arcade, were charged by the police and clubbed. The police once created great excitement by charging the Arcade, which was well filled with people.[2]

At 3:30 p.m. cars began returning to the Street Railway Stables. The foot officers cleared the crowds on Front Street, then six mounted officers escorted the cars back to the yard.

Chief of Police, Frank Draper, commented in the paper that he had one hundred and twenty men on duty at the start of the day, six of them mounted. He stated that it was the duty of the police to ensure that the cars could get through the crowds. He was quoted as being "well pleased with the men on duty; they acted quietly and determinably. The mounted men in particular, did good service in scattering the crowds."[3]

1   *Globe* Saturday March 13, 1886
2   *Globe* Saturday March 13, 1886
3   *Globe* Saturday March 13, 1886

The 1886 Toronto Street Railway Strike. Picture, William White, Toronto, 2001.

1886

Chief Constable Draper was determined to form a permanent mounted squad and recommended to the police board that they purchase seven horses for the seven sets of saddlery. He also requested an additional eight sets of saddlery which would be used on horses rented from the livery stables when the need arose. He could then field 15 mounted men and establish five or six permanent patrols.

In support of his request he wrote, "The cost of this would only be about $1,500 at the outset, and about the same sum for animal maintenance." He explained that people in the outlying districts had been complaining of the lack of police protection. "Residents at these points would then receive ample police protection, while the value of the mounted staff on special occasions, such as public funerals and processions, and street disturbances, would be difficult to over-estimate. Our experience in the past proves that in a street riot or crowd, one mounted man is worth ten on foot."[5]

Draper finally received permission to assign officers to full-time mounted duties. Routine orders during January announced that PC Watson and PC Goulding would take up mounted duties beginning January 26, 1886. They were to report for duty at 2:30 p.m. at Jim Bond's Stable and be attached to the second relief, coming off duty at 1:00 a.m. Horses rented from the stable would be ridden during their patrols.

PC Watson was to patrol Queen's Park, Avenue Road and Bloor Street to Jarvis Street. Constable Goulding's patrol was Spadina Avenue, College, Beverley and St. George Streets. They were instructed to take the names and addresses of all parties driving at an immoderate rate and to report same to the Deputy Chief Constable.

The full-time Mounted Squad had been organized by Chief Constable Draper and his subordinate officer, Constable George Watson.[6] Watson joined the Toronto Police Force in 1882 after having spent twelve years with the Royal Horse Artillery. On June 29, of that year, he became Acting Sergeant George Watson.

Watson failed to secure the permanent position in charge of the Mounted Unit. George Goulding was appointed to the acting sergeant position later in the year and permanently promoted to Patrol Sergeant on April 1, 1887. George Watson was eventually promoted to Patrol Sergeant in 1890, but it is not known if he continued to serve with the Mounted Unit.

On February 5, routine orders required that the Mounted officers submit a report to the Chief Constable every morning detailing all the activities performed during their shift.

Unfortunately these documents have not survived, they would have made interesting reading. The practice continues today in the form of the Unit Commanders *Morning Report*.

The most important event of 1886 was the Toronto Street Railway Strike. Street disturbances and labour strife were common occurrences at this time causing the police to hold weekly street skirmishing drill. In March, a violent one-week strike took place between the Street Railway Company and its employees. The 1886 written reports of the force stated, "The trouble extended over one week and the authorities were compelled to adopt severe measures in restoring order."[7]

The Board of Police Commissioners was pleased with the conduct of the police force during the strike. Board members were allied with the city's ruling class and were considered to be openly on the side of the Street Railway Company. The Toronto Police general orders dated March 15, 1886 states, "The conduct of the Force during the past week under very trying circumstances has been reported to the Board of Police Commissioners, and the Chief Constable is directed to announce that two days extra leave will be granted for this year to every Officer and Constable on the Force in recognition of this recent duty, and as a slight encouragement for the future." This was a very large reward in 1886.

The year's account of the force goes on to note that although the whole force performed well, the Mounted Unit deserved particular recognition: "In view of the excellent service rendered on this occasion by the mounted detachment, they can safely be regarded, for all time to come, as a necessary permanent branch of the service."[8]

The routine orders and the Toronto newspapers reported that Inspector Seymour was in command of the mounted detachment during the Street Railway Strike. This man must have been Sergeant Charles Seymour who joined the Toronto Police Force in 1870 and was promoted to sergeant in 1874. Seymour had previously served in Her Majesty's Service for 10 years. Seymour must have been very influential in the formation of the Mounted Squad, but probably too senior in rank to be permanently assigned to such a small unit.

The Police Board authorized the purchase of additional police horses for the Mounted Squad soon after the Street Railway Strike. Routine orders of June 1886 ordered PC Goulding and PC Nelson to attend the Canadian Pacific Freight Yard at the Queen's Wharf at 2:00 a.m. on June 30. They were to pick up police saddles from the police station on their way to the wharf and upon arrival, to assist PC Watson with the new horses. These animals had been purchased from a dealer in Woodstock, Ontario.

The first Toronto Police horses were described as:

Norval, 10 Year old Bright Bay Gelding.
    15.3 hands in height. Sold in February 1888.
Revenge, 7 Year old Dark Bay Gelding.
    15.3 hands in height. Sold in February 1887.
Bessie, 13 Year old Dark Brown Mare.
    15.2 hands in height. Unknown disposition.
Elsie, 9 Year old Mouse Grey Mare.
    15.3 hands in height. Sold April 1889.

A fifth horse, named "Fanny" was purchased in July. The Mounted Squad would not buy any more animals until October, 1887. The quality of these horses is suspect as they deteriorated or became unsuitable for police work very quickly. At least three of the horses were dispensed with within three years. Elsie was one of only three grey horses owned by the Toronto Police. The second was "Paddy," a mouse grey purchased in 1890 and sold in 1900; the third was "Magic," an iron grey purchased for the Wagon Service in 1909 and sold in 1915.

The new police horses were taken to the Eastern Stables on Sumach Street. Constables George Goulding and Thomas Bloodworth were assigned their upkeep. The stables opened at 6:00 a.m. each morning and closed at 7:00 p.m. The officer responsible for locking the door at night was to give the key to the live-in custodian.

A mounted officer passing the corner of St. George and Bloor Streets, c. 1890. This is the site where PC Tinsley began his pursuit of the window-sash wagon, described in the close-up story of his mounted career. The magnificent mansion in the background still stands today as a private club. Photograph, Strathy Smith Collection. SC 128-1-1118, City of Toronto Archives.

Constable Thomas Bloodworth (131), c. 1886.
Note the chain around the horse's neck in
place of the white rope.
Photograph, Toronto Police Museum.

By July, the Mounted Squad was staffed by five officers —an acting sergeant and four constables. Officers assigned to other units were used to supplement the mounted ranks for special occasions. On July 16 Constables Leggatt, Weston, Blake and Follis were ordered to report to the riding school each day at 7:00 p.m. Later in the month Constables Nelson, McLelland, Mulhall, Patton and McLearron were also ordered to report to the stables at 2:00 p.m. for riding instruction.

The Mounted Squad was on duty for the Orange Day Parade on the 12th of July. This was a very important Toronto event, one celebrated with a large procession through the streets. The July 13 *Globe* stated that the parade was led by the Public School Inspector mounted on a black horse, followed by 37 horsemen and 1,661 men on foot. It noted that a large force of police were on hand to control traffic and turn away carriages approaching the Orange Hall.

The *Globe* also described a woman located in front of the Orange Hall in a highly excited state. She danced as each band passed and cautioned the men to "stand firm and true": "She appeared to be acquainted with a large number of the marchers and shook hands with them as they passed, although the mounted officers did not seem to look on her with pleasure." The parade ended at the Exhibition grounds where many events took place. The paper reported "little drunkenness and almost no quarrelling."[9]

In his 1886 annual report Chief Constable Draper stated, "A mounted squad has been organized and equipped during the year and has rendered useful service in many ways. Their beats are chiefly confined to the outlying sections of the city, where their presence has imparted a sense of security to the residents of those localities, who seldom, if ever before, saw a policeman in their neighbourhood."[10]

The Chief Constable complained: "The situation of the stables is inconvenient (located at City Hall, Front and Jarvis Streets) being so remote from the western end of the city that in order to reach the furthest point the patrolman has, in going and returning, to ride 10 miles exclusive of the beat, making it impossible for one horse to cover the ground more than once a day. I would therefore suggest that stable accommodation be provided in some more central locality."[11]

The description of the Toronto Police Force prepared for the 1886 Colonial Exhibition stated "the detachment of mounted police has provided an excellent service on many occasions, especially during street disturbances and processions. It has clearly demonstrated the wisdom of establishing the unit."

Along with the establishment of the Mounted Squad, the Police Force also purchased its first patrol wagon for the transport of prisoners. Prior to this, wagons had been hired as needed from a local contractor. The wagon service became a separate entity from the Mounted Squad, although its horses shared stable accommodation.

The Men Who Formed the Mounted Unit

The following description of the Toronto Police Force is taken from the book *The History of Toronto and County of York, Ontario*, written by C. Blackett Robinson and published in 1885.

> *The City of Toronto is singularly fortunate in its police force, which is composed of as fine a body of men as may be seen in any similar corps in the world, and even perhaps in any military organisation. The majority of them have, previous to their Canadian experience, served in the Royal Irish Constabulary, and as they are thus individually well drilled and disciplined, the handling of the force, which is carried out on strictly military principles, becomes a comparatively easy matter.*
>
> *The physique of the men and their soldierly bearing evokes the admiration of all visitors to the city, and especially those from the other side of the border, accustomed to the anything but martial-looking patrolmen of the American cities.*[1]

---

1   Jackson, Basil. *To Serve and Protect, The History of the Metropolitan Toronto Police Force, 1834-1970*. Unpublished, 1970. Page 54.

The Police wagon service was established in 1886. Police patrol wagon, c. 1912. Photograph, Toronto Police Museum.

A Police Career in 1886

Great care was taken in recruiting men for the Toronto Police Force. To become a member you had to be male, of British descent, under thirty years of age and five foot ten inches without shoes. If you met the physical standards, you were required to pass an examination in reading, writing and arithmetic. All applicants were required to provide first-class recommendations regarding their character.

To be approved by the Board of Commissioners of Police, applicants were required to pass a thorough medical examination by the force medical officer. The pay for a new third-class constable was $1.35 a day. The first training sessions included instruction in the rudiments of drill, and studying the regulations of the force, the by-laws of the city and the criminal laws of Canada. After receiving enough training to perform the duties of a police constable intelligently, the recruit was issued a uniform and assigned to a division for regular duty.

Discipline was strict as officers would not condone any nonsense. All members of the force were liable to reduction in rank or class for a breach of discipline. Promotion from one class of constable to another had to be supported by reports of good conduct and efficient performance of duty not just length of service.

All members of the force were required to work seven days a week. Officers were entitled to fourteen days paid annual leave a year and constables ten days. Should a police officer become ill and require sick leave, one third of his pay was deducted. All members of the force were entitled to free medical care by the medical officer (police work was one of the few occupations at the time to receive this important benefit). Full pay was continued when a policeman was on sick leave due to an injury received while on duty.

Officers and men were clothed at department expense and they were possibly the best-equipped force in the Dominion. Every man was provided with one uniform suit a year, a baton, handcuffs, whistle, revolver, fire-alarm key and a small pocket lamp. Revolvers used were manufactured by David Bentley, Birmingham, England and carried only on night duty, or by escorts in charge of prisoners.

Training for police duties continued throughout a policeman's career with every member required to participate in military drill, and street skirmishing practice once a week. Skirmishing was prepared especially for the Toronto Police with a view to the speedy suppression of riots and street disturbances. A constable would be an integral part of these drills if lucky enough to become a mounted officer.

The pay scale for the Toronto Police in 1886 was as follows:

3rd class PC	$1.35 a day (under 12 months service)
2nd class PC	$1.60 a day (over 12 months, under 5 years service)
1st class B PC	$1.85 a day (over 5, under 10 years service)
1st class A PC	$1.90 a day (over 10 years service)
Sergeants	$2.55 a day (including Detectives)
Inspectors	$2.90 a day[1]

George Goulding, one of the first two officers assigned to full-time mounted duties in 1886. Goulding was promoted to acting patrol sergeant in 1886 and would be the officer in charge of the Mounted Unit until his retirement in 1910. Pictured as a patrol sergeant, c. 1886. Photograph, Toronto Police Service Museum.

1   From the description of the Toronto Police Force prepared for the Colonial Exhibition in London England, 1886.

 **1887** In 1887, the Mounted Unit was moved into No. 1 police station located on Court Street in an area previously used by the Toronto Fire Department. During the year there were strikes in the building trade, but all were peaceful. The Chief Constable reported that there was "No disturbance of a serious nature, a fact that was due to the good sense of the people as well as the preparations that had been made to suppress a popular outbreak."[12]

In June the city government held a parade to celebrate Queen Victoria's Golden Jubilee. Officers of the Mounted Unit attended the event keeping a discreet distance from the crowd. The sight of the policemen and their well groomed horses, standing motionless on the side of the busy streets was reported to have had a tranquilizing effect on the crowd. Despite people's daily familiarity with horse-drawn traffic the horses drew many admirers. Mounted men were under strict orders to return to the stable by nightfall before the public fireworks display began.[13]

The Police Department purchased "Harry," a new mounted squad horse in October.

The first two police ambulances were ordered during the year and the Police Ambulance Service was created. The horse-drawn ambulances were manned by police officers and would respond to any call for service. To ensure that everyone who needed an ambulance could get one, payment for the use of the ambulance service was optional. Ambulance horses were also purchased and stabled with the Mounted Unit horses.

 **1888** On January 21, 1888, the police surgeon submitted his 1887 annual report to the Board of Police Commissioners: "Twenty-five men were injured while in the discharge of duty, a large proportion of which were Mounted Men."[14] It would seem that then, as now, the Mounted Unit was one of the more injury-prone assignments within the police service.

In 1888, telephones were installed in all police stations and call boxes placed at strategic locations throughout the city. Mounted officers could report into their station while on patrol by using the call box system. With the advent of new communication systems, mounted officers could also be located and dispatched to disturbances very quickly.

The Mounted Squad horses were all comfortably stabled at Police Headquarters, No. 1 Station, Court Street. The Chief Constable was pleased with their performance throughout the year and stated "Their services continue to be most useful in escorting large processions, impounding stray cattle, and in other ways they are almost indispensable."[15]

The performance of Patrol Sergeant Goulding was brought to the notice of the Board of Police Commissioners. The condition of the horses and their immunity to sickness was credited to the care and attention that he bestowed upon them. The unit purchased three new mounts during the year. The *Globe* newspaper reported that the Police Department spent a total of $130.00 on breeches and boots for the mounted men.[16]

During the year, No. 3 Station was expanded and a roomy and well-ventilated stable and wagon house built. This station was located at St. Andrews Market, in the city's west end, and was for police wagon horses only.

1889 The Village of Parkdale was annexed by the City of Toronto and became No. 6 Police Division. The Chief Constable suggested to the Police Board that the Mounted Squad be increased by two officers so that a mounted officer could be posted to patrol Parkdale in Toronto southwest. One officer would be stationed at the new No. 6 Division Police Station, equipped as it was with stable accommodation. The other officer would be assigned to a new police station, then being built, which would also be equipped with a stable. The Chief Constable wanted to keep seven mounted officers at the Headquarters' stables.

The request for extra officers for the mounted service was turned down. Parkdale did not receive its permanent mounted officer.

Chief Draper was pleased to report no casualties among the horses and that they had been generally free from sickness, lameness and other problems. In his opinion, this "speaks well for the care and attention bestowed on them."[17]

Beginning in 1889 the Mounted Squad was officially referred to as the Mounted Service.

⬚ 1890

Chief Constable Draper assigned three mounted constables to No. 3 Station, St. Andrews Market. The move was made to reduce the travel time to the western beats. Patrol Sergeant Goulding and three Constables remained at No. 1 Stable, Court Street. Thus began the satellite stable system which remained until 1994.

Draper resigned during the year and was replaced by Chief Constable (formerly Colonel) Grasette who would lead the Toronto Police Force for the next 30 years. He was a firm supporter of the Mounted Service and helped to ensure its continuity through the changing times.

There were no deaths or casualties of a serious nature among the horses, although two were sold as being unfit for service. During the year, large crowds began attending Queen's Park on Sundays to listen to speeches. There had never been any trouble, but a strong police detail was always in attendance. Attendance at Queen's Park demonstrations remains a regular occurrence for officers of the Mounted Unit to this day.

A mounted officer and a foot constable "gossiping" at Queen's Park, c.1890. They may have been there to enforce the new "Sunday-in-the-park" Bylaw. The officers would have faced internal police charges had their patrol sergeant caught them in idle conversation. Photograph, Toronto Research Library, Toronto Parks. T-30635.

 **1891** The year began poorly for the Mounted Service, its utility was being questioned, and abolition advocated. Chief Constable Grasette responded to the criticism:

Such a retrograde step would be a distinct mistake. The few men on horseback, patrol more ground than twice their number on foot could cover, and their presence in the outskirts imparts to the residents a sense of security that it would be extremely undesirable to disturb.

The withdrawal of the mounted men from their present beats would possibly be followed by a demand that they should be replaced by foot police, which, if acceded to, would involve either a considerable increase to the force or a redistribution and removal of men from the central sections of the City. As I have said before, the services of a few mounted men are most useful in serving summonses in the country, impounding stray cattle, and attending race meetings and processions, while on the occasion of popular tumult they are invaluable.

The large cities of the United States and of Europe have mounted men as part of the police establishment, and although they may not find favour with that part of the community who might come in collision with them, I am satisfied the law abiding citizen regards them as an additional safeguard to life and property."[18]

The Chief Constable proved his point and the Mounted Service remained. This was only the first call to disband the unit. Over the years it would continually face calls for its reduction or elimination.

Cost of maintaining the Mounted Unit in 1891 was $1,425.00, salaries and uniforms excluded.[19]

One horse was cast as unfit for service during the year: nine were purchased, although some of the new animals must have been for police-wagon and ambulance service.

Officers were sent for first-aid training with the St. John Ambulance Service—the first year that formal instruction was given to these men, including those officially assigned to the police ambulance service.

City of Toronto Council passed a Sunday-in-the-Park Bylaw which stopped the political and religious speeches at Queen's Park. This action was one of the first examples of the repression of free speech which would occur in Toronto over the next fifty years. The Mounted Service would be used by the political, business and police leadership of Toronto to help repress views contrary to their own. The checks and balances we have in place today were not available in 1891, and the rights of the masses were few and far between.

The following story appeared in the Toronto Telegram *on April 6, 1915.*

First Mounted Constable

C.A. Chatterson returning to Winnipeg after funeral of father, Charles A. Chatterson, formerly of Toronto, passed through the city yesterday on his way to Winnipeg, after attending the funeral of his brother and father, who were buried the same day in Coburg.

Mr. Chatterson was formerly a Toronto Policeman and was the first mounted constable in the city. He will be remembered by many as the policeman stationed on King Street East, by the late Chief Draper, to stop the speeding of those who used to drive down in horse-drawn vehicles to the Woodbine race meets. He was also commended for his good work during the streetcar strike in 1886."[1]

Constable Chatterson was probably riding rented livery horses prior to the establishment of the full-time Mounted Squad in 1886. He may have been the first Toronto police officer assigned to ride horses in the execution of his duty, but he was not the first member assigned to full time mounted duties. The honour of being the first full time mounted officers must be split between George Goulding and George Watson.

1   *Toronto Telegram,* April 6, 1915.

 1892 The Sunday-in-the-Park Bylaw must have been effective as the chief constable reported no disturbances were worth reporting upon. The city continued its growth and mounted officers had their beats expanded to cover greater ground. By all accounts it was a quiet year at the Mounted Service with no horses injured, purchased or sold.

 **1893** The easier times continued into 1893 as the Mounted Service continued to provide police presence in remote areas, or in areas where footmen would be unable to cover the ground adequately. Four of the unit's horses were sold and replaced with others of a higher quality. New stables were added to No. 7 Police Station which was located on Ossington Avenue, north of Bloor Street West.

A portrait of Constable James Roe (36), c. 1895. Painted by H.C. Meyers of Toronto. James Roe was born in 1862 in Perth Ontario, joined the Toronto Police Department in 1887 and retired with rank of sergeant in 1922. Painting, Toronto Police Museum.

 **1894** Quiet times led to yet another call for the disbandment of the Mounted Service. In response to these demands, Chief Constable Grasette had this to say:

"The duties devolving upon the men employed as mounted constables have been discharged with continuous regularity, and their usefulness is now so fully recognized that a suggestion to dispense with the horses on the grounds of economy was immediately followed by largely signed petitions protesting against the proposition. The total cost of maintaining this force (salaries excepted), for the year was less than $1,100.00, or about $137.00 per man and horse."[20]

The Toronto Police purchased five bicycles during the year, to be used by constables assigned to check vacant houses and areas not currently patrolled by the police. The mobility offered by the bicycle was another threat to the existence of the Mounted Service. One hundred years later, the mobility of new style police mountain bicycles would be another reason to justify the reduction of the Mounted Unit. In 1994, the responsibility for park patrols was transferred from the Mounted Unit to the new divisional bicycle units.

1895 The Mounted Service continued its usual patrols throughout the year. Four constables were transferred out of the unit and replaced by four others who were sent for training. This was intended to extend the mounted experience to other members of the force as backup. Two horses were sold and two others purchased as replacements. The Chief Constable stated that "Sickness, sore backs, etc., have been conspicuously absent, indicating the care and attention that the horses received." [21]

Chief Constable Grasette requested that wooden floors in the stables at No. 1 and No. 7 stations be replaced with concrete or brick as more durable and sanitary. In October the unit purchased a regular-issue military saddle from the Militia Department. This may have been the first of the universal military saddles which are still in use by the Toronto police service.

1896 Mounted Patrols remained as the main police presence in the outlying areas of the city. In 1896 the Chief Constable reported that the residents of the outskirts were now more than ever dependent upon the mounted officers for their police protection. The unit cast three horses as O.W.O. (old and worn out) and purchased three replacements.

Chief Constable Grasette complimented the mounted officers on the care bestowed on the horses by reporting "No deaths have occurred; and the healthy condition of the horses is the best proof that they have been treated and ridden with care."[22]

A Toronto mounted officer, c. 1895. The officer is wearing the white issue summer helmet. Note that his mount has only a snaffle bit in its mouth. The horse has a mane, its tail has not been bobbed and it is carrying a universal style British military saddle. Photograph, Toronto Police Museum.

A Toronto mounted officer with some well dressed citizens at the gates to High Park, c. 1895.
Photograph, Toronto Police Museum.

▣ 1897

Chief Constable Grasette had been trying since 1889 to have regulations passed for the control of vehicular traffic, and he informed the Police Commission:

> *"Vehicular traffic on the main thoroughfares is now of such volume as to require systematic regulation. The bylaws relating to the subject seem to be framed on the old statutes of Upper Canada, and are too vague for the city of today. A large portion of the traffic that finds its way through the most crowded parts of King, Yonge and Queen Streets consists of coal carts, lumber wagons, drays, lorries, express vans etc., that have little or no concern there, and could just as readily use the less frequented streets and so relieve the congested parts.*
>
> *"Another feature of worthy consideration is the fact that very young children are, in many instances, entrusted to drive; and they are incompetent to control their horses, and are ignorant as well of the 'rules of the road,' which, indeed, many of their elders entirely ignore."[23]*

Despite the Chief's report not much was done and the bylaws regulating traffic were left vague and inadequate. During this period, regulation of traffic was an important part of the mounted officers' duties. In addition to its regular patrols, the Mounted Service were, "Considerably engaged during the year repressing immoderate riding and driving in the City."[24] A new fad known as "scorching" became a police concern. A scorching occurred when two youngsters raced their bicycles, often side-by-side, on city streets and sidewalks.

The Mounted Service remained busy providing escorts for processions. On June 22, 1897, a major parade was held to celebrate the Diamond Jubilee of Queen Victoria. Career development of officers continued as four constables were returned to regular duties at police divisions while four new constables were brought to the Mounted Service.

Three police horses died during the year and two new horses were purchased. On November 10, police-wagon horse "Sandy" was shot, probably due to an accident. The City of Toronto held a referendum to obtain public opinion on whether streetcars should be allowed to run on Sundays. The motion only just succeeded. It would be many years before other activities were allowed to take place on Sundays. Even playground equipment was secured by chains and padlocks to prevent children from contravening the Lord's Day Act.

Chief Constable Grasette, 1890-1920. Photograph, Toronto Police Museum.

Station duty staff, c. 1895. Photograph, Toronto Police Museum.

From the North West To the Mounted Unit

Peter Kerr joined the North West Mounted Police on April 18th, 1882. He enlisted as a constable and was assigned regimental number 704. While in the N.W.M.P. he was stationed at "D" Division, Lethbridge, North West Territories. He was a veteran of the 1885 Riel Rebellion and was awarded the North West Canada medal with Saskatchewan bar. He held the rank of sergeant when he resigned from the force after six years service on April 18, 1888.

Five days after resigning, Kerr was in Toronto to join the Toronto Police Force. He transferred to the Mounted Service and served with the force for about forty years. Kerr died in Toronto on August 14, 1945.

A mounted officer in winter dress, c. 1900. The officer is wearing a riding cloak with his regular police helmet. The Persian lamb winter hats have yet to be introduced. Photograph, Toronto Police Museum.

 **1898** During 1898, the Mounted Unit continued to provide patrols to outlying districts. The Chief Constable reported to the Board of Police Commissioners that their presence "gives a feeling of security to the residents there, prevents cattle from roaming at large, and preserves order over a wide and sparsely occupied district."[25]

Two horses were retired and two new ones trained in a field at the corner of Simcoe and Wellington Streets. The force requested that concrete floors be installed in the stables at Police Stations 3, 6 and 7 as the wooden floors were unsafe. Nothing came of the request, which would be made again the following year.

Toronto City Hall and Police Headquarters 1853-1899. Sketch, Toronto Police Museum.

 **1899** In his annual report the Chief Constable stated that the "very limited number of men forming the mounted patrol have covered the ground assigned to them effectively, extending protection and supervision to districts that might otherwise be without police."[26]

There were no casualties among the mounted horses which were all well cared for. Police Ambulance horse "Mand" died of colic on February 13.

The population of Toronto grew rapidly during the 1890s. By 1899, approximately 190,000 people lived in the city. The police force was still quite small with only 277 men working out of seven police divisions. Eight officers were assigned to mounted duties.

The City Hall at Bay and Queen Streets was opened during 1899. Police Headquarters were relocated to the building the following year.

A mounted officer, c. 1900. This officer is wearing a St. John Ambulance First Aid badge on his sleeve. Photograph, Toronto Police Museum.

THE MOUNTED SERVICE AT THE END OF THE CENTURY

Patrol Sergeant	1	Budget Est.	$1,300.00
Constables	7	Actual Costs	$1,014.76

Irish-Canadian Policemen of Toronto

When John Prince became Chief of the Toronto Police Force in 1858, he remodelled the force after the Royal Irish Constabulary. This new police department was a semi-military force with preference given to men with prior service in the military or the Royal Irish Constabulary. This structure was fitting for Orange Toronto, the Belfast of North America.

In the early 20th century, the stereotype Toronto policeman was a rugged Irish constable. By 1910, about 20% of the force was Irish born, with many other Canadians of Irish descent. Membership in the Orange Lodge was an important factor affecting hiring and promotion within the police service. In 1913, an observant officer estimated that three quarters of the force belonged to fraternal organizations, primarily the Orange Lodge.

Employment registers reveal that, during this era, the Police Commission preferred to hire new immigrants from the British Isles. Second choice was men from rural areas or small towns in Ontario—people with few personal or family ties to the community.[1] Unlike community policing done today, senior officers did their best to prevent familiarity with citizens of the community: they rotated the beats policeman covered, and fined them heavily if caught "gossiping" with citizens.

Applicants with employment history showing prior police experience had the best opportunity of being hired. Those classed as being skilled or semi-skilled workers were the next preferred group. On the basis of salary and housing, the life style of an average policeman was on par with a lower-middle class skilled worker.

Another factor in determining who would be hired was a man's religion which was listed in the back of the Chief Constable's Annual Report. Anglicans, Methodists and Presbyterians comprised approximately eighty per cent of the police department and held all senior officer positions. Catholics were under-represented in relation to the community they were to protect.[2]

Notes made by employment examiners show that politeness and respectfulness were highly rated traits as the Police Commission preferred skilled workers and rural recruits who they believed would accept the existing social order more than common urban labourers; the latter stood little chance of being hired.[3] The hiring policies and rules and regulations of the force prevented the men from becoming sympathetic with the working poor, those people who were likely to walk the picket lines and strike for social change.

1   Marquis, Greg. *Early 20th Century Toronto Police Institution*. Ph.D. Thesis submitted to the Department of History, Queen's University, Kingston, Ontario, November 1986. Page 202.
2   Leibaers, Jan K. *The Toronto Police Strike of 1918.* Major research paper submitted to Professor N. Rogers, September 1990. Page 28.
3   Leibaers, Jan K. *The Toronto Police Strike of 1918.* Major research paper submitted to Professor N. Rogers, September 1990. Page 39.

 **1900** The new century found the unit being called by its original name, the Mounted Squad. Three constables were sent back to regular police duties, to be replaced with three new men. The chief constable requested that two more officers be added to the unit, and if officers could not be permanently assigned to the unit, he asked that they be put on mounted duties for a minimum of seven months.

One horse had to be destroyed.

The Governor General visited Toronto in May and was provided with a mounted police escort. South Africa's Boer War was at its height and news announcements of major events relating to the conflict brought large crowds into the street; these were orderly, often waving Union Jacks at the announcement of British victories over the Boers.

By the turn of the century, the area around Toronto City Hall was a sprawling slum filled with decrepit housing: residents endured terrible living conditions. York Street was known as Toronto's toughest street. On October 6, the *Toronto Star* ran a story titled, "When the Police Have To Fight," describing some of the recent battles involving the police.

Two other "tough" areas named in the article were Lombard Street and "Cork Town," which was located between Trinity Street and the Don River. The article boasted about the fighting abilities and no-nonsense attitude of the quick-fisted policemen who kept order in these neighbourhoods, often with the use of a billie club. No doubt mounted officers were detailed to these areas to back up the foot patrolmen who had to control gangs of "insolent young blackguards" on Saturday nights."[27]

James Tinsley

James Tinsley was born in Hamilton, Ontario on May 4, 1872. When he was fifteen years old, a recruiting Sergeant of the North West Mounted Police came to Hamilton seeking recruits for service in Canada's West. James Tinsley applied, lying about his age, by stating he was eighteen years old. The recruiter told him that they usually only took twenty-one year olds, but with his parents' permission he would be accepted. James's older brother helped him to convince his parents to let him enlist. Accepted into the force in 1888, he was sent west—probably the youngest Mountie in Canada's history.

After five years service, Tinsley applied for discharge from the mounted police and returned to Ontario where he took a position as a superior at the Brockville Mental Asylum. He later joined the Brockville Police Force, and was awarded the Sanderson medal for bravery after being involved in a shoot-out on March 9, 1896 with a crazed man armed with a shotgun.

The gunman had gone on a rampage killing one man and wounding eight others. Tinsley confronted him armed with an old revolver the police had seized from a suspect years before. When the gun failed to fire, Tinsley took cover in the firehall where he borrowed a shotgun from a fireman. Then he confronted the man a second time and managed to disable him with a blast from his gun just as he himself was shot in the face and arm. Tinsley would carry a number of shotgun pellets in his body for the rest of his life as the hospital was unable to remove them all.

Resigning from the Brockville Police Force, after two years service, (with the rank of sergeant) Tinsley joined the Toronto Police Force on July 5, 1898 as a third-class constable. Almost immediately, he was transferred to the Mounted Squad. The following story of his mounted service was contained in his memoirs, written upon his retirement around 1951.

Mounted Duty

Long before Sunnyside Amusement Park was made and the [Lakeshore] Boulevard Drive was built there were no subways [through the railway embankment] leading from High Park, just plain level railway crossings to the old Lake Shore Road. At the south side of the road the lake water used to be very close to the road.

At that time I was on the Toronto City Mounted Police. I was ordered to train for this duty, as it was known I had previous experience. During the rigorous four months training I went through after joining the force, I brought my weight down to about one hundred and seventy five pounds. I claimed I was too heavy and tried to avoid joining (the Mounted Squad) because when I left the west I had made up my mind to have nothing to do with horses again.

It was no use. I had to do as I was told, and make the

best of it. As a matter of fact I rode horses for eleven years in Toronto, five years as a Constable and six years as a Patrol Sergeant. At the end of that time I was promoted to full Sergeant and attached to Number Four Division.

During my mounted service we had a couple of street-car strikes, Halloween fights with students, attended all important parades, also did duty at horse shows and [the] Canadian National Exhibition.

I rode a most intelligent horse called Rufus or Red [as] he was a dark red colour, and shone like gold. He used to follow me around like a dog. I could walk across Queen's Park and Red would go around on the roadway and meet me on the other side. He would not go on the grass or Boulevard unless someone offered him an apple and then he would go almost anywhere.

The Beatty children on St. George Street near Bloor Street, were in front of their home eating apples, I passed them on foot, my horse following on the roadway. When I got to Bloor Street, I looked back and my horse had disappeared, I went back and found him in Beatty's back yard and the household in a commotion, as the children had run into the house saying the Policeman's horse was chasing them. I explained he only wanted them to give him a piece of apple. I was sorry afterward as those children used to feed him apples daily, and I had dirty bits to clear away, when I reached the station.

One day a farmer with a wagon load of apples in barrels crossed Bloor Street going south on Huron Street. Old Rufus smelled those apples, chased after that wagon and I had to run almost to Harbord Street before I caught him.

During the winter a contractor was building a house on the south side of Bloor Street just west of St. George Street. This man was delivering a load of window sash from a lane in the rear, when one of the window sash fell off hitting his horse. The horse ran away, scattering window sash over the roadway.

The wagon hit a telegraph pole, broke the wagon reach, and the horse headed west on Bloor Street with only two front wheels.

I had just turned on to Bloor Street and Rufus and I took after the runaway. At Spadina Avenue the horse crossed on the wrong side of Bloor Street and continued west. The Spadina intersection was slippery and in crossing I lost ground, a streetcar stopped at Brunswick Avenue and a girl stepped off, those wheels missed her by inches, that girl was near death that day, I had the reins in my left hand and had

to grab that horse with my right when I got my balance and the chance.

He opened out away from the curb at Lippincott Street and I came alongside and got hold of the bridle, and stopped him right in the centre of Bloor Street and Bathurst Street Intersection. The owner offered me a reward, and I refused it, he afterward sent money to Chief Grasette, who returned it, with thanks, and notified me through my superior officers. I was satisfied as long as he learned about it.

One Sunday that winter I was reporting to the Patrol Box in High Park when I saw a runaway hack team going west on the old Lake Shore Road. There appeared to be a number of people in the sleigh, and the driver could not stop the horses. By the time I mounted and crossed the Grand Trunk Railway tracks, they were passing the west entrance of High Park, and just about there the driver fell off the sleigh.

I caught up to the team just about fifty yards from the Humber River. I got the neigh horse by the bridle, ran them around in a circle and finally got them stopped. The spool had come off the double trees and the trace was loose on the off horse and he was bleeding at the nose. The horses had been coupled up too short and their heels had been striking the sleigh at every jump.

The Driver, an old hand, had so much furs on he became exhausted and fell off. The sleigh contained a Mrs. Mcholes, her mother and three Mcholes children. They had started out from the Ocean House Hotel at King and Queen Streets, Mr. Mcholes, the ladies husband, was the proprietor of the Ocean House.

I understand the driver visited the Chief Constable's Office regarding my stopping his horses, again I was notified that the Chief Constable was very pleased.

My horse Rufus was getting old and commenced to stumble, so they put him hauling the police ambulance, While he was on duty at the Canadian National Exhibition, his driver must have tied him too loose, as the halter shank got over the top of his head, and he pulled back until he was strangled.

He was a grand horse and I really loved him. Shortly after that I was returned to foot duty and transferred to Number Three Division, where I remained until I reported to be a Patrol Sergeant and returned to mounted duty.

1901

In his annual report, Chief Grasette stated that "the usefulness of the mounted constables was more apparent than ever last year, when in addition to the ordinary patrols; escorts for Royalty and Vice Regal visitors were furnished at all public functions and other occasions."[28] The Duke of York's visit to the Canadian National Exhibition, which brought out huge crowds of well-wishers, was the biggest event to face the mounted officers.

Patrol Sergeant George Goulding, was promoted to Sergeant on November 1st, 1901. He was the officer in charge of the Mounted Unit since 1886 and remained at the unit after his promotion. The position of officer in charge of the unit had been upgraded to sergeant, indicating the growing prominence of the unit within the police structure.

In September the unit purchased 10 rawhide whips. These likely saw service the following year during the second Toronto Street Railway Strike.

1902

On Saturday June 21, 1902, the Toronto Street Railway employees went out on strike for more money and the recognition of a grievance committee. Although the strike was settled in three days, major riots broke out on the Sunday when the railway attempted to put its vehicles into service, despite the strike.

The *Toronto Telegram* reported the Police Commission had requested the assistance of the military and were to be supplied with 700 cavalrymen from Camp Niagara and 700 local infantrymen of the militia. The soldiers were never used for strike duty. The Mounted Unit supplied mounted escorts to protect wagons carrying the electricians that were sent out to recover abandoned streetcars. They also provided mounted escorts to wagons delivering food to the strike breakers. This practice ended after the unions threatened to punish the suppliers by calling the city's bakers out on strike.[29]

The following description from the *Toronto Telegram* describes the riot which began when police used a patrol wagon to move replacement workers into the Yorkville streetcar yards. "Seven mounted men with crops waving above the peoples heads charged the mob of several thousand. For three blocks the police fought its way through the thousands with the patrol wagon following."

"Meanwhile at the King Street Yards the crowd began throwing stones and breaking windows late in the evening. Police reinforcements were called in and a large number of mounted men and other police began to disburse the crowd. By 11:30 p.m. King Street was practically clear."[30]

A police ambulance in front of the University Avenue Armouries, c. 1902. Photograph, Toronto Police Museum.

The strike was one of the more momentous events of the year in Toronto. In his annual report the Chief Constable stated, "The Streetcar Strike was an occasion when the utility of the mounted police was more than evident. I consider eight men no longer sufficient for the duties that devolve on this branch of the service, and recommend an additional four to the Mounted Squad. The equipment should be increased to provide for at least 25 men if required."[31]

The *Toronto Star* reported that 20 police officers were mounted during the strike. This means that part-time riders were still being used when the situation required. The extra officers were probably former mounted officers who had been returned to regular police duties. The horses were rented livery horses, from the Police Wagon Service or Police Ambulance Service.

Fortunately it does not appear that there were any serious injuries resulting from the events surrounding the Street Railway Strike. Despite the fears of city administrators, the police were able to contain the situation and the military was not needed. The military call out may have been a precaution due to a fear that the police themselves sympathized with the strikers.

The *Toronto Star*'s description of the mounted policemen charging the crowd swinging black maria whips presents an image of extreme police violence, although in the context of the times, this was fairly mild compared with the confrontations that occurred in other jurisdictions across North America. During the Street Railway strike in Hamilton, Ontario in 1906, for example, the response of the Hamilton Police and the military was much more extreme than what occurred in Toronto.

On Halloween night, a large fight took place between students and the police force. It began when University of Toronto Students, parading through the streets singing varsity songs, met up with students from a rival college. The paraders started fighting each other, and then the police. Rioting lasted for about an hour and a number of students were arrested.

The Dean of the University claimed that the students had been marching through the school grounds, as they walked onto College Street *"they were ridden into by some mounted police, and a number were struck with rawhide whips, without warning. It is not creditable that the Chief of Police gave orders that could be construed into a warrant for such a cruel attack, which was more worthy of Cossacks than of the members of the police force of Toronto, which stands preeminent among such bodies."[32]*

The Police Commission launched an investigation which found the police to be at fault—a rare occurrence in those days. In his annual report Chief Constable Grasette requested the mounted unit be increased to 12 men with 25 sets of saddlery for emergencies. He finished off the report by stating that the saddlery was in fair order, but needed to be extensively repaired in the next year.

The Rescue of George Haley

Constable James Tinsley.
Photograph, Toronto Police Museum.

On December 2, 1902, Constable James Tinsley was riding his horse on Eastern Avenue near Booth Avenue. He saw a woman running down Booth Avenue towards the waterfront. There was obviously something wrong so he galloped his horse towards the trouble. When he reached the waterfront, he found that a seven-year-old boy had fallen through the ice into lake Ontario. Two other boys had managed to hook the victim's sweater with a long pole,

and this prevented the boy from sliding under the ice. There was nothing else they could do as ice was breaking up all around the drowning boy, preventing any rescue attempt.

Constable Tinsley ran to a nearby boat house and pried off the lock. He removed a boat and dragged it to the shore. He placed the two boys with the pole in the front of the boat and pushed it across the ice until they could grab the victim. When the rescuers got the victim to shore, he had every appearance of being dead. Constable Tinsley covered him with his coat, secured his tongue with his handkerchief and began artificial respiration.

Tinsley continued to perform artificial respiration. By the time a doctor arrived, the boy was groaning slightly. The doctor ordered the boy removed to a nearby house and used a clothes peg to secure the victim's tongue. The doctor and Constable Tinsley continued to take turns performing artificial respiration. The doctor finally said to Tinsley, "This boy is going to die as rigor mortis is setting in, we have done all we can do, is there anything you can suggest?"

Tinsley remembered how years before when he was a child his grandmother had put his sister in a tub of warm water and brought her out of a convulsion. He suggested to the doctor that they place the boy in a tub of warm water with some dissolved mustard and after they had given him a good rubbing, the young victim commenced to cough, spit out mouthfuls of water and cry. The boy fully recovered and was taken home later that day.

The Royal Humane Society awarded Constable Tinsley a parchment certificate, and his two young associates received bronze life-saving medals. Years later, off-duty Constable Moffat was talking to a man in Buffalo, New York. Moffat happened to tell his acquaintance that he was a Toronto Police Officer. The man asked if he knew a man on the force named Tinsley. Constable Moffat replied that Inspector Tinsley was his boss. The man responded, "Well my name is Haley, and your boss saved my life once."

Commenting on this story years later, the now retired Inspector Tinsley recalled Moffat's meeting with Haley and noted "that, my friends is the kind of thing that makes life worthwhile."

The 1902 Toronto Street Railway Strike

This excellent description of the Street Railway strike riots appeared in the *Toronto Star* newspaper, Monday June 23, 1902, and is quoted verbatim.

"STONE-ARMED RIOTERS BATTERED THE CARS"

Mob Attacked and Wounded Several Men at the King Street barns on Sunday.

Mobs set out yesterday to prevent the intention of the Street Railway Company to operate the service, and succeeded.

As a result of day's rioting, seven men have been arrested, nine more are known to have been injured, while a dozen were wounded and have been hid away. Each of the arrests was accompanied by a tumult, the police vans were stoned, nearly a dozen cars were wrecked, and the glass in all the city car barns suffered to a greater or less degree, while at the east end car barns, King Street, scarcely a pane is left in the front of the building.

The Most Serious Trouble

Men who attempted to run the cars were all more or less wounded.

The whole of the city's police force was kept on duty, many of the men not having had a full night's rest for several days. Twenty mounted men were also on hand.

The most serious trouble took place in the East End. At an early hour the barns on King Street on the corner of St. Lawrence, looked down on a crowd who were determined that any cars that came from that barn would have a warm reception.

Shortly before eight, the company started its first car. The mob had stones in its hands and its eye on the front doors. But with a neat little coup, the car came sliding around the side of the barn, instead of through the doors. The suddenness of the car's coming took the crowd off its guard, and although the windows were smashed nothing happened to the men in charge. The car got as far as Woodbine. All went well until the switch on Kingston Road was met, when it was discovered that someone had stolen the points, and the car ran up towards Norway Hill, followed by a mob pelting stones, eggs, and potatoes, the unfortunate motorman and conductor fled for the hills.

Car 866 was the point of attraction for the missiles of the now furious mob. With a full head of speed on, the man at the motor tore through the crowd, followed by hoots and stones. Opposite De Grassi Street, a stone felled the motorman, and he was carried into Dr. Rowan's surgery. Meanwhile the conductor had been pressed into service, and was bending low, dodging stones and other missiles. This car was likewise deserted, and the man in charge left as fast as his legs could carry him.

By this time the crowd seemed more ready for business. It had, so to speak, filled its pockets with stones. It watched more carefully lest it should let the fleeting car slip by without doing it full damage. Nearly five thousand people were along the streets between the bridge and the barns, and when the third car appeared, there was not a whole window. Two other cars followed, but they shared the same fate. Tinkle, tinkle, biff, bang, glass cracking, men shouting, and woman, too, and over and above all the cries, "Scabs, scabs! Kill them!"

Making Arrests

The police were busy. But what could a handful do against a mob of thousands?

A representative of the Toronto Star saw the streetcars after their peril-filled trip. Inside were many stones and much splintered glass. Stones in many cases, were as big as a man's fist, and would have carried death had they landed on a motorman's head.

Much excitement occurred in the north end. At 3:30, car No. 850 came out. The wheels had scarcely made a single revolution when a stone went through the window, and out again on the other side. A brace of eggs spattered over the outside. Blood was drawn just before the car reached the corner of Yonge Street. A small stone went through the window, and cut the motorman's nose. Two policemen jumped on the outside of the car and it turned down Yonge Street, with a shouting mob of young men following it.

A Night Riot in Yonge Street

There was a serious riot in Yonge Street, in the vicinity of Yorkville Avenue car barns, between 8 and 11 last night. At 8 a rumour spread that a patrol wagon was bringing up a load of scabs, and in a few moments an immense crowd gathered.

A few minutes later a roar from down the street betokened that there was something in the wind. Hardly had the cries warned the crowd than a few speedy wheelmen arrived and shouted confirmation of the news. "The patrol wagon is coming up with a load of scabs."

Hard on heels of the cyclists came the wagon, the horses stretched out in gallop. Around the wagon galloped a guard of eight mounted policemen, just as the wagon crossed Bloor Street the bombardment commenced. Rocks flew in a shower.

As the wagon pulled into Yorkville Avenue five of the guarding policemen fell back, and, suddenly wheeling, charged the crowd. For a moment the crowd gave back. Then some of the bolder ones broke through the thin line, and the situation looked grave.

The promptitude of the policemen alone saved them. Out came their blacksnake whips, and they rode into the crowds, slashing as fast as their arms would move. The effect was the crowd swept back like the turning of a tide."[1]

1   *Toronto Star*, Monday June 23, 1902.

A mounted officer in High Park, c. 1902. Photograph, Mike Filey collection.

 1903

The name of the unit was changed to the Mounted Unit in 1903. The police department purchased some new saddlery and equipment for the unit during the year. Stabling accommodation was also increased to allow for the expansion of the unit. Despite all the preparations and the Chief Constables request, no new officers were assigned to the unit. Colonel Grasette also recommended that a stable be built onto No. 2 Police Station.

Automobiles were beginning to appear on the city streets. By 1903 there were 103 cars registered in Ontario. Most were located in Toronto. The introduction of the automobile would have far-reaching effects on policing. The Mounted Unit would be instrumental in the regulation and supervision of problems caused by the introduction of the motor vehicle.

1904

On April 19th, a police constable on foot patrol noticed a fire in a downtown warehouse. He ran to an alarm box and summoned the Fire Department. By the time the firemen arrived, the blaze was out of control. The city's call for help was answered by Fire Departments from as far away as Buffalo, New York. Fire fighting equipment and men were sent to Toronto by special emergency express railway trains.

The police had a trying time restraining the large crowds pressing on the fire lines. The Mounted Unit was probably on duty through much of this time assisting with crowd control and the suppression of looters.

The Great Toronto Fire, as it came to be called, destroyed much of the city's manufacturing district. The final toll was 104 buildings destroyed, $10,000,000 in damage and 5,000 people put out of work.

On April 30th, the *Toronto Star* newspaper reported numerous complaints of cars exceeding the 10 mph speed limit. People also complained that drivers were staging impromptu races on Jarvis Street and other paved roads in the city. The *Star* reporter stated that "It is probable that the coming summer season will see not a few arrests in this connection. Seven mounted policemen, whose duty is to patrol the parks, may find something to do in chasing speeding vehicles."[33]

There is no record of what, if any traffic enforcement was done by the mounted officers during the year. The annual report only states that the usual mounted patrols and escorts were provided.

On September 11, police mount "Rufus" died while on duty at the Canadian National Exhibition. The horse had been stumbling while on mounted patrol. It was decided to transfer him to the Police Ambulance Service where he would work in harness rather than carry the weight of an officer. The ambulance crew improperly tethered him while he was tacked up and he became entangled in the tack. He either strangled himself or broke his neck while trying to get free.

A mounted officer patrolling the campus of the University of Toronto, c. 1900. Photograph, Toronto Public Library.

 **1905** Two more officers were assigned to the Mounted Unit during the year, bringing the total personnel to 10. The squad continued to patrol the outlying areas of the city and "in other ways demonstrated their usefulness."[34] The mounted officers were pleased with the Police Commission's decision to reduce terms for Third Class Constable by one year and the term for Second Class Constable by two years. As most of the mounted officers were Second Class Constables, this was a significant financial bonus.

The annual tradition of having the Mounted Unit lead the Santa Claus Parade began this year. Since its inception, the Santa Claus Parade has always been an important duty for members of the police service. The horses and riders of the Mounted Unit are always immaculately turned out, and a crowd favourite.

1906 The patrols of mounted officers were extended to those new districts which had been annexed by the city. Three horses were sold during the year and three remounts purchased. In his annual report the chief constable complained that the cost of suitable horses had risen by 30%.

During the year a patrol sergeant's position was added to the authorized strength of the Mounted Unit. This enabled closer supervision of the mounted officers and also provided a second-in-command to lead the unit during the absence of the person in charge. The position was filled by Patrol Sergeant Henry Gilks, who had been promoted to that rank on April 1st, 1905.

1907 It was a quiet year for the ten officers of the Mounted Unit as they maintained their regular patrols and continued to expand their beats into new areas. Two horses were sold during and two remounts brought into training.

From the Veldt to the Mounted Unit

On October 7, 1902, twenty-six-year-old George Cook and twenty-five-year-old George Thompson joined the Toronto Police Department as Third Class Constables. The two men had served together in the Royal Canadian Dragoons for three years and took their discharge at Stanley Barracks the same day. Then they walked down King Street to police headquarters where they both joined the police force.

The Royal Canadian Dragoons were with the first contingent of Canadians to go to South Africa at the start of the Boer War. Thompson was in South Africa for about fifteen months: Cook was probably with him. By 1908 both officers were serving as members of the Mounted Unit. With their cavalry experience they were a great asset to the force.

*Top:
PC George Thompson.*

*Bottom:
PC George (Thomas) Cook.*

*Photographs,
Toronto Police Museum.*

The Hamilton Street Railway Strike of 1906

The following account of the Hamilton Street Railway strike provides a comparison of how the authorities handled social unrest in other jurisdictions. Methods used by Hamilton police and soldiers sent to assist them were much more severe than those used by the Toronto police force.

On November 5, 1906, the Hamilton Street Railway workers went on strike over the failure of their employer to implement concessions won during an arbitration hearing. The company tried to use strikebreakers from Toronto to operate streetcars. The public firmly sided with the strikers and the dispute became more violent as it dragged on. Streetcars were derailed and damaged, buildings burned, and men, including police officers, were beaten and gun shots fired.

Things continued to deteriorate until on November 23 when a crowd of ten thousand angry citizens took to the streets. Things were made worse by the no-nonsense magistrate Colonel George Taylor Denison who used his position to force the Hamilton police into escalating the violence. "I had some trouble getting them to use their batons at first," he reported." "I rode behind them all night and kept busy urging them on by shouting 'give it to them'."[1]

That same evening, due to a request from the City of Hamilton under the Aid to Civil Powers Act, a special train left Toronto carrying 173 men of the Royal Canadian Dragoons, Royal Canadian Horse Artillery and an infantry unit from the Royal Canadian Regiment. The men and horses were loaded onto trains at the Stanley Barracks located at the Canadian National Exhibition grounds.

The soldiers arrived in Hamilton at 1:00 a.m. on November 24. The Hamilton Spectator of November 24, 1906 describes what happened next:

"While the police had driven one section of the crowd north to Gore Street, two squads of military had forced the other half south to King Street. The Dragoons led the way, followed by the infantry. The cavalry rode in double columns with drawn sabres up to King Street. The soldiers then divided into sections. The cavalry formed a single line across James Street to York Street, turning up York, scattering the crowd as they rode, using the flats of their sabres and their horses to disperse the crowd."[2]

The following day the soldiers sent out patrols, but there was no further trouble. Good discipline shown by the soldiers kept them from reacting to the insults and jeers from the Crowds. The *Hamilton Spectator* reported that "the police were more feared than the troops." The soldiers remained in Hamilton at the request of the city until the strike was settled on December 6.[3]

The picture of Canadian soldiers using the flat side of sabres to clear the streets of Canadian civilians is hard to imagine today. Toronto's Mounted Unit may have been the one police tool that prevented the city from ever having to use the military to maintain social order. Although the Toronto and Hamilton Streetcar strikes were very similar in nature, the exception was that there was less force used to maintain public order during the Toronto unrest.

1   Greenhous, Brereton. *Dragoon, The Centennial History of The Royal Canadian Dragoons, 1883-1983,* `The Guild of the Royal Canadian Dragoons, Belleville,Ontario, 1983. Page 194.
2   The *Hamilton Spectator* Newspaper, November 24, 1906.
3   Greenhous, Brereton. *Dragoon, The Centennial History of The Royal Canadian Dragoons, 1883-1983,* The Guild of the Royal Canadian Dragoons, Belleville, Ontario, 1983. Page 163.

The Royal Canadian Dragoons on parade, c. 1910. Photograph, Canadian National Exhibition Archives.

 **1908** The City of Toronto continued to grow with the continued annexation of new territory. Due to the expansion, some police horses were moved to stables closer to the outskirts to save time going to and from their posts.

The distances patrolled by the officers had become so great that a second patrol sergeant was added to the unit. One sergeant was responsible for the western beats, the other the eastern. Two constables were also added bringing the Unit's strength to thirteen.

A new police station opened on Pape Avenue, and was equipped with a stable and mounted officers permanently assigned. It would be used by the Mounted Unit until 1968 when the men and horses were moved to Sunnybrook Park. Pape Avenue mounted officers provided patrols to the annexed Town of East Toronto, which expanded the eastern boundary considerably.

An unusual amount of ailments during the year caused five horses to be off their normal good health. The Chief Constable complained in his report that "good saddle horses are getting very scarce, and the price is steadily rising."[35]

1909 By 1909, fifteen officers were permanently assigned to the Mounted Unit. George Goulding was promoted to the rank of Inspector and remained in charge of the Mounted Unit. The police were given new powers to regulate parades, processions and street traffic, and to enforce the observance of the rules of the road. Major renovations were made to the stables and wagon houses but costs of repairs were so high that the Chief Constable exceeded his budget.

Toronto continued to grow as it annexed the Town of West Toronto. In the east end, the city limits were extended to Victoria Park Avenue with the annexation Midway and East Toronto.

In his annual report the Chief Constable outlined the duties that the Mounted Unit had performed over the last year. His support for the unit was evident: "I regard this branch of the service as indispensable." He went on to complain that "good horses were increasingly scarce and higher in price. Lameness is much more in evidence since asphalt and other hard roads have become the rule rather than the exception."[36]

Composite picture of the Toronto Police Mounted Unit, c. 1908. Rear row: Thomas Cook, Walter McDermot, W. Fowler, Ernest Hobson, James Lawlor, James Tinsley. Front row: James Jarvis, George Thompson, Sgt George Goulding, Austin Mitchell, George Guthrie. Photograph, Toronto Police Museum.

The Mounted Unit, c. 1909. Note the length of riding crops some officers have attached to their saddles. Photograph, Canadian National Exhibition Archives.

A mounted officer at the "old" Woodbine Race Track, c. 1910. The expensive carriages and the formal dress of the drivers and footmen suggests this may be the Queen's Plate or other important race day. Photograph, McLethwaite Collection, City of Toronto Archives. SC-497-254.

Inspector Goulding speaking to two well dressed men in High Park. They are there to watch the Royal Canadian Dragoons conduct cavalry training manoeuvres in the park, c.1909. Photograph, Toronto Public Library, Timmis Collection, Volume 8, S249 page 27 #1043.

1910 Chief Constable Grasette's annual report opened with the comment, "One sergeant, one patrol sergeant and fifteen constables constitute this very limited but useful branch of the force, for the supervision and protection for the outskirts of the city." The Chief requested the Police Commissioners add an additional patrol sergeant and four constables to the Mounted Unit.

Inspector George Goulding retired during the year and the Chief Constable made special note of his many years of efficient and faithful service. On April 1, 1910, Patrol Sergeant Henry Gilks, a former member of the famous British Life Guards Cavalry Regiment and a twenty-three year veteran of the Toronto Police Force, was promoted to full Sergeant and placed in command.

Inspector Goulding, and later Sergeant Gilks, were also responsible for the Police Wagon Service and the Police Ambulance Service including horses assigned to the units. Although these police units shared some facilities, they were considered three separate entities much like today's Mounted and Police Dog Services, where two separate units serve under one administrative umbrella.

The working conditions of Toronto police officers improved substantially during the year when the Board of Police Commissioners granted every officer two regular days off a month. The board also promised this allowance would be increased to one full day a week some time in the future. Upon the death of King Edward VII, all members of the force were required to swear allegiance to the new King, George V.

The Chief Constable was determined that the police take better control of the streets. Motor vehicles were more common, and were creating greater congestion. Injuries caused by accidents were a substantial concern. The Mounted Unit was ordered to take a more active role in the regulation of traffic and a number of mounted officers were assigned to regulate traffic at busier intersections.

The City of Toronto continued to grow in size as it annexed the towns of Dovercourt and Earlscourt, which required a further extension of Mounted Unit patrols.

A mounted officer listening to a speech being made by the dignitary standing in the convertible automobile at the opening of the Hillcrest Race Track, Bathurst Street and Davenport Road, 1911. Photograph, City of Toronto Archives, William James Collection. SC 24 -8213.

1911 In his annual report to the Police Commission, the Chief Constable commented on the good job that the mounted men were doing with traffic regulation. The Department purchased its first motorcycle. Motorcycle officers helped relieve mounted officers of some of their traffic responsibilities.

John James McIntosh, Chief of Police, Town of North Toronto. He is mounted on "Victor" at the corner of Yonge Street and Montgomery Avenue, Spring 1911. "Victor" would become a Toronto police horse when the Town of North Toronto was annexed. Photograph, Toronto Reference Library. 980-32.

1912 By 1912, the Mounted Unit was staffed by 24 officers of all ranks. The men were distributed across the city, as near to their assigned beats as stable accommodation would permit. As well as providing traditional patrols to the outlying districts, the unit was assigned beats on some of the main thoroughfares and were responsible for the regulation and direction of traffic. Traffic had become such a concern that the first Traffic Squad was formed. Speed limits were increased to 15 mph.

April saw the opening of the new No. 11 Police Station, with its modern facilities, located on Markham Street near Bathurst and Bloor Streets. The stable at No. 11 was used until 1974 when the officers and mounts were moved to the Horse Palace at the Canadian National Exhibition.

Sergeant Henry Gilks was promoted to the rank of Inspector on April 1 and remained as officer in charge of the Mounted Unit. He led the mounted officers as they provided a number of ceremonial escorts during a Royal Visit in May.

Expansion in Toronto continued with the annexation of the towns of Moore Park and North Toronto. With the annexation of North Toronto, the unit took possession of a bay gelding named "Victor," the horse used by the former Police Chief of North Toronto. They also took possession of the tack and other mounted equipment formally owned by the town.

1913 The Mounted Unit continued to provide patrols in areas that could not be covered by constables on foot. Patrols from the No. 11 Division stable provided a police presence in areas where they were "much wanted." The Chief Constable reported that mounted constables were becoming even more useful as escorts for processions. He also said that traffic, to a limited extent, was regulated by mounted constables to "advantage."

Two horses were replaced with two remounts. The force found it difficult to get the "right stamp of horse," even when they offered to pay more.

The usefulness of the police horse was again questioned when the Toronto Police introduced the first motor-driven patrol wagons during the year. They also purchased two motor ambulances and sold off the old horse-drawn ambulances, although the wagon service retained a number of horse-drawn patrol wagons for emergencies.

Toronto Police Mounted Unit, c. 1914. Photograph, The Toronto Police Museum.

1914

On May 22, 1914, the Governor General, the Duke of Connaught, came to Toronto and inspected the Toronto Police Force. There were two panoramic photographs taken of the event. The first photo shows the Mounted Unit formed up behind rows of foot officers at Varsity Stadium. The second shows the Mounted Unit leading the marching foot police officers into the "Eyes Right" salute. Copies of the photo exist at the Police Museum, the City of Toronto Archives and the Archives of Ontario.

During the Inspection, the Duke addressed the force saying, "Colonel Grasette, officers and men of the Toronto Police, I desire to express to you my very great satisfaction at the very splendid turnout you have made today. I congratulate Toronto on having such a fine body of men, and what is better even than your splendid appearance, is, I am told, your high sense of the duties imposed upon you in a great city like Toronto."[38]

The Duke of Connaught is being escorted through the streets of Toronto, c. 1914. A Toronto Police mounted officer watches the procession pass by. The Royal Canadian Dragoon officer on the right of the carriage is having problems controlling his mount. The horse is probably reacting to a band that has started playing as the escort approaches the Duke's destination. Photograph, Toronto Public Library, Timmis Collection, Volume 3, S249 page 53B.

The Duke went on to say that, from his personal observations, the police were very popular with the people of Toronto.

On August 4, the British Empire, including Canada, went to war against Germany and her allies. The first Toronto Policeman called to active duty was Constable George Wright of the Mounted Unit. He received notice to hold himself in readiness to return to England on the day war was declared.[38a] Within days of the declaration, forty members of the force requested military leave, either to join the Canadian Army, or to return to Britain to fight as reservists.

In support of the war effort, the Police Department donated eighteen of the Mounted Unit's best horses to the military. An act which, with the enlistment of at least five mounted officers, left the Unit somewhat disorganized. On September 30, the *Toronto Telegram* reported that because of the gift of horses to the military, eight mounted men went on patrol on foot. Of the twenty-two officers assigned to mounted duties, fourteen still patrolled on horseback while the other eight walked beats. A number of citizens offered horses to replace those given to the army, but these were not saddle horses and thus were unsuitable for police work.[38b] Suitable remounts were found by the end of the year.

The shortage of horses in the military led the Chief Constable to accept that there would be a rise in the price of horses suitable for mounted constables. He also predicted a rise in the price of forage for the horses.

On the 1st of July, Constable James Tinsley was promoted to Patrol Sergeant and remained assigned to the Mounted Unit.

Chief Constable Grasette at the Duke of Connaught's inspection of the Toronto Police. Photograph, Toronto Telegram *May 22, 1914.*

The march past of the Mounted Unit at the Duke of Connaught's inspection of the Toronto Police Force, May 22, 1914. Photograph, Toronto Telegram.

German Scare in High Park

On November 5, 1914, three months after war was declared against Germany and its allies, the *Toronto Evening Telegram* reported that there had been quite a "German scare" near High Park the previous night. A motorist spotted five men on the Grand Trunk Railroad Bridge near the park entrance. The citizen felt that the men were acting suspiciously, and they might be German saboteurs attempting to blow up the bridge.

The motorist drove into the park and flagged down the mounted constable patrolling the area. The officer investigated, saw the men on the railroad tracks, dismounted from his horse, and climbed the railway embankment on foot. At the sight of the officer, the men fled. The officer fired two warning shots into the air. The sound of gunfire only made the men run faster which caused the officer to fire at the individuals but he missed them in the growing darkness.

Another officer arrived on the scene and tried to follow the men while the first officer rode to the call box and sounded the general alarm. The five men were never found and there was no damage to the tracks or bridge. It was later thought that the men were tramps waiting to board a train.

PC George Wright. The first Toronto policeman to go on active service. Photograph, Toronto Telegram, *August 1914.*

The Toronto Police Horses Go to War

When Canada went to war in August 1914, the people of Toronto responded with patriotism and war fever. City council offered to donate fifty or one hundred city horses to the Canadian artillery. Mayor Hocken received a telegram from Sam Hughes, the Minister of Militia, thanking him for the offer. Colonel Morrison, the director of artillery, told the minister that "no better or finer contribution could be made to the service."[1]

A special city council meeting was called to facilitate the donation. The law did not permit the city to give its property away so special legislation in the form of an Order in Council had to be obtained from the Ontario Cabinet at Queen's Park. The city received the required permission and by August 26 the first city horses were passed on to the military.[2]

Major McDougall the officer commanding the 9th Canadian Field Artillery inspected all of the police horses and picked eighteen of the best for service with the battery. The horses were turned over to his command on August 27, 1914. The fact that the horses all went to the 9th Canadian Field Artillery was fitting as it was known in the newspapers as "The Toronto Battery." A number of the horses became officers' chargers due to their fine training.[3]

At least four Toronto mounted officers, William Connor, Thomas Dundas, Ernest Masters and Charles

Chalkin enlisted in the 9th Battery along with the horses. They proudly gave their occupations as mounted police constables on their attestation papers. Constable F. Davis joined the 9th at the same time, but it is not known if he was a mounted officer. Connor was appointed Battery Sergeant Major and later commissioned as a lieutenant. He was killed in action at the Somme on July 4,1916.

The horses were transported by train from Toronto to Camp Valcartier near Quebec City. No doubt these well-trained mounts were prized by the officers and men of the unit. On October 3, 1914 they sailed for England with the 33,000 men of the first Canadian contingent. The ships arrived in England eleven days later. The horses remained in the cramped holds of the ships for a few days longer before being unloaded.

They were taken by train to Salisbury Plain where the Canadians were being trained for the ordeal ahead. They lived in crude stables exposed to the wind, terrible cold, and rain which fell in record amounts that winter. The animals must have suffered terribly.

In February 1915, the horses were sent to France where they were loaded on box cars and taken to the Ypres Salient in Belgium. The 9th Battery was "in line" on April 22, 1915 when the Germans launched the first poison gas attack of the war. Canadians held the line despite the severe losses inflicted by German gas, artillery, and infantry attacks.

The 9th Battery was in the thick of the fighting. Fortunately one of the members was a chemist by trade and recognized the smell of the chlorine gas. The men were told to urinate into their handkerchiefs and then to breathe through them. This saved the unit from the worst effects of the gas.

French Colonial troops on the Canadian left fled after the initial gas attack leaving a large gap for the Germans to attack through. The men of the 9th fired over open sights at the oncoming Germans. Loading and firing so fast that the guns overheated and breeches seized. Finally under small arms and artillery fire the guns were ordered to withdraw. The horses brought into this inferno by the drivers saved the guns from capture.

The Canadians managed to hold back the German advance through the night of April 22nd and the day of April 23rd. The 9th Battery was in continual action in an exposed position at a village known as St. Julien, which had been heavily shelled by the Germans since dawn. The 9th Battery and the small garrison holding the village were running short of ammunition.

At Canadian Headquarters at Mouse Trap farm, Brigadier General Turner advised the men of the situation at St. Julien and the danger involved. He told the men that he would not ask anyone to attempt to enter the village, but, if soldiers wished to try, he would not stop them. Every man of the 9th volunteered to continue on to the main battery position.

After hearing the response of his men, Brigadier General Turner decided to allow only the first two crews to attempt the mission. He ordered an aide to take the names of the volunteers: then they were off at the gallop. Jim Grey, a member of the Battery recalled that *"arriving in St. Julien safely, a very irate officer popped out of a doorway and ordered them to 'get those goddamned horses out of here!' Unhooking and dumping the contents of the 'pill boxes' in the middle of the road, the boys told the officer where to go and headed back down the road."*

A little later Lieutenant Stan Lovelace wrote in his diary *"A 5.9 blitz (Artillery barrage) came in the afternoon so we did a 'horse artillery' move to the rear of the wood at Potijze. We signaled for the horses, now depleted by at least a third—both my dear "Paddy," a Toronto Police horse, and Speckles had been killed. The drivers came up at the gallop— elbows waving as they forgot the proper methods of riding and rode like cowboys and Indians. God bless them, they were just showing the rest of us they were in this too."*

The Batteries limbered up as the German shells increased in frequency and accuracy. The first gun took off across the field, down a ditch, then flew up onto the road with the gunners hanging on for all they were worth.

Lieutenant Lovelace's diary states, *"This move was coming off with gusto, a shell cut down a thin tree about six inches in diameter between the wagons. Now the horses got into this too and didn't even pause but went over the tree like jumpers. But one gun and limber wheels hit that tree. The gunners couldn't hold on, but flew into the air like trapeze artists."*[4]

We can only guess how many of the Toronto Police horses became casualties at this point in the battle, which was only half over. It is probable that very few of the horses that left Toronto were still alive by the end of April 1915, although the loss of the horses paled with the 5,000 casualties suffered by the Canadian Division during the spring of 1915; those horses that did survive faced almost four more years of warfare.

A post-war newspaper reported that "Mischief," an old time High Park Pet, ridden by Charlie Chalkin died at the front as well as "Colonel," a great favourite of the Deputy Chief. One Toronto police horse did beat the odds and was still alive when the war ended on November 11, 1918.[5]

The Chief Constable reported in his 1918 annual report that "I have recently been advised from the front that one of the artillery horses, a gift from the police department, has survived the war after four years of unbroken service without mishap. It is proposed to bring the animal back to Toronto where he deserves to pass the rest of his days in peace."[6]

The Board received a letter from Brigadier General Gunn at its meeting of the 8th of April, 1919. The General stated that the former police horse, "Bunny," would be returned to Canada if the City would pay the transportation expenses. The Board agreed to pay all of the costs, but before the arrangements could be made "Bunny" was sold to the Belgian Government. The Canadian Army had decided that only horses used by senior officers would be repatriated.[7]

1   The *Toronto Star*. August 22, 1914.
2   The *Toronto Star*. August 26, 1914.
3   Unknown Toronto newspaper c. 1924 (Possibly *Toronto Telegram*).
4   McWilliams, James and Steel, R. James. *Gas! The Battle for Ypres*, 1915. Vanwell Publishing Limited, St. Catharines, Ontario, 1985. Page 136.
5   Unknown Toronto newspaper c. 1924 (Possibly *Toronto Telegram*).
6   Chief Constables Reports. 1918.
7   Police Board Minutes. 1919.
8   Unknown Toronto newspaper c.1924 (Possibly *Toronto Telegram*).

The City of Toronto horses donated for military service, August, 1914. Photograph, City of Toronto archives, William James Collection. SC 244-822.

THE HONOUR ROLE OF TORONTO POLICE HORSES
WHO DIED IN THE GREAT WAR 1914-1918

DOVER	14 year old dark bay gelding purchased in 1905
CRUSADER	12 year old dark brown gelding purchased in 1908
MISTAKE	10 year old dark bay gelding purchased in 1909
MISCHIEF	11 year old bay gelding purchased in 1909
MATHEW	12 year old dark bay gelding purchased in 1909
BARRIE	10 year old dark bay gelding purchased in 1909
BRAMPTON	11 year old dark bay gelding purchased in 1909
POSTMASTER	9 year old bay gelding purchased in 1910
VANITY	9 year old bay mare purchased in 1910
JURYMAN	10 year old dark bay gelding purchased in 1909
SHERBROOKE	8 year old bay gelding purchased June 22, 1911
ST. PATRICK	8 year old bay gelding purchased in 1912
ST. DAVID	8 year old bay gelding purchased in 1912
ST. PAUL	8 year old brown purchased in 1912
CORONER	8 year old bay gelding purchased in 1912
VANGUARD	6 year old bay gelding purchased in 1912
ANCHOR	4 year old dark bay purchased in 1912
CANADA	6 year old bay mare purchased in 1914

The ages listed above refer to the age of the horse when donated.

Letters From The Front

The following letter was written by Mounted Constable George Brown, to his wife in January, 1915 while on active service during the War.

He had been assigned to the Markham Street Stable and at the time the letter was written, he was serving in Belgium with the Royal Field Artillery.

We have travelled on through the north of France and Belgium and all through the battle of Ypres, which is suppose to be the biggest battle in history. Anyone who has not been there can have no idea of the dastardly work of the Germans. It is simply awful to see the fine French and Belgian towns that have been shelled to the ground. But the Germans have paid a terrible price for it. Our artillery is splendid and has accounted for tens of thousands.

I am now with a gun detachment and our work is to fire at the German aeroplanes. We are credited with having brought down 17 German Aeroplanes since we came out here; that is pretty good work, but say, we have had some narrow escapes. We have had the aeroplanes drop bombs within a few yards of us. I am afraid there would not be much of us had they been a few yards nearer, but the nearest touch we had was at Ypres. We were in action there one morning when suddenly the German artillery got the range on us and their shells were bursting all around us. We were in a farmyard at the time, and I can tell you it did not take us long to get out of that. Just as we were coming out, a shell fell a few yards from me and killed and wounded ten of our horses. I have a piece of the shell now, but we were very lucky, as none of our men were killed.

I have slept in some funny places since I have been out here—stables, haystacks, farmhouses. The best of all was a brewery. I saw Princess Patricia's Regiment come through the other day and I also saw a policeman from No. 3 Division, Claremont Street; they were going to the firing line [deleted by military censor] miles from here. We have been here about a month now having a rest, and we have earned it, for we have been in the firing line ever since we have been out here.

I would rather fight until I dropped than see my wife and child in the power of these dastardly Germans, and we don't spare many of them for when we get a chance we send them to Kingdom come.[1]

George Brown

George Brown was born in England in 1883. He enlisted in the Royal Field Artillery and served for three years, probably seeing service in South Africa in the early 1900s. He joined the Toronto Police Department in November 1908 and transferred to the mounted unit.

At the outbreak of war he immediately re-enlisted in the Royal Field Artillery and returned to England. He was in France by September 1914, about a month after the war started, and took part in the retreat from Mons and the first battle of Ypres. He was honoured as being one of Toronto's few "Old Contemptibles" (called by the German Kaiser as England's' contemptible little army, i.e., "unprofessional").

1   *Toronto Telegram.* 12 February 1915.

This letter was written by Mounted Constable Thomas H. Dundas to his former landlady, June 1915, while on active military service.

He had been assigned to the Police Stable No. 2, Agnes Street. He was serving in Belgium as a Bombardier in the 9th Canadian Field Artillery.

As for us signalers, we have a very nerve racking job. We have to keep communication by phone with the trenches and battery and the wires keep breaking all the time by shell fire, so a man is running under shell and rifle fire all on his own, and believe me it is so lonesome when the shells are bursting all about, no one to speak to, but we go out now in twos and it is not so bad. I am not ashamed to say that I was scared almost to death sometimes. I have been in another big fight since Ypres, but it was child's play compared to that. Believe me if a man were made of iron he could hardly stand what we came through at Ypres, such sights I never want to see again. I had some pretty close calls, was hit by pieces of shell, but they were all spent so did no damage. A chum and I were going to the trenches one evening when a shell burst about four or five yards off, and I was sure that was the finish, but all the harm it did was to cover us with mud. Some French soldiers standing near were surprised to see us come out alive.[2]

Thomas Dundas was born in Ireland in 1885. He joined the Royal Inniskillen Fusiliers when he was 16 years old and served in South Africa. After eight years of service he was discharged from the army and joined the Royal Irish Constabulary where he spent two years before emigrating to Canada where he joined the Toronto police department in 1912.

When war was declared in 1914 he immediately signed up for active duty and accompanied the Toronto police horses to Europe with the 9th Canadian Field Artillery. He became the most decorated Toronto police officer to serve in World War One. He was awarded the Military Medal (M.M.) for "Bravery in the Field" in 1916. He received the Meritorious Service Medal (M.S.M.) in 1918 "In recognition of valuable services rendered with the Forces in France during the present War." He was honoured with a Mention in Dispatches

(MID) in 1919 after his name was submitted by General Sir Douglas Haig as "deserving of special mention."

He served with the 9th Field Battery for the duration of the war being wounded twice and rising to the rank of Battery Sergeant Major. He returned to the Mounted Unit in 1919 and was assigned to the Court Street station. The military sent a formal request to the police commission asking that he be allowed to continue to serve with the militia after the war but the request was denied. After being promoted to Patrol Sergeant in 1928, he was transferred from the Mounted Unit. He was promoted to full sergeant in 1937 and retired from the police service in 1950 at the age of 65. He died at his cottage 4 months later.

Thomas H. Dundas, M.M., M.S.M., M.I.D., 1885-1950.

2 *Toronto Telegram.* July 16, 1915.

Letters From The Front

The following letters were written by Mounted Patrol Sergeant Fred Tucker to Detective George Guthrie of the Toronto Police Force while on active service with the 4th Canadian Mounted Rifles.

Writing from "any old place in France," Sergeant Major Tucker of the 4th Canadian Mounted Rifles, formerly sergeant in the Mounted Unit tells of his experiences after he arrived at the battle front.

I got it in the foot, but fortunately came out of the trenches the next day, and I was able to fix it up. I can't walk very good, but I can ride alright and I have a lot of that to do just now. I didn't report sick so escaped going to the base.

We have been having a rather hot time of it for three days. The shell fire was simply 'pure hell' on both sides. I was watching our fellows bombarding a town all the afternoon and in the evening they turned on Fritz's trenches. Of course, he came back just as our artillery slackened, and as he thought we had gone to bed he made a night attack. I was in a bay of the trench. Col. Black, Capt. Sifton, Capt. McRay and three men were in the two bays when a high explosive shell burst just over and between the two bays.

Everyone was hit but me. Poor Mack was killed, besides three men. I was knocked over but wasn't hurt. I was so mad that I picked up one of the poor fellows rifles, jumped on the parapet, laid down and blazed away till I couldn't see a German. The range was only 200 yards from our trenches, and the starlights they threw up made it as light as day.

On the way back I felt my foot stiff. I don't know how or when it happened, but when I took my boot off it was full of blood. I had no business there, for I don't have to go in the trenches, but a fellow likes to be with the boys. Poor chaps, sometimes it's up to their knees in mud, but they are cheery and full of fight.

The British have lots of guns and ammunition now. The Huns got busy a few days ago with gas, but the gas helmets helped, and then the wind changed and the gas blew back over the enemy.

For spite they made an attack and it is reported not one got back alive. This is a great game.

Tucker saw a lot of his old friends in the 3rd Battalion including several police officers who left the force to do their bit for their country. Connors was riding one former police horse, "Charlie," which was once the mount of Tucker when he was in Toronto.[1]

———————————

In another letter from France, to Sergeant James Reeves of the Toronto police force, Sergeant Tucker reveals more experiences. He had been on leave for nine days, and gone away before all leave was cancelled. "I just got back in time to see our boys take 1,500 yards of trenches. It was glorious hell while it lasted."

After describing the trenches, listening posts and the joys of being bombarded, he adds: "Our regiment is some regiment. You should see them in action. God bless them, I love them. There are only about 150 of us left of those that came over with us, but we are the same old 4th C.M.R. They call us the 'Fighting Fourth'."

Tucker wrote that he was the only staff member left who was with the regiment in Toronto, and that the unit now had its third commanding officer.

Of the Ross rifle, he wrote: "It's the best target rifle in the world, but no good in this game. I've seen a fellow actually jump on the bolt to open the block, and then couldn't load, when the Lee Enfield was working like a charm under similar circumstances. The sights are too delicate, and so is the magazine. I've seen hundreds of them split in the barrel. In other words, they won't stand the work in trench warfare."[2]

1   *Toronto Telegram.* 12 January 1916.
2   *Toronto Telegram.* 21 March 1916.

Patrol Sgt Fred Tucker

Fred W. Tucker was born Canada in 1869. He enlisted in the Royal Canadian Regiment and served in the army for 3 years. He joined the Toronto Police Department in July of 1897. He was promoted to Patrol Sergeant in 1911 and served with the Mounted Unit.

He enlisted in the 4th Canadian Mounted Rifles in November of 1914 and was appointed the Regimental Sergeant Major. He was wounded in June 1916 and recommended for the Military Medal for "Bravery in the field." After the war he returned to the police service and was promoted to the rank of full sergeant in 1919.

LACROSSE GAME RIOT

On Saturday July 31, 1915 a lacrosse game took place between the Maitlands and Riverdale Clubs at Cottingham Street Park. A player was injured and a number of crowd members took exception to the opinions of the referee. One individual in particular was warned off the grounds a number of times by the foot constable assigned to patrol the park. The man eventually assaulted a second officer and was arrested.

The situation deteriorated and the crowd became more hostile. One individual was arrested for "inciting a riot" after he was heard telling members of the crowd to "rush the cops" and to "put the boots to them." Three men were arrested including one who kicked a police horse.

After hearing the evidence the magistrate summed up his position by saying, "Rowdyism. We must put a stop to that." He sentenced the man who assaulted the officer to $20.00 and costs, or ten days, and the man who kicked the horse received a fine of $5.00 and costs, or ten days.

Toronto Telegram. August 3, 1915.

Letters From The Front

Ernest Masters

1   *Toronto Telegram.* June 25, 1915.

The following letter was written by Mounted Constable Ernest Masters while serving as Signal Sergeant, 9th Canadian Field Artillery. It was written to Police Constable Tom Ross, June, 1915.

The watch that you gave me was the means of saving my wrist from a nasty wound during the battle of St. Jullian [sic]. *The watch was smashed but my wrist escaped without a scratch.* PC Masters was formerly a member of the Toronto Police Pipe Band and finished the letter by thanking PC Ross for sending him a picture of the Pipe Band.[1]

Ernest Masters was born in England in 1882, joined the 3rd Dragoon Guards in 1899 and fought in the Boer War. He was awarded the King and Queen's South African medals and discharged from the Dragoons after four years' service.

He joined the Toronto Police Department on February 1, 1911 and soon transferred to the Mounted Unit, and also became a piper in the Police Pipe Band.

When war was declared in 1914, Masters immediately enlisted for active duty and accompanied the donated police horses to Europe with the 9th Canadian Field Artillery. He was later awarded a commission and promoted to lieutenant in the signal corps. Upon returning to Toronto at the end of the war, he resumed his prior duties as a member of the Mounted Unit.

On July 16, 1922, he was promoted to patrol sergeant while remaining at the Mounted Unit. Later that year he was made secretary of the Toronto Police Silver Band.

In 1924 he was stationed at the Keele Street stables attached to No. 9 Division.

 **1915** The patrol wagon service was pleased with its new motorized vehicles as the phasing out of horse-drawn wagons began. By 1915, only two horse-drawn vehicles remained as an emergency reserve, and these were seldom used. The plan was to purchase one more motorized vehicle following which the police draught horses would be sold. The last wagon horse was sold in 1917. One unfortunate horse never lived to see his forced retirement: "Horace" had to be shot during the year, probably as a result of an accident.

No. 5 Station was built at Davenport Road and Belmont Street. It became Mounted Headquarters and would be used by the unit until 1968, when men and horses were moved to Sunnybrook Park. The police department rented a stable in No. 4 Division which was used by the officers who patrolled the Dundas East and Sherbourne Streets district known as "Cabbage Town," due to the number of cabbages grown in the gardens of the Irish immigrants who lived in the area

World War I dramatically affected the manpower of the police force, it lost eighty-three men to active military service. The twenty men assigned to the Mounted Unit were able to continue their duties, but on a reduced scale.

The Police Department, and the Mounted Unit in particular, assisted the military in its activities in Toronto. A number of parades were organised to help instill *esprit de corps* in the recruits and to stimulate recruiting. The *Toronto*

Telegram reported, on August 27, that the Labour Day parade of September 1 would include both the city's union men and soldiers. The parade left Queen's Park, led by five mounted police officers, and wound its way through to the Canadian National Exhibition.

At its meeting of September 21, the Police Commissioners sued a Don Clarke for stopping payment on a cheque he had tendered to purchase police mount "Bouncer." There is no record of why Clarke stopped payment, or if something was wrong with the horse. The lawsuit did go forward, and there is no record of a final result.

The *Toronto Telegram* of November 3 reported, "The prompt action of the mounted police patrol on duty above the C.P.R. tracks on Yonge Street averted what might have been a serious accident." A team of horses yoked to a heavy wagon was parked on Summerville Avenue when a train frightened them. The horses "ran away" at top speed towards Yonge Street.

Mounted Constable Tomenson who saw the team, stopped all traffic on Yonge Street before turning the charging animals north on Yonge Street as he galloped along side. Leaning over, he grasped the loose reins and "at great personal risk brought the horses to a stand still near the top of the hill." Citizens who witnessed the event had nothing but praise for the officer.[38c]

Constable William G. S. Connor

William G.S. Conner
1885-1916
Photograph, Toronto Police Museum.

William Connor was born in Ireland in 1885 and later emigrated to Canada where he enlisted in the Canadian Field Artillery. He left the military after seven years service, joined the Toronto Police Department in 1912, and was soon transferred to the Mounted Unit.

In August 1914 he volunteered to accompany the donated police horses on active service with the 9th Canadian Field Artillery and was immediately appointed the Regimental Sergeant Major of the Battery.

He went to France with the 1st Canadian Contingent and was later awarded a commission and promoted to Lieutenant. On July 4th, 1916 he was the forward observing officer in the front line trenches directing the fire from his battery onto the German positions. Later in the day he was severely wounded and evacuated from the trenches: he died the following day.

He was recommended for the Distinguished Conduct Medal.

The Temperance Parade and Riot

Prior to and during the First World War, there was a strong temperance movement in Ontario. Society was divided between those who wanted to drink and those who wanted to ban liquor entirely. The war gave politicians and temperance supporters the excuse needed to consider liquor prohibition as a wartime contingency.

Many members of the armed services were opposed. Right or wrong, liquor provided the soldiers with an escape from the realities of the war. Social drinking was an important pastime for those serving at the war front and away from their homes, in Canada or abroad.

By March 1916, the temperance crusade had collected a petition requesting prohibition be instituted in the province. The huge document contained over 825,000 signatures. Arrangements were made to hold a parade through Toronto on March 8th, 1916, to advertise the cause; the petition would then be presented to the Premier and his Cabinet at Queen's Park. People arrived by train from all over Ontario to take part in the procession, singing and carrying signs against the evils of drink. Two hundred and seventy police officers were assigned to keep order along the route, plus thirty more assigned to duties at the government buildings and grounds of Queen's Park.

The parade began at the Y.M.C.A., 40 College Street, two blocks to the east of Queen's Park, and featured the petition displayed in a large wagon while members of the crowd were given banners spread between two wooden poles to carry. The largest named "The half-mile-long banner" was in reality, approximately 500 feet.

Even before the parade began soldiers convalescing at the Military Hospital on the south side of College Street began hooting and booing. They produced their own banner, "We fought for you, why deprive us of our liberty?" They attempted to fix their banner to the parade's water wagon as it passed by the hospital, but were prevented by prohibitionists. A number of other soldiers came forward and restrained their comrades before a fight developed. The soldiers began singing a popular ballad of the era, "How Dry I Am!"

As prohibitionists passed near City Hall, a crowd of soldiers at James and Albert Streets booed the participants loud enough to drown out the cheers of the marchers.

The parade passed the armouries on University Avenue where approximately 1,000 soldiers and anti-prohibitionists lined both sides of the street. Soldiers continued to boo and jeer, and the odd one entered the street to obstruct the marchers. The real trouble began when the University Chorus and student contingent reached the roadway between the crowd of anti-prohibitionists. Many soldiers became enraged that these able-bodied young men were not serving in the army and began to throw snowballs and ice, some badly cutting participants about the face. A number of soldiers rushed into the crowd and tore up the prohibitionists' banners. Those who resisted were beaten with the poles which had previously carried the banners (now shredded).

The *Toronto Star* reported, "A mounted policeman rode among the crowd in an attempt to restore order. A soldier grasped him and threw him from the horse."[1] The *Globe* elaborated in its coverage of mounted policeman Tufts, "who made efforts to stave off the impending scene, but was dragged from his horse and badly hurt. He bled freely from two wounds in the head where he was struck by pieces of ice."[2]

The melee lasted for approximately fifteen minutes with the police powerless to stop it. Eventually Colonel Donald Duncan of the 134th Battalion had the "Fall In" sounded by his bugler and the soldiers returned to the armouries. Only one soldier ignored the call and the army provosts arrested him.

The parade continued to Queen's Park where the representatives entered the building and presented the petition to the Premier and Cabinet Ministers. They declared the day a great success for the cause of prohibition. Two police officers, twelve marchers and several soldiers were reported injured. Many others were slightly injured by the ice projectiles.

Chief Constable Grasette reported, "Nothing like what occurred was ever even thought of when we made our arrangements for the demonstration. All our plans were made with a view to handling of the street traffic and allowing it to cross through the marchers without hindrance. A handful of policeman would not be able to do much with 3,000 soldiers which I am informed gathered outside the armouries."[3] "We could have put more mounted men on who could have ridden through the crowds when there was any sign of trouble, but I doubt even then, with so many soldiers, that they could have done anything. Besides, with soldiers so numerous in Toronto we don't want to antagonize them, so we made no arrest at the time."[4]

The *Telegram* reported that soldiers blamed the mounted police for the troubles. Private Johnson stated that the soldiers only planned to jeer the crowd as a friendly "Joah." "If the mounted policeman had not run a soldier down there would not have been any trouble."[5] In contrast to this, Reverend Byron Stauffer reported that "The police at first were entirely helpless, and those who could not get a view of the situation thought it was a joke. What finally saved the day was the arrival of the mounted police."[6]

The military were embarrassed by what had occurred at the armouries. They reported that the men who had taken part were really "civilians in Khaki" as they had not received any training or discipline. Despite the soldiers' opposition, the Ontario Temperance Act was passed and the sale and consumption of potable liquor was banned for the duration of the war.

On April 25, Drum Major H.J. Chessell submitted a claim to the Police Board for damages suffered on March 8 when a police horse knocked him down. The Commissioners decided that a tumult was in progress at the time and the constable was doing his best to suppress it. Under the circumstances, they did not recognize Chessell's claim.[7]

1   *Toronto Star*. March 9, 1916.
2   *Globe*. March 9, 1916.
3   *Globe*. March 9, 1916.
4   *Toronto Telegram*. March 9, 1916.
5   *Toronto Telegram*. March 9, 1916.
6   *Toronto Star*. March 9, 1916.
7   Board of Police Commissioners Minutes. April 25, 1916.

1916

Inspector Henry Gilks was forced to retire from the Toronto Police Force after 29 years of service. His position was temporarily filled by Patrol Sergeant Herbert Little. Little had served with the Cape Mounted Police in South Africa for four and a half years before coming to Toronto in 1905 to join the Toronto Police Force.

Five horses were retired. They were worn out during the year and not replaced. Other horses were also reported to be approaching the end of their service careers. On December 29th, 1916 Police Mount "Edgeley," a 14-year-old dark bay was retired from the department. It is doubtful that any other police horse enjoyed the retirement experience this lucky horse had. Edgeley was purchased by the Toronto millionaire Sir Henry Pellatt for the sum of $100.00.

In 1906 Sir Henry had erected a showpiece stable and carriage house on property he owned at the top of Walmer Road Hill. By 1913 he had built and moved into the famous Toronto Landmark known as Casa Loma. The stable housed his prize collection of Clydesdales and Percherons, and former police mount, "Edgeley," who was probably used as a charger by Sir Henry, a high-ranking officer in the militia.[39] Sir Henry was a big man and no doubt a load to carry, but lucky "Edgeley" was able to spend his final days in the most luxurious horse accommodation in Toronto. Today the castle and stable are open to public view, and are one of the city's most charming sights, both inside and out.

With every new year more automobiles increased the congestion on Toronto Streets. In 1916 alone, 22 people were killed in motor vehicle accidents. Parking was also becoming such a major problem that Chief Grasette called the downtown area an "open air garage."[40]

As a wartime austerity measure, the Provincial Government passed the Ontario Temperance Act, outlawing the sale and distribution of alcoholic beverages. The Act probably had little direct effect on the Mounted Unit, however it did place great demands on the short-handed police force, which now had to help enforce this sometimes unpopular prohibition. The province would remain "dry" until 1927 when the unpopular law was repealed.

The Belmont Street Police Station was used as Mounted Headquarters from 1915 to 1968. Known as No. 5 Division until 1957, it was then renamed No. 57 Division. Once the Mounted Unit moved out, the stables were converted into an ambulance station. Photographs, Sgt Lorna Kozmik, 1998.

The Honour Roll of Toronto Police Mounted Officers Who Served in The Great War 1914–1918

The following list is the most complete possible. Some mounted officers may have been missed due to absence of records. Those listed below, with their police badge number, were serving with the Mounted Unit at the time of their enlistment.

Patrol Sergeant Fred Tucker	4th Canadian Mounted Rifles
PC Peter Bartley (141)	Canadian Field Artillery
PC Amos Bell (324)	20th Canadian Infantry
PC George Brown (9)	Royal Field Artillery
PC William Carr (296)	Royal Canadian Dragoons
PC Charlie Chalkin (28)	9th Canadian Field Artillery
PC William Connor (239)	9th Canadian Field Artillery
PC Thomas Crosbie (401) D.C.M..	3rd Divisional Ammunition Column
PC Thomas Hugh Dundas (448) M.M., M.S.M., MID	9th Canadian Field Artillery
PC Ernest Masters (439)	9th Canadian Field Artillery
PC Thomas Mitchell (44)	Canadian Field Artillery
PC Thomas H. Williamson (144)	2 Central Ontario Regiment.
PC George Wright (397)	Royal Field Artillery

*Private Thomas H. Williamson
Joined the Toronto Police Department in 1915 and enlisted in the 2nd Central Ontario Regiment in 1918.*

*Trooper William R. Carr
Joined the Toronto Police Department in 1915 and enlisted in the Royal Canadian Dragoons in 1918. He was wounded by machine gun fire when the Canadian cavalry was called into action in the closing days of the war.*

*Gunner Peter Bartley
Joined the Toronto Police Department in 1915 and enlisted in the Canadian Field Artillery, and served in France with the 32nd Battery.*

Constable Charlie Chalkin

Charles Chalkin was born in England in 1887. He served with the Royal Army Medical Corps (Volunteers) for three years before emigrating to Canada.

He joined the Toronto Police Department in 1911 and transferred to the Mounted Unit soon after. He volunteered for active military service immediately at the outbreak of war, served with the 9th Canadian Field Artillery and accompanied the donated police horses to England.

He was transferred to the Canadian Military Mounted Police and was assigned to the Paris, France detachment. His duties included patrolling the streets of Paris on horseback to keep order among Commonwealth Troops.

At the end of the war, he returned to Toronto and was reassigned to mounted duties. Promoted to Patrol Sergeant in 1924, he was placed in charge of the Pape Avenue Stable. In 1939 upon retirement, he was still an active member of the Mounted Unit.

Photographs, Toronto Police Museum.

Charles Chalkin

Sergeant George Smith
Joined the police force in 1914 and was assigned to the Mounted Unit. He enlisted in the Canadian Field Artillery in 1915 and was discharged from the Army in 1919. He returned to The police department and mounted duties.

Private T. M. Mitchell
Joined the police force in 1913 and was assigned to the Mounted Unit. He enlisted in the Canadian Field Artillery in 1915 and was wounded on November 1, 1917 at Passchendaele.

The Chief Constable reported that the mounted officers continued their patrols, escorts and other details "without interruption by the weather or other causes."[41] The Toronto Street Railway employees went on strike during the year, but unlike the 1902 strike, no problems emerged.

On February 23, the Great War Veterans held their first major parade in Toronto and it was billed as a living plea for recruits. Three mounted officers led the parade and cleared the masses of people from the parade's path. Cheering crowds lined the route as the marchers paraded west on Bloor Street, south on Yonge Street and west on Queen Street to the armouries on University Avenue.

Herbert Little was promoted to full Sergeant on November 1, 1917 and remained in charge of the Mounted Unit. A sad event ensued when police mount "Ontario" died of pneumonia on September 7.

A new duty band was issued to officers; it was similar to that worn by the Metropolitan Police in London, England, and was worn on the left sleeve when an officer was on duty. A citizen could then determine if a uniform policeman was officially available to assist or not. This addition was important as officers were encouraged to wear uniforms while travelling to and from their shifts.

Two pictures of a mounted officer and a foot officer in Rosedale Valley Ravine, c. 1917.
Photographs, courtesy of Richard Gerry.

Sergt. T. D. Crosbie, 3rd C.D.A.C., formerly a member of the Toronto police force, and Sergt. C. L. Stubberfield.

Future Mounted Inspector Crosbie in France, 1916. Note the mud on his uniform.
Photograph, Toronto World, January 21, 1917.

The March King, John Phillip Sousa, (left) leading the United States Marine Corps Band up University Avenue, c. 1916. Mounted officers ride both sides of the street to keep the crowds back. The officer on the right appears to be Inspector Gilks. Note the man who is watching from the tree on the left. Photograph, City of Toronto Archives, William James Collection. SC 244-2246.

1918

The Mounted Unit was reduced to fifteen members due to the resignations of officers leaving for active military service. At the start of the year, an officer's working day was reduced to eight hours. This benefit was later withdrawn because of wartime manpower shortages. Military police maintained a detachment in Toronto and assisted the understaffed police force in matters to do with soldiers. A number of special constables were hired for limited duty, but the experiment had little success and was discontinued.

Serious rioting took place in Toronto in August. The police, taken by surprise, could not prevent a great deal of damage being done. A thirteen-day inquiry was held and a number of officers were removed from the force. None of the officers were members of the Mounted Unit.

On October 18, PC Raney of the Pape Avenue Stable was patrolling on Danforth Avenue when he saw a car that had been reported stolen from 39 Cecil Street. He confirmed the licence number against the list of wanted cars mounted officers were required to record. The *Toronto Telegram* reported that PC Raney "spurred after it" and gave chase along the Danforth. As the car began to increase the distance between them, PC Rainey dismounted and commandeered a car to continue the pursuit which he did as far as Coxwell Avenue and Queen Street East where he lost sight of the vehicle. The car was later found abandoned on Major Street.

With a sigh of relief heard around the world, the First World War ended on November 11th. When the Armistice was announced, the people of Toronto took to the streets to rejoice. Celebrations lasted most of the night, but very little trouble was reported. No doubt mounted officers were ready to respond to any repeat of the previous rioting.

The Police Commissioners received a claim for damages from a Reverend D.A. Hamilton of Sutton, Ontario. He asked for $12.40 for damage done to his car's electric battery (mounted on the outside of the car) caused by a kick from a mounted policeman's horse on Yonge Street. As Reverend Hamilton was on the roadway and not at a crossing, the Commissioners did not consider themselves liable and refused to pay.[41a]

The August 1918 Street Riots

On August 2, a number of returned soldiers and sympathetic citizens ran amok in the streets of Toronto. At approximately 5:45 p.m., a returned soldier got into a dispute with a foreign-born waiter at the White Star Café. There were strong anti-foreigner feelings among the soldiers and other residents of the city. The soldier left the café and at approximately 6:00 or 6:15 p.m. returned accompanied by a group of soldiers. They attacked the restaurant. The riot at the café was over by 7:15 p.m. and all was quiet.

Seventy-three policemen were on duty, policing a city of thirty-two square miles with five-hundred-and-thirty miles of streets. The situation was complicated by the fact that the police believed that a hands-off policy towards soldiers was in effect, leaving military authorities to take care of their own.

Rioting flared up again in the downtown at 10:00 p.m., and while the police did their best to disperse the crowds, a number of premises were damaged. At 2:00 a.m., carloads of soldiers and supporters drove into No. 6 Division and attacked restaurants in the Parkdale area.

The acting deputy chief constable had contacted the military authorities earlier in the evening, requesting assistance but the provost marshall said he would not act unless the Riot Act was read. Instead of sending the military police, the provost marshall sent one hundred soldiers armed with rifles and bayonets and twenty five rounds of ball ammunition each. The military commander also requested that a magistrate be assigned to read the Riot Act to the men.

Surprised police officers refused. They preferred to deal with the crowds, rather than have ball ammunition being used on the streets of Toronto. Why the military responded in this way was a mystery. The police and military police had experienced a good working relationship throughout the war.

Rioting flared again on Saturday at Court Street Police Station where a crowd of several thousand people gathered to demand the release of a man who had been arrested in the initial melee. The police reacted by sending officers from the station to disperse the crowd.

The *Toronto Star* described the dispersal of the crowd on Court Street. *The police made their first charge and in the next few minutes nearly a hundred civilians were laid out on the sidewalk bleeding and groaning. The officers used their batons mercilessly on everybody within reach. The crowd moved away reforming at Adelaide and Victoria Streets and growing in size as a group of veterans were giving the police a hard time. Just as it seemed the small number of foot police were powerless to stop the crowd a dozen mounted officers appeared on the scene and cut their way through chasing the mob along Victoria Street.*[1]

At this the leader of the veterans moved up near the Arcade and shouted to his companions to 'fall in'. Nearly a score had mustered, but they had hardly formed up when the mounted men rode amongst them, and one veteran received a crack on the head with the thick canes carried by the officers on horseback. This incensed the veterans and a general uproar followed.[2]

Soldiers and supporters became inflamed with anger and looked for bricks and other projectiles to throw. They moved up to Yonge and Richmond Streets as fast as they could. "The mounted men were going at a trot by this time and the crowd went helter-skelter in all directions. The horsemen took to the sidewalks and their brandished canes were sufficient warning for the tardy ones to get a move on."[3]

The crowd of several thousand continued to move north on Yonge Street followed by the mounted policeman who "put some pep" into the people by driving a wedge into their ranks. There were so many people that the crowd refilled the wedge as soon as they withdrew.[4]

The angry veterans reformed at "Shrapnel Corner" in the Yonge and College Streets area where the police charged into the mass striking many with their batons. "Mounted policemen rode in and added to the general confusion, as the mob rushed madly for the nearest door, alley or place of refuge available. A hail of bombs from some aerial aviator could not have made a more general stampede."[5]

While the *Toronto Star* reporter was interviewing victims of this charge, a second charge took place across the street. "The police on foot charged into the crowd using their batons freely, while mounted police rode along near the curb hitting out with their whips left and right."[6]

While all this was going on a second crowd of three or four thousand had gathered at Dundas and Terauley Streets. A veteran was speaking to the crowd about the returned men's grievances "until his speech was brought to an abrupt halt by the appearance of the mounted police.

There was a rush for shelter every time the officers on horseback made their appearance. Officers on foot could make little progress in such a crowd."[7]

Newspaper reports stated that the rioting continued until late in the night with the biggest battle occurring at Yonge and Queen Streets. It seems that by this time some of the police officers "lost their heads" and the scene degenerated into a "Police Riot." Foot police, backed up by mounted units, continued to use their batons to disperse the crowds leaving a number of innocent people injured. One man claimed he was struck on the head with a baton and badly injured. He went to the Court Street Station to complain and was told, "I had no right to be on the street at that time of night. I told the inspector that I was walking home peacefully, but all the satisfaction I got was a rough reply to 'beat it'."[8]

By the end of the night ten persons had been arrested and five hundred injured, thirty five suffering from serious injuries by police clubs. The *Toronto Star* reported that people alleged that "woman and children, in many cases, were badly beaten with clubs at the hands of police who were battling the crowd indiscriminately."[9]

Police Station No. 2 on Dundas Street. The crowd made three attempts to storm the station and free all prisoners. Drawing, Toronto Police Museum.

A synopsis of what took place on the night of August 3, 1918.

18:45:	Fight at College and Yonge Streets.
19:05:	Crowd raids the Court Street Police Station.
19:30:	Fight at Victoria and Queen Streets.
20:20:	Crowds raid the Dundas Street West Police Station.
20:50:	Fight at Yonge and College Streets.
21:30:	Second attempt to storm the Dundas Street West Police Station.
22:20:	Third attempt to storm the Dundas Street West Police Station.
22:50:	Fight at Elizabeth Street.
23:15:	Mob hurled back in fierce fight with police.
23:30:	Yonge Street cleared from Queen to Albert Streets.
00:15:	Fight at College and Yonge Streets.
01:15:	Fight on Yonge Street.
01:45:	Yonge Street cleared from Queen to College Streets.
02:15:	Yonge Street restaurants cleared out and closed.

The first Toronto police car, c. 1913. The mechanization of the police department may have led to the disbanding of the Mounted Unit. The need for horses in crowd management situations like the 1918 riot ensured that Toronto would continue to maintain a mounted unit. Photograph, Toronto Police Museum.

A number of mounted officers were injured during the riot including Patrol Sergeant Ernest Hobson who was struck on the head by a flying brick, Constable Robert C. Rogerson who had his horse rear up and fall on him injuring his thigh and Constable George Brown who was also struck by bricks.

The following night the police were out in force, determined to prevent a repeat of the riots. Police dispersed stone-throwing crowds without serious damage or injury reported.

A number of soldiers complained of being struck by police officers during the riots. An inquiry was called to look into the riots and two inspectors, one patrol sergeant and one constable lost their jobs. The Board of Inquiry also noted the meritorious performance of some officers during the riots. Five officers were promoted and seven others received merit marks.

The constable who was fired was active in the police union movement. Identified as a union man to the tribunal officers as he entered the room, they immediately ordered him dismissed before any evidence was heard for or against him. The newspapers reported that the tribunal officers felt he did not possess significant intelligence to be a police officer. The unjust treatment of this officer was the spark that led to Toronto's only police strike.

The liberal use of batons by the police would have a significant impact in Toronto. Just over a month after the inquiry was completed, Frank McCullough would be arrested for the murder of Detective Williams. It was Williams's alleged use of a baton that helped to generate public support for his accused killer and the rioting that preceded his execution.

The riot and inquiry also called into question the competency of Toronto's Police Commissioners. After the inquiry was completed, the *Toronto Telegram* ran daily stories criticizing the inquiry's process and detailing how other North American city police departments were administered. Within a year members of the police commission would be replaced and some reforms would begin.

1   *Toronto Star.* August 6, 1918.
2   ibid.
3   ibid.
4   ibid.
5   ibid.
6   ibid.
7   ibid.
8   ibid.
9   ibid.

Patrol Sgt Hobson of the Mounted Unit was praised in the newspapers for the testimony that he gave at the inquiry into the riot. He was promoted to full sergeant within days of the inquiry.

A mounted officer and foot officer standing in front of a call box, probably in High Park, c. 1918. The foot officer is wearing an arm band on his right sleeve with his badge number and a duty band on his left sleeve indicating that he is on duty. He is also wearing an external leather baton case on his right side. Photograph, Toronto Police Museum.

The 1918 Toronto Police Strike

Extensive dissatisfaction was prevalent throughout Canadian society in late 1918. Toronto Police officers, like other workers, had been coping with rapid price increases due to wartime inflation while having all requests for pay adjustments refused. In 1917 the Toronto Police Commissioners gave the officers a temporary war bonus, then voted to double their own salaries, while refusing the request of the force for a permanent raise.

Because of the wartime manpower shortages, the Police Commission cancelled the officers' weekly day off which extended their duties to seven days a week at increased hours, meaning weeks without letup. Wages remained the same despite the increased work schedule, while other minor grievances involving working conditions and promotion helped to alienate the lower and middle ranks.[1]

A number of secret meetings were held to discuss the formation of a union. A number of police forces in Canada had already become unionized. Constables organizing the Toronto union approached the Trades and Labour Congress and requested help. The Police Commission viewed any attempt to unionize as a mutiny rather than an industrial action.[2]

On December 3, 1918, a deputation of officers arrived at the Police Commission to request the Toronto Police Union be recognized. That did not happen due to the resistance of the Police Commission. Over the next few weeks the officers moderated their demands seeking an agreement. The Police Commission was prepared to create an end to union demands once and for all.

On December 17, the Police Commission invited twelve union members to a meeting and enquired if they planned to continue the attempt to certify a police union. The men answered in affirmative, and all were fired on the spot. Rank and file policemen held a meeting, and demanded that the officers be reinstated or the commissioners would face a strike. The twelve officers were not rehired and a four-day police strike began.

The only officers officially permitted to remain on duty by the strike committee were the mounted officers, charged with the caring of horses. In order to preserve public support, squads of striking police officers responded to police service calls dressed in civilian clothes. Picket lines were set up but no one who wanted to enter the property, including non-striking officers, was interferred with. Inspectors in charge of stations did not issue revolvers to those lower rank officers who reported to work despite the strike.

There were no increased problems across the city as a result of the strike partly because the striking policemen were very visible and responded to incidents. The other reason was the not-too-subtle message from military authorities who had mounted troopers from the Royal Canadian Dragoons paraded up and down Yonge Street.

The strike was ended by the Provincial Government when it appeared that other civic unions were about to walk out in support of the police. In one incident, a street railway driver refused to move his car until a non-striking policeman got off.[3] As a result of the agreement the twelve dismissed officers were rehired and a Royal Commission was appointed to look into all grievances.[4]

The Royal Commission rejected police unionism and the right to collective bargaining. Most of the grievances raised were dismissed or ignored. However, officers were permitted to form a police association to air their complaints. The new Toronto Police Association was not allowed to be affiliated with any union or The Trades and Labour Congress. The strike also led to changes in the personnel on The Police Commission which, despite the new faces, continued to favour management in industrial disputes for decades to come.

What would have happened had the police officers been allowed to form a union affiliated with The Trades and Labour Congress? Would police response to labour disputes during the 1920s and 30s have been different? Perhaps. We'll never know, but it might well have changed the future history of union/management relationships in the Province of Ontario.

1   Leibaers, Jan K. *The Toronto Police Strike of 1918.* Major research paper submitted to Professor N. Rogers, September 1990. Page 6.
2   Leibaers, Jan K. *The Toronto Police Strike of 1918.* Major research paper submitted to Professor N. Rogers, September 1990. Page 25.
3   Leibaers, Jan K. *The Toronto Police Strike of 1918.* Major research paper submitted to Professor N. Rogers, September 1990. Page 66.
4   Jackson, Basil. *To Serve and Protect, The History of the Metropolitan Toronto Police Force, 1834-1970.* Unpublished, 1970. Page 70.

The Winnipeg General Strike – 1919

Canada experienced civil unrest across the country following the end of the First World War. Both the returned soldiers and those who had worked hard and done without on the home front wanted the better life that they had been promised. Labour unrest and massive strikes were the result of this discontent. The largest, and by far the most important strike, took place in Winnipeg, Manitoba, in May 1919.

A general strike was called and some thirty thousand essential workers joined the industrial workers, and brought the city to a virtual halt. The city police sympathized with the strikers and were all dismissed from their jobs. The Royal North West Mounted Police and special constables took over policing duties in the city. A mounted troop of policemen was dispatched to the city and became the first R.N.W.M.P. mounted detail to be used in crowd control.

Authorities feared most that the strike leadership had been infiltrated by revolutionaries. Such fears were not totally unrealistic when you consider that Canada had troops in Russia at the same time trying to support the recognized Russian government fighting against communist revolutionaries. Tens of thousands of disenchanted war veterans roamed Canada: they would make superb fighters in any organized revolt.

The strikers planned to stage a large parade through the streets of Winnipeg on June 18. When it began, the mounted policemen were used to clear strikers from the streets. The situation degenerated to the point where some officers were pulled from their horses by demonstrators. Mounted policemen drew their revolvers and fired into the crowd to protect their dismounted colleagues from serious injury. A few days after this violence, the strike was called off.

The extreme bitterness of the event and the sheer numbers of people that heeded the call to walk out on strike upset and frightened the establishment right across Canada. It was this upheaval coupled with other post-war events that convinced men like Brigadier General Dennis Draper, the future chief constable of Toronto, that the labour movement (Communists especially) had to be subdued to preserve Canadian democracy and its British traditions.

During the industrial disputes of the early 1920s the R.C.M.P. (formerly R.N.W.M.P.) kept mounted troops for crowd control duties at nine strategic locations from Ottawa to Vancouver. By 1930, this had reduced to five mounted troops located at Rockcliffe (Ottawa), Vancouver, Edmonton, Winnipeg and Regina. These squads travelled to areas where industrial disputes or unemployment marches where taking place.

The Royal Canadian Dragoons also provided strike details during the 1920s. Mounted troopers were sent to help local police forces at a number of locations in Quebec and the Maritimes. The largest detail attended was the British Empire Steel and Coal Company strike on Cape Breton. The use of both military and police horses to maintain social order was reaching its peak in Canada during the post-war years.

R.N.W.M.P. mounted officers (later R.C.M.P.) on the streets of Winnipeg. Photograph, Manitoba Archives.

The Frank McCullough Riots – 1919

On November 19, 1918, acting Detective Frank Williams was murdered in Cross's Livery stable at King and Bathurst Streets. He had gone to the stable to investigate a report that two men in a rented buggy had tried to sell some stolen furs earlier in the day. Williams waited at the stable until the men returned with the rented buggy.

While investigating the men in a back office, a scuffle broke out and Detective Williams was shot and killed by Frank McCullough. During the scuffle, McCullough had been struck numerous times by Williams's police baton. When the case went to trial, McCullough claimed that he had fired his gun at Williams in self-defence as he thought Williams was going to beat him senseless.

The murder of the police officer came just after the inquest into the August 1918 riots. During the investigation, the police use of batons on defenceless citizens and wounded soldiers generated a distrust of the Toronto police within the community. Many citizens thought that the police were too quick to use their batons; and maybe McCullough had been justified in defending himself. Other factors including inaccurate portrayals of McCullough in the press made him a hero to the disenfranchised in Toronto.

At the end of the trial, Frank McCullough was sentenced to hang for the murder of Detective Williams. Some people felt that the sentence was unjust and protested at the Don Jail during the days leading up to the hanging. On June 12th 1919, large crowds began to gather in Riverdale Park in anticipation of the execution, scheduled for the following day.

The crowd outside the jail called for a reprieve of the sentence. The warden at the jail, Henry Addy, became alarmed at the crowd's size and mood. He telephoned Chief Constable Grasette requesting that police reinforcements be sent as he felt the crowd might soon storm the jail. Mounted officers were dispatched to the jail and began to patrol outside the prison fence.

Around midnight McCullough appeared at the window of his cell. The crowd went wild. The police made two unsuccessful attempts to clear the people from Riverdale Park. More mounted officers arrived at the scene from the outlying stables. "As the crowd became decidedly hostile in character, bricks began to fly above the heads of the police and the order to charge was given to the mounted men. The mounted police obeyed the order at the gallop, only to be driven back to the jail walls with volleys of missiles."[1]

Detective Frank Williams. Photograph, Toronto Police Museum.

Sixty additional foot police officers arrived at the jail and were taken inside the building. There were many returned soldiers in the crowd. Military police were also sent to the jail to assist the hard-pressed Toronto police officers with the soldiers.

As more foot officers arrived, they were assigned to work with the mounted men. "With their numbers strengthened, at last, by sheer persistency, rallying, the mounted police pushed a good portion of the crowd out onto Broadview Avenue at the back of the jail and onto Gerrard Street at the front. Here a pitched battle took place, ending in many arrests including returned soldiers."[2]

"The worst of the violence occurred at the intersection of Gerrard Street and Broadview Avenue. As the mounted police 'charged down Broadview and the crowd ran, a group at the intersection turned on the police and bricks, stones and milk bottles were flying in all directions'."[3] The enraged crowd tore a signboard from a building and threw it at the mounted officers as they advanced on the crowd.

The violence ended at 3:00 a.m. when the last of the crowd members dispersed or were arrested. Two mounted officers, Constables Raney and Milton had received head injuries and had fallen from their horses. Several foot officers were also injured in the riot.

At approximately 8:00 a.m., June 13, 1919 the sentence was carried out and Frank McCullough was executed. The hostility directed towards the Toronto police was a sure sign that changes had to be made with police service in the city. These changes were already underway as a result of the August 1918 riot inquest and the Royal Commission into the 1918 police strike.

The story of Frank McCullough is told in the book *No Tears to the Gallows* by Mark Johnson, an excellent account of the murder, trial and execution. The book also shows what happens when a police force loses its legitimacy in the eyes of a significant portion of the community that it serves.

1   Johnson, Mark. *No Tears to the Gallows.* McClelland & Stewart Inc., Toronto. 2000.
2   Johnson, Mark. *No Tears to the Gallows.* McClelland & Stewart Inc., Toronto. 2000.
3   Johnson, Mark. *No Tears to the Gallows.* McClelland & Stewart Inc., Toronto. 2000.

The Mounted Unit at Hart House, University of Toronto, 1919. Front: Patrol Sgt Fraser, Inspector Little, Patrol Sgt Crosbie. Photograph, Toronto Police Museum.

1919

Unlike the manner in which the Toronto Board of Police Commissioners dealt with some of the officers, it continued to show a fair amount of concern for the horses. At the meeting of March 4, the Police Commissioners discussed a letter from a Mr. Frank Stark who offered $30.00 to purchase police mount "Punch." The Board decided to accept the offer as the horse "was old and needed a good home."[41b]

A Mrs. Dunlop wrote to the Police Commissioners in April requesting compensation for damage to her dress, which was caused by a police horse kicking her in the knee when the street was crowded with people watching a parade of returning troops. The Board voted to give her a gratuity of $15.00 with no admission of liability.[41c]

The Third Canadian Battalion, the Toronto Regiment, arrived in Toronto on April 23, prior to being demobilized. They detrained at the Canadian Pacific Railway Station at Yonge Street and McPherson Avenue in midtown Toronto, where the Mounted Unit and a detachment of Royal Canadian Dragoons stood ready to escort the soldiers on a parade through the downtown streets of Toronto.

The band of the Governor General's Body Guard (later the Horse Guards) led the parade playing, "Pack Up Your Troubles." The Mounted Unit rode in front of the soldiers on their parade down Yonge Street. "Both sides of the street were lined with spectators; the windows were filled with people; more people stood on the house tops to watch; and there were even some men and boys perched in trees along the route."[42] This was probably one of the most thrilling parades ever led by a mounted officer.

The soldiers were taken to Queen's Park and then to Varsity Stadium where they were reunited, in some cases after a four-and-a-half-year absence, with their friends and family. Toronto's mounted unit also had the honour of leading the 75th Battalion through the streets of Toronto when it arrived home after three years overseas. Many more

The Mounted Unit at Hart House, University of Toronto, c 1919. The first troop is led by Sgt (later Inspector) Little and Patrol Sgt Fraser. The second troop is led by Patrol Sgt Crosbie.
Photograph, Toronto Police Museum.

parades would follow as soldiers arrived to be demobilized.

The price of horse forage and shoeing continued to increase with no end of the serious inflation in sight. The Chief Constable recommended to the Police Commission that the Mounted Unit be increased by at least three constables. He also recommended that a stable be built at No. 9 Station to facilitate patrols in the city's west end.

The Police Commission paid the cost of maintaining telephones in the homes of its inspectors in charge of divisions. At its meeting of July 15, the Board voted to cover the same cost at the residence of Sergeant Little, the officer in charge of the Mounted Unit to help him to remain in touch with the unit during his off hours.[42a]

The *Toronto Star*, August 21, reported that record crowds were expected at the 1919 Canadian National Exhibition and that Inspector Beatty would be in charge of the Toronto Police Exhibition detachment. Three sergeants would be assigned to the fair, one on station duty, one at the

Grandstand and the other at the east end loop (streetcar stop). Two patrol sergeants were assigned to patrol the exhibition grounds along with fifty uniform constables, fifty special duty plainclothes men, two police ambulance men and twenty detectives. The contingent would be rounded off with ten mounted men to patrol the grounds.

The Prince of Wales, the future Edward VIII, visited the Canadian National Exhibition in August and returned to the city in October. His visit to the "Ex" brought out the largest crowds the mounted officers had ever had to handle. Maintaining a passage through the crowds was a difficult task and the manner in which it was done brought official commendation.

The crowd was so thick, that after the Prince dismounted from his horse, he was compelled to climb a fence in order to leave the Exhibition grounds. He was provided with a number of mounted escorts during his stay in Toronto.[43]

The *Toronto Star* of August 26 reported that the large crowds, which had come out during the Princely visit, placed a severe strain on the personnel of the Toronto Police Force. On the 26th alone, the police furnished officers, including uniform constables, plainclothes men, detectives and the Mounted Unit for over a dozen events. August 25 had been an even busier day at the exhibition. The police also handled enormous individual crowds in different parts of the city.[44]

A more serious concern to the city administrators was the increasing unrest among trade union members and returned soldiers. The Chief Constable requested that the police force be increased in size to deal with potential problems as strikes were taking place all across Canada. The most vivid example was the Winnipeg General Strike where the entire City Police Force was fired for sympathizing with the strikers. Many citizens feared a general strike which would shut down the City of Toronto. The only major strike that did occur during 1919 was a thirteen day walk-out by Toronto Street Railway employees. There was no violence or other serious occurrences as a result of the strike.

New equipment was issued to Toronto Police officers, their first battery-operated flashlights and waterproof great-coats. No doubt the mounted officers were the most grateful recipients of the modern rubber raincoats. All officers were also issued with a police wallet and badge to be used for official identification purposes only. Officers below the rank of inspector assigned to motor vehicle duty, were issued a new type of forage cap (similar to the one worn today) . The "Bobby" style helmet remained part of the regular dress for mounted and foot patrol officers.

1920

Chief Constable Grasette resigned on December 18, 1920 and was replaced by Deputy Chief Samuel J. Dickson. One of the new chief's first accomplishments was the introduction of a system of semaphore signal lights for traffic control which were operated by a constable on foot. The new system relieved mounted men of their traffic point duties at most major intersections.

In his first report to the Board of Police Commissioners, Chief Dickson reported that the Mounted Unit horses and equipment had been kept in first-class condition. He felt that the men assigned to this duty showed a great interest in their responsibilities. Obviously a friend of the unit, he requested that this "important branch of the service" be increased thirty percent from its roster of 22 men.[45]

During the 1920s, mounted officers began referring to themselves as the "Senior Service," perhaps to express their feelings about the new motor vehicles which were beginning to take precedence within the force.

Sergeant Herbert Little was promoted to the rank of Inspector on May 1, 1920 and remained at the Mounted Unit as the officer in charge. Two horses were sold during the year and two remounts purchased at prices that remained about the same as the previous year. The price of feed was dropping.

The City of Toronto purchased land adjoining No. 9 Police Station on Keele Street, because the chief constable wanted a stable capable of equipping six horses attached to the station. This facility would house the men and horses charged with patrolling High Park and the surrounding area.

Toronto continued to rapidly grow in population with the post-war immigration boom. City council approved the hiring of 150 additional police officers to bring the total strength of the Toronto police force to 893 men. (The chief constable had requested that the force be brought up to a strength of 1,000 men to deal with the new growth and anticipated labour unrest.) There were a number of labour problems during 1920. The most notable occurrence being a three day Toronto Transit workers' strike.

◈ 1921 The Mounted Unit was increased in size with the addition of six more officers.

The police department also purchased eleven new remounts while disposing of only three horses. The price of horse feed declined considerably through the year. The chief constable reported to the Police Commission that Service horses had been free from sickness or accidents, and the equipment had been kept in excellent condition. He complemented work of the staff of the Mounted Unit and commented on their continued interest in their work.

The Chief continued negotiating to have a stable built at No. 9 Station. The west end of the city was expanding rapidly and he wanted mounted men stationed closer to their western posts. The police department issued a new revolver during the year—32 Calibre Colt Police Positive.

Mounted officers provided regular patrols at the Woodbine Race Track where they were active regulating the parking of automobiles. They also regulated the parking at the Canadian National Exhibition where they also did "valuable work patrolling the grounds." One newspaper reported that mounted officers "may often be seen riding the grounds of the Exhibition with a lost child in the saddle in front of them." The officers were also assigned regular beats as they patrolled the parks, the ravine districts and the outlying residential areas.[46]

"Pussyfoot" Johnson

On Sunday, April 10, 1921, the Temperance speaker "Pussyfoot" Johnson came to Toronto to speak at Massey Hall, and the Metropolitan United Church at Queen and Church Streets. Toronto was one stop on a North American tour that had been drawing huge crowds wherever Johnson spoke, and was no exception with thousands of people both for and against prohibition coming to the event.

Inside Massey Hall, a number of yelling matches took place between individual "Wets" and "Drys." Police were kept busy ejecting the most vocal of "Pussyfoot's" opponents from the building. On the street, the crowd of several thousand people continued to grow and to make their verbal opposition to the Ontario Temperance Act loudly known.

Deputy Chief Geddes, in charge of the police response, called out seventy foot officers, sixteen mounted men and twenty plainclothes men. As the police removed the ejected men from Massey Hall, the crowd of "Wets" filling Shuter and Victoria Streets was becoming increasingly agitated. The *Globe* reported that police managed to prevent serious problems from occurring outside Massey Hall. As tempers grew with the size of the crowd, a squad of mounted police cleared protesters and observers alike from Victoria Street starting at Queen Street, to as far north as Shuter Street.[1]

The *Toronto Telegram* reported that a number of police officers were struck by stones and other projectiles thrown by the more vicious elements in the crowd. Police arrested a few citizens on a charge of inciting to riot, but no civilians were reported injured.[2] To add to the confusion, the fire department responded to a false fire alarm called in at the corner of Yonge and Shuter Streets. Later in his career, Inspector Crosbie would tell a reporter that the largest crowds he had ever worked were those that came out for the appearance of "Pussyfoot" Johnson.

1. *The Globe*, Monday, April 11, 1921.
2. The *Toronto Evening Telegram*, Monday, April 11, 1921.

The Unemployment Parade

On Monday, April 25, 1921, a couple of rallies were held in Toronto sponsored by the Committee for the Unemployed, which was protesting the lack of jobs and a general dissatisfaction with all government remedies. Approximately seven hundred demonstrators met in the morning at the bandstand at the rear of Queen's Park. Representatives of the group attended a meeting with members of the Provincial Cabinet inside the building.

Later, about three thousand persons gathered in front of Toronto City Hall demanding to speak to the Mayor. A line of police officers on foot barred the crowd from entering the building. A representative of the Mayor came out of the building, advised the crowd that the Mayor was not in, and asked the protesters to put their grievances in writing. He assured the people that the Mayor would receive their complaints and would act accordingly.

The *Globe* reported that the angry crowd attempted to "break through the police cordon on the City Hall steps, but the line wavered, then held firm. Instantly a corps of mounted men appeared from the west [side of the building] and another squad from the City Hall entrance."[1] The police line held firm and the crowd was dispersed by the police officers.

The story changed a bit on April 26th when the *Toronto Telegram* reported, "A miniature repetition of the riots of 1919 was staged yesterday, when the police on guard in front of the City Hall during the unemployed demonstration charged the crowd with drawn batons. Simultaneously ten mounted policemen galloped forward." The three thousand crowd members "were sent flying east and west on Queen Street and down Bay Street."[2]

The police pursued the dispersing crowd through the streets breaking up any small groups that began to reform. What may have precipitated the melee were the actions of two detectives who had been assigned to mingle in the crowd and to arrest any ringleaders inciting misbehaviour. The detectives were recognised by crowd members and had to retreat to the police lines which became the focus of the crowd's anger. Demonstrators began to push forward. Deputy Chief Geddes ordered the crowd to disperse, but his voice was drowned out by shouts from the protesters.

Not pleased with what he saw happening, the Deputy Chief made a hand signal and, "Instantly the police, who were waiting for the signal, rushed forward in a solid line. The mounties galloped forward at either end of the charge." A few of the officers were knocked down and trampled, "but the officers as a unit were mostly on top, wielding their batons and using their fists with right good will."[3]

The reporter stated that the two police inspectors on duty tore the banners from the "army" of demonstrators and used the poles "with terrific effect on a lot of heads in the mob."[4] Within five minutes it was all over and the police were in full control of the streets. There were no reports of serious injuries, but some protesters were arrested.

A photograph of the fight on the steps of the City Hall was published on the front page of the *Telegram*. The newspaper highlighted the hands of the police officers and circled the batons they were holding. A police baton had been a factor in the Detective Frank McCullough murder case and the riots which preceded his execution in 1919. The police use of batons was clearly an issue that was not going away. Mayor Church later sent a letter to the Chairman of the Unemployed Committee regretting the fact that he had not been available to meet with their representatives.

1   *Globe*. April 25, 1921.
2   *Toronto Evening Telegram*, April 26, 1921.
3   *Toronto Evening Telegram*, April 26, 1921.
4   *Toronto Evening Telegram*, April 26, 1921.

A mounted officer (centre, top) patrolling along the old Lakeshore Boulevard probably during the Canadian National Exhibition. Photograph, Toronto Transit Commission Archives. 6202.

A mounted officer patrolling in front of the C.N.E. Coliseum building at the Royal Winter Fair. Photograph, City of Toronto Archives, William James Collection. SC 244-1198.

1922

The outlying sections of the city continued to grow, forcing the Mounted Unit to expand existing beats and add more, in order to provide protection to these areas. The Chief Constable reported that two or three horses and men had been found useful in the congested downtown sections of the city where they assisted in keeping traffic moving.[47] A Toronto newspaper reported that the horses assigned to regulate traffic at the fruit market were considered the luckiest, due to all the tidbits that they were given.[48]

In his annual report, Chief Dickson commented on the condition of the horses. Six had to be disposed of, being as no longer fit for service. They were replaced with six new remounts. The horses of the Mounted Unit had been free from accident or sickness through the year and all were in good condition. Two older horses, with many years service were nearing the end of their careers and were due to be replaced. All saddles and equipment were reported to be in "splendid condition."[49]

The sale of police horses was of great concern to the Board of Commissioners. They appear to have taken a personal interest in what became of former police horses and discussed their fate in detail. At its meeting of January 11th, the Board approved the sale of police mount "Warneford."[49a]

On May 25, the Commissioners approved the sale of "White Oak," "Thamesville," "Barrie" and "Girgil." At the same meeting, they also approved a newspaper ad advertising the sale of 18 old saddles which had begun to deteriorate in the store room.[49b] On November 30, the Chief Constable made a special request to the Board asking permission to sell a horse for "bad temper."[49c]

The police became more active in suppressing what they considered subversive activities. On May 25, Police Commissioners received a complaint from the leadership of the labour movement about police interfering with open air meetings.[49d] The complaint was disregarded and harassment of the labour movement would continue until the start of the Second World War in September 1939.

The stable at No. 9 Station was still under request to be built. Chief Constable Dickson also asked that a stable be built at No. 12 Station in North Toronto.

A Toronto newspaper article described how the mounted policeman made their arrests. "In the event of requiring to make an arrest the constable walks in front of the horse with his prisoner while the animal follows obediently." The offender would be taken to the nearest call box where the officer would summon the patrol wagon.[50]

1923

Inspector Herbert Little was transferred from the Mounted Unit to No. 10 Station on January 1st, 1923. He had been in charge of the Mounted Unit since 1916 and "under his command the unit was brought to a high state of efficiency."[51] Patrol Sergeant Thomas Crosbie was assigned to take command of the unit.

A newspaper article from the 1920s stated that Chief Dickson was very pleased with the results achieved by the Mounted Unit since he had ordered them to regulate traffic in the heart of the city. He was reported to be assigning as many men to this detail as there was funding available. The article goes on to describe the rush hour patrol.

The mounted policeman always attracts the eye, and their appearance on the downtown streets in the heart of the business section of Toronto, keeping the traffic open in the rush hours, has called particular attention to the smartness and efficiency of the Mounted Division of the Police Force.

The well-set-up officers and their beautiful horses draw forth many expressions of admiration while they dodge in and out among the traffic, relieving congestion at the busy spots. If a slow vehicle is holding up the general movement they make short work of getting it out of the way to let the faster ones go

by. At principle crossings they assist the "stop and go" officer in regulating the stream. They get improperly parked motor cars removed without much ado.[52]

During the summer, Constable Mosher was on patrol on Queen's Quay when he observed a runaway horse heading for the holiday crowd lined up at the entrance to the ferry docks. As the horse neared the crowd, PC Mosher was able to ride up to it and to reach over to affect its stop, just in time to avoid a calamity. A newspaper report stated, "His horse which had taken a gallant part in the smart work did not appear to be the least bit excited about it."[53]

The Chief Constable was finally able to report that the City of Toronto Property Commissioner had set aside funds for a new stable at No. 9 Station, and called for tenders to have the structure built to assist with the protection of the west end. He also felt there was a pressing need for a stable at No. 12 Station in North Toronto.

The Police Department ordered 23 mounted police "waterproofs" at the cost of $30.00 each. A very expensive purchase, but no doubt appreciated by the mounted officers who patrolled their posts in all weather. Police mount "Colonel" died during the year.

Stopping Runaway Horses – A Dangerous Duty

Before the introduction of the automobile, a horse was the most important means of transportation available in Toronto. Railways and ships transported goods outside of the city while horses towing wagons and sleighs transported them inside the metropolis. Not only were horses ridden, they were used for pulling streetcars, coaches, fire wagons, freight wagons, buggies and numerous other vehicles. Horses were still used for milk delivery in the 1950s – they even knew each house, where to stop.

The sheer number of horses in the city guaranteed that there would be the inevitable "runaway," and the introduction of automobiles and trucks in the last century increased these occurrences. Anything can cause a horse to "break and flee." Even the best-trained horse may balk at something, and, given the opportunity to run, it will. Even veteran police horses sometimes reach a point where they "runaway," and it may take all the skill the rider possesses to settle the horse down again.

The fear, commotion and danger caused by an out-of-control horse galloping down a crowded street can be well imagined. Add to this a wagon swinging wildly behind, and the prospect of injury, death and property damage is clearly evident. The runaway horse might also startle other horses causing them to bolt as well.

Dealing with runaway horses was an important police function, especially for mounted officers, who had an advantage in dealing with such situations. The New York City Police Mounted Unit was formed in 1874 specifically to handle the problem of runaway horses in the downtown area.[1] In 1891 thirty-three Toronto police officers were entered into the merit book for stopping runaway horses; not all of those men so honoured were on horseback.

A merit mark was the highest individual award of recognition that the Toronto Police Department had in those days. Liverpool, England had a police bravery medal that it bestowed on deserving officers. Many of those medals were awarded to police officers who stopped runaway horses.

Toronto Police horses were specifically trained to catch up to and stop runaway horses. Inspector Thomas Crosbie told a newspaper reporter that while he was still a constable, and riding police mount "Mayo" up Yonge Street, he saw a runaway team of horses drawing a wagon.

Crosbie started to chase the rapidly moving horses: the wagon crashed into another team that had been parked at the curb. The second team also took off in fright. With two runaway teams at mad gallop, Constable Crosbie manoeuvred "Mayo" so that he was wedged between the two teams which were running neck and neck.

Crosbie dropped the reins giving "Mayo" his head, while he leaned forward, reached down with both hands, and grabbed the bridle rein of each team. As soon as Crosbie got hold of the reins, "Mayo" put on the brakes, and although dragged on his hooves and haunches, managed to bring both teams of horses to a quivering halt.

"Mayo" had been involved in other runaway incidents and knew that when the master had secured the loose reins, it was time to stop. On another occasion the officer had the reins of the runaway in his hands: "Mayo" slid to a stop. The reins were jerked out of the officer's hands and the runaway continued its mad flight. Without hesitation, "Mayo" took off again in hot pursuit, this time making sure the horse would stop by pushing it into the curb where it was forced to come to a halt.[2]

The following article appeared in the *Toronto Telegram* of December 15, 1924, and describes how Constable Thomas Hugh Dundas stopped a runaway horse, probably saving a number of lives in the process.

Clattering comes the sound of swift moving hoofs on Adelaide Street, east of York, just as the noon whistles are sounding and downtown Toronto is hustling to restaurants and quick-serve counters. Startled pedestrians give one fleet look over their shoulders and then skip nimbly to doorways and other places of refuge, as a runaway horse heads full gallop for Bay Street, dragging behind it a driverless wagon which rocks crazily from side to side.

One man with a small child narrowly escapes from

being knocked down by the frightened animal, which in some way has managed to free itself from its bridle. It is even-betting that when the terrified beast reaches Bay Street there's going to be damage done to life and limb.

But while the crowd breathlessly watches the headlong careening of the runaway, there echoes behind the thud of the hoofs of another horse; this time ridden by a man in the blue uniform of the Toronto Mounted Unit.

The horse is "Mayo," whose bridle has not seldom been decked with the victorious rosette in local show rings, and the man on the chestnut mare's back is Constable Dundas, a former Irish Fusilier who later was destined to win the Military Medal when serving with the Canadian Field Artillery in the Great War.

And both "Mayo" and her rider know their job, although they have not much time in which to do it. A ticklish job it is, too, to stop a runaway without a bridle to grip, but the powerful chestnut, responsive to its rider's urging, overhauls the other horse and ranges itself alongside. Then into play comes the long whip the officer has drawn from its resting place on the right of the military saddle on which he is seated. Smartly he taps the maddened animal on its sensitive muzzle, for there is no other way to check its flight. And "Mayo" does her part too, for she shoulders her weight against her refractory equine brother's flank and pushes him inexorably towards the curb. Between rider and horse the runaway is brought to a quivering halt less than five yards from the busy intersection, and the excitement is all over.

An incident like the above is all in a day's work for the Toronto Mounted Police Unit.[3]

Another article from 1924 tells either the same story a little bit differently or describes a second incident involving PC Dundas and a runaway horse. It is also worth repeating to provide a vivid picture of a runaway horse and the bravery of PC Dundas and his mount "Mayo."

The wisdom of the police horses stopping runaway horses on the streets was exemplified in spectacular fashion a short time ago on Adelaide Street. A horse attached to a wagon became frightened near Simcoe Street and made a wild dash eastwards. As York Street was approached, the wagon struck an obstruction with such force that it was torn away from the crazed animal which increased its pace when freed of the load.

Constable Dundas, on traffic duty, urged his horse into a gallop for a wild race with the runaway and when he had about over taken it jumped from his mount and secured the runaway by the head in such a manner as to bring it quickly to a stand still. His own horse stopped ahead, within a few yards and with fine intelligence turned inwards to block the progress of the runaway had it kept going to the busy crossing of Bay Street not far away. Sergeant Crosbie says he has no doubt that other horses in the squad would have acted in a similar fashion, never-the-less the whole mounted force is proud of the incident which is only one of many in the history of the organization.[4]

*PC Thomas H. Dundas.
Photograph,* Toronto Telegram, *October 1916.*

1 *Toronto Star.* June 19, 1982.
2 *Toronto Telegram.* May 5, 1930.
3 *Globe and Mail.* December 15, 1924.
4 Unknown Toronto Newspaper (Perhaps *Toronto Telegram*). 1924.

Constable Thomas Dundas and "Mayo" stop a runaway horse on the streets of Toronto. Illustration, William White, 2001.

1924

The new stable with "modern fittings" was finally opened at No. 9 Station on Keele Street alongside the original police station built in 1889. West Toronto and High Park would be patrolled from the new facility. Chief Dickson continued to stress in his annual report that there was an "urgent" need for a stable at No.12 Division.

Patrol Sergeant Thomas Crosbie was promoted to full Sergeant on September 24th. He remained as the officer in charge of the Mounted Unit which was increased in strength to 30 officers of all ranks.

During the year, the mounted squad paid special attention to the downtown areas during rush hour, and were especially effective in enforcing the new no parking by-laws on Bay Street. A number of special escorts were given for noted personalities who visited Toronto, including the Prince of Wales.

The Chief Constable appeared before the Police Commissioners at their meeting on October 30th. He requested permission to sell a horse that was gradually going blind. The Commissioners approved the request and instructed the Chief to ensure that the horse went to a good home.[53a]

The Mounted Unit showed a number of horses at the Royal Winter Fair Horse Show held each year in November. A newspaper reported that the Toronto Mounted Policemen "drew from American show ring judges, the flattering tribute that they were the best turned out body of uniformed men that they had ever seen."[53] No small achievement as the cavalry of all nations were the premier riders at most horse shows, and were the Olympic competitors for many countries.

A Toronto newspaper reported that while the mounted officers were patrolling the outlying beats to which they were assigned, they were expected to keep an eye out for suspicious looking autos entering the city. Officers patrolled in the saddle for three hours, then received an hour break, then rode out again for a further three hours of patrol. At the conclusion of the day, the officers were responsible for looking after the needs of their mounts and held responsible for any neglect in the care of the horse.[54]

Another article reported, "In the early evening when they appear to be riding leisurely along the business thoroughfares they are really escorting bank messengers on the way from the banks to the clearing house and guarding untold wealth."[55] These bank messenger details were called "Red Feather Escorts" and were done by the Mounted Unit until the mid 1960s.

The *Toronto Telegram* commented on the condition of the horses and stables as follows; "The Constables take a tremendous pride in keeping their charges groomed to a height of efficiency not often equalled in the crackest of crack cavalry regiments, where grooming is a fine art. The saddlery and head stalls get plenty of attention too, for lots of elbow grease, as well as soap, had been expended on those which the *Telegram* inspected."[56]

The Mounted Unit attended every large gathering held in Toronto. The number of Mounted officers required was transferred from regular duty and assigned to these events. Officers usually patrolled quietly on the outside perimeter of the crowds, from where they could easily be called in when they were needed. During 1924, large meetings of the unemployed had been the main special duty call outs. All of the meetings were orderly and it was not necessary to use the mounted officers to disperse any of the crowds.

One newspaper reported a turbulent labour demonstration at City Hall in the 1920s. The mounted police were called in and side passaged their horses into the crowd: this proved to be most effective deterrent for aberrant behaviour. Sergeant Crosbie remembered the most difficult crowd he faced as the one that formed around Massey Hall when Temperance speaker "Pussyfoot" Johnson spoke. The streets were densely packed with people, not all of them fans of Mr. Johnson and "keeping a passage open was a difficult affair."[57]

The report that went on to note that outside police circles, many citizens think that the Mounted Unit should be increased due to its success in regulating traffic. One member of the unit stated, "One mounted officer is worth six on foot when it comes to relieving traffic congestion." Mounted policemen proved to be of great service during the extensive program of street railway rehabilitation, and were credited with having prevented many accidents when regular routes were diverted due to streets being torn up for repairs.[58]

A mounted officer helps a lady cross the road.
Drawing, The Toronto Star Weekly, *August 25, 1923.*

The Mounted Unit 1924

STATION	PERSONNEL AND HORSES	
Police Station No. 5 Mounted Headquarters Belmont Street	Sergeant Thomas Crosbie, Officer in Charge Constable Amos Bell, Stableman 6 Mounted Constables	7 Horses
Police Station No. 1 Court Street	Patrol Sergeant Robert Rogerson 5 Mounted Constables	6 Horses
Police Station No. 8 Pape Avenue	Patrol Sergeant Charles Chalkin 4 Mounted Constables	5 Horses
Police Station No. 9 Keele Street	Patrol Sergeant Ernest Masters 4 Mounted Constables	5 Horses
Police Station No. 11 London Street and Markham Street	4 Mounted Constables	4 Horses
Police Station No. 6 Parkdale	3 Mounted Constables	3 Horses

▣ 1925

The Chief Constable reported that all of the horses were in good condition and the saddlery and equipment was in first class order. Chief Dickson felt that the mounted officers should be commended for the excellent care that they had bestowed on the horses and kit.

On April 1st Constable Keen (648) was on mounted patrol at St. Clair Avenue West and Lauder Avenue. As he rode past a moving van parked on the south side of the street his horse bolted in front of a streetcar and was struck, knocking both rider and horse to the ground.

Witnesses carried the injured officer to a nearby drug store where he was treated by a doctor and then transported to hospital by police ambulance. He was admitted to hospital to be treated for a suspected fractured skull. His mount "Autumn," a six year old chestnut coloured horse, was removed to a veterinary hospital by horse ambulance. The horse was injured so severely that it had to be destroyed.

The Mayor of Toronto presented a letter to the Police Commissioners at their meeting on June 19th. It was from the Mayor of Philadelphia and it requested that the Toronto Police Department send twelve officers and mounts to Philadelphia in September 1926 to take part in the Sesquicentennial International Exhibition. The Board of Commissioners approved of the request and authorized the officers to attend. The following spring the Board directed the Chief of Police to write to Philadelphia to advise them of why the mounted officers could not attend the exhibition. There is no record of why the Board withdrew its permission for the officers to attend the Exhibition.[58a]

Ten horses were entered and exhibited in two classes at the Royal Winter Fair in November. There were 21 open entries in the classes. The police horses took the 1st, 2nd and 3rd prizes. The Chief felt that "the achievement reflects great credit on the officers and men concerned."[59]

The Toronto Police Commission received a letter on December 17th from the Toronto City Council. It read in part "That this city Council congratulates the Board of Police Commissioners, Chief of Police Dickson, Sergeant Crosbie, his officers and men on the splendid showing of police horses and general appearance of the mounted police force at the Royal Winter Fair; and also congratulates the officer commanding Stanley barracks, his officers and men for their splendid showing at the Royal Winter Fair."[59a]

A Toronto Newspaper reported that American visitors were so impressed with the Toronto mounted constables in the hurdling contests that on December 2nd Chief Dickson got offers to purchase 3 police horses. A Chicago man offered $1,000.00 for "Golden." A New York man offered $800.00 for "Sunshine" and a New England man offered $500.00 for "Connaught."[60] Needless to say the horses were not for sale even at these extraordinary funds. The Toronto Police were averaging between $50.00 and $75.00 for the horses that they sold around this time.

The Toronto Police Horse of the 1920s

The following article appeared in an unknown Toronto newspaper, probably the *Toronto Telegram*. It gives a fine description of some of the police horses of the times:

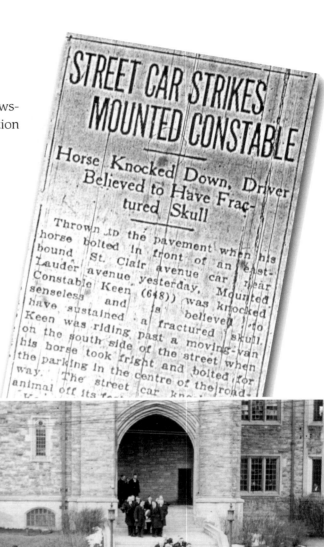

'The star of the stable is 'Shamrock,' the sergeant's (Thomas Crosbie) mount, called 'Billy' for short. While most of the horses in the squad have circus qualifications, 'Shamrock' excels in accomplishments. He will shake hands with a visitor and, when there is music about, he has to shake a leg. It was him that was dancing so prettily to the marching airs played by the bands in the military parade last Sunday.

A Kentucky bred horse, he is a lovely chestnut with a white nose, ten years old, sixteen hands high and is considered to be the most admired horse in the city, particularly by the children of whom he is very fond. He was purchased at the Thorncliffe Race Track and in his three years of service on the force has learned police work like a book. He follows the sergeant faithfully when told to do so and will answer a summoning whistle within the distance of its sound.

'Linwood' is another horse full of pretty tricks and much attached to Sergeant Masters. High Park visitors know this horse which follows a long way for an apple. 'Black Watch' another handsome brute, the mount of Constable Houston, has a host of friends in the western St. Clair district. This horse was purchased from a deaf and dumb man and while in training for police duties would lie down as soon as a saddle was put on. It was difficult to get it to rise because its former owner had been unable to speak to it and it did not understand conversation, but when it did commence to learn, it progressed speedily and is now one of the most intelligent beasts in the squad.

'Sunshine' a young dark chestnut animal ridden by Constable Mitchell is another prime favourite. Constable Mitchell is in charge of the training of new horses at present and 'Sunshine' is used as a model for the newcomers. The intelligence of every horse in the stables is far above the average.

A mounted officer keeping back the crowd at the funeral of Sir John Eaton at the Eaton New Church, St. Clair Avenue West. Photograph, City of Toronto Archives, William James Collection, SC 24-1020.

1   Unknown Toronto Newspaper. (Possibly the *Toronto Telegram*, 1924).

A photograph of the opening of the York Township streetcar line. The mounted officer in the foreground appears to be trying to keep the track clear of people for the cars' departure. Photograph, Toronto Transit Commission Archives, 3527.

Mounted constables lead the first Toronto Transit Commission streetcars into York Township, November 19, 1924. Photograph, City of Toronto Archives, J. Boyd Photograph, SC 266-6725.

Amos Bell

The position of Quartermaster is very important in the Mounted Unit. Not only does the quartermaster look after all of the unit's supplies, he also repairs and evaluates all of the equipment used. The position is usually given to a senior officer with a lot of equine experience. They must also have the aptitude to do the complicated repair work.

The unit's first quartermaster was Constable Amos Bell. He was responsible for the care of the stable as well as the supplies and was usually referred to as the stableman. Today, the job of stable manager and quartermaster are separate functions.

Amos Bell was born in Yorkshire, England on November 29, 1883 and joined the Toronto Police Force as Constable 324 on April 27, 1908. He was the perfect size for a mounted officer standing 5'10 3/4." He transferred into the unit sometime before the First World War.

On the 11th of February 1916 he enlisted in the 169th Overseas Battalion of the Canadian Expeditionary Force. He gave his occupation as mounted policeman on his attestation papers and changed his date of birth to make himself appear five years younger, a more acceptable age for active service.

He arrived in England on the 28th of October 1916 with the rank of corporal, then reverted to the rank of private at his own request to enable his transfer to be made to the 20th Battalion and front line service in France. He returned to Canada after the war and was discharged from the military on August 20, 1919 after three and a half years service.

After the war he returned to the Toronto Police Force and was reassigned to the Mounted Unit. By 1924, he was the stableman/quartermaster at the Belmont Street Station, the first identified quartermaster in the Mounted Unit.

Constable Amos Bell as a member of the 20th Battalion, C.E.F. Photograph. Toronto Police Museum.

1926

Trophies won by the unit during 1925 at both the Canadian National Exhibition Horse Show and the Royal Winter Fair were put on display at the Police Commissioners' meeting on January 7, 1926. The Commissioners were "proud of the achievement of the Mounted Squad."[60a]

The police department continued to increase the size of the Mounted Unit. By 1926 a total of 32 officers of all ranks were assigned to mounted duties. Chief Constable complimented the men again on the first class condition of the equipment. He also continued to press the Police Commissioners into building a stable at No. 12 Division, North Toronto.

Five horses that were no longer fit for police service were sold during the year and replaced with remounts. The Chief Constable was quoted as saying, "Having in mind the faithful service rendered by the animals, a good home was found for each one."[61]

The police entered the open competition at the Royal Winter Fair and won the First, Second and Third Place ribbons for the second year in a row.

Mounted officers hold back the crowd at the Canadian National Exhibition as the nine horse team of the Harris Milk Company passes by. Inspector Crosbie is in the centre in the forage cap, c. 1925. Photograph, City of Toronto Archives, William James Collection. SC 244-2240.

Mounted officers on duty at the Dunlop Trophy Bicycle Race which was an annual event on the Canadian National Exhibition Grounds, 1926. Photograph, City of Toronto Archives, William James Collection. SC 244-1013.

The Coldest Posting on the Police Force
Winter Dress of the 1920s

The position of mounted police constable is probably the coldest job in the police service. Officers and mounts are out for hours in extremely cold weather as horses must get out of the barn for their exercise despite the cold. In the days before the Mounted Unit had horse trailers, all officers had to ride to and from their details. This could involve riding for miles on the coldest days of the year and then remaining outside for hours at a demonstration or other event. The frozen officer would then have to ride back to his stable.

There were many private stables still in operation in the city. It would have been possible for the officers to find a friendly civilian stable that would allow them to come in and warm up. This would however have been a risky proposition because if the patrol sergeant had caught them, they would surely have been in trouble.

The mounted officers were provided with the warmest clothing that could be found. The following description of the Toronto mounted police winter kit appeared in the *Toronto Telegram*. "In Winter, all mounted officers wear a long blue cloak of Cossack design, which serves the double purpose of protecting the wearer and the most vital parts of his horse. The riders feet are encased in felt boots and overshoes, and a leather stirrup is substituted for the regular one of steel."[1]

Officers wore a Persian Lamb hat which was equipped with ear flaps that they purchased privately. A new hat cost $50.00, which was the equivalent of two week's pay. A used hat, if available, was $25.00. The posts that they were assigned to ride had specific routes that they had to follow in order to reach their call boxes on time. Imagine having to ride into the wind when the temperature was zero degrees Fahrenheit and the wind chill forty below!

The same basic equipment is still used today. Snowmobile boots have replaced the felt boots. Thermal underwear and other fabrics have improved the insulating power of the modern officers' clothing. Snowmobile gloves and leather gauntlets prevent fingers from freezing. Even with the modern clothing and equipment the mounted unit remains the coldest posting in the police service.

The frozen officers of the 1920s must have longed for the hot summer days ahead. Once these days arrived the officers would boil in their heavy box neck tunics. Toronto police officers were never issued with police uniform shirts. They were required to wear their tunics and helmets, and later forage caps all summer long. Would the sweltering officers ever day dream of the cold winter days ahead?

A Mounted Unit officer in winter dress, c. 1925.
Photograph, Author's Collection.

A Mounted Unit officer in Winter Dress, c. 1925.
Photograph, Toronto Police Museum.

1 *Toronto Telegram.* December 15, 1924.

Mounted officers patrolling Lakeshore Boulevard and Stadium Road at the opening of Maple Leaf Baseball Stadium, 1926. Looking east from the top of the stadium. Photograph, City of Toronto Archives, William James Collection. SC 244-1164.

Officers assigned to the London Street Station, c.1926. Photograph, Toronto Police Mounted Unit.

Right: A Mounted Unit sergeant and constable leave the Grandstand at the C.N.E. Horse Show, c. 1920. Photograph, Toronto Public Reference Library. T10524.

Big Men on Big Horses
The Mounted Unit in the 1920s

It was not easy to become a mounted officer in the Toronto police in the 1920s. A majority of constables were still walking the beat. The few plainclothes, motorcycle, scout car and wagon positions were filled by senior officers. The Mounted Unit was one of the few areas open to junior men who wanted to get off the beat. Only those with the best of qualifications would be able to make the transition from walking to riding.

The Toronto Police Force was full of military veterans, many of them with cavalry experience from before and during the First World War. Most of the Canadian-born recruits had come from rural backgrounds where they had grown up with horses. The Mounted Unit could afford to be picky when selecting recruits as more applicants than positions were available. There was a long waiting list of competent officers longing to be called to fill an opening.

Ninety percent of the officers in the Mounted Unit during 1924 had military experience. The *Toronto Telegram* stated that, "The flower of Britain's cavalry regiments is here represented, for in it are men who have worn the white buckskin breeches and steel cuirass of the Life Guards, and have done their mounted sentry-go on the King's Guard at Whitehall; men who have worn the red and black plumed brass helmet and scarlet tunic of the Queen's Bays; Men who have worn the gaudy jacket of the Royal Horse Artillery, that historic branch of the service whose proud privilege it is always to take the right of the line on a review, and last, but by no means least, men who through their soldiering have worn the dingy-hued khaki, the British Soldiers Fighting Dress."[1]

The Mounted Unit comprised many men whose military bearing and physical stature impressed all who saw them. A *Telegram* reporter stated that, "In appearance they recall Sir William Napiers famous description of Wellington's Dragoons—Big men on big horses." Their no-nonsense unit commander would stand for nothing less than perfection in his men. He was extremely proud of the Mounted Unit and had this to say about them;

"I have the finest body of mounted men on the continent and have had compliments paid them from all the large cities in the U.S. I was asked to go across the boarder to organize such a group more than once. It is a great compliment first to myself and men, and also to the city. There is a need for such a squad and we carry out innumerable duties, which otherwise would take many more footmen."[2]

The prestige of being a mounted officer increased when the new police Chief Dennis Draper was appointed in 1927. The big men on big horses were soon to be known as "Draper's Dragoons."

1   *Toronto Telegram.* December 15, 1924.
2   *Toronto Telegram.* Monday, May 5, 1930.

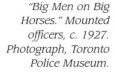

"Big Men on Big Horses." Mounted officers, c. 1927. Photograph, Toronto Police Museum.

A mounted officer patrolling eastbound on Adelaide Street at Bay Street, April 27, 1927. Photograph, Toronto Transit Commission Archives, 4846.

The Prince of Wales, the future King Edward the VIII arrives at Toronto City Hall. Inspector Crosbie can be seen in the background. Photograph, City of Toronto Archives, William James Collection. SC 244-1016.

George Young

These photographs are excellent depictions of mounted officers at work. They also show the enthusiastic crowds that sport celebrities attracted in the early part of this century. In the 1920s there were few non-sporting entertainment venues in Toronto. All of the bars had been closed and liquor was banned under the Ontario Temperance Act. Movie theatres and stage shows were frequented, but television had not been invented and radio was not yet in common use. Sporting events drew large crowds and large crowds drew the Mounted Unit.

George Young was a Toronto resident and a marathon swimmer. In 1927 he won the Catalina Marathon in California, being the first man to swim from the mainland to Catalina Island. He returned to a hero's welcome in Toronto and his City Hall reception is depicted in the photographs.

Mounted officers can be seen gently clearing a path through the crowds on Queen Street West as the car carrying George Young approaches the front of City Hall. Photograph, City of Toronto Archives, William James Collection, SC 244-1021.

A single mounted officer assists uniform and plainclothes foot officers who are pushing back the crowd on the front steps of City Hall. Photograph, City of Toronto archives, William James Collection. SC 244-1025.

Mounted officers have cleared the crowd and the car has arrived at the steps of City Hall. The horse manure visible on the ground would have been from the horses that cleared the crowd in front of the car. Photograph, City of Toronto Archives, William James Collection, SC 244-1022.

Inspector Crosbie and Chief Constable Dickson reviewing the troop. The first Police Church Parade, May 15, 1927. Photograph, Globe *Newspaper.*

1927 On April 1st, Sergeant Thomas Crosbie was promoted to Inspector, making him the youngest Inspector in the history of the Toronto Police Force. He remained assigned as the officer in charge of the Mounted Unit. The biggest event of the year was the visit to Toronto by the Prince of Wales. Large crowds turned out to greet the Prince and the Mounted Unit was engaged in crowd control duty and in providing royal escorts.

Four horses were sold during the year and five remounts were purchased. The Mounted Unit's complement included 32 horses.

Inspector Crosbie has dismounted to accompany Chief Constable Dickson on an inspection of the Mounted Unit at the first Church Parade of the Toronto Police, May 15, 1927. Photograph, Globe *Newspaper.*

A Unit of War Heroes

In the mid 1920s, ninety percent of the men assigned to the Mounted Unit had served in the military. Most had served with front line units during the First World War. A number of officers had been decorated with medals for specific acts of bravery. There was probably a higher concentration of decorated men in the thirty-man mounted unit than in any other police division in the city.

The following members of the Mounted Unit are known to have been awarded with medals for bravery.

Inspector Thomas Crosbie:	Distinguished Conduct Medal
Constable Thomas Dundas:	Military Medal, Meritorious Service Medal, Mentioned in Despatches.
Constable Charles Hainer:	Military Medal, Croix de Guerre.
Constable F.R. Hill:	Military Medal.
Constable R.C. Mosher:	Military Medal.

The medals worn by Constable Thomas Dundas. Photograph, Author's Collection.

The Padré finds one of "his boys" in the police motor cycle escort, P.C. Chas. F. Hainer, M.M., C.deG., 9th Howitzer Battery and 67th Battery C.F.A. Ven. Archdeacon (Col.) F. G. Scott, C.M.G., D.S.O., former Senior Chaplain of the First Canadian Division, was the "Happy Warrior" of the Re-Union. He was met with hand-shakes and cheers on every hand.

Police Constable Charles F. Hainer, M.M., C.de G. with Cannon Scott C.M.G., D.S.O., former senior chaplain of the First Canadian Division at the Canadian Corps Reunion 1934. P.C. Hainer was killed in an on duty motorcycle accident on September 18, 1943 after transferring from the Mounted Unit to the Traffic Unit.

Chief Constable Draper in front of Queen's Park with mounted, motorcycle and foot officers. All of the officers in the picture were Great War Veterans. Photograph, Toronto Police Museum.

Constable Charles Whitford and the Elizabeth Street Murder

On the evening of Wednesday March 30, 1927, a forty-two-year-old man named Fong Yong was walking up Elizabeth Street in Toronto's Chinatown. He had been suffering from mental illness for some time and had been receiving some treatment for his problems. At about five minutes to six he went into the grocery/ butcher shop located at 17 Elizabeth Street, lit his pipe and complained about a number of things to the proprietor.

For some reason he suddenly grabbed a sixteen-inch butcher knife from the butchers block and started for the door. As he left the store he slashed at a man cutting his clothes, but only slightly cutting the skin. He zig-zagged north on Elizabeth Street waving the knife and muttering in broken English, "I get 'em, me kill everybody."[1]

Eleven-year-old Elsie Macheska of Nelson Street was taking her brother's lunch to the Olympia Bowling Alley at Yonge and Gerrard Streets. He had to work late and would need the lunch. Poor Elsie was walking ahead of Fong Yong and as he started to pass her he stopped for a moment before plunging the butcher knife into the back of the defenceless girl. The blow penetrated her lungs causing a fatal injury. As the girl collapsed on the pavement her enraged assailant kicked her in the face. People who witnessed the assault began to flee in panic. Two more men were stabbed by Yong as he continued up Elizabeth Street. Both men suffered painful, but non life threatening injuries.

A number of citizens grabbed little Elsie and put her in a car. She was rushed to the hospital where she was immediately taken to the operating table but pronounced dead. Immediately after the first man was stabbed outside the grocery store a citizen ran to Bay and Queen Streets where a mounted constable was usually on traffic duty. The man ran up to Constable Charles Whitford and reported, "Bad Chinaman with big knife on Elizabeth Street, come quick, he kill."[2]

PC Whitford galloped his horse "Mayflower" towards the scene passing terrified people fleeing from the bloodshed on Elizabeth Street. The people running from the scene hurriedly updated him as he charged along Queen Street towards Elizabeth Street. As he rode up Elizabeth Street he saw Yong further along still waving the knife over his head. As the officer closed in, Yong reached out and grabbed another citizen.

Whitford drew his revolver and fired a shot at Yong from horseback. The shot missed, but the citizen managed to wrench himself free before being stabbed. Although the shot went wide a frightened onlooker beside Whitford fell on his face spooking "Mayflower," causing her to rear. Whitford fell, or slid off his horse and approached Yong with his revolver still drawn.

Constable Whitford shouted, "If you move I will kill you." Yong made a charge at the constable with his knife and Whitford punched him in the face. He then grabbed the assailant's knife hand and was struck with the blunt side of the knife. Whitford punched him in the head a second time and Yong fell to the pavement dropping the knife. After kicking the knife away, the officer managed to get physical control of the suspect after a short wrestling match. He was handcuffed and the two waited for the backup officers to arrive.

The press and police officers of the city had nothing but praise for Constable Whitford. He in turn directed most of the praise to "Mayflower." "She is a wonderful mare," he told the *Toronto Star*. "When I jumped off her last night, she just followed me along and as I dealt with the Chinese she came up on the sidewalk and kept walking up and down in front of the crowd, nodding her head back and forth until after I had the man handcuffed."[3]

Whitford described the arrest to the *Star* reporters: "I first saw Yong near the registry office and he was drawing the dull side of his knife over the neck of a man. Seeing he was about to wound the man I charged my horse toward him and pulling my revolver fired at him. Yong released his grip on the man and was about to run when I fired a second time and my mount reared in the air."

"I then took my feet from the stirrups, slid to the ground and ran towards the Chinese. Even after I had knocked him down he got hold of my arms with the strength of a man twice his size and build. It was only after a hard struggle that I was able to get him in a position where I could get the handcuffs on him."[4]

It would seem that Constable Whitford was very lucky. Although he describes "sliding" off the horse in the *Toronto Star* interview, the evidence suggests that he actually fell off striking his head as he did so. He told the *Toronto Telegram* that he was seeing stars after banging his head during his fall. He said it was fortunate he went off on the left side of "Mayflower" away from the assailant. Had he gone off on the right side he may have been defenceless and stabbed.[5]

There is no doubt that the prompt actions of Charles Whitford saved many people from injury or death. He became a hero and was remembered for his deed for many years after. Constable Charles Whitford, badge number 594, was born in Cornwall, England. When the First World War began he was working in Arizona, USA. He immediately returned to England where he joined the premier cavalry unit, the 1st Life Guards. Following an honourable discharge he came to Canada and joined the Toronto Police Force in December 1920.

The following eyewitness account appeared in the March 31, 1927 *Toronto Star*.

Like a Scene In Melodrama Of the Movies. A vivid description of the lurid scenes in Toronto's Chinatown last night was given to the Star today by F. Howard Annis, one of the passengers in the Toronto Whitby bus, which was starting from that vicinity.

As we turned into Elizabeth Street," he said "we found it in an uproar: men, woman and children running in all directions, shouting and screaming. Then they carried that little girl to within a short distance of the bus, and she lay there weltering in her blood, a terrible, pitiful sight.

Up the street we heard the galloping approach of the mounted constable. When bullets began to fly there was almost a panic among the passengers, for fear of stray shots penetrating.

When the whole thing was over it was a highly-excited bunch of passengers who were transported to Whitby and Oshawa to spread a hectic tale of Toronto's underworld.[6]

Elizabeth Macheska.
Photograph, Toronto Telegram, *March 31, 1927.*

Constable Charles Whitford and "Mayflower"
Photograph, Toronto Telegram, *March 31, 1927.*

1   *Toronto Star.* Thursday March 31, 1927.
2   ibid.
3   ibid.
4   ibid.
5   *Toronto Telegram.* Thursday March 31, 1927.
6   *Toronto Star.* Thursday March 31, 1927.

POLICE HORSE KNOWS HIS DUTY

Constable Charles Whitford (594) on his mount Mayflower, which he was riding when he rounded up Fong Yong, insane Chinese who ran amuck last evening on Elizabeth Street, stabbing an 11-year-old girl to death, then wounding four others. Whitford, aided by his horse, captured Yong at Louisa and Elizabeth Streets, but not until after he had fired two revolver shots at him. There were times, Whitford says, when Yong brandished the knife at the horse, narrowly missing the constable's legs. Whitford praises his horse for the intelligence it displayed when he dismounted to arrest his man, by walking before the crowd and keeping them back until other police assistance arrived on the scene.

Globe *Newspaper, March 31, 1927.*

 **1928** Chief Constable Dickson retired from the Police Department in February. He had been a firm supporter of the Mounted Unit through some troubled times. As automobiles became more prevalent in the city, many people questioned the wisdom of maintaining the Mounted Unit. During the 1920s, many major North American cities, did in fact, disband their mounted patrols in favour of mechanization.

If the mounted officers were worried about their unit's future under the new Chief Constable, they should not have been. On May 1, Brigadier General Dennis C. Draper arrived in Toronto to take command of the Toronto Police Department. The new Chief Constable became the biggest supporter the Mounted Unit ever had. He was an avid rider and would attend some details mounted on "Bruce," his personal police mount.

In his first annual report Chief Draper commented that the saddlery and other equipment was kept in excellent condition. Like Chief Dickson before him, he felt that this reflected credit on those concerned. Four horses were sold during the year and two remounts purchased bringing the total number of horses to thirty-four. Unfortunately police mount "Hillcrest" died in May.

The Canadian National Exhibition was the largest annual event in Toronto. Every year during the fair, mounted headquarters was moved to the Horse Palace. Officers patrolled the grounds and the parking areas that surrounded the Exhibition. In 1928, Inspector Crosbie and fifteen mounted officers worked exclusively at the Exhibition.

Horses were still quite common in the streets of Toronto. The city's Street Department still owned 400 horses in 1928, and busy times 200 more horses were leased from private owners. Full-time staff included a veterinary doctor and six blacksmiths. Every year more motor vehicles appeared on the street and the use of horses was slowly phased out. Simpsons' last Department Store delivery horse was sold in 1928 and all deliveries after that were carried by only motor vehicle.[62]

The Mounted Unit troop in line at the Annual Police Church Parade, c. 1928. Photograph, Toronto Police Museum.

Inspector Crosbie leading the troop past the reviewing stand at the Annual Police Church Parade, c. 1928. Photograph, Toronto Police Museum.

Inspector Crosbie of the Mounted Unit laying a wreath at the City Hall War Memorial on behalf of all Toronto Police officers, 1928. Photograph, City of Toronto Archives, Globe and Mail *Collection. 15386.*

An unidentified Toronto mounted officer, c. 1928 Photograph, Toronto Police Museum.

1929

By all accounts the 1920s were very good to the Mounted Unit. The Police Department had ignored those who questioned the unit's relevance in the modern age. The Mounted Unit had in fact been increased in size and was staffed by forty-one officers of all ranks and forty horses.

The unit continued to grow. Four horses were sold and ten remounts purchased. Patrol Sergeant Robert Rogerson was promoted to full sergeant and placed in second command of the unit. The police did not have an exercise ring or a training ring of their own during this era. The military permitted them to use its Riding School at the University Armouries to train both men and horses.

Mounted officers stopped wearing the "Bobby" style helmet, using instead a forage cap when on patrol. Foot officers continued to wear the helmet. Why the Mounted Unit discontinued wearing the helmet is not known, but the change was probably implemented by Chief Constable Draper for appearance reasons. It was an odd decision because the helmet might well have provided officers with some protection in crowd-control situations.

On Tuesday, August 13, there was a large confrontation between the police and members of the Communist Party at Queen's Park. It would be the first of many major clashes that took place between Toronto Police and groups which had been deemed to be subversive.

On August 29th the Toronto newspapers ran stories about gang fights which occurred in city parks. Several complaints from citizens that youths were brawling in the parks with baseball bats. The gangs were identified as the "East Enders" and the "West Enders." Mounted officers stepped up their park patrols to end these fights.

The Labour Day Parade was led by three mounted constables and two motorcycle officers. Eight weeks later, on October 29, Black Tuesday, the stock markets around the world crashed. Many of the people who marched in the Labour Day Parade would be involved in violent confrontations with these officers during the next few years. The 1920s decade ended with the start of the worst economic depression and social unrest Canada had ever seen.

Sgt Rogerson, c. 1929. Photograph, Toronto Police Museum.

A mounted officer stands by as a foot officer holds back the crowd at the University of Toronto during the visit of Queen Maria. Photograph, City of Toronto Archives. William James Collection, SC 244-1012.

The Red Riot

On Tuesday, August 13, 1929, members of the Communist Party of Canada planned to hold a rally at Queen's Park. Although the Communist Party was a lawful and recognised political entity, the Toronto Police Commission advised party members that they would not be allowed to hold their planned meeting. Police, detailed to Queen's Park, were ordered to prevent anyone from making speeches. The confrontation began when the police moved in to stop the organizers from speaking to the crowd.

How you interpret the day's events depends on which Toronto newspaper you read, as each gave differing accounts of events based on their "pro police" or "establishment" editorial policies. One described the dispersal of the crowds as police "*savagery.*" The *Toronto Telegram* did not deny the police were rough, but downplayed the police violence—explaining that a few inexperienced officers had "lost their heads." What is not in doubt is that the Red riot was a very violent occurrence, and probably set the tone of police-Communist Party relations for the next ten years.

The following description of the events of August 13 is based mainly on the reports carried in the *Toronto Telegram*. It was a beautiful summer evening and people began arriving at Queen's Park just after 6:00 p.m. No effort was made by the police to deter anyone from entering the park. At around 7:00 p.m. the mounted officers arrived and went directly to a courtyard at the rear of the Parliament Buildings where they were kept out of sight. The size of the crowd grew, by a few hundred people every minute or so.

Officers on foot patrolled the perimeter of the park and at around 7:15 p.m. three or four mounted officers began walking [their horses] through the crowds. By 7:30 p.m. there was a crowd of about 5,000 people gathered on the grounds. Only about 150 or 200 of these people were "Reds," the majority of the people were in the park for recreation or curiosity.

The "Red" speakers were just about to head for the podium to start their meeting when they were turned away by the police. Inspector Marshall, Inspector Alexander, Inspector Crosbie (of the Mounted Unit), Patrol Sergeant Gibbs and Chief Inspector Guthrie walked up on the stand and ordered everyone to leave the park in an orderly manner. Their orders could not be heard very well due to the noise of the crowd.

One of the "Reds" tried to get up on the stage, but was physically stopped by Inspector Marshall. A crowd of communist supporters then surrounded the Inspector. At this point a group of foot police charged into the crowd of 40 "Reds" and broke through to Marshall. A pushing and

The band shell at Queen's Park where the riot began on August 13, 1929. This picture was taken on August 27th. Mounted officers have been posted at the band shell to prevent anyone from gaining access to the podium as a Communist rally had been advertised. Photograph, City of Toronto Archives, *Globe and Mail Collection, 17707.*

shoving melee began. *'This was the sign for the mounted men to come pouring from the courtyard of the buildings. Fifteen came tearing across the greens, as though doing a charge of the light brigade."* [2]

At this point other police reinforcements, including motorcycle officers, also entered the park. Protestors became wedged between the line of foot police and the men on horses, while police motorcycles cut paths through the compressed crowd. It was inevitable that people would be hurt as not all citizens had a clear escape route.

The *Telegram* described the actions of the mounted officers under a subtitle, "MOUNTIES CHARGE," and went on to say: *"How the mounted men were able to prevent their horses from trampling people under, is still a miracle. Fifteen charging animals, looking ferocious to those on the ground, their front hoofs going high in the air in a deadly looking gallop, broke through the crowds and caused innumerable people to fall as they were pressed sideways.*

But the horses did not harm one person. There were persons who attempted to hurt the animals by taking a kick at the horses' legs. It was a dangerous practice on the part of anyone, but the mounted men deserve credit in holding their charges under a strong arm and preventing horses from hurting anyone." [3]

The police moved the crowd south to College Street. A group refused to move and gathered in the flower beds at the front of the legislative building. The *Toronto Telegram* described what happened next. *"Horses, motorcycles and police bore down on them and made them move on. A few more fist flew here and the mounted men, for the first time, drew their whips but as far as anyone could see they were not used on anyone. They were swung over the heads, or shoved into the back of one or two to keep them moving, but no one was struck."* [4]

The mounted men continued to drive the crowd away followed by motorcycle men who kept stragglers moving. The last of the crowds were pushed out into the oncoming traffic on College Street. Fortunately no injuries occurred. It was all over by 8:30 p.m.

Numerous complaints were made to the newspapers. One man claimed he was in the middle of the park when a mounted officer leaned over and held him by the ear, literally dragged him off his feet and carried him forward. As he was being dragged alongside the horse's hoofs, a plainclothesman came up and kicked him. [5]

Another man, an army veteran of forty years told a newspaper reporter that he was "feeling pretty sick," because of his experience with a mounted policeman during the "Red riot."

He had just got off the streetcar to visit a friend. He did not know about the rally until he saw the crowd being driven down the street by the police and a mounted man rode up beside him and struck him with a whip.

"'Stop! Don't knock me about. I am a hundred percent disability man. I know nothing about these communists. I'm going to see a friend.' I told him, but he said, 'Get the hell out of here' and struck me over the back with his whip. He then drove me along with the mob.

This photograph was taken after Queen's Park itself had been cleared of people on August 13. A line of foot officers backed up by a mounted officer are pushing the crowd down the street away from the park. *Photograph, City of Toronto Archives,* Globe and Mail Collection. 17511.

"I am feeling pretty sick today. I have had 40 years service in the army, and during and after the war I was for four years a special constable here. All the inspectors know me. Yet I was treated like that."[6]

The August 19th *Toronto Telegram* carried a clarification of the above story. The man stated that he had been misrepresented by another Toronto paper. He told the *Telegram* that he had telephoned Chief Draper to advise him of the error and attended at police headquarters to swear an affidavit as to what really happened. He said that he had been spoken to harshly and forced to move with the crowd, but under the circumstances the police were justified in doing so, and probably saved lives by keeping control of the situation.[7]

Chief Constable Draper referred all of the press inquiries to Inspector Marshall who had been in charge at the scene. Inspector Marshall denied any unnecessary force was used and stated, *"The story of police kicking people and of the mounted men riding roughshod over civilians is all imaginary. Certain measures had to be used to clear the park, but the story of people being trailed at the feet of galloping horses was untrue."[8]*

The Chief Constable attributed all complaints as communist propaganda and publicity. The Trades and Labour Congress said that it did not support the communists, but that the police were foolish in resorting to these methods to clear the park as it made martyrs of the victims. On August 15th the Congress passed a resolution asking for an inquiry into the melee. After listening to speeches and debating its response, the Congress came up with what appears to be, considering the circumstances, a moderate rebuke to the police and the Police Commission.

The Congress disassociated itself from the Communist Party, but stood up for the principle of free speech. They expressed concern that the Police Commission was adamant that these methods would continue to be used until all meetings held under the auspices of the Communist Party were suppressed. To the Congress the issue was as much about free speech, as police methods and police violence. The free speech section of the Trades and Labour Congress statement said, *"Whereas serious danger to the liberty of speech is threatened, and a long-standing British right is likely denied the citizens of Toronto, and other organizations whose views may not be accepted by the higher authorities of the state, and may be denied the right to carry on educational work in harmony with the evolution of a modern society."[9]*

Police Warning

An attempt may be made by those interested in the spread of Bolshevism and Communism propaganda to hold a public meeting in places of public resort in the City of Toronto. As such meetings are likely to disturb the public peace, it is the duty of the Officers of the Law to take such action as may be necessary to prevent any such meetings in public places.

The public is warned that it is unlawful for a group of people to forcibly attempt to hold a meeting in a place of public resort, and all parties who resort thereto for that purpose may be guilty of partaking in an unlawful assembly or riot, and may be prosecuted accordingly.

The public is further warned that it is the duty of every private citizen, under penalty of the Criminal Code, to assist the police officers of the city in maintaining the public peace, and, dispersing any unlawful assembly.

It is not the desire of the police authorities to have good citizens involved in any breaches of the law, and the co-operation of the public is solicited by remaining away from any places where parties are likely to congregate for the purpose of demonstration.

D. C. DRAPER,
Aug. 26th, 1929.   Chief Constable, Toronto.

The police advertisement from the Toronto Telegram *warning people not to attend Communist rallies.* Toronto Telegram, *August 26, 1929.*

The Police Commission announced on August 15 that there was no need to hold an inquiry into how the police disbursed the crowd. As far as the Commission was concerned, its order still stood that no Communist meetings were allowed in any city park, street or hall. The Communist Party would not be intimidated and planned another rally for Thursday August 22nd.

Chief Constable Draper did not view the issue as one of free speech, and released a statement on August 18th, where he said; *"The issue has erroneously been stated to be whether or not there shall be free speech in Toronto. The real question is whether we shall allow sedition to be openly taught and advocated in public in Toronto."* His statement continued, explaining the dangers and goals of the communist *"agitators."*

Draper then explained the police position, by saying *"The police will never interfere with any proper movement to bring about changes by constitutional methods, but the men engaged in this propaganda are utterly disloyal to Canada and every other civilized country. The same fight we are carrying on here is now being carried on in Paris, France, only along somewhat different lines. In China this party is being stamped out and its members deported. It probably would be terrible to contemplate Canada if this movement is not nipped in the bud. In fact, the budding stage is past. I can assure the board that no more force has been or will be used than is essential to prevent unlawful assemblies in public places."[10]*

Communist demonstration at the University of Toronto, October 19, 1929. Inspector Crosbie (foreground) and two mounted constables back up uniform and plainclothes officers who are preventing people from entering the grounds of the University. Photograph, City of Toronto Archives, Globe and Mail *Collection, 18378.*

The Chief obviously saw his duty clear, and that duty was total war with the Communist Party of Canada. He would fight this war with: detectives assigned to the "Communist Squad," motorcycle and foot officers; and the mounted officers, who were soon given the nickname "Draper's Dragoons."

The communist demonstration planned for Thursday August 22nd fizzled, and there were no more major communist meetings. On August 26th, the police department took out an advertisement in the local papers. The advertisement contained the large headline "POLICE WARNING." Members of the public were warned to avoid Communist meetings under the threat of arrest or forced dispersal.

On October 29, 1929, stock markets around the world "crashed" and the Great Depression began. The 1930s proved to be a trying time for the Toronto Police with hundreds of homeless and unemployed citizens filling the streets of Toronto. The economic downturn forced more people into the ranks of those wishing for social change and willing to take to the streets to get it. Across Canada, police officers were involved in violent confrontations with the disenfranchised. The image of police using violence to maintain the status quo will always be a major icon of these troubled times.

In his book, *The Great Depression*, Pierre Berton begins his story with a description of the August 13 Riot which he refers to as the start of "The Great Repression." After this street battle, people began to question the methods used by the police and the repressive laws Canada used to control the poor, the homeless and those asking for changes unpopular with the ruling class. Events like this, and the social disorder that continued through the 1930s, eventually led to social changes which brought Canada its welfare state, and eventually, the Charter of Rights and Freedoms.

1   *Toronto Telegram.* August 14, 1929.
2   *Toronto Telegram.* August 14, 1929.
3   *Toronto Telegram.* August 14, 1929.
4   *Toronto Telegram.* August 14, 1929.
5   *Toronto Telegram.* August 14, 1929.

6   *Toronto Telegram.* August 15, 1929.
7   *Toronto Telegram.* August 19, 1929.
8   *Toronto Telegram.* August 14, 1929.
9   *Toronto Telegram.* August 16, 1929.
10 *Toronto Telegram.* August 19, 1929.

Mounted officers escorting Communist demonstrators through the University grounds, October 19, 1929. Photograph, City of Toronto Archives, Globe and Mail *Collection. 18450.*

The Communists have left the University property. Inspector Crosbie is in the right of the picture and appears to be giving instructions to the officers. Photograph, City of Toronto Archives, Globe and Mail *Collection. 18437.*

Mounted Training in the 1920s

The mounted division was a desirable posting within the Toronto Police Department in 1924. There were more applicants than positions and the Inspector could be choosy about those he accepted. The following story on the training of mounted men was compiled from a number of 1920s era Toronto newspapers.

The only benefit to transferring to the Mounted Unit was the opportunity to work with horses and to be part of an elite unit. The rate of pay and hours of duty were the same as for the regular force. Officers did not just ride the horses, they were responsible for their bedding, feeding and grooming.

The weight and build of the officers was an important factor in who got to join the unit. "In the selection of men for the Mounted Squad Chief Dickson prefers men weighing around 165 pounds. This is considered a fair load for the horse to carry." If the officer weighed 160 pounds it would mean "that in full marching order their mounts are asked to carry approximately 200 pounds."[1]

The *Evening Telegram* of May 5, 1930 had this to say about the difficulty in getting posted to the mounted division:

The selection test for the mounted squad is a pretty stiff one. Not all who apply are taken on, and there is always a waiting list. First of all the candidate must have a minimum of one year's service on the force before he can be considered. Then he is put through an exhaustive riding test in the armouries to see if his horsemanship measures up to the required standard. Then, providing that he is found suitable, and there happens to be a vacancy, he is admitted on probation.[2]

One of the things they looked for in deciding if a candidate was "suitable" was prior service in the military. *With one or two exceptions all the members of the unit have seen active military service in the army. Military experience is considered an important qualification for the unit.*[3]

Once an officer had passed the initial riding test and been deemed suitable for the Mounted Unit he would undergo a two-month training course. The *Telegram* described the training:

The course is as tough as it can possibly be to turn out a perfect rider. The men must be able to walk, canter or gallop the horse without stirrups or reigns. They must be able to leap into the saddle from the ground with one hand on the saddle and without touching the stirrup. They are trained to change horses at the gallop.

The hardest of the training is leaping into the saddle. At first the men tend to land on the horses bare back at the hind quarters. This is a sensitive spot and will often cause the horse to start moving. The result is the man usually finds himself on the ground. The training is very thorough and Inspector Crosbie makes sure that it is. After the man is taught to ride he is taken to a stable and shown how to care for the animal and its harness.

The finishing touches are, the man is taught the theory of how to handle the public as a mounted officer. Inspector Crosbie states, 'I will stand for no impoliteness on the part of my men. I like discipline. The public are always right and there must be no argument. My men are instructed to follow the right course, but without undue sternness. They must be firm, but must be gentle at the same time. They must never talk back in a rough or ungentlemanly manner when spoken to.[4]

If the officer graduated from the riding school he would be assigned a horse and placed in one of the city's police stables. He would be expected to take excellent care of his kit and mount and to be immaculately turned out at all times. If he did not maintain the high standards of the mounted service he would be transferred out of the unit. There were many others waiting to take his place.

1   Unknown Toronto Newspaper. (Possibly *Toronto Telegram*, 1924).
2   *Evening Telegram* May 5, 1930.
3   Unknown Toronto Newspaper. (Possibly *Toronto Telegram*, 1924).
4   *Evening Telegram* May 5, 1930.

Constable Charles Whitford (left) and "Mayflower" with another officer at No. 11 Police Station, London and Markham Streets, 1926. Photograph, Toronto Police Mounted Unit.

An arrest on Spadina Avenue, February 1931. Photograph, Toronto Telegram.

Constable Christopher Leary (587) with a lost child at the Canadian National Exhibition. Photograph, City of Toronto Archives, Globe and Mail *Collection, 17701.*

Chief Constable Dennis Colburn Draper
1928–1946

Chief Constable Dennis Draper riding his police horse, "Bruce." Photograph, Toronto Police Museum.

Brigadier General Dennis Draper had no police experience when he was hired to be the Chief of the Toronto Police Department. The Police Commission passed over many competent officers within the department to select Draper for the job.

The Police Commissioners wanted a strict military disciplinarian in charge. The wealthy families, who actually controlled Toronto, wanted someone who could contain the Labour, Communist and Socialist movements. The Police Commission contacted the Department of National Defence in Ottawa and they suggested Brigadier General Dennis C. Draper (retired) for the job. Draper had just stood for election as a Conservative Party Candidate and had been defeated. He was then working in Quebec in the lumber industry.

By most accounts Draper was a poor Police Chief. The famous police reporter, Jocko Thomas, described Draper as being Toronto's most incompetent and clownish Chief.[1] The senior police officers resented the way that he was made Chief ahead of them. The men despised the harsh discipline that the new chief imposed. It is important to remember that Chief Draper did exactly what he was hired to do. The press, public and police may not have been happy with him, but those in power must have been elated with the job that he did.

When Draper took over the Toronto Police Force it was dominated by the "Irish." You had to be a member of a fraternal organization such as the Orange Order or the Masons to get anywhere on the job. Draper began to change this system of patronage and promotion by replacing it with his military style of patronage.

Draper started putting his stamp on the force the first day he arrived in Toronto. One of the constables picking him up at the railway station was wearing his World War I service ribbons. Draper looked at the ribbons and reputedly said, "A D.C.M. man (Distinguished Conduct Medal), what rank are you?" The officer replied that he was a constable and the new Chief asked him if that was not the lowest rank. The officer said that it was and the next day Chief Draper had him promoted to patrol sergeant.

Brigadier General Draper was himself a genuine war hero who had been awarded the Distinguished Service Order, twice. The citations for these awards are found in the London Gazette, 19 August, 1916. Temporary Lt. Colonel Dennis Draper, 2nd Canadian Mounted Rifles

"For conspicuous gallantry in the face of the enemy. He led reinforcements to exposed points, and twice drove off determined hostile counter attacks. Though himself wounded, he carried his mortally wounded C.O. from the firing line."

Bar to the Distinguished Service Order, Lt. Colonel Dennis Colburn Draper C.M.G., D.S.O. London Gazette, 7 July, 1918.

"For conspicuous gallantry and devotion to duty in several engagements. In an attack, when elements of his battalion reached the line of their final objective and held their position though both flanks were in the air, with the aid of two companies of another brigade he formed a defensive flank 500 yards long, and with great skill and coolness secured the left of the ground gained. He afterwards remained in the forward area until the evacuation of all his wounded had been organized."[2]

The Draper years, 1928 to 1946, became the golden years of the Mounted Unit. Chief Constable Draper was an excellent rider and kept his own police mount "Bruce" at Sunnybrook Park. Jocko Thomas, the famed *Toronto Star* crime reporter, states that at many of the crowd control sweeps done by the police, Chief Draper would be mounted and ride with the officers.[3] After a number of street clashes the press gave the Mounted Unit the nickname "Draper's

Dragoons." In the United States many of the mounted police units were referred to as "Black Hussars" or "The Cossacks of Capitalism."

His preference for men with military service stood the Mounted Unit in good stead with the Chief. Almost all of the men had military service and many of them had been decorated for bravery in the field. His mandate to control unrest in the streets also made the Mounted Unit one of his most valuable tools.

Of the four Toronto papers the *Toronto Star* was the most critical of Draper and his police force. Draper would not allow the *Star* in any police buildings. He referred to it as "The Red *Star* on King Street." The events of these times are described quite differently in each paper that you read. The other papers were much more forgiving of the police actions than the *Star*. In some cases the other papers were quite unsympathetic to the communists and other groups associated to the left, including labour.

These were very troubled times in Canada. Although "Draper's Dragoons" did deal with a lot of unrest in Toronto, things were much worse on the Prairies. R.C.M.P. Mounted Squads were involved in many very violent confrontations in Western Canada. The descriptions of these riots make the Toronto confrontations pale in comparison.

During World War II, Draper volunteered for active service. He took a military leave of absence and went to England to offer his services. His offer was declined due to his age and he returned to Toronto. He retired from the police force in 1946 after eighteen years as Chief of Police.

After Draper left the chief's office, the Mounted Unit would enter a quiet time with a reduced complement of officers. The booming post-war economy meant that there was very little of the social disorder that had lasted through the 1930s. The Draper years were good to the Mounted Unit and probably good for the majority of Torontonians. Many today question his methods, motivation and goals. What should be remembered is his one real rare quality, which is seldom seen today. He did exactly what he was hired to do, and whether his methods were right or wrong, he did his duty.

1 Thomas, Jocko. *From Police Headquarters.* Stoddart Publishing Company Limited, Toronto,1990. Page 33.
2 Riddle, David K. & Mitchell, Donald G. *The Distinguished Service Order Awarded to Members of The Canadian Expeditionary Force and Canadians in the Royal Naval Air Service, The Royal Flying Corps and the Royal Air Force, 1915-1920.* The Kirkby-Marlton Press, Winnipeg, Manitoba, 1991.
3 Thomas, Jocko. *From Police Headquarters.* Stoddart Publishing Company Limited, Toronto, 1990. Page 36.

1930

In 1928 the Kilgour family donated property it owned on Bayview Avenue to the City of Toronto. The land and buildings were assumed by the Parks Department and became Toronto's Sunnybrook Park. The Parks Commissioner offered the Mounted Unit the use of a number of residences and a barn in the new Park. There was also a riding school attached to the property, with plenty of room for breaking and training young horses.

The unit had been looking for many years for a suitable facility in which to conduct its training. Although Sunnybrook Park was located north of the city limits, a long ride from downtown, the Mounted Unit was grateful for the offer, and moved officers and horses there in early 1930. A small contingent of mounted officers and their families moved into the old buildings of the Kilgour Estate.

Inspector Crosbie moved his family into one of the houses, but continued to maintain an office at police headquarters. He was assigned a Ford Model "A" Touring Police Car to travel to work and visit all stables. Chief Constable Draper stabled his mount at Sunnybrook Park. The charger, "Bruce," was a huge animal and stood at least 17 hands high.

A new communications system, using patrol boxes and bell lights, was introduced in February. Call boxes and bell lights were strategically located throughout the city, and patrolling officers were required to report to their police stations at designated times throughout the day. This was known as the timed beat system. An officer's call in was recorded by the station duty operator. If the officer failed to call at the specified time, a patrol sergeant would come looking for him.

The patrol boxes were equipped with a light and a bell which could be activated from the station. When an officer heard the bell, or saw the light, he was to contact the station on the call box telephone. The station would then assign him a pending detail. Patrolling officers could also contact the station when requesting a patrol wagon after they made an arrest. An emergency assistance call device on the box summoned help.

Mounted officers were required to contact their respective stations while on patrol. There was even a call box placed on semi-rural Rosedale Valley Road, a No. 5 Division mounted post. Other specific Mounted Unit call boxes were located in High Park.

On May 5th, the *Toronto Telegram* newspaper ran a story headlined "Police Mounts Earn Rest After Years of Service." The article portrayed the strong bond formed between the mounted officers and horses of the Unit. Two older horses were being sold and the reporter came to the stable to see the horses off. "'Sorry old timer, but we must part,' a constable spoke to 'one of his best and most understanding pals.'"[65]

The paper reported that the mounts would be taken for their last ride and then shipped to the best homes that could be found for them, homes where they could live their lives out in peace. Horses would not be sold to peddlers, riding schools, delivery wagons or contracting firms. The horses would only go to private citizens who wanted a horse for light riding. Even after being sold the former police horses would be visited periodically by members of the Police Department. Inspector Thomas Crosbie visited his former mount once every other month.

The reporter went on to remark that it was no wonder officers bonded with their horses. They rode their mounts for eight hours every day, they cleaned them, fed them and looked after their needs when they were sick. Saddlery was cleaned and well looked after so as not to cause any sores

A mounted officer responds to Danforth Avenue after a test of new police call box system. He is speaking to former Chief Constable Grasette, Chief Constable Draper and Chair of the Police Commission, Judge Morrison. February 20, 1930. Photograph, City of Toronto Archives, Globe and Mail Collection, 19232.

or aches to the horse. The man and horse, came to understand each other well. The man would teach the animal tricks, and most horses were quick to learn.[66]

The Unit purchased two remounts to replace two that were sold. They also purchased an additional eight remounts, bringing the Mounted Unit's total horse strength to forty-eight mounts, the most it ever owned.

1930 was an election year and the Communist Party was actively campaigning. It had legal standing in the election, with nine candidates seeking seats. Attempts to campaign in Toronto were obstructed by the police and others who did not support their beliefs.

Pierre Berton described one of the confrontations at a Communist election rally: "A gang of toughs disrupted one meeting at Spadina and Dundas Streets, three mounted policemen and four uniformed constables stood by smiling."[67]

On October 1st, the unit was out in force to be part of the funeral parade for former Chief Constable H.J. Grasette, C.M.G.

He had served as Chief Constable from December 1, 1886 to December 18, 1920 and was always a good friend of the Mounted Squad.

A mounted officer walks the riderless horse behind the hearse at Chief Constable Grasette's funeral. The riding boots are reversed in the stirrups in military tradition. Photograph, Toronto Police Museum.

Inspector Crosbie on the right with the mounted escort at the funeral of former Chief Constable H.J. Grasette. Photograph, Toronto Police Mounted Unit.

The mounted unit formed up in "troop in line" outside the Horticultural Building at the Canadian National Exhibition, 1930. Photograph, Toronto Police Museum.

Sunnybrook Park

The Kilgour family owned the lands which make up today's Sunnybrook Park. The surrounding area was the location of the homes of many of Toronto's most prominent families. Some of these large estate homes still exist, although most are no longer in private hands.

Major Kilgour was a noted equestrian. He would host horse shows and foxhunts at his Sunnybrook Farm estate. His Foxhunts sometimes attracted as many as a hundred riders. The farm was one of the finest private equestrian centres in Canada. In 1928, the Kilgours donated the land and buildings to the City of Toronto.

In 1930, the Mounted Unit was offered the use of the main stable and a number of the houses within the park. The offer was accepted and the unit took over the old light-horse barn, which was equipped with an indoor riding ring. There was an outdoor riding ring located in the upper grounds where playing fields are now located. Today the light-horse barn houses the snack bar, the Parks Department's storage area and its drive shed.

In the 1930s, the park was still a long way from the city. Officers assigned to work at this location lived in the Park, forming their own Mounted Unit community. Inspector Crosbie was given the large house currently used by the owner of the Sunnybrook Riding Academy.

There was also a semi-detached house, since demolished, at the rear of the police barn. Constable Harvey Coathup, his wife and two boys lived in one half of the house while constable Tom Pogue, his wife and three children lived in the other. Both Coathup boys were later killed while serving with the Royal Canadian Air Force in World War II.

A number of single men's apartments were located on the second story of the police barn. These were occupied by Constables Tommy Burgess, Andy Cooper, Tom Frazer and Alvin Morrison. Officers' meals were prepared and served by Mrs. Crosbie at the Inspector's house.

The Units' Blacksmith travelled to the park to care for the horses. Veterinarian, Doctor Clark, would also attend them as needed. Inspector Crosbie kept his horse, "Shamrock" at the Sunnybrook Stable along with Chief Constable Draper's "Bruce." All new remounts received their accommodation and training at the Sunnybrook Stable.

In the late 1930s, Chief Constable Draper instituted a program where by all recruits to the Toronto Police Force were required to attend Sunnybrook Park for mounted training. The recruits were instructed by Inspector Crosbie and they learned to be competent riders, even if they never had any ambitions of becoming mounted officers.

The barn presently used by the Mounted unit had been the Heavy-Horse Barn on the Kilgour estate. This barn was turned over to the 9th Mississauga Horse Regiment in 1930. The 9th Mississauga Horse was later amalgamated with the Governor Generals Body Guard to form the Governor Generals Horse Guards.

Sunnybrook Estate, c. 1910. The barn in the centre was the heavy horse barn, given to the Mississauga Horse in 1930. It became the police barn in 1968. The house on the left was used by a constable's family in 1930 and by Inspector Johnson in 1968. Photograph, Mike Filey Collection.

Sunnybrook Estate from the west, c. 1910. The light horse barn that became the police stable in 1930 is in the top right. Inspector Crosbie's house is on the right. The police barn (1968) is top centre and Inspector Johnson's house is on the left. Photograph, Toronto Police Mounted Unit.

Sunnybrook Hospital was built during the Second World War, and all of the lands and buildings in Sunnybrook Park were expropriated by the Canadian Government. In 1943 the Mounted Unit was forced to vacate the park and turn the facilities over to the military. A large base was built at the site.

The current public playing fields area on the high ground at the end of the park road were filled with military buildings. All the buildings were torn down during the late 1960s with the exception of the current pavilion, which, was the officer's mess .

In 1967 the Federal Government decided to return the Sunnybrook land to Metropolitan Toronto, and it was officially returned to Metropolitan Toronto Parks Department in 1968. The Parks Commissioner advised the Police Commission on September 14, 1967 that two buildings in Sunnybrook Park would be made available for the Mounted Unit. One building was the old Mississauga Horse stable which was suitable for twenty-four horses. The other building was a residence which could be used by supervisory staff.

The Parks Commissioner needed to know within seven days whether the police would accept the buildings, so the necessary alterations to the buildings could be put into the 1968 budget. The Police Commission did accept the gift, and Inspector Johnson visited the site. He made these recommendations.

With reference to the proposed future operation of Sunnybrook Stables I recommend that consideration be given in the near future as to what stables will be closed and relocated at Sunnybrook. With respect to the above I suggest the following:

1. *That Sunnybrook Stables be operated as a combined headquarters, training and regular patrol stable.*
2. *That operations of Headquarters Stable (57 Stable, Belmont Street) and 56 Stable (Pape Avenue) be discontinued and horses and personnel relocated at Sunnybrook.*
3. *That sufficient additional stalls be acquired to accommodate additional horses from other stables at a future date.*

The Mounted Unit moved back to Sunnybrook in October 1968. Photograph, Toronto Police Mounted Unit.

Winter training beside the police stable in Sunnybrook Park, c. 1975. Photograph, Toronto Police Mounted Unit.

On examining the facilities of Sunnybrook with the Metropolitan Toronto Parks Authority I recommended the following alterations and additions required for the operation.

(a) Additions to the stable proper to accommodate office facilities for headquarters operations.

(b) Interior alterations to provide:

1. Twenty standing stalls and three box stalls.
2. Tack room for approximately 24 "kits" on wall racks.
3. Lunch and locker room (24 lockers)
4. Equipment storage room and workshop.
5. Washroom facilities.

Providing the above suggested facilities are obtained a good efficient operation will be feasible at Sunnybrook. When we considered the good facilities available for the training and the major park areas accessible from this point, this proposed move is certainly a step in the right direction. [1]

The Police Commission concurred with Inspector Johnson's recommendations and alterations were made to the building as follows: tack room, harness store and workshop, lunch and locker room, washroom facilities, a sergeant's office with public reception space and an inspector's office. The nine horses at Belmont Street and the seven horses at Pape Avenue were moved to Sunnybrook.

Inspector Johnson was offered use of the house in the park as private residence. Renovations were completed on the inspector's new abode on October 29th, and he moved into the park with his family. The renovations on the Sunnybrook stable began on September 9th and the Unit moved the men and mounts into the Stable on December 17th. The Belmont Street Stable and the Pape Avenue Stable were both permanently closed.

After the Program Review of the Mounted Unit in 1993, all remaining horses were moved from Sunnybrook to the Exhibition Stable. A plan was written to renovate the stable at Sunnybrook and return the horses there after work was completed. The unit commander, staff sergeant, clerk and quartermaster continued to work at Sunnybrook while the horses and operational staff were located at the Exhibition.

Plans changed and officials decided to renovate the Exhibition Stable instead of Sunnybrook. In November 1999, all police horses were returned to Sunnybrook during renovation of the Exhibition location. On July 24, 2000, the Toronto Police Mounted Unit moved out of Sunnybrook Stable and the building was returned to the City of Toronto Parks Department.

1 Unit Commander's Annual Report. 1967.

PC Merle Smith riding a remount on the hill overlooking the police stable, 1968. Photograph, James Lewcum, Globe and Mail.

The Mounted Unit Drill Team at Sunnybrook Stable in June 2000. The Unit moved out of the park the following month. Left to right: Staff Inspector Davis, PC Speirs, PC Mamak, PC Rowbotham, Sgt Spurling, PC Jones, PC Smith, PC Montgomery, Sgt Acott, PC Gilbert, PC Bradford, PC Decosta, PC Woods, PC Penney, Sgt Wardle. Photograph, Alex Robertson photography.

Mounted officers are patrolling Bloor Street West outside of Varsity Stadium, c. 1931.
Photograph, City of Toronto archives, William James Collection. SC 244-1714.

The Mounted Unit in 1930. This photograph was probably taken in Rosedale Valley Ravine. Left to right: Inspector Crosbie, Sgt Rogerson,
PC's McRae, Morrison, Hutchinson, Hunt, McMaster, Gallagher, Walker, Hall, Harvey, Houston, Fullerton, Creighton, Danson, Watt,
Chief Constable Draper, Judge Morrison, PC's Lepper, McCauley, Moore, Mclush, Lain, Cooper, Carr, Hill, Phillips, Dedlow, Murray, Coathup,
P/Sgt Chalkin, P/Sgt Masters. Photograph, Toronto Police Museum.

The Rosedale Barracks Fire

Early police mounts were taught to stand and wait for their riders when left alone. The following story, which appeared in the *Toronto Telegram* on Monday May 5, 1930, indicates just how effective that training was. While on general patrol riding police mount "Listowel," a mounted constable observed a fire in the Rosedale Barracks. The officer immediately rode the horse to a lower floor window of the structure. He stood up on the horse and pulled himself into a window to check the building for occupants. The horse then walked to the sidewalk where it waited for its rider. Nothing could shift the horse until its rider returned.

It is amazing that with all of the noise and confusion of a fire scene, a horse would stand and wait for its rider. "Listowel" was probably one of the more talented police mounts. The horse had also been taught to gently shake hands with young children.

1   *Toronto Telegram.* Monday May 5, 1930.

"Listowel" at the Rosedale Barracks fire. Illustration, William White, 2001.

1931

In his annual report, Chief Constable Draper reported that the Mounted Unit was making full use of Sunnybrook Park for training purposes. "A rigid schooling of men and horses, together with instruction in horsemanship, is being carried out."[68]

On February 25, a large rally took place at the corner of Spadina Avenue and Dundas Street, the heart of the clothing trade. The *Toronto Telegram* reported it to be organized by members of the Communist Party. Almost 4,000 attended to listen to organizers delivering speeches while standing on a pile of bricks.

A small contingent of foot police from the Claremont Street Station allowed the speakers to orate for one hour. At two o'clock, mounted officers moved into the crowd waving their riding crops above their heads while the officers on foot drew their batons. The crowd, pushed from the corner, began a pre-planned march to City Hall. The police headed them off at University Avenue and Queen Street and the marchers were forced to disperse into small groups on the side streets. By 4 o'clock there were no marchers to be seen.

The *Telegram* reported that "The horses used by the department showed the crowd that they would stand for no trouble, swinging right into people helping their riders. In one case a man thought that a very tall officer must have grabbed him to yank him round. It proved to be a horse which had 'collared' him using its teeth to hold him by the shoulder."[69]

Twelve persons were arrested on various charges and a twenty-seven-year-old lady was taken to hospital after being knocked off her feet by a police horse. One police officer was injured from being struck in the mouth with a brick.

At its meeting on February 26, the Police Commission accepted a request from the Toronto Police Association that every member of the Police Force with ten or more years' service be granted three weeks annual leave like other civic employees and firemen. Mounted Constable Percy Johnson (375) was awarded a Merit Mark "for the arrest of two automobile thieves, who drove a stolen car into another automobile last December at Harbord and Major Streets, causing serious injury to the driver of the second car."[70]

Four horses were sold during the year, one died, and were replaced by five remounts. The Mounted Unit took part in a number of open competitions during the year. Several trophies were won at the Canadian National Exhibition, The Royal Winter Fair, The Eglinton Hunt Club and the Toronto Open Air Horse Show.

The population of Toronto in 1931 had grown to 627,231. About one third of the workforce was unemployed as a result of the Depression. The risk of civil unrest and Chief Draper's continuing vendetta against the Communist Party ensured the viability of the unit through these tough economic times. Horses were becoming scarcer on the city streets. On April 7th, the Toronto Fire Department disposed of its last two horses, "Mickey" and "Prince."[71]

Mounted officers on crowd control duty at Dufferin Race Track, June 1931. Photograph, City of Toronto Archives, Globe and Mail Collection. 30345.

1932 Chief Constable Draper was very pleased with the training program being administered by Inspector Crosbie at Sunnybrook Park. He believed the facilities were increasingly valuable in maintaining the Mounted Unit at a high point of efficiency.[72]

The department cast three horses, two others died during the year and were replaced with five remounts. Several trophies were again won at the Canadian National Exhibition, The Royal Winter Fair, The Eglinton Hunt Club and the Toronto Open Air Horse Show.

The Police Department's annual Church Parade was held on October 30th. This important event usually rated a front page story and picture in most newspapers. Foot and mounted officers reported for duty immaculately turned out. The parade of marching officers was led through the downtown streets of Toronto by Chief Constable Draper, mounted on "Bruce," followed by the Mounted Unit on their impeccably groomed mounts.

No. 6 Police Station was opened at Queen Street West and Cowan Avenue in the Parkdale area and equipped with a stable used by the Mounted Unit until 1965, when the officers and mounts were moved into the Horse Palace at the Exhibition.

Further expansion took place when No. 12 Police Station was opened in North Toronto at Yonge Street and Montgomery Avenue. It was equipped with a stable manned by members of the Mounted Unit until the early 1940s.

No. 6 Station, Cowan Avenue and Queen Street, 1998.

The stable area of No. 6 station. The station is now used as a community centre, stable doors have been replaced by bricks, 1998. Photographs, Sgt Lorna Kozmik.

A mounted officer outside Maple Leaf Gardens, 1931. Photograph, Pringle & Booth Ltd.

A mounted officer can be seen behind the car holding back the crowd at the opening of the Eaton's College Street store in 1930. Photograph, City of Toronto Archives, William James Collection. SC 244-1641.

ronto Police and Organized Labour

e Police Commission presented itself and the force as disinterested parties in labour disputes, their sole interest stated to be the maintenance of order. It led police into violent confrontations with strikers.

The reality was that the members of the Police Commission were part of Toronto's ruling elite and favoured industry owners in labour disputes. The Toronto police were often used to help defeat many of the demands of the labour movement. In contrast to the upper class police commissioners, Toronto police officers were recruited from the working class. Their work, recreation, values and life styles were much like the working people of the city.

Strict discipline and firm control of the rank and officers was maintained by the Police Commission. The purpose was to ensure that the police would obey the laws and maintain social order by force if required. Seen in this light, Toronto policemen worked against what would seem to be their own class interests. Despite the sometimes rocky relationship between the constables on the beat and union demonstrators, the police on the street received support from organized labour.

Union moderates correctly identified their true foes– the members of the Toronto Police Commission. Union leadership reminded its striking workers that the average policeman, even if he abused strikers on the picket line, was a working man controlled by autocratic senior officers. They told their membership that the police constables did not enjoy being assigned to strike duty.[1]

During the turbulent 1930s, Chief Constable Draper's crusade against Communists, and organized labour was at its peak. Morale sagged as police officers grumbled about being constantly assigned to crowd-control duties. The force was beginning to suffer from the continual reports of police harassment of leftist groups and the suppression of free speech. The very legitimacy of the Toronto Police Force was beginning to be called into question.[2]

A strong empathy existed within police ranks to sympathize with strikers, the best example being the Winnipeg General Strike of 1919. The official history of the Royal Canadian Mounted Police states that it was the fear that local police forces could not be relied upon to maintain order in labour disputes that kept the federal government from disbanding the R.C.M.P.[3]

After the violent 1902 Toronto Street Railway Strike, a number of Toronto officers refused to eat in a restaurant that was kept by a motorman who had not participated in the strike. No discipline was taken against the officers, but they were transferred to other divisions.[4] This strike was fairly violent, police were injured, so they could not have supported the strikers. Yet some of the constables sympathized with the strikers who also had no union representation or collective bargaining rights. Officers had to rely on the goodwill of the police commission for salary increases and improved working conditions. The Trades and Labour Congress openly began to assist the police in 1916. The relationship between the Toronto Police Commission, and the rank and file police officers supported by the Trades and Labour Congress, came to a head with the 1918 police strike.

The Royal Commission that followed ended all hopes of police union membership and established a weak Police Association which was the predecessor of today's Toronto Police Association.

This history contains the story of a number of violent confrontations between the labour movement and the Toronto police force. Only the strikes where something went wrong were described in the newspapers, which were a primary source of the information for this history. Considering the time span of this history and the amount of strike action attended by the Mounted unit, the occasions where violence occurred are few and far between.

Compared to how other jurisdictions dealt with their labour unrest, the Toronto police were much more tolerant than some modern authors would have you believe. Violent confrontation that took place in the United States and Western Canada were much more severe than anything that occurred in Toronto. In the 1922 book, *Grey Riders*, the author states, "say 'State Policeman' to the average citizen and straight away he will conjure up the picture of an iron-faced man on a rearing horse, surging into a mob of strikers with flailing night stick or smoking gun."[5]

The Toronto mounted officers were certainly not adverse to using force to disperse crowds. At times the force used may have been excessive, but it was certainly much less than the violence which police used elsewhere.

Foot officers encourage demonstrators to "move on." Photograph, City of Toronto Archives.

Another photograph of the Mounted Unit escorting a demonstration. Photograph, City of Toronto Archives, Globe and Mail Collection. SC 266-26719.

Demonstrators being shadowed by mounted officers as they march to Queen's Park. Photograph, City of Toronto Archives, Globe and Mail Collection. SC 266-20072.

Mounted officers following at the rear of a demonstration. Photograph, City of Toronto Archives, Globe and Mail Collection. SC 266-23743.

1   Marquis, Greg. *Early 20th Century Toronto Police Institution.* P.H.D. Thesis submitted to the Department of History, Queen's University, Kingston, Ontario, November 1986. Page 99.
2   P. Marquis, Greg. *Early 20th Century Toronto Police Institution.* P.H.D.. Thesis submitted to the Department of History, Queen's University, Kingston, Ontario, November 1986. Page 129.
3   Horrall, S.W. *The Pictorial History of the Royal Canadian Mounted Police.* McGraw-Hill Ryerson Limited, Toronto, 1973. Page 179.
4   Leibaers, Jan K. *The Toronto Police Strike of 1918.* Major research paper submitted to Professor N. Rogers, September 1990. Page 40.
5   Van de Water, Frederic. *Grey Riders.* G.P. Putnam's Sons, New York, 1917. Reprinted by the Trooper Foundation, State of New York, 1992. Page 12.

...ia Avenue – The Centre of Dissension

During the 1930s, Spadina Avenue was associated more with the Communist Party and the Labour Movement than any other location in Toronto. Mounted policemen were a common sight on this street during the turbulent thirties.[1]

The area was inhabited by many Jewish people and immigrants. As the centre of Toronto's fashion industry, many people employed in the district laboured under terrible working conditions. Their rights were few so going on strike by withdrawing their labour, was their only hope for improving employment conditions.

Many living in poverty in the area felt politically disenfranchised in Orange Toronto. Socialists and Communists offered them a new hope as their needs were usually ignored by the mainstream political parties. Events that occurred in Toronto's fashion district during the decade helped to force the creation of the welfare state. It was the strikes, demonstrations and political activism that occurred principally on Spadina Avenue which led to legislation in 1935 which regulated pay, hours of work, and established a minimum wage.

The following photographs were taken in the area of Spadina Avenue and Dundas Street during a Communist rally and march on February 25, 1931.

A lone mounted officer stands watch at the corner of Dundas Street and Spadina Avenue. Photograph, City of Toronto Archives, Globe and Mail Collection, D23267.

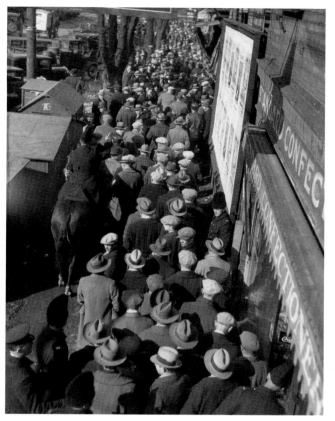

A mounted officer monitors the crowd as they walk on the sidewalk. Foot officers can be seen in the left and right of the picture. Photograph, City of Toronto Archives, Globe and Mail *Collection. D23269.*

A woman who was knocked over by a police horse is taken to hospital by the police ambulance. Photograph, City of Toronto Archives, Globe and Mail *Collection. D23273.*

A protester has been arrested and is being led to the patrol wagon by mounted officers. The mounted officer on the left hold his riding crop. Photograph, City of Toronto Archives, Globe and Mail *Collection. D23271.*

1933

The Great Depression was nearing its worst depth. Chief Constable Draper reported that owing to the unsettled industrial conditions, the demands made on the Mounted Unit had been very heavy throughout the year. He noted that the services provided by the unit had been very valuable in maintaining law and order.

Members of the mounted division patrol the downtown business district and perform essential service in eliminating traffic congestion. These officers also render valuable aid in facilitating the movement of traffic in congested areas during the rush hour periods.[73]

A large squatters' camp called a "Hobo Jungle" had grown up in the Don Valley just north of the Bloor Street viaduct. The railroads that ran nearby brought many transients who were "riding the rails," their prime source of moving to try to find a job. Hobos had left their cities, towns and farms in a futile search for a better life. The valley was full of homeless and often hungry people.

Mounted officers from No. 5 Stable policed this area by riding through the Rosedale Ravine and then north up the valley. It must have been a fairly dangerous and depressing area to patrol with so many desperate people living in squalor. The last police call box was located back on Rosedale Valley Road. Should patrolling officers encounter trouble, help would be a long time coming.

For members of the Toronto Police Force the Depression was probably not all that bad economically. Those people that had jobs saw their pay cheques going further due to deflation. The Police Commission enacted a rule which forbade police officers' wives from working—to try to create job opportunities for other families. Policemen were bringing home a steady wage and, depending on their performance, had secure jobs.

On June 3rd about 500 members of the Unemployed Workers Union held a rally in Trinity Park. It was violently broken up by police and some idea of the intensity comes from the story which appeared in the *Toronto Telegram.* "Meeting the 'ganging' tactics employed by the demonstrators, the police asked no quarter and gave none."[74] This story is more like the description of a clash between two opposing armies in the last war than the dispersal of a demonstration in a city park.

In July 1933, fifteen thousand people marched up Spadina Avenue to Queen's Park to protest the anti-Semitism of the new German government. Demonstrators were primarily Jews who were concerned with the horror of events taking place in Germany. This was likely the largest demonstration Toronto had seen to date.[75]

Six thousand attended another rally in Trinity Park on July 26. At 8:30 p.m., speakers from the unemployment groups and youthful members of the anti-war and anti-fascist groups started to speak. At 9:00 p.m. almost thirty policemen had arrived on horseback, foot and motorcycle.

The officers began to clear the park and the main group of "agitators" gathered at Queen Street West and Gorevale Ave. These demonstrators began to sing communist songs and shout slogans.

The police continued to push the crowds of people towards Spadina Avenue. A number of complaints appeared in the newspaper regarding the conduct of the police. The motorcycles used by police were equipped with a device that created a smoke screen of black smoke and nauseous gasses. A number of children were pushed to the ground during the dispersal, some reportedly near the hooves of the advancing horses.[76]

During the month of August, the Mounted Unit was busy dealing with the Swastika movement in Toronto's east end.

Last minute instructions from the sergeant. The Police Church Parade. October 29, 1933. Photograph, City of Toronto Archives, Globe and Mail *Collection. 31574.*

The Swastika movement climaxed their efforts with the riot in Christie Pits on August 16. The lack of a strong police presence at Christie Pits, despite warnings of possible problems, was partly to blame for the riot getting out of hand.

The left wing political parties in Toronto were quick to point out how their activities were over-policed while the right wing activities were not. That was probably true. Their complaint on August 15 was that police had deployed four mounted officers and numerous foot and motor-cycle officers in Allen Gardens in anticipation of a speech being made. Conversely when police had a clear warning of a possibility of violence involving right wing Nazis, the police response was minimal.

During a rally on August 17, a C.C.F. member of The Ontario Legislature asked why, "Draper and his Cossacks" broke up their recent meeting in Trinity Park "freely using batons and nauseating gasses in dispersing peaceful gatherings." The speaker demanded that the mayor ask why, "Only six policemen were present when the trouble broke out at Willowvale Park (Christie Pits), while the rest of the force was at Trinity Park unlawfully breaking up a peaceful meeting of citizens of Toronto."[77]

No doubt the members of the labour movement and the left wing parties were over-policed. It would seem that the right wing fascist parties were not viewed by Chief Constable Draper as much of a threat to society as was Communism.

Mounted officers at Spadina Avenue and Clarence Square waiting for the anti-Nazi march to begin. This was probably the largest demonstration that had occurred in Toronto, July 1933. Photograph, City of Toronto Archives, Globe and Mail *Collection. SC 266-30538.*

The anti-Nazi march begins. Members of the Swastika Club had to be aware of this march and the feeling of the Jewish community to the swastika and Nazi Germany. Photograph, City of Toronto Archives. SC 266-30538.

The Swastika Movement In 1930s Toronto

During the 1930s, Toronto was struggling through the Great Depression. The foreign born or those identified as being foreigners faced the wrath of some people who blamed them for their problems. In the Eastern Beaches area of Toronto, some local residents were fed up with what they saw as the invasion of their neighbourhood by foreigners every summer weekend.

Although the term foreigner was most often used to describe all the "undesirables" the main target of the protesters were Jews. Some of the younger Beaches residents adopted the swastika, the symbol of Hitler's Germany as their symbol of protest. There can be no doubt that they knew of the German dictator's treatment of Jews and what the swastika represented.

The leadership of the Swastika Club simply stated that the swastika was an old Iroquois good luck symbol and had no link to the political ideology. The club members had to have known that this symbol was repulsive to the Jews of Toronto. What became sure was that the Jewish Community was prepared to fight back against those who goaded them by brandishing swastika.

The Swastika Club members probably rallied or associated near the Balmy Beach Canoe Club. In August 1933, they began staging "Swastika Patrols" on the boardwalk to "clean up the beaches."[1] Soon after the Jewish community reacted to the use of the swastika. The *Toronto Star* reported on August 5 that the two sides where preparing for trouble on the upcoming weekend when three thousand Jews were scheduled to meet in Kew Gardens on Queen Street east of Woodbine Ave.[2]

The *Star* was right and a near-riot did occur as a number of club members had their swastika badges torn from their shoulders. Inspector Majury from No. 10 Police Division was able to quell the trouble and ordered the remaining club members to remove their swastikas. The problems continued throughout the summer with swastika members continually patrolling the boardwalk.

Gangs of young Jews from the city also patrolled the boardwalk looking for those wearing swastikas. The Beaches became a priority post for the mounted officers from Pape Avenue Stable. By mid-August the swastika groups had officially disbanded under the police pressure. Although swastikas were gone, the prejudice and discontent remained.

Willowvale Park is located at Bloor Street West and Christie Street and commonly known as "Christie Pits."

During the 1930s, it was the home of a group of young toughs known as "The Pit Gang." It was a tough area and dangerous for policemen to patrol on their own. On at least one occasion a foot patrolman was disarmed by members of the gang while on lone patrol. Mounted officers from No. 11 Stable patrolled the park in pairs.[3]

The park was used by baseball leagues and the games held there were usually well attended. On the night of August 14, 1933, a Jewish team was playing a team fielded by St. Peters Church. In the final inning of the game a group of people identified as gang members unfurled a large banner with the swastika symbol boldly displayed. After the game someone painted a large swastika and the words "Heil Hitler" on the roof of a park building.[4]

Another game was scheduled between the same teams on Wednesday August 16, the police should have been better prepared for what was about to occur. The events of the previous month should have foretold them that trouble was brewing. Close to one thousand Jewish spectators filled the park for the game. In the second inning a group of about thirty "Willowvale Swastikas" stood up and shouted "Heil Hitler." Small fights began to break out between the Jews and the swastika bearers.

The police officers in the park were able to contain the situation although minor fights continued. Once the game was completed, a large swastika banner was again displayed and with its unfurling, both sides clashed and a major riot exploded. Over the next six hours Jews, swastika-bearing gentiles, the toughies and police would battle both in the park and the surrounding streets. As time went on, more people came to the park to watch or join in the fighting. Truckloads of Jews came west from Spadina Avenue when the news spread through the neighbourhood that Jews were being beaten up in Christie Pits.

Every available police reinforcement, including the Mounted Unit, were called to help the small detail assigned to the park. The *Toronto Star* reported that the first mounted officers did not arrive at the park until 8:45 p.m. which was an hour after the first fists flew.[5] Metropolitan Toronto Police historian, Jack Webster, was a child at the time of the riot. He was in the park with friends and witnessed the rioting which took place. In his book, *Copper Jack*, he describes a number of incidents involving the Mounted Unit. "When he (Jack) turned to see a large contingent of mounted police charging full speed down the Christie Street hill and into the Pits, he decided it might be worthwhile to venture closer to the action."

He remained close to the mounted men who were in the centre of the park for most of the riot. "Order was only gradually restored, partly by mounted officers herding the crowd out of the park with their riding crops. Jack saw a mounted policeman strike one of the Pit Gang members. The member shouted, 'How come you don't hit the Jews?' 'Don't you tell me who to hit! Get out of this park, or I'll beat you to a pulp!' yelled the cop."

After the mounted officer was done with the Pit Gang member he turned towards Jack and his friends and gestured with his riding crop, "You young bastards, get on home or I'll give you a taste of this, too."[6]

The mounted officers tried to prevent people from entering the park and joining the fight but many were still able to get through. By 10:30 p.m. the horses were surrounding the trucks that were arriving with new combatants and escorting them out of the area before they could drop people off. By 11:10 p.m., the worst of the troubles were over despite large crowds who remained on Bloor Street and the side streets.

A number of people were injured during the riot and some arrests were made. The police were severely criticized for not being better prepared to deal with the problems that night and they started to take the swastika problem more seriously. The use of their dreaded symbol to provoke Jews and support Nazi Germany soon ended. Mounted patrols increased in all parks where problems could be expected.

The corner of Manning Avenue and Bloor Street West after the crowd has been pushed out of Christie Pits by the mounted officers. Photograph, City of Toronto Archives, Globe and Mail Collection. SC 266-30791.

1   Levitt, Cyril and Shaffir, William. *The Riot At Christie Pits.* Lester and Orpen Dennys, Toronto. 1987. *The Riot in Christie Pits.* Page 111.
2   Levitt, Cyril and Shaffir, William. *The Riot At Christie Pits.* Lester and Orpen Dennys, Toronto. 1987. *The Riot in Christie Pits.* Page 118.
3   Webster, Jack. *Copper Jack.* Dundurn Press, Toronto and Oxford. 1991. Page 12.
4   Levitt, Cyril and Shaffir, William. *The Riot At Christie Pits.* Lester and Orpen Dennys, Toronto. 1987. *The Riot in Christie Pits.* Page 153.
5   Levitt, Cyril and Shaffir, William. *The Riot At Christie Pits.* Lester and Orpen Dennys, Toronto. 1987. Page 162.
6   Webster, Jack. *Copper Jack.* Dundurn Press, Toronto and Oxford. 1991. Page 14.

1934

The activities of the Mounted Unit were a popular feature in all Toronto newspapers during the 1930s. On January 11, 1934, they reported Inspector Crosbie had resigned as president of the Toronto Police Amateur Athletic Association. On May 3, reports stated Constable Charles Whitford, while travelling in England, visited friends from the Great War who were in the Household Cavalry. Whitford remained a hero for apprehending the "crazed man" on Elizabeth Street in 1927.

On September 28, a story ran in the *Daily Mail & Empire* describing how a bootleg still had been found by a mounted policeman in an article titled, "Mounted policeman does some sniffing."[78] The Mounted Unit's involvement in the annual Police Church Parade rated coverage in October 28 editions.

Not only positive stories made the news as all incidents of civil disobedience, especially those which resulted in the active use of the Mounted Unit were covered. In his book, *The Great Depression*, author Pierre Berton stated that the Toronto Press used the term "riot" to describe any "parade, demonstration, rally, or work stoppage that brought out the police and threatened established order." Forty-three incidents were described as riots in the Toronto newspapers.[79]

In his annual report Chief Constable Draper reported that, *"The service rendered by the members of the Mounted Division has been a valuable aid in maintaining law and order. In addition to the regular street and traffic duty a great many special duties were carried out by the Mounted Division during the year. With respect to these special duties, speaking conservatively, the duty performed by each mounted man, had he not been there, would have necessitated the services of a number of foot patrolmen. Such service is particularly effective where the Force is operating with limited personnel. Members of this Division, with mounts, are permanently located at various strategic Division points throughout the City and are readily available for patrol duty in the areas best served by this type of police service."*[80]

Many of the localities patrolled by the mounted officers and special details that were assigned in 1934 are the same as those performed by the Mounted Unit today, 60 years later. It is interesting that the Chief Constable also reported that mounted officers had been used for 238 days of plainclothes duty. The men were assigned to both part-time and full-time plainclothes assignments. Some also became Acting Detectives. These duties were performed in the late fall and spring when the demand for mounted services was reduced.

The Mounted Unit established permanent patrols at the Isolation Hospital, now known as Riverdale Hospital. The officers were required in the area because relief workers were being employed at the Riverdale Park. There had been some disturbances caused by the workers and the mounted officers were to prevent any further problems from occurring.

The Communist Party had not been crushed by the continued police interference. A major clash took place on July 4 between Communist demonstrators and the Mounted Unit. Chief Constable Draper was certainly not a popular man with the Communists, labour movement or the unemployed. During a hunger march held on July 31, the crowd sang a song about "hanging" Chief Draper.

On Saturday September 22, the horse-racing season opened at Woodbine Race Track in the east end. Before races began, crowds gathered on the beach side of the track to look over the odds and lay their bets with bookies. Crown and Anchor games were also operated by some of the gamblers.

Four plainclothes men went into the crowd to procure evidence of offences, assisted by two mounted officers who had been assigned to help when arrests were to be made. When signaled, the Mounted officers moved in to split the crowd to provide a lane for the prisoners to be removed. These arrests were described in the September 24 *Globe* under the heading, "Big Crowd Scatters During Police Raid Near Race Course," "Mounted Officers Clear The Way."[81]

Mounted officers line both sides of Kingston Road at Woodbine Avenue as part of the honour guard at the funeral of three Toronto Firemen who were killed at an oil tank inferno, July 27, 1934. Photograph, City of Toronto Archives. Globe and Mail. *34206.*

The "Eyes Right!" at the presentation of the Toronto Police "Colours," University of Toronto, 1934. Photograph, City of Toronto Archives, Globe and Mail Collection. SC 266-28432.

Inspector Crosbie and Chief Constable Draper accompany the Lieutenant Governor on an inspection of the Mounted Unit. The Royal Winter Fair, November 23, 1934. Photograph, Toronto Mail & Empire.

SPECIAL DUTIES PERFORMED BY THE MOUNTED UNIT IN 1934

DUTY	JAN	FEB	MAR	APR	MAY	JUN	JUL	AUG	SEP	OCT	NOV	DEC	TOTALS
Strikes	386	257	167	86	129	147	96	300	90	16	22	32	1728
Maple Leaf Gardens	26	29	62	50	14	6	14	4	19	32	45	35	336
Massey hall	14	14	34	23	2	13	---	2	15	21	19	7	164
Arena	19	13	24	16	8	---	---	---	---	---	---	---	80
Isolation Hospital	68	44	50	46	32	---	26	39	4	---	---	---	309
Ball games	---	---	---	---	52	18	37	35	33	8	---	---	183
Sunnyside	---	---	---	32	48	38	27	23	14	---	---	---	182
Parades	---	---	---	---	51	---	51	---	2	---	79	---	183
Simcoe Park	---	---	---	---	---	48	66	48	2	60	---	---	224
Exhibition	---	---	---	---	10	7	---	164	144	---	73	6	404
Races	---	---	---	---	34	28	---	---	30	28	---	---	120
Meetings in Parks, etc.	---	---	---	54	77	36	31	10	19	---	---	---	227
Miscellaneous	20	11	31	16	25	3	2	8	---	---	---	3	119
Plainclothes Duty	---	---	61	24	---	---	---	---	---	---	---	153	238
TOTALS	533	368	429	293	459	385	355	654	363	184	238	236	4497

The Toronto Police Amateur Athletic Association

The physical and intellectual condition of Toronto police officers had always been a concern of the Board of Police Commissioners. For the educational development of the officers, they established the first police library in North America in 1878. It was considered one of the finest libraries in the city until the first Toronto Public Library was established seven years later. The books were available to all of the members of the force.

The Board also provided exercise rooms equipped with bar bells, boxing gloves and other physical education equipment. In 1883, a group of officers formed the Toronto Police Amateur Athletic Association and were encouraged by the Police Commission in the development of this organization and the participation of all police officers. In 1886, the force claimed some of the best amateur athletes in the country were members of the Toronto Police Department.[1]

Many members of the force took advantage of the team and individual sports offered by the Athletic Association. "Triple A," as it became known, was an excellent way to improve the physical fitness of the officers and their morale. The first Police Field Day was held in the summer of 1883 and proved to be a great success.

The annual tournaments, or Field Days, were always very well attended by officers, family, friends and the public. They were especially popular in the days when few entertainment venues were available across Toronto. The games became an important public relations tool for the police and was especially true when Chief Constable Draper was harassing Communist and the labour movement. The games were so popular that they assisted the force to maintain its popularity and legitimacy.

The Mounted Unit takes part every year by leading the march past of the "Police Force on Parade." Beginning in 1966 the Mounted Unit performed its musical ride at the games each year that a "Ride" was organized.

The Amateur Athletic Association has supported a number of baseball and hockey teams fielded by members of the Mounted Unit. They have also provided funding for equestrian competitions, golf tournaments, road races and other activities where members of the unit have been involved.

Individual officers who attend police Olympic events in other locations also receive financial assistance.

When the new mounted headquarters was built in 2000, the Toronto Police Triple A provided the majority of the funding to equip the building with a gymnasium. The Mounted Unit has been very fortunate to receive the support of the A.A.A..

Inspector Thomas Crosbie was president of the Toronto Police A.A.A. in the 1930s. In this photo he is standing on the right speaking to officials on the Annual Field Day. Photograph, Crosbie Family.

1 The 1886 Account of the Force.

Special Duties Performed by the Mounted Unit

OFFICER DAYS PER DETAIL

DUTIES	1935	1936	1937	1938
Strikes	2020	740	1222	1361
Maple Leaf Gardens	437	351	347	476
Arena Gardens	n/a	29	30	43
Maple Leaf Stadium	151	113	107	120
Massey Music Hall	156	124	87	111
Varsity Stadium	171	87	90	68
Varsity Arena	n/a	n/a	33	n/a
Ravina Rink	n/a	n/a	70	64
Ulster Stadium	n/a	16	7	11
Hunt Club	n/a	44	54	47
Sunnyside	179	143	164	85
Simcoe Park Beach	131	213	132	78
Cherry Beach	110	53	100	68
Park Meetings, Picnics, etc.	138	24	24	20
Parades, etc.	553	[251]	[304]	[391]
Military Parades	n/a	62	62	214
Fraternal Parades	n/a	42	24	56
Civilian Parades	n/a	147	193	121
Veterans Parades	n/a	n/a	25	n/a
Motor Show	n/a	28	28	28
Horse and Motor Shows	37	n/a	n/a	n/a
Races	119	n/a	n/a	n/a
Road Races	n/a	6	n/a	4
Woodbine Races	n/a	46	56	55
Dufferin Races	n/a	52	61	64
Exhibition and Winter Fair	366	[318]	[326]	[390]
Exhibition	n/a	252	260	318
Royal Winter Fair	n/a	66	66	72
Government House	n/a	5	14	n/a
City Hall Delegations	n/a	17	15	3
Parliament Buildings	n/a	9	7	11
Red Demonstrations	n/a	n/a	n/a	95
Demonstrations	123	44	n/a	n/a
Plainclothes Part Time	n/a	1574	1750	1780
Plainclothes Full Time	n/a	184	157	243
Acting Detective	n/a	130	n/a	n/a
Plainclothes Duty	920	[1888]	[1907]	[2023]
Weddings, Receptions, etc.	n/a	72	17	51
Funerals	n/a	57	49	86
Reserve Elections	n/a	6	n/a	n/a
Coliseum (Horse Show)	n/a	22	12	12
Don Jail	n/a	4	n/a	4
School Concerts, Socials	n/a	n/a	4	2
Jarvis St. Church Fire	n/a	n/a	n/a	6
Miscellaneous	92	n/a	n/a	n/a
TOTALS	5703	4753	5267	5777

Compulsory Mounted Training

In the late 1930s, the Toronto Police Force instituted a policy whereby every new recruit was required to take riding lessons with the Mounted Unit. The idea of giving every man mounted training would have appealed to the old cavalryman in Chief Draper. There were a number of reasons that the recruits were put through the equestrian training.

Commercial horses were still in use on the streets of Toronto, it would have been important that a city-bred policeman know how to handle horses in an emergency. Their training also gave Inspector Crosbie the opportunity to pick out the recruits he needed for his unit. The most important reason why the recruits received an equitation course was because of the belief that mounted training "builds character"—especially when conducted by former Battery Sergeant Major Thomas Crosbie.

The Royal Canadian Mounted Police had always used mounted training to build character in their officers. They continued mandatory training of all recruits until 1966 when it was discontinued as a cost-saving measure and as the practical need for mounted training was long past. They continued teaching men to work with horses because it was an important tool used by the college instructors to pass on the values and discipline required of new police officers. The riding master at Depot Division in Regina had this to say about providing compulsory mounted training to all of the recruits; "The Mounted Police horse is the equine detector of courage, or lack of it, in police candidates. Skilled tuition in equitation will replace timidity with boldness and develop a disregard for the inevitable bodily bruises which even the most proficient must experience. Handling horses promotes mental alertness and rapid acceleration of muscular reflexes."[1]

Inspector Crosbie and a police recruit class in Rosedale Valley Ravine, May 1930. Photograph, City of Toronto Archives, Globe and Mail *Collection. SC266 20074.*

A police recruit class receiving mounted training, Rosedale Valley Ravine, May 1930. Photograph, City of Toronto Archives, Globe and Mail Collection, SC266 20075.

The compulsory mounted training which was given to all new recruits in 1937 was described by former Police Chief James Mackey in his book *I Policed Toronto*:

A course in horse-back riding at the stables on Bayview Avenue was also included as part of our learning process. The course was fairly extensive and included riding in the arena, taking the horses over several jumps, as well as cantering, trotting and galloping in the open fields. I wasn't too expert at any of this, especially jumping. I usually wound up hanging onto the horse's neck after going over a jump. This poor horsemanship netted me the nickname 'the cowboy'. Hugh Hopperton, our stomach painting victim, would somehow manage to wind up facing the rear end of the horse, holding onto the tail! Kind of fun if you didn't fall off. Inspector Crosbie, the officer in charge, didn't think we were too funny. Every time we went over a jump he would crack the whip to make the horse jump a little higher.[2]

The mandatory mounted training of recruits ended in Toronto by 1940. Due to the war the police force was only recruiting cadets and temporarily attached constables. They wanted to get these men on patrol as soon as possible to replace all of the officers who had left the force for active service overseas. By the time the war was over and regular recruiting began again there was a new chief constable who was not as pro mounted as the chiefs of the past.

1   Kelly, William and Kelly, Nora. *The Horses of the Royal Canadian Mounted Police*, A Pictorial History. Doubleday Canada Limited, Toronto. 1984. Page 122.
2   Mackey, James. *I Policed Toronto*. Self Published, Toronto. 1985. Page 16.

1935

The importance of the Mounted Unit in the eyes of Chief Constable Draper is evident from his annual reports. He was including full descriptions of the duties performed by mounted officers backed up with the charts showing all the special duties which they were assigned. A number of major cities had disbanded their Mounted Units and some people suggested that Toronto should get rid of theirs. In response, Draper was promoting the unit in the best way possible, by showing exactly what they were doing, and why they were indispensable in those troubled times.

During the month of March the Police Commissioners, as well as all other civic administrators had their budget cut. Two of the ways suggested to save money was to postpone the implementation of the radio patrol plan and to disband the Mounted Unit. During the debate the *Toronto Star* reported that the "Inspectors of divisions claimed one mounted man in an emergency was worth from six to ten foot constables."

The following is extracted directly from Chief Constable Draper's annual report:

Officers and men of the Mounted Division have been detailed for duty in connection with the various strikes occurring through the City, because of the effectiveness of the Mounted Constables for such service, and to permit the greater number of foot patrolmen that would have been necessary to continue on regular patrol duty. The same statement will apply equally as well with respect to other special duties shown, Parks, Beaches, etc., Mounted Constables constitute the most economical and efficient type of police service for these duties.

In general, the territory patrolled by the members of the Mounted Division represents districts not covered by foot patrol and districts which by their nature, can more thoroughly and economically policed by mounted men that by foot patrol. If the same territory was covered by foot patrol, three or four times the number of men would be required, as these beats average from two to three miles in length.

If the above was not enough justification the Chief concluded by saying "In my opinion, the services of the Mounted Police in marshalling crowds generally are indispensable. During the past year the work performed by this branch of the service clearly demonstrates that there is a sphere of police effort to which the Mounted Division are peculiarly suited and indeed it would be impossible to substitute their accomplishment effectively with foot patrol or other branch of the service."[83]

The strength of the Mounted Unit was forty-seven men of all ranks and forty-six horses. The parks and ravines were patrolled by the mounted officers until 11:00 p.m. During the summer months, the eastern Beaches were patrolled regularly and two mounted officers were on duty in the area until 11:00 p.m. The beach patrols were probably partly in response to the troubles caused by the right wing Nazi movement which was fairly strong in this area.

On January 4th, the *Toronto Mail and Empire* reported that the mounted officers were "keeping tabs on traffic" in the downtown area. Being assigned a traffic point in January would have been a very cold assignment.[84]

An example of the labour strike duties performed by the unit at this time can be found in the Saturday January 26th *Globe* Newspaper. The story appeared under the heading "WILD STREET BATTLE BROKEN UP BY POLICE...Strikers and Strike Breakers Mix It Up on Adelaide West and Mounted Men Ride Amid Bricks and Jeers."[85] A picket line had been formed at the Standard Garment Company, the only nonunion garment plant in Toronto. The company was still in operation with strike-breakers working inside the plant. When the police escorted the strike-breakers out of the building and into waiting cars the crowd erupted in anger.

The crowd became violent and "stones, bricks and other missiles flew threw the air, and yells, jeers and the crash of breaking glass echoed along the street, mounted police rode through a mob of several hundred demonstrators."[86] Once the scabs were out of the plant and escorted away the crowd regrouped and broke into the rear of the

The Mounted Unit was called in to maintain order at Maple Leaf Gardens when large crowds showed up to attend the 1935 Liberal Rally. Photograph, Alexandra Studio.

building. The strikers destroyed material and machines until the reinforced police entered the building to evict them.

The *Telegram* estimated that the crowd contained 1,000 persons and reported that there were no injuries in the forty-five minute melee. At one point when it looked like the crowd was going to turn on the police, batons were drawn, but put away when the crowd yielded. A few people were arrested for throwing missiles on the street, but there were no arrests for damaging the interior of the factory. The crowds lingered on Adelaide Street West between Spadina Avenue and Widmer Street until they were finally disbursed by the police.[87]

On March 6th police mount "Mayo" died. "Mayo" had become famous for his exploits in stopping runaway horses in the downtown core. He was also a favourite in the horse show ring and earned his riders many awards.

The Mounted Unit was a very desirable posting in 1935. Thirteen young constables were given a thorough course of training in equitation during the year. The officers were all volunteers who took the training on their own time after completing their regularly scheduled police duties.

On May 21st, 1935 a dispute between a bookie and a client escalated into a large brawl. The *Globe* newspaper described the story under the headline "Gamblers Battle On Woodbine Beach." The paper reported that plainclothes men were unable to get to the people who were causing the

trouble due to the large crowds. Mounted constables then split the crowd and moved the people on. The paper stated "Fists were flying and punches were exchanged freely before the police raided the crowd." Fearing that further fights would break out the police cleared the crowd from the back of the racetrack.[88]

The officers were active in mounted competitions throughout the year. They competed at the Toronto Open Air Horse Show, The Eglinton Hunt Club, The Canadian National Exhibition and the Royal Winter Fair Horse Show. The showing by the officers was reported to be a credit to the Toronto Police Department and the City of Toronto. The officers were allowed to compete at the shows in uniform with their mounts, but had to do so on their own time.

The effects of the Great Depression are evident in the Chief Constable's annual report. He was quick to mention that both the competitions and the mounted training was an "off duty" event. The troubled year ended with a major clash between the jobless and the police on December 19th. The Mounted Unit was involved in dispersing the crowd of unemployed people, who must have gone home to a very depressing Christmas.

The Mounted Unit leading the Warriors Day Parade at the 1935 Canadian National Exhibition. Photograph, City of Toronto Archives, Globe and Mail *Collection. SC 266-41053.*

The Mounted Unit in 1935

LOCATION	STAFF	GENERAL DUTIES
No. 1 Stable Court Street	7 Constables 7 Horses	Patrols in No. 1 and No. 2 Divisions Traffic, Disturbances, etc.
No. 5 Stable Mounted H.Q. Belmont Street	4 officers 1 Stableman 5 Constables 9 Horses	Patrols in No. 5 and part of No. 12 Divisions. Ravines, Parks, etc.
No. 6 Stable Cowan Avenue	7 Constables 7 Horses	Patrols in No. 6, No. 3 and No. 9 Divisions. High Park, Sunnyside, Exhibition Park and Traffic Enforcement.
No. 8 Stable Pape Avenue	7 Constables 7 Horses	Patrols in No. 8, No. 10 and No. 4 Divisions Traffic and Beat Duty, Simcoe Park, Cherry Park and the Waterfront.
No. 11 Stable Markham Street	5 Constables 5 Horses	Patrols in No. 11, No. 9 and No. 7 Divisions. Wynchwood Park, Royce and Willowvale Parks. Traffic and Beat duties.
No. 12 Stable Montgomery Avenue	3 Constables 3 Horses	Patrols in No. 12 Division. Traffic and Beat Duty.
Sunnybrook Park	1 Stableman 5 Constables 8 Horses	Beat Duty, Sunnybrook park and Surrounding Districts.
Totals :	7 Stables 4 Officers 2 Stableman (Constables) 39 Constables 46 Horses	

Inspector Crosbie with "Jock," the horse fancied by Chief Constable Draper. "Jock" had been purchased shortly before this picture was taken. The horse had been trained to count out its age by pawing the ground, which it is doing in the photograph.

The near ideal proportions of a 1930s city police horse are seen in this portrait.
Photograph, Toronto Star. *May 17, 1930.*

1936 Chief Constable Draper, in his annual report, left no doubt that he valued the work of the Mounted Unit. He backed up the justification of his belief by including statistical data from the previous year. The Mounted Unit continued its regular patrols of the parks, ravines and beaches patrolling these areas till eleven o'clock at night. The mounted men were also detailed to the strikes occurring throughout the city.

The Chief Constable estimated that if foot patrol men replaced the mounted officers on the beat, it would take four foot patrol officers to replace one mounted officer. The mounted police were "a most effective branch of the service in the control of parades, demonstrations and the handling of crowds."[89]

Inspector Crosbie moved his office from Police Headquarters to Mounted Headquarters located at No. 5 Police Station. Two mounted officers were assigned to duty as stablemen, one went to Mounted Headquarters, where in addition to his other duties he was in charge of stores and repairs of all saddlery and equipment.

The other stable man was at Sunnybrook Park where he took care of all the sick and injured horses. He also assisted in the training of all the new remounts and was also responsible for the care of "Bruce," Chief Draper's horse.

A mounted officer on duty at a parade. Photograph, City of Toronto archives, Globe and Mail *collection. SC 266-26890.*

Another photograph of the parade. Photograph, City of Toronto Archives, Globe and Mail *Collection. SC 266-26904.*

This photograph was captioned as being of a Communist demonstration. The sign carried by the crowd identifies the marchers as the Macedon Peoples League. This may or may not have been a Communist organization. The press and the police of the time labelled almost all demonstrations as being Communist. Photograph, City of Toronto Archives, Globe and Mail *Collection. SC 266-33195.*

During the year mounted officers performed plain-clothes duty, including acting detective duty, for a total of 7,624 hours. This must have been in a training capacity to help prepare officers for promotion, the forerunner of today's lateral transfers and career development programs.

Inspector Crosbie took leave in the summer to attend the Vimy Pilgrimage with his family. Almost 6,000 veterans of the Great War and their families made the trip to Europe. Men and mounts continued to perform at equestrian competitions on their own time, attending shows at the Eglinton Hunt Club, Canadian National Exhibition, Royal Winter Fair Horse Show, etc.

The annual Church Parade was held on October 4 and included three hundred and fifty officers who formed up at the University Avenue Armouries. Chief Constable Draper led the parade riding his charger to the music of the Police Pipe Band and the Toronto Police Silver Band. The parade marched to City Hall where Acting Mayor William Robbins and the former police commissioner Judge Morrison took the salute. A wreath was then laid at the base of the Cenotaph in remembrance to those who had fallen in the Great War. Many of the participants wore their service medals and decorations.

The *Daily Mail and Empire* described the scene at the Cenotaph. "The white-gloved police constables, their buttons shinning against the blue of their uniforms, and the mounted officers drawn up in immobile ranks behind them presented a spectacular scene. The perfectly groomed mounts entered into the spirit of the occasion by standing still as statues during the ceremony."[90]

The Mounted Unit then led the parade west on Queen Street East to Jarvis Street, and then to St. Paul's Anglican Church. The parade route was lined with large crowds and hundreds of civilians took part in the service. A minute of silence was held for members of the Toronto Police Force who had been killed in the line of duty. The Silver band played the "Dead March from Saul" and buglers sounded the Last Post and Reveille.

New technologies continued to bring changes to Toronto. The City's first police radio system was introduced with forty radio equipped police cars hitting the streets. In the private sector, the Eaton's Department Store delivery fleet became totally mechanized and the last of the their chestnut coloured delivery horses were sold off.

This photograph was captioned "Mounted police to the rescue." It was taken at the Orange Day Parade on July 11th, 1936. This photo was never published and there is no record of what type of altercation broke out. Orange Day was a very big event in Toronto and the parade was always very well attended. Photograph, City of Toronto Archives, Globe and Mail *Collection. SC 266-40738.*

The 1930s Toronto Police Recruit

The minimum height and weight for a Toronto police officer in 1936 was 5'10 1/2" and 160 lbs. None of the recruits in the December 1936 class were under 6'1." The starting wages for a constable was $28.50 per week. From this the department deducted 9% for the pension fund and 5% for the relief fund. The new recruit had to buy the large Persian wool winter hats themselves. A new hat cost anywhere from $45.00 to $75.00, or if you were lucky you might find a used one for as little as $20.00.[1]

1   *I Policed Toronto.* Page 13.

1937 The Mounted Unit was very busy through the year with strikes, parades and special duties. As well as crowd control, officers continued to maintain their regular patrols. During the summer the Toronto Islands were policed by mounted officers. Their horses were very important there as no motor vehicles were permitted on the islands. The importance of the unit continued to be stressed in the chief constable's annual reports.

On June 18th Constable Archie Houston testified in court, in what may have been the first impaired driving arrest made by a mounted officer. He testified, while on Sunnyside Avenue, he heard "a motor racing wildly. There were two ladies in the motor car. The accused was in the front seat behind the wheel. The car was driven up Glendale Avenue. I followed on my horse." He further testified that, "She smelled strongly of liquor and acted stupid." She was convicted of the offence and sentenced to 7 days in jail.[92]

The Toronto Police Department used a teletype system which distributed information to the various police stations. This included descriptions of criminal suspects, stolen property, stolen cars, etc. Officers, going on or off duty, were expected to read all messages and note such things as stolen licence plate numbers or wanted suspects in their memo books. An officer who put a parking ticket on a stolen car without recovering the car was in for big trouble from his superiors. Mounted Unit officers recovered 67 stolen cars throughout the year.

The Mounted Unit once again excelled in open equestrian competitions. Officers competed on their own time at the Toronto Horse Show, Eglinton Hunt Club, Canadian National Exhibition and Royal Winter Fair Horse Show. They collected an impressive five firsts, three seconds, five thirds and one fourth place finish. The Church Parade was held on October 3rd, 1937.

These two photographs were taken at a community picnic during the 1930s. Photographs, Toronto Police Museum.

◈ 1938

Patrols continued to be made to the ravines, parks and the eastern beaches, by the Mounted Unit. Crowd control remained its major function and its effectiveness was again recorded in the Chief Constable's annual report.

On August 20, the *Globe and Mail* ran an article entitled, "Toronto Demonstrates Horse Indispensable in Policing a City." It told how Chief Draper, a horse lover himself, is one of the staunchest supporters of the "oft-criticized mounted policeman." He fought for the unit not for sentimental reasons, but because he believed it is one of the most important branches of the police service.

Montreal had disbanded its mounted unit, but reinstated it when they found they could not get along without policemen on horses. Detroit's Mounted Unit consisted of a half dozen scraggly nags. After they saw the effectiveness of Toronto's mounted unit a few years before, they began increasing their unit strength to seventy-six horses and project to have one hundred and twenty-five by 1940.

The forty-six men of Toronto's Mounted Unit were reportedly the envy of every police department in North America. "The mounts' good manners and uncanny habit of doing the right thing at the right minute without apparent guidance from the rider is admired not only by Torontonians but visitors from the British Isles and the United States."

The article further credited the performance of the horses to the training they received at Sunnybrook Park. The key training tool was, "Infinite patience and firm-but-kind training. No horse attached to the department ever had a sound thrashing since it was selected from a farm in Ontario."[93]

In the 1930s, the first day of May was a special day around the world. May Day was celebrated by school children, with games and the selection of the Queen of the May. It was also a day of celebration for the Communist Party and the labour movement with a large parade being held in Toronto. Those taking part in the parade were certainly no friends of Chief Draper.

Chief Constable Dennis Draper, C.M.G., D.S.O. Photograph, Toronto Police Museum.

Each year Toronto Police routine orders laid out the plan for dealing with this parade. The Mounted Unit was a big part of the police plan and members of the unit were detailed to strategic locations throughout the city. The police considered the possibility of public disorder quite high and were well prepared for any eventuality. However, it seemed their planning was effective, or the suspicions of the police unfounded, as there was little or no trouble associated with these parades.

On July 4, three or four different political factions held meetings in the city. Adrien Arcand, a fascist leader from Quebec, held a rally at Massy Hall in an attempt to form a fascist coalition in Canada. Shuter Street was lined by blue uniformed fascist supporters wearing arm bands with a flaming torch in place of the Nazi swastika. The police were on scene to prevent any clashes between factions.[94]

A counter demonstration of anti-fascists was held at Yonge and Albert Streets, drawing a crowd of two thousand people to the intersection; four demonstrators were arrested. Minor skirmishes broke out in the crowd and one lady who shouted, "Heil Hitler," was struck over the head with a cane. The *Toronto Telegram* reported that the, "Speakers harangued the crowd from 8:00 p.m. until police decided that it was time to scatter the throng, and shouts of 'down with fascism' were heard as constables, both mounted and on foot, drove the crowd before them."[95]

Pierre Berton's book on the Depression says the crowd also chanted "Down with the brutal police; they are fascist tools!" He describes the scene: *More of Draper's troops arrived on horseback, forcing their steeds into the middle of the crowd. One woman was struck on the head and knocked to the sidewalk. A newspaper reporter who went to her aid was himself knocked down by a passing horse. Part of the crowd fled into a nearby store; others ran down Yonge Street. For the rest of the evening the police patrolled Shuter Street, keeping the crowd moving and away from Massey Hall.*[96]

Just over a year later, Canada would be at war with the fascist regimes of Europe. Canadian fascists lost the "open" support they had allegedly been receiving from the police. Ironically, in three years Canada would be allies with Communist Russia in the fight against the fascists. Toronto's open war against Communism came to an end with this alliance despite the fact that Chief Draper would remain in command of the Toronto police for another four years.

Former Inspector George Sellar joined the Toronto Police Force as a constable in 1938. There were 20 men in his recruit class and all were required to take a riding course at Sunnybrook Park. After training, he was assigned to No. 1 Station on Court Street for foot patrol duties. One day while on patrol, Inspector Crosbie stopped him to ask what he thought about joining the Mounted Unit.

A rare photograph that was probably privately taken while waiting to provide an escort at the Old Woodbine Race Track. The officer with the cigarette in the foreground is probably Sgt Rogerson. The officer with the pipe appears to be PC Andrew Cooper. If Inspector Crosbie had come by and caught the officers smoking in public view they would have paid dearly for their indiscretion.

A casual photograph from Woodbine. Photographs, Toronto Police Museum.

Inspector Crosbie had probably approached him due to his light weight, one of the methods the Inspector used to recruit suitable applicants that caught his eye. George agreed to transfer to the Mounted Unit and was assigned to the stables at the Court Street Station. Part of his permanent beat was to patrol the fruit market every morning. He left the Mounted Unit after a few years to get more involved in general policing duties and rose through the ranks and retired as the officer in charge of the Homicide Squad.

Inspector Sellar remembered that members of the Mounted Unit were given one hour for lunch while all other police officers received a half-hour. This was to give the horse a longer break between patrols. It would also allow the officers time to warm up on frigid days. The annual Police Church Parade was held on October 2nd.

During the year, members of the mounted division and their mounts competed on their own time, at various shows, winning a total of five firsts, five seconds, four third, and four fourth place prizes in open competition.

Left: Constable Hugh Banks in the late 1930s. He enlisted in the Canadian Army during Word War II. He was wounded and lost a leg in combat. Both his son and granddaughter later joined the Metropolitan Toronto Police Force. His son, former Superintendent Don Banks, donated the Hugh Banks Memorial trophy which is presented each year to the officer who wins the Canadian National Exhibition Police Class. Photograph courtesy of the Banks Family.

Constable Hamilton Hutchinson. He enlisted in the North Irish Horse during WWI. During the German offensive of March 1918, he manned his machine gun until he exhausted all his ammunition and was forced to surrender. He was sent to a prison camp in Poland until the war ended. Once released from prison, without adequate food or clothing, he had to walk across Europe in order to reach the Allied lines and safety. He later emigrated to Canada and joined the Toronto Police Department. Photograph, Toronto Police Museum.

1939

The Mounted Unit continued to provide patrols on all of its established beats. It was probably a fairly quiet year for special duties as Chief Constable Draper did not include a detailed schedule of special assignments in his annual report. The usefulness of the unit was questioned in 1939 and disbanding the unit was discussed. Fortunately the chief constable again fought off the detractors and his beloved unit survived into the next decade.

There were two very big events during the year. The first was the Royal Visit to Toronto made by King George VI and Queen Elizabeth. On June 7th, their Highnesses were taken on a twenty mile tour of the city. The entire force was called out for the day. The second major event was the start of the Second World War in Europe and Canada's declaration of war on Germany which soon followed the outbreak of fighting. As the city went on a war footing, the annual Police Church Parade was not held.

No horses would be sent to war this time, however many police officers, including Chief Draper, requested and were granted leave to join the military. A number of mounted officers left for active military service. Constable Hugh Banks went overseas and was wounded losing a leg. Constables Jack Ogle, Bud Williamson and George Martin all became aircrew in the Royal Canadian Air Force. As no nominal roles exists showing the units to which officers were assigned, it is impossible to determine who else from the Mounted Unit went overseas.

The Toronto Police Force formed a special flying column composed of veterans of the Great War.

The column included foot officers as well as a special mounted section under the command of Inspector Crosbie. The purpose of the "flying column" was to take instant action against any war-inspired trouble arising in the city.

During the year members continued to compete on their mounts in open competition at the Canadian National Exhibition Horse Show winning two firsts, two seconds, two thirds and two fourth place prizes.

One of the effects of the war was the rationing of gasoline and tires so many companies returned to the use of horses. Both Eatons and Simpsons returned to horse-drawn delivery vehicles for the duration of the war.

No. 8 Stable, Pape Avenue. This stable was used by the Mounted Unit from 1908 to 1968 and became an ambulance station when the horses moved out. When this picture was taken in 1998 the stable features, such as the I-beam used to raise hay to the hayloft were still visible. Photograph, Sgt Lorna Kozmik.

Constable Jack Ogle patrolling the parade route during the 1939 Royal Visit. Within a year he will have enlisted in the Royal Canadian Air Force where he was Awarded the Distinguished Flying Cross (D.F.C.). Photograph, courtesy of the Ogle Family.

A well turned out mounted man awaits the arrival of the King and Queen, May 22, 1939. Photograph, City of Toronto Archives, Globe and Mail *Collection. SC 266-58611.*

The King and Queen arrive at City hall. A troop of Royal Canadian Dragoons stand in the background while mounted officers can be seen patrolling the parade route. Photograph, City of Toronto Archives, Globe and Mail *Collection. SC 156-6.*

The Police "Flying Column." Formed to take instant action against any war-inspired trouble, arising in Toronto.

Top left: Inspector Crosbie of the Mounted Unit confers with Inspector Marshall commanding the foot police.

Top right: The Foot Contingent.
Bottom right: The Mounted Contingent.
Photographs, Toronto Telegram.

 # 1940

The manpower of the mounted unit was only slightly reduced in 1940 even though the force was understaffed due to the war. The Chief Constable's report was very similar to prior years. The unit maintained its park and suburban patrols as well as attending all major functions. Mandatory mounted training of new recruits had come to an end.

To help alleviate the manpower shortage, the force hired its first police cadets. To be hired an applicant was required to be between the ages of seventeen and twenty-one. Upon reaching twenty-one they were sworn in as constables. "Temporarily Attached Constables" were also hired. Most men hired in this capacity were veterans of the Great War, although some younger men, who had been deemed unfit for military service, were also hired.

Their employment was for the duration of the war. The program, was more successful than the one tried during the First War, when "specials" were hired, but soon let go. Some "attached constables" served over seven years, vacating their positions in 1946 when the soldiers returned from overseas. No cadets were assigned to the Mounted Unit during the war and probably none of the temporary constables worked with the unit.

The Mounted Unit in front of the Horse Palace, c. 1940. This photograph may have been taken during the 1940 Musical Ride. The Horse Palace did not become a permanent stable for the Mounted Unit until 1968. Photograph, Canadian National Exhibition Archives.

On August 9th, Constable Geoffrey Rumble left the unit to enlist in the Royal Canadian Artillery. He eventually rose to the rank of Regimental Sergeant Major and was then commissioned as a Captain. He returned to the police force after the war, but was not assigned to mounted duties. He retired from the police force with the rank of Inspector.

Due to the demands of the war the Royal Canadian Mounted Police had to cancel its Musical Ride. The Canadian National Exhibition had scheduled the Mountie's Musical Ride for the grandstand show. After receiving the news the executive of the fair approached the Toronto Police Commissioners. They requested that the Toronto Mounted Unit take the Mounties place and perform a musical ride. The police agreed to the request and the Mounted Unit organized its first musical ride which was performed at the grandstand show. The show was put on each night of the Exhibition between August 24th and September 7th. Members of the unit competed with their mounts on their own time at the Canadian National Exhibition Horse Show winning one first, one second, one third and one fourth prize in open competition.

The Mounted unit leads a Victory Bond parade in the summer of 1940. Photograph, City of Toronto Archives, Globe and Mail *Collection. 68609.*

🔲 1941

The Mounted Unit provided its regular park, ravine and beaches patrol during the year. The Chief Constable stopped reporting on the special duties performed by the Mounted Unit. This was probably because there were very few to attend. The war had led to full employment and there was little if any labour unrest.

The Communists were no longer treated as the threat that they had been since Russia and Canada had become allies in the war. The war had not yet affected the manpower of the unit as it was still staffed by forty-three men and forty-six horses. Mounted officers competed at the C.N.E. Horse Show in open competition, winning one first, one second, one third and one fourth place prize.

The Mounted Unit in 1941

LOCATION	STAFF	GENERAL DUTIES
No. 1 Stable Court Street	6 Constables 6 Horses	Patrols in No. 1 and No. 2 Divisions Traffic, Disturbances, etc.
No. 5 Stable Mounted H.Q. Belmont Street	4 Officers 1 Stableman 5 Constables 9 Horses	Patrols in No. 5 and part of No. 2 Divisions. Traffic, Parks, Ravines, etc.
No. 6 Stable Cowan Avenue	7 Constables 7 Horses	Patrols in No. 6, No. 3 and No. 9 Divisions. High Park, Sunnyside, Exhibition and Traffic Enforcement.
No. 8 Stable Pape Avenue	6 Constables 5 Horses	Patrols in No. 8, No. 10 and No. 4 Divisions Traffic and Beat Duty, Simcoe Park, Cherry Park and the Waterfront.
No. 11 Stable Markham Street	5 Constables 5 Horses	Patrols in No. 11, No. 9 and No. 7 Divisions. Wynchwood Park, Royce and Willowvale Parks.
No. 12 Stable Montgomery Avenue	5 Constables 5 Horses	Patrols in No. 12 Division. Traffic and Beat Duty.
Sunnybrook Park	1 Stableman 3 Constables 9 Horses	Beat Duty, Sunnybrook park and Surrounding Districts.
Totals :	7 Stables 4 Officers 2 Stableman (Constables) 37 Constables 46 Horses	

The two photographs show mounted officers on duty during parades at the Canadian National Exhibition. The officer has been posted to watch the crowd and insure the parade route remains clear.

Photographs, Canadian National Exhibition Archives.

1942 The quiet times continued through 1942. The Mounted Unit was reduced to thirty-nine men of all ranks and forty-six horses. No major incidents were in the year-end report.

1943 In October 1943 the Mounted Unit was told that it would eventually have to move out of Sunnybrook Park as the Federal Government had expropriated the land for the military (part of the park would be used to build Sunnybrook Military Hospital which was to provide medical treatment to returned soldiers). A large military base was also built on the plateau above the police stable, where the playing fields now stand.

The Mounted Unit continued to be reduced, finishing the year with thirty-four men of all ranks and forty-five horses. A quiet year in Toronto, according to the Chief Constable's annual report.

1944 The Mounted Unit maintained its regular patrols during the year covering the parks and ravines until eleven o'clock at night in the summer. The Eastern Beaches were patrolled regularly by officers from No. 8 Stable. The Mounted Unit maintained forty-six horses although only thirty-six officers of all ranks were assigned to the Unit.

One mounted officer was assigned to the detective division, probably a lateral transfer, for career development.

1945 The Sunnybrook Stable was closed during the year and the buildings turned over to the military. With the loss of this facility, all sick and injured horses were taken to Mounted Headquarters on Belmont Street.

Even with the loss of Sunnybrook and reductions in manpower, the Unit continued to maintain forty-five horses on staff, the highest ratio of horses to men ever. It was difficult for horses to get the regular exercise to which they were accustomed. To make matters worse, none of the horses could be turned out on their own because there were no paddocks available.

With the exception of the former patrols from Sunnybrook Park, all regular patrols were maintained. Constable John Watt was promoted patrol sergeant during the year.

As the war drew to a close, the Toronto Police Department began hiring full-time officers again. Inspector Crosbie inspected each recruit class to select those graduates he felt had the physical build to be mounted men. He interviewed each officer to determine potential interest in mounted training. Should the officer prove to be a suitable candidate he was told he could volunteer for transfer to the Mounted Unit for training, and possibly permanent assignment.

In November the Police Force retired the "Bobby" style helmet. All Toronto police officers would wear the forage style hat. The white version of the "Bobby" helmet would be revived in 1966 as part of the Mounted Unit's ceremonial dress uniform. In the 1990s, the white "Bobby" helmet was selected as the head gear for the Chief of Police's Marching Unit.

PC Fred Anketell (centre) at the Dufferin Race Track, c. 1942.

Constable Fred Anketell, c. 1942. Photographs, courtesy of Sgt Dennis Grummett

 **1946** Brigadier General Draper retired as Chief Constable of Toronto and was replaced by his Deputy, John Chisholm. The new Chief had spent most of his career in investigative functions which meant he knew very little about the Mounted Unit.

Without Chief Draper to fight for them, the Mounted Unit was finally reduced in size to twenty-eight men of all ranks and thirty horses—back to its 1921 strength. The No. 12 Stable located at Yonge Street and Montgomery Avenue was closed. With the exception of the continued North Toronto beats the Unit continued its regular patrols of ravines, parks, beaches and downtown.

The first reported incident of labour unrest in years occurred when the Seaman's International Union (S.I.U.) went on strike in July. In 1946 the Port of Toronto was much more important and busier than it is today. Certainly mounted details were involved in monitoring the seamen's walkout. The strike was peaceful in Toronto, but elsewhere violent confrontations took place.

The 1946 Police Horse Auction

The Board of Police Commissioners ordered the Mounted Unit reduced in size in line with its policy of increasing the mechanization of the police force. On April 22, eleven police horses were sold at auction. The auction hall was so crowded that a special clearing had to be made through the crowd in order to get the horses into the auction box.

Inspector Crosbie was extremely upset that the horses were being sold to the highest bidder rather than being retired to the best possible home, but the new Chief of Police insisted that the horses be sold at auction. Inspector Crosbie was ordered to attend the auction but refused to wear his uniform as he was so ashamed at the manner in which the horses were being "retired."

The first horse brought into the ring was "Polly." As she quietly trotted up and down the ring the auctioneer asked to start the bidding at $150.00. The crowd was quiet for a few minutes until the first bid was accepted by a quiet nod from a member of the crowd. The bidding then commenced and continued until the horse was sold for $380.00.

Some excitement occurred when an eight-year-old bay gelding named "Monty" entered the ring. "'Monty' danced up and down the ring and gave a brief exhibition of rearing." A newspaper article stated that "Monty" was not used to crowds, but was a proven jumper. It is odd that anyone would say that a police horse was not used to crowds.

The organizers then asked Mrs. Ron Gray to mount "Monty" and give a demonstration ride to offset any bad impressions "Monty's" antics had caused. After letting the lady on his bare back "Monty" spun around throwing the lady off. A saddle and bridle was put on the horse. A stable boy rode him up and down the ring and the bidding commenced.

This was probably the only time that Toronto Police Horses have been sold where the price realised was more important than the future well being of the horse.

The following horses were sold with prices realised.[1]

Polly	$380.00	Monty	$210.00	Ajax	$570.00
Pixie	$500.00	Superman	$150.00	Dunkirk	$285.00
Captain	$375.00	Windsor	$330.00	Golden Glow	$480.00
Glenalton	$350.00	Lady Imp	$310.00		

1 *Toronto Telegram*, April 23, 1946.

1947

The Mounted Unit continued to function with twenty-eight men and thirty horses. Regular patrols were continued except that the officers patrolled to 10:30 p.m. The Police Force was quickly becoming the only civic department, still employing horses. The Toronto Street Department sold its last 25 horses and became totally mechanized.[98]

1948

The Unit soldiered on through the year doing its regular duty with twenty men and twenty-nine horses. Patrol Sergeant John Watt was promoted to Sergeant during the year and became second in command of the Unit.

The description of the Mounted Unit in the chief constable's reports had been reported in a standard format for almost ten years. It provides very little information about the value of services provided by officers and horses. The 1940s were a very quiet time for the mounted officers and it was a long time before any complimentary statements were made about them. Finally in his 1948 report, Chief Constable Chisholm wrote;

"The citizens of Toronto are justly proud of the Mounted Division. The services of this branch of the Force was most outstanding during the year, and in dealing with parades and riots the Mounted Police are invaluable."[99]

The Toronto Police Association requested that the officers' working agreement be changed to permit them to work five and a half days per week (all officers currently served six days a week usually with Sundays off). The Association also requested a one-hour lunch break for all officers, such as the mounted men had been receiving for some time, rather than the half hour then in use.

An officer and his mount check out what was billed as "the latest replacement threat to the Toronto police horse," A new Jeep purchased for the traffic unit. July 3, 1947. Photograph, Toronto Telegram *Photograph Collection, York University Archives and Special Collections, Neg. #1693.*

"Surprise! Surprise!"

That might well be an ideal name for this colt born a few days ago to mare Black Bess purchased from a farmer early this year by the Toronto Police Department for its Mounted Division. Neither purchaser nor former owner had any idea the sale would be two for the price of one. Admiring the new arrival is Guy Chalk, 9, of Dixie rd., at the farm of Charles Hemstead.

Photograph, Toronto Telegram.

1949

The Mounted Unit continued its usual patrols during the year. A scout car was assigned to the unit and was used by the Inspector and supervisors to visit the men.

The city grew quickly during the post-war years reaching almost 747,000 persons, and covering an area of 35 square miles with 576 miles of streets and 157 miles of public lanes. Including the Toronto Islands, the city contained over 2,000 acres of parkland. The Mounted Unit's role was primarily parks patrol.

The authorized strength of the Toronto Police Force increased to 1,267 officers of all ranks, although actual size of the force was 1,240 members. Headquarters was located at 149 College Street. The city was divided into twelve police divisions, each commanded by an inspector.

The Toronto Police Force required 75 cars, 2 Jeeps, 3 patrol wagons and 68 motorcycles to fulfil its mandate. The "Senior Service" was beginning to appear quite insignificant in numbers with only 27 officers and 29 horses in the Unit. Many officers must have wondered what the future would hold for the Mounted Unit in this rapidly growing environment.

A tourist article of the time titled, "Toronto Calling," had this to say about the Toronto Police Mounted Unit:

But perhaps the most colourful part of the force is still the Mounted Division with its 27 police and 29 horses with an Inspector in Charge. These smartly uniformed men with their well-groomed horses of the cavalry type are much admired by our citizens and by visitors to our city as they lead a parade or patrol our streets. Their duties include the patrol of parks, ravines, and beaches, disturbances, traffic, etc.[100]

On the night of September 16, the cruise ship S.S. *Noronic* caught fire and burned in Toronto Harbour. Although the ship was still tied to the dock, 119 persons died in the tragedy. A temporary morgue was established in a building at the Canadian National Exhibition. Mounted officers were assigned to crowd-control duties at the scene for days following the fire. Large crowds of curious onlookers lined Queen's Quay to get a view of the doomed vessel.

Just before the *Noronic* burned, Constable Thomas Frazer returned to mounted duties after being off work for an extended period due to an injury suffered while on duty. He was assigned to crowd control duties at the fire scene and was on patrol on Queen's Quay when someone in the crowd threw a brick or other object. The horse was struck on the nose and reared up so high it fell over backwards landing on the officer, causing serious back injuries. Constable Fraser eventually returned to mounted duties and remained a working mounted officer until he retired from the force ten years later.

Inspector Crosbie can be seen riding his mount during a parade to honour Toronto's ice-skating "Queen," Barbara Ann Scott on her return to Toronto. Photograph, Jack Judges, Toronto Telegram.

The Mounted Unit in 1949

LOCATION	STAFF	GENERAL DUTIES
No. 1 Stable Court Street	4 Constables 4 Horses	Patrols in No. 1 and No. 2 Divisions
No. 5 Stable Mounted H.Q. Belmont Street	2 Officers 1 Stableman 6 Constables 9 Horses	Patrols in No. 5 and part of No. 12 Divisions. Traffic, Parks, Ravines, etc.
No. 6 Stable Cowan Avenue	1 Officer 4 Constables 5 Horses	Patrols in No. 6, No. 3 and No. 9 Divisions. High Park, Sunnyside, Exhibition and Traffic Enforcement.
No. 8 Stable Pape Avenue	1 Officers 5 Constables 6 Horses	Patrols in No. 8, No. 10 and No. 4 Divisions Traffic and Beat Duty, Simcoe Park, Cherry Park and the Waterfront.
No. 11 Stable Markham Street	4 Constables 5 Horses	Patrols in No. 11, No. 9 and No. 7 Divisions. Wynchwood Park, Royce and Willowvale Parks.
Totals :	5 Stables 4 Officers 1 Stableman (Constable) 23 Constables 29 Horses	

The Rank of the Structure
Toronto Police Force in 1949

Chief Constable	1	Detective Sergeants	36
Deputy Chief Constable	1	Patrol Sergeants	68
Chief inspector	1	Detectives	25
Inspector of Detectives	1	Acting Detectives	17
Inspectors	22	Constables	857
Sergeant of Detectives	10	Police Women	5
Chief Identification Officer	1	Police Matrons	3
Sergeants	43	Civilians	149

Mounted officers on Queen's Quay making sure the crowds keep away from the fire-ravaged S.S. Noronic. Photograph, Canadian National Exhibition Archives.

Frank joined the Toronto Police Force in 1934 when he was twenty-four years old. After completing his training, he served at No. 2 Station on Court Street. A few years later, probably in 1937, he transferred to the Mounted Unit. Frank served there for seventeen years before transferring to traffic to become a motorcycle officer. He retired from the police force in 1971 after thirty-seven years of service. He died in November 1994 after a long illness.

Sometime around 1937, Frank heard that the Mounted Unit was looking for volunteers to take mounted training. He had no riding experience, but weighed 175 pounds, which was the weight required. The constables in his class received their training at Sunnybrook Park. During his training, Frank was issued with a used set of riding boots which he wore during his entire career at the Mounted Unit.

PC Frank Allen and Queen, c. 1938.
Photograph, courtesy of the Allen Family.

Inspector Crosbie taught the class in a very disciplined fashion. He remembered the Inspector being much like the Sergeant Major which he had been in the first war. When a man fell off his horse, Inspector Crosbie walked up to him and said, "Who the hell told you to get off that horse?"

When he first served in the Mounted Unit, policemen received only one day off a week. It was not until 1950 that policemen were given two days. Mounted Headquarters assigned all days off. A particular day could be requested but there was no guarantee that it would be approved. Frank did not receive annual leave during the summer in his first twenty-five years.

Officers worked two shifts, days from 9:00 a.m. to 5:00 p.m., (Frank was not positive of this shift, it may have been 7:00 to 3:00 or 8:00 to 4:00), and afternoons from 3:00 p.m. to 11:00 p.m., switching from days to afternoons and back again every two weeks. When necessary, hours were changed by Headquarter's memo.

Mounted Headquarters assigned beats which required officers to telephone in to receive their day's duty at the beginning of each shift. Each officer was required to ride a specific beat and be at certain points at specified times, thus making it easier for the patrol sergeant to be in touch. Call boxes were located along the routes patrolled. Astride the horse, the officer would bend down and pull the call box lever; once in contact, he would give the division station his badge number. Sometimes the regular routine would be changed, in order to move the officer to a strike or some other event of greater importance. Should there be no change in duties, the box was closed and the patrol resumed. No portable radios in those days to make an officer's life easier and service response more instantaneous.

Officers were expected to issue parking tickets from a regular ticket book. Summonses required the license number and details of the vehicle to be noted in a memo book. Later a summons form was typed at the station and mailed to the accused. Specific quotas for issuing tickets or summonses were not required.

The Mounted Unit men rode in all kinds of weather wearing tunics year-round. Officers' badge numbers were secured at each shoulder. Special large-skirted riding raincoats protected rider and horse. In winter, felt boots were worn with galoshes over top that held spurs. To keep the horse warm, riding cloaks had a flared bottom that fitted over the horse's backs. Corduroy breeches kept officers from freezing, as did tall Persian wool hats that often were hard to keep on. Each officer was required to buy one of these hats which cost between $25 and $75, a lot when Frank's family's grocery bill was only $7.00 a week.

Frank was a member of the 1940 Musical Ride trained by Inspector Crosbie. Performances were given almost every night at the Grandstand, of the Canadian National Exhibition. At that time, officers did not carry a lance, like today or wear special uniforms.

During his tenure in the Mounted Unit, Frank was assigned (without recourse as to location) to No. 8 Stable, (Pape Avenue), No. 11 Stable, (Markham and London Streets), and No. 6 Stable, (Cowan and Queen Street West).

At No 6. Stable, Frank was assigned to patrol High Park and had a predetermined route. Once in the park the planned route brought the officer to a specific point that had to be reached at a certain time. A call box in the park, was used to report to the station. Time allowed for one circuit of the park before returning to the stable for lunch, eaten in the saddle room.

Patrol Sergeant Gallagher visited the men on their beats and specified a time to record his visit in their memo book. Patrol sergeants seldom rode horses; a patrol car was their usual mode of transportation.

Officers on patrol carried a leather billy or sap in their back pocket and a riding crop on the right side of the saddle. They did not have a handcuff pouch like foot officers, so Frank secured his handcuffs in the braces under his tunic. At the end of each shift, officers turned in their guns to the Divisional Sergeant of the police station where the stable was located. These were stored in a gun locker and reissued the next working day.

Mounted officers had the option of travelling to and from work in civilian clothes or uniform. Overalls were worn when mucking out the stables or grooming a horse. Men on foot patrol wore the "Bobby" style helmet but mounted officers wore a stiff forage cap. Frank kept his soft forage cap, like the motorcycle men, which he sometimes wore—against the rules.

Chief Constable Draper had his own horse, one that he rode on special occasions. Small by police standards, it was kept at Sunnybrook Park. During the winter, it would spend most of its time being turned out, and its hair would grow so long until it looked somewhat like a bear.

Frank was offered a place to live, with his family, in Sunnybrook Park but he turned it down as being too far from everything. Sunnybrook was well in the country at that time, and without amenities. Living there

meant quite a walk out to Bayview Avenue to catch public transportation.

The Mounted Unit led many parades during the year. Usually the Inspector would lead the Unit, followed by two officers whose job it was to move people back to the safety of the street curb so the main body of mounted men could follow. One of the largest parades attended every year was the Police Church Parade, usually held in October. Men assembled at the armouries on University Avenue before marching to the church.

The Mounted Unit performed extensive crowd-control duties. Seldom were there problems, but when there was, men would ride into the crowds with whips drawn (although they were rarely used). In his seventeen years as a mounted officer, Frank could not recall having to strike anyone, even with his smaller riding crop. Instead, when necessary, officers used the size and weight of their horses to push people along.

A constable at Mounted Headquarters took care of the equipment and material stores, and did leather work. Any problem with a horse was directed to the Patrol Sergeant and, if necessary, a veterinarian would be summoned. Horses were ridden to the blacksmith shop when they needed to be shod. Some were held by the bridle, but most blacksmiths needed little, if any, help.

Most horses were bay or chestnut coloured as the force owned very few blacks. The great care these horses received was well reflected in the shine of their coats and hooves, and the brightness of their eyes. No trucks or trailers existed for transporting horses so they were required to be ridden wherever they were required. Mrs. Allen recalled Frank arriving home frozen and exhausted after having to ride his horse from the Pape Avenue Stable in the east end to the Cowan Avenue Stable at the far reaches of western Toronto where he had been transferred. It was during the depths of winter when Frank took that

PC Frank Allen in High Park, c. 1945.
Photograph, courtesy of the Allen Family.

memorable ride down the length of Queen Street into a freezing west wind.

Frank never patrolled the Toronto Islands. At night, red reflectors were attached to stirrups to attract motorists attention. Frank did not remember any accidents between horses and cars during his service. A thick felt pad fit under the saddle to protect the horse's back and the leather of the saddle.

People really liked police horses and their wonderful appearance. Every rider kept their brass bosses shined. The white rope and breast plate were examples of first class care. Mounted officers were always well turned out.

Bill Ganson and Andy Russell trained horses in Sunnybrook Park. Frank recalled that "remounts were always ticklish, especially when they had not seen or been in traffic." When his mount "Queen" was sold, Frank was given a remount. Travelling north on Yonge Street, Frank and his mount entered an area where there were a lot of elevators at Shaftsbury Avenue. Frank wanted to expose his horse to this new environment, for the experience. At that moment, a large truck drove by with its canvas top flapping in the wind. The horse reared and fell over backwards across Frank's leg. A fast-thinking citizen

grabbed the reins until Frank got to his feet. He immediately checked over his horse which appeared to be uninjured, although shaken. Somewhat bruised himself, Frank mounted up and the two started off again. Frank was not seriously hurt and, to his good fortune, this was the only injury he suffered on the job.

As time went on fewer officers chose to become part of the Mounted Unit. During 1950, John Watt, who had been a Patrol Sergeant when Frank first joined the unit, took command. Frank remembered Watt as a good man and easy to talk to at any time duty required.

Frank was forced to leave the Mounted Unit because of a physical incapability of riding due to increasing symptoms of multiple sclerosis. Frank's condition continued to deteriorate until he was eventually confined to Providence Villa and Hospital in Scarborough.

When the author talked to Frank Allen in 1993, he had spent ten years in the hospital. During the discussion, it was clear that even after a 40 year absence from the Unit, where he had served the citizens of Toronto for over 17 years, Frank still carried many fond memories of being one of Toronto's Finest, a Mounted Police Officer.

PC Frank Allen in winter dress, c. 1940.

PC Frank Allen, c. 1940.
Photographs, courtesy of the Allen Family

1950 No. 1 Police Stable on Court Street was closed during the year. It had been the oldest stable of the unit, in use for 63 years and was the oldest Police division in operation. All men and mounts were distributed to other stables in the city. With the closing of Court Street no mounted officers patrolled in No.1 or 2 Divisions, which encompassed the downtown core. The Unit directed most of its patrols to the ravines, parks and Eastern beaches, with duty time reduced to 10 p.m. in the summer months.

Constable Ed Johnson was assigned as a horse trainer soon after his arrival at the unit in 1949. No facilities were available for training horses at Mounted Headquarters where the remounts were stabled. Early in the 1950s, an area was found on Yonge Street where the Rosedale Subway Station now stands where they could work new horses. To get there, trainers rode their own horse and ponied their remounts.

New horses were walked through city traffic and across busy Yonge Street every day they were taken for training.

Once subway construction began at this site, the officers could no longer use it for training. Instead they took an hour or more ponying their horses to Whitewoods Stable on Pottery Road, which had the only riding ring available to the police. The training ring was located where Fantasy Farms now stands. The old Whitewoods Stable building became part of Todmorden Mills Historic Village. Once horses could be ridden, training could be undertaken in the Rosedale Ravine.

The Toronto Police Commission refused to grant its police officers the five-and-a-half-day work week which their Association had requested earlier. The issue was sent to arbitration and the officers received a welcomed Christmas present when the labour arbitrator granted them a five-day-week on December 26. The horses would also be given two rest days a week.

A mounted officer at Toronto Island, c. 1948. Photograph, Toronto Police Museum.

1951 Inspector Crosbie became ill while working the 1950 Royal Winter Fair. He never fully recovered from this illness and was admitted to hospital in March. He died soon after. The Mounted Unit provided a full mounted escort at his funeral. Sergeant John Watt was promoted to Inspector and placed in charge of the Mounted Division. There were no patrol sergeants left on staff.

On November 5, 1951, three men escaped from Toronto's Don Jail: Edwin Alonzo Boyd, William Jackson and

Leonard Jackson. All three were bank robbers and were soon to become famous as the "Boyd Gang." The Don Jail is located on the edge of the Don Valley near Broadview Avenue and Gerrard Street, and provided the men with an excellent escape route. Mounted officers were then, as they are now, one of the best means of searching this extensive area. The officers scoured the valley floor for any sign of the three escapees but to no avail. They had managed to flee the area and began robbing banks again.

A mounted officer with a child outside of the Canadian National Exhibition Stadium, c. 1950. Photograph, Canadian National Exhibition Archives.

The Mounted Unit, c. 1951. Inspector John Watt is in the centre and PC Ed Johnson third from the left. Photograph, Toronto Telegram *Photograph Collection, York University Archives and Special Collections, Neg. # 1697.*

The stable area of old No. 11 Division in 1998. This facility was used by the Mounted Unit from 1912 until 1974. The Ambulance Department assumed use of the building after the police moved. The old hayloft door and I beam hoist can still be seen.

The front doors of old No. 11 Division, 1998. The corner of London and Markham Streets near the corner of Bathurst and Bloor Streets.

Photographs, Sgt Lorna Kozmik.

 **1952** Patrols of the ravines, parks and eastern beaches were extended to 10:30 p.m. during summer months. It was another quiet year for the Mounted Unit. The Toronto Argonaut Football Club won the Grey Cup on December 1st. The Mounted Unit was involved in escorting the victory parade through the cheering, people-filled downtown streets of Toronto.

On March 6th, 1952, Sergeant of Detectives Edmund Tong was fatally wounded by Steve Suchan and Leonard Jackson of the Boyd Gang. On March 23, 1952 the Mounted Unit provided a mounted escort at his police funeral. The Boyd Gang members were soon apprehended for a second time and lodged in the Toronto Don Jail. Police officers were assigned to the patrol the outside perimeter to increase security and prevent another jailbreak.

On September 8 the Boyd Gang did it again. Boyd, Suchan and the two Jacksons escaped from jail. Once out of the prison, the gang members disappeared into the ravine beside the jail and successfully fled north, up the Don Valley area. Mounted officers were again sent to patrol but the prisoners were long gone. All were later captured. Leonard Jackson and Steve Suchan were executed by hanging at the Don Jail for the murder of Sergeant of Detectives Tong. Edwin Boyd was sentenced to prison and paroled after serving twelve years.

Chief Constable John Chisholm 1946-1958

Chief Constable Chisholm replaced the very pro-Mounted Unit Chief, Dennis Draper. Inspector Crosbie appears to have lost a lot of his influence once Draper left. It was Chief Chisholm who ordered him to sell the police horses at auction to the highest bidder. By the mid 1950s the chief became very positive about the Mounted Unit in his annual reports. This may have been because he was worried that those planning the creation of the new Metropolitan Toronto Police would want to disband the Mounted Unit.

1953 The Mounted Unit was no longer able to service all of its patrol areas due to reductions in staff. The regular mounted beats in No.'s, 4, 7, 9, 10 and 12 Divisions were discontinued. With only twenty-six men of all ranks, and twenty-seven horses the Unit had to consolidate mounted posts.

The Greater Toronto area consisted of thirteen individual municipalities. Toronto had grown so much that its surrounding towns abutted on each other, creating many administrative problems and duplication of services due to the conflicting interests of local governments. Toronto was no longer allowed to annex other municipalities as it had done in the past.

In order to address these issues, the Provincial Government formed the first regional municipal government in Ontario by creating the Municipality of Metropolitan Toronto. Political power was shared between local councils and the new regional level of government. Some services were left locally while other services were controlled by the

Council of Metropolitan Toronto.

Policing remained a local responsibility, temporarily, under the separate control of the municipal or township government. While the amalgamations of the police forces was being considered, the possible effect on the Mounted Unit remained unknown.

During the 1953 Canadian National Exhibition a serious outbreak of polio caused great concern in Toronto. Three officers assigned to the Exhibition were struck down with this terrible disease. One was Patrol Sergeant John Ogle, formally of the Mounted Unit, who had left for active service in the Royal Canadian Air Force in World War II.

While recuperating in Sunnybrook Hospital, the Governor General of Canada came to visit and pinned a belated Distinguished Flying Cross on John's chest. John had won the medal during the war, but had not received it.

The disease left him crippled and he was forced to use two canes to walk around. John Ogle was assigned to the employment office where he finished his career.

Constable Walter Metcalfe, c. 1953. Metcalfe served in the Royal Canadian Air Force in World War II and was awarded the Distinguished Flying Cross. He joined the Toronto Police Department after the war. Metcalfe took a military leave of absence during the Korean War and served his country for a second time, rejoining the police after his discharge from the military. Upon retirement from the Metro Toronto Police, Metcalfe immediately joined the Toronto Port Police. When the Toronto Port Police was absorbed into the Metro Toronto Police he became a serving member of the force once again, as well as a police pensioner. Metcalfe retired from the Metro Police for the second time at age sixty-five. Photograph, Toronto Police Museum.

▣ 1954

For a short time during the year the Mounted Unit was operating with only Inspector Watt and twenty-six constables. The officers were busy during the year working 249 hours of overtime. All of the overtime was taken as time off. The members of the unit exhibited horses at the Canadian National Exhibition and the Royal Winter Fair. They were highly commended by fair officials on these occasions.

The Mounted Unit was now concentrating its patrols in green belt areas. There was no longer any mention of regular post duties in the annual reports. The officers were still responsible for traffic enforcement and other beat duties, but this was done while they were patrolling to their assigned parks.

The Metropolitan Toronto Council appointed an advisory committee in September to look into the feasibility of amalgamating the thirteen police forces and fire departments within the boundaries of Metropolitan Toronto.

SPECIAL DUTIES 1954 AND 1955

DUTIES	1954 PCs	1954 Hours	1955 PCs	1955 Hours
Parks and Ravines	2862	22580	3177	25308
Coliseum	334	2016	383	2904
Races, Woodbine and Dufferin	213	1589	180	1440
School Crossing	156	738	199	1592
Parades	117	627	85	237
Red Feather Escort (Money escort)	97	373	99	331
Strikes	112	207	268	303
Automotive Building	24	192	n/a	n/a
Bank Supervision	41	82	48	96
Municipal Election	7	70	n/a	n/a
School Games	10	68	20	160
Plain Clothes Duty	7	56	56	448
Labour Meetings	9	45	n/a	n/a
Maple Leaf Gardens	10	38	21	168
Sunnyside	5	30	n/a	n/a
Central Technical School	6	28	n/a	n/a
Exhibition	n/a	n/a	136	1088
TOTAL	**4010**	**28639**	**4612**	**34075**

A rainy day at No. 8 Stable, Pape Avenue, c. 1955.
Photograph, Toronto Police Museum.

⊞ 1955

The annual report for 1955 presented more detail than usual about the operation of the Mounted Unit. A constable working at No. 5 Stable was assigned, on a part time basis, to duty as a stableman. In addition to his patrol and stable duties, he was in charge of stores, saddlery repairs, and attended to sick and injured horses.

Constable Ed Johnson was promoted to Patrol Sergeant on March 17 and became second in command of the Unit. A patrol car was assigned to the Mounted Unit to be used by Inspector Watt and Patrol Sergeant Johnson to visit all stables and officers on patrol.

The report noted that the posts in the ravine (Rosedale Ravine), Don Flats, Cherry Beach and other parks were patrolled by mounted constables until 10:00 p.m. It went on to say: *In addition to the above-noted regular posts patrolled by members of the Mounted Division, special duties were performed during the year at: various parks throughout the city, the Coliseum, school crossings, the Woodbine and Dufferin Race Tracks, the Canadian National Exhibition, strikes, parades, the Maple Leaf Gardens, and school games. Members of the Mounted Division also performed special duties as money escorts, in plainclothes, and in providing bank supervision.*[101]

Members of the Mounted Unit worked 335 hours of overtime during the year, all of which was paid back with time off. Officers exhibited horses at both the Canadian National Exhibition and Royal Winter Fair where they were again highly commended by officials at both shows.

Officers were issued with a special shoulder patch for the first time, a red felt triangle with a blue horse rearing in the centre. "Toronto City Police" was embossed across the top. It was the only cloth insignia ever issued by the Toronto Police Force.

ARRESTS MADE by the Mounted Unit IN 1954 AND 1955

OFFENCE	1954	1955
Drunk	25	31
B.L.C.A.	8	8
Theft	3	0
Vagrancy	2	1
Ability Impaired	1	3
Drunk Driving	1	0
Indecent Exposure	1	0
Cause Disturbance	0	1
Careless Driving	0	1
Obstruct Police	0	1
TOTALS	**42**	**47**

SUMMONS ISSUED by the Mounted Unit 1954 AND 1955

	1955	1954
Right or Left Turns	903	923
No Name and Address	581	726
Defaced Markers	528	665
Autos, No Lights	291	307
Bicycles No License	285	33
Stop Streets	263	162
Disobey Traffic Signal	140	124
Highway Traffic Act, General	120	62
Vehicles Unattended	101	0
City By-Laws	53	369
One Way Streets	46	90
No Driving Permits	30	19
No License Plates (Current Year)	19	0
Dogs at Large	9	0
Parking (General)	5	25
Pass Stationary Street Car	4	3
Careless Driving	2	8
Obstruct Crosswalk	2	0
Defective Equipment	0	32
Unnecessary Noise	0	13
TOTALS	**3382**	**3561**

1956

The Mounted Unit continued its patrols in the green belt areas of the city. Consideration was given to purchasing a double-horse trailer to save time in getting officers to their patrol posts.

The Chief Constable's Annual Report listed the special duties performed by the Mounted Unit. For the first time in years, mounted officers were not required to attend strike details or events at Maple Leaf Gardens. Although, the Unit continued to supply officers for money escorts.

Some may have questioned the value of maintaining the Mounted Unit, especially considering the lack of labour unrest or large demonstrations. Chief Constable Chisholm stated his opinion about this issue in the annual report. "There are various schools of thought in regard to the use and value of Mounted Police Officers, but in spite of the highly mechanized age in which we live, I am of the opinion that there is still a definite place for a reasonably-sized Mounted Detail.

"Having in mind the pending merger of the Police Forces of Metropolitan Toronto, I am a strong advocate of retaining the Mounted Division at its present strength of 28 men and 28 horses... To sum up, a Mounted Police Detail is always a pleasant addition to any large parade and its members are well received by the public generally."[102]

Throughout Toronto, 310 police call boxes and bell lights remained in operation as the main means of communication for the patrolling mounted officers; the six boxes in High Park were also used by park personnel.

Royal escorts conducted at the Queen's Plate Horse Race were the responsibility of the Governor General's Horse Guards Regiment. The Mounted Unit provided officers and horses at these duties to help bolster the ranks of the Horse Guards. Thus began the Mounted Unit's tradition of mounted officers taking part in these official functions while wearing the uniform of the Governor General's Horse Guards: for the next 20 years the Unit would assist the Horse Guards in this way.

1956 was the last year of the City of Toronto Police Department. When the force was formed in 1834, it policed a small market town of less than 10,000 people, but by 1956 the population had increased to 643,791. The Mounted Unit, and its traditions, had been an important part of Toronto's social history through these years of growth.

Changes happening within the policing community would prove benefit to the Mounted Unit. Membership in the new Metropolitan Toronto Police Force would bring new responsibilities and a resurgence of the Unit's size and stature.

THE MOUNTED UNIT IN 1956

LOCATION	STAFF	GENERAL DUTIES
No. 5 Stable Mounted H.Q. Belmont Street	2 Officers 7 Constables 9 Horses	The Rosedale Ravine, Don Flats, Reservoir Park.
No. 6 Stable Cowan Avenue	8 Constables 8 Horses	High Park, Exhibition Park.
No. 8 Stable Pape Avenue	6 Constables 6 Horses	Riverdale Park, Greenwood Park, Cherry Beach.
No. 11 Stable Markham Street	5 Constables 5 Horses	Wynchwood Park, Royce Park and Willowvale Park, (Christie Pits).
Totals :	4 Stables 2 Officers 26 Constables 28 Horses	

The Metropolitan Toronto Police Service 1957–1997

Sgt Edwin Johnson is the right front marker as the Mounted Unit passes Judge C.O. Bick, Chairman of The Metropolitan Toronto Police Commission, Mayor Nathan Phillips stands on his right, during the march past at the Metropolitan Toronto Police Amateur Athletic Association Field Day. Photograph, Toronto Police Museum.

1957

January 1, 1957, the Metropolitan Toronto Police Force was officially created, as thirteen municipal police forces of Metropolitan Toronto were amalgamated into one large regional police force. The Mounted Unit was little affected by the organizational changes taking place, and continued to patrol its old posts within the City of Toronto.

The format of the Chief Constable's report changed, and included less information about special units within the force. Fortunately, the unit commander of the Mounted Unit continued to submit an annual report to the deputy chief responsible for specialized units each year. Many of these reports survived, and provide details on the duties performed by officers of the new police force.

1958

A 1958 Chevrolet Scout Car was assigned to the Unit with the radio call sign, "Car Fifty-Five." Also purchased was a 1957 Mercury Panel Van and horse trailer, which allowed the Unit to transport horses more quickly to their destinations.

Regular mounted patrols were maintained within the City of Toronto, and no new patrolling areas were established in any of the former municipalities comprising the new Metropolitan Toronto. The Mounted Unit provided a number of officers and horses, in Governor General's Horse Guard's Uniforms, to assist with the major military escorts of the year.

On July 4, Constable Patrick Woulfe, on patrol in High Park checking the parking lots, found a small trickle of blood dripping from a car. He discovered the body of Chief of Police John Chisholm who had shot himself some time earlier in the day. Chisholm's unfortunate death was attributed to the pressures involved in the formation of the new police force, and the resulting power struggles amongst senior officers and politicians.

Mounted Unit officers assigned to ride with the Governor General's Horse Guards at the 1958 Queen's Plate.
Left to right: Sgt Ed Johnson, PC Jim Lewis, PC John Wear, PC Merle Smith, PC Bob Quinn, PC Robert Boardman.

The thirteen Toronto area Chiefs of Police from the police departments that were combined to form the Metropolitan Toronto Police force in 1957. It may have been the pressure involved in forming this new police service that led to the premature death of Chief of Police John Chisholm on July 4, 1958. Veteran Toronto Star crime reporter Jocko Thomas wrote in his book, From Police Headquarters, that John Chisholm was probably Toronto's most competent chief of police.
Photograph, Toronto Police Museum.
To Serve and Protect, Vol. I..

Front Row: (l-r) Andrew Hamilton (Etobicoke), Harry A. Smith (East York), Robert Alexander (York), John Chisholm (Toronto), Roy D. Risebrough (North York), Joseph Thurston (Acting Chief, Forest Hill), Wilfred McLellan (Scarborough). Back Row: William R. Weatherup (New Toronto), Fred H. Herman (Mimico), Robert W. Smyth (Long Branch), James Lovell (Swansea), Arthur Webster (Weston), Clarence Anderson (Leaside).

The Mounted Unit leading the funeral parade for Chief Constable John Chisholm. The officers are riding westbound on Queen Street West at Sorauren Avenue, July 1958. Inspector John Watt is leading, 1st Row: Sgt Ed Johnson on "Major," Frank Lepper on "Marie," (unidentified), 2nd Row: Gordon "Red" Collinson, Bill Boardman, unidentified, unidentified, 3rd Row: Jim Lewis, unidentified, unidentified, unidentified, 4th Row: unidentified, Pat Woulfe, unidentified, Merle Smith. Photograph, Janik Photo's. LE6-0110.

Constable Thomas Frazer

Constable Tom Frazer as a member of the Toronto Police Department, c. 1955.

Tom Frazer as a member of the Metropolitan Police Force, c. 1960. Note the shoulder flash and M.T.P. dress saddle blanket. Photographs, Toronto Police Museum.

The following article appeared in the Toronto newsletter of the International Police Association in the late-1960s. It was written by Tom Frazer, an old-time mounted man, and is a fine example of the bond between a mounted man and his horse.

"Her name was Princess, born about 1937 and joined the Toronto Police Department in 1942. I broke her out at Sunnybrook Park and then she was sent into the city. I got her back in the late forties and we were inseparable up to the day she was retired from the force. I could not see her sold to someone who would not take good care of her, so, I decided to purchase her for myself and was successful in doing so on the second try.

I sent her to a farm near Milton but it was not to her liking so I had her transferred to the Double Horseshoe Ranch in Whitchurch Township under the care of Mr. Don Whitehead. We had an agreement that if ever he wanted to dispose of her that I was to be notified. It was unnecessary because she had found her Horse Heaven and soon became one of the family. Don was approached on many occasions by persons wanting to purchase Princess but his answer was always the same, she will never leave here alive, a promise which he kept and which ended with her death on January 15, 1966.

Don and his daughter rode her for the first few years but for the last six years she has never had a saddle on her back or a bridle in her mouth. She lived the life of 'Riley' and in the last few years I have had more time to spend with her at the farm. Going over old times, she seemed to understand such things as the parades we used to do together. Every major and most minor parades she was in the lead; the 12th of July, Holy Name, Grey Cup and many, many more. The one she really enjoyed was the Santa Claus Parade. She loved the children and would put her head into the crowd to be petted by them as we moved along the route. Then there was the Exhibition and the Royal Winter Fair where she never failed to win a ribbon or a cup in competition with other police horses.

She was tops! She liked tagging. I would throw the reins over her neck and start to make out the tag, when she heard me tear off the tag she would look around for traffic and when clear, would move out along the side of the auto and stop at the windshield and lean over so that I could place the tag under the wiper and then immediately move off to the next car. When on duty at Christie Pits many a prisoner she led over to the patrol box by the sleeve of his coat and she would not let go until the Scout Car arrived and she turned the prisoner over to [the] officer.

She collapsed on January 15th at the ranch and could not get up, but with great heart and pride she never gave up. My good friend Don called me and I knew she must be in a bad way. When I arrived at the ranch about 1:45 p.m. I think she heard me and was trying to get up and come to me. As I knelt beside her and took her head on my lap she quietened right down. I stayed with her until she passed away at 3:00 p.m. She died peacefully and I knew that I had lost the best friend I have ever had. I loved that old gal and she loved me. Princess was the oldest police horse on the department and the most faithful. I will never forget her.

I cannot speak too highly of Don Whitehead and his family for the love and care that they shared with Princess.
'Good Old' Tom Frazer.

Inspector Johnson and the Mounted Unit leading a parade up Yonge Street, c. 1965. Photograph, Toronto Police Museum.

1959 A second truck and two horse trailers were purchased for the Mounted Unit. This added mobility allowed for extended patrols to the five municipalities outside the City of Toronto. Horse trailers selected were a 1957 Riche and a 1957 Beaufort.

Problems took place at a number of soccer games which were being held at Fred Hamilton Field. The Mounted Unit was credited with "saving the day" on a number of occasions when tempers got out of hand. During the year the Mounted Unit provided 18 escorts at parades. They investigated 6 persons, did 49 paid duties, issued 5,146 parking tags and applied for 4,501 summonses.[1]

The mounted officers assigned to the Royal escort for Queen Elizabeth II at the 1959 Queen's Plate. Rear: Ivan McAnsh, Bill McGauchie, Ken Porter, Ed Johnson. Centre: Ted Lloyd, Harrell, Merle Smith, Bob Quinn, Kevin Dowling. Front: Roy Cardy, Gordon Collinson, Bill Currie, Pat Woulfe, Frank Lepper. Photograph, Toronto Police Mounted Unit.

1960 The Mounted Unit continued providing regular patrols in the parks and ravines within the boundaries of the City of Toronto. The total strength of the unit decreased by two during the year leaving twenty-nine officers of all ranks. A major shake up of personnel occurred when one officer resigned and seven transferred out of the Unit. Five new constables transferred to the Mounted Unit and one officer, Jim Davis, was hired.

In his annual report, Inspector Watt requested that the unit be increased by one Patrol Sergeant and three constables. Ed Johnson had been promoted to full sergeant on March 22nd leaving no patrol sergeants in the Unit. A new patrol sergeant was needed to provide improved supervision to the stables spread across the city. New constables were necessary because of the possibility

mounted patrols would be extended into new areas of Metropolitan Toronto.

Inspector Watt and Sergeant Johnson worked Monday to Friday. There was no mounted supervision on weekends. Usually only three mounted officers worked on Sundays as the rest of the unit were on their day off. Officers on duty cleaned stables and vehicles rather than ride horses.

The Island Stable was manned by three constables from May to October. Members of the Mounted Unit worked a total of one hundred and fifty-nine hours overtime during the year. They performed a number of special duties including taking part in twenty-two parades and fifty special events for the United Appeal. A number of officers were injured during the year and, as a result of these mishaps, members of the Unit missed a total of one hundred and forty-nine days of work.

1961

The main patrols of the Mounted Unit were concentrated within eight parks in the City of Toronto. During the summer, the Unit began to send out truck and trailer details to provide coverage to suburban parks. A proposal was made to the Police Commission to open a new stable in Scarborough. Additional patrol sergeant, four constables and four horses were requested to work from the proposed stable.

There was desperate need of training facilities. The Canadian National Exhibition allowed the use of show rings located in the Horse Palace and Coliseum on a part time basis. Use of these facilities was limited, however due to events taking place at the Exhibition.

Ultimately, the Unit lost the use of the Exhibition facility because of increased event activity, and major reconstruction work. No other training facility was available. The Unit Inspector reported that both men and horses required from four to eight weeks in the riding school. "It will be increasingly difficult to train, especially the horses, without the use of the rings."[2]

A 1960 Chevrolet Patrol Car was acquired to be used by supervisory staff to visit the officers. A 1957 Panel Van described as being in poor condition was employed for full time use. A second mounted van used by Central Garage, was borrowed by the Unit as needed.

During the year, two constables resigned from the police force, and three transferred out of the Unit. An additional eight new officers transferred in. No notation is available about where these new officers received their training. Members of the Unit were off for a total of one hundred and five days due to injuries received on duty. Officers worked a total of one hundred and twenty seven and a half hours of overtime.

Between August 8 and 14, a special team of mounted, foot and motorcycle officers were assigned to patrol High Park in response to citizen complaints of indecent acts. Mounted officers arrested thirty-two persons for sex offences during the assignment.

It is interesting to note that the Unit still used surplus cavalry equipment from World War I. While on patrol, Constable Jim Davis was stopped by a man who identified himself as a veteran of the Canadian Field Artillery from the First World War. The man commented on the tack that Jim was using, noting its similarity to the tack he had used fifty years before. Jim asked the man to look at the bottom of his stirrup irons on which were stamped "C.F.A. 1914," (Canadian Field Artillery, 1914 issue.)

The Metropolitan Toronto Police Riot and Emergency Squad was formed during the year—it would later be renamed as the Emergency Task Force (E.T.F.). Mounted officers would have a close association with this new unit right through the turbulent 1960s.

Mounted officers at the Prince's Gates of the Canadian National Exhibition, c. 1960. Left to right: PC Sandwell, Sgt Johnson, PC Smith, unidentified, PC McConnell, PC Davis. Photograph, courtesy of Jim Davis.

1962

The lack of a proper training facility was still the Mounted Unit's major problem. The Inspector reported that many of the new personnel had little or no previous experience with horses and required more training than the experienced recruits of the past. Training rings at the Canadian National Exhibition were used but these were not always available. As a result, some horses and men being sent into the streets without proper training.[3]

Another concern was the lack of proper stabling facilities. Existing buildings did not allow the Unit to provide proper care for sick and lame horses. Some had to be boarded out to private stables in the country. The Inspector suggested that the force purchase a training farm for the Unit. Properly equipped with the necessary stabling and training facilities such a farm would enable the Unit to provide its horses with the necessary care and attention.

There continued to be a large turnover of personnel. Two constables resigned from the police force, and four constables transferred from the unit. The Unit increased in size with fifteen new constables being transferred to mounted duties finally building to its prior strength of pre World War II levels. The average age of all horses was eight years.

A new police station and court house was built in the (former) Township of Scarborough at the corner of Birchmount Road and Eglinton Avenue East. The facility included the first new police stable to be built in fifty years. The No. 4 District Stable located at No. 41 Division was equipped with one box stall and six standing stalls. The officers and mounts assigned to this building would provide the first regular mounted patrols outside the City of Toronto.

The majority of the Mounted Unit patrols were concentrated in eight parks within Toronto, plus an additional three in Scarborough. From May to October, five mounted officers were assigned to the Island Stable. The stableman/quartermaster position was once again made a full time position. The constable assigned worked at No. 57 Division Stable (the new designation of old No. 5 station), which remained headquarters of the Mounted Unit.

A new 1963 Chevrolet Panel Van was issued to pull the existing horse trailer. One truck and trailer was stationed at No. 16 Division (old No. 6 stable, Cowan and Queen) for moving horses within the City of Toronto. A second truck and trailer was stationed at No. 4 District Stable in Scarborough for transporting officers and horses to and from Scarborough parks. The Scarborough truck and trailer was also used for extended trips to the country to purchase and/or sell police mounts.

Mounted officers attended sixteen parades and twelve United Appeal events, and the A.R. Clarke Tannery Strike in No. 8 Division. During the Shriners' Convention, the Unit took part in two parades and provided special coverage on the Exhibition Grounds. Special details were also provided for the Grey Cup Parade and weekend, and the football game at the Canadian National Exhibition Grandstand.

The Queen Mother was the special guest at the Queen's Plate Race at the New Woodbine Race Track. A detail of sixteen horses and men paraded in Governor Generals Horse Guard uniforms.

In fall 1962, Judge C.O. Bick and Chief of Police James Mackey travelled to Scotland to study the use of police dogs. Incidents which had taken place in Hamilton, Ontario, and New York City, convinced them that dogs should never be used for crowd control. Presentations seen in Scotland failed to change their minds.

In his book, *I Policed Toronto*, Chief Mackey commented on the Mounted Unit and crowd control: *As far as I could see, it was the horses that were the real asset to our department in crowd control, rather than dogs. Many of the disturbing groups would use electric prods and throw ball bearings and marbles on the road to try to upset them [the horses], but they still did an excellent job for us. From the demonstrations put on for Judge Bick and me in Glasgow, my opinion on this matter was unchanged.*[4]

A mounted officer seen patrolling an isolated path somewhere in Scarborough. Photograph, courtesy of Jim Davis.

Constable Roy Cardy and "Bruce" from the front cover of the Metropolitan Toronto Police Annual Report of 1962. Roy Cardy served with the Mounted Unit from 1951 to 1979 when he retired and became an ordained Anglican Minister. His new career took him to a parish in northern Alberta. He is also the Chaplain of the Canadian Mounted Police Association. Photograph, Toronto Police Museum.

SPECIAL DETAILS IN THE 1960s

SPECIAL DUTIES	1960 Days	1961 Days	1962 Days	1963 Days	1964 Days	1965 Days	1966 Days	1967 Days
C.N.E.	112	247	107	131	108	n/a	n/a	n/a
Royal Winter Fair	22	33	5	31	12	n/a	n/a	n/a
Stanley Park	126	69	n/a	n/a	n/a	n/a	n/a	n/a
School Crossings	115	0	n/a	n/a	n/a	n/a	n/a	n/a
Strikes	59	118	621	n/a	1272	n/a	n/a	n/a
March Past	45	48	n/a	n/a	n/a	n/a	n/a	n/a
United Appeal Escorts	30	50	n/a	n/a	n/a	n/a	n/a	n/a
Coliseum Sportsman Show	26	24	n/a	n/a	n/a	n/a	n/a	n/a
Search Details	19	0	n/a	n/a	n/a	n/a	n/a	n/a
School Games	17	12	n/a	n/a	n/a	n/a	n/a	n/a
Election (Schools)	11	0	n/a	n/a	n/a	n/a	n/a	n/a
Banks	10	35	n/a	n/a	n/a	n/a	n/a	n/a
Escort (G.G.H.G.)	10	18	n/a	n/a	n/a	n/a	n/a	n/a
Horse Shows	7	19	n/a	n/a	n/a	n/a	n/a	n/a
Plain Clothes Duties	0	58	n/a	n/a	n/a	n/a	n/a	n/a
Parades	0	56	n/a	n/a	n/a	25	n/a	n/a
Grey Cup Game	0	7	n/a	n/a	n/a	n/a	n/a	n/a
Varsity Stadium	-0	4	n/a	n/a	n/a	n/a	n/a	n/a
Other Special Duties	N/A	N/A	146	59	n/a	690	497	475
TOTALS	**609**	**798**	**879**	**221**	**1392**	**715**	**497**	**475**

ARRESTS IN THE 1960s

CHARGE	1960	1961	1962	1963
Drunk	43	36		
Vagrancy	4	2		27
Indecent Exposure	3	0		2
Breach, Liquor Control Act	5	3		
Impaired Driving	2	0		13
Mentally Ill	1	0		
Common Assault	1	1		1
Uttering	1	0		
Theft	1	5		11
Break & Enter, House	0	5		1
Break & Enter, Shop	0	4		
Assault, Bodily Harm	0	3		1
Cause Disturbance	0	2		
Robbery	0	2		
Improper Driving	0	2		
Careless Driving	0	1		
Warrant of Committal	0	1		1
Attempt Suicide	0	1		
Gross Indecency	0	1		23
Breach of Probation	0	1		1
Fail to Remain	0	0		1
Drive Under Suspension	0	0		1
Attempt Auto Theft				1
Assault, Police	0	0		1
Indecent Assault Male	0	0		1
Mischief	0	0		1
Possession	0	0		3
Intimidation	0	0		1
Trespass by Night	0	0		1
Escape Custody	0	0		1
TOTAL ARRESTS	**61**	**70**	**59**	**143**

ASSORTED STATISTICS FROM THE 1960s

	1960	1961	1962	1963	1964	1965
Stolen Autos Recovered	3	10	10	6	15	n/a
Wanted Autos Located	0	1	4	5	10	n/a
Persons Investigated	2	28	56	434	599	n/a
Paid Duties Mounted	147	54	59	20	42	n/a
Paid Duties Foot	n/a	n/a	n/a	438	308	n/a
Tags	7898	8472	6297	11236	16571	n/a
Summons	4682	6955	6849	7860	6567	8348
Cautions	n/a	n/a	n/a	315	n/a	n/a

The Mounted Unit In The 1960s

The following excerpt is from a report sent to the Police Public Relations office on July 9, 1964.

There are six permanent stables and one temporary stable, located in the Metropolitan Area. All the stables are attached to Police Division Stations with the exception of the temporary stable which operates on the Toronto Island during the summer months. The largest stable has eight standing stalls and one box stall. The smallest, four standing stalls.

The area patrolled by mounted details includes the congested area of Toronto proper and the suburbs of Scarborough. The basic duties of this unit are the patrolling of parks, ravines and residential areas. Our patrols also cover the traffic congested areas of the City and enforce the traffic laws of the City and its bylaws. The main function of this unit is in regard to crowd control duties at major disturbances, parades, labour disputes, sports events, large fires, and any events where large crowds gather.

The unit operates on a two relief system. The first relief is from 7:45 a.m. to 4:00 p.m., and the second relief from 2:45 p.m. to 11:00 p.m. Mounted patrols end at 10:00 p.m. in the summer months and 6:30 p.m. during the winter. All stable maintenance, care of horses and equipment is performed by mounted personnel, time being allowed for same. Mounted details ride to and from their beats and park areas. In the case of distant park areas, patrols are moved by horse trailer units.

THE MOUNTED UNIT IN 1964	
Inspector	1
Sergeant	1
Patrol Sergeants	3
Constables	41
Horses	41
One police car	
Two vans	
Two horse trailers	

ARRESTS IN THE 1960S			
1964	**1965**	**1966**	**1967**
90	155	82	104

Training The 1960s Mounted Recruit

The following is from a report submitted by Inspector Johnson in 1965 or 1966.

The training of the mounted constable is just as important (as the horse), with a great deal depending on the ability and character of the man himself. The qualities desired in a new recruit are patience, an even temper and self-confidence. He must be willing to do some manual labour, take pride in his turnout and watch his weight. Above all he must like horses and the work that goes with them, and, on completion of his training, be able to ride any horse assigned to him. At the present time the training period for recruits is from four to six weeks. For the inexperienced man joining the unit today, this is not really sufficient, however, when proper training facilities are obtained the training period will be extended to at least two months. Even this seems little when compared with the cavalry man's training of six to nine months in the riding school.[2]

The lack of a proper training facility and the fact that many of the recruits had riding experience in the mid 1960s meant that they only received a short period of instruction. In 1964 the new recruits to the unit received a four to eight week course in basic cavalry training. By 1978 many of the new recruits had never before been in contact with a horse. The equitation course had to be lengthened to where it now took about three months for a recruit to earn his spurs.[2] The recruit courses conducted today are fifteen weeks.

1   Johnson, Inspector E.S., *Report on Training 1965.* 1966.
2   *Sunday Star* September 1, 1985.

1963 The Mounted Unit assigned regular patrols to eleven parks and patrolled twenty-five other parks on a casual basis. Inspector John Watt retired after thirty-nine years of service. Sergeant Edwin Johnson was promoted to Inspector on July 8, and became Officer-in-Charge of the Mounted Unit. Constable John Wear was promoted to Patrol Sergeant. The new Inspector requested that one more patrol sergeant be transferred to the unit to help improve supervision.

A number of changes occurred in constable ranks as five officers resigned from the force and one officer transferred out of the Unit. These men were replaced with eight new officers who had requested transfer into mounted duties. In addition to providing training to the new officers, the Unit began training all mounted officers in "Cavalry Troop Drill" at the Coliseum Ring of the C.N.E. grounds. Training began in the fall. It was deemed necessary because of major riot and crowd control duties. The training was very successful and the unit planned to continue it as soon as proper facilities became available.

A mounted officer at the High Park Zoo. Photograph, Toronto Police Museum.

During the summer, Mounted Unit officers assigned to the High Park Stables patrolled in plainclothes from 8:00 p.m. to midnight. The Inspector's annual report stated: *This system resulted in a thorough cleanout of perverts from High Park with a total of about sixty persons being charged with Gross Indecency and Vagrancy 'Section E'.*[5]

The High Park Stable had a full-time mounted staff periodically assigned over the years. When officers were not there full-time, the stable was used by officers patrolling the park from the Cowan and Queen Stable, or in later years, the Canadian National Exhibition Stable. Officers could rest, water and feed their horses in the stalls and take their own lunch break. The stable was located in the Parks Department Works Yard and in use until 1995, when the Unit was asked to surrender the facility because of the necessity for renovations.

The High Park Stable in 1998. Photograph, Sgt Lorna Kozmik.

An unidentified mounted officer with mount "Barney," talks to off-duty PC Ralph Cole at the London Street Stable. Photograph, Toronto Police Museum.

The unit received a new 1963 Ford Scout Car and a 1963 GMC Panel Truck. The Inspector recommended that a six horse van be acquired to facilitate the transportation of horses to the outlying districts. The Mounted Unit had forty-two horses on staff. During the year, officers attended twenty-seven parades, and twelve special details for the United Appeal.

When a horse needed to have its shoes reset the officer would ride his mount to a local blacksmith shop. The rider would wait while his horse was being "shod." In order to reduce the time lost by having officers waiting for their horses, a new mobile blacksmith was hired, and began visiting the police stables on November 1st, 1963. The system proved very effective by reducing the police man hours involved in "shoeing" to almost nil. "A noticeable improvement in the quality of the "horse-shoeing" is also quite evident."[6] The new Blacksmith was Konrad Myiers. Konrad would keep the contract for the next 25 years, before retiring in 1988.

PC Jim Davis patrolling St. Andrews Road in Scarborough. The patrols from the new No. 4 District Stable provided a police presence in areas that had never before been accessible to the police. Photograph, courtesy of PC Jim Davis.

The Beatles Come to Toronto

The Beatles provided one of the biggest entertainment phenomena the world had ever seen. Their first North American tour took place in 1964. Pandemonium reigned at every location they performed, and Toronto was no exception. The Mounted Unit supplied thirty horses to assist with crowd control during their visit. The Beatles came to Toronto in 1964, 1965 and 1966. At each visit, the Mounted Unit provided large details to control the masses of fans who came out to greet them.

The following first hand description of one of the Beatles visit is from the book written by former Chief of Police, James Mackey, *I Policed Toronto*:

> At the time the Beatles were the top rock group, they had a concert scheduled for Maple Leaf Gardens. The crowds that followed them were unbelievable. At the King Edward Hotel where they were lodged, it was necessary for us to put a large detail of men in the hotel. We used our Mounted Unit on King Street to keep the crowds away from the building.
>
> Young girls were going out of their minds! They were screaming and frenzied! When the group was escorted to the Gardens it was necessary to surround them with the mounted men as well as foot patrol officers. The crowd was in such a state of hysteria it was incredible!
>
> Outside the Gardens we had a truck on location with a stand mounted on the back and I was able to observe all the happenings from that position. Inside I went to the top of the arena to observe this mass of frantic humanity! It was our sincere hope of spotting trouble before it could become acute.
>
> While this was an exceptionally wild night with many arrests for drugs and a few other incidental infractions, our men did an excellent job of protecting not only the Beatles, but the public itself, from itself! It certainly was an interesting time in my life meeting all the very different types of people in our world.[1]

St John Ambulance officers remove a fainting fan. Photograph, Globe and Mail.

1   Mackey, James. I *Policed Toronto*. Self Published, Toronto. 1985. Page 124.

Outside the King Edward Hotel, August 1964. Photograph, Globe and Mail.

The Beatles arrive at the King Edward Hotel. Photograph, Toronto Sun Syndicate.

1964

The Mounted Unit had trouble attracting recruits in 1964. Three members of the unit resigned from the police force and nine transferred to other divisions. The Inspector reported that replacement constables were hard to find. The Unit was able to convince thirteen replacement officers to transfer to its service, but still did not have a sufficient supply of candidates awaiting transfer on file.[109]

The Inspector stated that should it be necessary to add additional personnel to the Unit, a better system for acquiring men should be put in place. He recommended that probationary constables should be able to apply directly for transfer to the Mounted Unit upon completion of their Police College and divisional training.

The Inspector also requested that another patrol sergeant be transferred to the Mounted Unit as it was short of supervisors, especially during annual leave periods. The duties of the patrol sergeants included general supervision, training of personnel, and relieving at Mounted Headquarters.

Another trailer and van was requested to enable faster movement of more men and horses. The need for the additional transport was evident during a strike alert earlier in the year. Having to ride to and from the details used a lot of man hours needlessly. One cruiser was used for supervision

The Inspector's "pride of Unit" and the Unit's progress over the year was evident: *The increased activities of the Mounted Unit this past year resulted in a general improvement to unit morale and efficiency. Greater use was made of our equine strength with valuable experience gained by both horses and personnel. The events of this year certainly proved that the Mounted Unit operates most effectively as a 'riot and emergency' force.*[7]

The unit patrolled eleven parks on a regular basis and twenty-five more as possible. The new No. 43 Division Police Station was opened on Lawrence Avenue East in Scarborough. The No. 43 Division unit commander requested mounted patrols for the Highland Creek area. The area was patrolled on a casual basis using the truck and trailer from the No. 4 District Stable to bring men and horses into the area.

Mounted officers' day shift was 7:45 a.m. to 4:00 p.m. "Afternoons" began at 2:45 p.m. and ended at 11:00 p.m. The actual patrols ended at 10:00 p.m. in the summer and 6:30 p.m. in winter. The Toronto Island Stable was staffed by five mounted officers from May to October.

A proposal was made to obtain full-time stabling at the Horse Palace at the Canadian National Exhibition grounds as a permanent facility there would solve the training facility needs of the unit.

The Toronto Maple Leafs won the Stanley Cup and the Mounted Unit provided twenty-seven horses to control the crowds at the team's reception at City Hall. The Beatles also visited Toronto for the first time and thirty horses assisted in crowd control at Maple Leaf Gardens. There were also two major labour demonstrations at City Hall and Queen's Park: twenty-five horses were provided on each occasion. Seventeen smaller parades were also escorted in Toronto and Scarborough. Mounted men also attended twenty-four parades and forty special details for the United Appeal.

MAJOR DETAILS OF 1964

DETAIL	No. of HORSES
The Garrison Parade	9 Horses
The Lions Parade (International)	22 Horses
The Grange Parade	12 Horses
The Warriors Day Parade	9 Horses
The Labour Day Parade	6 Horses
The Santa Claus Parade	18 Horses
The Grey Cup Parade	18 Horses
The Governor General's Escort	10 Horses
The March Past (Police Games)	20 Horses
The Stanley Cup Parade	27 Horses
The Beatles	30 Horses
City Hall Labour Demonstration	25 Horses
Queen's Park Labour Demonstration	25 Horses
Also 17 Minor Parades.	

The biggest event of the year was the Toronto Newspaper Strike. The entire police force was put on daily strike alert to deal with this labour dispute.

In 1964, the Metropolitan Toronto Police Force Mounted Unit was the largest in Canada. Toronto had a total of forty-one police horses with an average age of eight years. The Montreal Mounted Unit was one or two horses smaller. Vancouver had thirty horses and Halifax had nine horses. The Unit continued to grow with the purchase of eight remounts. The average age of the new horses was four years. Seven older horses were retired during the year.

The Mounted Officers were equipped with a new parade uniform in the form of White Gauntlets, Red Cap Band (normal colour at this time was dark blue), white lanyards and a wider red stripe on the riding breeches. The blue and red dress saddle cloths finished off the appearance by covering over the yellow felt numnahs. The new equipment gave a distinctive and military effect to the parade turn out.

The visibility of horses while patrolling at night has always been a concern. The Unit has been fortunate in that there have been very few mishaps involving patrols after dark. In an attempt to increase officer visibility, a battery operated stirrup light was issued. It was hoped that the new light would allow officers to ride later at night with more safety.[8]

PC Pat Woulfe in the new mounted unit dress uniform in front of Casa Loma. Mounted officers were assigned to patrol the grounds of castle during the summer months as a public relations gesture. Woulfe joined the Toronto Police Department in 1957. He had previously served with the North Yorkshire police in England and the British Army in Germany. He was immediately assigned to the Mounted Unit and spent his entire career at the Unit rising to the rank of staff sergeant. He retired in 1993 after 36 years of mounted service. Photograph, Toronto Police Museum.

The 1964 Toronto Newspaper Strike

STRIKE-SMASHING POLICE COSTING METRO $40,000 A WEEK

The Printers' Story . . .

NUMBER 14   TORONTO, ONT.   OCT. 17, 1964

METRO Police Force is spending about $40,000 a week to help smash a union.

The money is spent in overtime (to be taken in extra holidays later), in cancelled leave, and in work not done elsewhere.

The money won't show on the police budget—but it shows up on picket lines whenever Toronto Typographical Union, on strike against the three Toronto newspapers, tries to publicize its cause.

And the bill, of course, will be paid by the taxpayers.

About 600 men are on call, 200 on special duty, with 25 on "secret work" connected with the strike.

Goon squad

The contingent includes a "goon squad" of police in plain

These horsemen are waiting behind O'Keefe Centre to smash any effective picket line put up by Toronto printers.

In July 1964, the Toronto Typographical Union went on strike against the three major Toronto newspapers. The cause of the strike was management's implementation of new technologies which led to the loss of the printers' jobs. The newspaper industry suffered through many disputes as labour-intensive processes of the business were modernized.

The newspapers and the unions had conducted unsuccessful negotiations on the technology issue since December of 1962. They reached agreements on three occasions, but these were later rejected. As the strike dragged on, problems on the picket line increased, especially when management continued to issue newspapers using replacement workers. There were a number of violent incidents. The police became involved in the dispute.

On October 9, the *Toronto Star* attributed the following quote to a union negotiator: *The 'few isolated acts of violence' in the three months-long Toronto newspaper strike demonstrate the remarkable peacefulness of the 1,000 pickets involved.*[1]

Despite the optimistic opinion of the union leader, the Metro Toronto Police Force thought the situation serious enough to issue a "Strike Alert." The mounted portion of the "Strike Alert" procedure was as follows:

The Mounted Unit has a six-day a week patrol of between 25 and 30 mounted policemen, who will leave Divisions 16 and 14 and Divisions 57 and 56 at 7:00 a.m., each day: one half of the unit will rendezvous at Spadina and Lakeshore, and the other half will rendezvous at Yonge and Lakeshore. (A call to M-1 will result in the transportation of 4 mounted constables, by trailers, to any point in Metro). The two trailer units known as "M1" stood by at 32 Division in North York with a foot cordon of riot squad officers. The foot officers involved were members of the Emergency Task Force.

At 10:00 a.m., each day, if peace is maintained, these units will return to their respective stables. Each unit is radio-equipped, and an officer on patrol in a scout car (M-1) will supply assistance when requested to do so.

During the strike the printers union published their own newspaper called the "Printers' Story," which printed an account of the strikers' point of view, and the police response to it. Headlined "Strike-Smashing Police Costing Metro $40,000 A Week," the paper described how the strike was costing taxpayers $40,000 a week in police over-time, cancelled holidays and re-assignment from other duties. According to the paper the tax payer was footing the bill to have the police smash their union on behalf of the publishers.

It noted there were six hundred policemen on call with two hundred more on special duty. An additional twenty-five men were assigned to "secret work" connected to the strike. Allegedly this included a "goon squad" of plainclothes police who would try and provoke trouble on the picket lines.

"A dozen Mounted Police, horses champing at the bit, stand behind O'Keefe Centre six days a week, waiting to smash any picket line that might be put up around the *Star* or *Globe and Mail*." Another group of men and horses were stationed near the *Telegram* where they "can charge into and demolish any picket line there." There were also more horses in Willowdale ready to rush to the assistance of any commercial printer who may be picketed.

The article alleged that pickets had been brutalised by the police. The week before, a picket line had been placed around a commercial printer. A *Printer's Story* reporter wrote "Police moved in and smashed it, kicking men and manhandling them." The police were accused of working for the publishers, assisting them to carry on business while making the nine hundred strikers look like hooligans in the public eye.

Two mounted officers are patrolling the downtown core during the Printer's strike. The officers are on standby for crowd control, as the horses are not wearing breast plates. Photograph, Stan Turnbull, Toronto Typographical Union Archives.

Another article featured David Archer, president of the Ontario Federation of Labour. At a Massey Hall rally, Archer stated that the labour movement must be prepared to break the law. "There comes a time when if a man is to stand erect, to remain a man, he must disobey the law." Archer was commenting on injunctions that limited picketing at the newspapers. "If the police force is used to enforce injunctions limiting picketing, they are serving the interests of management, thus, the court and the police are used against the interests of this country. The ones who are guilty of violence are the people who hire strike breakers and try to beat down the legitimate demands of the people."[2]

Worker bitterness permeates these articles. The workers firmly believed that they were being treated unfairly by their employers. After the picket line confrontation, the newspapers went to court and were granted injunctions limiting the number of people the union could have on a picket line. The picket line was the only really effective tool the union had in this dispute. With the implementation of computerised printing, employers did not need the printers to return to work in order to publish. The only strategy the printers union had was blocking the passage of the trucks, thus hindering the papers' circulation.

Once the injunction was in place limiting the union's right to picket, massive police presence was not needed. The union saw the police function in this dispute as clearly on the side of the publishers. In fact they accused police of provoking the violence on the picket line which led to the court injunction that ended the picketing.

1   *Toronto Star*, October 9, 1964.
2   *The Printer*, Fall 1964.

A mounted officer escorts striking printers north bound on Queen's Park Circle. Photograph, Toronto Typographical Union Archives. #1695.

A mounted officer watches the members of the Toronto Typographical Union and their supporters a they demonstrate at Queen's Park. Photograph, Toronto Typographical Union Archives.

A young mounted officer escorts striking printers and their supporters past the Toronto City Hall, 1964. Photograph, Toronto Telegram Photograph Collection, York University Archives and Special Collections, Neg. #1699.

A Police mount watches the protest at Queen's Park. Photograph, Toronto Typographical Archives, Stan Turnbull.

A symbolic picture of a striker protesting the use replacement workers from the United States in front of a statue of George Brown, the founder of Toronto's Globe Newspaper *and a Canadian Nationalist. The relaxed state of the protest line can be deduced from the fact the mounted officer in the rear of the statue is watching the crowd dismounted. Photograph, Stan Turnbull, Toronto Typographical Union Archives.*

November 11, 1964, Rememberance Day. A mounted troop advances towards the picket line at the rear of a newspaper building. The officers are probably moving in to ensure that the day's paper can be loaded onto trucks for delivery. Although it is a crowd management detail the officers are wearing their rain gear. Photograph, Toronto Typographical Union Archives.

🏵 **1965** The Mounted Unit was given temporary stabling facilities at the Horse Palace at the Canadian National Exhibition in April. The stable at Cowan and Queen Streets was closed down and the officers and mounts moved to the "Ex." It was a poor and inadequate set up for both horses and men. The unit commander reported that "the building was cold, damp and poorly ventilated and this, combined with excessive dust, affected many of the horses. A number were infected with colds which were very difficult to cure."[9]

The facilities for the officers were very poor and there was no permanent heating equipment available. It was hoped that this problem would be solved when the Unit moved into its winter quarters, being built in an area completely closed off from the rest of the building. During the Exhibition and the Royal Winter Fair, the Unit was required to move to another area of the Horse Palace. Horses, harness, stable equipment, lockers, furniture and appliances were shunted about from one place to another for the duration of the events.

The training of the personnel and horses improved with the greater use of the C.N.E. facilities, as the Unit received periodic training in Riot and Troop Drill in the Coliseum Ring. The Inspector requested that an additional sergeant and patrol sergeant be assigned. The sergeant would be given the function of "Riding Master," similar to that of the R.C.M.P. and would be responsible for all in-service, recruit and remount training. The extra patrol sergeant would increase the general supervision of the constables. The Inspector also recommended hiring a civilian stable man to replace the police officer assigned to the job at the C.N.E. stable.

For as long as anyone can remember, Mounted Headquarters had been moved from No. 5 Station to the C.N.E. Horse Palace for both the Canadian National Exhibition and the Royal Winter Fair. The establishment of the new facility meant that such a move was no longer as important.

The Mounted Unit carried on effectively during the year concentrating on its special functions of riot and emergency duties, crowd control, parade escort and ceremonial duties. Eight horses were purchased and eight other horses sold due to their age and condition. The Mounted Unit, had authorized strength of forty-two horses.

On May 30, 1965, members of the Canadian Nazi Party held a rally at Allen Gardens. Many former victims of Nazi oppression joined thousands of others to protest this, the 1st meeting of the newly formed Nazi Party. A near riot took place when, John Beattie the leader of the Nazi Party showed up.

During the anti-Nazi rally, one demonstrator was charged with obstructing police after he punched a police horse in the face. The man was convicted and sentenced to 30 days in jail. Another horse and rider had to be treated after a bottle of acid was thrown on them by a demonstrator. A search of a car turned up a supply of marbles which a protester believed could be used against the horses.[10]

The Mounted Unit was an important factor in quelling the disturbances at Allen Gardens. When the original troubles began, the mounted detail on scene did an excellent job and was commended by the senior police officers present. As a result of the May disturbances, mounted coverage of Allen Gardens was provided for the remainder of the summer.

The Beatles returned to Toronto and the Mounted Unit sent six horses to Malton Airport to assist with crowds upon their arrival. A mounted detail of twenty-three horses was provided at Maple Leaf Gardens and at the King Edward Hotel, where the Beatles stayed.

In June, Her Majesty, the Queen Mother Elizabeth attended the Queen's Plate Horse Race at the New Woodbine Race Track. A mounted detail of twelve horses and men was attached to the Governor General's Horse Guards, in Horse Guard uniforms to assist in the escort.

Toronto's New City Hall opened in September. A mounted officer was assigned to work in Nathan Phillips Square, daily until the end of October. A new ceremonial dress uniform was issued to the officers and used for the first time at the City Hall detail. It was reported to have received a great response from the public and civic authorities.

The Unit also purchased five dress saddle cloths with a new design. This new style cloth has remained unchanged for thirty-six years and is still in use today.

Horses were required to have rubber pads on their feet in order to walk safely on the concrete surface of the square. The pads were no longer made in Canada and a special order had to be sent to England. It was been estimated that the mounted officer on duty at Nathan Phillips Square had his picture taken 3,000 times each three hour shift.

THE MAJOR DETAILS OF 1965

The Orange Parade	9 Horses
The Eagles Parade	7 Horses
The Warriors Day Parade	9 Horses
The Labour Day Parade	9 Horses
The Garrison Church Parade	9 Horses
The Santa Claus Parade	18 Horses
The Grey Cup parade	18 Horses
The March Past (Police Games)	23 Horses
The Beatles	23 Horses
17 Minor Parades.	

Twelve officers and their mounts entered competitions at the Canadian National Exhibition Horse Show and the Royal Winter Fair. The officers competed in the new ceremonial dress uniform. The new uniforms were also worn at the opening and closing ceremonies at the Royal Winter Fair.

The age of modern communications finally arrived with the arrival of seven portable radios. The unit was issued with four of the "new carryphone sets" and three of the old style "R" sets. Officers without radios would still have to rely on the old call boxes to receive details or contact the station. A new six-horse van was also being constructed for the unit.

PC Grist showing "Buck's" new rubber shoes for use at the City Hall Detail and Nathan Phillips Square. Photograph, Toronto Telegram Photograph Collection, York University Archives and Special Collections, Neg. #1691.

Above and below: officers preparing for patrol, c. 1965. The officer in the foreground is putting on a head kit while those in the rear are clipping the mount.

Photographs, Toronto Police Museum.

The six-horse transport known as the "Blue Goose." Photograph, Jim Davis.

1966

There was a resumption of troubles at Allen Gardens. On June 19, John Beattie and his Nazis attempted to hold another rally but Beattie was drowned out by the boos and catcalls of the crowd of fifteen hundred people who showed up to protest against his organization and their meeting. Beattie was eventually removed in the back of a police patrol wagon before the crowd got out of hand. As a preventative measure, the Mounted Unit gave special attention to patrolling Allen Gardens for the balance of the year.

In his book, *I Policed Toronto*, former Chief of Police John Mackey wrote about the Allen Garden troubles:

"Unfortunately the Nazi movement did not end with WWII. Nazi organizations sprung up in many major cities in Canada and the United States, and Metropolitan Toronto was no exception. A man named John Beattie headed this organization in Toronto and used Allen Gardens, a public park, to preach his anti-Semitic propaganda. A crowd of about 1500 people gathered here to listen to Beattie in 1966. This particular gathering seemed to bring matters to a head. Practically everyone in the crowd was Jewish. As Beattie proceeded with his propaganda the throng surged toward him in a threatening manner and we had our hands full to keep them away from him. Our mounted officers moved in and were able to separate them and there is no doubt that they saved Beattie's life. From that time on we heard very little of Beattie. Occasionally he would show up at a demonstration, but it never amounted to anything much."[11]

In appreciation of the actions taken to suppress the Toronto Nazi movement, the Israeli government planted 100 trees in Israel in honour of the Metropolitan Toronto Police Force. In personal recognition, the Israel Consul in Toronto presented Chief Mackey with the Israel Medal on behalf of the Israeli government.

The number of suitable constable applicants interested in joining the Mounted Unit increased dramatically, and soon the Inspector had a working list of fifteen constables wanting to transfer to the Unit. Horse strength remained the same with seven horses being purchased with an average age of seven years to replace seven that were retired.

A major change occurred in the supervision of the unit when Patrol Sergeants Quinn, Wear and Boardman all resigned within a two-year period, to be replaced by the promotion of Constable Sandwell and the return of Patrol Sergeant McAnsh. Quinn's new responsibilities were at raceways testing racehorses for drugs and he was later joined by other mounted officers who had left the police force.

The new six-horse van was delivered in June. All officers were instructed in how to operate it and to train the horses to load and off-load efficiently. The Inspector requested more supervision within the Unit as it had been necessary during the summer months to use acting ranks, which were not as effective as men in permanent supervisory positions. Inspector Johnson requested a sergeant and patrol sergeant be added to the Unit as well as six constables.

The new winter quarters provided by the Canadian National Exhibition at the Horse Palace was more satisfactory than before. Nevertheless, the police mounts experienced problems, due to improper ventilation, heating, excessive dust and dampness, when they were relocated to the second floor during the Exhibition. Contagious ailments brought in by private horses during the C.N.E. Horse Show and the Royal Winter Fair, required a great deal of veterinary treatment.

During the Royal Winter Fair, the entire compliment of horses contracted a severe "cole virus" and were disabled for nearly two weeks. Unhealthy conditions at the Horse Palace also affected the men. Eight officers were off sick at one time from colds and flu caught during the Royal Winter Fair. To rectify the situation, the Inspector recommended that the force obtain permission to remain in their winter quarters year round. While the C.N.E. executive tentatively supported this measure, the Royal Winter Fair officials had yet to agree.[12]

The Beatles returned to Toronto for their third and final visit, and the Mounted Unit brought out twenty-five horses for crowd control. Horses were used at Malton Airport, Maple Leaf Gardens and the King Edward Hotel. A major strike by civic employees' during the year caused the Unit to put large details into the streets while keeping the remainder of its officers in reserve. The Unit also participated in twenty-four parades.

The City Hall Square detail was continued in April with four officers on duty from 9:00 a.m. to 9:00 p.m. daily. Later the actual time each officer spent on the square was increased, so that only three officers, with proper time off, manned this detail.

A ceremonial detail of one patrol sergeant and eight constables attended the march into Varsity Stadium during a rehearsal for the unveiling on City Hall Square of Henry Moore's "The Archer." Allegedly, the controversy surrounding this sculpture led to the defeat of Mayor Givens in the next election.

The Yorkville Village area became a major problem for the police with the arrival of warm weather. Yorkville hippies took to blocking off streets to try to keep vehicular traffic out of the popular area. In early June, a strong police presence was brought into the district to keep a lid on the sometimes-bizarre happenings of the Saturday night crowds. When hippies again attempted to shut out traffic, mounted and foot police moved in and reopened Yorkville Avenue while having to make a number of arrests. The streets remained cleared by the police sweep, allowing traffic to again flow unhindered through the Village. Mounted officers from the Belmont Street Stable remained on hand right throughout the summer.

On July 25, fifty hippies from the Yorkville area marched to Nathan Phillips Square to protest against police brutality. Without a permit, they were in contravention of a bylaw and were moved from the square by foot and mounted officers.

During the month of August, hippies revived their attempts to close the Yorkville area to vehicles by staging a number of sit-down protests. Mounted officers stayed back from the crowd while foot officers removed and often arrested the protesters. Offenders were sometimes carried to paddy wagons and taken to the station. At least two major sit-ins occurred on Yorkville Avenue during that time.

In December 1965, Inspector Johnson had been given permission, by the Chief of Police, to form a Musical Ride. The Unit began training in the Coliseum Ring on January 10 and would later put on thirteen performances throughout the year.

The Inspector felt that the time had come to reorganize the Unit in new facilities. He recommended that a sixteen-horse stable be built in the downtown area close to the new City Hall. A second thirty-horse training and patrol stable equipped with an indoor and outdoor ring was recommended to be located just outside the downtown. The Mounted Unit would relocate all its personnel and mounts to these two locations and operate a few seasonal stables like the Island Stable during the summer months.

This was the last year officers were stationed permanently at the High Park Stable. Officers assigned to patrol the park rode out from the C.N.E. Police Stable. If a downtown facility was built, it would be of immense value to the unit and significantly increase the time officers could spend patrolling the downtown. Reduced response times in emergencies would also have been a major benefit.

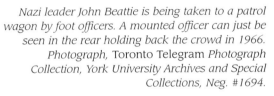

A mounted officer watches as Anti-Nazi demonstrators advance in Allen Gardens on June 19, 1966. Photograph, Toronto Star, F. Lennon.

Nazi leader John Beattie is being taken to a patrol wagon by foot officers. A mounted officer can just be seen in the rear holding back the crowd in 1966. Photograph, Toronto Telegram Photograph Collection, York University Archives and Special Collections, Neg. #1694.

PC William Moncur and "Queen" at the New City Hall Photograph, Toronto Police Museum.

The Farncomb Kidnapping

On May 11, 1967, at 8:15 a.m., six year old Mary Farncomb left her Alexandria Avenue home and started walking to her kindergarten class at John Ross Robertson Public School. She had been asked to come to school early to assist the teacher with a special project. A short time later a neighbour called Mary's parents to say that she had seen the little girl in company with a husky man near St. George's United Church at about 8:40 a.m.

Mary's mother called the school and was told that Mary was not there. Police were notified of the girl's disappearance and a search of the immediate area was started. About 10:00 a.m., her parents received a telephone call from a man demanding a $10,000.00 ransom be paid for her safe return.

A massive police operation was begun to deal with the crisis. The suspect stated that he would phone back again at 4:00 p.m. to provide further information on how the money was to be received by him. All available officers were called in to assist with the search and investigation.

About 11:00 a.m., Inspector Edwin Johnson, Sergeant Jim Pedlar and Constable Jim Davis of the Mounted Unit were driving northbound on University Avenue in the Inspector's car. Sergeant Pedlar spotted a man and a girl who fit the description of the parties, walking on the street near the Hospital for Sick Children. They made a U-turn and drove toward the pair. As the officers got out of the car the man let go of the little girl's hand, told her to "keep on walking," and ran off into a construction site.

Inspector Johnson ran after Mary, caught her and picked her up. The girl was frightened and emotionally upset, but physically unharmed. Sergeant Pedlar and Constable Davis split up, with Davis following the suspect while Pedlar went around the outside of the construction fence. The suspect saw Davis coming after him and bolted for the south exit running into the arms of Sergeant Pedlar who arrested him.

The suspect had approached Mary and told her the school principle had sent him to meet her. The man talked to her while they walked towards the school. Once they reached the school doors the man told Mary there was someone he had to see and asked her to come with him. The man took her to a subway station where they boarded a train and headed downtown.

The twenty-three-year-old suspect was charged with kidnapping the little girl. The accused was convicted and sentenced to seven years in prison.

On Friday May 12, 1967, Chief of Police James Mackey issued a special routine order to the members of the police force: *The Board of Commissioners of Police and the Chief of Police join in sincerely commending all ranks of the Force (and in particular, Inspector Edwin Johnson, Sergeant Alexander (Jim) Pedlar and Police Constable Albert (Jim) Davis (1713), all of the Mounted Unit) for their outstanding police work on Thursday May 11, 1967, following the abduction of a six-year-old girl, Mary Farncomb, in No. 53 Division.*

The girl's parents, Mr. and Mrs. Farncomb, have asked the Chief of Police to convey to all ranks of the force their heartfelt appreciation of the diligent and effective efforts put forth yesterday, which had such a happy culmination for them.[1]

Sergeant Pedlar was named May's policeman of the month, by the Toronto Junior Board of Trade. The Metropolitan Board of Commissioners of Police awarded an official commendation to Sergeant Pedlar and Constable Davis at its meeting on December 19, 1968. The commendation was for "Keen observation and intelligence in effecting the arrest of Andy Schewk on a charge of Kidnapping."

*Facing page: Mary Farncomb with Sgt Pedlar.
Note the special Centennial hatband worn by Sgt Pedlar.
Photograph, Bruce Reed, Toronto Telegram Photograph Collection,
York University Archives and Special Collections.*

1   *Police Routine Orders*, Friday May 12th. 1967.

1967

Canada's Centennial year. The Mounted Unit was involved in numerous special activities across all of Metropolitan Toronto. To help celebrate Canada's first century, a special badge was worn on the tunic of all members of the Metropolitan Toronto Police. A centennial hatband was also issued and worn for the duration of the year.

Forty-three horses were on strength and fifty-four officers of all ranks. Six horses, with an average age of six years were purchased, and six others sold due to age or condition.

It was a big year in sports in Toronto as the Maple Leafs Hockey Team won the Stanley Cup. The Mounted Unit supplied a large contingent for the victory parade and a City Hall reception given for the team. A large mounted presence at Maple Leaf Gardens was required for a concert by the "Monkees." The unit also took part in fifty parades during the year and provided a ceremonial escort at the opening of the Canadian National Exhibition for William R. Allen Q.C., Chairman of Metropolitan Toronto Council.

Smaller mounted contingents covered the visit of Rabbi Feinberg to Massey Hall, the visit of the King of Greece to the Granite Club and the attendance at the C.N.E. of the President of Italy. Numerous demonstrations took place at Queen's Park and the new City Hall, and regular demonstrations happened at the Yugoslav Consulate.

The Musical Ride was organized and trained for a second year but practice time involved in preparing the "Ride" had to be considerably reduced. About half of the Unit took part in the training. The Ride put on a total of fifteen performances at various locations during the year. Due to the Ride and other commitments, the Unit was forced to cut back its park patrols. High Park, the Island and Scarborough Parks still received mounted coverage. Hours at the City Hall detail were reduced by beginning at 12:00 noon but still closing at 9:00 p.m.

American involvement in the Vietnam War continued to incite protest movements across the world. In the United States, people took to the streets to demonstrate their opposition to the war. A number off anti-war groups were active in Toronto keeping the Mounted Unit busy assisting with the peace marches and rallies that centred on demonstrations held outside the U.S. Consulate on University Avenue.

Yorkville remained a priority post of the Mounted Unit for a second year. The neighbourhood was a five-minute walk from Mounted Headquarters on Belmont Street making it possible for mounted officers to patrol it constantly. The unit commander's annual report simply refers to the activities of the "Hippies in Yorkville" as one of the major tasks of the Mounted Unit.

A ceremonial escort at the Canadian National Exhibition. PC Mac Lyons is the right front marker and Inspector Johnson is on the right wheel of the Landau.

Photographs, Toronto Police Museum.

Inspector Johnson leads the unit past the reviewing stand at the Police Field Day.

The Yorkville area continued to attract large crowds of youth from the suburbs in the evenings and on the weekends. It was also very congested with traffic, as many drivers came to Yorkville to see the hippies for themselves. The hippies maintained a continual campaign to shut Yorkville Streets to traffic and *Maclean's* magazine reported that there were riots when the police tried to clear hippies off the streets of Yorkville.[13] A group of Toronto lawyers prepared a book showing how to defy the police yet remain within the law, and distributed it to Yorkville hippies.

The Toronto Board of Education conducted a five-day course which taught eleven mounted officers to drive the new six-horse van. A two week advanced equation course was conducted at the C.N.E. during the winter.

The Royal Winter Fair agreed to allow the Mounted Unit to remain in the permanent winter quarters at the Horse Palace. There were no contagious diseases or illness contracted by the horses. The C.N.E. promised that it would build a permanent brick wall to separate the police stable from the rest of the Horse Palace.

The stable at No. 56 Division (old No. 8 Stable), required extensive repairs if it was to remain open. A proposal for Sunnybrook Stable to be reopened for police use meant 56 Stable, and 57 Stable on Belmont Street, could be closed. Nine horses were stabled on Belmont Street and seven on Pape Avenue.

Ready for patrol at Sunnybrook Stable. Photograph, Toronto Police Museum.

1968

The anti-Vietnam War protest movement continued to grow in the United States. Riots and civil disobedience experienced in the major cities in the United States was a major cause for concern in Toronto. The Mounted Unit was held in esteem by police management, and Police Commissioners hoped to avoid the problems that were occurring across the United States. They believed that the Mounted Unit's proactive and successful history in crowd management would prevent similar occurrences from happening here.

Protests at the United States Consulate occurred almost every weekend during the late 1960s. The Mounted Unit had sixteen horses on standby at the Consulate for every demonstration. When these protests turned ugly and horses were used to restore order, Inspector Johnson estimated that each mounted officer was worth many men on foot.[14] During these demonstrations, a number of horses were poked, stabbed, pelted with rocks and hit with sticks.[15] On October 26, 1968 a detail of thirty horses combined with foot officers was required to control a serious situation involving five thousand Vietnam War demonstrators.

The mounted officers began serious crowd control training with the Emergency Task Force Riot Squad. At this time the E.T.F. was the force's special duty squad, with the formation of a riot squad as one of its many functions. During the training, E.T.F. officers would act as an unruly crowd with flags, signs and fireworks. This training exposed police foot officers to the horses, and provided the horses with exposure to the sights they would see while working within crowds.

In a magazine interview done in the summer, Inspector Johnson spoke of the value of horses in crowd control. He stated that a mounted officer was worth ten foot officers in a crowd. People were afraid that they would get stepped on or kicked by the horse. Johnson went on to explain how the horses would only kick when provoked or startled, and would not step on anyone except by accident.

Johnson stated that he couldn't remember a Toronto Police Horse ever kicking anyone, but a few demonstrators had their feet stepped on when a horse's vision was blocked. In a number of cities, police horses had been attacked by angry crowds. That had not happened in Toronto. A Montreal Police Horse died during the summer of 1968 after being attacked with a razor. It was soon after, that Montreal restricted its Mounted Unit to Mount Royal and stopped using horses for crowd control.[16] (In 1995, the Montreal Urban Community Police visited the Metropolitan Toronto Police Mounted Unit with a view to getting horses back to proactive crowd management. Montreal began to use horses for this purpose in the summer of 2000.)

THE MOUNTED UNIT IN 1968

STABLE	PERSONNEL
Sunnybrook Stable	Inspector
Mounted Headquarters	5 Officers
	23 Constables
	20 Horses
	6-Horse Van
	1 Scout Car
C.N.E. Stable	14 Constables
	13 Horses
	2-Horse Trailer
13 Division Stable	5 Constables
Markham Street	5 horses
4 District Stable	6 Constables
Eglinton Avenue East	6 Horses
	2-Horse Trailer
Island Stable (Summer Only)	5 Constables

MAJOR MOUNTED DETAILS OF 1968

Event	Horses
Visit of the Premier of Greece	3
German Consulate	4
Allen Gardens (Beattie)	20
Visit of Prime Minister Trudeau	10
Allen Gardens (Beattie)	10
Vietnam Peace March	28

Labour Disputes

Company Name	Location
Frigidaire Plant	Scarborough
Thermatex of Canada	North York
American Standard	York
Goodyear Plant	Etobicoke
Square D Company	York
Beer Precast	Scarborough

Other Details

24 Parades
24 Additional Labour Disputes
7 Major Demonstrations.

The social disorder of the late 1960s led to the resurgence of mounted units all over the world. In 1968, the New York City Police Department had four hundred horses; the Metropolitan Police in London, England had two hundred and ten horses.

The Musical Ride gave eleven performances during the year. Members of the Unit attended twenty-four parades and twenty-four labour strikes. A ceremonial escort was given to Ontario Premier John Robarts at the opening of the Canadian National Exhibition.

The Mounted Unit operated with fifty-three officers of all ranks, with two open vacancies for constables waiting to be filled. There were forty-three horses at the Unit. Six horses were retired and six remounts purchased. Constable Pat Woulfe was promoted to Patrol Sergeant on April 23.

Renovations on the Sunnybrook Park facilities began on September 9, making it possible for the Mounted Unit to be moved into the stable on December 17. The Belmont Street Stable at No. 57 Division and the Pape Avenue Stable at No. 56 Division were both permanently closed.

Headquarters staff also moved to work out of Sunnybrook Park. The Inspector, Supervisors, and Quartermaster were all accommodated in the new facility. A house in the park grounds was offered to the Unit for use of the officer in charge. Renovations were completed on the Inspector's house on October 29 and he was able to move into the park with his family.

The move to Sunnybrook Park required that the Unit request another truck and trailer for horse transport. Regular patrols in the areas previously covered by No. 56 and 57 Division officers were discontinued. The Inspector requested that consideration be given to building a new stable in the eastern part of the downtown area of the city.

Facilities at the Canadian National Exhibition Stable continued to be very poor. The C.N.E. was unable to provide permanent walls in the building due to a budget shortfall. Temporary walls were unsatisfactory during the winter months. Every year the horses caught colds and similar ailments from other animals in the building. The lunch and tack rooms at the Exhibition were in terrible shape. Dust and dirt from the stable area had free access over the top of the temporary partitions. It was impossible to keep clothing and equipment clean and to secure the area. A permanent masonry structure was desperately needed.

The Mounted Unit moving back to Sunnybrook. Note the parked panel van and horse trailer. Photograph, Toronto Police Museum.

Left to right: Inspector Ed Johnson, Sgt Jim Lewis, "Major," Wayne Jackson, Andy Bathgate, "Prince," Cy Hawley, Hugh McConnell, "Lancer," Derick Williams, "Nancy," Al McKechnie, "Buccaneer," Larry Shepherd "Roy." Photograph, Toronto Police Museum.

A mounted officer introduces his mount to professional wrestler "Whipper" Billy Watson and an unidentified youth. The youngster is probably that year's "Timmy," the youth representative of the "March of Dimes." Photograph, Toronto Police Mounted Unit.

Three well turned out mounted officers waiting at Yonge and Queen Streets to lead a parade. Photograph, Toronto Police Museum.

Trudeaumania

In 1968, Pierre Elliott Trudeau became the youngest Prime Minister in Canada's history. His personal appeal incited an excitement and admiration usually reserved for music or film stars. The crowds that attended his public appearances were much different than those that appeared to see other political leaders. The media soon referred to this excitement as "Trudeaumania." The pictures on this page are from a ceremonial escort provided to the Prime Minister during one of his visits to the Canadian National Exhibition.

The escort riding through the crowds.
Photograph, Toronto Police Mounted Unit.

The arrival at the drop-off point.
Photograph, Gilbert A. Milne & Company.

Approaching the destination.
Photograph, Gilbert A. Milne & Company.

Mr. Trudeau leaving the carriage. Inspector Johnson is in the background. Photograph, Toronto Mounted Unit.

The Big Vietnam Peace March

Groups opposed to the Vietnam War were planning a worldwide weekend of protest in October 1968. In Toronto, a rally was scheduled to take place at Queen's Park on Saturday October 26th. The protesters stated that after the Queen's Park assembly they would march down Yonge Street to New City Hall where they would hold another rally before marching to the United States Consulate on University Avenue.

Two rival anti-war groups sponsored the protest marches for the day. Both groups planned to meet at Queen's Park around the same time. The Vietnam Mobilisation Committee wanted to march to New City Hall via Wellesley Street, Yonge Street, and then along Queen Street to Nathan Phillips Square. The other group, the N.L.F. (National Liberation Front) was content to march down University Avenue to the United States Consulate.

The Police Commission advised the protesters that they would not be allowed to march down Yonge Street and refused to issue them a parade permit. The Police suggested alternate routes for the march, but these were rejected by the organization committees. The protestors insisted that they be allowed to march down Yonge Street. One of their leaders explained their position by saying it was "because the Streets of Toronto belong to the people, not the police"[1] Both sides dug in their heels and made plans for the big day.

The protests began at midnight on Friday, when a group of American draft dodgers, known as the "American Exiles," began picketing the United States Consulate. About 10:00 a.m., members of the Edmund Burke Society began a counter protest across from them. The Edmund Burke members wanted the United States to drop nuclear bombs on the North Vietnamese. Both groups picketed peacefully, ignoring each other.

At about 1:00 p.m. the two anti-war groups began to gather at Queen's Park. Each faction began making speeches through loud hailers, competing against each other to see who could attract the larger crowd. After about an hour the N.L.F. began marching south on University Avenue. There were 100 marchers.

After the N.L.F. left, the Mobilisation Committee then began its march along College Street. When the marchers reached Elizabeth Street, they ran into a line of about 24 foot police officers. The Police Superintendent in charge of the detail told the demonstrators to disperse, but they kept on marching towards the thin blue line chanting anti-war slogans and "We want Yonge Street."[2]

As the crowd got closer, the officer in charge called for the Mounted Unit and the riders appeared from around the corner. The mounted officers rode past the foot officers and approached the demonstrators in single file. When they reached the front of the marchers they spun their horses sideways knocking over a few of the demonstrators and forming a solid wall of horses. Those marchers who tried to get through the line of horses were grabbed by foot constables and arrested.

As the horses side-passaged into the crowd, marchers were forced to either back up or head southbound on Elizabeth Street. Deputy Chief Harold Adamson stated that "At every point we contacted demonstrators we tried to give them a line of backing down without losing face."[3] The crowd refused to co-operate and the police blocked their access to Yonge Street.

Mounted officers form a barrier to hold the crowd on the sidewalk during an anti-Vietnam war protest in 1968. The officer in the foreground is very off-balance as he turns to see what the crowd is reacting to. The Sergeant behind him is wearing an old style box neck tunic. Photograph, Toronto Telegram *Photograph Collection, York University Archives and Special Collections, Neg. #1689.*

The *Telegram* reported that "The iron-shod horses, stamping nervously, moved the demonstrators on the sidewalk in a matter of minutes."[4] The crowd was now walking southbound on the sidewalk of Elizabeth Street.

A group of motorcycle policemen came out of concealment and drove alongside the crowd, preventing it from moving onto the road. When the protestors reached Gerrard Street, they turned east towards Yonge Street, but were again, forced southbound on Bay Street. The Mounted Unit patrolled Bay Street keeping the marchers on the sidewalk.

Marchers taunted the police with cries of "Pigs, Pigs, Fascists bastards." There were a few scuffles and a few arrests during the march to New City Hall, but nothing serious. The *Telegram* reported that the police kept "cool" despite the taunts and no one was injured. Once at the Hall the protesters listened to anti-war speeches.[5]

At the other demonstration on University Avenue, Inspector Magahay of the Emergency Task Force was the police officer in charge. He was able to convince the Edmund Burke members to cancel a planned march in front of the pro Viet Cong N.L.F. as it arrived at the US Consulate. Both of the groups remained in separate areas and ignored each other. Had the Burke's interfered with the N.L.F., there probably would have been a violent confrontation.

At about 3:20 p.m., Inspector Magahay called for reinforcements. He wanted to remove a number of men with loud hailers who were making speeches from the elevated flower beds. A few scuffles broke out and the police were having trouble with the crowd. Reserve patrol wagons were sent to the scene and "a dozen mounted policemen galloped over from the square. Within 10 minutes the demonstrators had been pushed into a mass on the east side of University Avenue."[6]

It started to rain and the majority of the crowd dispersed on its own. About a hundred protesters reformed at Queen's Park but were removed by the police. The demonstrators then went to No. 52 Division police station at 149 College Street to protest the police action. They returned to the U.S. Consulate and finally went to Hart House at the University of Toronto where they sat on the floor and discussed what happened. Thirty-four protesters were arrested during the day.

A newspaper editorial reported that "it was only the remarkable restraint of the police that prevented pandemonium and probable injury." Although the paper didn't entirely agree with the police methods that day, it blamed most of the problems on a small group of "Trotskyists" who tried to hijack the march, against the knowledge of many of the participants, and hoped to create a violent confrontation with police.[7]

1 *Toronto Star*. Monday October 28, 1968.
2 *Toronto Telegram*. Monday October 28, 1968.
3 *Toronto Star*. Monday October 28, 1968.
4 *Toronto Telegram*. Monday October 28, 1968.
5 *Toronto Telegram*. Monday October 28, 1968.
6 *Toronto Star*. Monday October 28, 1968.
7 *Toronto Telegram*. Monday October 28, 1968.

A view of the line of horses. Inspector Johnson can be seen on the left in front of the officers. The row of foot officers are visible behind the horses. Photograph, Toronto Police Museum.

The horses start to force the crowd southbound onto Elizabeth Street from College Street. Photograph, Toronto Police Museum.

Mounted officers pass through the crowd in half sections at Gerrard Street. The officers then rode south on Bay Street keeping the crowd on the sidewalk. Photograph, John McNeill, Globe and Mail *Newspaper.*

A mounted officer stands by to assist the foot officers who are making an arrest. Bay and Centre Streets, Oct. 28, 1968. Photograph, Toronto Telegram Photograph Collection, York University Archives and Special Collections, Neg. #1974-002/284.

A police horse "cutting a show" on University Avenue in front of the United States Consulate. The officer is surrounded by members of the National Liberation Front. Note that the officer has his raincoat attached to the back of the saddle and his saddlebag clipped to the side of the saddle. Photograph, Doug Griffin, Toronto Star.

◉ **1969** The last year of the decade was a quiet time for the Mounted Unit. There were no big demonstrations or crowd control situations reported in the city, and only a few minor labour disputes that required the attendance of mounted officers. Those who attended were on a stand-by basis only. The Unit continued to provide mounted details to various sports events and parades and to help police crowds at the Canadian National Exhibition. The Anti-Vietnam demonstrations continue at the U.S. Consulate.

The Musical Ride gave five public performances during the year. Musical Ride training was carried out at Sunnybrook Park. Ceremonial escorts were given at the Canadian National Exhibition for Prime Minister Trudeau and a visiting American astronaut. The new stable at Sunnybrook provided patrols in the Central Don Valley and connecting parks. Street patrols were also sent out of the park to areas as far away as Avenue Road.

The unit purchased nine remounts during the year with an average age of four years and a cost of $400.00. Only five horses were disposed of, as one horse died and four were sold. The Metropolitan Toronto Police had forty-nine horses on strength. Training of both men and remounts had improved since the move to Sunnybrook. In warm weather, the training of horses and personnel could be done in the outdoor riding rings. Winter training was still conducted in the indoor rings at the C.N.E. Horse Palace.

The Inspector reported that the authorized strength of the unit should be increased from forty-eight constables. During the year, manpower shortages required the closing of one or two smaller stables to adequately staff the Musical Ride. The Mounted Unit had enough horses for its commitments, but not enough men.

Stable accommodation at the C.N.E. remained in terrible condition, very dirty, poorly ventilated, difficult to maintain and keep secure. Police horses continued to become sick from the diseases of other animals brought to the C.N.E. or Royal Winter Fair.

The Exhibition Board planned for the following renovations when the money became available:
1. Building the lunch room and tack room areas with brick or cement block.
2. Installing adequate plumbing and heating equipment.
3. Permanently partitioning the stable area from floor to ceiling (to separate the Police Stable from the remainder of the building).

The move to Sunnybrook Park removed a number of officers from downtown patrol and put them on park patrol. Traffic enforcement of the unit decreased and the total number of tags and summonses issued dropped significantly. One new truck and trailer was received during the year to enable better deployment from Sunnybrook Stables. Constable Jim Stafford was promoted and transferred out of the unit, but would later return as a staff sergeant.

A quieter time at Nathan Phillips Square. Constable Bill Smith riding "Major" talks to a lady at the south side of the square, c. 1968. Photograph, Toronto Police Museum.

Inspector Johnson (in forage cap) and three mounted constables in winter dress lead a Vietnam Mobilisation Committee march down Bay Street on Nov. 10, 1969. Photograph, Toronto Telegram *Photograph Collection, York University Archives and Special Collections, Neg. #1974-002/284.*

Training Constable Jim Davis

During the 1950s, members of the Mounted Unit rode in a number of major events with the Governor General's Horse Guards Cavalry Squadron. (Albert) Jim Davis, a member of the Horse Guards, had ridden the point position during these escorts with Sergeant Ed Johnson of the Mounted Unit. He obviously impressed both Sergeant Johnson and Inspector Watt as he was asked if he would like to become a member of the Mounted Unit.

Inspector Watt took Jim to the police employment office where he told the staff that Jim was to be hired as a constable and assigned to the Mounted Unit. The employment office followed his instructions and Jim became one of the very few, if not the only, mounted officer to start his police career at the Mounted Unit.

Within two days of being hired, Jim was patrolling in uniform at Belmont Street Stable. He was sent out on the road unarmed, as he had not yet been to the Police College to receive training. He could not be given a gun until he had attended recruit training at the Police College. One of his daily assignments was to ride to Balfour Park at lunchtime. A number of children had been accosted in the park while walking home from school for their lunch, and patrolling the park became a daily mounted detail.

The unarmed and untrained Davis made his first arrest in the park when he took custody of a man for indecently exposing himself. After two months of mounted patrol, Jim attended the Police College and was then assigned to three months foot patrol duty in No. 1 Division (Court Street Station). He then returned to the Mounted Unit where he remained until he retired in 1994.

Jim first started riding when he enlisted in the Governor General's Horse Guards in 1950. After joining the police force he was allowed to continue his commitments to the military, and he remained active in both the militia and equestrian activities of the Guards. Jim rose to the rank of Regimental Sergeant Major and was then commissioned with the rank of Captain. He was appointed Ringmaster of the Royal Winter Fair and held this position for twenty-five years. Jim finally retired from the military in 1982, but remained in close contact with members of the Horse Guards.

Jim was the Mounted Unit's riding and vehicle operations instructor between 1965 and 1970. He returned to regular patrol duties at the No. 4 District Stable (Scarborough) in 1970 and remained there until he was once again appointed Training Constable in 1980s and returned to training the unit's recruits.

Jim remembers the 1960s and 70s as being the busiest and greatest years for the Mounted Unit. He saw it grow from twenty-four horses and officers to over sixty horses and eighty officers and regain the status that it had held during the 1930s under Chief Constable Draper. Jim and other members were kept busy policing the many crowd control details, parades and searches to which the Unit was assigned.

Constable Jim Davis wearing the Mounted Unit's new dress uniform, 1964. The red cap band, wide-stripe breeches and white gauntlets had just been introduced.
Photograph, courtesy of Jim Davis.

Some of the major details that stick out in Jim's mind were the bitter anti-Vietnam War demonstrations at the U.S. Consulate and the lengthy newspaper strike of 1964. In 1965, the Toronto Maple Leafs won the Stanley Cup. During the victory parade the crowd swarmed out into the street and the hockey players never did reach City Hall for their official reception. The Mounted Unit had not been asked to assist with this parade, so there were no horses to help the overpowered foot officers. That was the last parade held during that era without a mounted escort.

Jim was the driving force who cleared the way for Toronto mounted officers to attend the police equestrian competitions in the United States. He also designed and managed the Mounted Unit's competitions at the Royal Winter Fair and Canadian National Exhibition. Since his retirement, Jim and his wife Linda continue to assist the Mounted Unit with its internal competitions. They also help at out-of-town horse shows. Jim, and another retired mounted officer, Paul Dean, founded the Canadian Mounted Police Association.

Jim's reputation as a mounted police trainer is known around the world. He provides annual training to the mounted unit of the Barbados Police.

He has assisted a number of other Caribbean countries with the purchase of Canadian horses. When the Peoples Republic of China decided to form a Mounted Police Unit, they looked to Canada to obtain proper training. In April 1997, Jim was flown to China where he provided new mounted police officers with a two-week course in equitation. Jim has also been to the United States to provide training to American mounted officers.

During his 32 years of military service and 34 years of police service, Jim was honoured with many awards: the Canadian Decoration, the Centennial Medal, the Queen's Jubilee Medal, the Canadian Chief's of Police Long Service Medal and the Canadian Police Exemplary Service Medal.

Searching the railway track in Scarborough after a bus/train collision, 1975. Note the reflective gaiters on the mount's front legs. Photograph, courtesy of Jim Davis.

At the National Police Equitation Competition, Washington D.C., 1996. Left to right: Jim Davis, Linda Davis, Sgt Bill Wardle, PC Bob Bowen. Photograph, Author's Collection.

1970

The social unrest of the mid-1960s began to return in 1970. The Mounted Unit attended fifteen major demonstrations and assemblies during the year. Thirty horses were provided at some events, one being the largest demonstration, an anti-war protest on May 9, although it was rivalled by a Pop Festival on June 26 and 27.

There were six major labour disputes in 1970. Mounted officers were required to attend at strike scenes on one hundred and forty occasions. The unit sent mounted officers to thirty-six parades in Metropolitan Toronto and a mounted contingent and the Pipe Band took part in the St. Catharines Wine Festival. Six performances of the Musical Ride were performed for the public. The Ride's biggest night was at the Military Tattoo at the C.N.E. performed under lights to a crowd of fifteen thousand people.

The Mounted Unit purchased eight new remounts with an average age of three years. Seven horses were sold leaving the unit with a strength of fifty horses. The Inspector reported that he was having no trouble finding suitable horses at the right price. The manpower of the Mounted Unit was increased by three constables bringing the unit to an authorized strength of fifty-four.

Patrol Sergeant James Pedlar was promoted to sergeant and remained at the Mounted Unit. The Inspector was concerned with the lack of supervisory staff and requested an extra patrol sergeant. He also requested four additional constables be assigned to the Unit to bring their strength to sixty constables. During the summer, No. 13 Division Stable (London and Markham Streets) was closed to supply men for the Musical Ride.

All mounted personnel and horses participated in weekly training sessions at the Canadian National Exhibition Stable. This involved equitation; cavalry troop drill and crowd control training. The Emergency Task Force participated in the training when they were available.

Renovations were finally completed at the Canadian National Exhibition Stable providing space permanently separated from other users at the Horse Palace. The area was much more comfortable for both men and horses.

The Mounted Unit Christmas card, c. 1970.

Below: The Mounted Unit leads a parade down Yonge Street in the mid to late 1960s. Officers are wearing shirts with white gloves.
Photograph, Toronto Police Museum.

Our Main Function Is Crowd Control

In an interview with John Maclean of Southam Business Publications, Inspector Johnson spoke of the Mounted Unit and crowd control:

Our main function is crowd control duty. The Mounted Unit is the force's best weapon in crowd control because one horse can do the job of ten men on foot. We have been used a great deal in crowd control and we've become involved in the odd riot. In times like this, the horse is the backbone of the crowd control forces of the department.

The emergency task force and mounted unit displaying their crowd management equipment, 1973. Photograph, Toronto Police Service.

The May 1970 Riots Reprinted with permission, *Toronto Sun* Syndicate

On Saturday May 9, 1970, a large peace rally was held at the United States Consulate on University Avenue. The United States had just invaded Cambodia and large demonstrations were taking place all over the United States. On May 4, four students at Kent State University were killed and many others wounded when members of the Ohio National Guard fired their rifles into a crowd of demonstrators.

The Toronto rally was held to protest the invasion of Cambodia and the killings at Kent State. The Toronto demonstration got out of hand and the Mounted Unit was called in to assist the foot officers in controlling the crowd. On Monday May 12, the *Toronto Telegram* ran the following story.

Patrol Sgt Pat Woulfe at the front of the United States Consulate on University Avenue, May 9, 1970. Photograph, Franz Maier, Globe and Mail Newspaper.

Mounted officers clear the crowd from University Avenue in front of the United States Consulate, May 9, 1970. Photograph, Toronto Telegram Photograph Collection, York University Archives and Special Collections, Neg. #1974-002/284.

CHIEF DEFENDS RIOT CONTROL:

'We will use horses again if necessary'

Metro Police Chief Harold Adamson today defended use of mounted police-men in breaking up the City's worst anti-Vietnam war riot Saturday and promised they would be used again if necessary.

Several innocent spectators were knocked down by the horses on Univer-sity Ave. in the wild-swinging melee between police and about 3,000 demon-strators in front of the U.S. Consulate.

Leaders of the anti-war movements protested the use of horses which push-ed among their ranks, po-lice who removed identi-fication badges and over-reacted to the demonstra-tion.

Restraint by police cooled Wash

There were 91 arrests after the protesters chas-ed by police ran rampant

Metro Police Chief Harold Adamson today defended use of Mounted Policemen in breaking up the City's worse anti-Vietnam war riot Saturday and promised they would be used again if necessary. The horses on University Ave. knocked down several innocent spectators in the wild-swinging melee between police and about 3,000 demonstrators in front of the U.S. Consulate.

Leaders of the anti-war movements protested the use of horses which pushed among their ranks, police who removed identification badges and over-reacted to the demonstration. There were 91 arrests after the protesters chased by police ran rampant through the streets as far as Yonge and Albert Streets, smashing store windows as they ran.

Chief Adamson said the situation would have been worse without the horses. 'They were used because people wouldn't move,' he said. 'Nobody was seriously hurt and our men did a fine job.' Police Commissioner Alderman Hugh Bruce said he was not asking for a special inquiry or investigation into the way the Metro Police handled the demonstrators on Saturday. He said he would ask the Chief to produce a report collating the numerous incidents involving police and the demonstrators during the demonstration.

The crowd had been demonstrating peacefully moving around in an orderly circle. 'The problems began when someone jumped on a policeman's back. Another officer went to his aid and was hit with a piece of wood from one of the demonstrator's signs. It was then that the mounted men moved in to help them." Paint was thrown at the building and the Consulate windows were broken. The officer in charge decided

Constable Jim Davis and "Barney" move in to clear protestors from the centre median of University Avenue. May 9, 1970. The protestors were digging up tulip bulbs and rocks from the garden and throwing them at the mounted officers. Photograph, Toronto Telegram Photograph Collection, York University Archives and Special Collections, Neg. #1974-002/284.

to split the crowd because, 'far more violence would have taken place it we hadn't.

Deputy Chief Simmonds said horses were jabbed with sticks and hit with stones. Steel ball bearings were thrown under their hooves. The deputy blamed the demonstrators for their 'defiant attitude.' Acting Deputy Chief Harold Genno said demonstrators seemed determined to not to let the day go by without a confrontation with the police'. He said he was surprised that three bus loads of demonstrators from New York State were able to get across the border.

SIDEARMS OFF

Police removed their sidearms before they went on the demonstration detail. This was a precaution in the event of trouble. They didn't want pistols falling into the wrong hands if they fell from holsters. When the clash took place, they removed their badges before moving in to engage the war protesters. Hugh Crothers, a Metro Police Commissioner, said he was sure this was not done to prevent identity of police in the event of charges of brutality. 'If one of them got hit on the badge it could pierce his chest,' Mr. Crothers said.

Executive Alderman Tony O'Donohue, who went to see the riot first hand said he thought the police handled themselves well. He said, however, that their order to break up the demonstration at 6 p.m. might have had some influence in making matters worse. 'Its not nice to be called a pig. I'm very satisfied with the way the police behaved,' he said.

Alderman Hugh Bruce, also a member of the Police Commission, said the conduct of the police was 'admirable.' The overtime pay for the Metro policemen during Saturday's demonstrations will cost more than $7,000.

RUBY ARRESTED

Clayton Ruby, a 28 year old lawyer who was on hand to arrange bail for any demonstrators arrested was one of those arrested himself. He complained he had been held more than three hours without opportunity to contact another lawyer.

The protest was organised by several anti-Vietnam war groups. They gathered outside the consulate to complain about U.S. troops in Cambodia and the four Ohio University students shot to death by the Ohio National Guard. The first trouble started when there was a clash between the anti-war demonstrators and the Edmund Burke Society members who support the U.S. action in Vietnam.

The march was organized by the May Fourth Movement, a Rochdale College group describing themselves as 'a collection of anarchists, freaks, students and communists.' Bill King, of the May Fourth Movement, said after: 'We believe the majority of the police at the demonstration are ashamed and embarrassed by the department as a whole.' He demanded to know what 'pig' had ordered police to remove badges to prevent identification.

The crowd moves back as the officer advances. Note the people running away in the background. May 9, 1970. Photograph, Toronto Telegram *Photograph Collection, York University Archives and Special Collections, Neg. #1974-002/284.*

Jeff Goodall, of the Edmund Burke group, said his members were there 'simply to defend democracy and civilization.' He said the main trouble stemmed from the May Fourth Movement and the Maoists. 'Those May Fourth guys, particularly, were talking pretty tough,' he said.

The protests outside the consulate began about 2 p.m. At first, there was no trouble. But as more and more protesters arrived there was growing unrest and tension. Police tried to hold groups on both sides of University Avenue. About 6 p.m., a loud speaker boomed out: 'This demonstration is over. I suggest you all go home.' When the crowd failed to disperse, police moved forward on horseback. Bottles, eggs, dirt and paint descended among the police.

Mounted officers are assisting the foot officers to push the crowd away from the United States Consulate. A horse descends the court house steps as the officers move the crowed through the plaza at the court building and to Nathan Phillips Square. May 9, 1970. Photograph, Toronto Telegram *Photograph Collection, York University Archives and Special Collections, Neg. #1974-002/284.*

It took more than an hour for police to force the crowd from the Consulate to the courthouse across the street. Traffic on University Ave. was blocked more than once as the melee swirled.

The anti-war group burned an American flag, then ran toward Nathan Phillips Square chanting: 'Agnew, Nixon...how many kids did you kill today.' The also yelled 'Power to the people...join us!' Police rushed reinforcements to Yonge and College Streets. Horse and Motorcycle units were dispatched to Yonge and Queen Streets. Five windows at the T. Eaton store were smashed, but there was no looting. Police were given orders to use nightsticks if necessary to bring the crowd under control.

FILM SEIZED

Several newspaper reporters and cameramen were shoved and harassed in the mix-up. Police ripped film from one television news photographer. Police said afterward that they had attempted to arrest 'agitators' only; those people urging others to resist police. A teenage girl, repeatedly screaming 'pig' at a policeman, was arrested. Police worked with two patrol wagons. Each suspect was photographed before being placed inside.

Forty-four persons were charged with causing a disturbance, nineteen with assaulting police, twelve with carrying offensive weapons (knives, rocks, sticks, etc.), ten with obstructing police, three with public mischief, one with having liquor in a public place, one with common assault and one with theft.[1]

1 *Toronto Telegram.* Monday May 12, 1970.

The crowd is now concentrated in Nathan Phillips Square. The mounted and foot officers are pushing the crowd to effect a final dispersal. The posture of the mounted officers indicates they are facing resistance. Photograph, Toronto Telegram *Photograph Collection, York University Archives and Special Collections, Neg. #1974-002/284.*

Constable Warren Pollard at Sunnybrook. Photograph, Toronto Police Museum.

🪷 1971

The Mounted Unit was involved in many crowd management details throughout the year, the biggest assignment being the visit of Premier Kosygin of the U.S.S.R.. The unit supplied forty horses throughout the two-day period of his visit. Mounted details were used to cover events at the Science Centre and at the Inn-on-the-Park Hotel. In his annual report, Inspector Johnson stated that he felt that the presence of the Mounted Unit had prevented a major riot situation from occurring at the Kosygin demonstration.[16a]

All available mounted personnel were called in to work the detail. The Central Don Stable loaned the Mounted Unit twenty stalls so that all of the unit's horses could be stabled at the park. This was the only time in recent history that all of the unit horses were stabled in one location.

There were other major crowd events during the year. The biggest ones were known as the two "Amchitka" demonstrations. The first occurred on November 6, to be followed by a second later in the month. Toronto residents joined people all over the world in the "Blast Demo" protesting the Amchitka Nuclear tests. Mounted officers were on scene of both these peaceful demonstrations which took place at Nathan Phillips Square.

Regular street posts and park patrols continued during the year. Mounted officers provided escorts for all marching parades in the Metropolitan Toronto area. The Musical Ride gave six public performances.

Six additional remounts were purchased and five horses were sold. The equine strength of the unit was now fifty-one horses. Inspector Johnson was able to acquire four police cadets to work primarily on security and stable duties. No additional constables or supervisors were transferred to the Unit and the Inspector repeated his request for another supervisor. He also asked for an additional six new constables to bring the Unit strength up to sixty constables. During the summer, No. 13 Division Stable (London and Markham Streets) closed to supply personnel for the Musical Ride.

Officers participated in weekly training sessions at the Canadian National Exhibition Stable. The training was designed to enhance equitation skills and prepare officers and mounts for crowd management details. The Emergency Task Force participated in the training when they were available.

The Visit of Premier Kosygin – What Really Happened

In October of 1971 the Soviet Premier, Alexei Kosygin was invited to Canada to meet with politicians and business leaders. His visit was considered a high security risk as police in Ottawa located two live bombs and 11 Molotov cocktails after a demonstration there. A member of the Edmund Burke Society had attempted to attack the Premier. Large demonstrations were held in Ottawa, Montreal, Edmonton and Vancouver when Kosygin appeared in those cities.

The Premier's safety was the largest concern for officials planning the Toronto Visit. The police gathered a lot of intelligence information before the Premier arrived. They had estimated crowd sizes; ethnic and political compositions and possible intentions of the crowds. Security plans were based on these estimates.

The Canadian Manufacturers Association invited Mr. Kosygin to a dinner in the Great Hall of the Ontario Science Centre. The dinner was to be held on the evening of October 25, 1971. The Premier would then stay overnight at the Inn-on-the-Park Hotel. One third of the Metropolitan Toronto Police Force, 1,222 officers, were assigned to security details at the Inn-on-the-Park or the Science Centre. There were 710 regular officers at the Science Centre, backed up by 91 auxiliary officers and 318 men stationed on Don Mills Road.

About 17,000 people showed up that night in protest. A number of different factions were present but most of the demonstrators were peaceful and co-operative. One confrontation between the police and a small group of protesters occurred outside of the Science Centre on Don Mills Road. This led to a number of allegations of police brutality, especially on the part of the mounted officers.

On December 1, 1971, Judge Ilvio Anthony Vannini was appointed to head a Royal Commission of Inquiry into "The Conduct of the Public and the Metropolitan Toronto Police on the 25th of October, 1971."

The Judge listened to the evidence of 212 witnesses and prepared a report based on the testimony of what he heard and other evidence presented to him.

Early in the evening Constable John Lunn was riding police mount "General" in the area of the Inn-on-the-Park. The horse was wearing rubber shoes, as it was normally a City Hall horse. It was raining out and the pavement was wet. "General" slipped on a painted white line on the roadway and fell, breaking PC Lunn's leg. A demonstrator came forward and identified himself as a doctor and treated PC Lunn's injury until he was taken away by ambulance.

The events that took place that night have become obscure with time. Many officers who were there are convinced that the Mounted Unit saved the day and prevented a much larger, more violent confrontation. This is probably true, although Judge Vannini had some criticisms of the Unit's actions.

Many of the newspaper articles of the day contained accounts highly critical of the police actions. These were based on the statements of demonstrators, most of whom were also heard at the inquiry. What really took place that night? I believe that the following narrative contained in Judge Vannini's report under the title "The Mounted Unit ...The Manner and Extent of its Use" is the fairest description of the events of October 25th, 1971.

"Inspector Johnson has been with the Force for 26 years. The last 23 years were with the Mounted Unit of which, he has been in command for the past 9 years. Prior to the Second World War, he served as a Regular Army cavalryman for 3 years with the Royal Canadian Dragoons. Inspector Johnson is a highly experienced, dedicated and

DIARY OF A DEMONSTRATION

'Using mounted police prevented a riot during Kosygin's visit here'

★ Police prevented a riot without using unnecessary force during the demonstration while Soviet Premier Alexei Kosygin was dining in the Ontario Science Centre on Oct. 25, says a special Metro police report to City Council. Here are excerpts from the report, presented Wednesday:

Acting Staff Superintendent Victor Telford's report.

On Monday, Oct. 25, 1971, I was in charge of security at the Ontario Science Centre for the visit of Soviet Premier Alexei Kosygin.

Magahay's emergency task force men assisted him.

There can be little doubt that a number of the more militant groups had a co-ordinated plan to break through the police lines and rush the Science Centre with the hope of gaining entrance to the banquet.

I firmly believe that if I had not taken the action I did in having the mounted unit move these militant demonstrators when I did, we would have had a riot at the steps and entrance to the Science Centre, with many people injured.

At no time did I ever see police

conscientious police officer with considerable expertise as a rider and trainer of both horses and riders for use in crowd control and with considerable experience gained from the actual use of the Mounted Unit in many and varied crowd situations.

At the meeting held on October 19, of Senior Police Officers, Chief Adamson of the Metro Toronto Police Force made the decision and ordered the Mounted Unit to assist in crowd control as part of the security arrangements for Premier Kosygin at both the Inn-on-the-Park and the Science Centre, and the Emergency Task Force for use in the personal security of the Soviet Premier on his way to and from the Science Centre.

From this, Inspector Johnson concluded that the Emergency Task Force would not be available to assist the Mounted Unit in crowd control as was done occasionally, if not as a matter of course, in the past. At 4:40 p.m. and after consultation with and upon the direction of Acting Superintendent Telford, Inspector Johnson took up position with 20 mounted men along the front of the Fountain Area at the Science Centre.

At 5:30 p.m., and in anticipation of Kosygin's arrival at the Science Centre at 5:45 p.m., Inspector Johnson moved the entire Unit up in broken-line formation facing east on Don Mills Road from the southerly limit of St. Dennis Drive to a point just south of Rochefort Drive and immediately behind the police line along the east curb.

These returned to the front of the Fountain Area shortly after Kosygin and his party entered the Science Centre at 5:45 p.m. Thereafter there were 20 mounted men in somewhat close formation opposite the street entrance on Don Mills Road and along the front of the Fountain Area.

From the time that the crowd began to continually increase at the intersection of St. Dennis Drive and Don Mills Road. From 6:00 p.m. onwards, Inspector Johnson spent most of his time on his mount in the opening of the street entrance, with his two section leaders close behind him. From time to time, he moved to the centre strip or medium of Don Mills Road for a better view and appraisement of the situation at the opposite intersection.

At 6:30 p.m. Inspector Johnson consulted with Acting Superintendent Telford at the centre strip about the growing build-up at the intersection and the Acting Superintendent instructed him to be alert and ready in case he was called.

The Inspector then conferred with his section leaders and formulated the plan that if the Mounted Unit was called in to assist they would enter the crowd at its weakest point on St. Dennis Drive, clear it of all demonstrators by dispersing them off onto the sides and then going in behind

the crowd at the northeast corner where it was the thickest—estimated at some 25 to 30 deep, and relieve the pressure there from behind. From 7:00 o'clock on Inspector Johnson remained on his mount in the intersection at the centre strip opposite the median to be closer to and in full view of and on the alert for any command for assistance from Acting Superintendent Telford.

As the police line at the northeast corner swayed back and forth, and the bulge then developed, the Inspector observed the manual signal from Telford, who was on the line with his men, ordering him forward. The Mounted Unit's purpose, Telford testified, was to split the crowd to relieve the pressure on the line; to not seek out troublemakers but to move them along, and to not chase any wrongdoers in the crowd.

Upon the verbal command given to him by Telford, Inspector Johnson in turn and by pre-arrangement with his two section leaders, who were then in line formation with seven other mounted officers, ordered and led them forward—10 in all, toward the crowd.

They crossed the intersection at a controlled trot with

The Mounted Unit contingent at the Inn on the Park. Photograph, Toronto Police Museum.

their riding crops in their saddles. Made aware of their approach from the noise they made as they trotted across the pavement, the crowd and consequently the front line of policeman moved back, i.e., eastwards, some 10 to 15 feet or more on St. Dennis Drive. The second and third line of policemen across the mouth of St. Dennis Drive made way for them by stepping back, thereby exposing the front line of policemen and the crowd to the approaching horsemen who came to a halt momentarily a few feet back from the front line of policemen who maintained their position in the line across the front of the crowd along the full width of St. Dennis Drive.

At this time, the front line of policemen stood on the white line marking the easterly limit of the cross-walk across St. Dennis Drive and the first two or three of the horsemen who were in the lead, one of whom was Inspector Johnson, came to a halt within the cross-walk. By then, also, the pressure on the curve of the curb at the northeast corner which had caused the bulge had subsided as the attention of the demonstrators and the police who were there was diverted and became transfixed on the horses at the mouth of St. Dennis Drive.

As the horses approached and then stood in this position more candles and plastic holders and other objects were thrown over the crowd toward the foot police in the lines and the mounted officers, striking some but for the most part passing over them and landing on Don Mills Road as cameras flashed in quick succession to record the fast-moving events.

Apart from the objects that were thrown and the verbal abuse that was being hurled at them, the crescendo of the shouting and excitement of the crowd, there was then no positive single or collective act of hostility on the part of the crowd. Any resistance by the crowd at this time was not only an impassive one but involuntary because of the mass of bodies that was compacted on the street and on the sides thereof making it difficult for them, without any prior warning, to extricate themselves even if they wanted to, as quickly as the police might have expected them to do.

And the crowd may have stopped in their retreat as it did because the horses came to a halt a

few feet in front of them, thereby being led to believe that the riders did not intend to drive their mounts into the crowd. When the crowd at the front of the police line on St. Dennis Drive made no attempt to withdraw or disperse more than the 10 to 15 feet it already had, Inspector Johnson ordered his mounts forward with their riding crops out at the ready.

And he did so within a matter of seconds after his mounts had come to a halt in front of the crowd, without adequate warning or order to them to withdraw or to disperse and unaware that the dangerous situation which existed moments before at the curve of the curb in the northeast corner had suddenly and completely subsided or, as one of his riders put it, had been defused.

As he advanced across Don Mills Road and entered the crowd, Inspector Johnson believed that the Emergency Task Force would not be available, or made available, to assist the Mounted Unit with the crowd because of the decision that had been made the day before to assign that Force to assist in the personal security of the Soviet Premier.

Of this Inspector Johnson testified, 'I was leaving that up to the Field Commander but we felt that we would not have the support of the E.T.F. like we usually have in these operations.'

After giving his opinion that it would be 'very unwise' and 'very much against our policy to send foot men into a crowd to pull out protesters' because of the great danger to the men, he said that 'usually the procedure in a crowd is to disperse the crowd and then the E.T.F. or other footmen (move) behind us and apprehend the people' and after the

Mounted and foot officers face the growing crowd on Don Mills Road. Photograph, Don Dutton, Toronto Star.

horses have split a crowd and moved them to a predetermined position, to move in 'to maintain the line and also—apprehend the protesters regarding arrests and so on.'

Finally Inspector Johnson conceded that, having later pushed this particular crowd to the north side then, 'in the normal circumstances (had) the E.T.F. been there and followed us in, they would have maintained that line and we would have fallen back.' Of the availability of the E.T.F. and the assistance it usually gives the Mounted Unit in crowd control, one of his riders testified, 'I knew that they were not going to be fulfiling their normal role with us, their sometime normal role with us, should I put it that way, to come into the crowd.'

In describing the role he said, 'Well, they normally operate along with the horses, virtually as an arresting body. We go into the crowd, they come in with us, usually behind us, and we usually pass through their line in fact. They then follow us up and act virtually as a mopping-up unit. They mop up the demonstrators that come through our line. If there is anybody causing particular trouble, we try to pass them through the horses and the E.T.F. follow up from there.'

With the belief, for the reasons given, that the E.T.F. would not follow his unit in to assist them as they usually did, Inspector Johnson led his men into the crowd with their riding crops out and at the ready to protect themselves and their mounts. Because the crowd was bigger at the northeast corner and the objects that were being thrown appeared to come from the back of that area, the Inspector ordered seven of his mounts to the north curb and the other two to the south curb of St. Dennis Drive.

Inspector Johnson entered the crowd on a firm but controlled walk of his mount. Having easily made an opening with minimal resistance, four or five of the other riders who were behind him followed through in somewhat single file at a quicker but controlled walk approaching a semi-trot toward and along the north curb of St. Dennis Drive. The remaining 2 or 3 riders, who were at the rear of the line, swung their mounts towards and proceeded at a quick but controlled walk approaching a semi-trot over the curve of the curb at the northeast corner and onto the lawn toward and into the crowd to the east of a sign located thereon.

As the first of the four or five other riders proceeded 60 to 80 feet easterly along the north curb of St. Dennis Drive they turned and proceeded northerly onto the lawn in wedge formation, advancing at a quick but controlled walk against and pushing the crowd toward and back to the most southerly of the spruce trees.

Although Patrol Sergeant Patrick Woulfe was aware that the original thrust of the horses east on St. Dennis Drive had not only cleared the street to the boulevard on each side, but had also relieved the pressure at the northeast corner, he nevertheless ordered and led his group of six mounts onto the north lawn without further instructions from his superior officers because, as he explained, 'I knew this was the plan' whose purpose 'was to divide that crowd up into smaller groups.'

At this time on this lawn were most of those who were originally there at 7:00 o'clock—a crowd some 25 to 30 deep, and the larger part of the demonstrators who had been dispersed from St. Dennis Drive on the first thrust of the horses easterly thereon.

As the horses advanced upon them in this manner most of the demonstrators scurried or ran to get out of their way and in doing so several stumbled or tripped and fell to the ground and several were accidentally struck by the horses and knocked to the ground. A few stood their ground. Others struck or attempted to strike at the riders or their mounts with their placards or umbrellas either in protest of the action of the horsemen or in self-defense.

With the quick manoeuvring of the horses and the ensuing scramble of the people to get out of their way, two mounts—one following the other, suddenly and unexpectedly came upon the cartons of candles and of plastic candle stick holders that were piled neatly in the form of a quadrangle on the lawn well back from the east curb of Don Mills Road and just north of the sidewalk on the north side of St. Dennis Drive. The mounts were unsuccessful in their effort to hurdle them. In attempting to do so they sent two young girls who were crouched within the quadrangle scurrying for their safety and knocked the cartons over with their hooves,

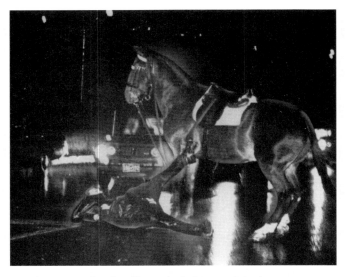

PC John Lunn's foot is still caught in "General's" stirrup. The horse had fallen to the ground breaking PC Lunn's leg. Photograph, Dennis Robinson, Globe and Mail.

scattering the contents on the lawn and one, if not both, of these horses immediately returned to trample over them.

With seven horses advancing in wedge formation in a northerly direction on the lawn at a controlled semi-trot the crowd was forced back toward and up against the apartment building and split to the west and east of the clump of spruce trees which were located on the lawn close to the northeast corner. In distances they were forced back some 125 feet to the apartment building with the front of the crowd being 50 to 60 feet from the north curb of St. Dennis Drive and extending easterly some 250 to 300 feet from the east curb of Don Mills Road.

As Inspector Johnson entered the crowd slightly north of the centre of St. Dennis Drive the two riders to his right who had been directed by him to the south side of the street confronted the crowd head on and when it didn't give they swung their mounts at a trot in a circular or semi-circular manoeuvre in the intersection and directed them at a quicker walk than the others approaching a semi-trot toward the crowd which quickly dispersed to the east and over onto the south side of the street.

In the meantime, having made the original opening in the crowd on the north side of St. Dennis Drive and the seven riders having gone through it, Inspector Johnson swung his mount to the south to assist the two riders on that side, if needed. Except for Inspector Johnson who never removed his riding crop from his saddle, all the other riders removed theirs on his order before entering the crowd and held them either by the side of their mount, upright, or in a swinging, flaying motion in the direction of the scurrying and running demonstrators in front or to the side of their mounts.

As the horses came among them in this fashion the shouts of 'shame, shame, Gestapo' rose from and a barrage of missiles, consisting mostly of candles or plastic candleholders, either singly or as a unit, were thrown at them from the crowd. Except for a small number of stragglers, St. Dennis Drive was rapidly cleared by these quick manoeuvres and the crowd then stood on the curb, boulevard and narrow lawn on the south side and on the wider lawn about 50 to 60 feet north from the north curb of the street.

With this the seven mounted officers on the north lawn, who by now were standing facing the crowd, were ordered to withdraw to St. Dennis Drive. As one of the riders put it, 'I saw the other horses falling back and we had achieved, as far as I was concerned, what we had set out to do at that time (and) I fell back with them.'

As they stood on the south side of St. Dennis Drive several cartons, boxes and more candles and candleholders were thrown in the direction of the mounts and their riders.

In so withdrawing from the north lawn they left the crowd up by the apartment building with no foot policemen to hold them there if indeed it was the plan of the police that the crowd was to remain or be kept there. When the mounts returned to the south side of St. Dennis Drive some 75 to 100 demonstrators from the crowd advanced in a disorganized manner southerly across the lawn, some with their placards and others carrying their umbrellas, shouting and yelling their remonstrations at the mounted officers on the street.

This movement was interpreted as a hostile, menacing and threatening advance upon the mounted officers with the result that the same seven officers who were earlier on the north lawn were ordered to advance against this group of advancing stragglers. With this order to advance Inspector Johnson hurried to the mouth of St. Dennis Drive and manually ordered four of the mounted officers who were standing in reserve at the street opening to the Science Centre on the east side of Don Mills Road forward and joined them on their thrust northeasterly onto the north lawn to assist the seven mounted officers who were by then advancing northward on the lawn.

One of these four riders immediately withdrew his mount back across Don Mills Road when it slipped on the wet grass because of its rubber shoes and balked at the debris of cartons and their contents on the lawn. Ten horses now moved against the straggling group of advancing demonstrators and toward the others in the crowd at the back of and on the north lawn at a firm, controlled walk with some moving quicker than others and with some riders with their crops by their side or at the ready and others swinging and flaying theirs at the demonstrators in their way, pushing them further back than on their first thrust on the lawn.

As with the first thrust some of the demonstrators deliberately attacked some of the horses with their placards and umbrellas and attempted to unseat several of the riders and other demonstrators sought to protect themselves from the horses advancing upon them and as a result one arrest at least, if not two, were made.

But unlike the first thrust no demonstrators were knocked or fell to the ground. This time, also, two riders drove their mounts at a trot and in a circle around a spruce tree, swishing their crops at several persons who took cover under it. Another rider trotted his mount at a high speed across the front of and from the west to east end of the crowd that was backed up against the apartment building.

Two riders proceeded northerly on the lawn to the front on the west side of the apartment building a distance of 125 to 150 feet from the north curb of St. Dennis Drive, chasing and pushing the crowd further north than hitherto and into the ground level alcove verandah of the apartment building.

The one arrest that was made on the lawn at the northeast corner was of a young university student—one Bohdan Petyhyrycz, who is alleged to have attempted to unseat a rider. Observing the scuffle between them a traffic foot policeman came to the assistance of the rider and in turn became involved in a wrestling, tumbling scuffle with the young demonstrator falling to the ground between the horses which were moving about them. In the end seven mounted riders came to the assistance of the foot policeman and either directly participated in subduing the demonstrator or by surrounding the two of them to keep the other demonstrators from interfering.

It was after this young demonstrator had finally been subdued and was being held forcibly by a rider and the traffic policeman, when Inspector Magahay appears for the first time on the lawn to assist in this arrest. Indeed, two other traffic foot officers came to assist and the three traffic officers then conducted the youth under arrest to the police wagon in front of the Science Centre to the east of Don Mills Road.

Inspector Magahay and the three traffic officers were the only foot men to come to the assistance of the Mounted Unit in its two thrusts and the manoeuvres on the north lawn. On his own initiative Inspector Magahay ordered out his 47-member E.T.F., who up until then were in the cafeteria of the Reception Building, to assist the Mounted Unit and this only after the four mounted officers were ordered forward by Inspector Johnson to assist the seven other mounted officers on their second thrust onto the north lawn.

Upon arriving at the intersection of Don Mills Road and St. Dennis Drive, the E.T.F. secured the curve of both curbs and the extension of the curbs easterly on St. Dennis Drive for approximately 20 feet and from there across the width of the street in an inverted "U" formation.

The crowd at the northeast corner and on the north lawn on St. Dennis Drive having been dispersed and pushed back in the manner and to the extent that it was, the eleven mounted officers standing on the north lawn withdrew for a second time to St. Dennis Drive and after rejoining the remaining two riders that were always on the south side, withdrew to their original position in front of the fountains.

In moving out of St. Dennis Drive, the E.T.F. and the other foot men who were there opened up to let the Mounted Unit by and then re-formed across the street.

As the remaining foot policemen quickly bolstered the re-formed line across the mouth of St. Dennis Drive the Emergency Task Force withdrew to the Science Centre.

After the tumult subsided following the withdrawal of the Mounted Unit, many of the elderly and the older demonstrators forsook Kosygin's departure from the Science Centre and returned to their homes humiliated and hurt more in their pride than to their person from the Mounted Unit being used against them and leaving the younger ones to continue their demonstration of protest on Kosygin's departure from the Science Centre.

The crowd that remained were permitted to return onto St. Dennis Drive and at the corners thereof with Don Mills Road where they remained in peaceful protest until Kosygin left at 9:30 p.m. to return by the same route to the Inn-on-the-Park.

As with Kosygin's expected arrival, so too with his expected departure, the Mounted Unit took their position in a display of straight in broken line formation just east of the median facing the crowd on the east side of Don Mills Road.

As with his arrival, Premier Kosygin and his party left the Science Centre without an incident. With this the demonstrators dispersed to their homes as peacefully as they had arrived to protest his visit and to make known their opposition to Soviet Communism."

Mounted officers ride into the crowd at Don Mills Road and St. Dennis Drive. Photograph, John McNeill, Globe and Mail.

◈ 1972

The biggest news at the Mounted Unit during the year was the ongoing Kosygin inquiry. Many of the mounted officers who were on scene that night were called to give evidence before the Royal Commission.

It was a fairly quiet year as the Unit maintained its regular patrols. Mounted officers attended a total of fifteen demonstrations. Large mounted details were supplied for the two visits of Prime Minister Trudeau. The Rolling Stones performed at Maple Leaf Gardens and a large contingent of mounted men were on hand for crowd management. Small mounted details attended eight separate labour disputes in the suburbs. The Unit provided mounted escorts for forty-two different parades.

The Musical Ride was performed for the public on nine occasions. The Inspector recommended that the "Ride" only accept invitations to perform at large venues as the size of the crowds at a number of the performances did not justify the amount of time that was used to prepare for a small audience.

In the spring, the force purchased a new six-horse "low-bed" trailer and also ordered a new tractor unit to pull it, the trailer was delivered later in the year, and the Unit gained the ability to transport eighteen horses.

An additional patrol sergeant was appointed. The Inspector was committed to increasing the size of the Unit. He requested that still another patrol sergeant be appointed along with eight more constables. The Inspector asked that all eight officers be transferred to the Unit simultaneously so that they could be trained together. Should these officers be forthcoming, No. 13 Stable could be kept open during the Musical Ride season.

The Mounted Unit received a pleasant surprise in the summer when one of the new horses, a mare named "Selkirk," proved to be pregnant. A filly was born in September, to be named "Nancy." She was retained by the force and used until about 1983 when she was retired due to lameness. At the end of the year the equine strength had increased to fifty horses, including the youngster.

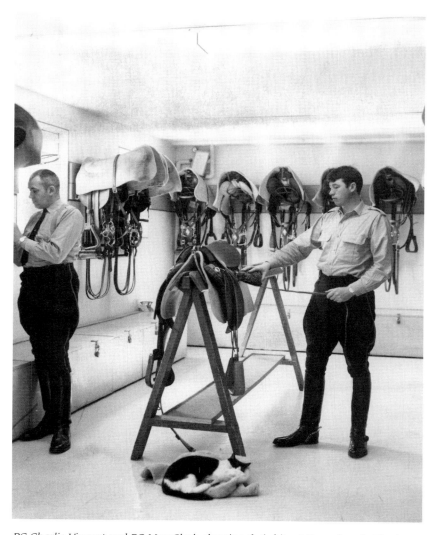

PC Charlie Vincent and PC Moe Clark cleaning their kits at Sunnybrook. The barn cat is sleeping at their feet. Photograph, Toronto Police Museum.

PC Charlie Vincent carries his saddle while PC Don Vincent (no relation) sweeps the floor at Sunnybrook. Photographs Toronto Police Museum.

1973

This was a very quite year for the Mounted Unit with officers attending just eleven peaceful demonstrations and three labour disputes. The Unit participated in forty parades throughout Metropolitan Toronto and the Musical Ride put on five public performances.

A number of requests for Park patrols were submitted to the Unit from police District Commanders. Due to personnel shortages only the "Belt Line" in the North Toronto area and Morningside Park in Scarborough were accommodated.

The biggest event of the year was the one week visit of Queen Elizabeth the Second to Toronto. The entire Unit was involved in the many mounted details required. On June 26th, a mounted escort of thirty horses and men accompanied the Queen on her route from the Royal York Hotel to the New City Hall. Also on June 26th, Patrol Sergeant Sandwell and twelve constables wore the Governor General's Horse Guards uniforms as part of the fifty-man escort that rode with the Queen to Queen's Park.

On June 30th, twelve mounted officers and horses under Sergeant Lewis formed part of the Governor Generals Horse Guards escort at the Queen's Plate at Woodbine Race Track. A special escort of six horses was sent to the Queen's rest area in Caledon Ontario. Her Majesty enjoyed an hour and a half ride around the Eaton Estate on police mount "Maureen" with Inspector Johnson.

Members of the Unit who rode with the Queen, were Inspector Edwin Johnson, Patrol Sergeant Ivan McAnsh, Constable Gerry Haywood and Constable Croutch. Four other constables were assigned to groom up four police mounts equipped with English Tack for the Queen, Prince Phillip and two Royal aides. No cameras were permitted and officers had to take their own lunches and drinks for the two days they worked at the "rest area."

The Inspector reported that the Unit budget would need to be increased the next year. The price of feed was expected to rise by at least 40% and the tack and stable supplies up to 20%. Some items already purchased from the United Kingdom had increased in price by 50%.

The Chief of Police authorized an increase in the horse strength of the unit to fifty-five horses. Two horses had to be destroyed during the year and three horses were retired. The unit purchased five remounts bringing the equine strength at the end of the year to fifty horses. The Inspector requested that Unit personnel also be increased to sixty-five constables in 1974.

In May, a new constable, Tom Matier, was assigned to ride one of the remounts, "Queen," on the regular rider's day off. There was a heavy thunderstorm taking place and the officer was looking for some shelter for himself and his mount. As he was riding eastbound on Queen Street West, three woman came out of the Sheridan Centre Hotel complex. All three opened umbrellas at once.

The motion of the umbrellas and the popping sound they made when opened, caused "Queen" to back up across Queen Street. PC Matier regained control of "Queen" and tried to move her back to the curb. As she neared the three woman, "Queen" backed up again onto the street car tracks. She was struck by a streetcar before the officer could get out of the way. The officer suffered minor injuries and the horse received a severe cut to the haunches.

"Queen" was taken back to the Canadian National Exhibition stable where she was examined by the unit veterinarian. When the cut had healed, the officers tried to hand walk "Queen" in the stable. The horse would become agitated and kicked out to prevent anyone from getting close to her. The veterinarian did further examinations and discovered that the horse had received a bone tumor, a fracture to her back, in the accident. On August 9th "Queen" was destroyed.

The police force ranking system was modified in 1973. The rank of patrol sergeant was dropped: all patrol sergeants became sergeants. Former sergeants were given the title of staff sergeant. Constable Warren Pollard was promoted to sergeant during the year and transferred to a regular police division.

Constable Mike Best investigates the lack of horsepower under the hood of a car stalled on University Avenue. While he checked the car, owner Mrs. Wylo Lavelle held the reins of his horse. May 10, 1973. Photograph, Franz Maier, Globe and Mail.

PC Tom Matier stops to make a phone call on patrol. Photograph, Globe and Mail.

PC Jim Davis and "Chieftain" watch as a police serviceman changes the tire on a horse trailer. Photograph, Shane Harvey, Toronto Sun.

PC Tom Matier assigned to the City Hall detail at Nathan Phillips Square. Photograph, Toronto Police Museum.

Two mounted officers assist a Volkswagen Beetle across the picket line at the Consumers Gas workers' strike in 1970. Photograph, Toronto Telegram Photograph Collection, York University Archives and Special Collections, Neg. #1699.

Cadet Brian Shaw and "Buccaneer" patrolling Sunnybrook Park, January 10, 1970. Young people between the ages of 17 and 20 who were interested in a police career could join the police force as a cadet. They were full time civilian employees with peace officer status. If their work performance was satisfactory they would be sworn in as constables when they turned twenty-one years old.

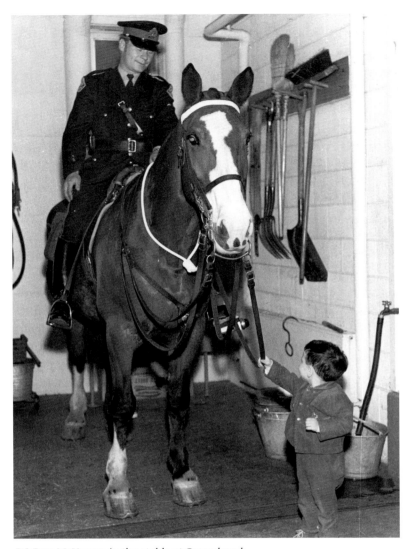

PC Martin Zakrajsek and "Major" at Nathan Phillips Square with PC Mike Sale who is modelling a turn of the century police uniform and bicycle.

Photographs, Toronto Police Museum.

PC Bert McKeown in the stable at Sunnybrook.

PC Mac Lyons at a pro-police rally in 1973. Photograph, Globe and Mail.

The Royal Visit 1973

On June 26, 1973, the Mounted Unit provided a ceremonial escort for Queen Elizabeth II. Officers accompanied her from the Royal York Hotel to a reception at Nathan Phillips Square.

The Mounted Unit also provided one sergeant and twelve constables wearing the uniform of the Governor General's Horse Guards, for the Royal Escort at the Queen's Plate.

The Royal Escort at Yonge and Queen Streets.

The Queen also requested a riding break during her visit to Canada. Inspector Johnson had police mount "Maureen" transported to the Eaton Estate north of Toronto, and the Inspector accompanied the Queen on an hour and a half ride around the estate.

The Queen arrives at Nathan Phillips Square.

The Royal Escort in "Troop in Line" for the Royal Salute.

The Royal Escort at Woodbine Race Track. Photographs, Toronto Police Mounted Unit.

1974

1974 was another quiet year for the Mounted Unit. There were no demonstrations or labour disputes that required its attendance. Small details were assigned to the Toronto Island Ferry Docks for the Rock Music Festivals that took place on the Island, but there were no problems. The fallout from the Kosygin inquiry may have been part of the reason for the low mounted profile.

The Mounted Unit assigned officers to patrol the Metropolitan Toronto Zoo properties and Morningside Park in eastern Scarborough. Additional officers were assigned to No. 4 District Stable so that these patrols could be conducted on both the day and afternoon shifts. Officers transported horses by truck and trailer to reach to these patrol areas.

The Metropolitan Toronto Zoo requested that the Mounted Unit permanently station officers in one of their stables. An agreement was reached and the Zoo began to renovate two buildings for the Unit's use. Zoo officials wanted the mounted officers to supplement its own Security Police Force. At one point, the Zoo had its own squad of Mounted Security Police officers, but this was discontinued after a few years.

The Mounted Unit officers assigned to the Sunnybrook Stable began regular truck and trailer delivery of horse patrols to the parks in North York. These patrols were conducted on both day and afternoon shifts and, were directed at parks where problems had been reported.

The Musical Ride gave performances at four locations during the year. Twelve officers rode with the Governor General's Horse Guards at the Queen's Plate, escorting the Queen Mother in Horse Guard uniform. The Unit participated in thirty-three different parades during the year and provided a number of eight-man escorts at the World Festival Tattoo at the Canadian National Exhibition Grandstand. All of the major football games in the city had mounted paid-duty officers assigned.

No. 13 Police Stable at London and Markham Streets was closed down after sixty-two years of use by the Mounted Unit. Officers and mounts were moved to the Canadian National Exhibition Stable after mounted patrols in the area were discontinued.

Eleven mounts were purchased and seven horses retired. Four of the retired horses were cast due to the "heaves" which was becoming a major problem for the Unit. Once a horse gets the "heaves" it can not be cured. There are medications that mask the problem, but the best solution is to move the horse out into the country where it can live out its life outdoors. Stabling horses in an enclosed area, within the dirty city environment increases the suffering. At the end of the year the equine strength of the unit was fifty-five horses.

The March 6 issue of the *Scarborough Mirror* contained an interview with Constable Jim Davis of 4 District Stable. The story reported that Davis was using a stop watch to time cars and stop speeders while on horseback in Scarborough. Davis talked about speed traps and reported that mounted officers always think of safety first and never endanger the horse or themselves when stopping vehicles. The main job of the Scarborough Unit was to deter drinking, drug use and vandalism in Scarborough Parks.[17]

A staff development program was initiated by the Mounted Unit to assist officers in enhancing their police experience, and become better qualified for promotion in rank. It was becoming hard for members of the Unit to be promoted because promotion boards wanted officers with a broad range of experience.

One sergeant and two constables were sent out on lateral transfers during the winter months. (Lateral transfers are designed to help the officers develop their policing skills). In his annual report, the Inspector stated that it was important that all mounted supervisors be experienced horsemen. He felt more consideration should be given to mounted personal at promotional selection boards. He concluded his report with, "If we are to maintain our present high standards for the future, the experience and quality of future Mounted supervisors is most important"[18]

Constable Robert Heenan, successful at the promotional board, was promoted to sergeant and remained at the unit.

The police force purchased a used nine-horse trailer and ordered a new tractor to pull it. A 1974 Ford van and two horse trailer were also ordered for the new No. 2 District Stable which was then under construction.

Another summons is issued. Constable Jim Davis and "Barney."
Photograph, Steve Behal, Scarborough Mirror.

The Zoo Stable

The Metropolitan Toronto Zoo was built on land which had once been part of a country estate called "Valley Halla," built by a Doctor Jackson, who had made his fortune selling Jackson's Roman Meal, a breakfast cereal/porridge. Jackson built the home for his wife, who died before it was completed.

The original mansion survives today, tucked away in the Rouge Valley at the end of a long country lane. The beautiful old home sits empty, but remains fairly well maintained. It is sometimes used as a movie set by film companies who value the impressive home and its rural setting.

The Doctor's old riding paddocks are still visible beside the house and some fencing survives. The original gatehouse and ground-keeper's cottages are located beside the old police stable and are in daily use by Zoo staff. The two buildings used by the police were formerly calf barns on the estate. These had low interior walls, with stanchions located two feet off the ground for securing the calves in their stalls.

The Mounted Unit maintained the Zoo stable from 1974 to 1981 when it was closed as a result of personnel shortages. By the mid-80s, it was apparent that the stable would not be reopened and its buildings were returned to the Zoo. The old police stables were converted into living quarters for the use of the Chinese Zoo keepers who came to Toronto with the Panda Bear Exhibit in the late 1980s.

Ten years later, an old farmhouse was moved to the site for the use of environmental groups, working to preserve the Rouge Valley system. The area has now been designated as a National Park. The fragile environment of the Rouge Valley cries out for continued mounted police patrols. The growing popularity of mountain bikes has caused an increase in damage to paths and sensitive growth areas. Toronto's "Garbage Crisis" has led to increases in illegal dumping of industrial and residential waste. Random mounted patrols are still provided in this area to help ensure continued preservation of one of Toronto's last natural settings.

PC Ken Cassidy at the Zoo Stable. Photograph, Toronto Police Mounted Unit.

Sgt Peter Quan of the Metropolitan Toronto Zoo Police Mounted Unit and PC David Hadlow of the Metropolitan Toronto Police Mounted Unit. Photograph, Toronto Police Museum.

The Island Stable

In a 1975 interview with John Maclean of Southam Business Publications, Inspector Johnson used the Island Stable as an example of a Mounted Unit success:

> *The main thing with a Mounted patrol is the prevention of crime. The mounted man on patrol is the same as a man walking the beat. He can be seen. As an example, on Centre Island when they started developing the island parks, there was a great deal of trouble. Then they asked for mounted patrols and in a very short time, in the one year that followed, crime of assault and other offences were cut down to practically nothing. Most of this is credited to the fact people could see that a mounted officer was on patrol.*

Mounted officers patrolling Toronto Island during the annual Toronto Police Association Picnic. Photograph, Toronto Police Association.

Mounted officers returning from a search for a missing boy in Claireville Park, Etobicoke. PC Bill Mathers is on the left. January 31, 1975. Photograph, Globe and Mail *Newspaper.*

PC Clarence Sauve and PC Jim Davis in front of No. 41 Division in Scarborough. Photograph, Toronto Police Museum.

1975

On January 7th, the Mounted Unit officially took possession of the two buildings that the Metropolitan Toronto Zoo had prepared for them. The horses, tack and men were all moved into the stable and the unit began to provide mounted patrols both within Zoo property and in the Rouge Valley park system. Since the Zoo Stable was not attached to a police station, a cadet or constable had to be assigned to work a midnight shift security detail. There was also a stableman assigned to the building on day shift.

On November 4th, the new No. 2 District Stable was opened at No. 22 Division located on Dundas Street West in Etobicoke. Its officers patrolled some street beats as well as in the parks located in Etobicoke. This was the first time regular mounted patrols were sent out into this area of Metropolitan Toronto.

On June 4th, police mount "Colonel" was sold to the Barrie Ontario Police Department. By prior arrangement a mounted officer resigned from the Metro Toronto Police and was hired by the Barrie Force to perform mounted duties within their City. The Barrie mounted patrol carried on for some time before it was cancelled and the officer put on regular vehicle patrol.

The Musical Ride performed to maximum crowds at the Scottish World Festival. The Inspector wanted to see the "Ride" continue, but its existence was a drain on the Unit's resources. The Unit's staff development program continued as eight constables were sent to the Emergency Task Force and territorial divisions. Sergeants were also allowed to go out on laterals.

The unit sold four older horses during the year and purchased seven remounts, paying between $400.00 to $625.00 for each horse. The sergeant's scout car was replaced with a 1975 Ford Pinto. New equipment was purchased for night riding; this consisted of a "britching harness" with reflectors for the rear of the horse and a reflector for the animal's "breastplate." This equipment was worn in conjunction with the "reflective gaiters" on the horse's legs and "stirrup lights."

THE MOUNTED UNIT IN 1975

LOCATION	HORSES
Sunnybrook Stable	18 Horses
Mounted Headquarters	
North York	
C.N.E. Stable	23 Horses
Toronto	
4 District Stable	6 Horses
Scarborough	
Zoo Stable	6 Horses
Scarborough	
2 District Stable	6 Horses
Etobicoke	
Island Stable (Summer Only)	4 Horses
Toronto	
TOTAL	**59 Horses**

PC Jim Davis with the Tractor and Nine Horse trailer which was used from 1974 to 1987.
Photograph, courtesy of Jim Davis.

PC James Barger in front of the new police complex in Etobicoke which included No. 2 District Stable. Photograph, Toronto Police Museum.

PC David Hadlow inside the new No. 2 District Stable. Photograph, Toronto Police Museum.

On duty at the Princes' Gates during the C.N.E.. Photograph, Toronto Police Museum.

 **1976** Social peace prevalent during the 1970s continued throughout the year. No major demonstrations or labour disputes disturbed the people of Metropolitan Toronto. A major detail of the year was the 1976 Olympic Soccer Games which were held at Varsity Stadium on Bloor Street. A mounted detail of sixteen officers was assigned to patrol the area every day a game was played.

During the Canadian National Exhibition, the Unit provided four officers on the day shift and four officers on the afternoon shift to patrol specific points. All were dressed in ceremonial uniform, tunic, tie and helmet during this very warm time of the summer. Officers discontinued wearing ceremonial dress uniform in 1982, when they manned these details in regular attire.

One officer patrolled the Princes' Gates and Marine Museum parking lot while a second patrolled the fountain area in front of the C.N.E. administrative building. A third officer was stationed at the Dufferin Gate and baseball park, and a fourth patrolled Manitoba Drive, from Strachan Avenue to west of the Food Building.

 **1977** The 1970s proved to be a very positive time for the Mounted Unit. Personnel reached ninety-eight officers of all ranks, with fifty-nine horses quartered in five police stables. No major demonstrations occurred and only one labour dispute in April, at the Becker Milk Company Plant, Warden Avenue, Scarborough, required mounted intervention.

During the strike, the plant remained in operation and the Mounted Unit was used to escort trucks in and out of the Beckers' compound. The Member of the Provincial Legislature for Scarborough-Ellesmere Riding visited the strike scene. David Warner, N.D.P. Metro Affairs Critic, asked the Solicitor General to order the police to stop using horses at the site. The Member told the *Toronto Star*; "there shouldn't be mounted police. It just isn't safe—either for the strikers or for the policeman on foot to have horses around those big trucks when they come out of the plant. When I was there a horse knocked a policeman off balance. Thank goodness he wasn't hurt, but he could have been." The member stated that he counted twenty-five policemen on foot, fifteen motorcycle officers and three mounted police officers at the scene. There were about sixty people on the picket line and "they were not unruly."

The Solicitor General refused to order the withdrawal of the horses. No persons were injured during the strike as a result of the actions of mounted officers. Mr. Warner also asked the Solicitor General to order the Milk Marketing Board to cease delivery of its products to Beckers for a period of

The Mounted Unit had grown in strength to eighty-five officers of all ranks, and sixty-one horses. The fact that the unit was spread far and wide over Metropolitan Toronto meant supervision was becoming an increasing problem. In order to facilitate a better supervisory system, the Unit was divided into two troops; each headed by a staff sergeant. Each staff sergeant had three sergeants reporting to him and supervising the constables on patrol. The Inspector commented in his annual report that the new system was proving successful as, "Supervisors now have closer contact with their men, resulting in improved evaluation and discipline."[19]

The Musical Ride operated for the tenth year entertaining the public with seven performances.

A second scout car was assigned to the Mounted Unit for the use of the Inspector, and also to be used by mounted supervisors on weekends. Five constables and one sergeant were allowed lateral transfers during the winter. On February 3, Constable Bill Macey was promoted to Sergeant and remained to help supervise the Mounted Unit.

one week. He felt if the deliveries were stopped, pressure would be put on the company to negotiate a settlement.[20]

Park patrols were the main function of the Unit with special attention being directed against people driving motorcycles in the parks or on private property. This proved a continual problem for the Mounted Unit until the Provincial Government passed the Off Road Motor Vehicles Act ten years later. This Act gave police powers which virtually eliminated these incidents within one year of its enactment.

On the night of April 11, PC Richard Vandusen was riding "Roy" westbound on the main road in Sunnybrook Park. Another mounted officer accompanied him. Both horses wore their proper reflective gaiters, breastplate reflectors and britching harnesses used for night patrolling.

A car was driving on the road, towards the officers. As it neared them, a pick-up truck moved out to pass. Constable Armstrong and "Prince," who were on the curbside of the road, managed to get out of the way. "Roy" was struck by the truck and thrown back approximately fifteen feet. Constable Van Dusen took the impact on his left leg and was thrown against the cement curb. "Roy" fled the scene and was later caught by a citizen and walked back to the police stable.

Constable Van Dusen was transported to hospital by ambulance and treated for a cut to his left elbow and an injured leg. "Roy" suffered lacerations to his legs, and his saddle was destroyed. The driver was charged with improper passing under the Highway Traffic Act.

On Saturday May 14, Constable Mackevicius, on police mount "Joan," was on regular patrol in Étienne Brûlé Park in Etobicoke when he came across two Metro traffic officers who were in the Humber River attempting to rescue an elderly woman who had fallen into the freezing water. Constable Mackevicius rode "Joan" into the river several times to assist with the rescue and to carry blankets to the officers, as they worked to try to keep the woman warm.

She was given artificial respiration by the officers and transported by ambulance to St. Joseph's Hospital in critical condition. The river is full of jagged rocks at this point and "Joan" suffered two cuts to her feet. No record exists of whether the lady recovered from her ordeal.

On July 31, Police Mount "Regent," evidenced signs of colic. Despite the best efforts of Sergeant Sandwell and other mounted officers, the horse could not be saved and was put down by the veterinarian. One other horse also died during the year. The Mounted Unit replaced twelve horses including the two that died. The Inspector purchased nine remounts at an average price of $700.00.

The Mounted Unit's new organization under the troop system worked well. The Inspector proposed that permanent supervision at all stables be instituted, and suggested a new "Corporal" rank be created for stable supervisors.

The Parks Department approved plans to renovate the Island Stable, providing three standing stalls and one box stall. These improvements would enable the Unit to use the facilities for longer periods of time. Major renovations were also done to the Canadian National Exhibition Stable, to provide officers with separate lunch and work areas.

The Musical Ride put on numerous performances during the year, including fourteen separate shows at the Royal Winter Fair. Two Sergeants and five constables took on lateral transfers during the winter months.

For years the Metropolitan Toronto Police Association had been requesting that all officers be issued with short sleeve shirts for summer wear. The traditional code of dress for officers required them to wear a long sleeve shirt; tie and shoulder cross strap year round. The Police Commission refused to issue short sleeves because it felt that members of the public would be offended by the tattoos which some officers wore on their arms.

Finally in June 1977, officers were issued new blue short sleeve shirts: the grey-coloured long sleeve shirts were retired from service. The men still wore ties and cross straps, but the short sleeve shirts made patrolling much cooler. The Police Commission refused to issue new blue long sleeve shirts for the winter, but these were ultimately issued in the late 1980s. Many mounted officers have returned to long sleeve shirts in the summer because they provide for added protection from the ultraviolet radiation of the sun.

Passing time at the Beckers Strike, Left to right: PC Tom Low, (unidentified), PC Jim Croutch, and PC Peter Scribner. Photograph, courtesy of Jim Davis.

Mounted Officers assisting a truck across the picket line during the Becker's Milk strike. Photograph, courtesy Toronto Star, Dick Loek.

A relaxed looking group of officers standing by at the Becker's strike. Mounted, PC John Brooks and PC Jim Davis. Mounted Unit Sgt Ernie Sandwell is on foot at right. Photograph, courtesy of Jim Davis.

BEDDING

Total Unit Cost (62 Horses)
Per Year	$14,600.00
Per Month	$1,216.00

Cost per Horse
Per Year	$235.00
Per Month	$19.60
Per Day	$0.64

FEED

Total Unit Cost (62 Horses)
Per Year	$57,000.00
Per Month	$4,750.00

Cost per Horse
Per Year	$920.00
Per Month	$76.00
Per Day	$2.50

SHOEING AND SUPPLIES

Total Unit Cost (62 Horses)
Per Year	$14,600.00
Per Month	$1,216.00

Cost per Horse
Per Year	$235.00
Per Month	$19.60
Per Day	$0.64

A picturesque scene of PC Al McKechnie and "Dolly" in Sunnybrook Park. Photograph, Hugh Wesley, Toronto Sun.

1978

The Mounted Unit was not involved in any sensational events during the year. Crowd-control duties were at a minimum with the usual small details detached for entertainment events at the Canadian National Exhibition and Varsity Stadium. The Unit attended many small parades throughout Metropolitan Toronto, and provided large contingents for the Grey Cup Parade and Santa Claus Parade. The City Hall detail began duties on May 15 and operated until October 31st. This post was covered by three constables from 12:00 noon to 9:00 p.m.

The Musical Ride presented seven public performances. High interest remained within the Unit in the "Ride" because it provided valuable advanced training for personnel. The Mounted Unit had sixty-one horses on strength in 1978. The Inspector reported that horses which met police standards were becoming harder to find, but he "had his eye on a few he wanted to purchase next year."[21]

Retraining classes commenced in the fall to maintain equitation standards for younger members of the Unit. These two-week classes involved personnel who had been with the Unit for at least four years. A special class was also scheduled for senior men who had recently been assigned with remounts. It was getting difficult to find men with sufficient experience and ability to take over inexperienced remounts from the trainers, and work with them to develop the high requirements required for these horses to perform regular street duty.

A number of building alterations were made to the office and personnel areas of Sunnybrook Stable. Smoke detectors were installed in all stables except for that at the C.N.E.. An automatic watering system was ordered to be installed in all stables by the end of the year, it would prove a welcomed labour-saving improvement, as men would no longer have to carry water to the stable by hand. The Parks Department delayed renovations at the Island Stable until the fall of 1979.

The Inspector expressed concern that the Unit not lose its cadets, who provided night stable security at the Zoo, C.N.E. and Sunnybrook Stables, as these buildings were not attached to police stations and would be left unsecured. Should the cadets be taken off strength, constables would have to be diverted from patrol duties to replace them. The Inspector requested an additional sergeant be assigned to the Unit to assist with supervision

Mounted Unit horses continued to experience problems due to "the heaves." Two horses were put down during the year due to the advanced nature of their ailment. No mention was found in reports of what improvements were attempted to improve air quality within all stables. Three other horses were sold.

Faced with an increasing health problem, the Mounted Unit experimented with a new feeding system which proved successful in the smaller stables. The Unit decided to use "Purina Complete Feed" throughout the ranks, replacing hay, oats, bran and the mineral supplement previously used. The Inspector reported that, the Unit "had seen marked improvement in the condition of these horses, particularly those suffering from respiratory problems such as the heaves. There was also a noticeable reduction in the amount of manure. The cost was about the same for the two feeding systems."[21a]

 **1979** There were no major events involving the Mounted Unit during this year. The 1970s ended on a quiet note. Mounted officers attended crowd control details at two anti-police demonstrations during the year and at a large Rock Concert at the Canadian National Exhibition Grandstand.

Members of the Unit attended forty-one parades and the Musical Ride performed for the public on six occasions. The Unit sent officers to thirty schools and other locations for public educational purposes. Paid duty officers worked at forty-nine sports events and large picnics.

During most of the 1970s, the Mounted Unit assigned officers to divisional patrol areas. This allowed an officer to patrol wherever he wanted within the designated area. On March 19, 1979, the Unit reverted to the old beat system whereby officers were assigned specific routes, to follow, and patrol. All variations had to be approved by the supervising sergeant.

The first reason cited for the change was that horses were not receiving sufficient exercise and exposure to traffic. The second reason was the lack of enforcement being done by the officers who were reminded that they were to enforce traffic and parking bylaws and to investigate suspicious persons.

At the No. 4 District Stable, the garage area was converted into a lunchroom for officers. The Island Stable was in poor condition but the Parks Department remained undecided about what to do, so renovations were again delayed.

Three horses were retired due to age and three horses were disposed of due to lameness or chronic ailments. There were few suitable horses offered as replacement: the high price paid for horsemeat was blamed for this lack. With prices as high as seventy cents a pound, farmers sent good horses as well as poor to the meat market. The Inspector felt that he might have to begin paying over one thousand dollars for a good horse in the future.

The new feeding system led to healthier horses, and respiratory disorders such as "the heaves" and some chronic blood disorders were no longer a problem. Cost remained on par with the earlier hay and oats system.

During the Musical Ride's performance schedule, No. 4 and 2 District Stables were closed due to personnel shortages. The Inspector recommended that in 1980 the Ride be discontinued, should the Unit's personnel shortage not improve.

The smaller ratio of men to horses was becoming a concern.

The Mounted Unit had fifty-nine horses on strength. The Inspector reported that,"The number of patrol personnel on strength is insufficient to our present horse establishment on the road. Horses must be exercised on a regular basis and even with men riding two horses per day it is difficult to provide the necessary exercise with the personnel on hand."[22]

The Unit relied on the good will of private citizens and members of the department to provide pasture land in the country for sick or lame horses. The Inspector recommended that a stable and pasture of its own be acquired close to Metropolitan Toronto. He felt that some of the horses ailments and injuries could be corrected with a stay on good pasture land.

Sgt Harry Highet examines an officer's horse. Photograph, Hugh Wesley, Toronto Sun.

The Inspector ended his annual report by stating, "The morale of the unit is fair considering the investigation going on at the present time. It's a shame that we have to go through this but I am sure that as in the past, the Unit will come out on top."[23] The investigation referred to was the "Productivity Report" which would be just one of many internal police force reviews that the Unit would face in the future.

By the end of the decade, the Metropolitan Toronto Mounted Unit was the largest mounted unit in Canada, and second in North America only to the New York City Police Department Mounted Unit.

Front cover of the Police Association Magazine, *February 1978.*

The Mounted Unit rehearsing its March Past for the annual Metropolitan Toronto Police Amateur Athletic Association Field Day. The officers would also perform a Musical Ride during the evening. The Field day being held at the Exhibition Stadium at the C.N.E. Its astroturf surface was very slippery and required great skill to perform the Musical Ride successfully. 1977 was the first year officers wore short sleeve blue shirts, and the last year that they would wear leather cross straps.

Photographs, Toronto Police Museum.

PC Shawn Blackmore receiving a citizenship award from the City of Toronto.

The 1980 Productivity Report

The 1980s got off to a bad start with the release of "Mounted Unit, A Productivity Sub-Committee Report." by the Police Inspection Unit. The report looked at the Unit's productivity and made a number of recommendations, often comparing the function of the Mounted Unit to that of police divisions and traffic units.

The report found that the mounted officers were on the fringes of policing. It stated that many of the officers did not see themselves as actually being police officers or that their job involved law enforcement. As a standard, the report used the concept that a police officer should divide time into thirds: one-third preventative patrols, one-third answering calls for service, and one-third enforcement functions. The Inspection Unit found the time of the mounted officer was divided ninety percent into preventative patrols and ten percent enforcement.

The Productivity Report was a fairly scathing report in its conclusions, and should have been a wake up call to the officers on the Mounted Unit. The Inspection Unit basically concluded, that with the exception of the Scarborough Stable, the Mounted Unit was not contributing any measurable productivity to Toronto's police force. The report, may have been correct in the fact that more could and probably should have been done, by Mounted Unit officers, however at the same time, the Inspection Unit did not fully comprehend the value of the mounted officer.

Nine recommendations made in the report were as follows:

1. Phase out the use of both the Island and Zoo stable and police these areas with a mobile mounted squad that can be moved in when desired by the District Staff Superintendent.
2. Consider No. 2 and 4 District Stables to be non-permanent and staff them only during those months of the year when, in the opinion of the Staff Superintendent, this service is of some value.
3. The resources of the Mounted Unit are insufficient to patrol all parks; therefore, this service must be limited to requests for service from Unit Commanders.
4. Each District Staff Superintendent to consider as a high priority, the integration of horse patrols with foot patrols in areas of high density and high crime.
5. The Mounted Unit be prepared through training to respond to any request for service from the Community Services Bureau particularly in the ethnic and government assisted housing areas.
6. A portion of the Mounted Unit be developed as a highly trained tactical squad with emphasis on a crowd control capacity.
7. Mounted Unit shifts be re-examined and become flexible enough to provide their support at any time on any day their service is needed.
8. The Mounted Unit personnel be required to submit a daily activity log for continuous assessment by the unit commander and his supervisors.
9. Civilians be phased into the mounted operation in the capacity of grooms, exercise riders and night watchmen in sufficient numbers to maximize the patrol time and with regard to the limitations of the animals.

The report also stated that the City Hall Detail should be discontinued and the Musical Ride, which had already been discontinued, should never be resurrected.

Inspector Johnson fought back. He sent a stern memo to the Commissioners pointing out the errors that the report writers had made. Of the nine points listed above he agreed with only points numbers four and seven. Johnson felt that civilian watchmen could be hired, but, not civilian stablemen or grooms. The points made in the Inspector's rebuttal were valid and for the most part, must have been accepted by the Command Officers.

The elimination or reduction of the Mounted Unit has been a constant theme throughout its history and particularly since the 1980 report, which marked the end of the "good times" for the Unit which had been at its peak in the 1970s. Since 1980, Toronto's Mounted Unit has experienced gradual reductions in personnel and in horses.

1980

The Mounted Unit reached its peak in manpower and horses by 1979. The new decade started off with a report on the productivity of the Unit by members of the Inspection Team and this launched the Unit into what would become a very difficult decade.

Mounted officers lost a good friend with the retirement of Chief of Police Harold Adamson. The new administration was not horse-orientated and remained very "conservative on the matter of horses at demonstrations."[24] Criticism leveled at the force because of the Kosygin Royal Commission was foremost in their minds. When horses were assigned to demonstrations, it was usually on an out-of-sight basis.

The authorized strength of the Mounted Unit totalled eighty-six officers of all ranks and sixty horses. The Unit had the horses, but were short two constables. By the end of the year, the Unit's last cadet left, and would not be replaced. The Inspector requested either the cadets be returned or civilians be hired to replace all officers taken off patrol to fill the jobs done by cadets. This request was never granted.

Special mounted patrols were sent regularly to the Regent Park area of 51 Division and the Eastern Beaches. The Beaches patrol was part of a "summer patrol and enforcement program" being run by 55 Division, the local police station. The program was very effective and Mounted Patrols were reported to be appreciated by the public. As always, the various parks continued to be patrolled, and officers dealt mainly with drunks, disturbances and vandalism. Escorts were provided for thirty-eight parades.

Emergency crowd-control details were provided at three rock concerts. Eleven horses were sent to Ontario Place after a Teenage Head concert got out of hand. During the Canadian National Exhibition, twenty horses helped to police the crowds at the Who concert. Fifteen horses were called to help suppress the riot that occurred when the Alice Cooper concert was cancelled.

The 1980 Metropolitan Toronto Police annual report noted with regard to the above incidents, "Mounted assistance was requested by the senior officer in charge at the scene, when the situation became out of control. The prompt arrival of Mounted Officers supported by foot personnel brought these riot situations under control with little violence or injury." It further reported: "Complimentary letters were received from Ontario Place Officials and Senior Officers at the scene commending the actions and conduct of our mounted details."[25]

The Musical Ride was disbanded due to the reduction of mounted personnel. The Inspector wished to have more use made of the Mounted Unit by the different police districts, not just for preventative patrols but for more crowd control functions. In his report the Inspector said, "The horse is our most effective means of crowd control for both peaceful and violent situations. With the recent rock concerts this year the 'horse' proved himself again, and according to reports, 'saved the day' on these three occasions."[26]

As to the productivity of the Mounted Unit, the Inspector stated that the specialized function of the mounted officer restricts the type of enforcement he can do. He did not think it was fair to compare his "workload" to that of an officer in a traffic unit or a division. Considering the special duties that the Mounted Unit was involved in, their overall productivity was "very good."

THE MOUNTED UNIT IN 1980

(As per the Inspection team Productivity Report)

STABLE	COMPLEMENT	COVERAGE	ENFORCEMENT	COST
Toronto Island	4 Constables 4 Horses	Toronto Island May to October	Low	$43,000.00
City Hall Detail	5 Constables 5 Horses	Nathan Phillip Square	Low to none	$64,000.00
Zoo Stable	8 Constables 1 Cadet 6 Horses	Metro Zoo Rouge Valley & Parks	Low to none	$225,000.00
4 District Stable	6 Constables 6 Horses	Parks & Ravines	low	$150,000.00
2 District Stable	6 Constables 6 Horses	Parks & Ravines	low	$150,000.00

Productivity figures for the 1970s are not available, but it is assumed that the numbers for 1980 were higher than in the previous years.

One incident of note occurred at the Exhibition Stable during the summer as two officers reported off duty. They had just left the stable when they observed three men who appeared to be breaking into cars in the parking lot across the street. One officer returned to his locker to retrieve his revolver, then they moved to apprehend the suspects.

The men fled at the officers' approach, and a foot chase began. The armed PC caught one suspect and a struggle took place. During the fight, the officer's gun discharged: the suspect was shot in the armpit and through the shoulder. The suspect and his two accomplices were charged with theft under $200.00. All of the evidence was consistent with the shooting being accidental, due to the struggle. The officer was cleared of any wrongdoing.

One of the more popular members of the Unit was Constable Kevin Burns, whose wife had recently died of cancer leaving him to raise their two children alone. Constable Burns was at the farm of another mounted officer helping him to train two horses to work on wagon harness. Something startled the horses while he was working with them. Burns was unable to get out of the way. He was run over by the charging animals.

An emergency ambulance run was set up, and every major street along the route was blocked off to assist its rapid ride to hospital. Unfortunately Constable Burns was pronounced dead soon after his arrival at the Toronto General Hospital.

THE DAILY SCHEDULE IN THE 1980s

DAY RELIEF 07:00 - 15:00

06:45 - Report for duty (stable duties, groom)
08:00 - Turn out to post
11:15 - Stables for lunch
12:15 - Stables, tack up and stable duties
12:30 - Turn out, resume patrol
14:30 - Stables, tend to mount and clean kit
15:00 - Report off duty

AFTERNOON RELIEF 15:00 - 23:00

14:45 - Report on duty (stable duties, groom)
16:00 - Turn out to post
18:30 - Stables for lunch
19:30 - Stables, tack up and stable duties
18:45 - Turn out, resume patrol
22:30 - Stables, tend to mount and clean kit
23:00 - Report off duty

STABLE ACCOMMODATION IN 1980

Sunnybrook Stable	21 Stalls
C.N.E. Stable	28 Stalls
4 District Stable	7 Stalls
Zoo Stable	7 Stalls
2 District Stable	8 Stalls
Island Stable	4 Stalls
Total	75 Stalls

THE MOUNTED UNIT IN 1980

Inspector	1
Staff Sergeants	2
Sergeants	6
Constables	
Stablemen	9
Quartermaster	1
Horse Trainers	2
Rider Trainers	1
Regular Duty	60
Total Constables	73
Cadets	2
Total Unit	84

1980 PRODUCTIVITY STATISTICS

ARRESTS	1980	1981
Criminal Code	32	72
Criminal Code ,Traffic	21	21
Liquor Offences	125	70
Juveniles	22	48
TOTAL ARRESTS	200	211
Parking Tags	10,108	11,298
Summonses	1,319	1,240
Persons Investigated	2,132	2,496

The Alice Cooper Riot

On August 19, 1980 rock star Alice Cooper was scheduled to perform at the Canadian National Exhibition Grandstand. The warm up bands played to a full house awaiting the star's appearance. At the appointed time, the announcer worked the crowd up in anticipation of the star's arrival. Alice Cooper did not arrive at the stadium, and cancelled his Toronto performance at the last minute. The crowd, "psyched up" for their idol's arrival, was told that Cooper would not appear.

To complicate matters, the Metropolitan Toronto Police Association was involved in a labour dispute with the Police Commission, which meant officers involved in a job action refused to do Paid Duties. This left only a skeleton crew of regular duty officers on hand at the stadium.

When the crowd heard of Cooper's defection, they began to throw chairs and other debris at the stage. Police on the scene had to brave these missiles, and remain on the stage to prevent the crowd from gaining access to the large speaker towers. At one point, a group of youths pushed against the towers, they almost fell onto the masses of people milling around on the stadium floor. Quick action on the part of the officers in clearing the stage probably saved many people from serious injury.

Within minutes, a full-scale riot broke out. The small number of officers on stadium duty were not able to contain the situation and the police radio room broadcast a citywide call for reinforcements. Officers from all over Metropolitan Toronto headed for the scene. Mounted officers from the C.N.E. Stable were at the stadium almost immediately after the "assist call" was sounded. Other mounted officers were rapidly moved in from outlying stables.

The press reported a number of arrests, several injuries and thousands of dollars in damage. Fortunately the small staff of both mounted and foot officers inside the stadium took a firm hand in dealing with unruly members of the crowd. The riot was contained quickly before it could spread through the entire Exhibition grounds. The Mounted Unit received many letters and calls of appreciation for a job well done, from police officers, Canadian National Exhibition officials, and from the public.

Three mounted officers back up foot patrol officers who are making an arrest at the Alice Cooper riot. Photograph, Jack Dobson, Globe and Mail *Newspaper.*

The Police Applicant of 1980

PC Jim Bradford and "Sandy" in High Park.
Photograph, Toronto Police Service

Applicants to the Metropolitan Toronto Police Force had to pass basic conditions of age, 18 to 21 years old for cadet, 21 to 35 years old for constable. A minimum grade twelve diploma and citizenry of Canada or of Great Britain was required. Male officers were required to be a minimum of 5'8" and weigh a minimum of 160 pounds. Female applicants had to stand 5'4" and meet a minimum weight standard.

Applicants who fit these qualifications were given oral and written examinations, a complete medical, eyesight tests, physical strength and endurance tests, and a psychological evaluation. About 40% of all candidates were eliminated at this stage.

Successful candidates underwent a thorough background check of themselves, parents, in-laws and previous employers; fingerprints and records were checked for criminal history. Applicants who remained in the process after these checks, went before a review board where another three to four percent of candidates were eliminated.

After all the tests and checks were completed only 8.5% of the original applicants in 1979 made it to Police College. If they passed the courses at the College, these men and women faced an eighteen-month probation period of employment from the date of being sworn in as a probationary constables. After three years of good conduct, they become first-class constables, qualified to apply for transfer to the Mounted Unit.

The Gay Bath House Raids

In June 1981, the Metro Police raided three Gay Bath houses in the downtown area. A number of people were charged as "Keepers of Bawdy Houses" and others as "Found-Ins." The raids generated significant negative feelings in the Gay community and non-supportive editorials in the press. Leaders in the Gay community organized anti-police demonstrations and marches to protest the raids and charges.

The command officers of the police force ordered the Mounted Unit to remain on standby, behind the New City Hall during demonstrations. The Unit was not to be used for crowd control except in an emergency. As a result, they were not called out early enough to prevent the pending confrontations.

On Saturday June 20, a very large rally and march by Gays, became disrupted by a number of anti-homosexual protesters. The anti-Gay group attacked some of the protesters with broken pieces of wooden fencing. The first Gays to be attacked simply raised their arms to defend themselves. They began to fight back after a few of their number were knocked to the street by flying pieces of wood thrown by the Gay bashers.

Foot police moved in and restored order, but fights began to break out again. One lady was alleged to have had her leg broken in the melee. The anti-homosexual group picked up momentum as the night went on. At least two persons were arrested for assaulting police. Finally, five mounted officers were given permission to ride to the scene to assist the foot officers. Foot and mounted officers were able to control the crowd until the end of the protest.

When the demonstration ended, Gay protesters slowly broke up into smaller groups and moved off in different directions. One of the groups began to move down Yonge Street with police on either side holding the Saturday night crowds on the sidewalks. The *Toronto Star* reported that "there seemed to be little property damage and no major injuries in the forty-minute clash."[1]

Photograph on facing page: Relations between the Gay community and the police have improved dramatically since 1981. Today the annual Gay Pride parade is one of the biggest events in Toronto. Mounted officers are assigned to help manage the parade crowds every year. Photograph, Toronto Star.

1   *Toronto Star.* June 22, 1981.

1981

The Mounted Unit attended a number of potential crowd control events but were only actively involved a few times during the year. Mounted officers took part in fifty parades and provided small escorts for dignitaries at the Scottish World Festival. The largest escort of the year was at Woodbine Race Track where twenty-two horses escorted Lieutenant Governor John Black Aird into the stadium for the running of the Queen's Plate Race. Other ceremonial escorts were provided at the Royal Winter Fair. Mounted officers were also sent to fifty-five community events at schools and other social functions.

An increase occurred in the number of requests for park patrols from the different Police District Commanders. In response, the Unit started to provide more mobile park patrols to outlying areas. Officers worked a special late afternoon shift and travelled to and from the different complaint areas on a random basis. These patrols proved to be very effective and in line with the 1980 Productivity Report.

The personnel situation at the Unit did not improve. The Metropolitan Toronto Zoo Stable and the Toronto Island Stable were closed permanently. This allowed the Inspector to staff the remaining four stables with sufficient personnel. The Mounted Unit also started to receive information from the Records Bureau which reported various occurrences taking place in parks. Constable Paul Dean began working as a crime analyst to help determine where mounted patrols were most needed. A large pin map was obtained and the different crimes plotted using colour-coded pins. Officers could tell at a glance where the trouble spots were before setting out on patrol.

Probably as a result of the Productivity Report, workload numbers of the unit increased, and the Inspector noted this in his annual report. "Enforcement increased during the summer months, particularly with regard to arrests and summonses in Metro Parks. More problem areas were covered by mobile patrols operating during prime time on a special 7:00 p.m. to 2:00 a.m. shift."[27]

Mounted officers submitted a fairly substantial workload with 11,000 parking tickets issued, 1,200 summonses, 2,496 persons investigated and 211 persons arrested. During the summer months, the Unit assigned two mounted officers to patrol Yonge Street from 8:00 p.m. to 2:00 a.m. each night.

The Mounted Unit disposed of six horses during the year due to age and chronic ailments. Five remounts were purchased with the price per horses ranging from $1,050.00 to $2,000.00, demonstrating how difficult it was becoming to find the right horses at the right price.

The original concept of the lateral transfer system was to enable officers to leave the Unit for six months to gain job experience for promotion purposes. Constable Tony Smith gained the necessary experience for promotion through these transfers and was promoted to Sergeant during the year. In 1981, the lateral system was amended to make it mandatory that the Mounted Unit send officers to the field to help staff police divisions during the winter. Inspector Johnson was concerned that staff reductions during the winter reduced the horses' exposure to traffic and other distractions, thus leaving them more susceptible to respond in an unpredictable manner:

"The efficiency of both horse and rider depends on continuous exposure to traffic, parades, crowd control duties and other special activities." The Unit was forced to send two sergeants and sixteen constables out on temporary transfers. In order to provide horses with the necessary exposure, the Inspector recommended that only one sergeant and eight constables be sent out on lateral transfers during the winter months.[28]

On the way to a parade. Left to right: PC's Peter Cousins, Dennis Rowbotham, Al McKechnie, Fred Lloyd. Photograph, Toronto Police Mounted Unit.

1982 The future of the Mounted Unit was still in doubt in Spring 1982. The Metropolitan Toronto Police Commission hired the consulting firm of Hinkling and Johnson to study police operations. It was hoped that the $400,000.00 study would streamline and reorganize the structure of the Metropolitan Toronto Police Force. The Mounted Unit was hit hard by the report, but fought back and survived the massive cuts recommended.

Had the Hinkling and Johnson recommendations been fully implemented, the Mounted Unit would have been cut back to about twenty horses. Due to a public outcry, massive cuts were avoided but the Board of Commissioners of Police still recommended that the equine strength be reduced. Staff Inspector Johnson was ordered to shrink the unit to forty-two horses by the end of 1984. This was a one-third reduction from the Unit's strength of sixty horses beginning in January 1982. By the end of 1982, the Mounted Unit reduced its horse population to fifty-two.

The Unit was also reduced by attrition as two officers retired during the year and another two transferred from the unit, not to be replaced. The Unit had four fewer officers and the Inspector felt that there should be a majority of least ten more officers than horses. Inspector Johnson told a *Globe and Mail* reporter, "We're a little concerned about being reduced, I think they're going to be sorry in the future."[29]

The Mounted Unit was spread thin. In addition, the Musical Ride was revived during the summer, lessening the number of officers available for regular patrol. The "Ride" only gave two public performances during the year. It may have been worth staging the Ride for its training benefits, but it certainly was not worth the manpower invested for only two events.

During the summer, two mounted officers patrolled Yonge Street each night from 7:00 p.m. to 3:00 a.m. The Unit also sent mobile park patrols to police the problem areas in parks. The reduction in staff, reached a point where the Inspector began to refuse smaller public relations details in order to focus on getting out the maximum number of park patrols. Despite these shortages, members of the Unit attended a number of small parades and community events. Officers continued to be assigned to the City Hall detail from April to October.

One of the primary functions of the mounted officers on park patrol was the enforcement of laws dealing with off-road motor vehicles. Continuing complaints poured in about people operating these machines on both private and public property. By-law contraventions and trespassing were the only offences, however, that could bring a charge. Penalties involved in these charges never deterred the people riding such vehicles in the wrong places.

It was also difficult to catch motorcyclists riding unsafely. During the summer, such occurrences reached a climax in the Morningside and Highway 401 area of Scarborough. Residents had had enough of the noise and dangerous driving associated with the trail bikes in their local park. Three area residents tried to scare the bikers away themselves with walking sticks, but ended up being arrested and charged with Possessing Weapons Dangerous to the Public Peace. The residents were later granted absolute discharges in court after pleading guilty to the reduced charge of causing a disturbance.

The Mounted Unit hockey team. Front row: Steve Devost, Howie Peers, Greg Ladner, unidentified, John Dower, Steve Niemirowski. Rear row: Roy Smith, Mike Brooks, unidentified, unidentified, Ken Cassidy, Peter Spurling, Nick Spearen, Mike Roberts, unidentified. Photograph, courtesy of Jim Davis.

The Hinkling-Johnson Report

August 1982

The following is an extract from the Hinkling-Johnson Report:

Recent data indicates that the Metropolitan Toronto Police Force has between fifty-five and sixty horses available for routine and mounted patrol duty. The full cost of the Mounted Unit is approximately $3.5 million for fiscal year 1982. Most of this cost is made up in uniformed officers' wages and benefits. The Mounted Unit has three primary functions:

- *Crowd Control.*
- *Park and ravine patrol.*
- *Visibility.*

CROWD CONTROL

In terms of crowd control, there is little dispute that horses can be used very effectively. A Metropolitan Police Force internal sub-committee reported that:

"Mounted horses are plainly visible and probably beneficial in this (crowd control) preventative role, if for no other reason than the size and strength of the horse. On the other hand, when at strikes or demonstrations, the physical power of the horse, when combined with the authoritarian power of the officer, make a formidable team that many citizens find intimidating. In this day and age, the horse and rider are construed to be a show of force that carries resentment and a perceived justification to react with opposing force which results in violence."

Essentially we agree with their statements and add that this function could also be provided with a much more limited stable than the existing level of fifty-five to sixty. Further, crowd control that requires horses have not been a particular problem in Toronto in recent years.

PARK AND RAVINE CONTROL

Horses are also perceived by many citizens to be effectively used in park and ravine patrol. However, it is our view that this is a false perception. Granted they have high visibility, which gives people a sense of security and in some instances acts as a deterrent. In reality though, they are only effective if they happen to randomly encounter an incident in progress.

In providing these functions, the mounted officer is out on patrol for a period of three and one half hours during the summer months for each 8-hour shift. During the winter months, the time on patrol drops to about three hours per eight-hour shift. While on patrol, the mounted officer rarely (if ever) answers a call for service, rarely (if ever) make out an occurrence report, and rarely (if ever) undertakes investigations. In some instances, however, mounted officers do enforce minor parks by-laws and some parking violations.

VISIBILITY

In a productive and efficiency sense, a Mounted Unit is relatively ineffective. However, a mounted patrol officer parading in front of City Hall is good for tourism; the horse/officer combination makes a nice photograph with the City hall as background. Children are very impressed by mounted officers, which is beneficial by it in terms of public relations. Generally, adults also like the image of mounted officers. There is something about a mounted uniformed officer that most citizens' feel is beneficial. It adds a sense of history and culture to the city as well as a certain ambience that few can argue with. There is a cost associated with the Mounted Unit that must be taken into consideration. In our opinion the Mounted Unit is a luxury that the government of Metropolitan Toronto can afford —even in these troubled economic times. However, the Mounted Unit should not be considered necessary to fulfil any of the six primary policing functions: Response, Education, Crime Solving, Prevention, Law Enforcement, Referral.

It is likely that the citizens of Metropolitan Toronto, for emotional reasons, will wish to retain the Mounted Unit in order to maintain a presence at City Hall, visibility in some parks, and for ceremonial functions. We believe that it is appropriate for Metropolitan Toronto to support a scaled-down Mounted Unit external from the regular policing budget and therefore we recommend that:

40. The Metropolitan Toronto Government budget funds for the Mounted Unit separately from the normal police budgeting process.

For park and ravine service requirements some jurisdictions make use of motorcycles specifically designed for grass, dirt and trail riding, and deploy them out of a division as a result of a call for service or a complaint. In our opinion this is a much more effective use of police personnel than random mounted patrol.

The public relations, parade and crowd control functions could be performed with a reduction in the Mounted Unit — perhaps to less than one-third of the current strength, with a resulting cost savings of approximately $2 million. In this regard, we recommend that:

41. The Metropolitan Toronto Police Force scale down the Mounted Unit program to approximately one-third of its current strength.

"Last horse laugh: Why is this police horse smiling? Because a flood of public protest caused Metro Police to reconsider a proposal to do away with half of Toronto's Mounted Force."
Photograph and caption, Toronto Star.

So What Happened?

When the report was released Police Chief Jack Ackroyd announced, "that based on the report, there are substantial cutbacks in the Unit's future." In a speech to the International Association of Coroners and Medical Examiners he announced that due to the report the Unit would probably be cut in half. Predictably, Inspector Johnson was extremely angry not only about the report, but in the manner the report was prepared. With thirty-seven years of police experience, he was not about to be silenced.

He openly spoke to reporters giving his views on the report and pointing out its shortcomings. He told the *Toronto Star,* "The people who prepared that report never even visited any of the four mounted units in Toronto to find out how we operate or what we do. The only contact I had with them was one very brief telephone conversation, when they wanted one figure. How they can reach this decision based on that shocks me."[1]

In the article Johnson pointed out how the number of charges laid in the parks by mounted officers had been almost double in 1982. The number of reported crimes in parks had also increased and mounted officers had been redeployed from some ceremonial duties to provide more park coverage. At this point the *Star* canvassed a number of politicians and only one, June Rowlands, a future Police Commissioner and Mayor, were in favour of retaining the Unit at its current strength. Chief Ackroyd wanted the Unit to be downsized to between thirty to thirty-five horses.

The *Toronto Star* pointed out how other North American Cities were in the process of re-establishing their own Mounted Units. New York City Police expanding its mounted unit by 20% after public protests occurred in response to plans to disband the force.

The *Toronto Star* took up the cause of preserving the Unit and helped to gather public support to save it. A number of articles appeared pointing out the value of the mounted officers and the experience of other cities. The *Star* opened a phone line where citizens could call the paper and give their opinion as to whether the Unit should be reduced or left intact.

"Metro has a message for Police Chief Jack Ackroyd: We need all our horse patrols—badly. *Star* telephone lines were flooded yesterday as hundreds of callers urged the chief to trim his budget anywhere else, but not from the 75-man, 55-horse unit that costs $3 million a year. Save our horses, at all costs, was the nearly unanimous verdict."[3]

Members of the public also called the Chief's office and the Police Commission to let them know how they felt. The Chief reported that even his mother–in–law had called to tell him to leave the horses alone.[4]

Public support and the newspaper coverage proved too much for the Police Board and the Police Command Officers to ignore. Pressure applied by the *Toronto Star* and the citizens of Metropolitan Toronto was enough to make the powers that be reconsider implementing this aspect of the Hinkling-Johnson Report. The unit was not cut back and survived intact, actually increasing in size, over the next ten years.

At the Canadian Association of Chiefs of Police Conference held in Moncton, New Brunswick in August 1982, the Deputy Chief of the Los Angeles Police Department was a guest speaker. He stated that the L.A.P.D. had recently returned to the use of horses. Their police force believed that a few officers on horseback could provide control equivalent to many officers on foot. He attributed the move to "something we learned from our Canadian colleagues many years ago." Obviously a reference to the Metropolitan Toronto Police Mounted Unit as it was the only mounted unit active in crowd control in Canada.

1 *Toronto Star.* June 13, 1982.
2 *Toronto Star.* June 13, 1982.
3 *Toronto Star.* June 20, 1982
4 *Toronto Star.* June 20, 1982.

 **1983** The Mounted Unit continued to be reduced through attrition. Official authorized strength was still listed at seventy constables, although officers who retired or transferred from the unit were not replaced. There were only fifty-five constables shown on the roster by the end of the year. Horses were reduced to forty-eight; the goal continued to be to lessen their number to forty-two.

The chief of police continued his support for reducing the size of the Mounted Unit. After being forced to shelve the Hinkling and Johnson recommendations to cut the Unit's size by two thirds, Chief Ackroyd subscribed to a new plan. The *Toronto Star* reported on Jan 28 that the Chief planned to reduce the Unit to thirty-seven horses from its current strength of fifty-nine.[32] (Actually fifty-two horses remained in the Unit at the time of the article).

The Chief suggested that an additional five horses be cut from the previously agreed number of forty two.

The Inspector purchased three horses and disposed of eleven others during the year. There were no horses ready to be sold due to age or disability. Some pressure came from senior management to dispose of more horses, but the Inspector resisted selling sound horses just for the sake of meeting earlier down-sizing targets. After all the training and experience that had gone into these animals, it did not make sense to part with them so quickly.

Inspector Johnson continued to fight the cuts stating in his annual report that for 1984, the Unit should have at least forty-five horses. This permitted the deployment of at least forty horses for future major crowd control events.[33] The unit had enough vehicle transport to move nineteen horses to their assigned details. The nine-horse tractor trailer conveyance was over twenty years-old and in poor condition.

Colour party and lead section of the March Past at the Toronto Police Athletic Association Field Day.

Left to right: PC Paul Dean "Charlie," Sgt Bill Macey "Bruce," PC Steve Kemley "Joe."

Left to right: Bert McKeown "Ann," Bob Wright "Trooper," Mike Roberts "Paddy," Greg Robertson "General."

Photographs, Toronto Police Museum.

The Mounted Unit sent officers to twenty-two different "crowd control" events during the year. A Musical Ride was organized and performed in public on three occasions. In sports, the Toronto Argonaut's football team won the Grey Cup. The game was played in Toronto and mounted details patrolled the stadium grounds during the game. There was a large party on Yonge Street after the Argo's win and mounted officers were busy policing the crowd well into the early morning hours.

Demonstrations continued at Litton Systems of Canada Ltd. The Unit sent details of fourteen horses to the plant on four different occasions during the year. The Litton Plant was located on a wide area of open grounds. It was ideal to have the mounted officers patrol the peripheral of the plant and to place the foot officers along the front fence where the bulk of the demonstrators were located. A number of the demonstrators managed to climb the fence but, were quickly arrested. The annual reports stated "It was evident that the presence of the horses helped prevent more violent attempts to invade Litton Properties"[34]

The Mounted Unit also provided officers for crowd control duty at the Argo's ticker tape parade and City Hall reception. A detail of ten mounted officers led the parade up Bay Street to Nathan Phillips Square. By the time they reached Queen Street, the crowd was so large the horses began to actively move the people out of the way so the parade could reach the Square. They managed to escort all of the parade vehicles and participants to the reception area without incident.

Considering the amount of people, noise, ticker tape and other distractions, the horses performed superbly. There was a lot of activity on the Square with some "rowdies" pushing and shoving and causing a few minor problems. A number of citizens approached Inspector Johnson and commented on the excellent performance by both the mounted and foot patrol officers.

In addition to the Argo victory parade, the Mounted Unit escorted fifty-four other parades during the year. Mounted details attended the Music Festival parade in Burlington, Ontario and the Whitby Dunlop's Parade in Whitby, Ontario. In addition to the regular Park Patrols, sixteen continuous complaints were dealt with, most of which involved motorcycle riding in the parks, drinking and people causing disturbances.

In a 1983 interview with the *Globe and Mail,* a Concert Production International administrator told the paper "the horses are good to have when the band is gone and the kids still want more." C.P.I. as it was known would hire a few mounted paid duty officers for each of its C.N.E. events. The horses would patrol the periphery of the field to discourage lawlessness. He went on to say "The mounted cops are great, more open, more sociable"[35]

On February 4th, a constable of the 4 District Stable was injured at the intersection of Kennedy Road and Eglinton Avenue East. His horse "Andrew" went down on the pavement crushing his leg. In his annual report the Inspector doubted that the officer would be able to return to the unit due to the extent of the injury.[36]

A new computer system was installed at Mounted Headquarters giving the officers access to the R.C.M.P. Criminal Information system. It helped to facilitate investigations and brought the officers a little bit closer to mainstream policing. The new C.P.I.C. terminal replaced the old police teletype system.

Sgt Pat Woulfe, (centre) holds onto a civilian horse that escaped from a horse auction on the Canadian National Exhibition grounds. Photograph, Hugh Wesley, Toronto Sun.

1984 The Mounted Unit continued to maintain its mobile park patrols and street beats. The Musical Ride gave three public performances. These would be the last Musical Rides performed by the Unit until 1990. The Unit continued to supply officers for the City Hall details, local parades and public relations events.

The biggest event of the year occurred on Friday, September 14th, when the Pope came to Toronto. Every mounted officer was called into work for what was probably the largest undertaking the Unit had ever been assigned. Mounted officers monitored the entire route travelled by the Pope. They were strategically placed in areas where crowds might gather. Mounted details were also assigned to the Papal residence for the duration of his stay.

On Saturday, September 15th, the Pope held a mass at Downsview Air Force Base. The Mounted Unit provided a large contingent of personnel to help police the event. Some estimates placed the crowd size at one million people. There were no problems during the Pope's visit to the city.

On September 29th, Queen Elizabeth visited Toronto. The Mounted Unit provided a number of mounted details during the Royal visit. The Queen attended a special Tattoo in her honour at the Canadian National Exhibition Grandstand. Mounted escort for this event was provided by the Governor General's Horse Guards.

As the landau carrying the Queen entered the stadium, the military fired off a Royal Salute using cannons located near the stadium. Normally a salute would not have been presented until the Queen was out of the landau and the horses had safely left the field. The premature salute caused the horses pulling the landau and the escort horses to "spook." Fortunately they were quickly brought under control, and the escort was completed successfully.

The last day of the Canadian National Exhibition usually resulted in rowdiness during the night and this became progressively worse each year. The end of the 1984 "Ex" found gangs of youth roaming the grounds, looting vendors' booths and vandalizing other property.

To counter this trend the police force began to assign more officers on duty at the "Ex" during the final night; this included a large contingent of mounted officers deployed on the grounds. Troubled events like this seem to feed off themselves, ultimately becoming an attraction to those bent on trouble making. People hear the stories of the "fun" from the year before, and more show up looking for a repeat of the action.

Closing of the Canadian National Exhibition would become an important mounted detail for the next ten years. Closing the Exhibition Grounds early, with a large police presence patrolling the grounds ended the tradition of anti-social behaviour.

PC Jim Bradford on patrol in Etobicoke.
Photograph, Toronto Police Museum.

The Mounted Unit was asked to do more about the problem of motorcycles in parks. A story in the *Toronto Star* on July 21 reported arrests of citizens and the Mounted Unit's response to the illicit use of motorbikes. A second story appeared on July 27 describing the problem: "Mounted Police, trail bikers clash in Scarborough." Officers from 4 District Stable paid special attention to the area and, between June 17 and July 25, they investigated forty-six individuals riding motorcycles in the area. Twenty-five people were charged with trespassing and twenty-one issued with cautions. The *Star* also reported that area residents were concerned with the possible cutbacks to the Mounted Unit. [30]

One of the most contentious events of the year took place at Litton Systems in Etobicoke. This high-tech company produced guidance systems for American cruise missiles. The Canadian Government had given the United States permission to test these missiles in northern Canada, a decision which was protested across the country, and which caused the Litton Systems Plant to become the focal point of anti-cruise missile protests in Toronto.

On November 11, Remembrance Day, a large protest was planned for outside of the Rexdale factory. Sixteen horses were detailed to the plant for crowd control. The police had information that the protesters were planning to storm the factory property, and enter the building. Horses were used proactively, with foot details to keep the crowd from the property. The Inspector reported, "It was evident that this show of force disrupted the plans of the demonstrators to enter the Litton Property."[31]

Over the next few years Litton Systems became the scene of many mounted crowd control duties. A domestic terrorist group based in Squamish, British Columbia eventually set off a car bomb on the front lawn of the factory. A number of police officers were seriously injured in the blast. Legitimate protest groups ceased holding their demonstrations at Litton Systems, and disassociated themselves from this act of violence.

The rock group, The Who, returned to Toronto for another concert at Maple Leaf Gardens. A number of young people had been trampled to death at a previous Who concert in Cincinnati, which caused the press to give extensive coverage to the Toronto appearance. Eight officers were deployed at the Gardens by the Mounted Unit to assist with crowd control.

The Unit supplied horses at eighteen other crowd-management details during the year. On one occasion a call for assistance came from Paid Duty Officers at Maple Leaf Gardens, an AC DC concert was in progress and the crowd was going "wild" causing major concern about what would happen when people started exiting the building.

Four mounted officers managed to make it to the Gardens and started to patrol Carlton Street. A number of windows were broken out on the upper levels of the stadium and people began to hurl projectiles at the horses and officers on the street below. At the end of the show the crowd poured onto the street, and surrounded numerous cars and streetcars. They began rocking cars violently in an attempt to roll them on their sides with the occupants still inside. Finally cars and streetcars were rescued from the tumult and escorted through to safety by the mounted officers who were then ordered to clear Carlton Street—which they accomplished despite the trail of projectiles and firecrackers thrown at the horses. The officer in charge of the detail notified Inspector Johnson that had it not been for the prompt action of the mounted men, the situation could easily have degenerated into a riot.

A remount trainer, was badly injured during the latter part of 1984. He was riding a remount in Sunnybrook Park when it began raining. Slowly he started putting on his raincoat, because his horse had never been exposed to the coat before. The horse bolted cantering across the grass. When it reached the roadway and stepped on the pavement the horse slipped and fell, crushing the officer's leg. The constable was transported to Sunnybrook Hospital by ambulance. His leg was badly broken and required immediate surgery. After a short stay at home, he returned to duty at Sunnybrook Stable still wearing a cast. He continued to train remounts at the Unit despite a permanent disability caused by the fracture, until his retirement.

PC Jim Bradford and "Brutus," August 1982.
Photograph, Fred Thornhill, Toronto Sun.

PC Jim McAleer checks a parking meter to see if it is working properly before writing a parking ticket. The horse is on the sidewalk because of heavy traffic on Eglinton Avenue East. November 2, 1984. Photograph, Edward Regan, Globe and Mail Newspaper.

Mounted Unit Baseball Team Front row, Left to right: Peter Scribner, Greg Robertson, Bill Wardle, Ken Whalley, Mac Lyons. Rear row, Left to right: Jim Davis, Ken Cassidy, Mike Roberts, Roy Butler, unknown, Lenny Kotsopoulos, Mike Brooks.

A Mounted Unit van and two-horse trailer.

Photographs, Author's Collection.

PRODUCTIVITY DURING A THREE MONTH PERIOD IN 1985	
Summonses	207
48 Hour Reports	17
Parking Tags	2,417
Arrests	15
Person Investigated	467
Accidents Investigated	6

1985

The Mounted Unit had a busy year, providing mounted details for crowd control duties at forty-two demonstrations, entertainment and sports events. Mounted officers were sent to pro and anti-abortion rallies taking place at the Morgentaler Abortion Clinic on Harbord Street. These demonstrations and counter demonstrations continued until a court order was granted restricting what the anti-abortionists could do. A number of mounted details were sent to the Litton Systems factory, which was still attracting anti-cruise missile demonstrators.

The Ontario Jockey Club asked the Mounted Unit to assume responsibility for operating the landau carriage used to carry important guests at special events, and the Lieutenant Governor at the opening of Parliament. Constable Nick Spearen was sent on a training course to learn to drive and harness the landau teams.

On June 20th, five Metro Toronto police horses were sold to the Jockey Club for training on the landau. These horses were deleted from the unit strength, but kept and used by the Mounted Unit for regular patrol when not required for landau duties. Unfortunately, police mount "Prince" died of Colic on June 22nd while training for landau duty at the Canadian Carriage Driving Centre. Once the training was complete, the horses were returned to the Unit barn where they continued to receive weekly training in harness. The landau officers drove the carriage for the Queen Mother at the Queen's Plate, the opening of the Provincial Legislature and provided eight escorts at the Royal Winter Fair.

The arrangement with the Jockey Club meant that the Unit was now at its mandated strength of forty-two horses. In addition, the Unit still had access to the five Jockey Club horses. Personnel strength of the Unit dropped to sixty-four officers of all ranks.

Staff Inspector Edwin Johnson retired after forty years of police service. Staff Sergeant Robert Heenan was promoted to Inspector and remained at the Mounted Unit as the officer in charge. Sergeant Patrick Woulfe was promoted to staff sergeant and Constable Barry Gerard was promoted to sergeant. The transfer request of Constable Cathy Farrell was accepted and held on file at the Unit. When an opening became available she would be transferred to the unit to become Toronto's first female mounted officer.

The Mounted Unit provided escorts for fifty parades in Metropolitan Toronto. It also sent officers to participate in two out-of-town parades: the Unionville Festival Parade was led by two mounted officers, and Constable Ken Cassidy was sent to the Barrie Race Track for the International Police Sulky Drivers Race against M.S. Mounted officers also attended seventy-two public relations events including local

ROYAL STROLL
PRINCESS ANNE is closely guarded as she makes her way to the trustees' lounge for the running of the Canadian Oaks at Woodbine yesterday. She also received a royal salute.

PC Bob Bagshaw salutes as Princess Anne leaves the landau at the Queen's Plate. Inspector Heenan is giving a sword salute in the background. Photograph, Toronto Sun.

fairs, street parties, school details, etc.

The Mounted Unit was becoming more involved in high priority policing details. Officers were being assigned to regular patrols of high crime areas. Mobile park patrols continued to patrol problem areas within the park system.

The Unit participated in crowd control training with foot patrol officers from 14 Division and 52 Division. Most of the demonstrations attended by the Mounted Unit were also policed by members of the divisional foot patrols. The combined training sessions gave foot officers a chance to work with the horses and provided a "crowd" for the horses to work. The Unit conducted 2,301 visitors through formal tours of its stables. Many more people dropped in for informal tours of the facilities.

The Unit Commander of 42 Division requested that mounted officers pay special attention to complaint areas within his division's parks. The five officers at 4 District Stable patrolled these areas, charged sixty-seven persons with Liquor License Act Offences, and cautioned twenty-three others. They dealt with the motorcycle complaints by stopping and charging eighty-three trail bike riders with various offences. At the end of the summer, the 42 Division

Inspector reported that residents of his division were very pleased with the police response to their complaints.

On Tuesday October 15th, Constable Clarence Sauve was killed in an accident on Gerrard Street East while driving his motorcycle to work at the C.N.E. stable. Sauve had joined the force in 1967 and served with the Mounted Unit since 1973. He was very well known in the French speaking community and founded the French Council of the Knights of Columbus, in addition to organizing French athletic leagues. The forty-three year old officer was survived by his wife and two children, the oldest of which, Alain, was a Metropolitan Toronto Police Cadet.

PC Clarence Sauve

The Inspection Audit Team of the Metropolitan Toronto Police Force visited the Mounted Unit again during 1985. Their final report was released in February 1986. Inspector Heenan felt that although most of his officers viewed the visit with trepidation, it was in fact good for the Mounted Unit. The Audit Team's report turned out to be very positive, especially when compared to the 1980 Productivity Report or the Hinkling and Johnson Report. The Audit Team even recommended the number of mounted constables be increased from fifty-five to sixty, and made positive recommendations regarding the use of horses in crowd control. It stressed the importance of good communications between the Mounted Unit and the different police divisions, attendance at demonstrations, and the need to have the crime analyst point out where the mounted would have maximum effect. The report pointed to the successful accomplishments and productivity of the Unit when its resources were deployed properly, and provided examples of how continuous complaints for things like break and enters had been eliminated after mounted patrols were been placed in the areas at the peak break and enter times.

One interesting proposal made in the report was to have the Mounted Unit assume policing duties on the Toronto Islands. This would have freed up the personnel from 52 Division who were assigned there. The Unit would have been increased in size to accommodate the extra duties involved.

Unfortunately, the plan was turned down. In 1993, the Marine Unit did exactly what the Mounted Unit had been asked to do in 1985 and took over the policing of the Islands. Accordingly, The Marine Unit was increased in staff after the 1993 Program Review Team review. The Mounted Unit was reduced in size that same year.

PC Jim Bradford grooming his mount. Photograph, Toronto Police Museum.

Police Mount Casey

Horses have very distinct personalities, and the individuality of some police horses made them legends within the Mounted Unit. During the 1970s and 80s, "Casey" was one such horse.

"Casey" was very intelligent and feared nothing. He was a very dominant horse, with a mean streak that could be unleashed instantly on an unsuspecting horse or police officer.

When "Casey" was with other horses, he would stand quietly, until his rider relaxed, waiting for the right moment to lunge out and attack another horse. "Casey's" brother, "Stormy," was also a police horse but the two could not work together. As soon as they came into close proximity, "Casey" would attempt to kick or bite his sibling.

"Casey" liked to torment officers of the Mounted Unit. Officers always needed to be on guard around him. "Casey" enjoyed chasing officers out of his stall during muck out. His favourite pasttime was biting policemen; few mounted officers of that era did not experience a nip from "Casey's" teeth.

On August 29, 1986, "Casey" was being ridden along the Lakeshore just west of the C.N.E. grounds. The ground gave way underneath him, causing "Casey" to fall into a sinkhole up to his neck. The horse had to be rescued by the fire department which dug a trench so he could walk out. Any normal horse would have panicked in this situation. "Casey" calmly waited to be freed, showing no signs of distress.

Despite these vices, "Casey" was a top police horse. Once he left the stable "Casey" knew he was on the job. He would modify his behaviour, and never attempted to bite a child or adult that came to pat him on the street. In crowd management, "Casey" would lead other horses into any situation.

When the time came to sell "Casey," mounted officers working nearby came to watch him leave. As "Casey" was being led to the trailer, he stretched forward and bit the officer leading him.

It seemed such a fitting way for "Casey" to say goodbye.

Photograph, Fred Thornhill, Toronto Sun.

"Casey" comes out of the hole. Paul Greenaway standing left, has pulled so hard that Casey's headkit has come off in his hand. PC Ray Roushias standing centre and PC Don Mawson standing on the right. Photograph, Peter Lee, Toronto Star.

1986

The Metropolitan Toronto Police Mounted Unit had been in continual operation for one hundred years. A number of initiatives were planned to help celebrate the Unit's centennial. Constable Roy Butler produced a documentary video about the history of the Unit, and the video unit of the force also prepared a presentation for in-house viewing and for use in divisional training sessions. For the first time in many years, a group photograph was taken of the mounted officers.

Constable Roy Butler co-ordinated the production of a 100th Anniversary limited edition print—a historical collage depicting different scenes from the Mounted Unit's first hundred years. Noted equestrian artist, Eileen Bordessa, painted the collage and the original was presented to Inspector Edwin Johnson at his retirement party. Each member of the Unit was also presented with a commemorative belt buckle with their badge number engraved on the back.

The Mounted Unit received a plaque commemorating its 100th Anniversary from Captain Mark Phillips, husband of England's Princess Anne. The presentation took place in August during the Loblaws Classic Horse Show at Sunnybrook Park. In return, the Inspector presented Captain Phillips with one of the Limited Edition 100th anniversary collages. The Mounted Unit received further tributes at the Canadian National Exhibition, The Royal Winter Fair, Ontario Jockey Club events and the Metropolitan Toronto Police Games.

The Mounted Unit inducted its first female officer in its continuing "endeavours to be progressive."[37] Constable Cathy Farrell was transferred to the unit. A major media blitz accompanied her arrival. Female washrooms and change rooms did not exist at any of the stables. A number of alterations had to be made to buildings to accommodate female officers who had received approval to transfer to the Unit.

The horse-drawn landau carriage was used extensively during the year. Lieutenant Governor Lincoln Alexander rode to the opening of the Provincial Legislature in the landau accompanied by a mounted escort: the landau and a mounted security escort were also provided for Princess Anne and the Governor General of Canada, Madam Sauvé. Premier of Ontario, David Peterson, was provided with a landau escort at the World Dressage Championship in Newmarket, Ontario.

A number of other dignitaries visiting Toronto were also provided use of the landau and mounted escorts, including special guests of the Royal Winter Fair. Six constables were assigned part-time landau duties.

The Unit received over three hundred requests to attend various parades, special events and crowd-control details. Thirty-three high profile crowd-management events were attended, including rock concerts, an anti-apartheid demonstration, the Caribana festival and the visit of the Premier of Italy. Mounted officers were sent to one-hundred-and-eight community relations details during the year and escorted fifty parades in ceremonial dress. Approximately sixty-five hundred people were given tours of the stables during the hundredth anniversary year.

Mounted officers serviced more continuous complaints than ever, the majority about disturbances and the illegal use of trail bikes in parks. Officers issued 935 summonses, a twenty-six percent increase over 1985. A total of 9,416 parking tags were issued, an eighty-three percent increase over the previous year. While on patrol, officers investigated 1,521 persons for various reasons.

Mounted Unit crime analyst, Constable Paul Dean, correlated crime statistics and complaints with regard to parks, advising the sergeants of noticeable trends to which assigned personnel could respond. One example of an identified trend was in Allen Gardens where twenty robbery offences and eight assaults occurred during the year. This became a priority patrol for the unit. On many occasions, however, officers were taken off these details to provide other services such as searches, crowd control, etc.

The force sold its aged, unreliable nine-horse tractor-trailer, replacing it with two new Ford dual-wheel pick-up trucks and four-horse trailers. Having two smaller vehicles available instead of one large one, improved deployment options available to the Unit.

INJURED ON DUTY 1980-1985

Duties	No.	No's. Resulting in time off work
Training	8	2
Patrol	13	4
Grooming	5	3
Stable Duties	20	5
Reoccurring	7	2

JULY 1985

PC Dave Hannaford at the Police Association Picnic on Centre Island. Photograph, Toronto Police Association.

THE MOUNTED UNIT IN 1986

LOCATION	PERSONNEL	
Mounted Headquarters	Inspector	1
Sunnybrook Park	Staff Sergeants	2
	Sergeants	6
	Constables	23
	Horses	17
C.N.E. Stable	Constables	22
	Horses	18
2 District Stable	Constables	5
Etobicoke	Horses	6
4 District Stable	Constables	5
Scarborough	Horses	5
TOTAL:	64 officers of all ranks	
	46 Horses	

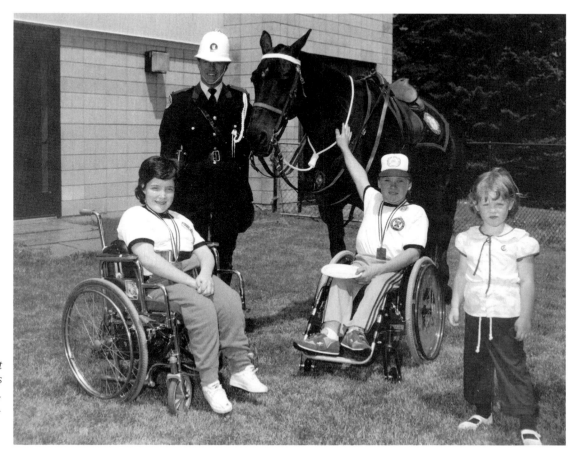

PC Clarence Sauve and "Sally" at the Variety Village Special Olympics in Scarborough. Photograph, Toronto Police Museum.

Constable Roy Butler modelling an 1886 era Toronto Police uniform at Black Creek Pioneer Village. Photograph, Toronto Police Museum.

Constable Roy Butler organized most of the activities which took place during the Mounted Unit's 100th anniversary celebrations. Here he is wearing a 1957-era Metro Police uniform and 1960s Mounted Unit tack. Photograph, Toronto Police Museum.

Captain Mark Phillips at the Loblaws Classic Horse Show with Deputy Chief Scott (centre) and Inspector Heenan (right). Photograph, Toronto Mounted Unit.

The staff of the 4 District Stable in Scarborough. Left to right: PC Greg Woods, PC John Machnik, PC Bill Wardle, S/Sgt Pat Woulfe, PC Ron Gilbert, PC Ken Cassidy, PC Jim Davis. Photograph, Author's Collection.

The Mounted Unit's 100th Anniversary photograph, taken in Sunnybrook Park in April 1986. Photograph, Toronto Police Service.

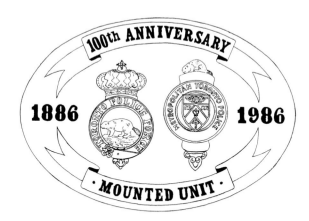

Above: the Mounted Units 100th Anniversary logo. This design was used on all official stationary, insignia and belt buckles that were issued during the year. The centre of the logo displays the two styles of bit bosses used by the Mounted Unit. The bit boss on the far left was used from 1886 until 1965. The one on the right was introduced in 1966 with new ceremonial dress uniform and saddle blankets.

Back row, mounted: Don Vincent, Bob Sutton, Jim McAleer, Peter Scribner, Bob Green, Bob Wright, Fred Lloyd, Ken Cassidy, Tom Matier, Nick Spearen, Bert McKeown, Bill Mathers, Rick Vandusen, Mike Roberts, Mike Best, Andy Currie, Paul Dean, Charlie Gleed.

Middle row, standing: Greg Woods, Jeff Rogers, Jon Van Hetveld, Rick Mamak, Bill Wardle, Peter Cousins, Bill Lyons, Jim Bradford, Lenny Kotsopoulos, Ron Gilbert, Steve Devost, Steve Niemirowski, Dennis Rowbotham, Al Parks, Cathy Farrell, Dave Dalziel, Ray Roushias, Greg Ladner, Tony Pietrantonio, Steve Derbyshire, Graham Acott, Bob Bagshaw, Paul Greenaway, John Dower, John Machnik, Ken Whalley, Mike Brooks, Don Mawson, Conrad Myiers (Blacksmith).

Front row, sitting: Sgt Malcolm Lyons, Sgt Tony Smith, Sgt Warren Pollard, S/Sgt James Stafford, Inspector Robert Heenan, S/Sgt Patrick Woulfe, Sgt Bill Macey, Sgt Barry Gerard, PC Jim Davis.

Absent: Sgt Al Read, Nick Nisavic, Al Bowman, Jim Barger, Greg Robertson, Roy Butler, Dave Curtis, John Feather, Doug Miller, Al McKechnie.

Exercising mounts in Sunnybrook Park. Left to right: PC Dean, PC McAleer, PC Dower, PC Hannaford.

Left to right: PC McAleer, PC Dean, PC Hannaford, PC Dower. Photographs, John Mahler, Toronto Star.

The Mounted Unit's first female mounted officer, PC Cathy Farrell. Photograph, Blue Line Magazine.

The Metropolitan Toronto Police Association recognizes the Mounted Unit's 100th anniversary.
Photograph, Toronto Police Association.

The Mounted Unit's 100th Anniversary collage. The pictures depict significant events that took place during the Mounted Unit's first century of operation. Painted by Eileen Bordessa.

The Anti-Apartheid Demonstration

PC McAleer and Sgt Sandwell working the crowd at the Anti-Apartheid demonstration.
Photograph, Keith Beaty, Toronto Star.

A large anti-Apartheid demonstration took place at the University of Toronto in February 1986 when the South African Ambassador to Canada, Glenn Babb, came to the campus to defend his country's policies. The *Toronto Star* reported that two mounted police officers were called in after a few demonstrators tried to remove the metal barriers separating the crowd from the hall where Babb was speaking. The officers pushed back the crowd of three hundred people amid flying snowballs and shouts of "Prussians!"

The Star reported, "When it seemed that the protesters were about to topple the fence, five mounted police came out from behind the rear of the building and two rode into the crowd, forcing the startled demonstrators to scatter." Snow balls came from the rear of the crowd, but those near the fence moved back to get away from the horses.

The other horses then moved in and formed a barrier between the crowd and the fence. A University of Toronto math professor was incensed by the use of horses. "I think it is disgusting for them to ride into us with horses. Where are the people who believe in free speech? They only believe in free speech for criminals." The police defended the use of the horses on the grounds that the barrier had to be maintained. Had the fence come down numerous people might have been hurt.

No members of the crowd were injured during the demonstration. One man who pulled a riding crop from a mounted officer's hand was taken away by police, but released with no charges laid. After the police had cleared the crowd from the fence, protestors moved to the side of the building where they hoped to disrupt the meeting inside by shouting and striking the building with hands and sticks.[1]

1   *Toronto Star.* February, 1986.

The Mounted Unit and Crowd Control
The Preventative Approach

The Inspection team report released in February 1986 had this to say about crowd control:

Crowd Control details have historically been a no-win situation for the Force as a whole, but especially the Mounted Unit. There is no doubt we will displease at least one side of the issue regardless of the decisions made. For this reason we must be ever mindful of the purpose of police intervention at scenes of civil disobedience or demonstrations, i.e., to keep the peace and prevent crimes.

The most difficult decision for a commander in these situations when the peace is breached, is to implement the right level of intervention that will restore order.

The Audit Team, through experience and acquired knowledge, believes a deficiency exists in deployment strategy when the prevention aspect is ignored or downplayed to the point where only 'calling in the cavalry' and force will restore order.

Using mounted personnel in a strategic, planned manner addresses both the prevention and control factors in crowd control. While our recommendation is addressed to the Mounted Unit, we believe it necessary to involve persons with expertise in many areas of policing to develop a viable procedure.

The main point was that we were not using the mounted unit to prevent problems. The mounted was only being used to solve the problems once they had occurred. The Audit committee recommended that when an event is anticipated, the mounted men should be deployed in small numbers even before the crowd arrives. Their numbers should be increased as the crowd increases. This would accomplish three main purposes:

1. *The crowd, from its inception, sees mounted officers patrolling the area of the gathering. This then is not an unusual show of force but simply the police officers assigned to this detail. They are then an accepted complement of police control.*
2. *The mounted officers would analyse the crowd and its makeup as they gather. The mounted officer has several advantages over the foot patrolman, he can see into the crowd from his position on his mount, where the footman is limited to the first few rows of people. From this vantage point the mounted officer can survey the crowd for any signs of trouble, including an early warning of everyone armed with offensive weapons.*
3. *Although it is hard to define or measure, there is a certain rapport that builds between a mounted officer and the citizenry. People will approach a police officer on horseback where they would not approach a foot patrolman. This rapport also develops in large crowd/demonstration situations. It does not, however, have an opportunity to develop when the mounted unit is called into a situation which has already turned ugly. This can best be described as calling in the cavalry.[1]*

The above observations helped to bring the Mounted Unit into a more proactive mode in its crowd control details. This was a positive move for the Mounted Unit, the Police Force, the people being policed at these events, and all the citizens of Metropolitan Toronto.

1   *Internal Audit.* 1986.

1987 This was one of the Mounted Unit's busiest years with over three-hundred-and-fifty formal requests for mounted officers' assistance received. A mounted presence was provided at one-hundred-and-twenty different public relations duties and escorts at forty-three parades. The number of continuing complaints about activities in parks dropped, probably do to the effectiveness of mounted patrols during the previous years.

The Mounted Unit produced a "Public Order – Mounted Guideline" for the use of field officers. It was developed to provide senior officers, and other members of the police force, with an outline of what the Mounted Unit could do to assist them. As more officers became familiar with the role of the Mounted Unit, the demand for its services increased. The Unit received seventy-four requests for crowd control assistance and twenty-four for help in missing persons searches.

The landau and mounted escort were provided to Lieutenant Governor Lincoln Alexander at the opening of the Legislature. Prince Andrew and Sarah Fergusson, the Duke and Duchess of York, visited Toronto in July. Mounted officers assisted with crowd control at their reception at the New City Hall, in addition to providing mounted security escort and the landau for their attendance at the Queen's Plate Race.

The Mayor of Scarborough requested increased mounted patrols within her city. The Metropolitan Toronto Zoo also requested that the Mounted Unit provide more patrols in its vicinity. A number of incidents had occurred around the Zoo property: one young child was injured by a Zoo animal while trespassing at the perimeter fence. As a result, the Mounted Unit's authorized strength was increased and the additional constables were sent to 4 District Stable to strengthen Scarborough park patrols, paying special attention to the Zoo.

Constables Bob Bagshaw and Greg Vanderhart were allowed to travel to Washington, D.C. to compete in the National Police Equestrian Competition, the first time that members of the Unit had been permitted to compete outside of the city. Both officers placed well in a field of ninety competitors.

Members of the Metropolitan Toronto Auxiliary Police Force made application to be assigned to the Mounted Unit. Unit management debated the idea, before forming a

PC Doug Miller at Sunnyside Beach, February 25, 1987. Photograph, Dick Loek, Toronto Star.

structured policy for the involvement of auxiliary officers. The unit commander agreed to begin interviews with interested auxiliary officers who were qualified equestrians.

Twelve officers took a special "A" Class licence course which qualified them to drive the new four-horse vehicle combinations. The International Chief's of Police conference was held in Toronto: mounted officers performed an obstacle course for their entertainment during a tattoo at the C.N.E. Coliseum.

The year ended with about fifty-five thousand people attending the annual New Years Eve party at Nathan Phillips Square. Fights broke out and eighteen stores on Yonge Street were looted when the mood of the crowd turned ugly. Some $100,000.00 worth of merchandise was stolen, during the night. About sixty persons were injured and twenty-one arrested for various offences. Mounted officers were used to disperse the unruly gangs of people. The *Toronto Sun*, January 2, reported that one rookie constable was attacked by members of the crowd when he tried to make the first arrest of his career. He "was knocked down, roughed up and had his uniform torn before being rescued by two policemen on horseback."[38]

Sergeant Ernest Sandwell retired and Sergeant Anthony Smith was promoted to staff sergeant. Sergeant David Hannaford and Sergeant Scott McConachie, both former mounted constables, replaced them.

PC John Machnik and "Andrew" make a new friend at the Variety Village Special Olympics. Photograph, Toronto Police Museum.

One of the new dual-wheel pickup trucks, with its four-horse trailer. Photograph, Toronto Police Museum.

PC Mike Brooks chasing a fan off the field at the Blue Jays home opener. Photograph, Dale Brazao, Toronto Star.

QUEEN'S PLATE

The Queen's Plate July 19, 1987. Staff Inspector Heenan is riding on the wheel. Sgt Warren Pollard is the front right marker. PC Bob Bagshaw and PC Jim Bradford are on the rear seat. PC Nick Spearen (left) and PC Steve Devost are riding postillion. Photograph, Toronto Sun.

PC Wardle riding "Susan" and PC Cassidy riding "Caesar" return from a search for an escaped prisoner. Photograph, Norm Betts, Toronto Sun.

Police officers detailed to search a park after the body of a young murder victim was discovered. Photograph, Jim Garnett, Toronto Sun.

The Postal Strike June 1987

In June 1987, Canada Post's outside workers went on strike. In response, the Post Office hired replacement workers. Mounted officers were used to assist buses carrying these people through the picket lines. Vehicles carrying the mail in and out of the sorting plants had to be escorted as well. There were numerous altercations during the strike as the horses had to keep the driveways clear using force. Fortunately no serious injuries occurred during the dispute.

Later that same year, the inside workers at Canada Post struck. Again the Corporation used replacement workers to keep the mail moving. There were no major confrontations involving the Mounted Unit during this second postal dispute. Several labour union leaders were upset that police horses had been used during the June strike. The Mounted Unit was asked not to send horses to the Labour Day Parade. No mounted officers have participated in the Toronto Labour Day parade since.

An angry striker attacks a police horse and mounted sergeant. He is arrested a short time later and taken into custody.

Photographs, Paul Henry, Toronto Sun.

A striking postal worker challenges a police horse to a fight.

Foot officers form a cordon to allow vehicles to enter the Eastern Avenue sorting station. Mounted officers patrol beside them to prevent confrontations between the strikers and foot officers.

Photograph, Toronto Sun.

Escorting Lieutenant Governor Lincoln Alexander to the opening of the Legislature at Queen's Park. Nov. 3, 1987.
Left to right: PC Bob Bagshaw, PC Jim Bradford, S/Sgt Pat Woulfe. Photograph, McKenna, Globe and Mail.

Deputy Chief Bill Kerr and Staff Inspector Bob Heenan leading a parade up Yonge Street. Deputy Chief Kerr received his mounted training as a member of the R.C.M.P.. He was the first Toronto Police Command Officer to ride with the Mounted Unit since the 1930s. Photograph, Author's Collection.

1988 Three-hundred-and-sixty-five formal requests for mounted officers were received in 1988, a twenty-five-percent increase over the previous year. The officers were in great demand at public-relations events and parades. The main focus of the Unit continued to be a high police visibility in neighbourhoods, and the enforcement of the laws in the park system. The success of the mounted patrols led to a further reduction in the number of continuous complaints the police received regarding people causing disturbances, liquor offences and motorcycles in parks.

Toronto hosted the G-7 world leaders at their Economic Summit in June. There was a very high security risk associated to the event; a number of major demonstrations were anticipated. To prepare for the expected events, members of the Unit were sent for a special two-day training course taught by members of the new Public Order Unit. Horses and officers began receiving more crowd management training at the Unit level as well. The majority of the demonstrations which occurred during the G-7 summit were peaceful, and the Mounted Unit was actively involved on only a few occasions.

In 1988, the Unit began embarking on a program to improve equitation skills. This required a search for greater expertise which extended beyond Toronto. Sergeants Barry Gerard and Al Read, and Constable Steve Devost, were sent to the Canadian Police College in Ottawa, to the Royal Canadian Mounted Police Riding Clinic. The Mounties also sent two of their instructors to Toronto to conduct a Mounted Clinic for six members of the Unit.

The landau maintained a busy schedule providing Postillion escorts at a number of events. In June, the landau and mounted officers provided the dignitaries at the Canadian Carriage Association with an escort. The Mounted Unit provided the landau and a security escort for Princess Margaret at the Queen's Plate Race at Woodbine Race Track. The landau was also used at the 100th Anniversary celebration of the Ontario Agricultural and Food Ministry. A mounted escort and the landau were sent to Hamilton Ontario for the American Federal Bureau of Investigation Convention. The landau also provided seven escorts at the Royal Winter Fair including one for Her Royal Highness, Princess Anne, The Princess Royal.

On February 11, Konrad Myiers retired as the contract blacksmith. Konrad had been fifteen when he started work as a blacksmith apprentice fifty years before in his native Germany. Konrad lived outside of Toronto and would drive into the city to shoe police horses. It took him two days to

Police Chief Jack Marks (above). Marks was on hand to send off retiring police blacksmith Konrad Myiers. Photograph, Bill Sandford, Toronto Sun.

Police mount "Susan" making friends in the trailer. Photograph, Author's Collection.

cover all of the stables and he would usually sleep in his van at one of the barns. Konrad was very popular with members of the Unit and a large party was held in his honour after his retirement.

Gerry Haywood a former mounted constable, turned blacksmith, was awarded the new shoeing contract. Gerry had been one of the Mounted Unit's horse trainers before he resigned from the police force to practice blacksmithing full time.

Staff Sergeant Stafford retired during the year, to be replaced by Staff Sergeant Jim Jones. Sergeant Bill Macey transferred off of the Unit and Sergeant Howie Peers replaced him. By the end of the year, there was one auxiliary police officer riding the Units' horses and three more auxiliaries waiting for transfer to the Unit. All three would have to complete three years of service with the Auxiliary Force before being advanced to the Unit.

During a troop training session at the Canadian National Exhibition Stable police mount "Brigadier" kicked police mount "Princess," who suffered a compound fracture to her leg. Officers were able to restrain "Princess," and immobilize the leg as best they could, but the veterinarian was called, and "Princess" had to be put down.

Constable Gerry Haywood as a member of the Mounted Unit.

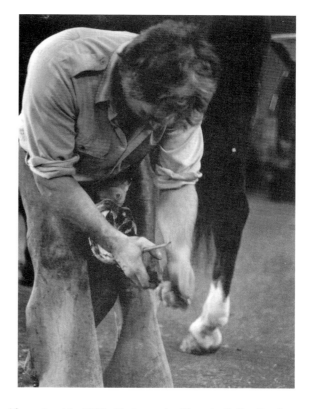

Former Mounted Unit constable Gerry Haywood was awarded the blacksmith contract in 1988. Photographs, Toronto Police Service.

Patrolling the lake front.
Photograph, The Toronto Sun.

Start your engines... Constable Allan Bowman and "Charlie" enjoy a laugh yesterday as they stand by a race car driven by Mike Hardt. Several race cars were on hand at the C.N.E. to help promote the Molson Indy weekend. July 18-20. The event was run in and around the C.N.E. grounds.
Photograph, Hugh Wesley, Toronto Sun.

PC Jim Patterson and "Andrew," with PC Bill Wardle and "Susan" wading in Lake Ontario at Rouge Beach Park.

Exercising horses on the beach is an excellent way of thoroughly cleaning the horse's feet.
Photographs, Author's Collection.

Top Right: officers preparing to rehearse the escort at the 1988 Queen's Plate.

Top Left: PC Jim Bradford and PC Nick Spearen ready to begin the rehearsal on the landau.

Photographs, Author's Collection

Left: A police horse rearing up during the Caribana Parade on University Avenue.

This is an extremely dangerous situation and the officer should remove the horse from the area immediately. Any horse who shows a tendency to rear up at events is sold off as being unsuitable for police work.
Photograph, Tibor Kolley, Globe and Mail.

The G-7 Economic Summit

One of the most important events in Toronto during 1988 was the G-7 Economic Summit. The leaders of the western world came to Toronto for G-7 meetings in the last week of June. The G-7 Summit was immediately followed by the annual Anarchist Convention, planned for the July 1st weekend. The Metropolitan Toronto Police, Royal Canadian Mounted Police and the Ontario Provincial Police all were involved in the policing of this event. A lot of planning and preparation was done to ensure the success of the Summit and the safety of the world leaders attending.

There had been major threats to public order and terrorist activities during G-7 Summits in other counties. A new Public Order Unit was recruited from qualified members of the Metropolitan Toronto Police Force. These officers received advanced training in crowd-management tactics, crowd psychology and other related topics. Most of the training was based on the public order drill of the Metropolitan Police in England. Mounted officers trained with the Public Order Unit and also received a special public order course taught by Public Order Unit instructors.

Days off were cancelled and the entire Mounted Unit was called to work during the Economic Summit. The only officers not on duty were those on annual leave. At least one officer voluntarily changed his leave dates to be part of the detail. Officers worked up to eighteen hours each day in extremely hot weather.

In this photograph mounted officers are training with the members of the Public Order Unit under the Gardner Expressway. Front row, Left to right: PC W. Lyons, PC T. Matier, PC R. Bagshaw, PC J.Davis, PC G. Ladner. Rear row: PC J. Rogers. Photograph, Toronto Police Service.

Fifty mounted officers were divided into troops and assigned to several of different sites throughout the city. The extraordinary planning that was done ensured that there were no major problems during the summit. Some peaceful protest marches took place and the anarchists caused minor problems on the last day. Horses were used to disperse these groups once public safety was threatened. All told Toronto's G-7 Summit was a very successful event for the Government of Canada, the City of Toronto and the Metropolitan Toronto Police Force.

The south end detail standing by near the summit meeting sites on Front Street.

The G-7 Conference. PC Don Vincent maintains his composure as he side passes "Star" into a crowd of masked anarchists outside the United States Consulate. The protestor in the foreground has grabbed hold of the reins in a failed attempt to take control of the horse. PC Vincent has attached both of the reins to the curb portion of the universal bit in "Star's" mouth. This was probably because "Star" had just come out of training a few months prior to this incident, July 5, 1988. Photograph, John McNeill, Globe and Mail.

The north end detail. PC Wardle, PC Acott, PC Bagshaw, PC Pietrantonio, PC Brooks, PC Niemirowski, Sgt Pollard, PC Dower, PC Vanderhart.

Passing the time at the summit, PC Acott, PC Wardle, PC Vanderhart and PC Bagshaw. Photographs, Author's Collection.

1989 Mounted officers continued mobile patrols of problem areas within park systems. A number of police divisions requested high visibility mounted patrols be conducted in their high crime areas. During the year the Unit received three-hundred-and-forty requests for its mounted services.

Officers were also sent to fifty-two different events for crowd control duties and attended forty-four demonstrations. Only one labour dispute during the year required the attendance of members of the Unit, but members of the Unit did attend 154 public relations details. Officers of the Unit led forty-three parades, in addition to providing ten security escorts for dignitaries.

Major renovations took place at the Sunnybrook Stable. Officers moved all office and change-room equipment into rented trailers while a two-story addition was added to the building to provide a larger office and reception areas. The change rooms were also enlarged, and a proper female washroom was added. This new facility was a great improvement over the cramped quarters that the Unit once used.

Winter patrol in Scarborough. Photograph, Author's Collection.

Mounted officers rehearsing for a landau escort and mounted security detail. Front row, Left to right: PC Ken Cassidy, PC Tom Matier, PC Lenny Kotsopoulos, PC Peter Cousins. Photograph, Toronto Police Mounted Unit.

Police Constable Robert Wright

On March 27th, 1990, the Mounted Unit was conducting a troop training exercise in the indoor ring at the Horse Palace. During the training constable Robert Wright collapsed in the saddle and fell to the ground. He ceased breathing and officers rendering first aid were unable to find a pulse. Constable Peter Cousins immediately began C.P.R. and tried to keep Bob alive with the assistance of other officers until an ambulance arrived, but he never regained consciousness.

Bob Wright was probably the hardest working and well-liked member of the Mounted Unit. He had exceptional riding ability and took first-class care of the horses. His appearance was always immaculate: he maintained high standards for himself and expected the same of others.

He was a native of England and had served in Algeria in the early 1960s as a member of the French Foreign Legion. He joined this elite military force under an assumed name as the British government frowned on its nationals serving France. He is mentioned in a history of the Legion as Bob White, the quiet Englishman. He was fluently bilingual and kept up his language skills by reading French language newspapers.

After he left the Foreign Legion, Bob became an airline steward and travelled the world. He later immigrated to Canada where he joined the Metropolitan Toronto Police Force on September 12th, 1967, as constable number 2903. He transferred to the Mounted Unit soon after joining the force.

Bob was assigned to ride a chestnut mare by the name of "Princess." He had been given the horse because she required an extremely competent and patient rider. She was known to be difficult to ride, but Bob accepted the challenge and began to work with her. Before long they had established a close bond as Bob took the time to slowly correct her bad behaviour.

Constable Robert "Bob" Wright at the New City Hall. Photograph, Toronto Police Service Museum.

On October 28, 1988, "Princess" was kicked by another horse during troop training in the indoor ring at the Horse Palace. She received a compound fracture to the leg and was put to sleep by veterinarians from the Humane Society. When Bob died less than two years later, it was at the same spot in the ring where he had lost his beloved "Princess."

The members of the Mounted Unit purchased two plaques to commemorate Bob's service with the unit and they were hung with framed photographs of him at the Canadian National Exhibition Stable and Mounted Headquarters. "A fine mounted man, a perfect gentleman who will be truly missed."[1] Bob Wright set the example of what every mounted officer should be.

1 *Memorial plaque*, Mounted Headquarters.

1990

In February, Inspector Robert Heenan was promoted to the rank of Staff Inspector. Along with the promotion came the responsibility of forming the Police Dog Services Unit. The Metropolitan Toronto Police Commission had approved the purchase of police service dogs, permanently assigning officers to the new unit. The management of the Mounted Unit was given the task of establishing and administering this new police function.

The management of Police Dog Services remains under the direction of the Mounted Unit Inspector. The name of the Mounted Unit was later officially changed to Mounted and Police Dog Services. This book, however, records only the mounted officers' story. The important and often exciting events in which the Police Dog Services have been involved merits a separate history.

1990 was a busy year at the Mounted Unit with a 12.3% increase in details over 1989. Officers continued to focus their efforts on high crime areas and mobile park patrols.

At the request of the Chief of Police, William McCormack, the Musical Ride was revived under the direction of Staff Sergeant Woulfe. The Ride presented performances at The Metropolitan Toronto Police Amateur Athletic Association Field Day, the Canadian National Exhibition, and the Royal Winter Fair.

There were numerous protests during the latter part of 1990 and early 1991 because of the Kuwait crisis. These included rallies at the United States Consulate, and marches through downtown streets. There were very few problems. A number of sit-ins took place which temporarily disrupted traffic, but these were short-lived as mounted officers maintained a visible presence, and took appropriate action when necessary.

The Mounted Unit and Police Dog Services had a very successful year at the promotion boards. PCs Gord Graffman, Jim Patterson, Tod Whitfield, and Dave Dalziel all achieved the rank of sergeant but were promoted off the Unit. Constable Ed Reed of the Police Dog Services was also promoted but remained at the Unit.

The Mounted Unit acquired its first full-time civilian employee. Leslie Dainard would perform the clerical duties previously done by police officers. The clerk was also responsible for much of the paper work of the Police Dog Services.

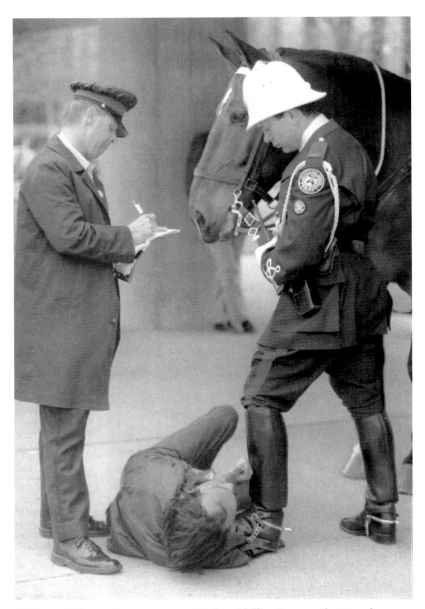

PC Doug Miller making an arrest at Nathan Phillips Square. *Photograph, Veronica Henri,* Toronto Sun.

1990 STATISTICS

DETAILS	1990	1991	1992
Public Relations	174	208	226
Parades	43	34	39
Crowd Control	65	55	88
Searches	38	32	19
Demonstrations	43	55	52
Escorts	8	8	7
Musical Rides	8	8	7
Lectures	3	10	1
Strikes	n/a	5	4
TOTALS	**382**	**421**	**443**

Modern Mounted Officers

THE CRITERIA FOR SELECTING OFFICERS FOR MOUNTED DUTY HAS BEEN THE SAME FOR YEARS. THEY MUST BE A FIRST CLASS CONSTABLE, MEANING THEY HAVE AT LEAST THREE YEARS EXPERIENCE IN REGULAR POLICE DUTIES. MOST APPLICANTS TO THE UNIT HAD A MINIMUM OF FIVE YEARS OF POLICE SERVICE.

Recruit class graduation at Sunnybrook Park, 1992. Left to right: PC Bob Bowen, PC Larry Bullock, PC Dawn McCauley. Photograph, Toronto Police Mounted Unit.

Weight should not be more than 180 pounds. In a 1964 magazine interview, the reporter described Inspector Johnson as "6'4," lithe and slim as are many of the riders. Regulations set 195 pounds as the maximum weight, and so far no members had eaten themselves out of the ranks."[1] Officers keep their weight in line for the sake of the horses.

On average, the fitness level of mounted officers is above average for police service. Most work out regularly and about one third of the unit's personnel take time to test for the voluntary Ontario Police Fitness Award each year. Officers wishing to transfer to the Mounted Unit must pass a physical fitness test at the Police College before they are accepted for training.

Officers do a lot of physical work at the Mounted Unit. Horseback riding itself is a good form of exercise. In one 1983 newspaper article, Inspector Johnson stated that he felt "The men of the Mounted Unit are the fittest on the force."[2]

The Mounted Unit was one of the last areas in the police force to accept policewomen into its ranks. The amount of physical work involved was one reason cited for refusing to allow females in the unit. Finally, in 1986, as part of the Unit's continuing "endeavours to be progressive," a female constable was introduced into the Unit for training.[3] More female officers have been accepted since and today women compose about fifteen per cent of the Mounted Unit's personnel.

A police officer wishing to transfer to the Mounted Unit must apply personally to the Unit Commander. The Commander, or his designate, will explain the functions of the Unit and the duties required of the officer should he or she be successful in their application. Applicants the Inspector deemed as suitable must complete a Mounted Unit application.

Most officers have had no previous riding experience. In fact, many Inspectors avoid recruiting officers with previous equestrian instruction. One of the former trainers, Constable Michael Best explains why, "We don't normally take 'experienced' riders in the Mounted Unit. Our men receive 120 hours of equestrian-related training in total, of which 80 hours is indoors and the balance outside. The primary reason for not taking experienced horsemen is that the intensive training period leaves no time for 'unlearning' bad habits."[4]

Once an application is accepted, the applicant must attend the Police College for a physical fitness test. A Mounted Unit supervisor checks the personal employment file. Applicants passing the physical test, with an exemplary service record, are invited to attend at the Unit for a fifteen-week equitation course during the winter months. A mounted officer assumes the recruit's place in the field division for the duration of the training course.

The 1986 Inspection Unit report recommended that mounted officers be sent to the field for ten weeks during the winter to get exposure to police work. To replace them, officers wishing to transfer to the Mounted Unit from the field would be brought in for mounted training. Thus mounted officers would receive updated police training while providing the mounted Inspector with a pool of qualified candidates for future openings.

Mounted Unit recruits are put through a gruelling course in equitation as they are trained in a balanced style of military riding by serving officers on the unit. They learn to become competent at the walk, trot, canter, side pass, pivot and reverse. Recruits spend a number of half days in the classroom learning different theories and studying equine topics. They are required to write a series of written examinations during the training and to achieve a minimum pass mark. Recruits are also subjected to equitation tests to measure their progress during the course.

By the end of training a recruit must be able to demonstrate his or her riding abilities both in the riding ring and on the street. The current recruit courses emphasize policing from horseback. The recruit is placed in a number of policing situations designed to prove competence and ability to get the job done while on horseback.

Should a recruit pass the riding examinations, he or she is given a final written examination. When successful in all aspects of the course, recruits receive their mounted diplomas at a formal graduation ceremony.

Recruits must return to their original police divisions. Their applications are kept on file at the Mounted Unit until a suitable vacancy occurs. The officer is notified of the opening and asked to submit a formal transfer request, after which he or she is soon accepted into the Unit.

The real learning begins however, once an officer becomes a full-time member of the Unit. In 1981 Inspector Johnson said, "Experience is the only way for the officers to learn, just like the horses." Inspector Johnson believed it took five years to make an officer a fully trained member of the Mounted Unit.[5]

PC John Feather on winter patrol. Photograph, Toronto Sun.

1 Unknown Magazine Article.
2 *Globe and Mail.* October 22, 1983.
3 Unit Commanders Annual Report. 1986.
4 *Toronto Star*, Sunday September 1, 1985.
5 *Unit Commanders Annual Report.* 1981.

The Queen's Plate

Photographs, Toronto Police Mounted Unit c. 1990.

Horses Injured On Duty

Very few police horses have been injured while on patrol. This is a tribute to the training of both horses and the riders. Police horses function in an environment that is contrary to their natural instincts. They are trained to remain in situations where their inborn impulse is to run.

Riders must always be aware of the conditions around them. Factors they must consider are; volume of traffic, speed of vehicles, road condition, etc. Riders must always look ahead to observe what is unfolding of interest and concern to their horse. When there is construction work or pedestrian activity they must assess what effect this may have on the mount. Riders quickly become aware of what activities bother their horses. Then they work with the horse to overcome its fears.

Some injuries are not preventable. In the photograph PC Jim Davis points out the injury to the leg of police mount "Susan" after an irate driver intentionally drove into her after receiving a $20.00 parking ticket.

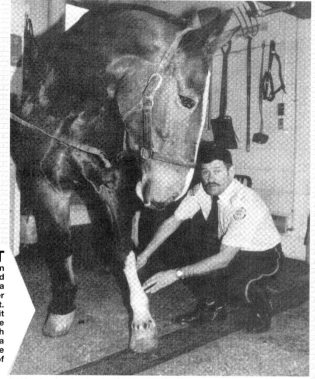

IT WASN'T A FAIR FIGHT
Const. Jim Davis examines the leg of Susan of Four District's mounted unit. She suffered a swollen leg yesterday after she was hit by a car at Eglinton Ave. E. and Kennedy Rd. after Davis gave the driver a $20 parking ticket. The man crumpled the parking tag, threw it away and drove his car into the horse. He then left the scene. police said. Charged with criminal negligence in the operation of a motor vehicle and failing to remain at the scene of an accident is Melvin Poyser, 45, of no fixed address.

Photograph, Toronto Sun.

 **1991** The Mounted Unit had another busy year as details increased 10.2% over 1990. On July 6, the *Toronto Star* headlined a story, "Park rowdyism becoming serious," which described problems taking place in the parks within Metropolitan Toronto. The Parks Commissioner wrote to the Chief of Police, asking that the police do more to ensure the safety of people and property within the park system.[39] Mounted officers began to work a late afternoon shift so that they would be in the parks when many of the problems took place.

Members of the Unit working at mounted headquarters were asked to pay special attention to a public housing project in 54 Division. The area was plagued with drug dealers and those crimes that accompany drug presence. Area residents were victimized by robberies, disturbances, assaults, in addition to numerous gunshots heard during the night time hours.

Mounted officers moved into the area to provide a more visible police presence. Their patrols helped to assure residents of their safety and to scare off undesirables. Crime rates in the neighbourhood dropped, and the Mounted Unit was commended by the Chief of Police on a job well done.

The final night of the 1991 Canadian National Exhibition was the busiest the Unit had ever seen. Large gangs of youths roamed the fair grounds looting vendor stalls and causing mischief. Mounted officers were ordered to clear the grounds just after dark. All the troublemakers were forced out onto Strachan Avenue.

Unfortunately there was a pile of bricks and rock on the corner of Strachan Avenue and Manitoba Drive. The crowd began to throw bricks at the Unit's horses. There were so many bricks flying through the air it appeared as if it was snowing. Pop cans were also stolen from a hot dog vendor and these, too, became missiles. Sergeant Howie Peers received an injury when he was struck in the face with one of the cans. Constable John Feather had his breeches ripped and leg cut open by a flying piece of concrete.

A number of other officers were struck with objects, but not injured. The crowd was quickly moved away from the location by the Mounted Unit, and officers spent the next hour dispersing groups of youths who were smashing windows and trashing streetcars.

Staff Inspector Bob Heenan retired from the Police Service in 1991. Staff Sergeant Jim Jones was promoted to Inspector and placed in charge of the Mounted and Police Dog Services.

Public Order Unit training with foot officers and ambulance personnel. Mounted Left to right: PCs Peter Febel, Doug Miller, Laura Lowson, Ted Gallipeau, Terri Douglas, Sgt Tod Whitfield. Photograph, Toronto Police Service.

The Santa Claus Parade. Left to right: Sgt Al Read, PC Bill Lyons, PC Greg Vanderhart, PC Mike Best, Staff Inspector Bob Heenan, PC John Feather, PC Cathy Farrell, PC Tony Pietrantonio, PC Paul Dean, PC Ray Roushias, PC Jim Patterson, PC Mike Brooks. Photograph, Toronto Police Mounted Unit.

Mounted officers back up police service dogs from three separate police services during a search for an escaped prisoner in the Don Valley. Mounted left to right: PC Larry Bullock, PC Jim Patterson, Sgt Howie Peers. Photograph, John Berry, Toronto Sun.

Paul Greenaway and The Guildwood Bank Hold-Up

On the afternoon of April 26th 1991, an individual armed with a sawed-off shotgun entered a branch of the Bank of Montreal in Scarborough. The man threatened the staff with his weapon and demanded cash, which he was given. PC Paul Greenaway of the Mounted Unit was inside the branch conducting some personal business at the time. The officer was off duty and unarmed.

Constable Greenaway remained silent watching the suspect's movements. After the bandit received his money, he walked past the officer to exit the bank. As he walked out the doors, the suspect placed his weapon in a bag that he was carrying. Constable Greenaway moved quickly to take physical control of the man once the weapon was in the bag, and not readily accessible. After a brief struggle, the suspect was subdued and held by the officer until the police officers responding to the bank alarm arrived.

Constable Greenaway was awarded with a Merit Mark by the Board of Commissioners of Police. The Canadian Bankers Association presented Constable Greenaway with the Canadian Bank's Law Enforcement Award. This award which is in the form of a gold medal was first instituted in 1972 and had only been awarded 149 times.

Constable Greenaway, his wife Susan and two other medal winners were flown to the Canadian Police Chiefs Convention in Victoria, B.C. where their Medals were presented to them.

PC Paul Greenaway in ceremonial uniform, 1994. Photograph, Toronto Police Museum.

PC Doug Miller and PC Jon Vanhetveld on "Rusty" at the Police Christmas Party. Photograph, Toronto Mounted Unit.

PC Jim Patterson on "Andrew" and PC Bill Wardle on "Susan" leading the Scarborough Canada Day Parade. Photograph, Author's Collection.

 **1992** The mounted patrols of parks and high crime areas continued to be the main focus of the Unit. There was a 5.2% increase in the number of mounted duties performed by mounted officers. It was a busy year in crowd control as well. On May 4, a demonstration at the United States Consulate turned violent and Toronto experienced what became known as the Yonge Street Riots.

The Musical Ride was organized for a third year and performed at The Metropolitan Toronto Police Amateur Athletic Association Field Day, the Fergus Highland Games, the Canadian National Exhibition and the Royal Winter Fair.

Often a Unit horse would cast a shoe or a shoe would come loose. The horse had to be "stood down" until the contract blacksmith arrived at the stable for the weekly visit. During the winter, Sergeant Howie Peers and PC Karl Seidel were sent to Seneca College for a fifteen-week blacksmith course. As a result, these officers were able to provide emergency shoeing services and keep horses on the road. The officers also received intensive instruction on the causes of lameness, diseases of the hoof and corrective shoeing. Both officers graduated with high honours and were included on the Dean's Honours list.

Inspector Jim Jones was promoted to the rank of Staff Inspector, and remained in charge of the Mounted and Police Dog Services. During the winter, former mounted Sergeant Dave Hannaford, was killed in a snowmobile accident in Northern Ontario. He was working at 22 Division at the time of his death.

During the spring and summer, the neo-Nazi group, the Heritage Front, became more active, or, at least, more visible in the Toronto area. On a number of occasions mounted officers were called to locations where the Heritage Front was holding rallies. Sometimes confrontations developed, particularly when anti-Nazi groups staged counter demonstrations nearby. The anti-Nazi groups united together into an organization called the Anti-Racist Action (A.R.A.).

On the morning of Sunday, October 25, at one a.m., hundreds of thousands of people poured into the downtown streets. The Toronto Blue Jays baseball team had just beaten the Atlanta Braves in the 11th inning of the final game to win the World Series for the first time. Yonge Street was closed from Bloor to Queen Streets to allow the fans to celebrate on the roadway.

A large contingent of mounted officers helped to patrol the area and the horses did remarkably well considering the noise, fireworks and other distractions that such a large, celebratory crowd always entails.

The St. Patrick's Day parade. Left to right: Sgt Al Read, PC Jeff Rogers, PC Paul Greenaway, PC Jim Bradford, PC Dave Curtis, PC Jim McAleer. Photograph, Author's Collection.

Although the crowd was very loud and boisterous, it was also well controlled and law abiding. Very few problems occurred during the celebrations which lasted until about five a.m.

On the evening of November 13, the neo-Nazi group, Heritage Front, held a meeting at a restaurant located on Bloor Street West at Gladstone Avenue. Members of the A.R.A. had heard about the meeting and surrounded the building. The potential for a violent confrontation could not have been greater.

The local division placed an emergency call for mounted officers to assist them with the crowd. The *Toronto Sun* reported that, "More than three dozen Metro Police officers, including seven on horseback, escorted about 125 members of the Heritage Front through a crowd of Anti-Racist Action Demonstrators. A.R.A. members chanted 'run Nazi scum' and 'garbage' at Heritage Front members. Some swung picket signs and others chased rally participants down the street, hurling obscenities."[40] This was the last major confrontation between the Heritage Front and the A.R.A. during 1992. The friction between these groups would continue into 1993, becoming more aggressive with time.

Many people believe Toronto is the most culturally diverse city in the world. Some ethnic groups in the city have long standing disputes with other ethnic groups over issues in their former homelands. On a few occasions, the police have had to become involved to help keep certain events orderly and to preserve the peace.

On Sunday December 6, members of the newly formed country of Macedonia were given permission to raise their new flag at Mel Lastman Square in the City of North York. Members of the Greek Community, who also view themselves as Macedonians, showed up to disrupt the flag raising. The dispute was over the use of the Macedonian name.

About three thousand members of the two Macedonian communities, "Kicked, punched and hurled insults at each other."[41] All available mounted officers were sent to the site as well as members of the Public Order Unit. Mayor Lastman tried to reason with the

Parade time!
The Blue Jays victory parade rolls ahead tomorrow.
It leaves the Royal York Hotel at 1 p.m. and goes west on Front, north on York, west on Wellington, south on Peter and into the SkyDome. There will be a ceremony inside the Dome at 2 p.m. with free admission.

PC Peter Scribner and "Colonel" at Yonge and Dundas Streets, after the Blue Jays victory. Photograph, Michael Stuparyk, Toronto Sun.

PC Jim Patterson and "Andrew" at Rouge Beach Park. Photograph, Author's Collection.

A mounted officer holds back one side of the Macedonian factions that attended the flag raising at Mel Lastman Square, December 6, 1992. Photograph, Ken Faught, Toronto Star.

crowd, but he too was assaulted. A number of police officers were attacked and a few crowd members were pepper-sprayed by foot patrol officers to bring them under control. The Mounted Unit was used to separate the Macedonian groups.

This is one example of the many situations in which mounted officers find themselves. Usually ninety percent of all mounted details end with no confrontation, and everything amiable. In this instance however, a simple flag raising almost generated into a riot when the rival group appeared on the scene. It is almost impossible to predict which demonstrations, parades or community events may be marred by violence or disputes, sometimes still simmering from "the Old Country."

Demonstrations occurred at the American Consulate almost every weekend. The civil war in the former Yugoslavia brought many diverse groups to the Consulate to let the American Government know their position. The only time there were problems at these demonstrations was when members of opposing factions would show up to either disrupt the current demonstrations, or to express their own counter point of view.

PC Kelly McCoppen patrolling in rush hour. Photograph, Paul Henry, Toronto Sun.

The Yonge Street Riots – May 4, 1992

On Monday May 4, a rally was held at the U.S. Consulate on University Avenue to protest the acquittal of the Los Angeles Policemen charged with the beating of a black man named Rodney King. The beating had been captured on video and widely broadcast around the world. Riots broke out in Los Angeles after the acquittal of the police officers involved. Tensions were also high in Toronto as a member of the Metro Toronto Police Force had shot and killed a black man the previous Saturday.

Some four hundred people attended the rally. A small number of foot patrol officers and ten mounted officers were assigned to work the demonstration. A number of fights broke out when a few "skinheads" showed up to stage a counter protest. The crowd grew more and more agitated as time went on.

Finally, demonstrators left the Consulate and marched to the New City Hall chanting the slogan "no justice, no peace." The crowd had swollen to a thousand protesters. On arrival at Nathan Phillips Square, some people attempted to storm the doors of the New City Hall. Mounted officers formed a line in front of the doors and prevented the crowd from getting in. Officers were pelted with missiles and numerous windows were broken. The *Toronto Sun* reported that one mounted officer was surrounded and his horse hit on the head with a large rock.

With their attempt to get into the New City Hall frustrated by mounted officers, the crowd headed for Yonge Street, where it began to march north smashing one hundred shop windows, looting stores, overturning vendors carts, and causing other mayhem and mischief. Windows of one sporting goods store were smashed and a shotgun taken. Fortunately it was quickly recovered and no shots were fired.

A police car moved ahead of the crowd using its public address system to warn the public of the approaching danger. The crowd swarmed up to Bloor Street, turned westward, then south on Bay Street. By the time it reached Charles Street, one street below Bloor, mounted officers had been authorized to disperse the mob using a minimum of force.

Officers rode into the crowd, breaking it up into small groups, forcing people down side streets. The rest of the night was spent dispersing groups as they formed on Yonge Street. No members of the crowd were injured by actions of Unit horses. Police mount "Trillium" was almost knocked unconscious on Bay Street when a brick struck her. Her legs buckled, but she managed to recover, suffering only a cut to the face.

Police mount "Dora" was struck in the eye with a brick. She was sent to the Veterinary College in Guelph where she underwent surgery. A portion of the pupil had to be removed. Her vision continued to deteriorate and "Dora" reached a point where she could not be sent out at night due to the deleterious effects car headlights had on her vision. In 1995 "Dora" was purchased by her assigned rider, Constable Deb Poulson, and moved to a farm where she continues to live in peace.

A young girl stands in front of the troop of horses once order was restored. Photograph, Toronto Sun.

The following day both the Premier and Solicitor General of Ontario praised the police for the restraint they showed during the riot. Thirty-two persons were arrested during the rampage. Thirty-seven police officers were hurt in the riot and three police horses received noticeable injuries. The following day Yonge Street looked like a war zone and property damage estimates totalled a half-million dollars.

The next night, groups of youths were back roaming around the downtown area looking for trouble. A few more windows were broken, but the police were prepared and nothing like the riot of the night before was allowed to take place. The Mounted Unit was again committed in strength. The one serious incident of note is that Molotov cocktail gasoline bombs were thrown. This was a first in Toronto. Fortunately nobody was injured, and the fires burned out on the pavement.

PC Cathy Farrell holds a get well card while PC Nick Spearen holds a dozen carrots that concerned citizens sent to "Dora." Note the patch over Dora's left eye. Despite the best treatment possible, she never fully recovered from the injury and was sold to her assigned police rider. Photograph, Toronto Police Association.

After the injury suffered by "Dora," Toronto Police horses were issued with protective visors. Photograph, Carol Robbins.

 **1993** At the end of January all of the Mounted Unit's personnel were given the opportunity to attend a two-day seminar in the Veterinary College at the University of Guelph. The staff of the college gave a series of lectures particularly relevant to the care of police horses.

On January 18, Constable William Wardle was promoted to Sergeant and Sergeant Allan Read was made acting staff sergeant. Later in the year, Sergeant Tod Whitfield returned to the Unit and Sergeant Scott McConachie transferred out of the Unit. Personnel strength of the unit had decreased to the point where 4 District Stable was closed down and the officers and horses transferred to the Sunnybrook Stable. Mounted officers continued to patrol Scarborough Parks from the Sunnybrook Stable.

On January 25, members of the Heritage Front were scheduled to appear in court at 361 University Avenue for a hearing into a Human Rights complaint. At previous hearings, anti-racist protestors had demonstrated at the courthouse; confrontations took place which required police horses to separate the two factions. At the January 25 hearing, about 500 demonstrators tried to prevent the Heritage Front from entering court and a violent melee resulted.

The Mounted Unit deployed all of its available horses for the Victoria Day Fireworks Display in May. Horses were assigned to the Ashbridges Bay fireworks display in the Eastern Beaches. There had been minor problems in the past and the police were well prepared to prevent any repetition of the former problems. There was also a fireworks display at Ontario Place.

Large crowds of young people had gathered outside Ontario Place in both the parking lot and on C.N.E. property. There were many gang members observed in the crowd who were looking for trouble. Foot officers assigned to the Ontario Place Fireworks display called the Mounted Unit requesting that horses be sent to assist them.

Four horses arrived from the Beaches to help manage the crowds. One young man was stabbed to death in an Ontario Place parking lot. Mounted officers helped to contain the scene and to move the hostile crowd members away. After the stabbing, more mounted officers were sent from the Beaches and the combined mounted force moved the crowd back to the streetcar loop in the C.N.E. grounds. No more confrontations took place once mounted officers started to move the crowds.

Unfortunately events like this seem to set a kind of tradition amongst those looking for trouble, because of the thrill they bring. This event was no exception. As a result, Victoria Day Fireworks would be accompanied by problems for the next few years.

The Mounted Unit was finally able to obtain eye protection for their mounts. As a result of the injuries suffered by "Dora" during the May 1992 riots, the Unit purchased face shields for its horses. The horses accepted these shields, and they did not adversely effect horse or tack in any way.

The Queen's Plate Race took place on Sunday July 11. Guest of honour was Chief Justice Lamer of the Supreme Court of Canada. The Mounted Unit provided an escort and landau. Performances of the Musical Ride were given at the Metropolitan Toronto Police Amateur Athletic Association Field Day, the Fergus Highland Games, the Canadian National Exhibition and the Royal Winter Fair.

In order to promote Musical Ride performances at the Canadian National Exhibition, it was decided to hold a preview night a few weeks before the opening of the "Ex." With the co-operation of the C.N.E., the Coliseum was booked for a free evening show open to the public.

The show was a great success and included a historical outline of the Mounted Unit, the Royal Canadian Mounted Police Mounted Arms display, a mounted obstacle course, a police dog demonstration and the Musical Ride. Officers from Detroit, Rochester, Munroe County in New York State, the New York City Police, and the Governor General's Horse Guards took part.

The night was dedicated to Staff Sergeant Patrick Woulfe and Sergeant Warren Pollard. Both officers had recently retired from the unit after many years of

Toronto officers attending the Detroit Police Mounted Unit's 100th Anniversary. Left to right: Sgt Barry Gerard, PCs Mike Best, Ron Gilbert, Bob Low.

dedicated service. Pat Woulfe had joined the Mounted Unit in 1957 and served for a total of thirty-six years.

In October, the Toronto Blue Jays won their second World Series by beating the Philadelphia Phillies after an exciting come-from-behind win. This year the celebrating crowds were much larger, with estimates of up to one million people partying on Yonge Street. It was the biggest crowd of its type that Toronto had ever seen.

The police force had a well-prepared crowd-control plan, and there were very few problems. The Unit's horses again proved their value in working with crowds, keeping the celebrants under control until well past dawn.

During the summer and fall, officers of the Program Review Unit reviewed Mounted Unit operations, with the result that the Unit faced severe cutbacks and changes in its mandate. This year marked the Unit's last Musical Ride performance. The last escort of the year was that given to Princess Margaret at the Royal Winter Fair. This would be the final time the landau was driven by members of the Mounted Unit and pulled by police horses.

Opening Yonge Street after a celebration. D Platoon, c. 1993. PC Rowbotham, PC Mamak, PC Poulson, PC Roberts, PC Ladner, Sergeant Ingwersen. Photograph, Toronto Police Mounted Unit.

PC Roy Smith and PC David Miller on duty at the Police Christmas Party. Photograph, Toronto Police Mounted Unit.

Members of E Platoon at an anti-Police demonstration. PC Al Parks, PC Bob Bagshaw, Sgt Warren Pollard, PC Steve Niemirowski, PC Bill Wardle. Photograph, Author's Collection.

The Court House Confrontation

On Monday, January 25th, 1993, the leadership of the Heritage Front white supremacist organization was to appear in a Toronto courtroom in response to a Human Rights Complaint filed against them. At an earlier hearing, a few weeks earlier, anti-racist protesters formed a ring around the courthouse and the Mounted Unit had been used to help clear a passage to permit Heritage Front attendance at the hearing.

Anti-racist groups planned to hold another demonstration at the courthouse during this second court appearance. Early in the morning, approximately five hundred protesters gathered at Queen's Park for a rally. They then marched down University Avenue to the court building. The police officer in charge of the detail requested that the Heritage Front members enter the Court House through an entrance that would avoid a confrontation with the protesters. The request was refused.

Thirty members of the Heritage Front insisted on marching into the court right past the protesters. Heritage Front members, surrounded by a dozen foot police officers, walked across Nathan Phillips Square chanting slogans and playing "Dixie" on a loud speaker. Anti-racist demonstrators retaliated with their own chants.

When the two groups were about one hundred yards apart, the nine mounted officers on scene moved forward to prevent the two groups from coming in contact. As the Heritage Front moved in closer, a number of missiles were thrown at police officers and at Front members. Horses held the crowd of protesters back as the Heritage Front passed the narrow space between the rear of the horses and a fence line.

The Heritage Front members moved into the courthouse without injury, the anger of the crowd redirected at the police, and people marched to police headquarters to continue protesting before dispersing on their own. One foot policeman received a separated shoulder, and two members of the crowd were reported to have been injured in the melee.

This would be the first of many confrontations between the anti-racist groups and the Heritage Front that took place in 1993. Mounted officers were in attendance at most demonstrations and counter demonstrations during the year.

The only other times there was violence between these groups was when the meetings were spontaneous and the mounted unit was not present.

January 25, 1993. Photograph, Geoff George. Toronto Sun.

January 25, 1993. Photograph, Moira Welsh. Toronto Star.

The Canadian National Exhibition Presentation Night

The Mounted Unit wanted to promote its Musical Ride performances at the Canadian National Exhibition. In order to do this, a police horse show was staged a few weeks before the opening of the "Ex."

The show included a historical outline of the Mounted Unit, the Royal Canadian Mounted Police Mounted Arms display, a mounted obstacle course, a police dog demonstration and the Musical Ride.

This was the first variety-type horse show ever sponsored by the Mounted Unit.

PC Jon Vanhetveld on "Toby" singing the national anthems.

PC Nick Spearen driving the landau with guests of honour, the president of the Canadian National Exhibition, the Chair of the Police Services Board, Susan Eng, and Chief of Police William McCormick.

The special guest of honour, winner of the name the horse contest.

Left and right: PC Peter Febel competing In the obstacle course.

Right: A R.C.M.P. officer stabs a dummy during a portion of the Mounted Arms display.

PC Tony Pietrantonio driving the practice wagon with "Billy."

Right: the Mounted Unit "Kick Off" began a Drug Awareness Campaign during the show. These stickers were given out during the evening and at public-relation details that followed.

Don't Horse Around With Drugs!

Metropolitan Toronto Police Mounted Unit

The Musical Ride, Above: the "Carousel."

Above: the "Gates."

Above: the "Charge." Photographs, PC Howard Rosenberg, Toronto Police Service.

The 1993 Program Review

In 1993, the Chief of Police created a new unit within the police service, the "Program Review." This unit was to look at the various units, divisions and bureaus of the police service and "right size them." The economic recession which had been in effect since 1990 was beginning to affect the police budget drastically. The size of the force had been shrinking through attrition, and a new retirement package was introduced to further save money. The police force felt redeployment was one way to bolster the personnel of field units.

The Program Review Committee recommended that the Mounted Unit be cut by just over one third of its strength. The Police Commission and chief of police approved this recommendation. As of December 31, 1993, the unit was reduced as follows:

Constables:	59 to 37
Sergeants :	6 to 5
Staff Sergeants:	2 to 1
Horses:	48 to 30

The mandate of the Mounted Unit was changed. Officers were to concentrate on high visibility policing details in the downtown core and high crime areas. Short term special projects in outlying areas could be taken on, but the Unit was no longer to perform regular park patrols, perform the Musical Ride, or be involved in driving the landau, although the Unit would still provide mounted security escorts for V.I.P.'s.

By mid-November, the Police Commission announced these results to the public. On November 19, the *Globe and Mail* headlined the Unit's reduction in an article titled,"The day music died on the police ride." Two members of the Police Commission, Brian Ashton, and Dennis Flynn, voted against the cuts. Ashton was quoted as saying, "We're getting to the point where we're beginning to tear down all our traditions."[1]

The Chief of Police stated that he was opposed to reductions in the Mounted Unit, and only signed the recommendations because his three deputy chiefs supported the cutbacks. Chief McCormick was quoted in the *Globe and Mail*, "I am diametrically opposed to (cutting) a unit that has not only served us extremely well, but is extremely necessary from the point of view of demonstrations, control and parks in the areas that we have in Metro Toronto."[2]

This time, however, there was no outpouring of public support. No newspapers came to the aid of the Unit, probably because of the way the cuts were presented. The police force emphasized the fact that the Musical Ride and the Landau were being terminated so that officers from these functions, rather than from patrol functions, would be returning to the field units.

Without the public or media support which had been so strong in response to earlier calls for cutback, restructuring of the Mounted Unit took place quickly. The reduced Unit took up its new mandate and carried on.

1 *Globe and Mail*. Friday November 19, 1993.
2 *Globe and Mail*. Friday November 19, 1993.

HORSING AROUND ON THE WAY TO THE FAIR

PC Tony Pietrantonio and PC Nick Spearen driving the practice wagon during training for the 1993 Royal Winter Fair. As a result of the 1993 Program Review, the Mounted Unit relinquished landau duties. Photograph, Jeff Goode, Toronto Star.

Questioning The 1993 Cutbacks

One columnist, *Toronto Star* journalist Rosie DiManno penned a column questioning the wisdom of the cutbacks, but to little avail. Reprinted with permission *Toronto Star* Syndicate.

WHY HOBBLE HORSE UNIT?

The riders sit impressively astride their mounts, their navy riding cloaks – set off elegantly with gold piping – fanning out over the horse's hind quarters. The thick fabric of the uniform is cumbersome but warm, designed primarily to shield the animal's kidneys in chilly weather; the rider is protecting the horse.

Equine coats are rich and glossy, the evidence of vigorous grooming. Bridles and reins jangle merrily. And there's the occasional snort and shudder of communication – horse-talk.

They have been arranged according to shadings of colour. First comes Staff Inspector Jim Jones on his lustrous ebony beast, then the phalanx of black mounts, followed by the bays, with one lovely chestnut bringing up the rear.

At precisely 1 o'clock, they set of across Bloor St. looking beautiful. Clippity-Clop, Clippity-Clop. Such a soothing sound, amid the clatter of downtown traffic.

This is one of those ceremonial occasions for the Mounted Unit of the Metro police, and the continuation of a tradition. It's the mounted police who each year lead the Santa Claus Parade though the streets of Toronto. That, we are assured, will not change. "This will not be the last time that we lead the parade," insists Jones. "There will be a Mounted Unit around for a long time yet."

Certainly the mounted unit, which has been in existence since 1886, has survived other cost-saving schemes before. But last week, as part of an attempt to shave the bloated police-operating budget, the police services board accepted a proposal to bounce 23 officers and 12 horses from a total complement of 42 horses and 59 police constables. The officers would be reassigned to cruisers, although the efficacy of more cops in cars is entirely debatable.

Criminologists argue that crime prevention will have to rely increasingly on the principle of community policing, and the mounted unit is about as community-orientated as law enforcement can get. It's a user-friendly detachment of officers. And, while the unit may be known primarily for its ceremonial appearances – particularly the Musical Ride, which will likely disappear as a result of this $1.5 million cost saving measure – the officers on horseback are cops first and foremost. The Mounted Unit conducts routine patrols, just like their counterparts on foot or in a car. They are invaluable for crowd control and in searches of missing children or Alzheimer patients who have gone astray.

"We are told that there are more efficient ways of doing what they do," says police commissioner Brian Ashton, who is hoping to find private funding to keep the Musical Ride alive.

"But in certain situations, I can't think of anything more useful than a cop on a horse. I'm not sure that police horses should be considered a frill." No officer will be laid off under the plan, although those who will be reassigned have yet to be identified. The police association has no official say in this internal process. "But we'd hope that management would not be autocratic about this and that they'd consider seniority," says association president Art Lymer.

The scheme would appear to save money, on the surface, but how sensible is it, really, to shuffle around officers who have spent years in this specialized discipline, not to mention selling off their highly trained mounts? The horses, a mixed Clyde-Hackney breed, are usually purchased as 3-year-olds, just halter-broken, and may spend their entire period of service yoked to one officer. And breaking up is hard to do.

"I've spent 10 wonderful years here," says Constable Paul Greenaway, after hanging up his tack at the unit's Sunnybrook Stables. "I love the horses and I would love to have retired here. But who knows what is going to happen?"

Greenaway, who as a youngster considered becoming a jockey, has spent most of the past decade riding recently retired "Red." "Looks like maybe we'll be going out together. The association has no input in who gets moved. I think it's going to turn into a personality contest."

As the equine unit shrinks, the canine unit will expand. "I know we need the dogs," concedes Sergeant Tod Whitfield, who joined the Mounted Unit originally in 1988. "They do good work in apprehending criminals."

Dogs are cool, horses are passé.

Happy trails.

PC Dave Miller and Lenny Kotsopoulos at a protest on Bloor Street. A few minutes earlier fights had broken out and one protester was arrested after he tried to remove a policeman's gun. Photograph, Warren Toda, Toronto Sun.

PC Vicki Montgomery and Sgt Bill Wardle, 1993. Photograph, PC Howard Rosenberg.

PC Pat Penny on "Sarge" and Derrick Speirs on "Regent" lead a parade into Fort York. Photograph, Sgt Lorna Kozmik.

Sgt Bill Wardle and "Sutherland" on Shutter Street. Photograph, PC Howard Rosenberg.

 **1994** The reduced Mounted Unit began the new year by moving all its horses, constables, and sergeants to the Canadian National Exhibition Stable. No. 2 District Stable was closed and the Sunnybrook Stable, void of horses, was manned by the staff inspector, staff sergeant, clerk, and quartermaster. Surplus horses were sold for $1.00 each to the Governor General's Horse Guards.

Two of the major recurring themes in the Unit's history had surfaced again. The reduction may have been expected, but what was not anticipated was that the Unit was no longer expected to patrol the outlying areas, parks in particular. Instead of providing a police presence in the suburbs, the Unit would concentrate on high crime and high visibility policing in the downtown core.

The Provincial Government introduced its Social Contract during the spring to reduce spending in reaction to the economic downturn. To avoid laying off government workers, the Social Contract required every government worker to take unpaid days off over the next three years. Members of the police force were also required to take these "Rae Days," named after Premier Bob Rae. The Social Contract generated additional protests and demonstrations for the Mounted Unit to police, but not as many as expected. All of these proved peaceful.

The Victoria Day fireworks display at Ontario Place on May 23 was marred by a disturbance caused by rampaging youths. Citizens in the crowd told police officers that "Their real motive for attending the fireworks display was 'hoping for someone to get killed'."[42] Just like the previous May.

The Mounted Unit leading the funeral parade for murdered Police Constable Tod Bayliss, June 22, 1994. Staff Inspector Jim Jones, 2nd row: Sgt Tod Whitfield, PC Karl Seidel, PC Fred Lloyd, 3rd row: Sgt Bill Wardle, PC Vicki Montgomery, PC Graham Acott, PC Peter Febel. Photograph, Toronto Sun.

Those youths causing the problems never paid the Ontario Place admission. Instead, they remained on the C.N.E. side of the fence chanting, "Its getting dark, its getting dark."[43] As night fell, foot and mounted officers were pelted with bottles and stones, in addition to having fireworks fired at them and their horses. Foot officers were compelled to move back across the bridge to Ontario Place, leaving the mounted officers alone on the Exhibition side. Once authorization to act was given, mounted officers dispersed the unruly part of the crowd.

During July, the World Cup of Soccer was played in the United States. The two finalists were Italy and Brazil. Toronto's large Italian population supported the Italian team with oversize street parties on St. Clair Avenue West after each win. The smaller Brazilian community was joined by the Portuguese community to form a large body of support for the players from Brazil, and these celebrated on College Street near Bathurst Street.

On July 17, Brazil won the final game to take home the World Cup. Both communities partied in their receptive areas until well into the morning. College Street, and St. Clair Avenue West, were shut down as more than 100,000 individuals took to the streets to celebrate. All throughout the World Cup, mounted officers actively policed all post-game celebrations.

The July 18 *Toronto Sun* reported, "The Battle is over. The War goes on," in describing the rivalries between team supporters. "Nowhere were emotions more frazzled than at St. Clair and Lansdowne Avenues, where police on horseback, and officers shoulder to shoulder, kept the fans of the two teams apart."[44]

The Regent Park area of 51 Division near Toronto's downtown was plagued with drug dealers, prostitutes, drug users and assorted criminals during the early summer months. Residents associations had asked the police to do more to combat this increase in crime. The Mounted Unit was requested to assist divisional officers in this special project.

Constables Bob Bowen, Greg Vanderhart, Bob Low and Ted Gallipeau were assigned to work a special detail in the area beginning August 1. The officers focused on the criminal element, making a number of outstanding arrests. This increased pressure drove most of the criminal element out of the neighbourhood, giving its seven thousand residents a well-deserved break from a situation which had been endangering their community.

The *Toronto Star* published an article on the project on Sunday August 14: "The officers come from all units—bicycle, emergency task force, drug squad and, perhaps most effective of all in frightening off the undesirables, the mounted police."[45] This project was a great success and generated much positive feedback from members of the community, politicians, and the press.

The 1994 National Mounted Police Competition was held in Washington, D.C.. Constable Peter Febel and police mount "Billy" won the McCarthy Trophy taking first place in the obstacle course. The trophy was brought back to Toronto and kept on display throughout the next year. It was the first time the McCarthy trophy had left the United States.

Sergeant Jim Patterson returned to the Mounted Unit in October, assuming the duties of Sergeant Peers who became a full-time training sergeant. Enhanced equitation courses were developed: eventually all members of the unit began taking advanced riding lessons during their day shifts.

Left: PC Steve Noble and guests with the plastic horse at a Mounted Unit Open House.
Above: Historical display at a Mounted Unit Open House, Canadian National Exhibition Stable,

Photographs, Author's Collection.

Photograph, Dick Loek, Toronto Star. *PC Greg Ladner and "Harry" on winter patrol in Coronation Park.*

 **1995** The Mounted Unit provided a large contingent for the Victoria Day Fireworks display at Ontario Place. As in previous years, an unruly crowd gathered and one mounted officer was shot in the chest with a Roman candle. The crowd was contained and there were no serious injuries.

Ontario's Provincial election during the spring, saw the Progressive Conservative Party voted into power, on an election platform which involved reducing the deficit by downsizing government and reducing spending. Many social programs and individuals would be affected by the new government's plans.

Almost immediately there was an increase in the number of demonstrations at Queen's Park, a continual stream of protests that seemed to repeat themselves almost daily, through the summer and fall.

On Wednesday, September 28, a large group of protesters tried to storm Queen's Park during the reading of the throne speech. A number of police officers and individuals were injured on the front steps of the Legislature building. A squad of foot officers trapped by the crowd in front of the Legislature doors was assisted by the Mounted Unit, who split the crowd and eased pressure by forming a barrier at the bottom of the stairs.

While on stable duties, Constable Paul Greenaway was kicked in the leg by police mount, "Smokey." The officer's leg was badly broken and he fell to the ground in the stall. "Smokey" continued to kick at Constable Greenaway as he tried to get out of the stall. Acting Sergeant Arlene Fritz was able to pull the constable to safety before he suffered even more serious injuries. Greenaway returned to full-time mounted duties after a six-month recovery.

Auxiliary PC Connie Mahaffey and Staff Inspector Jones after PC Mahaffey became the 1st Auxiliary officer to complete the 15-week basic equitation course. Photograph, courtesy Connie Mahaffey.

A Police Dog Services (P.D.S.) officer and mounted officers deployed in High Park to search for parts of a human body after investigators recovered a man's leg from one of the ponds. Standing: PC Landers (P.D.S.) and Sgt Bill Wardle. Rear: PC Tom Matier "Royal," Auxiliary PC Knapp, PC Jim Bradford "Bruce, PC Larry Bullock, PC Jeff Rogers "Chummy," PC Susan Aitken. Photograph, courtesy Susan Aitken.

Crowd management training with the Public Order Unit. Photograph, Toronto Police Service.

1996

Anti-government protests continued at Queen's Park. The most violent demonstration took place in the spring when student protestors broke through the Legislature Doors and entered the building. Concrete garbage can holders were used as battering rams to destroy the doors which were one hundred years old. Once inside the entrance hall, protesters sat down in the lobby and did not attempt to penetrate into the Legislative Assembly Room.

The majority of students at the demonstration remained outside, evidencing no desire to enter the building. Mounted officers realized that these students posed no threat to anyone and remained off to the side, as there was no need at this point for active crowd management. Students who remained outside continued their peaceful protest. Others, who had stormed the building, (actually the minority) were arrested or removed peacefully from the lobby by foot officers.

The Ontario Public Service Employees Union (O.P.S.E.U.) went on strike during Spring 1996 at over one-hundred-and-fifty locations in Metropolitan Toronto. Protests were peaceful and very few incidents requiring police action occurred. At the opening of the Spring Session of the Legislature, strikers allegedly tried to bar elected Members of the Legislature from entering Queen's Park. Ontario Provincial Police (O.P.P.) were in charge of crowd management, and assisted Members of the Legislature to cross the picket line. Toronto mounted officers on the scene were held on stand-by, and not asked to assist.

A number of confrontations occurred and complaints were made about the incident. A Royal Commission was called to look into the events of the day. Following this incident, the Legislature instituted its own security service to police Queen's Park.

On August 20, the Mounted Unit celebrated its 110th Anniversary by inviting officers from a number of American and Canadian mounted units to Toronto to join in the celebrations. During the day, some guests were taken on a mounted tour of the city. In the evening, the Unit hosted a Mounted Police Show at the Canadian National Exhibition Coliseum as part of the Exhibition's horse-show program.

The lead half section at the Queen's Plate. During a break in the rehearsal Sgt Bill Wardle and PC Bob Bowen listen to instructions. Photograph, courtesy Helen Curtin.

Pages 4-5, 10, 13 and 24-26

DAY OF INACTION ... Metro Police — including this mounted contingent in the financial district — stood on the sidelines yesterday as several thousand protesters took to the streets against the Harris government. The protest's biggest impact was on public transit, closed by illegal pickets.

The front page of the Toronto Sun *following the "Days of Action" protest. PC Greg Vanderhart and "Duke" in the foreground. PC Greg Ladner on his right. Photograph, Craig Robertson,* Toronto Sun.

The Unit was complimented in September when it was invited to send instructors to the National Police Equestrian Colloquium in Lexington, Kentucky. Sergeant Howie Peers and PC Graham Acott attended the course and trained the American officers in crowd management techniques. The organizers and participants were very pleased with the quality of instruction received. Sgt Peers and PC Acott were honoured at the end of the course, as they were made "Kentucky Colonels" by the Kentucky Governor .

On October 25, a coalition of labour organizations sponsored a one-day strike known as the "Days of Action," one of a series of general strikes taking place in major urban centres across Ontario to protest the policies of the Provincial Government. Estimates of crowd numbers vary, but the protests were limited in size and very few problems were reported.

The following day, the Progressive Conservative Party held its annual convention at the Metro Toronto Convention Centre. A protest march was organized and groups from across the Province came to Toronto to take part in the parade. It began at Coronation Park near the C.N.E. grounds, and passed the Convention Centre, ending at Queen's Park where a number of speeches were made.

Law enforcement's major concern was a potential confrontation at the Convention Centre as the marchers passed. However, march organizers had a number of marshals stationed outside the Convention Centre standing alongside the barricade erected by police. They did an excellent job in keeping the parade moving, thus preventing the small minority intent on causing problems from doing so. While there was huge public turnout for the parade, everything was peaceful with no confrontations taking place anywhere along the parade route.

Toronto officers attended equestrian competitions in Prince George's County, Maryland; Nassau County, New York; Hartford, Connecticut; and Livingston County, New York. Numerous trophies and ribbons were brought back from these events. The members of the Unit deservedly earned the reputation as the team to beat.

Crossing the Rouge River while on park patrol. Photograph, Author's Collection.

Warrior's Day Parade, Canadian National Exhibition. Photograph, Author's Collection.

The Volunteer Program

Left to right: E. Szabo, K. Leaver, C. Robbins, H. Wollis, H. Curtin, G. Kondo, J. Dvorakova. Photograph, Toronto Police Mounted Unit.

The 1993 program review of the Mounted Unit resulted in a dramatic reduction of Unit personnel. By 1996, there were not enough officers available to exercise the horses regularly. In order to have every horse ridden daily, the officers would ride two a day. This meant officers spent additional time in the barn preparing the horses for patrol, while the horses were only getting ridden for half a day. This was insufficient exercise: as a ten-mile ride is considered "light work" for Commercial Grade horses.

Sergeant Howie Peers explored the feasibility of developing a volunteer rider program. Civilian volunteers would be allowed to ride Unit horses in the exercise ring at the Horse Palace. A number of volunteer applications were accepted for a trial period. Each volunteer had to commit to riding a minimum of twice a week, and each had to pass a riding test supervised by Sergeant Peers. Only advanced riders with proven ability were accepted into the program.

The volunteers met all expectations and the program was expanded to include ten riders. At the height of the volunteer program, officers were back to riding one horse daily, and the horses were getting significantly more exercise. The program proved to be beneficial both to the Unit, and to the volunteers who were able to enhance their equestrian skills at no financial cost to themselves.

In 1997, the Unit began accepting volunteers who were massage-therapy students. These volunteers were able to apply their skills in helping horses that were prone to lameness or stiff muscles.

The Mounted Unit has also included a volunteer equestrian class during the annual police horse show at the Canadian National Exhibition.

The volunteer program fits in well with the strategic plan of the Toronto police service. The use of civilian volunteers is encouraged all through the service. The Mounted Unit helped to lead the way by implementing an initiative which corresponded directly with the goals and objectives of the police service.

Below: A casual picture of Mounted Unit volunteer riders.
Top, Left to right: E. Szabo, H. Wollis, J. Dvorakova.
Bottom, Left to right: K. Leaver, H. Curtin, G. Kondo, C Robbins.
Photograph, Toronto Police Mounted Unit.

The mounted detail at the New Year's Eve Party at Nathan Phillips Square December 31, 1996.
Left to right: unidentified, PC Greg Ladner, PC Peter Febel, PC Peter Spurling, Sgt Dale Guest, PC Dave Miller, PC Pat Penny.

1997

On February 20, two mounted officers responded to a call regarding an assault in progress at Spadina Avenue and Queen's Quay. The suspect in the assault was sitting in a T.T.C. bus that was parked in the streetcar loop. The mounted officers boarded the bus with two officers from 52 Division. They were speaking to the accused when, as the *Toronto Star* reported, the man "suddenly stood up and produced 'an object', which was later determined to be a hammer."[46]

One of the officers from 52 Division fatally shot the man as he threatened them with the hammer. A thorough investigation of the circumstances surrounding the shooting was conducted by the Province's Special Investigations Unit (S.I.U.). The independent investigators determined that the officer was justified in using his firearm to defend himself and the others on the bus.

The high quality of training and the reputation of the Toronto Mounted Unit were well known throughout North America. The excellent showing of Toronto's horses at competitions helped to promote this fact. In April the unit provided a training course for Constable Derrick McGougan of the Calgary, Alberta Police and Officer Scott Sorensen of the Reno, Nevada Police.

In June, Constables Bob Bowen and Graham Acott attended the Police Public Safety Day in Laval, Quebec. These officers joined members of the R.C.M.P. and a number of Quebec officers in putting on displays of mounted police competence.

The same weekend Sergeant Dale Guest and PC Peter Spurling journeyed to Rochester, New York to take part in a competition marking the 20th Anniversary of the Rochester Police Mounted Unit.

On Saturday April 20, social activists organized a protest to take place at 88 Carlton Street. The aim of the protesters was to gain entrance to an abandoned apartment building sitting vacant while the owner waited for permission to demolish it. Some 60 squatters had been evicted from the building the year before.

The *Toronto Sun* reported, "An unruly mob of labour-backed protesters clashed with police yesterday while trying to break into an abandoned building and claim it as housing for the homeless. With nightsticks in hand, a dozen officers struggled to push back a throng of about 200 demonstrators."[47]

Mounted officers move in to help the foot officers at 88 Carlton Street. Photograph, Boris Spremo, Toronto Star.

Mounted officers at the scene moved in and assisted foot police in moving the crowds back from the building, and escorting prisoners to the patrol wagons. There were no injuries.

On June 30, Queen Elizabeth II and Prince Philip attended the Queen's Plate Race. The Mounted Unit provided a full ceremonial escort for the royal couple. Staff Inspector Jim Jones and Acting Staff Sergeant Patterson were invited to attend a reception at the racetrack and were presented to the Queen.

On Friday July 25, the Mounted Unit Drill Team and the Pipes and Drums performed in the Police Tattoo held at the Port Perry Fair Grounds. The officers were well received and named the highlight of the show.

Caribana Weekend found larger crowds of people than anticipated on Yonge Street. The Mounted Unit was sent in to back up foot policeman assigned to patrol the street. At about 4:00 a.m. Saturday, a man was shot to death on Yonge Street near Elm Street. There were large crowds of people at the scene at the time, and Mounted Officers moved in to clear the crime scene of spectators. Then, officers returned to general patrolling, in hopes of preventing further problems.

Toronto's Entertainment District, located north of the Sky Dome continued to grow in popularity causing the Mounted Unit to dedicate one entire shift of officers to police the area on Thursday, Friday and Saturday nights. These officers provided a highly visible police presence throughout the area, especially between 1:30 a.m. and 3:00 a.m. when patrons left the nightclubs.

On Tuesday August 20, 1997, the Mounted Unit held its annual competition and show at the Canadian National Exhibition Coliseum. A number of different classes were exhibited including a demonstration of the "Bag Game." Honoured guests in the Royal Box were retired Inspectors Geoffrey Rumble, a mounted officer from the 1930s, and former mounted unit commanders Ed Johnson and Bob Heenan. One officer was injured while riding at the show. He was taken to The Toronto Hospital and treated for a broken pelvis and internal injuries.

Late in the year, a large demand was made for the services of the Mounted Unit as all major teacher's unions went on strike to protest changes to the education system. A number of sizable demonstrations required the attendance of mounted officers particularly when the teachers were joined by labour organizations to protest policies of the provincial government.

Soon after the teachers returned to work, the postal workers went on strike. Unlike the postal strike of 1987, the Post Office used no replacement workers, a decision which greatly lessened potential problems on all picket lines. Mounted officers were deployed to assist with a number of peaceful parades held by the striking workers and their sympathizers.

One strike that did involve the Mounted Unit was at a company in Scarborough. Striking workers and their supporters unlawfully entered the company's building and

PC Bob Bowen and Sgt Wardle with two R.C.M.P. officers at the National Police Memorial Service on Parliament Hill in Ottawa. Photograph, Author's Collection.

refused to leave. The company obtained a court order which directed workers to leave the premises. Should they not leave voluntarily, the Sherrif was instructed to order police to evict them.

Both the Public Safety Unit and Mounted Unit were called out in preparation for possible eviction of the workers. Fortunately, however, a negotiated settlement resulted in the workers leaving the building and there was no confrontation. The strike was resolved soon after the workers vacated the factory.

On Wednesday, November 19, former President of the United States, George Bush, attended a ceremony at the University of Toronto where he was awarded an honorary degree. About 300 protesters demonstrated outside the building. When Bush attempted to leave the building, his motorcade was surrounded by demonstrators. Mounted officers were called in to clear the crowd, which they did without incident.

A number of small incidents took place in Vancouver during the same week, as rioters protested the visit to Canada of the President of the Peoples Republic of China. The following weekend, he arrived in Toronto for a conference. The Mounted Unit attended the Metro Convention Centre to assist with anticipated crowd control problems, but the protests were peaceful, and there was no repeat of the violence that taken place in Vancouver.

The Unit's final crowd control detail of the year was New Years Eve, when mounted officers were deployed at Mel Lastman Square in North York, on the Yonge Street Strip below Bloor, and at New City Hall for the annual concert. Extremely cold temperatures kept crowds off the streets, which made a very quiet night for all.

A/S/Sgt Al Read, Sgt Howie Peers and Chief of Police David Boothby. Sgt Peers gave Chief Boothby riding instructions to prepare him for riding in special events and parades. Photograph, Toronto Police Service.

SPECIAL DUTIES

	1994	1995	1996	1997
Public Relations	48	50	104	136
Crowd Management	25	37	65	26
Demonstrations	35	22	57	75
Searches	6	10	21	20
Strikes	5	0	2	3
Public Order Training	1	2	5	1
Parades	7	6	20	19
Escorts	1	1	1	1
Totals	**128**	**128**	**266**	**281**

Right and below: PC Greg Woods "Tammy" and PC Paul Greenaway "General" attending the annual blessing of the animals at Saint James Cathedral.

Photographs, Michael Hudson Photography.

The 1997 Queen's Plate

Above: Escorting the landau to the drop off. Photograph, Michael Burns Photography.

Left: The troop just prior to the "Eyes Right" salute. Photograph, Author's Collection.

The Queen and Prince Phillip exit the landau. The Toronto police are no longer responsible for driving the landau. Royal Canadian Mounted Police officers and horses are brought to Toronto from Ottawa to drive the carriage. The landau is taken to Woodbine by former Toronto mounted constable, Nick Spearen. The Toronto Mounted Unit supplies 20 officers as escorts. The Ontario Jockey Club pays all costs including officers' salaries. Photograph, Author's Collection.

The Toronto Police Service 1998–2000

The teacher checks out "Toby" during a school visit.
Photograph, Author's Collection.

1998 As of January 1, the Municipality of Metropolitan Toronto became history and the new City of Toronto was created as the six separate municipalities of Metropolitan Toronto were combined under one level of municipal government. The Metropolitan Toronto police Service became the Toronto police service.

On January 26, the Mounted Unit dispatched a number of officers to 33 Division to help search for a missing elderly man. While walking down a ravine hill, police mount "Harry" slipped in the snow and slid to the bottom. His rider injured his knee requiring extensive surgery and has been unable to ride since. The body of the missing man was located about 100 feet from where "Harry" had fallen.

Mounted officers attended all major demonstrations and other crowd-management events. When not involved in special details, the Unit concentrated its patrols in the downtown core.

Beginning in May, the Entertainment District detail was reactivated, and the area was patrolled from 7:00 p.m. to 3:00 a.m., Thursday, Friday and Saturday nights.

The Royal Canadian Mounted Police celebrated their 125th Anniversary in 1998. The Mounted Unit was requested to represent the Toronto police service by participating in a series of tattoos hosted by the R.C.M.P.. The Unit's Drill Team participated in those held in Toronto, London, and Collingwood Ontario. The R.C.M.P. absorbed all costs and even provided accommodation for both horses and riders.

On August 10, the Mounted Unit led the funeral procession for slain police officer William Hancox. Police officers and other emergency service workers from across North America came to the funeral. The funeral cortege was more than two kilometres long. Within days of the murder two female suspects were arrested for the killing and later sentenced to life in prison.

Halton Regional Police requested the Drill Team to be part of their 25th Anniversary Tattoo, which was to take place on August 22 in Burlington, Ontario. A few days prior to the tattoo it became known that the Annual National Anarchist Convention was taking place in Toronto. A major demonstration was planned for the day of the Tattoo. Halton Regional Police were informed that the Drill Team might not be available, depending on the demonstration.

The night prior to the protest, mounted officers observed a gathering of anarchists in a west-end park. Two people dressed in police-type uniforms were walking on stilts with dummy horse bodies attached to their waists. They were sidepassing through the crowd pretending to strike participants with riding crops. It appeared to be a type of training exercise, or they were acting out a skit. The fact that the crowd could be training to confront police horses was a concern to the officers creating the plan to deal with the demonstration.

The Mounted Unit assigned 18 horses to help police the demonstration that assembled at Trinity Bellwoods Park in 14 Division and marched eastbound on Queen Street West. Both foot and mounted officers patrolled the parade route. The crowd marched to the front doors of 52 Division police station where they held an anti-police demonstration that included the two fake police horses and riders. The demonstration broke up peacefully at 4:00 p.m. and the drill team members left for Burlington.

The officers arrived at the site at 5:45 p.m. and immediately changed into their ceremonial dress uniforms. Some of the civilian volunteers had gone to the site earlier in the afternoon and ensured the field was properly marked, water and other needs procured for the horses. By 6:00 p.m. the officers were mounted and standing by to escort former Lieutenant Governor Lincoln Alexander into the stadium for the opening ceremonies. Good planning and the dedication of the officers and mounted unit volunteers ensured that they were able to police a major demonstration and still represent Toronto at the Halton Police Tattoo.

In October the Royal Winter Fair and the Toronto Sun newspaper announced that they would donate a horse to the Mounted Unit. The Sun ran a "name the horse" contest with a computer donated by Compaq Computers as the prize to the person who sent in the winning name. The winning entry was "Sunshine Boy" submitted by Mr. Craig Dyer of Shelburne, Ontario. The horse was presented to Chief of Police David Boothby during the Royal Winter Fair.

The rehearsal ride on the morning of the Queen's Plate. Photograph, Author's Collection.

Hay, Sunshine!

He's a horse with a mission – and a name. Sunshine Boy was the winning entry – submitted by Craig Dyer, left – in our contest to find a fitting moniker for the Toronto Police mounted unit's newest recruit. Sunshine Boy got to chum up with the boss, Police Chief David Boothby, at last night's presentation at the Royal Agricultural Winter Fair.

Story: Page 7

Mr. Craig Dyer, winner of the "Name The Horse Contest" with Chief David Boothby and "Sunshine Boy." Photograph, Stan Behal, Toronto Sun.

1999

At 8:00 p.m. on January 13, a fire broke out in the Medieval Times building at the Canadian National Exhibition. There were a dozen show horses in the stable, located in the rear of the historic building. The police radio room called in the alarm to Exhibition Stable, notifying the Unit officers of the fire. Fortunately it was lunchtime: all of D Platoon was in the building. Officers grabbed lead shanks for the horses and raced to the rescue.

Mounted officers and a few staff from Medieval Times entered the building and removed the horses. It was not an easy task because these horses, had rarely seen the outdoors, and rescuers were required to lead them through a maze of fire trucks and fire hoses which seemed to be everywhere. Outside, the temperature was 18 degrees below zero, extremely cold for horses used to a warm indoor environment. With some difficulty, all horses were safely transferred to the Horse Palace, and bedded down beside the police stable.

The last professional hockey game to be played at Maple Leaf Gardens took place on Saturday February 13. By game time, large crowds had turned out to witness the event. The Gardens was sold out and the crowds waiting outside were so large that Carlton Street had to be shut off to vehicular traffic to accommodate them. As the night went on, the crowd became louder and more boisterous .

Mounted officers were deployed on each side of the Gardens main doors: they also assisted streetcars safely through the crowd. The officers were called in to clear the front of the building when police inside the Gardens became

Sgt Bill Wardle leading "Gonzo" away from the fire scene at Medieval Times. Photograph, Ken Faught, Toronto Star.

concerned that the weight of the crowd pushing on the glass doors would cause the doors to give way or the glass to break and seriously injure someone. People were safely cleared from the sidewalk and horses were used to hold the crowd back until foot officers relieved them.

When fans began to leave the arena at the end of the game, crowds outside the Gardens tried to gain entry to the building. The crush of people trying to enter the arena, stopped the flow of those exiting. Crowds were increasingly compressed in the stairwells and on escalators inside Maple Leaf Gardens. It was a very dangerous situation for those people who could be caught in the crush.

The horses moved in again to clear the sidewalk. Once clear, the horses set up corridors through which people could exit the building. As the crowd left the building, horses cleared Carlton Street, opening it to traffic. Horses also prevented a possible accident from occurring inside the building by providing people an exit path for leaving the Gardens. The actions of the Mounted Unit during the final game at Maple Leaf Gardens is one of the best examples of why the police horse remains indispensable.

PC Moreen Smith hangs on while "Teddy" rears up after being "spooked" at Maple Leaf Gardens, February 13, 1999. Photograph, Rick Madonik, Toronto Star.

The Mounted Unit was called upon to help police a number of demonstrations held by Toronto's Kurdish community. Similar demonstrations in Ottawa and Montreal had turned violent. One R.C.M.P. officer in Ottawa was set on fire when a Molotov cocktail was thrown at him. Protestors in Toronto were peaceful and, except for a few minor incidents, no problems occurred.

Activists for the mentally ill and other community members staged demonstrations to voice their concerns over the Edmund Yu shooting on Queen's Quay. A Coroner's inquest into the shooting took place during the year and protests continued for its duration.

Toronto's Serbian community had been holding demonstrations at the U.S. Consulate for many years. By February, troubles in the Balkans were growing at an alarming rate. The size and frequency of the demonstrations increased as the problems worsened. Mounted officers were always assigned to help monitor these protests.

During the first week of April, a "Right to Life" Conference was held at a hotel on Dixon Road in Etobicoke. The abortion issue often brings out strong opposed factions, and on Saturday April 7, a number of different groups organized a mass demonstration to protest the conference. Some 500 pro-choice protestors were bussed to the conference site for the demonstration.

Public Safety Unit officers from both the Toronto Police Service and the Peel Regional Police Service surrounded the hotel. Dixon Road was closed to traffic to allow protestors to march on the street. After half an hour of peaceful protest, missiles began to be thrown at the hotel, and police officers manning the barricades. Some crowd members tried to penetrate police lines and enter the hotel. Foot officers tried unsuccessfully to force the crowd back. Mounted officers were called in: the horses were able to clear the barricades, and move the crowd off the roadway onto the opposite side of the street.

Protestors were directed back to their busses, and were driven away. Once this event was finished mounted officers loaded their horses on trailers and sped to the U.S. Consulate to deal with a large Serbian demonstration taking place on University Avenue.

PC Moreen Smith and "Regal" patrolling the lake front on a quiet day. Photograph, Patti Gower, Globe and Mail.

On June 27, the Mounted Unit provided ceremonial escort at the Queen's Plate. This proved to be Staff Inspector Jones' last escort as he retired from the service at the end of July. Jones was presented with police mount, "Trillium," as a retirement gift. Staff Inspector Karl Davis replaced him upon transferring to the unit from the Court Bureau. Staff Inspector Davis took riding lessons with the recruit class during the fall and winter.

Social activists held a number of demonstrations during the year, the most notable an assembly at a homeless camp, set up in Allen Gardens during the summer. At 5:00 a.m. on

Sgt Dennis Grummet and "Toby" patrolling after a snow storm. Photograph, Jim Rankin, Toronto Star.

August 10, the police moved in to remove the illegal campers from the park. The same groups also held a number of noisy protests during the Toronto Film Festival in September. Mounted officers attended all these events.

The Mounted Unit hosted its Annual Police Horse Show at the Canadian National Exhibition. During the "Bag Game" police mount "Teddy" lost his footing and fell to the ground injuring two officers. Both men were transported to hospital by ambulance. One officer suffered a separated shoulder and a knee injury, which required surgery to repair before he could return to duty.

The Toronto Police Service was becoming increasingly involved in United Nations peacekeeping missions around the world. PC Peter Febel volunteered to take part in one of these humanitarian efforts. He received training at the Canadian Police College in Ottawa, and was sent to Kosovo where he worked with police officers from around the world, as well as the German military.

In September, four mounted officers attended the National Mounted Police Competition in Virginia Beach, Virginia. Out of a field of over 100 competitors, team members finished as follows: PC Vanderhart 1st, PC Mamak 4th, Sgt Wardle 8th and PC Sonsini 12th. The Toronto team took the first-place team award. PC Vanderhart and "Lincoln" won the McCarthy trophy.

Military delegates to NATO held their annual conference in Toronto on September 22 and 23. A number of demonstrations and protests were held in response. A very large security detail was organized to ensure the safety of NATO delegates, demonstrators and the public. All protests were peaceful and no incidents marred the conference's success.

During the afternoon of October 20, a mounted officer was seriously injured while on patrol at the C.N.E.. Police mount, "Major," lost his footing and fell to the ground crushing her foot. The officer was transported to hospital and required extensive surgery.

The reputation of the Toronto Police Mounted Unit continued to spread within the policing community. Consistently fine performances at horse shows and positive coverage in the media attracted attention. Further training courses were requested and provided to police officers from the Ontario Provincial Police, and police forces from Chatham, Kingston, Walkerton and Calgary.

The Royal Winter Fair and the *Toronto Sun* newspaper ran another "Name The Horse Contest." During the Fair police mount "Winter Sun" was donated to the Mounted Unit. Retiring Police Chief David Boothby also donated a horse to the Mounted Unit. Chief Boothby was a strong Unit supporter and often rode police horses at ceremonial details. The new horse was named "Boot," a former nickname of the retiring chief.

In November the Mounted Unit moved all its horses and officers to Sunnybrook Stable and the 2 District Stable. Officers worked out of these locations while the Exhibition Stable was renovated and converted into the new Mounted Headquarters. There was much positive

feedback at the community level when residents saw the police horses return to the neighbourhood. There was also great disappoint-ment expressed when citizens learned that the horses were only present on a temporary basis.

The "bag game." A visiting American mounted officer describes the "bag game" as ice hockey on horseback. The "bag game" is designed to accustom the officers and horses to the rough-and-tumble world of mounted policing. Photograph, Author's collection.

WORKING OUT ... Const. Peter Febel of the Toronto Police mounted unit rides his horse Sabre through high snow drifts at the CNE grounds yesterday. With more snow expected to fall on Toronto in the next few days, Febel wanted to get his steed used to working in lots of white stuff.
— Fred Thornhill, SUN

PC Peter Febel and "Sabre" playing in the snow. Photograph, Fred Thornhill, Toronto Sun.

The Serbian Demonstrations of 1999

Riot police face rocks, Molotov cocktails at U.S. consulate: P. 4-5

COPS HURT AS WAR HITS T.O.

— Dave Thomas, SUN

The second night. Toronto Sun Photographs, March 26, 2000. Inset Photo, Dave Thomas, Toronto Sun, main photo, Canadian Press.

Members of Toronto's Serbian community had been holding demonstrations at the U.S. Consulate for many years. With few exceptions, these protests were very well organized and peaceful. There would only be problems when members of rival communities showed up to hold counter protests.

The number of demonstrations increased as fighting between Serbians and Albanians in Kosovo attracted greater world attention. On March 24, member nations of NATO began a bombing campaign in Kosovo in an attempt to force Serbian president Slobodan Milosevic back to the negotiating table.

Serbians in Toronto reacted to the bombing by holding an afternoon demonstration at the U.S. Consulate. The Mounted Unit's afternoon shift attended the demonstration and all was peaceful. At 4:00 p.m., the protest broke up and organizers advised the police that they would be resuming their demonstration at 7:00 p.m. The mounted officers were cleared from the scene and asked to return to the Consulate at 7:00 p.m.

The mounted officers split up to patrol the downtown core. They met up again at Queen and Simcoe Streets at 6:30 p.m. to prepare for the second demonstration. At 6:40 p.m., foot officers at the Consulate put out an emergency call for help. Five mounted officers immediately left for the scene.

A large crowd of Serbians had taken over University Avenue in front of the building. There were few foot patrol officers on scene, and no crowd barriers available to keep the crowd off the street and away from the building. Officers decided to allow the crowd to remain on the street until additional police resources were available. The mounted officers could have easily cleared the street, but there were not enough foot officers available to keep people from returning to the roadway.

The mood of the protestors had changed dramatically since the afternoon. Serbian marshals tried to maintain control of the crowd and to co-operate with the police, but the crowd was growing rapidly in size and mounted officers were forced continually to back up to make room for the expanding mass of people. Every time the horses moved, even away from the crowd, the crowd's anger would be directed towards the officers. Youths tried to provoke the police verbally, and finally someone in the crowd began throwing firecrackers at the horses.

One Serbian marshal attempted to divert the crowd's attention away from the police and towards the Consulate who he said, represented the real enemy. One youth shouted, "They are bombing us too, we hate them as well."

The Canadian military was also involved in the Kosovo bombing operations. Some crowd members were redirected their anger at the Canadian Government towards the Toronto Police Officers.

Crowd members began throwing eggs, rocks and paint bombs at the Consulate. The *Toronto Star* reported, "One man who tried to calm the crowd and stop the escalating violence was pelted with eggs. 'This is not the way,' he said as he tried, along with a few others, to stop protestors from throwing large rocks which they lugged to the demonstration in plastic bags."[1]

By 8:00 p.m., there were over 1,000 demonstrators on University Avenue. Almost every window in the front of the Consulate was broken, and the building was covered with paint. There were not enough police officers on scene to move the crowd safely back from the building. All the officers could do was monitor the mass and wait until help arrived. Some crowd members covered their faces with bandannas and balaclavas.

The crowd burned an American flag and at 9:00 p.m., began throwing flares onto the Consulate roof. Someone started a bonfire outside the front doors of the building. A fire department truck was called to the scene. When the

The first night March 25, 1999. Left to right: PC Correia, PC Greenaway, PC Smith, Sergeant Wardle, PC Vanderhart. Photograph, Rick Madonik. Toronto Sun.

firemen arrived, crowd members began throwing rocks at the firemen. The fire fighters retreated behind their vehicle as the rocks continued to land all around it. A few minutes later, the crowd surged forward and began to march on the fire truck shouting and screaming.

Mounted officers advanced to prevent the crowd from reaching the truck. The horses forced the crowd members back and cleared the front area of the Consulate. Officers and horses were under a constant barrage of rocks, steel candleholders, sticks and anything else that the mob could throw. Demonstrators also attacked the horses with their sign poles and flagpoles. Firemen followed the horses into the crowd to put out the fire. Once the fire was out, the Unit's horses did a second sweep of the front of the Consulate before returning to the fire truck to protect the firemen.

Horses and riders were covered in candle wax. A number of officers suffered cuts and bruises from rocks and sticks. Some crowd members continued to throw missiles, but active use of the horses convinced many demonstrators to leave. By 10:00 p.m., there were only about one hundred crowd members left, and these were gone by 11:00 p.m..

The next night the police were determined to prevent any reoccurrence of the violence. The Mounted Unit assigned 16 horses to the detail and the Public Order Unit was called out to monitor the crowd on foot. Barriers were set up, and the 1200 protestors who came to the Consulate were kept away from the front of the building. Everything remained peaceful until about 10:00 p.m., when the first of three Molotov cocktails was thrown at the building. Crowd members were soon throwing other projectiles as well. A small fire started inside the Consulate, but was extinguished by Public Order Officers. A fourth Molotov cocktail was thrown at mounted officers and struck police mount "Bruce" on the leg. Fortunately the bomb failed to ignite, and the gasoline poured out onto the roadway.

The *Toronto Sun* reported that "Molotov Cocktails, rocks, sticks and slingshots were wielded outside the battered University Avenue building as about 1,200 protestors denounced the NATO bombings and missile attacks on Yugoslavia."[2] Once the violence

began the Mounted Unit was asked to disperse the crowd and the horses advanced north bound on University Avenue pushing the crowd to Dundas Street. Most crowd members left the area at this time. A few youths stayed behind and began throwing rocks at the foot officers who were watching them.

The horses made another advance north bound and dispersed the reminder of the crowd ending the violence for the night. Two police officers on foot suffered serious injuries in the riot. A number of mounted officers were also injured, including some struck with ball bearings fired by slingshots. Mounted officers and horses were also covered with paint thrown at them by crowd members.

The Serbian community continued to hold demonstrations at the Consulate every day until the 17th of June. Crowds would average 500 people each weeknight and 1,000 people on Saturdays and Sundays. There were no further acts of violence. Crowd marshals regained their influence, and demonstrators were self-policing once again. Each night the organizers would select a different Foreign Consulate upon which to march. Crowds would form at the U.S. Consulate, then parade to the British, German or Italian Consulates where speeches would be made. Then the demonstrators would return to the U.S. Consulate and disperse.

Mounted officers attended each and every demonstration, monitoring the crowds and following them to their destinations. The strong police presence, and the cooperation of the Serbian organizers, insured that the protests remained peaceful and public safety maintained. It is a credit to all concerned that through three months of daily demonstrations, there was never a repeat of the rioting that occurred on the 24th and 25th of March.

1. Toronto Star, *March 25, 1999,*
2. Toronto Sun *March 26, 1999.*

A Molotov cocktail explodes on the front of the United State Consulate. Photograph, National Post.

Spencer, The "Draught" Horse

On June 12, 1998, PC Rick Mamak was hand walking his remount "Spencer" on the C.N.E. grounds. The horse had only been out of training for five months. Mamak stopped outside the stable to allow the horse to graze on the grass. Suddenly, "Spencer" bolted away, and ran onto the Go Train Station platform across the street, jumped onto the railway tracks and began to trot westbound. Go Transit was notified, and all rail traffic on the line was stopped.

"Spencer" trotted west for about half a kilometre before he turned around and began trotting back to the stable. PC Mamak stood on the track waiting to grab the lead shank as "Spencer" approached him. Then "Spencer" stood on his lead shank breaking it off, turned to the left and ran up a hill into an industrial complex before disappearing.

A few minutes later, "Spencer" walked through an open door into the Upper Canada Beer Store on Atlantic Avenue. The *Toronto Sun* reported that Sue Greenbank, who worked in the brewery's retail store, said she was on the telephone when their receptionist ran in to warn her about the four-footed customer. 'Sure enough. There's the huge thing walking through the door, and heads straight for the hospitality bar'."[1]

Store staff called the police and a mounted officer returning from court heard the call over his radio and raced to the store, where he recovered "Spencer." The horse was probably attracted to the store by the odours of the brewing process. "Spencer" entered the store through a door designed for humans. It was very fortunate he did not panic once he was inside.

PC Mamak explained the incident to the *Sun* by saying, "I guess he was thirsty, they wouldn't serve him 'cause he's only three and a half."[2]

PC Rick Mamak and "Spencer." Photograph, PC Derrick Speirs.

1 *Toronto Sun*, June 13, 1998.
2 *Toronto Sun*, June 13, 1998.

The C.N.E. Stable Prior To The Renovations

The need for renovation was evident in these photographs. The entire police facility was rebuilt over the winter of 1999-2000.

Left: Stable.

Left centre: Sgt Spurling in the office.

Bottom left: Tack room.

Below: The locker room.

The Toronto Mounted Unit at the International Monetary Fund meeting in Windsor, Ontario. Photograph, Sgt Dennis Grummett.

2000

The Mounted Unit has many supporters within the community. Citizens often visit the stables to see the horses or watch the officers ride. One of the staunchest fans is Dorothy Keith, who stopped by regularly at the stable to watch the recruit classes and troop-training sessions. Dorothy recalled memories of seeing Chief Constable Draper riding his mount along St. Clair Avenue West. When Dorothy heard about the donation of police mount "Boot," she asked if she could also donate a horse to the Toronto police service. Appropriate approval was obtained and Dorothy donated police mount, "Keith."

In March, Julian Fantino became the new Chief of Police: he began his service with a 90-day review of the operations of the entire police service. Members of the review committee visited the Mounted Unit, interviewed officers and examined the operations. The 90-day review made changes within the police service, but had no specific impact on the Mounted Unit.

As part of the review, the Chief met with community groups from every police division within the city. Mounted officers attended all seventeen meetings providing a visible presence, and answering any questions community members had in regard to the use and purposes of police horses. In addition to the chief's meetings, mounted officers were assigned to 195 other community events during the year as well as 33 major crowd-management details.

Those demonstrations that took place during the first half of 2000, were all very peaceful. Anti-poverty groups were active as well as the Serbian community, which held one major demonstration on the one-year anniversary of the bombing raids by NATO forces.

Staff Inspector Davis recognized the training value of the Unit's Drill Team and gave permission for its reactivation. Volunteer officers were selected in March and training began. The first public performance was in April, as part of the graduation ceremonies for the classes at the Sunnybrook Riding Academy.

On May 4, the Ontario Police Memorial was officially opened at Queen's Park. Officers from all over Canada and the United States came to Toronto to take part in the ceremonies. The Mounted Unit led all of the participants in a parade up University Avenue to the site for the dedication. Mounted officers from the Ontario Provincial Police, Chatham Ontario Police and Cleveland Ohio Police also took part in the parade.

The organization of American States was holding its annual meetings in Windsor, Ontario, during the week of June 4th. Major security concerns were associated with this conference. Earlier in the year there had been major rioting in Seattle, Washington, during an International Monetary Fund meeting. A similar meeting in Washington, DC, had seen huge crowds of protestors, but the city's Metropolitan Police were prepared for the worst and the crowds were contained.

All indications were that the same groups which had protested in Seattle and Washington planned to come to Windsor. Windsor police requested the assistance of the Toronto Mounted Unit. Ten horses were dispatched to assist the police with crowd control. Good planning by the police, and hard work by Canada Customs officers ensured the success of the conference. The Customs officers prevented many protestors from entering Canada, in addition to seizing any items that might be used as weapons at the demonstrations.

The entire conference area was sealed off with high fencing. A large contingent of foot officers from the Royal Canadian Mounted Police, Ontario Provincial Police, Peel Regional Police and Windsor Police manned the barricades. The Toronto police mounted officers were also very visible. As a result, the protests that took place were well managed and except for a few incidents, the event was peaceful.

On June 15, social activists held a demonstration at Queen's Park. This was probably the most violent demonstration ever held in Toronto. This event was supposed to kick off a summer of protest in the city. The planned follow up demonstrations did not occur, at least to the extent their leaders had hoped, so Summer 2000 remained a relatively quite one after June 15.

The "Lincoln" Horse

In February the Mounted Unit purchased a new remount. Members of the police service were invited to participate in a contest to name the horse. Potential names for the new remount were submitted to staff Sergeant Weaver, and members of the Unit selected their favourite entry. A former mounted officer, Arlene Fritz, submitted the winning name. The horse was called "Lincoln" in honour of former Lieutenant Governor, Lincoln Alexander.

After his initial six months of training ""Lincoln"" was assigned to PC Greg Vanderhart. Greg was responsible for continuing "Lincoln's" training and exposing him to as many new experiences as possible. In early August, Greg took "Lincoln" to a mounted police competition at the Erie County Fair in Buffalo, New York. "Lincoln", the brand new police horse placed first in the obstacle course.

Greg also rode "Lincoln" in the Unit's in-house competition at the Canadian National Exhibition. To everyone's surprise, "Lincoln" placed first again. This horse, still considered in training, outperformed the other Toronto police horses.

In September, Greg took "Lincoln" to the National Mounted Police Competition in Virginia Beach, Virginia. "Lincoln" placed first in the obstacle course and won the McCarthy trophy, the top mounted police award in North America. Greg and "Lincoln" also won the third place "uniform competition" award and were part of the first place Toronto team.

Less than a month later, October 20, stable manager, PC Vandusen, observed that "Lincoln" was showing signs of colic. Veterinarian Dr. Ralph Watt was called and immediately rushed to the stable. After initial treatment by mounted officers and Dr. Watt "Lincoln" was transported to the veterinary hospital in Guelph, where he underwent emergency surgery. A portion of his bowel was removed. The horse required further surgery later in the week and spent almost a month in hospital. During his stay in hospital, "Lincoln" received a number of special visitors including his namesake, Lincoln Alexander.

"Lincoln" was released from hospital and returned home to the Mounted Unit. He required extensive medical care for the next four months. After this recovery period "Lincoln" was able to return to full police duties.

Former Lieutenant Governor Lincoln Alexander with PC Arlene Fritz, PC Greg Vanderhart and "Lincoln." Photograph., Toronto Police Service.

Winter patrol in Sunnybrook Park. Horses remain one of the best methods for conducting searches in rough country. The Mounted Unit is called out regularly to assist in searches for missing persons. Photograph, Toronto Police Service.

PC Ron Gilbert and "Stuart" patrolling Sunnybrook Park.

Staff Sgt Roger Weaver with Toronto Sun Ambassadors in the advertisement announcing the name the horse contest in 1998. This horse would soon be known as "Sunshine Boy." Photograph, Toronto Sun, October 20, 1998.

Two mounted officers in front of the Toronto Eaton Centre. The high visibility provided by the horses makes them ideal for patrol in urban environments. The Unit's horses are popular both with tourists visiting Toronto and with our local residents. Mounted officers are usually the only contact visitors will have with the Toronto Police. Tourists' perception and memories of Toronto may have a direct correlation to this experience. It is important to keep every contact positive. Mounted officers always have to be aware that they are ambassadors for their community. Photograph, Toronto Police Service.

The "eyes right" march past at the Queen's Plate. Photograph, Michael Burns.

On June 25, the Mounted Unit provided the ceremonial escort for Chief Justice Roy McMurtry at the Queen's Plate. Staff Inspector Davis rode in the Landau as the Chief Justice's Aide de Camp. Sergeant Wardle rode in the escort as acting staff inspector. Sergeant Patterson rode as acting staff sergeant.

The Drill Team was invited to participate in the Canadian Olympic Trials at the Hendervale Equestrian Complex located in Milton, Ontario, on the 22nd and 23rd of July. The Mounted Unit planned to put on four demonstrations during the two days. A few days prior to the show, the police learned that a demonstration was planned at the Old City Hall Courts on the Saturday, because some people were slated to appear for bail hearings from charges associated with the riot of June 15.

Officers planned their duties so they could police the demonstration and then attend the Olympic trials. The demonstrators were peaceful and dispersed on their own at 11:00 a.m. After the protestors were gone, Drill Team officers loaded their horses onto a combination of trailers and travelled to Milton in time to present the Drill Ride.

Renovations at the Canadian National Exhibition Stable were completed by midsummer, and officers and horses moved back to the facility on July 25. This was the first time in over 100 years that the entire Mounted Unit's personnel were housed within one facility.

The Caribana Festival took place the first weekend in August. Large crowds of people congregated on Yonge Street each night. Horses were required to police the street until dawn, in addition to assisting foot officers at a number of venues through the night. The Caribana Parade was very well organized and ended early. People attending the parade were very orderly and well managed, so the horses assigned to the parade route did not have to do any proactive policing.

The Mounted Unit's annual horse show took place at the Canadian National Exhibition on August 21. The Drill Team, and the Pipes and Drums, gave three presentations of the Ride during the C.N.E.'s duration.

The three top riders from the Unit's obstacle course class traveled to Morris County, New Jersey, to represent Toronto at the National Police Equestrian competition. Once again, three Toronto officers finished within the top ten positions. Toronto officers also attended mounted police competitions in Kingston, Ontario, Buffalo, New York and Massachusetts.

Sergeant Bill Wardle and Duke at the 2000 Queen's Plate. Photograph, Michael Burns.

In September a special project was implemented to increase the Mounted Unit's presence in 51 Division. Two mounted officers were assigned to patrol the area exclusively for one month, when not assigned to crowd management details. Officers, PC McCarthy and PC Heard, spent fourteen working days in the area, making five criminal arrests. They laid twelve provincial offence charges and investigated seventy-eight individuals. The biggest pay-off to the community was crime prevention value provided by the enhanced police presence of the mounted officers.

The International Association of Women Police held its annual convention in Toronto, in September. Mounted officers from other jurisdictions who were attending the conference were invited to accompany Toronto officers on mounted patrol. The Mounted Unit provided ceremonial details throughout the conference.

On September 26, major demonstrations were held around the world protesting the policies of the International Monetary Fund. Toronto protestors planned to form up at the U.S. Consulate and march into the financial district. Some European demonstrations which had taken place earlier in the day had become violent. The Mounted Unit assigned a large contingent of officers to help police the Toronto demonstration, and there were no incidents.

On the weekend of October 21, the provincial Progressive Conservative Party held its annual policy convention at the Metro Toronto Convention Centre. Large demonstrations were expected and permits had been issued to a number of different groups who wanted to hold protests at the event. A park across from the Convention Centre was provided for the use of the demonstrators. With the exception of a student march on the Friday, there were very few participants at these planned demonstrations and no problems, occurred.

Chief of Police Julian Fantino at the grand opening of Mounted Headquarters. Photograph, Craig Robertson, Toronto Sun.

The Queen's Park Riot, June 15, 2000

Activist groups planned a series of anti-poverty demonstrations for the summer of 2000. The first of these protests was scheduled for June 15, 2000. The protestors planned to form up at Allen Gardens and then parade along Carlton and College Streets to Queen's Park. When they arrived, their representative would ask to address the Legislative Assembly. The *Toronto Star* reported, "That privilege, occasionally granted to foreign heads of state, is denied to ordinary citizens."[1]

Police were prepared for the demonstration with twelve horses available and a number of Public Safety Unit squads on call out. Marchers began assembling in the morning, and it was clear from the equipment and materials many crowd members were carrying, that their intentions were more aggressive than the police had anticipated.

Many in the crowd wore helmets, masks and protective eye goggles. New devices were seen, including a mattress with handles fashioned to be used as a barricade. Many protestors also carried heavy bags which officers suspected were loaded with potential projectiles. The protestor's signs were constructed with two by four pieces of wood.

Six mounted officers and a number of foot officers shadowed the march to Queen's Park. The demonstrators arrived at Queen's Park peacefully while crowd leaders made speeches on the front lawn of Queen's Park. A representative from the protest then walked up to the front doors of the Legislative Building and demanded to be allowed in to speak to Members of Provincial Parliament in the Legislative House. His request was refused and the man returned to the main body of the crowd.

The *National Post* described the next few moments: "What started as a peaceful march through the city's streets quickly became a violent, chaotic melee. Protestors rushed the police barricades in an attempt to storm the Legislature, prompting a swift and firm response as officers drove the mob back with truncheons and shields. The protestors hurled rocks at officers and attacked police horses with wooden planks. Many of the group of 500 came prepared, wearing gas masks and goggles."[2]

The initial charge by the protestors was unexpected and the crowd overpowered police officers manning the initial line of barricades. At least one Molotov cocktail was immediately thrown onto the steps of the legislature exploding beside the police officers lined up there. As the first line of barricades was pushed over, mounted officers standing by on the west side of the building began their advance.

Horses were used to move the crowd from the second barrier to protect the officers there. Horses and officers were bombarded with hundreds of projectiles including rocks, paint bombs, sticks, banner poles, smoke bombs and ball bearings. Within seconds of moving into the crowd, one officer had a bone broken in his right hand.

Crowd members attempted to use police barricades and bicycles to obstruct the horses. A number of foot officers were struck by projectiles and had to be evacuated by other officers.

Order was restored in less than an hour, as horse and foot officers worked together to move the crowd away from the front of the building.

Approximately 1,000 people were involved in the demonstration and riot. Many were identified as members of Anarchist groups from across Canada. A total of eighteen persons were arrested that day and twenty-nine officers and eight horses suffered injuries. Nine of the twelve mounted officers involved were injured. This was probably the most violent demonstration in the history of Queen's Park.

The Toronto media and general public were very concerned about the injuries Unit horses suffered during the riot and concerned citizens showed up at Sunnybrook Stables with treats for the horses.

Organizers of the protest at Queen's Park had billed it as the first of many such demonstrations scheduled to take place during the summer. No further demonstrations took place.

1 *Toronto Star.* June 16, 2000.
2 *National Post.* June 16, 2000.

Photograph, Chris Bolin, National Post.

The Grand Opening Of The New Mounted Headquarters

The Mounted Unit on parade at the grand opening of their new Headquarters.

Police Chief Julian Fantino and Police Commission Chair Norm Gardner prepare to cut the ribbon at the opening of the new Mounted Headquarters. This photograph includes both the Mounted Unit personnel and the civilian contractors who were involved in the design and the construction of the headquarter facility. Three former Mounted Unit Staff Inspectors are also in the photograph. Photographs, Alexander Robertson Photography.

Mounted Unit farrier, Alex Picard, is on the extreme left of the photograph. To his right is Norm Sutherland, the Mounted Unit's civilian station operator. The officers in forage caps are members of the recruit class who were receiving their Mounted Unit training. Photograph, Toronto Police Service.

Police Chief Julian Fantino, Police Services Board Chair Norm Gardner and Staff Inspector Carl Davis prepare to cut the ribbon at the opening of the new Mounted Headquarters. Photograph, Toronto Police Service.

The Drill Team performance in the exercise ring.

PC Pat Penney and "Sarge" lead the troop back to the barn.

Left: Dorothy Keith with Chief Julian Fantino. Insert: Dorothy Keith and Staff Inspector Karl Davis with police mount, "Keith." Earlier in the day, Toronto's newest police mount, "Dorothy," had been introduced to those attending the grand opening. The horse was named after Mrs. Keith in appreciation of her involvement with the Mounted Unit.

The end of a long day. Constable Steve Derbyshire cleaning his kit in the new tack room.

All photographs, Toronto Police Service.

The *Toronto Sun* newspaper and the Royal Winter Fair donated another horse to the Mounted Unit during the Fair. The name chosen during the 3rd "Name The Horse Contest" was "Royal Sun." The Drill Team gave two presentations at the Fair.

On December 6, the official opening of the new Mounted Headquarters took place. Chief of Police, Julian Fantino and Police Services Board Chair Norman Gardner cut the ribbon officially opening the facility. The Mounted Unit invited members of the media and also invited guests into the building for a tour of the facility and a presentation of the Drill Ride. The general public was invited into the stable in the evening for tours and another presentation of the Drill Ride.

Just before Christmas, a member of the recruit class was seriously injured when he fell from his mount during a training exercise and broke his leg. The officer underwent surgery and had a steel plate placed in his leg at the fracture site.

The year ended with a busy New Years Eve, as mounted officers assigned to the Entertainment District Detail worked until dawn.

EVERYONE LOVES ...
THE TORONTO POLICE HORSE!

Left: Sgt Peter Spurling and Sgt Bill Wardle returning from a demonstration at the United States Consulate. The staff of Hooters Restaurant pay special attention to police mount "General." Photograph, courtesy of Hooters Restaurant.

VALLEY

Yavuz Photo ©

2000

The Future

Now we have entered a new century, and he proud traditions of the Mounted Unit continue "To Serve and Protect." This history illustrates the professionalism and devotion to duty of the officers and horses of Toronto's Mounted Police.

The Mounted Unit has always been, and will continue to be, the most effective means of crowd control available to police. Containment of those violent confrontations which have occurred over the years continually demonstrates the effectiveness of the police horse.

The future of the Mounted Unit cannot be predicted. Constant cutbacks and the prospect of total elimination will always peer over the Unit's shoulder. The year-by-year accomplishments of the Mounted Unit more than justify the continued maintenance of this elite Mounted Police Service. I hope that this book will help to show those accomplishments and educate the reader as to the importance of maintaining police-horse services in Toronto.

After 19 years as a mounted officer, I had the fortune, or I might say at times, misfortune, to be promoted to staff sergeant and transferred from the Mounted Unit. I can no longer build and promote the mounted unit from within, my fondest duty.

I hope this publication will help the police officers assigned to mounted duties see just what an important role they are meant to serve within by the expectations of the extraordinary people who served before them as members of the Toronto Mounted Police.

Commanders of the Mounted Unit

The Boss. Staff Inspector Edwin Johnson leads the Mounted Unit during a performance of the Musical Ride. The Inspector was known to the troops as "Big Ed." His equestrian skills, love of the Mounted Unit, and standard of leadership will probably never be matched. Photograph, Toronto Police Museum.

Inspector George Goulding
1886 – 1910

George Goulding was one of the first of two Toronto police officers assigned to full-time mounted duties. Born in England in 1848, he served in the British military for almost five years, probably in a cavalry regiment. Goulding joined the Toronto Police Department on November 21, 1877.

The six-foot-one constable moved to the Mounted Unit in 1886 and was made an acting Patrol Sergeant later that same year. He was officially promoted to patrol sergeant on April 1, 1887 and full Sergeant on November 1, 1901.

Goulding's promotion to Inspector happened around 1909. He continued as Officer-in-charge of the Mounted Unit in addition to being responsible for other duties within the police service. The Chief's Constable's Annual Report of 1910, announced Goulding's retirement from the police

department and paid tribute to his years of service with the Unit. A 1924 newspaper article spoke of "Acting Inspector Goulding, who during his long period of service became a very familiar figure in Toronto."[1]

On November 22, 1923, former Inspector Goulding appeared before the Police Commission meeting with a number of other former officers with a request for an increase in their pensions. There was no inflation protection in those days and he was still receiving the same amount of money per month that he had been receiving since 1910. The rapid inflation of the war years had taken its toll on the officers' income. No record of the decision was made.

Photograph, c. 1908. Toronto Police Museum.

Inspector Henry H. Gilks
1910 – 1916

Henry Gilks was born in England in 1858. Before coming to Canada, he served for two and a half years in England's premier cavalry regiment, Her Majesty's Life Guards. He stood only 5'11," and was one of the shortest men on the Toronto Police Department (of six-foot men) when he joined the force on March 19, 1887. Gilks probably came to the Mounted Unit as constable before 1900.

He was promoted to Patrol Sergeant April 1, 1905, Sergeant on April 1, 1910, when he also became Officer-in-charge of the Mounted Unit. Gilks was promoted to the rank of Inspector on April 12, 1912.

In April 1916, he appeared before the Board of Police Commissioners charged with making a false statement to the Chief Constable. Gilks admitted to the offence and advised the Board he had been addicted to alcohol for over two years. The Board demoted him immediately to the rank of sergeant, and also ordered him to resign from the police force forthwith. Gilks immediately submitted his resignation.

The following week he appealed to the Board asking that he be allowed to retire with the rank of Inspector as his pension would be based on the rank held when he retired. Despite 29 years of faithful service, this request was denied and Henry Gilks retired on a sergeant's pension.

Photograph, 1916 James Collection #125, City of Toronto Archives.

Inspector Herbert W. Little
1916 – 1924

Herbert Little was born in England in 1879. He served in the Cape Mounted Police in Cape Province, South Africa for four and a half years. He came to Canada and joined the Toronto Police Department on September 11, 1905, becoming Constable Number 52.

Little probably transferred to the Mounted Unit some time after 1910, and was promoted to Patrol Sergeant on December 1, 1913. On May 1, 1916, he replaced Inspector Gilks as the Officer-in-Charge of the Mounted Unit. Little was made a full sergeant on November 1, 1917 and promoted to Inspector on May 1, 1920.

He transferred from the Mounted Unit in 1924 and placed in charge of a police Division. During the 1930s, he ran No. 11 Division. Little retired in 1936 after thirty and a half years of police service.

Photograph, Toronto Police Museum.

Inspector Thomas Douglas Crosbie D.C.M.
1924 – 1951

Thomas Crosbie was born in Dumfries, Scotland on January 1, 1888. His first public service job was working as a guard with the Glasgow South West Railway in Scotland. He later joined the Glasgow City Police Department. While on duty at a soccer game at Hamden Park, he was beaten up so badly by members of the crowd that he was not expected to live. The police brought his father to his bedside in the expectation that Crosbie might die, but he made a miraculous recovery and continued to serve as a member of the Glasgow Police. The British Colonial Office had posted a recruiting poster at the police station, advertising for experienced officers to join the Singapore police. Crosbie resigned from the Glasgow police in 1910 and booked passage to Canada, the first stop on his trip to Singapore.

His travels brought him to Toronto where he married the daughter of a local blacksmith, Mary Hornshaw. Crosbie's marriage, and the fact that he was running out of money caused him to postpone his Singapore dream. Crosbie joined the Toronto Police Force on June 15, 1910, as Constable Number 401. He walked the beat for a year and a half before transferring to the Mounted Unit in 1912. He was 5' 10 3/4 inches in height, perfect size for mounted duty.

In 1915 Crosbie joined the 9th Battery of the Canadian Militia and was sent to Kingston for non-commissioned officer training. The 9th Battery was the home service militia unit of the 9th Canadian Field Artillery, which the Mounted Unit horses and officers had joined in 1914 for active overseas service.

Photograph, Toronto Police Museum.

On January 3, 1916 Crosbie enlisted for service overseas with the Third Divisional Ammunition Column of the Canadian Expeditionary Force. When he arrived in England on March 25, 1916, he held the rank of Farrier Sergeant. On April 15, 1917, he was promoted to the rank of Battery Sergeant Major.

Crosbie was awarded the Military Medal for bravery in the field after being cited for carrying wounded men from the field of battle at Arras, France, in August 1918. The award was later upgraded, in February 1919, to the Distinguished Conduct Medal, second for valour to the Victoria Cross.[2]

The Distinguished Conduct Medal citation is as follows: "Battery Sergeant Major Thomas Douglas Crosbie #311373 3rd Divisional Ammunition Column, Canadian Field Artillery was awarded the Distinguished Conduct Medal 'For gallantry and devotion to duty. About 9:00 a.m. on 28th August, 1918, a large enemy shell landed in a dump located on the Arras-Cambrai Road between Arras and Faub St. Sauveur, killing seven men and wounding five of the dump personnel. He was blown twenty to thirty feet by the explosion and wounded slightly, but with great gallantry and utter disregard for personnel safety he immediately got water and put out the burning ammunition and prevented more casualties. Notwithstanding his wounds and the severe shock he had received, he continued to issue ammunition until relieved. His example throughout was most inspiring to the men'."[3]

On September 30, Crosbie was admitted to the 9th Canadian Field Ambulance with a number of fractured bones and shrapnel wounds. He was transferred to England for further medical treatment and found unfit for further active military service due to his wounds. Crosbie carried metal shrapnel in his body the rest of his life. As a result of his injuries, he qualified for a pension, but was not able to apply because, had he accepted it, he would have been considered unfit for further police service. He suffered from these wounds for the rest of his life.

Crosbie returned to Canada and was discharged from the military on March 30, 1919. He returned to the Toronto Police Force and his position at the Mounted Unit. On July 16, 1919, he was promoted to the rank of patrol sergeant, and to the rank of sergeant on September 19, 1924, when he was placed in charge of the Mounted Unit.

Thomas Crosbie became the youngest inspector in the history of the Toronto Police Force when he was promoted to the rank, on April 1 1927, in his 39th year. (His son Douglas was the first to break his father's record when he became the youngest inspector on the Metropolitan Toronto Police Force in 1957, at age thirty-three. Douglas had previously been a member of the Forest Hill Police and became an inspector when his department was amalgamated into the new

Battery Sgt Major Crosbie, 1919.
Photograph, Toronto Police Museum.

Metropolitan Toronto Police Force).

Inspector Crosbie was known as a strict disciplinarian. The following quote shows what he expected from his mounted officers. "I will stand for no impoliteness on the part of my men. I like discipline. The public is always right and there must be no argument. My men are instructed to follow the right course, but without undue sternness. They must be firm, but must be gentle at the same time. They must never talk back in a rough or ungentlemanly manner when spoken to."[4]

In 1929, Crosbie moved his family into a city-owned house in Sunnybrook Park where the Mounted Unit training facility was being established. During the 1930s, he was the President of the Toronto Police Amateur Athletic Association. At the start of the Second World War, he took a six-month leave of absence to work as a drill instructor for the Royal Canadian Air Force. Crosbie instructed recruits in foot drill at the Toronto Manning Depot located in the Coliseum Building at the Canadian National Exhibition.

Inspector Crosbie was a qualified horse show judge and often helped to adjudicate classes at the Royal Winter Fair and other events. He also purchased all of the department horses, the majority bought came from the Hagersville area. Once he bought a mare not knowing that she was pregnant. When the pregnancy was discovered, the horse was put on a farm until its colt was born. The colt was kept by the department. The Inspector took a lot of ribbing by people who said it was typical of a Scotsman to get two horses for the price of one.

The Inspector insisted on personally training every mounted officer to his own high standards. When mounted training was mandatory, he would select permanent staff from the recruits he trained. When the mandatory mounted training was discontinued, Crosbie would inspect every recruit class, selecting men with the physical stature required for mounted duties. He would then call the recruits in for an interview and, if he liked their qualifications, would invite them to be members of the Unit.

Inspector Crosbie also visited the prospective home of every retiring police horse. When the new Police Chief John Chisholm reduced the size of the Mounted Unit in 1946, Inspector Crosbie was forced to sell the Unit's horses to the highest bidder at auction, rather than to the best possible home. He was disgusted that money was more important to the force over the well-being of its horses. When his protests regarding the auction were ignored, Inspector Crosbie refused to wear his uniform to the auction.

During the 1950 Royal Winter Fair, the Inspector fell ill. He returned to work for a short time before taking ill again. Crosbie was admitted to The Toronto General Hospital where he died in March 1951. At the time of his death, he was still Inspector-in-Charge of the Mounted Unit, and had accumulated a total of forty-one years with the Toronto Police. The Police Force provided a full mounted escort at his funeral.

Thomas Crosbie's obituary reported that he gave this city one of the finest mounted divisions on the continent. "His fame as a trainer brought thousands of letters from horse lovers in the United States and Canada, offering him large sums of money to train their horses."[5]

Constable Crosbie at the Mounted Unit 1919. Photograph, courtesy of the Crosbie Family.

Inspector John Watt
1951 - 1963

John Watt was born in Aberdeen, Scotland in 1898. During the First World War he joined the Gordon Highlanders and was assigned to the Transport Section. He served in France as a "Wagoneer," driving horse drawn ammunition wagons to and from the front lines.

After the war, Watt immigrated to Canada and found work as a farmer. He joined the Toronto Police Department on June 2nd 1924, and walked the beat at No. 5 Division, Belmont Street. He transferred to the Mounted Unit in 1929, by 1931, he was working at No. 12 Stable.

Police Routine orders for February 5th, 1938, recognised Constable Watt #257, of the Mounted Division for his outstanding work in recovering forty-four stolen cars during the previous year. Inspector Watt's son remembers that his father would bring home a list of the licence numbers of stolen cars every night so he could memorize the details and search for the cars the following day.

Watt was promoted to Patrol Sergeant in 1945. He remained at the Mounted Unit, becoming the second in command in 1948 when, he was promoted to full Sergeant. He was promoted to Inspector in 1951, when he became the officer-in-charge of the Mounted Unit.

John Watt retired on June 8, 1963, after thirty-nine years of police service. His horse "Sandy" retired on the same day. The fifteen-year-old "Sandy" was turned out into the pastures of a farm near Bowmanville to live out his final days. Inspector Watt had first seen "Sandy" as a two-year-old at the Royal Winter Fair, and as soon as the horse came up for

Photograph, Toronto Police Museum.

sale bought him. "Sandy" remained the Inspector's horse for thirteen years.

After his retirement, Inspector Watt worked as a Sheriff's Officer at the University Avenue courthouse. He continued to ride a former police horse named "Lady," which he kept at his sons' farm. John Watt also paid regular visits to his old friend and comrade "Sandy," in Bowmanville.

Wagoneer John Watt of the Gordon Highlanders is standing on the right, c 1917. Photographs, courtesy of the Watt Family.

Inspector Watt and "Sandy" leading a parade in 1959. Police mount "Sandy" and Inspector Watt both retired on the same day.

Inspector Edwin S. Johnson M.M., M.I.D.
1963 - 1985

Edwin Johnson was born in Australia and immigrated to Canada with his family as a child. He spent most of his boyhood in Toronto and was left an orphan at a young age. Johnson joined the Royal Canadian Dragoons in 1937 when he was seventeen years old. The Royal Canadian Dragoons was a mounted cavalry regiment, which continued to use horses until 1940.

Johnson learned military riding with the Dragoons and was a member of their famed Musical Ride. Later, the Metropolitan Toronto Police Musical Ride would be Inspector Johnson's creation and it utilized many of the movements from his Dragoon days.

During World War II, Johnson went on active service with the Royal Canadian Dragoons, where he held the rank of Sergeant. The Dragoons were assigned to armoured scouting missions and Johnson served with them in England, Italy, where he was wounded, and Northwest Europe.

He was awarded the Military Medal for bravery in the field during an action that took place on May 4, 1945. Sergeant Johnson was in charge of a dismounted section of tank troops, assigned to "B" Squadron. They advanced on a hamlet called Grabestede, where they were ordered to check buildings at the roadside for enemy activity.

As they approached the village the squadron came under enemy fire from the German rear guard who were protecting a railroad bridge behind the buildings. Sergeant

Photograph, Toronto Police Mounted Unit.

Johnson's commanding officer submitted the following citation when recommending Johnson for valour:

"... came under heavy small arms fire and mortar fire. The dismounted personnel were pinned to the ground due to the close nature of the country, which in this area had numerous buildings and hedges, the armoured cars could not locate the exact location from which the fire was coming.

"Showing complete disregard for his own safety, Sgt Johnson ran to the lead armoured car and climbing on top pointed out targets to the crew commander, leaving himself fully exposed to the enemy's fire. Whilst the car was engaging the enemy, Sgt Johnson ran to the bridge, and still under heavy small arms and mortar fire, removed the charges, thus preventing this vital bridge from being blown."[6]

Johnson was also awarded with a mention in dispatches for consistent valiant conduct during his military service.

After the war Johnson returned to Toronto and was discharged from the army. He joined the Toronto Police Force on December 1, 1945, and served in No. 10 and No. 1 Divisions until transferring to the Mounted Unit in May 1949.

He was almost immediately made a horse trainer and began working with remounts. On March 17, 1954, Johnson was promoted to patrol sergeant, becoming second in command of the Unit. He was later promoted to full sergeant, and made Inspector on July 8, 1963. At 6'4," he was given the appropriate nickname of "Big Ed."

A *Globe and Mail* newspaper writer describe him thus "The inspector's, an ironed-willed type whom the men refer to as 'boss,' probably with affection as well as respect. When he picks up a ringing telephone, the caller will be left in no doubt as to who has answered: 'Inspector Johnson' he barks. He, too, is big, and the back of his neck is lined with deep creases, the long furrows of service."[7]

Salem Alaton, a writer who interviewed Johnson in 1983, paid him a superb tribute. After discussing the Mounted Unit, The Hinkling-Johnson report and mounted units from other police departments, Alaton concluded:

"This is Toronto, however, and Johnson has to retire within three years. He probably can't be replaced. He's an old hawk who was orphaned during the depression, joined the army and then became a policeman before the ink on Germany's surrender was dry. He's given the unit its musical ride—now one display a year rather than eight—and he looks like he could box the ears of the Chief of Police himself.

"After he's gone, the unit will have to stay on constant alert, lest the ambivalence within and without run riot."[8]

Staff Inspector Edwin Johnson and "Duke." C.N.E. stable, c. 1980. Photograph, Toronto Police Museum.

PC Edwin Johnson, c. 1952. Photograph, Toronto Police Museum.

Inspector Ed Johnson leading the troop at the Queen's Plate, c.1980. Photograph, Toronto Mounted Unit.

Staff Inspector Robert Heenan
1985 – 1991

Robert Heenan was born and raised on a farm in York Region, just north of Toronto. He grew up around horses and, as a teenager, drove a horse-drawn milk wagon around Toronto. He joined the Canadian Army in the early 1960s and served with the Princess Patricia's Canadian Light Infantry, rising to the rank of quartermaster sergeant. After a tour of duty in Germany, he took his discharge and returned to Toronto.

Heenan joined the Metropolitan Toronto Police Force on August 16, 1966. He served in No. 52 and 54 Divisions before he transferred to the Mounted Unit on January 8, 1968.

Heenan completed a number of training laterals and was promoted to the rank of sergeant on May 14, 1974. He was permanently assigned to the Mounted Unit, but continued to accept temporary assignments to other units to broaden his experience.

Robert was promoted to staff sergeant in April 1980, and remained at the Mounted Unit for the duration of his career. He was appointed Inspector on August 6, 1985 and Staff Inspector in February 1990. Robert Heenan retired from the police force in August 1991 after completing 25 years of service.

Photograph, Alexander Roberston Photography.

Constable Robert Heenan carrying the Canadian Flag in a parade on Queen Street at Yonge Street, c. 1969. Photograph, Toronto Police Museum.

Staff Inspector Robert Heenan leading the troop into the "eyes right" at the Queen's Plate, c. 1988. Photograph, Toronto Mounted Unit.

Staff Inspector James Jones
1991 – 1999

Jim Jones was born in Scotland and served with the Glasgow Police Department before immigrating to Canada. He joined the Metropolitan Toronto Police Force in 1965, but resigned soon after. He was reappointed to the Police Force as a third-class constable on January 10, 1967.

Jones served in 23 Division until he was promoted to the rank of Sergeant on June 11, 1974. He then served in 22 Division as a uniform sergeant and as a detective. He later transferred to headquarters Fraud and Forgery Squad. Jones was promoted to staff sergeant on August 7, 1984 and transferred to the Homicide Squad. After a year's service in Homicide, he returned to the Fraud Squad where he applied for transfer to the Mounted Unit.

Jones' transfer was accepted and he came to the Mounted Unit on November 24, 1987. Since he had no prior mounted experience, he participated in that winter's recruit training course. Jones was promoted to inspector on August 27, 1991, and staff inspector on March 10, 1992. Staff Inspector Jim Jones retired in July 1999, after 34 years of service.

Photograph, Alexander Robertson Photography.

Staff Inspector Jim Jones with the winners of the Presentation night name the horse contest, 1993.

Staff Inspector Jim Jones and members of the Mounted Unit kick off the 1996 Santa Claus Parade. As the Mounted Unit passed, they sent in "the clowns" to clear the way for the Pipe Band and St. Nick.

Photographs, Toronto Police Service.

Staff Inspector Karl Davis
1999 to date

Karl Davis was born in Hamilton Ontario and joined the Metropolitan Toronto Police Force as a constable in 1972. He served in 53 Division until 1979 when he was promoted to sergeant and transferred to 55 Division. In 1986, Davis was promoted to Staff Sergeant and returned to 53 Division. He was later transferred to 5 District Public Affairs.

In October 1989, Karl Davis was promoted to Inspector and was assigned as the Unit Commander of 53 Division. His next assignment was at the Court Bureau where he served until August 1999 when he was appointed as officer-in-charge of Mounted and Police Dog Services.

Photograph, Canadian Mounted Police Association.

Chapter 6

The Horses of the Toronto Mounted Police

The first horses used by the Toronto Police Department were Hunter style, readily available, and inexpensive to buy. Toronto's first police horses came from Woodstock, Ontario. In later years remounts would be purchased from locations all over southern Ontario. In the 1930s, Inspector Crosbie purchased many horses from the area around Hagersville, Ontario. Recently, most of the Unit horses have been purchased in the area between Lindsay and Guelph.

The breed of horses purchased by the Metropolitan Toronto Police over the last forty years is know as the Commercial Grade or Grade horse, also known as Trooper Horses or Canadian Crosses. These have been crossbred, and they are an animal with a mixture of a heavy draft breed (Percheron, Clydesdale or Belgian) and lighter breeds (Hackney, Standardbred, Thoroughbred, Coach, etc). This mixture produces a large, well-formed, cold-blooded horse with a gentle disposition.

The horses are selected by the officer in charge of the Unit from various breeders. Their age at purchase is usually three to six years, they must be 15.2 hands to 16.2 hands in height, approximately five feet tall from the hoof to the shoulder. Unit horses should weigh between one thousand two hundred pounds and one thousand three hundred and fifty pounds. The Toronto Police Service will only purchase horses classed by colour as Bays (Brown), Blacks or Chestnuts. The Mounted Unit purchases both geldings and mares, but prefers to buy geldings. Horses are purchased on a two-week trial basis. During this period, the animals will be examined by a veterinarian and carefully scrutinized by the training staff. If the horse is deemed sound and suitable for police work, it will be assigned an inventory number and renamed.

An ideal Toronto police horse in 1930. It was described as having a Troop Horse head with strong lines, a heavy jaw, thick muzzle and glaring eye. Photograph, Toronto Star, May 17, 1930.

The Unit's senior constables assigned to train remounts spend between six months and a year with a "green" horse. The Mounted Unit has started purchasing horses with some preliminary training, which cut the training period by almost half. When the trainer brings the horse to the point where it is ready for regular duties it is turned over to another senior constable for street work. The learning process continues with the new officer. It takes from three to four years for a horse to be considered fully trained.

The average age of retirement for a police horse is between sixteen and eighteen years. The Unit commander maintains a file with the names of people interested in purchasing a former police mount. In 1985, the waiting list was one hundred and fifty people.

When a horse was ready for retirement, a prospective purchaser is selected from the waiting list and questioned about what he or she intends to do with the horse. A supervisor from the Unit visits the site where the horse will be kept. If the stable accommodation is suitable, and the applicant deemed capable of giving proper care to the horse, it is sold for a nominal fee.

Unfortunately some police horses never make it to retirement, but are put down or die from natural causes. The most common cause of death is illness. A number of police mounts have been put down due to "colic" or other ailments.

In the old days, horses to be put down were shot by the officer in charge of the Unit. Police mount "Rockwood" was shot by Sergeant Goulding after contracting septic poisoning in the leg. On November 8, 1915, Police Wagon Service Horse "Horace" was also shot. Other horses like "Division" who died on October 2, 1909 from a concussion to the brain succumbed as a result of accidents.

Fortunately today, the Unit's veterinarian has more humane ways of destroying a horse. When any animal has suffered a severe injury, a police officer is entitled to use their firearm to destroy it if it is in extreme pain and humanity demands that instant action be taken. No Toronto police horse has been destroyed in this manner in living memory. Most accidents involving police horses are responded to by the Humane Society Ambulance and the Toronto Ambulance Service.

Over the last ten years or so, the Toronto police lost mounts "Prince" and "Alex" to colic, "Regent" to illness and "Princess" to a broken leg caused by a kick from another horse.

The training and selection of the Mounted Unit's horses was changed very little over the years. The following information was collected from a number of Toronto newspaper articles of the 1920s and 30s:

"The police horses are purchased green, from the country, in the neighbourhood of Toronto. The police are always looking for suitable remounts. When Chief Dickson

NO WHIPS ARE CRACKED, NO VOICES RAISED, OVER THESE HORSES

Training police horses at Sunnybrook Park, December 1937. Left to right: 1. Teaching a horse to canter. 2. Inspector Crosbie displays the training bit. 3. An officer training a horse to passage sideways in order to move crowds out of the way. Photographs, Toronto Star.

gets word of a suitable horse he notifies Deputy Chief Geddes who takes a veterinarian and Sergeant Crosbie in his car with him to go look at the horse. 'The deputy is a keen judge of the type of horse flesh the force needs and takes a lot of pleasing'. Only moderately priced horses are purchased for the unit. They are developed through the best care until their money value is much enhanced."[1]

From the *Evening Telegram:* "The horses are carefully chosen from farms throughout Ontario. The horse must be four years old or older. They must be 16 hands or higher and have plenty of bone and substance. A short back is best because it will carry weight better. A good long neck, or long reign as it is called, is preferred as it helps give carriage and grace. A veterinarian makes sure the animal is in sound order."[2]

Another article stated, "The majority of the police horses were bred in rural districts. Their average age on purchase is around 5 years. The traits looked for are; short backs, powerful quarters, good boned hocks and good riding necks, they should be 16 hands give or take an inch. The horses are purchased by Sergeant Crosbie or by the official veterinarian with the final approval coming from Chief Dickson."[3]

"The Toronto Police Department has specialised in bay, chestnut and black horses since its inception."[4] (A few grey horses were purchased in the early days.) The *Telegram* writer describes the horses as "Splendid representatives of the weight-carrying hunter breed, plus more than the average equines brains, and schooling."[5]

The training that the early police horses received is much like the schooling received by horses purchased by the unit today. Most officer-trainers working at the Mounted Unit learned their trade from other members of the unit. The theory and skills of horse training are passed down from one trainer to another. Methods used have a successful track record of over one hundred and ten years.

In the 1920s the training the Toronto police horses received was similar to that given to the remounts by the "Rough Riders" in the cavalry. Remounts were stabled in Police Station No. 5 at Belmont Street and Davenport Road. Since the police did not have a riding ring of their own, most of the training was done in the Rosedale Ravine. The military would sometimes allow them to use the riding school at the University Avenue Armouries.

Patrol Sergeant Quinn gives instruction to recruits PC Jack Bent on "Joe" and PC Larry Balsdon on "Norval," c.1962. Photograph, Toronto Telegram Photograph *Collection, York University Archives and Special Collections, Neg. #1698*

Inspector John Watt, officer-in-charge of the Mounted Division, Toronto Police Force, wrote the following essay. It appeared in the 1st quarter of 1956 issue of *Police News* Magazine, a publication associated with the Police Association of Ontario. Reprinted with permission – Ontario Police Association.

Biography Of The Mounted Police Horse

Casual observation of large cities with streets over-crowded with motor vehicles, tends to create the impression that this is a horse-less age and that under existing conditions, that the useful animal is doomed to disappear.

Statistics based upon census show, however, that while the normal rate of increase has not been maintained there are still a large number of horses in the country. These facts would seem to indicate that the doom of the horse has not yet been sealed and that he will continue to abide with us not only because he is useful, but also because from time immemorial he has earned and held the affection of mankind.

If the literature of a subject is an indication of public interest, and then the horse truly ranks high, for it has been estimated that more than 2,000 books relating to this animal have been published in England and an equal number elsewhere. No special effort has been made by the library to collect books on the horse for the reason that other government agencies specialise on that subject. Yet, there are deposited in the library nearly 1,000 volumes devoted exclusively to the horse, while the number containing references to it is countless.

The celebrity that has attended the horses of all ages that have carried successful generals in battle has led to their selection as models by artists and sculptors - but unhappily monuments are rarely erected until long after the generals and their horses have passed to the great beyond.

Many horses of military leaders such as "Bucephalus, " the charger of Alexander the Great, "Maringo" the famous horse of Napoleon, and "Copenhagen," the favourite mount of the Duke of Wellington, are well known in history.

The horse has been the companion and servant of man in nearly all his migrations and conquests and had always played an important part in the development of that civilization which is based upon intelligent cultivation of the soil.

From earliest times the horse has been known to exist on the high table lands of Asia. The use of horse chariots prevailed in Egypt as far back as the history of that country has been made known through monuments and ancient inscriptions.

The horse as depicted in the fifth century BC bears much resemblance to the wild horse of Asia in size, the shape of the head and neck, and the peculiar short, upstanding mane. From this early period the horse as pictured in the geographical areas now occupied by modern nations, began to show an increase in size and weight, and gradually assumed some of the conformation by which we now classify the several breeds of modern horses.

It is a remarkable fact that all history, ancient and modern, is more a recital of war and conquest than of industrial and commercial progress. Therefore, it is not surprising that the war horse is depicted, almost to the exclusion of any other, in the writings, pictures and sculptures of the ancients.

During the periods of peace, and with increasing populations, the needs of the agriculturists for farm animals began to take form, and the improvements in draft animals proceeded with that of war horses and gradually has come to be by far the most important. In all recorded history, trials of strength and speed have tempted men to train both themselves and their horses to enter the competitions, which, in ancient times played a great part in the affairs of state and nation.

The development of the horse has followed many lines, each indicating a purposeful end in view. The horse that is destined to seek its food on the open range, without shelter from the storms of winter and the midday rays of the sun in summer, accommodates itself to the conditions of its environment - the weak perish and the hardy survive.

Nowhere else in the world have draft animals been developed comparable in the slightest degree to the French Percherons, the British Shire, Clydesdales and the Belgians. Breeders the world over turns to them when seeking to improve their heavy breeds of horses.

Nearly every country has some particular breed of horse, on which the nation's pride is concentrated, even though it is an undersized horse or pony. There are always legends as to feats of endurance, speed or exhibitions of superior intelligence, to keep alive the sentiment of a community in which horse breeding plays an important role.

The saddle horse as known for many years was a horse of many gaits and of such refined training that he would change from one to the other at the indicated desire of his rider. The most important, as regards the Mounted Police Horse, are the walk, trot and canter gaits. Little difficulty is experienced in the training of Police mounts as much depends on the handling, and we find the majority of horses will respond to gentle treatment.

The horse best suited for police duty should stand 16 hands (a hand being 4 inches) and weighing 1300 to 1400 pounds. The breed preferable being part Clydesdale, Hackney or Coach. The Clydesdale is noted for good flat bone, considered cold-blooded, and a good weight carrier. The Hackney or Coach adds style and performance, the age of purchase being three, four or even five years. but at time of writing, one cannot pick or choose; we have to be content with conditions that exist and be governed accordingly.

At the commencement of training, the horse is allowed to get used to the conditions of his environment, fed, watered and talked to at regular intervals, after which the start of training commences the first thing being breaking or hardening the mouth. The method used is a rubber bit being inserted into the mouth securely attached to the bridle or halter to keep it in place. The horse gnaws or chews on the hard rubber to its heart's content, thereby hardening the gums in readiness for the steel bit.

The next move is the breaking tackle which consists of a flat broad saddle and girth, to which is attached a set of

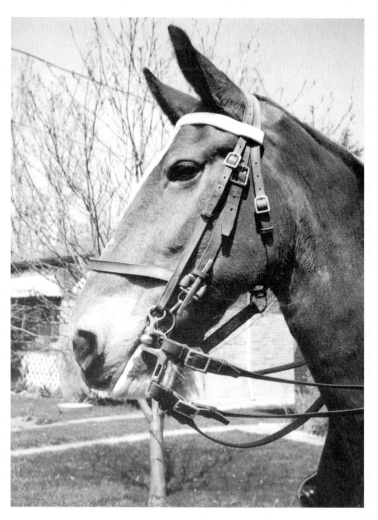

long lines. The horse is put through a period of training controlled by the line in a walk, trot and canter movement. After a period of ring work, it is surprising how quickly the horse responds to the various movements.

The next phase is getting the mount used to carrying weight, after being used to the saddle. The method used is sandbags of equal weight attached to each side of the saddle. After a few days of this treatment, the breaking tackle with long lines are used to teach the horse to side pass, back up, or any movement being taught. In order to strengthen the muscles of the neck and to teach the horse to carry its head erect, a strap is used, attached to the crown of the bridle along the neck and fastened in front of the saddle.

Then comes the most trying of all, getting the horse used to someone sitting on its back. This movement is generally started in the stable stalls. Some respond quickly and others take much longer, depending on the temperament of the horse. After the mount gets used to all the various requirements, including the rider on his back, it has to get used to the leg movement (instead of the long lines used in the first phase of his training) to teach the various movements of turns, sidepassing, etc. It is then taken out with an older horse to get used to traffic conditions, noises and anything that might occur during a day in the city.

In conclusion, I may say that the rider is held responsible for his mount and equipment. Once a horse has a steady rider, it is surprising how they get used to one another and form a team. It is necessary occasionally to change the horse and rider due to temperamental difficulties. The rider may take a dislike to his mount and the mount to the rider. Changes have to be made so that complete harmony will prevail.

The Indispensable Police Horse

On August 20, 1938, the *Globe and Mail* published an article entitled, "Toronto Demonstrates Horse Indispensable in Policing a City," which described Chief Constable Draper, a horse lover himself, as one of the staunchest supporters of the "oft-criticized mounted policeman." He fights for the unit not for sentimental reasons, but because he believes that it is one of the most important branches of the police service.

Montreal disbanded its Mounted Unit, but reinstated it when they found they could not get along without horses. Detroit had a mounted unit consisting of a half dozen scraggy nags. After they observed the effectiveness of the Toronto Mounted Unit a few years before, they began increasing their unit to a 1938 strength of seventy-six horses and projected to have one hundred and twenty five by 1940.

The forty-six-man Toronto Mounted Unit was the envy of every police department in North America. The article states, "The mounts' good manners and uncanny habit of doing the right thing at the right minute without apparent guidance from the rider is admired not only by Torontonians but visitors from the British Isles and the United States.

"A visit to the training school at Sunnybrook farm leaves one convinced that the main reasons for the almost perfect co-ordination between horse and rider are infinite patience and a firm but kind training. No horse attached to the department has had a sound thrashing since it was selected from some farm in Ontario.

"A green horse is bought when it is about 3 years old. Under the direction of Inspector Crosbie, who has been part of the Mounted Division for twenty-nine years, hours are spent walking, trotting and cantering the youngster in the schooling area before a saddle is even thrown over him. After three months he is ready for the noise and rumble of downtown traffic."[1]

(1) *Globe and Mail*, August 20, 1938.

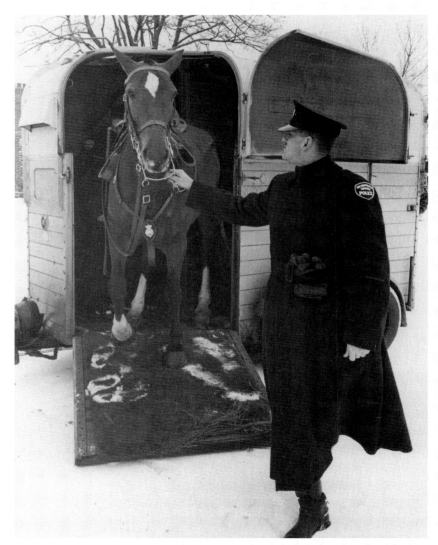

Police horses also have to be trained to enter, stand and ride peacefully in horse trailers for long periods. This is not always an easy task for them or their mounted trainers. Officers must use great care when transporting horses. One bad ride can completely sour a horse from ever travelling in a trailer. In this photograph from the 1960s, PC Jim Davis gently leads "Jay" off a front loading Rice Trailer. Notice that he is wearing a winter issue forage cap and has not had the reflective striping added to his riding cloak. Photograph, Toronto Star.

Recruits are taught to remain balanced while standing on the saddle, c. 1970.

More balancing exercises. c. 1970.

The recruits are also put through stretching exercises to reduce injuries and assist them with learning to balance, c. 1970.

Photographs, Toronto Police Museum.

Horses would be taught to stand still and behave in those situations when a horse would normally be startled—a streetcar or band passing, a loud bang, etc. The horse was trained to allow the rider to mount from either side and to obey the rider's aids of hands, body, legs and spurs. Remounts were taught to jump over low obstacles and to passage freely and easily from right to left and left to right, passage being one of the methods used to disperse a crowd.

A special bit was used so that the horse would respond to the slightest twist of the rider's hand. The horse was taught to carry the rider, without reigns or stirrups, at the gaits of walk, trot, canter and gallop. In 1938, a reporter for the *Globe and Mail* wrote an article praising the Toronto Police horses and their riders. The reporter commented on the kindness and patience shown to the police horses by their police officer trainers.[6]

In the days when horses were a common sight on Toronto streets, police horses were trained to stop runaways. To train the new horse, a mounted officer would ride an experienced police horse at a gallop without reigns or stirrups to simulate an out-of-control horse running away. The trainer would chase the runaway on the rookie horse, and when it caught up to the runaway, the trainer would teach the remount to cut in so that the runaway was driven into the curb.

One newspaper reporter provided the following description of the training horses received in 1924 after interviewing Sergeant, later Inspector, Crosbie; "Sometimes it takes as long as six months to train a young horse for police work and even after that period the horse cannot always be considered reliable. Three hours a day is devoted to the training, with patience and kindness accompanying all phases of the instruction. The horse is taught to respond to a faint pull on the rein and slight pressure by the rider's leg until he becomes proficient in the side pass, so that when he is called upon to keep a crowd back he will do it with the head or flank."

Inspector John Watt, officer-in-charge of the Mounted Division, Toronto Police Force, wrote the following essay. It appeared in the 1st quarter, 1956 issue, of *Police News Magazine*, a publication associated with the Police Association of Ontario. Reprinted with permission – Ontario Police Association.

Efficiency With Kindness

The Value of the Police Horse

"The extraordinary value of horses lies in controlling, not only an orderly crowd—but still more so an unruly mob of people whose temper and conduct may become inflamed with great and hazardous rapidity. Unless law and order prevails, riots could take a dangerous and ugly shape. We must be most grateful to these horses and riders who are capable of controlling crowds and regulating traffic under treacherous conditions and on the varying surfaces of modern roads. Needless to say, the man and the mount must have full confidence in each other to perform their difficult role, and also the handiness of the horse is by no means a minor factor.

Numerous occasions have given ample proof of the efficiency and value of the Mounted Police in controlling excitable sightseers. The patience and unfailing good humour they invariably display, with the tranquil methods they employ, enhance their popularity with the general public—for whom the sight of a Police horse on patrol is always cause for admiration.

The mount goes through the training stages from lunging to a course of long reining on the cavesson (by which the muscles and tendons are developed and strengthened to prepare it to carry weight). This also facilitates teaching responsiveness to the aids when the time comes to backing. Through this period the mount is gaining confidence, learning to understand and obey the voice, all-important factors in view of the severe tests he will have to undergo in the "Scare school." When the regular remount training is completed and he has graduated successfully through the riding school. Having proved capable of carrying out all such movements such as reining back, striking off at a canter on a desired leg at the indication of

Inspector John Watt with an unidentified senior officer, c.1960. Photograph, courtesy of the Watt Family.

his rider, etc., the recruit horse is gradually introduced to the various alarms. These range from flag waving to umbrellas being flapped in his face, accompanied by every conceivable element of surprise and noise; from bands, bagpipes and pneumatic drills to sirens in order to pass the final test for reliability on the busy thoroughfares. To be a custodian of crowds at ceremonial functions, political demonstrations and disturbances, he will have learned to ignore fire and smoke, and to stand imperturbably.

The training schedule includes a considerable amount of loose-rein riding, not only to give balance, but to teach the young horse to move forward freely without attempting to pull, and as preparation for creating a light mouth and confidence—as usually he has to be ridden with one hand. The police horse must get accustomed to being held up in traffic and in very congested circumstances, particularly for traffic duty in busy thoroughfares. An average sure-footed horse will, if he has been properly balanced and ridden collectedly with his hocks well under him, learn to keep his feet on all surfaces.

The proper shoeing of the police horse to enable it to cope with the numerous road surfaces is most important. Various types of feet demand different methods in the art of farriery, but the general principle is to keep frog pressure, maintain a healthy frog and prevent the heels becoming contracted. Studs are let into the heels of the shoes to foster grip.

A good steadfast eye, with breadth between the eyes, and ears carried upright and alert, invariably indicates a generous horse. Other requirements are for a horse of between 16 to 16 1/2 hands, showing quality and weight, with a good sloping shoulder to ensure the saddle being well placed, head well set with nice liberty of rein; depth through the heart, a well-ribbed middle section, strong loins with good quarters well let down into muscular gaskins standing on good, firm, unblemished legs and feet.

The selected horse would be walked and trotted on firm ground to examine for a good striding walk, clean action and surefootedness. His outlook has to be that of a well-balanced horse, for balance carries weight; having been lunged for wind, the final test would be to have him led back for a veterinary to examine eyesight, as defective vision which causes shying would be most dangerous in a Police horse. A horse shies invariably through fright, but there are some frightening elements that even training cannot offset and which will startle the most reliable veteran, such as the sudden flapping of a tarpaulin in a passing vehicle or the flapping of curtains at the back of a van.

There must always be Mounted Police. Mechanisation cannot take their place. In a disturbance, the Mounted Constable is equivalent to ten-foot police. From his height he can regulate crowds and traffic, make gangways speedily, and go practically anywhere in support of the foot police."

Inspector Ed Johnson watches a Mounted Unit trainer as he lunges a remount, The Horse Palace, C.N.E., c.1968. Photograph, Toronto Police Museum.

A Report On Horse Training

The following training report was submitted by Inspector Ed Johnson in 1965 or 1966.

"The most important element in maintaining this Unit is the training of horses and personnel. In a traffic-congested city such as this, managing a horse, especially a young horse, requires skill and caution. Both horses and personnel require more training than was necessary, say, ten or fifteen years ago. The training period for a remount is from six months to a year, depending upon the age and temperament of the horse when purchased. About one half this period is spent in the riding school, where, after being broke to bit and saddle, the horse is taught to walk, trot, canter and passage, in response to the aids of the rider. On completion of this phase, the horse then proceeds to the street, in company of an older horse to become accustomed to the strange sights and sounds of city traffic. When the trainer feels his horse has sufficient confidence he proceeds on his own and gradually works his horse into the more congested areas of the city. A great deal of patience is required by the rider in all phases of police-mount training. Even when the horse is handed over to a regular constable, he still requires patience, kind handling and confidence from his rider."

Merle Smith tries to mount a new horse. Smith was one the Mounted Unit trainers in the mid 1960s. November 21, 1964.

Working the horse on the lunge line. November 21, 1964.

Photographs, Toronto Telegram Photograph Collection, York University Archives and Special Collections, Negs. #1692 and #1690.

"When he has become manageable to a fair degree he advances to the more exciting work of learning how to stop a runaway horse as well as being taught how to stand after the rider has dismounted, how to follow in response to a soft word and how to come when called if he has been left standing. If he has demonstrated a tendency to back, that has to be overcome before he can go on the job. The training is very thorough and as a result the police horse seldom if ever gets flustered in a crowd. But keeps as cool as his rider who can guide him perfectly with a delicate touch on the lines and pressure of the knee denoting desired direction which is quite understood by the animal. A policeman never backs his horse into a crowd, all the work being done by movement forward and sideways. Sergeant Crosbie states with pride that there is no record of anyone in a Toronto crowd ever having been injured by a policeman's horse."[7]

In regards to stopping runaway horses the article stated:

"They are drilled in that sort of thing at the training school and seem to like it,' remarked Sergeant Crosbie. 'Of course they do not pick it up at once and some are much easier to teach than others. Occasionally horses are acquired which have never had a collar on and they are troublesome but they train all the better after a start has been made. Constable Mitchell, on putting them through their work, never raised his voice or uses a whip or spur. The confidence of the animal is obtained and then all runs smoothly. When a horse is turned out as fit for duty its first work is done in the quiet districts, then it advances to the light traffic areas and then becomes gradually used to things."[8]

As in cavalry training, the voice plays an important part in the horse's training. A good example was "Shamrock," the Kentucky-bred chestnut that Sergeant Crosbie rode. One article in the *Telegram* said that Shamrock was the most admired horse in Toronto. It described his ability to respond to voice commands.

"Here's a horse that his rider tells to go into a certain stall, or to come out. To turn around, to walk sideways or to assume that position of attention which is insisted on by discerning show ring judges–and the horse does all these commands as dutifully as the well-trained soldier."[9]

Before being purchased by the police department, "Shamrock" had won a number of ribbons at horse shows in the United States. He would shake hands on request and follow its master around like a well-trained dog.

The trainers begin working on the new horses right away. The first step, acclimatizing them to their new surroundings and the people in the barn. Once the trainer

Inspector Johnson adjusts a recruit's head kit while inspecting the troop at their graduation ceremony, c. 1970.

The recruits perform a "drill ride" at their graduation., c. 1970.

Photographs, Toronto Police Museum.

had the horse's confidence, he began to work it on the lunge line. Inspector Crosbie reported that "hours are spent walking, trotting and cantering the youngster in the schooling area before a saddle is even thrown over him." It would take about three months before the horse was first exposed to the "noise and rumble of downtown traffic."[10]

The initial training of the horse took about six months, after which the horse was turned over to another officer to begin street patrols and another six months before it was considered ready for all situations. The horse must be proven safe to use in all sorts of circumstances and accustomed to all sorts of noises without becoming startled. It must stand when left by his rider and follow when called. Before the remount could be put on regular duty, Sergeant Crosbie had to personally inspect its abilities before passing it as thoroughly schooled.

The final test took place right at the Belmont Street Stable. Neighbourhood children were invited to the barn to play with the new horse. The Inspector even permitted his own children to climb on the horse's legs. When the horse stood still and allowed the children to play around him he was considered ready to go to work.

The *Telegram* reported that the mounted men took great pride in teaching their horses tricks. The biggest horse in the department was over seventeen hands and worked at the Pape Avenue Stable. The horse had been taught to salute on command by lifting his foreleg. He would give his age when asked by pawing the ground. The horse would also nod for yes and shake his head for no.

Police horses have always received first class care. When they leave the barn, they are well groomed, with any ailment treated. The assigned officer was responsible for the care and condition of his mount. In 1930 the *Telegram* reported, "The men get to love their horses and woe betide the one who attempts to ill-treat a horse. The men would sooner suffer injury to themselves than [see it happen] to their horse."[11]

Not all of the police horses were well mannered. "The most vicious horse ever acquired was "Colonel." On one occasion he jumped over a stall to go after a man he did not like. It was necessary to put sandbags on his saddle for a long, long time before he got accustomed to putting weight on his back. He later became one of the most quiet and loveable of all. He was Deputy Chief Geddes favourite horse."[12] "Colonel" later went overseas with the draft of horses donated to the military and was killed at the front.

The average police horse served from five to six years, but many stayed for much longer. Police mount "Fidelity," a fifteen-year-old bay mare had served ten years at the time of the story and was described as "looking fit for another ten." She reportedly knows the proper hour in which she is to be fed. A bran mash was served once a week and "Fidelity" knew the night on which it comes and demonstrates her impatience "by her pleading whinnies."[13]

The horses would eventually reach the stage where their usefulness to the police had passed. This could be due to lameness, illness, age or just plain O.W.O. (Old and Worn Out). In the 1920s the sale of the horses was handled much like it is today.

Training constable Greg Ladner exercising a remount on the C.N.E. grounds. Photograph, Stan Behal, Toronto Sun.

Training The Police Horse in 1978

PC Andrew Currie and PC Don Vincent were two of the Mounted Unit's horse trainers in 1978. The following are extracts from an interview which appeared in The City, The *Toronto Star Sunday Magazine*. May 21, 1978, written by Gunter Ott "What Has Six Legs and Writes Parking Tickets?"

"The more experienced riders train young horses, while the older horses train young inexperienced riders."

Currie trains the new horses, called remounts, through association, gentleness, patience and repetition. He sees the task as almost an encounter with aliens, Martians maybe. 'You want to communicate but you lack a common language and interests' he says seriously. Currie's voice was described as having that soothing croon that calms a nervous horse.

Every day he enters the remount's stalls and eventually they come forward to nuzzle his hand. Slowly he introduces the horses to the weight of the blanket and finally to that of the saddle. 'You can't force them to learn faster than they are able, but usually within three to six months they're used to a man on their back and can move forward and back according to the trainer's command.'

The horse is then taken by an experienced rider into the park at Sunnybrook or the C.N.E. grounds where he can adapt to the noise and feel of the street. Here the rider must be alert to the needs of the horse because it will tell him through skittishness what conditions it fears.

It may be a manhole cover or the gravely growl of a cement mixer, but the rider must recognize the fear promptly and spend time helping the horse adjust. A policeman can't afford to have a less-than-confident horse out in the midst of traffic.

'On the street the rider has to be careful because people don't have the same respect and awareness for the horses that they used to have,' Currie said. 'They forget that the horse is not just another car and often drive up too close for comfort.'

Training the horse to accept noise is a long slow process that can take years. Only when both horse and rider feel they are ready for the street do they start out on regular patrols.

More from Currie on green halter broken horses: 'A halter broken remount has about as much training as a dog on a leash.' First thing the horse has to get use to is the bit. 'You have to convince the horse to open his mouth.' This is accomplished with much patients and kindness.

'We baby them at first, give them affection, try to give them confidence, they've got to be trained to be gentle, not aggressive.'

A horse that shows any signs of being vicious or high strung will be weeded out. We constantly pat the horses to get them used to being touched. 'We keep them docile. We don't want to make a riot out of a peaceful demonstration,' said Andy Currie.

After the horse gets used to the bit, it is introduced to the breaking harness and, at the same time it gets its main and feet clipped. Only the forelock will be left to identify the horse as a remount. After about three months if all goes well the forelock will be cut off. The horse will now be schooled in the double military bit The horse still needs much street training.

'It takes about a year for the animal to become reliable in the street,' said Don Vincent, 'you'd be amazed at what will scare them. A horse will go past 20 manhole covers and then panic at the twenty-first.' He explained street cars are another problem 'They're the noisiest dang things—and then suddenly the doors fly open."[1]

---

1 The City, The *Toronto Star Sunday Magazine*. May 21 1978.

"When it is time to sell a horse, Sgt Crosbie selects a home from a list of applicants. The sergeant must be satisfied the horse will live out its days in comparative comfort. Most of the horses are sold to good farms. Chief Dickson insists that the horse be well taken care of and considers this more important than the price obtained. He believes that the horses are entitled to pension as a form of reward for faithful service."[14]

One former police horse, "Countess," was sold to the jail farm and reported to be living a good life. Its companion at the farm was an old Fire Brigade horse. "Countess" apparently objected to being put in harness, but enjoyed being ridden around the farm.[15]

When the Sunnybrook Park Stable became available in 1930 the Mounted Unit had a top notch training facility. The grounds proved to be excellent for turning out trained horses. Bill Ganson and Andy Russell trained the horses at Sunnybrook Park in the 1930s. Unfortunately the police lost the facility during the Second World War and once again had to train at the Belmont Street Station.

In the early 1950s the remounts were stationed at Belmont Street. At first there was an area where the Rosedale subway station now stands where the horses could receive some training. Later the remounts had to be ponied (led by an officer on an experienced horse) by the trainer to Whitewoods stable on Pottery Road. This was a half-hour ride one way. The officers had to cross both Davenport Road and Yonge Street to get there

By 1961, the Mounted Unit was in desperate need of training facilities for the unit. The Canadian National Exhibition had been giving them use of the show rings located in the Horse Palace and Coliseum for short periods of time. Major reconstruction work was being done on the grounds and there had been an increase in the activities being held on the property. As a result, the Mounted Unit had to discontinue using the rings.

In his 1961 report, Inspector Watt stated that the horses required from six to eight weeks in the "Riding School." It would be increasingly difficult to train the horses without the use of the training rings.[16]

The horse-training problems of the Mounted Unit ceased with the acquisition of the Canadian National Exhibition Stable in 1965 and the Sunnybrook Stable in 1968. In winter the horses were schooled in the indoor ring at the Exhibition Stable. In the warmer weather the trainers and remounts moved up to Sunnybrook Park.

The remount trainers were assigned to work the day shift with weekends and holidays off. Their days off could be changed to cover any special details when the need arose. They were responsible to the Inspector for the actual training, progress and problem solving concerning their respective mounts. They were under the daily supervision of the sergeant or patrol sergeant who was supervising at the time they were on duty.

PC Dawn McCauley riding at her recruit graduation at Sunnybrook Park. Photograph, Toronto Police Mounted Unit.

The Mounted Unit had always used serving officers to train its staff. There is no record of any officers being sent to other police forces or training centres before the middle 1980s. In the past, many officers would have received mounted training in the cavalry before joining the police force. Very few mounted recruits have had previous training since the Second World War.

A few officers have attended equitation courses and seminars on their own time. Some enrolled in the equitation program that was offered at Humber College during the 1970s. Unfortunately this program has since been discontinued. Many others took private lessons or attended horse shows and other events to gain more knowledge.

In the late 1980s the Royal Canadian Mounted Police began accepting officers from Toronto in their annual two-week equitation courses. At least two spots were reserved for Toronto Police officers each year. Toronto police are now teaching all of their recruits and serving officers the more balanced R.C.M.P. riding and moving away from the foot forward cavalry riding of the past.

Toronto officers have also been sent to courses sponsored by the National Mounted Training Group in New York State and the Mounted Police course in Lexington, Kentucky. The Lexington police have asked Metropolitan Toronto Police Mounted Unit to teach the crowd control segment of the one-week course.

In 1994, the Mounted Unit hired Linda Whelden of the Sunnybrook Riding School to instruct the members of the unit in equitation. Every member of the unit attended a one-week course. The three member training team continued to receive weekly lessons from Linda and they, in turn, gave lessons to members of the unit.

The Mounted Unit has become very progressive in regards to training. Training Sergeant Howard Peers was sent to England in the summer of 1995 for a course with the Metropolitan Police of London, England. Their Mounted Unit is probably the premier crowd management unit in the world. They also have very high standards of equitation.

The crowd management philosophies of the British Police have been adopted in Toronto. Members of the unit are being instructed in the methods used by the British Police. Our focus on education and development is ensuring that the Toronto Police Mounted Unit continues to be one of the most professional police Mounted Units in North America—and the world.

Outside Training

PC Greg Vanderhart at the R.C.M.P. school in Ottawa. Photograph, courtesy PC Greg Vanderhart.

Trainers were to work their respective mounts through all phases of training, which included stable manners, clipping and trailer training in their initial stages. During their advanced stage of training, remounts were to be taken on their first parade, crowd-control duty, or other mounted unit functions. They had to experience these events with the trainers before they could be handed over to regular mounted personnel.

Training horses is a very demanding and physical job. It is almost inevitable that the trainers will be unseated at one time or another. The risk of injury is high. They have to have a gentle hand and endless patience. It is also in some ways a very thankless job. Regular members of the unit are sometimes quick to tell trainers the faults in a horse. They are seldom praised for the excellent job that they routinely do in producing excellent street horses.

Above and below: Resistance training at the Horse Palace. The horses are exposed to mock crowd management situations as part of their regular training.

Photographs, Toronto Police Mounted Unit, 1998.

Stable Safety

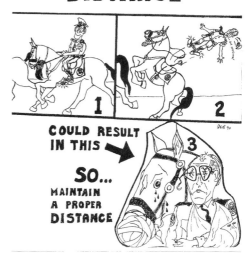

Sketches by PC Jim Bradford.

The Mounted Unit has one of the highest rates of on-duty injuries in the police service. Working with horses can be a very dangerous occupation. The cartoons shown above, sketches of actual incidents, were informally drawn and posted at the C.N.E. Stable. Although not officially sanctioned, they serve an important purpose.

The cartoons reaffirm safety standards in a humorous way by demonstrating how human error can result in an injury. Human error or inexperience causes most Unit injuries.

It is important that an officer be assigned to a mount that he or she has the experience and ability to ride safely. All Unit injuries are investigated and preventative measures sought to prevent a reoccurrence.

Officers should never forget they are working with animals, they should never become complacent around horses.

Horse Stories ...

"OOPS" Becomes a Police Horse

by Paul MacQueen

The Toronto police buy three or four new horses a year. Some are purchased from dealers, some come from farmers and others come from families. I asked one family that sold us a horse, which I knew they loved, how they felt about him becoming "Stuart," of the Toronto Mounted Police. Here is their reply, written from the horses point of view:

"Some of us with the Mounted Unit have had an interesting life outside of policing, before we learned to "Serve and Protect."

I, for example, began my life with a young girl named Amy MacQueen. I have not always been known as "Stuart." My mother was a quarter horse and could turn on a loonie. She planned to have a foal by a quarter horse stallion that could turn on a dime. But, alas, she fell for a Belgian stallion. I came into the world, to be known as "Oops," an accident.

At the age of 8, Amy made a deal to clean my stall for a year if she could own me. My master knew that Amy could not afford one of his reining horses, but her argument had some advantages. So, when I was 6 months old, Amy became not just my friend but my owner. I learned to wear harnesses, pull a cart, drag a log from my saddle horn, to walk, trot and canter on command; and before I was 3, we had competed at a small fair.

During the winter I was 2, Amy and I would ride through the snow-covered fields near Guelph together. Though she hung on tightly, it was clear to Amy's father that I was too much horse for her at that young age. He decided to look for someone more experienced for me, and for a horse with a little more experience for Amy, on which she could compete in eventing.

I was fortunate when my family sold me to the Toronto Police. They had received another offer for me—one with a little more money, but the Toronto Police gave Amy first right of refusal when it came to my time to retire. They also promised Amy she could come and see me any time she wished. Amy even helps at some of the shows we compete in like the C.N.E. and Can Am games. She has become great friends with some of my riders, although sometimes she distracts me slightly at the competitions. I am glad Amy and her Dad keep in touch, although I hope she never sees me in some of the darker sides of my work as I "Serve and Protect" in Toronto.

Amy's new mount, a flashy gray mare, has served her well and is expecting a foal from a grandson of Secretariat. (They say he was a chestnut and looked just like me.)"

With thanks to Paul and Amy MacQueen.

Amy with a young Oops "Stuart" at the family farm. Long before the family considered selling the horse to the Toronto Police. Photograph, courtesy the MacQueen Family.

Amy and Oops "Stuart" soon after she began riding him. Photograph, courtesy the MacQueen Family.

PC Ron Gilbert and "Stuart" talk to Amy McQueen at the Can Am Police Horse Show at Sunnybrook Park, July 1998. Photograph, courtesy the MacQueen Family.

"Regal's" New Job

by Helen Curtin

Police mount "Regal" served Toronto Police Service for 4 1/2 years. I first met "Regal" while he was still in training. As a volunteer exercise rider, I looked at this tall, 17.2 HH, good looking, lively guy with a special "I want to ride him" glint in my eye. I soon got the chance and discovered that "Regal" wasn't easy. He was always aware of every change in his surroundings, spooky, sensitive, but when you got his attention he would try his big heart out to respond the way you asked. These qualities proved difficult in the real life, practical world of the Mounted Unit. "Regal" did not tolerate different riders well. He could be stubborn, and even refuse to get on the trailer when not handled just so. The 'spooks' proved difficult and very dangerous in the busy downtown traffic. Then there was the incident where "Regal" spooked badly on the Bathurst Street bridge, and leapt into the horse and Officer beside him almost sending the Officer flying over the bridge rail to the tracks and passing GO Train below. "Regal" just wasn't very well suited to the job of a police horse.

PC Bob Bowen and "Regal" at the Collingwood Horse Show, 1998. Photograph, Carol Robbins.

My continual interest and appreciation of "Regal" was rewarded with the opportunity to buy him in October 2000. I was happy to offer him a new home and career—a rare opportunity, as "Regal" was young in retirement terms, at 9 years old. "Regal" immediately adapted to the rolling green hills and daily frolics in a paddock at Joker's Hill in King Township. The comings and goings of tractors and feed delivery trucks were easy for him to accept, compared to streetcars and cement mixers, but I had more in mind. Working with the Joker's Hill coach, Ken Denouden, we embarked on a program to see if "Regal" could become a jumper. Lo' and behold, with gradual and patient work, "Regal" made his debut in the spring of 2001 at the Palgrave Horse Show in the Beginner Hunter Division. With continued coaching, "Regal," although a little unorthadox compared to the lighter and more finely bred show horses, emerged from his first season standing in 7th Place overall in the Division, we will be the recipients of a lovely year end award.

There are a number of wonderful behaviours "Regal" has brought with him from his former career. Regardless of the commotion around him, "Regal" will stand and park. He does not think of kicking at other horses, no matter how close they pass. He is entirely comfortable being ridden in a crowd of horses. You can't chase him. If you try and encourage "Regal" to run around and release some energy while he is turned out, he will not run away. You can wave your arms, or even flick things at him, but he only comes closer. If you persist and annoy "Regal" he will walk right over you—a direct result of the crowd control training.

Helen Curtin and "Regal" clearing a jump at a competition in the horse show circuit. Photograph, David Brooks.

In 2002, "Regal" is headed back to the jumper ring. The fences are a little higher, the pace a little faster, the turns tighter. If he can do it, that will be wonderful, if it proves not to be his cup of tea, it doesn't matter, "Regal" will always have a wonderful home with me and we will happily venture into new and different activities. Hmmm, maybe he would like fox hunting.

"Bruce" the *King of the Barn*

by Kristen Guest

Retired police mount "Bruce" gallops around his new pasture seconds after being turned out in his new country home. Photograph, Sgt Dale Guest.

Over his 15 year career with the Mounted Unit, police mount "Bruce" pulled the Queen's landau, escorted governor generals, competed at the police nationals—and even beat out an R.C.M.P. team in a jump-off as part of the 110th Anniversary celebration. He participated in the Musical Ride, Drill Team, World Series and Grey Cup celebration parades, and he was on patrol for the closing of Maple Leaf Gardens. Despite his colourful career, though, Bruce is still best remembered as "king of the barn."

When "Bruce" was acquired from the Mennonites as a three-year-old in 1984, he was assigned to PC Jim Bradford who remained his rider until Bruce's retirement in 1999. Bruce was also trained to work in harness and was a member of the ceremonial landau team in the 1980s. Independent, forward and athletic, Bruce was an excellent police horse well suited for crowd control duties and police competitions.

Bruce was a dominant member of the police herd. He was not afraid of any horse, or person, and would take advantage of any opportunity to assert his authority within the barn. He would kick or bite any horse that he felt was a threat to his position in the horse hierarchy. Officers soon learned what horses could not ride beside Bruce. As a member of the Musical ride Bruce could only ride beside passive horses, or he would spend the entire ride trying to bite or kick his section mates. The officers assigned to Bruce had to be vigilant when riding him and working on the ground around him. Those that became complacent might find themselves in the middle of a horse fight, or worse, nursing a wound caused by one of Bruce's favourite past times, biting policemen.

Bruce's attitude didn't always endear him to everyone— but he did find a fan in Sergeant Dale Guest, who came to the Mounted Unit in 1996. Dale liked Bruce's independent spirit, which made him an excellent mount for leading his platoon during demonstrations. Both Bruce and Dale also liked to race and did so at every opportunity. Dale decided that he wanted to purchase Bruce when he retired, but in 1997 he got some competition. Kristen Leaver, a volunteer rider for Metro, also adopted Bruce as her favourite.

Dale and "Bruce," note the mane "Bruce" has grown in retirement. Photograph Sandra MacKenzie.

By the time Bruce was retired due to arthritis in 1999, the question of who would get to adopt him was happily resolved. Dale and Kristen had become a couple and together they decided to bring him home to their farm north of Toronto. Turned loose for the first time, Bruce showed that injuries aside, he still loved to run.

In the spring of 2001, Bruce performed one last ceremonial duty—as "best man" at Dale and Kristen's wedding. Bruce now goes for an occasional ride in the country, but spends most of his time out at pasture with his horse friends—and is still "king of the barn."

Kristen, Dale and "Bruce." Photograph, Sandra MacKenzie.

"Bess"

Police mount "Bess" was almost 20 years old when she was retired and purchased by the Witherspoon family. She immediately embarked on a new career as a show horse. Stephanie Witherspoon has ridden Bess in competitions all over Ontario. She has successfully used the horse in a number of different disciplines including Dressage and Hunt classes.

Stephanie and "Bess."

All photographs, courtesy of the Witherspoon Family.

"Bess" and Stephanie in the Dressage Ring.

"Bess" and Stephanie show perfect form while clearing a fence.

Bridles On.
A recruit class tacks up
at the CNE Stable.

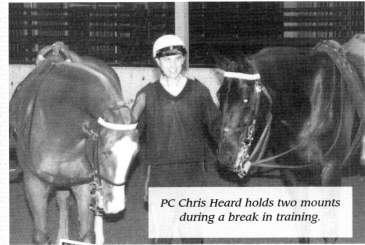

PC Chris Heard holds two mounts
during a break in training.

Right: Tied out to graze, Sunnybrook
Park, c. 1970. Photograph, Author's
Collection.

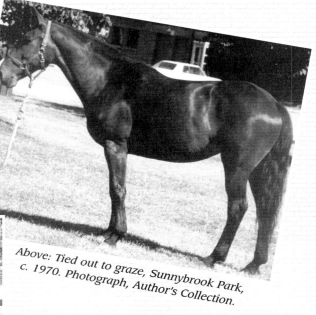

Above: Tied out to graze, Sunnybrook Park,
c. 1970. Photograph, Author's Collection.

Above: "Susan" enjoys the paddock
at 4 District Stable in Scarborough,
c. 1985.

Right: A police
horse enjoys a
gallop on the
track at Woodbine
Race Track.

"Susan" in the paddock at
4 District Stable in
Scarborough, c. 1985.

Police mounts receive
constant veterinary attention.
Dr. Ralph Watt and a young
assistant give an injection to
a mount at the CNE Stable.

The Names of the Toronto Police Horses

The Toronto Police horses are named by the officer-in-charge of the Mounted Unit. In most cases the horse is given a recycled name. The reason for this is economy since there are nameplates and equipment labelled with the name used by a previous horse.

This certainly causes confusion when "time on" mounted officers are talking about horses. There is talk of the "old Tom" or "the old chestnut Tom." To simplify matters the horses will also be identified in conversation by associating it to the officer who had ridden it, such as "Smith's Tom." Through its history the unit has ten or more horses with the more common names such as "Prince," "Queen," "Billy," "Regent," etc.

A list of the names used to identify Toronto police horses has been compiled. There is no master record of names kept so therefore there are probably some omissions. The list also contains the names of horses purchased for the police wagon service, ambulance service and police prison service. I have included them too, although they were not "mounted" horses, they were cared for by the mounted men and were under the care of the officer-in-charge of the Mounted Unit.

There are some interesting patterns to the names used by the Inspectors. The ambulance service used horses named "Doctor," "Bandage," "Coroner," "Fireman." The prison van used such horses named "Matchless," "Matchmaker," and "No Good." There was a period when the names of towns in Ontario were used for the horses. During the First World War patriotic names, such as "Kitchener," "Verdun," "Neutrality" and "Victory" were used.

During the 1920s, a great variety of different names were used. By the 1960s the unit was basically recycling the same names over and over again. Inspector Heenan named a number of horses after retired officers during his tenure. Such as "Sutherland" after former Inspector Edwin Sutherland Johnson, and "Connie" after the unit's former blacksmith, Konrad Myiers. A number of other officers were also honoured in this way.

Since 1998 the unit has been participating in contests with the Royal Winter Fair and the *Toronto Sun* newspaper. People are given the opportunity to submit names for the horse that is to be donated to the Mounted Unit from these two organizations. The Mounted Unit has also hosted internal competitions within the police service to pick out a name for our new horses.

Some horses are still named after specific events. Police mount "Spencer" was named after Diana Spencer the Princess of Wales. He had been purchased during the week that she died and was given her name as a lasting tribute.

When a remount is purchased it is given a name and a regimental number by the police service. The number begins with the year of purchase and the order of purchase. For example the first horse purchased in 1986 would be M.T.P.86 - 1. The fifth horse purchased would be M.T.P.86 - 5.

Until the 1990s, horses had the police force initials and regimental number tattooed on their upper lip. The initials used in the regimental number stood for T.P.F. (Toronto Police Force) or M.T.P. (Metropolitan Toronto Police). It is no longer felt that the tattoo is necessary to verify the identification of the horse. The tattooing process is painful and its identification value does not justify the discomfort to the horse. Most individuals who own horses today have microchips imbedded within the horses if they desire a means of permanent identification.

An old style stall nameplate. Photograph, PC Derrick Speirs.

General

The Horses Who Have Served With the Toronto Police Force

Illustrations by PC Kris McCarthy.

Chief

Trooper

Abby
Acton
Actor
Actress
Admiral
Ailsa Craig
Alex
Amtracite
Andrew
Anne
Archer
Arrow
Aspinwall
August
Autumn
Badger
Bangle
Barney
Barrie
Barron
Barroness
Beauty
Belle
Belmont
Bess
Bessie
Billy
Black Beauty
Blackie
Blacksmith
Blackwatch
Bob
Boot
Bonnie
Bonny Scotland
Bounser
Bracelett
Brampton
Brigadier
Briton
Bruce
Brutus
Buccaneer
Buck
Budea
Byng
Caesar
Cambridge
Canada
Candy
Casey
Champ
Charger
Charles
Charneford
Chatham
Chester
Chief

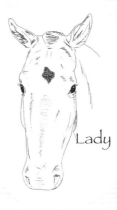
Lady

Boot

Chieftan
Chummy
Clancy
Colleen
Colonel
Connaught
Connie
Coronation
Coroner
Countess
Crowe
Crusader
Daisy
Dan
Dandy
Diana
Dick
Dilver
Division
Dobbin
Doctor
Dolly
Donna
Dora
Doreen
Dorothy
Dover
Dragoon
Duchess
Duke
Dungannon
Edgeley
Elizabeth
Ellismere
Elsie
Emblem
Emblematic
Emperor
Empress
Erindale
Fidelity
Firebird
Fireman
Freddy
Gallops
General
George
Georgetown
Ginger
Girgil
Glen
Golden
Golden Glow
Goldie
Goldon Rod
Harry
Havelock
Hazel

Hector
Hillcrest
Hodgson
Horace
Hussar
Ivan
Ivanhoe
Jack
Jarvis
Jay
Jean
Jeanni
Jessie
Jim
Jim McNeil
Joan
Joe
Jubilee
Julie
Juryman
Kate
Keith
King
Kitchener
Konrad
Laddie
Lady
Lady
Lady Bird
Lancer
Lazarus
Lexation
Lincoln
Listowel
Longboat
Lorraine
Louise
Louvain
Lucknow
Lucy
Mack
Majic
Major
Mand
Marathon
Marie
Matchless
Matchmaker
Matthew
Maureen
Mayfair
Mayflower
Mayo
Millie
Mischief
Mistake
Misty
Molly

Smokey

Royal
Sun

Duke

Montgomery
Monty
Moon Shadow
Mystic
Nancy
Nellie
Neutrality
No Good
Norval
Ontario
Oxford
Paddy
Patience
Patricia
Pearl
Peggy
Peggy McNeil
Pickering
Picton
Postmaster
Primrose
Prince
Princess
Princeton
Prudence
Queen
Red
Red Cross
Regal
Regent
Renfrew
Revenge
Rinwood
Rob Roy
Robin
Rockwood
Roger
Rolston
Rosedal
Roy
Royal
Royal Sun
Royal York
Rufus
Rusty
Sabre
Sally
Sam
Sandy
Sarge
Scarboro
Selkirk
Shamrock
Shelton
Sherbrooke
Silver
Simcoe
Skirmisher

Spencer

Teddy

Smokey
Spencer
St. David
St. George
St. Patrick
St. Paul
Star
Stewart
Stormy
Strategy
Stuart
Sunrise
Sunset
Sunshade
Sunshine
Sunshine Boy
Susan
Sutherland
Tammy
Teddy
Tempest
Tempest
Thamesville
Thorndale
Timmis
Toby
Tom
Trillium
Trinity
Trooper
Vanguard
Vanity
Verdun
Victory
Virgil
Viscount
Warneford
Watford
Westminster
White Oak
Winston
Woodstock
Wyndham

Winston

Chapter 7

The Equipment and Regalia of the Toronto Mounted Police

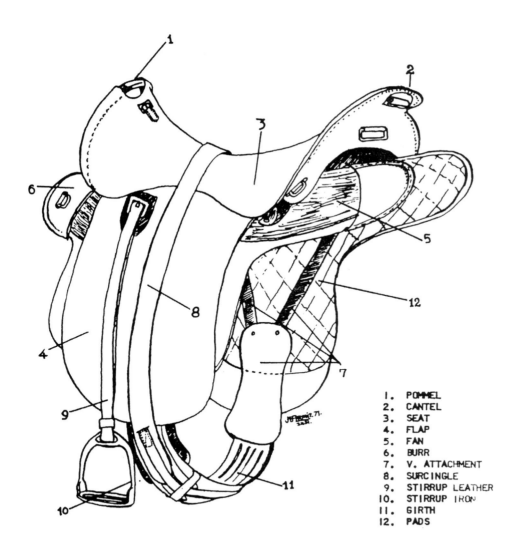

1. POMMEL
2. CANTEL
3. SEAT
4. FLAP
5. FAN
6. BURR
7. V. ATTACHMENT
8. SURCINGLE
9. STIRRUP LEATHER
10. STIRRUP IRON
11. GIRTH
12. PADS

This sketch of the Universal cavalry saddle was made as a training aid by Mounted Unit Constable Alisteir McKechnie.

The Saddle

The saddle used by the Mounted Unit is the Universal Trooper Saddle of the British Army. As cavalry troopers spent most of their day on horseback, the saddle was designed to be comfortable for extended periods. It is ideal for police work as mounted officers also spend many hours in the saddle each day. The Universal saddle has a very deep seat which tends to help hold the rider in place. The saddle's solid design and high arches has probably prevented many officers from becoming unseated.

In summer, officers ride with nickel stirrups, although the Unit is gradually switching over to stainless steel. In winter, officers use wooden stirrups covered with leather.

It is interesting to note that until the 1960s, the Mounted Unit was still using surplus cavalry equipment from World War I. One day, while on patrol, Constable Jim Davis was stopped by a man who identified himself as a veteran of the Canadian Field Artillery from the First World War. The man commented on the similarity of the tack that Jim was using, to that which he had used 50 years before. Jim asked the man to look at the bottom of his stirrup irons, stamped C.F.A. 1914,— short for Canadian Field Artillery, 1914 issue.

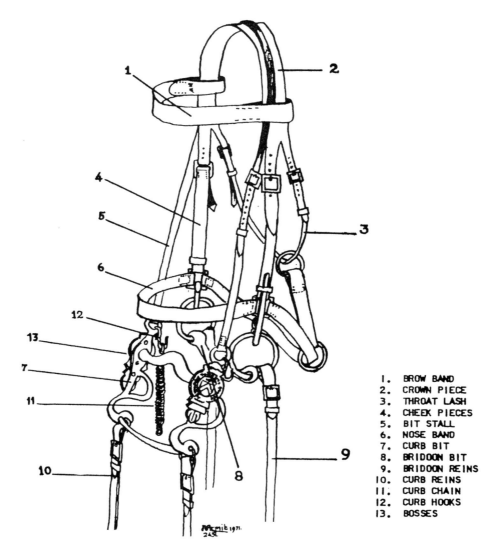

1. BROW BAND
2. CROWN PIECE
3. THROAT LASH
4. CHEEK PIECES
5. BIT STALL
6. NOSE BAND
7. CURB BIT
8. BRIDOON BIT
9. BRIDOON REINS
10. CURB REINS
11. CURB CHAIN
12. CURB HOOKS
13. BOSSES

Mounted Unit Constable Alisteir McKechnie made the above sketch of the cavalry style head kit as a training aid.

The Head Kit

The Mounted Unit uses a British Army double bridle with bridoon and curb bits. Officers ride predominately on the bridoon or snaffle bit, considered fairly mild on a horse's mouth. The curb bit is more severe, and gives the officer extra leverage should he or she have trouble controlling the horse.

The head kit was originally designed to become a halter at night. Cavalry troopers could take off the snaffle bit, then undo the curb bit that was held on by one strap.

Once the bits were out, the remaining leather became a halter. The white rope could then be used to tie the horse's halter to the nightlines.

The design of this head kit makes it very versatile and ideal for police work.

The Mounted Unit's training staff has the option of using a few different bit combinations while the horses are being trained. Recruit classes use milder bits while being taught how to ride. Mounted Unit volunteers also ride with milder bits.

The goal of any Unit officer should be to help his or her mount maintain a soft mouth. A gentle bit, and the soft use of the hands, will accomplish this while greatly enhancing the performance of the mount.

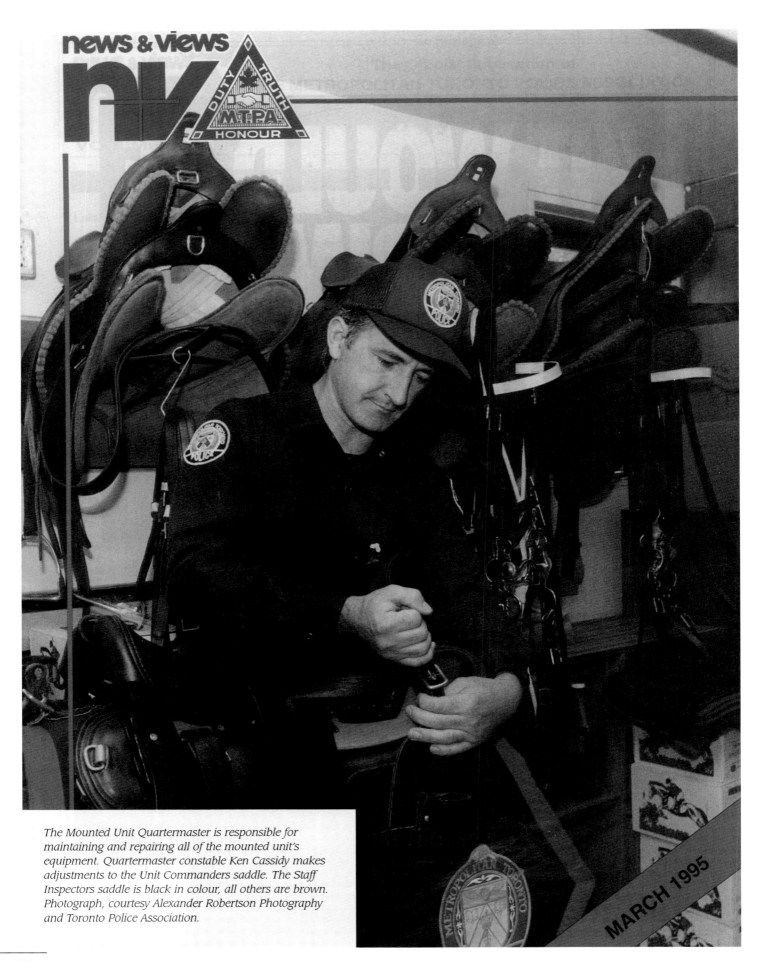

The Mounted Unit Quartermaster is responsible for maintaining and repairing all of the mounted unit's equipment. Quartermaster constable Ken Cassidy makes adjustments to the Unit Commanders saddle. The Staff Inspectors saddle is black in colour, all others are brown. Photograph, courtesy Alexander Robertson Photography and Toronto Police Association.

MARCH 1995

Above: A great place to work, the smile says it all. PC Gino Sonsini holds his head kit prior to tacking up his mount. Mounted officers take pride in the condition of their uniform and equipment. The appearance of the Toronto Police horses and officers is second to none.

Below: The Universal saddle and dress blanket. A sheepskin cover has been added to the girth to protect a sensitive area on the horse's stomach. Photograph, PC Derrick Speirs.

Top left: Officers are responsible for the condition and cleanliness of their issued equipment. Training Constable Larry Bullock cleans his kit at the end of his shift.

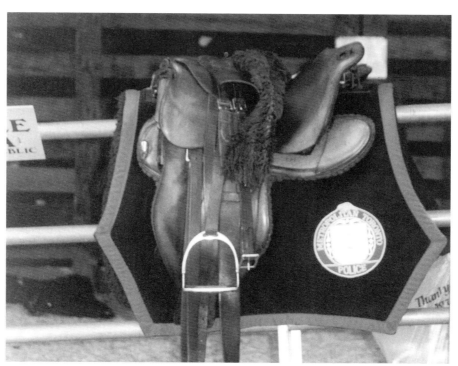

The Numnah Pad

The numnah pad is placed between the saddle and the horse's back. Its purpose is to protect the horse's back from the saddle. Toronto Mounted Police used felt numnah pads. The Staff Inspector and Staff Sergeant still use these pads on their kits. In the 1970s however, regular patrol officers were issued a thick brown, synthetic numnah pad.

If a horse has a sensitive back, or is engaged in a period of strenuous work, such as musical ride rehearsals a blanket is also used for protection. Sometimes, sheepskin is also placed around the horse's girth to prevent injury.

The White Rope

The white rope around the horse's neck always raises questions from people on the street. It is looped around the horse's neck and tied with a "hangman's knot," before being clipped onto the bottom of the head kit. The original purpose of the white rope was to give the cavalry troopers something to tie their horses up with at night. Today mounted officers continue to ride with the rope partly for appearance reasons, and also to provide a means of securing a horse in an emergency should they have to abandon the mount on the street.

Bit Bosses

The Mounted Unit began using custom bit bosses in 1886, soon after the Unit's formation. Bosses were mounted on the sides of the curb bit and on the horse's breastplate. These custom bit bosses were used until 1966, when a new boss was issued. It was inscribed Metropolitan Toronto Police, and had the municipal seal in the middle. The police service's name change in 1998 may lead to a new issue bit boss in the future.

Sketches of the two styles of bit boss and breastplate badge used by the Toronto police Mounted Unit. On the left is the 1886 issue Toronto Police Force boss. On the right is the 1966 issue Metropolitan Toronto Police bit boss.

The 1886 issue bit boss. The brass emblems need to be polished daily to maintain their luster. Photograph, PC Derrick Speirs.

The white rope can be seen around this horse's neck. PC Walter Metcalfe on Rosedale Valley Road, c.1953. Photograph, Toronto Police Museum.

The Lance

Lances used by the Mounted Unit are made of bamboo imported from Pakistan. They are difficult to locate for purchase and expensive when they do become available. The majority of the lances still in use with the Mounted Unit were purchased from the Canadian Government as war surplus cavalry equipment in the 1960s. These lances are at least 80 years old. They are nine feet long and weigh between 4-4.5 pounds. The parts of the lance are known as the point, butt, pole, point of balance and sling.

The Pennant

Cavalry has always carried pennants coloured specifically to the squadron to which troopers were assigned so that in the confusion of battle, a trooper could look around and ride to where pennants of his troop were visible. The pennant of the Mounted Unit, introduced in 1966, is composed of the colours of the Metropolitan Toronto police service.

All cavalry pennants have a red stripe at the top. The reason for this is so the blood of the stabbed enemy will not stain the flag. The Mounted Unit's pennant is red, dark blue and yellow in descending order.

In 1992, in honour of Canada's 125th birthday, Walter Shanley of Sunnybrook Riding Academy purchased eighteen pennants displaying the "Canada 125" logo. These pennants were donated to the Mounted Unit, to be used by the Musical Ride. The pennants are carried at all ceremonial details.

A photograph showing a Metropolitan Toronto Police bit boss mounted on both a curb bit (left) and a breast plate (right). Photograph, Author's Collection. (Alex Thompson.)

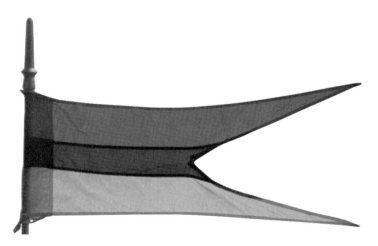

Above: The pennant of the Toronto Police Mounted Unit. Photograph, PC Derrick Speirs.

Left: The author and "Tom." Note the bamboo lance with the white 1992 "Canada 125" pennant attached. Photograph, Toronto Police Mounted Unit.

Dress Blankets

Dress blankets used by the Toronto Mounted Police have always been dark blue with a wide red stripe around the edges. During the 1930s, and continuing through to 1956, the Toronto Police Department used a crest with the initials T. P. D. at the back. The initials were changed to M. T. P. in 1957. The current Metropolitan Toronto Police crest was added to the blanket in 1966.

The 1957 Metropolitan Toronto Police dress blanket insignia.

The improved 1966 dress blanket insignia.
Photographs, Leslie Bluestein.

A mounted officer in spring/fall dress, c.1900. He is wearing a dark blue "Bobby" style helmet and box neck tunic with identifying numbers attached to the epaulets. His riding breeches have a red stripe down the leg. He is using the Universal style cavalry saddle with nickel stirrups and military head kit. The white rope can be seen around the horse's neck. The tack being used by the officer is identical to that being used by the Mounted Unit 100 years later. Photograph, Toronto Police Museum.

Head Dress

Officers of the Toronto Police used the British style "Bobby" helmet from the mid-1800s until 1946. A dark blue helmet was worn in the fall, winter and spring, while a white helmet was worn in the summer. The white helmet was retired in 1919.

Mounted officers stopped wearing "Bobby" Helmets in the late 1920s when they were issued with forage caps. The forage cap was modified over the years, but remained in regular use until 1993 when it was replaced with a safety helmet issued for use on the street.

In 1966, a white "Bobby" style helmet was issued to members of the Unit as part of the new ceremonial dress uniform. Members of the Musical Ride were issued with police crested baseball hats to wear during ride practices. Eventually these too were discontinued and replaced by the safety helmet.

During the 1920s, officers were required to purchase a Persian wool hat for wear in the winter months. The hats were removed from service about 1940 and were replaced with a winter forage cap. In the mid-1960s, a Persian wool hat, or "wedgey" as it was known, was brought back into service. This hat was withdrawn from daily use when the Yukon style winter hat was issued to all members of the

Toronto Police "Bobby" style helmet.

police service in 1984. The "wedgey" was retained by the Mounted Unit for dress details.

In 1998 the crested baseball cap became the standard head dress for all members of the Toronto police service. The baseball cap was replaced the following year with a new style forage cap.

A mounted officer in summer dress, c.1900. The officer is wearing a lighter weight summer box-neck tunic. The white summer issue "Bobby" helmet was used until 1919. Note the Saint John Ambulance first aid badge on his left sleeve. Photograph, Toronto Police Museum.

This photograph of PC Frank Lepper was taken in 1956 just prior to the formation of the Metropolitan Toronto Police Force. Note the dress saddle blanket with T. P. D. sewn onto it. PC Lepper is also wearing the red triangular 1955 issue mounted unit patch on his shoulder. Photograph, Toronto Police Museum.

Top left: Police issue forage cap. Year 2000 pattern. This is a lighter weight version of the previous forage cap.

Top right: 1960s issue "Wedgey" style winter hat. Photograph, PC Derrick Speirs.

Bottom right: 1986 Yukon-style winter hat.

Bottom left: Female officer's hat, issued from 1976 to 1991 when all officers began wearing the forage cap.

All badges are 1971 issue Metropolitan Toronto Police cap badges.

Photographs, PC Derrick Speirs.

A mounted officer c.1928. The forage cap has replaced the "Bobby" helmet. Guns are now worn in external holsters. Photograph, Toronto Police Museum.

The 1966 issue ceremonial dress helmet with a 1971-issue cap badge. Photograph, PC Derrick Speirs.

The mounted officer on the left is wearing the old style Snake belt. The officer on the right, PC Leary, is wearing the new issue Sam Browne belt that included a cross strap. The officers are wearing two different styles of box neck tunic. Both officers have their raincoats attached to the front of their saddles. c.1930. Photograph, Toronto Police Museum.

Winter patrol in Scarborough, c.1963. PC Wear is riding "Bonnie" and PC Davis is on "Jay." The officers are wearing winter issue forage caps with a second issue Metropolitan Toronto cap badge attached. They are wearing riding cloaks with the first issue shoulder patch. Yellow reflective piping has not yet been added to the cloaks. Note that the white ropes are not worn in the winter. Photograph, Toronto Star.

Left: The 1999 crested baseball cap, was withdrawn from regular service after one year. Mounted officers are still permitted to wear the hats when dismounted during rest breaks at public order management details.

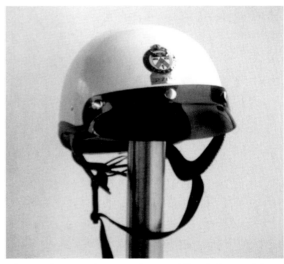

Left: The second issue public order management safety helmet. "Riot" style helmets were first issued in 1988.

Photographs, PC Derrick Speirs.

Above: The 1993 issue Lexington riding helmet. This helmet is used by mounted officers during general patrol and training, and has saved many officers from serious injuries.

The MOUNTED UNIT

The officers of the Mounted Unit are shown here as they paraded for inspection in front of the University of Toronto's Hart House in 1913.

From a modest beginning with 5 horses and 7 officers who were "expert horsemen with cavalry experience", the Mounted Unit has grown almost tenfold.

The Unit was formed in 1886 to stop a rash of "wild riders and drivers" who frightened the residents of Toronto's outlying areas – north of Bloor Street.

The public's longstanding affection for the Mounted Unit has fostered a special relationship between its officers and citizens. This is supported by the Unit's frequent public appearances, the Police Games, and the Musical Ride.

When the city's citizens first saw Toronto's Mounted officers during Queen Victoria's Golden Jubilee celebration parade in 1887, they stated in no uncertain terms "their admiration for the straight-backed officers on their fine-looking steeds".

Today's duties include searches (particularly in inaccessible areas such as parks and ravines), general patrol and traffic duty, parades, and ceremonial duties.

Horse and rider enjoy their greatest advantage in crowd situations, like concerts, sporting events, strikes and demonstrations. From a vantage point some 9 ft. above the crowd, Mounted officers can safely direct and control an unruly mob, thereby enhancing the safety and security of both foot officers and the public.

Mounted officers are fully trained police officers who ask to become part of the Mounted Unit. Officers and horses train each winter in jumping and cavalry drill, equestrian skills, crowd control and V.I.P. escorts.

Large, well-boned horses with even temperaments are required for police work. Horses are purchased between 2 and 6 years of age, and may continue in service for 15 years before being sold into private hands.

The Toronto Police Museum

The Toronto Police Museum is located in the front lobby of Police Headquarters at 40 College Street. The museum maintains a display dedicated to the history of the Mounted Unit. It includes a black fibreglass horse that is a scale copy of former police mount "King."

Many other displays contain artifacts also relevant to the Mounted Unit. Numerous photographs and artifacts help document its proud history.

Left: Part of the Mounted Unit display at the Toronto Police Museum. Photograph, Toronto Police Museum.

HORSIN' AROUND

Mounted Const. Peter Scribner waits as his horse Colonel, checks out the new pony in town and Police Cadet

Doug Kavanagh props up the phoney pony's rider. The mannequins are part of the police museum that's just

moved to the first floor at Metro Police headquarters, 590 Jarvis St. It opens officially this Monday.

Left: PC Peter Scribner and "Colonel" watch as police cadet Doug Kavanagh lifts a mannequin into the former Police Headquarters located at 590 Jarvis Street. Prior to its move to 40 College Street, the Police Museum used the plastic chestnut horse and mannequin in ceremonial dress to represent the Mounted Unit. Photograph, Fred Thornhill, Toronto Sun.

The Ceremonial Dress Uniform

PC Pat Woulfe wearing the 1965 ceremonial dress uniform that demonstrates the new issue of wide-striped breeches and red cap band. The saddle blanket contains sewn M. T. P. initials. Constable Woulfe is wearing a set of white leather gauntlets and the first issue of the Metropolitan Toronto Police shoulder patch. Picture taken at Casa Loma, where Mounted Unit provided an officer in ceremonial dress to patrol the grounds during the summer months.

The Badges

The Toronto Police Department began using a large maple leaf shaped helmet plate in the 1860s. The badges were mounted on the front of "Bobby" style helmets. The constable's plate had a black back ground with a silver beaver in the middle, capped with a Queen's Crown on its back. The Queen's crown was changed to a King's crown in 1902 after Queen Victoria died. The sergeant's helmet plate was silver and the senior officer's helmet plate gold

In 1906, Senior officers were issued with forage caps and a custom-made City of Toronto Cap Badge. Later they received collar dogs with the City of Toronto Seal. When mounted officers were issued with forage caps in the 1920s, they wore a smaller version of the helmet plate as a cap badge.

In 1919, officers were issued with a round wallet badge to be carried for identification purposes. The constables' badge had the badge number in the centre while all other ranks had their rank stamped on the badge. These badges were withdrawn from service in 1956. It was not until 1981 that another wallet badge was issued.

In 1954, rank and file officers were issued with a custom-made City of Toronto Cap Badge engraved with badge number or rank. In 1957, the officers were all issued with new numbered Metropolitan Toronto Police badges. In the early 60s, the numbered badges were recalled and the officers were issued with plain unnumbered badges. A plate with the badge number was issued to enable officer identification. This was worn on the breast pocket. In 1971, the breast numbers and old style cap badges were withdrawn from service and a new style numbered badge was issued.

Left: is a constable's helmet badge. The helmet plate on the right is a senior officer's. When forage caps were issued in the late 1920s constables and sergeants were issued with smaller versions of the helmet plates for use as cap badges.

Senior officer's collar dog with the City of Toronto seal.

1906 issue Senior officer's cap badge.

1954 Issue Toronto City Police cap badge. This badge was a sergeant's issue, S - 21. Photograph, Leslie Bluestein.

1957 issue Metropolitan Toronto Police badge. Photographs, PC Derrick Speirs.

One of the issues of the 1918 Toronto police strike was the issuing of wallet badges. This sergeant's wallet badge was issued in 1919. Photograph, Leslie Bluestein.

1971-97 issue Metropolitan Toronto Police badge.

1998 issue Toronto Police badge.

381

The Insignia

Toronto Police officers wore a box neck tunic until the 1930s. Prior to 1900, constables had their badge number pinned to the collars of their jackets. Patrol Sergeants wore a "P.S." and Sergeants wore an "S." After 1900, the numbers were moved to the epaulets. When open neck tunics were introduced, number insignia remained on the shoulder epaulets. These numbers were eliminated in 1956. Epaulet numbers for all ranks below senior officer were reintroduced in 1980. After World War II, patrol sergeants began wearing traditional military sergeants' stripes; sergeants began wearing sergeant stripes with a crown on top. In 1971, the rank system was reorganized; all patrol sergeants became sergeants, and all sergeants became staff sergeants. Their insignia remained the same.

In 1955, mounted officers were issued with a red felt triangle shoulder patch emblazoned with a blue rearing horse and the words Toronto City Police. This was the only patch ever issued by the Toronto City Police Department. At one time, mounted officers also wore a shoulder epaulet that said Toronto Police. It is not known when this was in use, but it was probably in the 1930s.

The Metropolitan Toronto Police Force issued three styles of shoulder patches during its forty-year history. Patches for ranks from constable to staff sergeant have a white boarder around the crest. Senior officers have a gold boarder. A Mounted Unit special unit patch was issued in 1992 to be worn on the left sleeve of the tunic or patrol jacket.

Officers were issued with a good conduct badge for every five years of service. These are now called service badges. The badge is a small maple leaf worn on the left sleeve of the tunic or patrol jacket. Since the 1890s, Toronto police officers have been wearing St. John Ambulance first aid badges on their left sleeves. After twenty years of service, officers may be recommended to receive the Canadian Police Exemplary Service Medal from the Canadian Government.

1955 issue Mounted Unit shoulder patch. Photograph, PC Derrick Speirs.

This crest was a prototype developed in the mid 1950s. It was never issued to the officers. Photograph, PC Derrick Speirs.

Rank insignia from the 1920s. Inspector's Rank Pip, Sergeant's "S," Patrol Sergeant's "PS," and Constable's number.

1965 issue breast number.

This Toronto police epaulet was probably used by mounted officers in the 1930s or 40s. There is no record or photographs to confirm when it was used. Photograph, Leslie Bluestein.

1957 cadet patch.

1957 Metropolitan Toronto Police shoulder patch.

Mounted Unit insignia worn on left sleeve of tunic or patrol jacket. Above left: Senior officer's gold version. Above right: Other ranks white version.

Photographs, PC Derrick Speirs.

1966 Black and white shoulder patch.

1978 Coloured shoulder patch.

1998 City of Toronto police services shoulder patch.

The 1966 ceremonial dress uniform. The officer is wearing the new "Bobby" style helmet and ceremonial tunic. Gauntlets have been traded for white felt gloves. A crested saddle blanket has also been issued along with a new-style shoulder flash. Picture taken at Nathan Phillips Square. Photographs, Toronto Police Museum.

Crest created by members of the Unit for unofficial use on baseball hats during the Mounted Unit's 100th Anniversary in 1986.

Belt buckle issued to each mounted officer in recognition of the Mounted Unit's 100th anniversary in 1986.

A strip of service leaves representing fifteen years. A service leaf is issued every five years for good conduct, and is worn on the left sleeve. Photographs, PC Derrick Speirs.

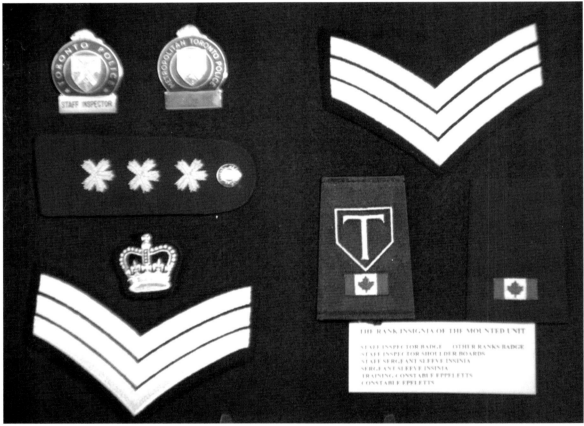

Saint John Ambulance first aid sleeve badges. Above: 1st issue. Below: Current issue. Photograph, PC Derrick Speirs.

Rank insignia display from Mounted Headquarters. Top left: Toronto Police Staff Inspector cap badge. Metropolitan Toronto Police cap badge for other ranks. Middle: Staff Inspector rank epaulet. Bottom left: Staff Sgt sleeve insignia. Top right: Sgt sleeve insignia. Bottom centre: Training constable epaulet. Bottom right: Constable epaulet. While on duty, badge numbers are attached to epaulets. Photograph, PC Derrick Speirs.

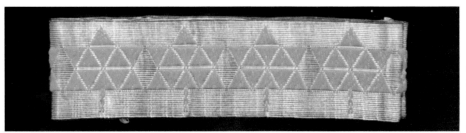

Hatband worn during Canada's Centennial year, 1967. Photograph, Leslie Bluestein.

Button worn on the breast pocket during Canada's Centennial year, 1967. Photograph, Leslie Bluestein.

Police constable Deb Poulson in summer dress in front of Queen's Park. She is riding police mount "Dora" who would lose the sight of one eye after being struck by a rock at the Yonge Street riots in 1992. PC Poulson purchased the horse when it was no longer fit for police duties. Photograph, Toronto Police Museum.

The traditional picture of the horses head and crossed lances which was created during the first Musical Rides and has now become the unofficial symbol used on stationery by the Toronto Police Mounted Unit.

SAMPLE COSTS

1917:
3 pairs of spurs, 12 spur straps...cost $24.70.

1919:
Two saddles and Bridles...cost $90.40.

1923:
Mounted riding cloaks...$35.00 each
New pattern forage caps...$2.50 each
Shoulder numbers...10 cents each
Blue Helmets...$3.50 each
Riding boots...$20.00 each
23 mounted police waterproofs...$30.00 each
Riding Breeches...$12.00 each.

1974:
The military equipment and tack for each horse came from England and cost $1,400.

PC Peter Scribner in winter dress at Sunnybrook Park, c.1980. Photograph, Toronto Police Mounted Unit.

FORMAL   SPRING & FALL   SUMMER

WINTER   CEREMONIAL   RAINWEAR

MOUNTED OFFICERS' UNIFORMS IN 1986

Photographs, Metropolitan Toronto Police, 1986.

A selection of identity plates removed from Mounted Unit equipment. Some equipment is assigned to a horse by name, as evidenced by the "Jack" and "General" plates. Other equipment is assigned a kit number, which in turn is assigned to an officer or a horse. The low number on plate number "40" indicates this is a kit number. The larger number is an officer's badge number which means that the kit is assigned to a specific officer. Photograph, PC Derrick Speirs.

The official logo of the Metropolitan Toronto Police. Pictures, Toronto Police Service.

The 1962-1982 issue Police Long Service Medal. Awarded to police officers by the Canadian Association of Chiefs of Police in recognition of 20 years of exemplary service. A bar is worn on the ribbon to denote 30 years of service.

The 1982 issue Police Exemplary Service Medal. Awarded to police officers by the Government of Canada in recognition of 20 years of exemplary service. A bar is worn on the ribbon to denote 30 years of service.

PC Greg Vanderhart with the Toronto Police flag. This flag is used by the officers performing ceremonial details outside of Toronto. Photograph, PC Derrick Speirs.

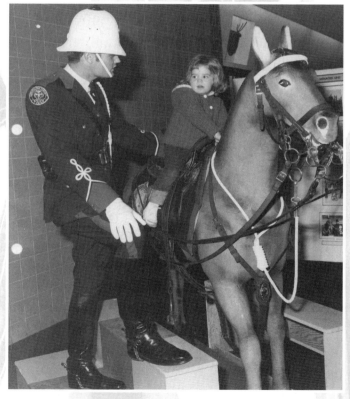

PC Jim Croutch with Mounted Unit equipment used for shopping mall demonstrations and "Police Week" displays. Picture taken at the Sherway Gardens Police Week display, 1973. Photograph, Toronto Police Museum.

Chapter

The Musical Ride and Drill Team

The British cavalry is credited with developing the first Musical Ride, which they used to make enhanced training interesting. The Ride helped relieve the boredom of the routine duties required by military life. It also gave the military a spectacular display for special events and regimental field days. It is believed that the first Musical Ride was performed by the 1st Regiment of Life Guards in England in 1882.

It was however, the Prussian cavalry which first developed the modern cavalry movements used in Musical Rides. It is fitting that the dress uniform worn by the Metropolitan Toronto Police mounted officers includes the "Bobby" style helmet. The design of the British Bobbies helmet was based on the Prussian military helmet.

In 1892 a party of ex-British cavalrymen had been performing a "private" musical ride for money at the Chicago World's Fair. When the Fair ended the ride was disbanded and a number of the members came to Toronto and joined the Royal Canadian Dragoons at Stanley Barracks. These men developed a musical ride and in 1894 they gave their first public performance in Toronto.

The Dragoon's ride continued until 1938 when the regiment was mechanized and the horses retired. In 1934 a Royal Canadian Mounted Police Rough Rider, Sergeant Soame, was attached to the Dragoon's Musical Ride for training. Sergeant Soame returned to the R.C.M.P. and developed their musical ride in 1937 based on what the Dragoon's had taught.[1] It should be noted that the R.C.M.P.'s founding force, the North West Mounted Police, had been performing Musical Rides as early as 1886.

Inspector Edwin Johnson enlisted in the Royal Canadian Dragoons in 1937 and was a member of their musical ride. He was part of the last performances ever given by the Dragoons that took place at Madison Square Gardens and the Royal Winter Fair in 1938. The Metropolitan Toronto Police Musical Ride, which Inspector Johnson developed in 1966, was based on his knowledge from his Dragoon days.

The Royal Canadian Dragoon Musical Ride at the Canadian National Exhibition, 1910. The Toronto Police Musical Ride movements were based on the ones learned by Inspector Johnston when he was a member of the Royal Canadian Dragoons. Photograph, Metropolitan Toronto Reference Library T13867.

The 1940 Canadian National Exhibition requested that the Toronto Police put on a musical ride at the grandstand during their nightly military tattoo. The R.C.M.P. Musical Ride had been scheduled to perform, but they cancelled due to war time man power shortages. Inspector Crosbie went to work and trained the Toronto mounted officers to do a musical ride. Patrol Sergeant Ernest Masters was appointed Ride leader. There were a number of cavalry veterans at the unit who had done musical rides during their military service and they helped with the training.

The officers attended "Ride" training at 2:00 p.m. each day and trained on their own time. The mounted unit obtained dress blankets to wear over their felt numnah pads for the first time. The officers did not carry a lance nor did they wear any special uniforms during the ride performances.

There is very little information about this "Ride" available. The August 26, 1940, *Toronto Telegram* only gives this minor mention of the ride in a column about the Military tattoo. It appeared under the sub title "Police Give Musical Ride." The article stated that "The musical ride by the Toronto Mounted Police was one of the features which received well merited applause."[2]

There is some information to indicate that the "Ride" may also have been performed at the Toronto Police Amateur Athletic Association field day and at the Royal Winter Fair.

In December of 1965 the Chief of Police gave Inspector Johnson permission to organize and train a sixteen man musical ride. The training commenced on January 10th 1966 in the coliseum ring. The training was conducted for two hours a day and then the officers were assigned to regular patrols, given horse transport training or assigned to stable duties.

Officers Inspector Johnson selected for the "Ride" were described by him as being "Interested in it, not too heavy, of smart military appearance and good horsemen." Over half of the unit participated in the musical ride training.[3]

The excellent co-operation and efforts of all personnel involved made the ride a success. The police Pipe Band worked along with the Mounted Unit from the start. They not only provided the necessary music, but, added pageantry and military distinction to the "Ride."[4]

The two main ride leaders were Patrol Sergeant Jim Lewis and Police Constable Bert Boardman. Bert was probably one of the biggest assets to the Inspector as he had previously served with the Household Cavalry in Britain. Regiments of the Household Cavalry are famous for their musical rides.

The Musical Ride of the Metropolitan Toronto Police was performed on an annual basis from 1966 to 1979. It was reorganized in 1982 and discontinued after 1984, resurrected once again in 1990 and permanently disbanded in 1993 after the program review of the Mounted Unit.

The 1991 Musical Ride and the Metropolitan Toronto Police Pipes and Drums in front of the fountain at the Canadian National Exhibition. Photograph, Author's Collection.

The Movements of the Musical Ride

The sixteen horses of the Musical Ride are divided into four sections of four horses each. Eight black horses comprise the 1st two sections while eight bay horses make up the other two sections. In the following diagrams the black ovals represent the black horses while the white ovals represent the bay horses.

The Movements of the Musical Ride in the sequence as they are performed.

(A) March In (B) Troop in Line (C) Musical Ride, March

1. Centre Pass
2. Figure of Eight
3. Maltese Cross
4. Shanghai Cross
5. Double Shanghai Cross
6. Bridle Arch
7. Sections – Single File
8. Diagonals
9. Turnstile
10. Extended Sections
11. Sections Incline or 11a. Maze
12. Four Small gates or 12a Jumps

13. Double Carousel
14 Two Large Gates
15. Star
16. Circle
17. Dome
18. Circle
19. Line Up
20. Charge
21. Rally
22. Carousel
23. March Past
(D) March Out

The march in

The line up

The march off

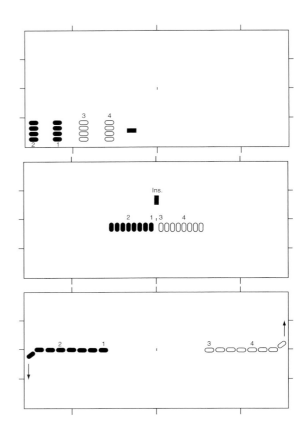

Inspector Johnson leads the musical ride into Exhibition Stadium during the 1973 Canadian National Exhibition. Photograph, Toronto Police Museum. The March In

The Centre Pass

The Figure of Eight

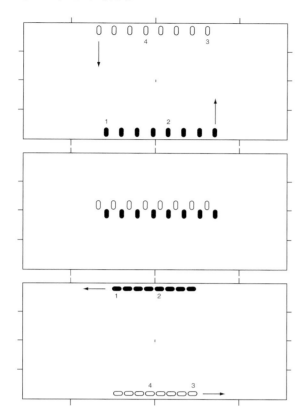

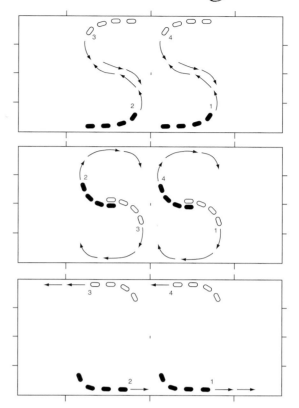

The Centre Pass

The officers have just past through each others ranks in the first movement of the musical ride at the 1973 Canadian National Exhibition. Photograph, Toronto Police Museum.

The Maltese Cross

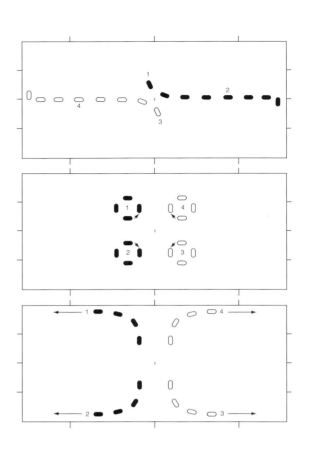

In this picture from the 1973 C.N.E. the officers are riding out of the movement called the Maltese Cross. To form this design the troop breaks down into four equal circles in the shape of a Maltese Cross. Photograph, Toronto Police Museum.

The Single Shanghai Cross

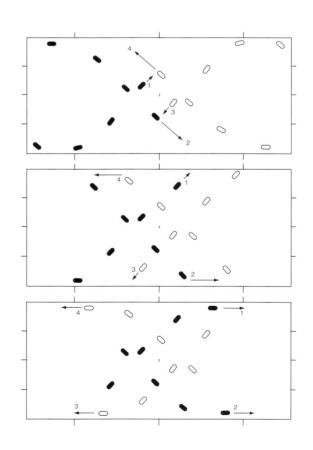

The four sections of four horses ride off of the quarter markers and pass through each others ranks. This photograph was taken at the 1973 Canadian National Exhibition. Photograph, Toronto Police Museum.

The Double Shanghai

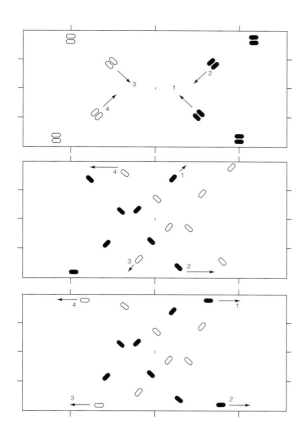

DISTANCES

It is very important that officers maintain a proper following distance during the movements of the Musical Ride. The following definitions are used;

1. Nose to tail – two feet from the lead horses tail to the following horses nose.
2. Half a horse – four feet from the lead horses tail to the following horses nose.
3. Horses length – eight feet from the lead horses tail to the following horses nose.
4. Horse and a half – twelve feet from the lead horses tail to the following horses nose.
5. Three horses lengths – twenty-four feet from the lead horses tail to the following horses nose.

During the Single Shanghai Cross the officers must maintain a horse and a half. The Double Shanghai Cross requires three horse's lengths. Any deviation may place horses on a collision course that requires evasive action that is usually obvious to those watching.

The Bridal Arch

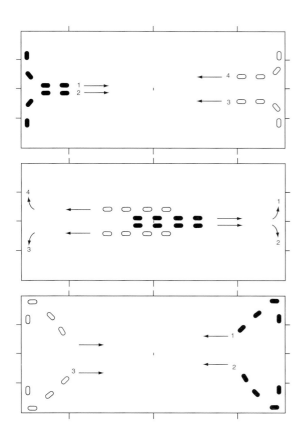

The black troop rides with their lances engaged through an archway created by the lances of the bay horses. Picture taken at the Canadian National Exhibition, 1973. Photograph, Toronto Police Museum.

Sections Single File

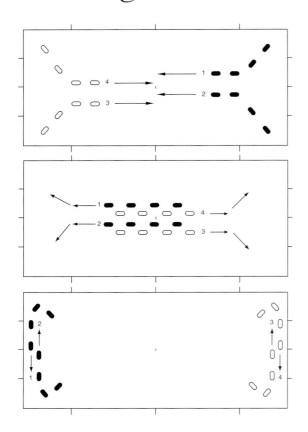

Diagonals

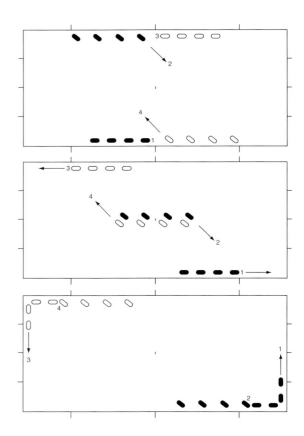

Turnstile

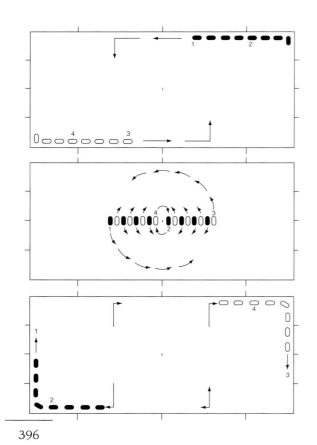

Extended Sections

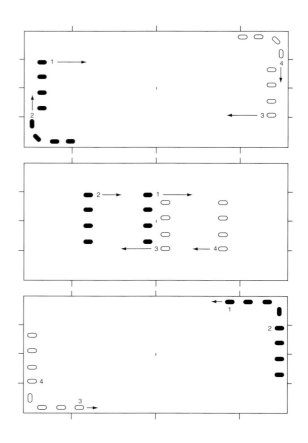

Sections Inclined

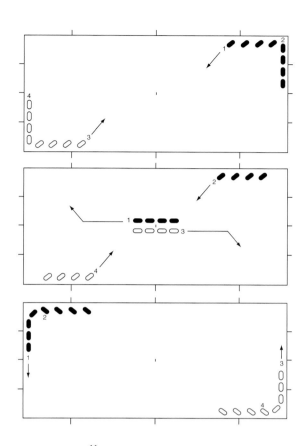

Four Small Gates

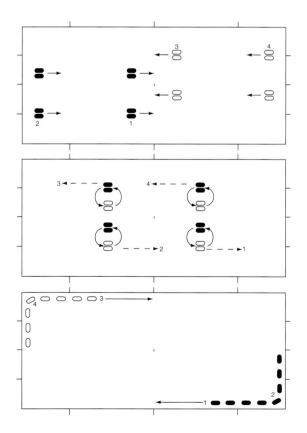

Maze

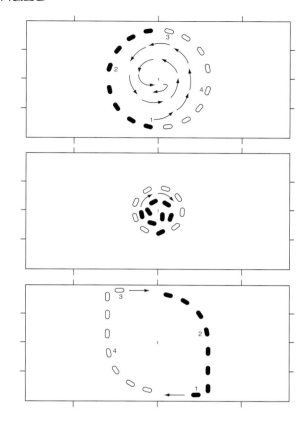

THE MUSIC AND GAITS OF THE MUSICAL RIDE

The Pipe Band selects the tunes that accompany the Musical Ride based on the horse's gait in the particular movement. The horse's gaits have individual beats, which are based on the number of times the horses feet touch the ground in each movement.

1. Walk – four beat movement
2. Trot – two beat movement
3. Canter – three beat movement

Movement	Gait	Tune
The March In	Walk	"The Maple Leaf Forever" (Or another Quick March as selected by Pipe Major)
The March Off *	Trot	"The Keel Row" or any Strathspey
The Carousel	Canter	"Bonnie Dundee"
The March Out	Walk	"Scotland The Brave" "The Black Bear"

*All movements between the March Off and the Dome are done to the Strathspey. There is no music played during the charge.

Jumps

Double Carousel

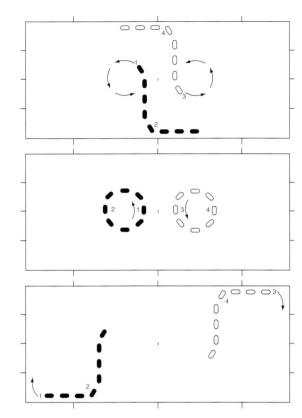

A rare picture of a discontinued musical ride movement c. 1966. Two officers would drop their lances to form an 'X Jump' between them. A third horse would pass between them going over the jump. This movement was removed after a number of lances were damaged. Photograph, Toronto Police Museum.

Jumps

Two Large Gates

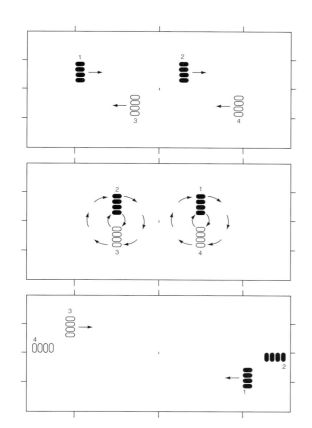

This photograph was taken just prior to a movement called "the gates." The troop has broken down into four sections of four. They will eventually form two sets of revolving gates of eight horses each when they reach the quarter markers. Dress rehearsal at Gore Park, April 1967. Photograph, Toronto Police Museum

The Star

The four sections have come together at centre field to form "the star." Dress rehearsal at Gore Park, April 1967. Photograph, Toronto Police Museum

The Circle and Dome

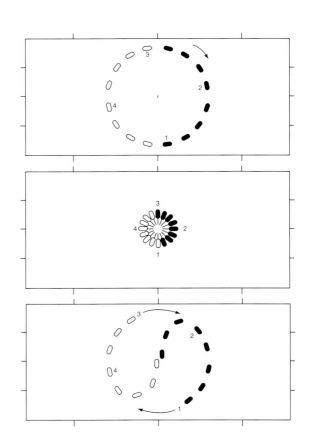

The officers have just finished turning their horses into the centre of the ring to form the movement called "the dome." Dress rehearsal at Gore Park, April 1967. Photograph, Toronto Police Museum

On the signal of the "Ride" leader the officers remove their lance and perform a lance drill that creates the shape of a dome in the centre of the field. Dress rehearsal at Gore Park, April 1967. Photograph, Toronto Police Museum.

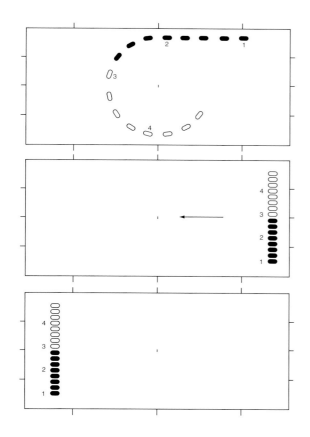

The line up before the charge. This photograph was taken at the 1973 Canadian National Exhibition. Photograph, Toronto Police Museum.

In this photograph the charge is being done in two ranks. In later years the officers formed a single troop of 16 horses to create a more impressive charge. Dress rehearsal at Gore Park, April 1967. Photograph, Toronto Police Museum.

The Rally

The Carousel

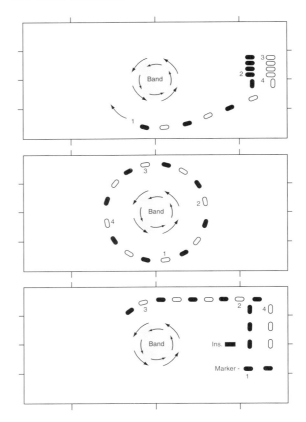

The officers rehearsing the Carousel without the Pipe Band at Canadian National Exhibition Stadium. The Musical Ride of the Metropolitan Toronto Police was performed on an annual basis from 1966 to 1979. It was reorganized in 1982 and discontinued after 1984, resurrected once again in 1990 and permanently disbanded in 1993 after the program review of the Mounted Unit.

The March Past

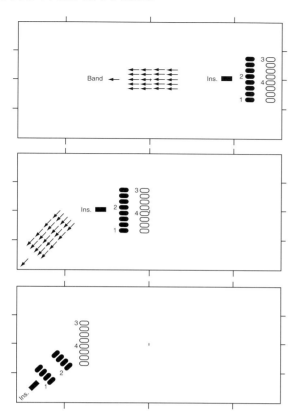

A tired looking officer takes a break during a Musical Ride practice. Photograph, Toronto Telegram Photograph Collection, York University Archives and Special Collections, Neg. #1696.

Original advertisement for the 1966 Musical Ride.

THE 1966 MUSICAL RIDE

The 1966 Ride Leaders; Patrol Sergeant Jim Lewis,
Constable Bert Boardman, Constable Pat Woulfe.

THE 1966 MUSICAL RIDE SCHEDULE

Date	Event
January 10	Commence training.
January 26	Special performance for Deputy Chief Simmonds.
February 9	Special performance for Magistrate C.O. Bick and Chief of Police James Mackey
April 30	Special performance for members of the police department, press and television
July 18	Commence Training for Canadian National Exhibition Horse Show.
August 10	Special performance in outdoors ring for press, television and M.G.M. News and the C.B.C.
August 22	First public appearance with 6 performances given at the Canadian National Exhibition.
September 27	Special performance for the International Police Association Convention.
November 12	Special matinee performance at the Royal Winter Fair.

1966 MUSICAL RIDE PERSONNEL

P/Sgt Lewis (4432)	PC Macey (53)	PC Sutton (1345)
PC Gleed (228)	PC Whitaker (709)	PC Claus (80)
PC Woulfe (168)	PC Leeson (754)	PC Moore (1739
PC Boardman (161)	PC Green (1707)	PC Smith (1072)
PC Mottram (1692)	PC Schewk (1286)	PC Shepherd (1772)
PC James (1363)	PC Davis (1713)	PC Pollard (635)
PC Vincent (221)	PC Byrne (490)	PC Sandwell (1481)

Jim Lewis was the first Musical Ride leader. He joined the Toronto Police Department in 1950 and was transferred to the Mounted Unit in 1951. He retired as a staff-sergeant in 1980.

11 Year old Keith MacLaggen shares his Doctor Pepper with "Bruce" after a Musical Ride practice.
Photograph, Toronto Telegram *Photograph Collection, York University Archives and Special Collections, Neg. #1688.*

THE 1967 MUSICAL RIDE

1967 was Canada's Centennial year. The unit put on a number of Musical Rides for special events and Centennial functions. Almost half of the officers on the unit participated in the training and performances. The need for practice sessions was considerably reduced due to the enthusiasm and effort of so many personnel involved.

The Musical Ride was very successful during a second year. Inspector Johnson made a request in his 1967 Annual report; "In view of the enthusiastic response and large crowds on hand at our various displays this year, I recommend that some 'out of town' requests be considered in the future. It is, of course, assumed that the costs involving transport, the sponsor would carry accommodation, feed, etc., and that the only cost to the Department would be in wages and man-hours. The advertising would offset this, in my opinion, for the Department and the Public Relations gained."

The additional horse-transport required would be obtained by rental at the sponsors expense as was experienced on some occasions this year."[5]

The Inspector wanted to take the Ride on the road. Unfortunately, this was not permitted, as the Police Commission did not want that many officers out of town at one time, being concerned the unit would be short-handed in the event of an emergency. The officer-in-charge of the 1967 Musical Ride was Patrol Sgt James Pedlar. Ride leaders were PC Pat Woulfe and PC Charles Vincent.

MUSICAL RIDE PERFORMANCES IN 1967

Date	Event	Location	# of Rides
February 23	Special performance for Chief Mackey	C.N.E.	1
April 18	Special Performance for B.B.C. film crew	C.N.E.	1
June 24	Strawberry Festival	Kipling Acres	1
July 3	Markham Centennial	Markham	1
July 22	Police Field Games	Varsity Stadium	1
August 10	Ontario Public Safety Convention	Coliseum	1
August 21	C.N.E. Horse Show	Coliseum	6
September 9	East York Centennial	Cedarvale Park	1
September 15	Scarborough Centennial	Thompson Park	2
September 28	Markham Fair	Varsity Stadium	2

Total of seventeen public performances.

1967 MUSICAL RIDE PERSONNEL

PC Gleed (228)	PC MacDonald (2621)	PC Clarke (1801)
PC Woulfe (168)	PC Davis (1713)	PC Bathgate (320)
PC Mottram (1692)	PC Byrne (490)	PC Cardy (410)
PC Vincent (221)	PC Haynes (1868)	PC Buffett (190)
PC Lowe (184)	PC Stafford (1614)	PC Lloyd (968)
PC Neath (1511)	PC Claus (80)	PC Lees (1682)
PC Macey (53)	PC Smith (1072)	PC DeBoer (1038)
PC Whitaker (709)	PC Shepherd (1772)	PC Bland (1918)
PC Cairns (824)	PC Pollard (635)	PC Green (1707)
PC Leeson (754)	PC Bond (1353)	PC Sheridan (149)

Staff-Inspector Edwin Johnson was the driving force behind the Musical Ride. He led the ride into each performance as the officer-in-charge.

The March In. The ride begins with the officers entering the performance area in sections (four horses). Picture taken of a dress rehearsal of the musical ride in Gore Park, 1967. The officers are in ride order just prior to marching onto the field to perform the musical ride. Photograph, Toronto Police Museum.

The "Centre Pass." The first movement of the ride was called the "Centre Pass." The Black and Bay troops pass through each others' lines at centre field. Dress rehearsal at Gore Park, April 1967. Photograph, Toronto Police Museum.

THE 1968 MUSICAL RIDE

It was estimated that twenty thousand people saw the Musical ride at the Royal Winter Fair alone in 1968. The officer-in-charge of the 1968 musical ride was Patrol Sgt James Pedlar. Ride leaders were PC Davis (1713) and Patrick Woulfe (168).

MUSICAL RIDE PERFORMANCES IN 1968.

Date	Event	Location	# of Rides
April 22	Ontario Traffic Conference	C.N.E.	1
June 18	International Municipal Parking Congress	Fort York	1
June 22	Strawberry Festival	Kipling Acres	1
June 26	Ontario Chiefs of Police Convention	Barrie, Ontario	1
July 20	Police Field Day	C.N.E. Grandstand	1
October 4	Markham Fair	Markham	1
November 16	Royal Winter Fair	Coliseum	5

Total of eleven public performances.

1968 MUSICAL RIDE PERSONNEL

PC Gleed (228)	PC Clarke (1801)	PC Green (1707)
PC Woulfe (168)	PC Bathgate (320)	PC MacDonald (2621)
PC Lowe (184)	PC DeBoer (1038)	PC Davis (1713)
PC Neath (1511)	PC Croutch (947)	PC Byrne (490)
PC Macey (53)	PC Jackson (1903)	PC Haynes (1868)
PC Whitaker (709)	PC Haywood (2732)	PC Stafford (1614)
PC Cairns (824)	PC Lyons (2750)	PC Shepherd (1762)
PC Leeson (754)	PC Currie (1872)	PC Pollard (635)
PC Wilson (1803)	PC Heenan (2118)	PC Sheridan (1490)
PC James (3026)	PC Schewk (1286)	

PC Jim Davis was one of the ride leaders during the 1968 Musical Ride.

PC Mac Lyons was a member of the 1968 Musical Ride. He was a Unit Personnel Riding Instructor and was eventually promoted Sergeant.

THE 1969 MUSICAL RIDE

The officers-in-charge of the 1969 Ride were Patrol Sgt James Pedlar and Patrol Sgt Patrick Woulfe. Ride leaders were PC Bathgate (320) and PC Neath (1511).

MUSICAL RIDE PERFORMANCES IN 1969

Date	Event	Location
June 21	Strawberry Festival	Kipling Acres
July 1	Dominion Day	Cedarvale Park, East York.
July 26	Police Field Day	C.N.E. Grandstand.
August 19	Public Festival	Thompson park, Scarborough.
September 14	Toronto Historical Society	Old Fort York.

1969 MUSICAL RIDE PERSONNEL

PC Gleed (228)	PC Clarke (1801)	PC Williams (1834)
PC Lowe (184)	PC Bathgate (320)	Cadet Seeley (3251)
PC Neath (1511)	PC DeBoer (1038)	PC Claus (80)
PC Macey (53)	PC Croutch (947)	PC McKechnie (2305)
PC Davis (1713)	PC Jackson (1903)	PC Moncur (3019)
PC Byrne (490)	PC Haywood (2732)	PC Vincent (221)
PC Haynes (1868)	PC Lyons (2750)	PC Smith (1072)
PC Stafford (1614)	PC Currie (1872)	PC Wilson (1803)
PC James (3026)	PC Heenan (2118)	PC Stewart (2991)

PC Bob Heenan was a member of the 1969 Musical Ride. He would be a ride leader in 1975 and would be Staff-Inspector Heenan when the Musical Ride was revived in 1990.

PC Bill Macey was a member of the 1969 Musical Ride. He was promoted to Sergeant in 1976 and became the officer-in-charge of the Musical Ride. He was one of its biggest advocates.

The officers are practicing their dressing during a rehearsal of the "Gates," c. 1966. Photograph, Toronto Police Museum.

THE 1970 MUSICAL RIDE

The Musical Ride was performed in public on six occasions. Its biggest night was at the Military Tattoo at the C.N.E. when it performed under spotlights to a crowd of 15,000 people. Officers-in-charge of the ride were Sgt James Pedlar and Patrol Sgt Patrick Woulfe. Ride leaders were PC Bathgate (320), PC Croutch (947), and PC Neath (1511).

MUSICAL RIDE PERFORMANCES IN 1970

Date	Event	Location
June 20	Strawberry Festival.	Kipling Acres
July 1	Dominion Day	Cedarvale Park, East York.
July 21	Greenwood Race Track	
August 10:	Conservation Convention	York University
September 6	Military Tattoo	C.N.E. Grandstand.
September19	Public Festival	Highview Park, Scarborough

1970 MUSICAL RIDE PERSONNEL

PC Lowe (184)	PC Currie (1872)	PC Norris (139)
PC Neath (1511)	PC Heenan (2118)	PC Pollard (635)
PC Macey (53)	PC Wilson (1803)	PC Schewk (1286)
PC Byrne (490)	PC James (3026)	PC Lunn (2498)
PC Stafford (1614)	PC Claus (80)	PC McKeown (2351)
PC Clarke (1801)	PC Moncur (3019)	PC Mathers (2941)
PC Bathgate (320)	PC Vincent (2708)	PC Dillon (2088)
PC Croutch (947)	PC Best (1772)	PC Lyons (2750)
PC Haywood (2732)		

PC Edward "Ted" Lloyd served in the Royal Canadian Navy during WW II. He joined the Toronto Police Department in 1951 and transferred to the Mounted Unit in 1953. He was appointed Unit quartermaster and served in that capacity through the 1970s until retirement in 1983.

PC Fred Lloyd joined the Toronto Police in 1974. He transferred to the Mounted Unit in 1975 and served with them for 20 years. Fred was one of the most skilled Musical Ride leaders.

This father and son gave fifty combined years of dedicated Mounted Police service to the people of Toronto.

THE 1971 MUSICAL RIDE

The officers-in-charge of the ride were Patrol Sgt Ernest Sandwell and Patrol Sgt Patrick Woulfe. The Ride leader was PC Bathgate (320). Inspector Johnson made the following observations about the Musical Ride in his 1971 Annual Report;

"The training and operating the ride is difficult at times, when it conflicts with other unit commitments. If some of the one day commitments (such as East York Dominion Day) were excluded, man-hours in training would be reduced considerably. Only large events, such as the C.N.E. Military Tattoo and special requests, should be considered in the future"[6]

PC Alisteir McKechnie was a member of the 1971 Musical Ride. He would be the Sunnybrook stable manager in the 1980s.

MUSICAL RIDE PERFORMANCES IN 1971

Date	Event	Location
June 13:	Woodbine Race Track	
June 19	Strawberry Festival	Kipling Acres
July 1	Dominion Day	Cedarvale Park, East York.
July 19	Greenwood Race Track	
July 22	Horse Show Display for World Authorities	Sunnybrook Park.

1971 MUSICAL RIDE PERSONNEL

PC Lowe (184)	PC Lyons (2750)	PC Schewk (1286)
PC Neath (1511)	PC Currie (1872)	PC Lunn (2498)
PC Macey (53)	PC Heenan (2118)	PC McKechnie (2305)
PC Hill (1921)	PC Wilson (1803)	PC Haynes (1868)
PC Green (253)	PC D'Arcy (2070)	PC Best (1772)
PC Blackburn (2703)	PC Claus (80)	PC McKeown (2351)
PC Bathgate (320)	PC Moncur (3019)	PC Mathers (2941)
PC Croutch (947)	PC Vincent (2708)	PC Pollard (635)
PC Haywood (2732)		

PC Paul Dean would become a Musical Ride member in 1972. He had previously served in the Royal Military Police and the Metropolitan Police in England. In the 1980s he would be appointed Mounted Unit Crime Analyst. He retired in 1995 and helped to form the Canadian Mounted Police Association.

THE 1972 MUSICAL RIDE

The officers-in-charge of the 1972 Musical Ride were Patrol Sgt Ernest Sandwell and Patrol Sgt Patrick Woulfe. The Ride leaders were PC Bathgate (320) and PC Neath (1511).

MUSICAL RIDE PERFORMANCES IN 1972	
Location	**Event**
Woodbine Racetrack	Queen's Plate
Kipling Acres	Strawberry Festival
Cedarvale Park (East York)	Dominion Day Festival
Greenwood Racetrack	Opening of Harness Racing
C.N.E. Grandstand	Police Field Day
C.N.E. Grandstand Military Tattoo (4 Nights)	
Total of nine public performances.	

1972 MUSICAL RIDE PERSONNEL

PC Lowe (184)	PC Lyons (2750)	PC Haynes (1868)
PC Neath (1511)	PC Currie (1872)	PC Smith (507)
PC Dean (3460)	PC Heenan (2118)	PC Wright (2903)
PC Bamlett (2468)	PC Wilson (1803)	PC Green (253)
PC Brooks (3254)	PC Norris (139)	PC Bayley (2165)
PC Murphy (3328)	PC Vincent (2708)	PC Haywood (2732)
PC Bathgate (320)	PC Best (1772)	PC Mathers (2941)
PC Croutch (947)	PC McKeown (2351)	PC Schewk (1286)

PC John Brooks was a member of the 1972 Musical Ride.

Another view of "the star." Gore Park dress rehearsal, April 1967. Photograph, Toronto Police Museum.

THE 1973 MUSICAL RIDE

The officers-in-charge of the 1973 Musical Ride were Sgt James Pedlar, Patrol Sgt Warren Pollard and Patrol Sgt Patrick Woulfe. Ride leaders were PC Don Vincent (2708) and PC Mike Best (1778).

PC Don Vincent

PC Mike Best

PC Don Vincent and PC Mike Best were the Musical Ride Leaders in 1973.

MUSICAL RIDE PERFORMANCES IN 1971

Date	Event	Location
June 16	Strawberry Festival	Kipling Acres
July 2	Dominion Day	Cedarvale Park, East York
July 28	Police Field Day	C.N.E. Grandstand.
September 22	Highview Park Festival	Scarborough.

1973 MUSICAL RIDE PERSONNEL

PC D'Arcy (2070)	PC Haywood (2732)	PC McKeown (2351)
PC Heath (1162)	PC Lynn (1690)	PC Mathers (2941)
PC Dean (3460)	PC Currie (1872)	PC Schewk (1286)
PC Gorrie (710)	PC Cole (2925)	PC Ruddock (1057)
PC Brooks (3254)	PC Wilson (1803)	PC Smith (507)
PC Matier (3467)	PC Norris (139)	PC Roberts (3423)
PC Damijonaitis (1700)	PC Vincent (2708)	PC Green (253)
PC Crouch (947)	PC Best (1772)	PC Bayley (2165)

"The Carousel." During a performance, the Pipes and Drums are invited to march out into the centre of the field after the charge. They eventually form themselves into a wheel with the pipers forming the outside circle and the drummers forming the spokes. On a signal from the bass drummer the mounted officers move off at a canter and form a circle moving clockwise around the band. On the same signal that starts the mounted portion of the movement, the band begins to circle in a counter-clockwise direction. Dress rehearsal (without pipe band) at Gore Park, April 1967. Photograph, Toronto Police Museum.

THE 1974 MUSICAL RIDE

Officers-in-charge of the 1974 Musical Ride were Sgt Ernie Sandwell and Sgt Patrick Woulfe. The Ride was led by PC Don Vincent (2708).

MUSICAL RIDE PERFORMANCES IN 1974

Date	Event	Location
July 1	Dominion Day	Cedarvale Park, East York.
July 18	Greenwood Race Track	
July 27	Police Field Day	C.N.E. Grandstand.

1974 MUSICAL RIDE PERSONNEL

PC Foster (2328)	PC Johnston (3510)	PC Smith (507)
PC Heath (1162)	PC Lynn (1690)	PC Roberts (3423)
PC Fynes (1833)	PC Currie (1872)	PC Green (253)
PC Wright (2903)	PC Cole (2925)	PC Clarke (1801)
PC Brooks (3254)	PC Vincent (2708)	PC Blackmore (1743)
PC Matier (3467)	PC Best (1772)	PC Schewk (1286)
PC Damijonaitis (1700)	PC McKeown (2351)	
PC Westcott (2631)		

THE 1975 MUSICAL RIDE

Officers-in-charge of the 1975 Musical Ride were Sgt Ernest Sandwell, Sgt Robert Heenan and Sgt Bill Fordham. They were assisted by PC Bill Macey (53). The "Ride" was led by PC Don Vincent (2708) and PC Foster (2328).

Musical Rides are very demanding on both horses and riders. Working in such close quarters increases the risk of collision and contact between the horses and riders. In some movements, like the "Centre Pass," it is inevitable that officers will bang knees as they pass through the ranks. Musical Ride training is extremely valuable in preparing both horses and riders for the crowd-management situations they will deal with during their police service. In this photo PC Shaun Fynnes checks "Glen" for any sign of injury after a fall. The only damage was a small cut on the right rear leg. Photograph Dave Cooper, Toronto Sun.

MUSICAL RIDE PERFORMANCES IN 1975

Date	Event	Location
June 21	Strawberry Festival	The Kipling Acres
July 2	The Shriners Convention	C.N.E. Grandstand.
July 26	The Police Field Day	C.N.E. Grandstand.
August 14 to 17	Scottish World Festival Tattoo	C.N.E. Grandstand, 4 performances.

1975 MUSICAL RIDE PERSONNEL

PC Foster (2328)	PC Johnston (3510)	PC Roberts (3423)
PC Thompson (3313)	PC Lynn (1690)	PC Green (253)
PC Fynes (1833)	PC Cole (2925)	PC Bayley (2165)
PC Wright (2903)	PC Vincent (2708)	PC MacKenzie (2611)
PC Brooks (3254)	PC McKeown (2351)	PC Macey (53)
PC Matier (3467)	PC Schewk (1286)	PC Smith (507)

THE 1976 MUSICAL RIDE

Officers-in-charge of the 1976 Musical Ride were Sgt Warren Pollard, Sgt Bill Macey and Sgt Patrick Woulfe. The Musical Ride was led by PC Robert Wright (2903) and PC Michael Best (1778).

Sergeant Warren Pollard, was one of the officers-in-charge of the 1976 Musical Ride.

MUSICAL RIDE PERFORMANCES IN 1976

Date	Event	Location
June 12	Strawberry Festival	Kipling Acres
August 3	Olympics for the disabled	Woodbine Race Track.
August 7	Police Field Day	C.N.E. Grandstand.
August 21 to 22	C.N.E. Horse Show 4 performances	Coliseum

1976 MUSICAL RIDE PERSONNEL

PC Best (1778)	PC Cole (2925)	PC Foster (2328)
PC Thompson (3313)	PC Vincent (2708)	PC Damijonaitis (1700)
PC McConachie (2374)	PC McKeown (2351)	PC Mackevicius (614)
PC Wright (2903)	PC Thomas (1865)	PC MacKenzie (2611)
PC Brooks (3254)	PC Huddleston (3382)	PC Kirkley (3024)
PC Matier (3467)	PC Brewer (4669)	PC VanDusen (2322)
PC Sauve (2890)	PC Green (253)	PC Johnston (3510)
PC Willis (3927)	PC Kelly (1595)	

THE 1977 MUSICAL RIDE

The officer-in-charge of the 1977 Musical Ride was Sgt Bill Macey. Ride leaders were PC Bob Wright (2903) and PC James (3026).

PC James McAleer was a member of the 1977 Musical Ride.

MUSICAL RIDE PERFORMANCES IN 1977

Date	Event	Location
June 11	Strawberry Festival	Kipling Acres
August 6	Police Field Day	C.N.E. Grandstand
August 20 to September 5	C.N.E. Horse Show	5 performances
November 11 to to 19	The Royal Winter Fair	14 performances.

1977 MUSICAL RIDE PERSONNEL

PC Brooks (3254)	PC Cassidy (4812)	PC Huddleston (3382)
PC James (3026)	PC McAleer (5755)	PC Brewer (4669)
PC Armstrong (284)	PC Lloyd (5736)	PC Green (253)
PC Wright (2903)	PC Switzer (307)	PC Willis (3927)
PC Moyes (5764)	PC Gillmore (4377)	PC Damijonaitis (1700)
PC Matier (3467)	PC McKeown (2351)	PC Mackevicius (614)
PC Gill (48)	PC Hadlow (1772)	PC Lyons (2750)
PC Byrne (490)	PC Bagnall (2958)	PC Kirkley (3024)
PC Kelly (1595)		

"Slinger" – On the Musical Ride

Reprinted with permission *Toronto Star* Syndicate

On Wednesday May 25, 1977, the popular *Toronto Star* Columnist named "Slinger" had this to say about the Musical Ride:

"CHARGE! One of the most splendid and infrequent sights in the city is the Musical Ride of the Metro Police mounted unit. The last time I saw them perform was at the opening ceremonies for last summer's Olympics for the disabled. In dress blues and white helmets, the 16 constables on their eight matched bays and eight matched blacks make you think of the Lancers in India, The Khyber Pass, the British Raj, the sun never setting and all that sort of thing. And for all those people in town who think the musical rides are the preserve of the R.C.M.P., the one fault with the Metro riders is that they appear too infrequently. A better public relations gimmick would be hard to come by. Their first show this summer will be Saturday afternoon, June 11, at the Kipling Acres Strawberry Festival, 2233 Kipling Ave. The Metro Police Pipe Band will as usual accompany them. The unit began training yesterday morning and will continue to do so for 5 1/2 hours a day, five days a week until the show. The police figure the whole thing is good training for both the horses and men. And why don't they appear more often? By the time you get the musical riders and the pipe band on parade, you have about 50 police officers pulled out of regular duties that also have to be paid. It's worth it."[1]

1 *Toronto Star*, May 25, 1977.

"The Charge." The 1967 Musical Ride. Left to right: PC Charlie Gleed "Dick," PC Leeson "Blackie," PC Bill Macey "Glen," PC Neath "Chummy," PC Charlie Vincent "Roy," PC Montram "Duchess," PC Pat Woulfe "Lancer." Photograph, Toronto Police Museum.

The 1977 Musical Ride during a rehearsal for the Police Field Day at the Canadian National Exhibition Grandstand. Photograph, Toronto Police Museum.

THE 1978 MUSICAL RIDE

The officer-in-charge of the 1978 Musical Ride was Sgt Harry D'Arcy. Ride leader was PC Bob Green (253).

Sergeant Harry D'Arcy was the officer-in-charge of the 1978 Musical Ride.

MUSICAL RIDE PERFORMANCES IN 1978

Date	Event	Location
June 17	Strawberry Festival	Kipling Acres
August 5	Police Field Day	C.N.E. Grandstand
August 19 to	C.N.E. Horse Show	C.N.E. Coliseum
August 20	4 performances	
September 1	C.N.E. Agricultural Day	C.N.E. Coliseum

1978 MUSICAL RIDE PERSONNEL

PC Brooks (3254)	PC Spearen (2437)	PC Huddleston (3382)
PC Mountjoy (4774)	PC McAleer (5755)	PC Brewer (4669)
PC Armstrong (284)	PC Lloyd (5736)	PC Green (253)
PC Renny (3804)	PC Durling (2975)	PC Willis (3927)
PC Bolongo (1478)	PC Gillmore (4377)	PC Mackevicius (614)
PC Matier (3467)	PC Stewart (3422)	PC Lyons (2750)
PC Gill (48)	PC Hadlow (1772)	PC Kirkley (3024)
PC MacKenzie (2611)	PC Smith (6768)	

THE 1979 MUSICAL RIDE

Officer-in-charge of the 1979 Musical Ride was Sgt Bill Macey. Ride leader was PC Robert Wright (2903).

MUSICAL RIDE PERFORMANCES IN 1979

Date	Event	Location
June 26	Strawberry Festival	Kipling Acres
August 11	Police Amateur Field Day	C.N.E. Grandstand.
August 16 to 19	Scottish World Festival Four performances	C.N.E. Grandstand

1979 MUSICAL RIDE PERSONNEL

PC Mountjoy (4774)	PC McAleer (5755)	PC Roberts (3423)
PC Rogers (2058)	PC Lloyd (5736)	PC Brewer (4669)
PC Byrne (490)	PC Durling (2975)	PC Wright (2903)
PC Bolongo (1478)	PC Fontaine (6089)	PC Desjardins (3831)
PC Matier (3467)	PC Cassidy (4812)	PC Kirkley (3024)
PC Gill (48)	PC Wojnicz (6665)	PC Smith (6768)
PC Spearen (2437)	PC Barnett (3718)	PC MacKenzie (2611)
PC Byrne (490)	PC Mathers (2941)	

NO MUSICAL RIDES WERE PERFORMED IN 1980 OR 1981.

THE 1982 MUSICAL RIDE

Officer-in-charge of the 1982 Musical Ride was Sgt Bill Macey. Ride leader was PC Bert McKeown (2351).

MUSICAL RIDE PERFORMANCES IN 1982

Date	Event	Location
June 26	Strawberry Festival	Kipling Acres
August 11	Police Amateur Field Day	C.N.E. Grandstand.
August 16 to 19	Scottish World Festival Four performances	C.N.E. Grandstand

1982 MUSICAL RIDE PERSONNEL

PC Robertson (138)	PC McAleer (5755)	PC Thomas (1865)
PC Rogers (2058)	PC Lloyd (5736)	PC Roberts (3423)
PC Bradford (1752)	PC McKenzie (3560)	PC Abrames 6848)
PC Thomas (1865)	PC Mawson (7272)	PC Wright (2903)
PC Matier (3467)	PC Cassidy (4812)	PC Derbyshire (6585)
PC Gill (48	PC Dean (3460)	

PC Tom Matier was a member of the 1982 Musical Ride. He would later become a Mounted Unit Personnel Riding Instructor.

THE 1983 MUSICAL RIDE

Officer-in-charge of the 1983 Musical Ride was Sgt Bill Macey. Ride leader was PC Fred Lloyd (5736).

1983 MUSICAL RIDE PERSONNEL

PC Robertson (138)	PC Lloyd (5736)	PC Lyons (2730)
PC Rogers (2058)	PC Scribner (3529)	PC McKeown (2351)
PC Gerard (6785)	PC Mawson (7272)	PC Hannaford (5892)
PC Mamak (6040)	PC Roberts (3423)	PC Spearen (2437)
PC Matier (3467)	PC Wright (2903)	PC Feather (2327)
PC Gill (48)	PC Dean (3460)	

Rehearsing "The Charge." Note protective rubber caps over the sharp points of the lances. The officer on the extreme right is PC Bert McKeown, on his right is PC Robert Wright. Photograph, Jim Russell, Toronto Star.

The 1982 Musical Ride at Sunnybrook Park. Photograph, Toronto Police Mounted Unit.

THE TRAINING VALUE OF THE MUSICAL RIDE

Sergeant William Macey (#53) submitted the following report to Inspector Johnson around 1980. It is probably the best "Musical Ride" report ever written. It was included in the appendices of the 1986 Inspection Unit Audit Team Report. The Audit Team was convinced of the training value of the ride and recommended its retention.

THE MUSICAL RIDE

by William Macey – Ride Sergeant

"The Metropolitan Toronto Police Pipe Band accompanies the horses and riders of the Metropolitan Toronto Police Mounted Unit to form the 'Musical Ride'. The Ride performs at various functions each year on behalf of the board of Commissioners of Police and the Chief of Police.

After each performance many letters are received by both the Chief of Police and (then) Mounted Unit Commander, Inspector E.S. Johnson, all very complimentary, praising the Ride for its smartness and perfection. Everyone enjoys the colours of the uniforms, combined with the music of the pipes and drums, and especially, the gleaming groomed horses.

Comments have been made that it must take years of practice for the horses and men to reach the perfection they display. The question arises: 'Is it worth all the time and trouble that it must take?'

The answer to this question is that the Ride is a great training event for both men and horses. In fact, the same men and horses are not used each year. The time involved is not as long as people would expect. For the first Ride of the year, twenty days; the second Ride is given fifteen days, any other Rides ten days or less if they are close together.

Every year six new horses are used in the Ride, which helps complete their training. It enables them to settle down when under stress, to stand still while under very bright floodlights; to be able to work in close formation with other horses making many complicated manoeuvres during which each horse will unavoidably receive a knock of two from either a lance butt, another riders boot, or the tail of another horse. The horse learns not to retaliate by kicking or biting back when receiving unexpected knocks.

When the new horse first works with the band, terror shows in its eyes and instinct tells him to run away. All the horses have to be comforted by their riders to learn to accept the fact that no matter how close they get to the band, they will not get hurt. They all learn to take confidence from their riders. This holds them in good stead when, later in their cases, they have to attend a big demonstration.

Even after they are used to the band, at first dress rehearsal they have to learn to overcome their fear once again because of the addition of the swirling tartan kilts and the high headdress worn by the bandsmen. Also, a full band is present, which is twice as big in numbers than at the earlier rehearsals. By the time the actual performance arrives the new horses perform as well as the older more experienced ones.

The Ride uses a total of sixteen horses for a performance, plus two spares dressed ready in case of a last minute injury. (Nine black horses and nine bay horses are used.) The lead horses and the two spares must be the most experienced (not the oldest in age) and reliable horses.

Sgt Bill Macey at a pro-Police rally at Nathan Phillips Square, 1973. Photograph, Toronto Police Museum.

Likewise, sixteen men ride in the actual performance, with two spares making a total of eighteen. It is excellent training for them, as it greatly improves their 'horsemanship' and their discipline. They learn to develop pride in striving for perfection; how to handle their horses in the most distracting situations and to develop pride in their appearance and their horse, even if they have to perform in the rain. They become a team, trying as hard as they can so they do not let the Ride down.

The Ride training improves the officer's 'seat', reining, use of the legs, and aids when making the transition through the various gaits required during the ride (walk, trot, canter, and jumping) including how to mount and dismount while carrying a lance. Every movement made in the Ride requires great concentration by each rider. Keeping the pace of the Ride, dressing to the side, covering-off to the front, excellent timing when turning into a new movement and making sure the horse is on the correct lead, all require excellent horsemanship. Top priority is for each rider to know and maintain the required distance from the horse in front of him, and in some cases the horse behind him. If one or more horses have to pass through a gap of eight feet between two other horses when they are all at a trot or canter, and the gap is not provided, you can imagine the disaster for both horse and rider—either man or beast could be seriously injured by the resulting collision. There are more than twenty complicated patterns used during the Ride, all at either the pace of trot or canter, most requiring exact distances of between four to eight feet between the horses.

During the training each man takes a turn at riding the lead position. He may be required to ride the lead position on the day of the performance if an unexpected injury or sickness occurs (the spare man will then fill the vacant secondary position). This is good training, since every man must learn the exact timing and responsibility required in a lead position. Each man helps his 'team mate' to achieve perfection.

Both the men and horses have to be transported to the performance area. This is very good training, for each man and horse has to learn to load and unload in different, and sometimes difficult, places and situations. They have to be familiar with all the various means of transportation used by the Mounted Unit, two-horse trailer, six-horse trailer, and nine-horse trailer. Twenty horses and riders, plus all the necessary equipment for the men and horses must be loaded. They have to arrive safe and sound, fully equipped, on time, ready to perform. There is no guarantee that on the day of the performance the weather will be ideal, sunny and dry. The Ride must perform to the audience regardless of the type of weather.

If required to perform on wet slippery grass, the rider must remain calm and make sure that the horse keeps his head up to keep him from slipping or stumbling. He must put the horse on the correct lead ready for the turns. This must be achieved earlier when conditions are slippery. This aids the training of both men and mounts.

Horses must be kept in tip-top condition. The men learn how to adjust the amount of feed required by the horse (depending on age, weight and extra work). The practice area usually gets very dusty or muddy depending on the weather, therefore, the men have to wash the sheath of the geldings and the teats of the mares more often than when on regular street patrol. Tails have to be washed more often. The usual 'pulling', mane and leg clipping (normal procedure) is maintained. The tension on the day of the performance helps develop self-discipline and patience in what is learned. All the extra effort by each member of the ride turns into good team spirit and the pressure, shared fairly, develops good esprit de corps.

I must say that the 'Ride' is well worthwhile. It produces pride, training, discipline in the officers, and good training, good manners, good health for the horses. The end product is an excellent 'Musical Ride', which is enjoyed fully by the public, therefore great for public relations. Visitors from other cities and countries say they enjoy the spectacle and enquire if it would be visiting their home town area.

I understand that since Inspector E.S. Johnson started the present 'Musical Ride' combined with the Pipe Band in 1966, various offers have been received by (then) Chief of Police H. Adamson for the 'Ride' to perform in various parts of the American Continent and the British Isles. Perhaps as our city grows, and the police manpower is at full strength, the Metropolitan Toronto Police Musical Ride will be able to attend these world-wide functions. What a great boost for our city and public relations.

The Mounted Unit Musical Ride is only one function of our training, but I hope you now understand that it is a very important and worthwhile part."[1]

1 Metropolitan Toronto Police, *The 1986 Inspection Unit Audit Team report on the Mounted Unit.*

The Pipes and Drums of the Metropolitan Toronto Police and the Musical Ride under the command of Sgt Bill Macey. Sunnybrook Park, 1982. Photograph, Toronto Police Mounted Unit.

THE 1984 MUSICAL RIDE

Officer-in-charge of the 1984 Ride was Sgt Patrick Woulfe. Ride leaders were PC Fred Lloyd (5736) and PC Bert McKeown (2351).

Sgt Pat Woulfe was the officer-in-charge of the 1984 Musical Ride.

MUSICAL RIDE PERFORMANCES IN 1984

Date	Event	Location
July 1	The Loblaws Classic Horse Show	Sunnybrook Park
July 2	The Loblaws Classic Horse Show	Sunnybrook Park
September 23	Heritage Day	Old Fort York.

1984 MUSICAL RIDE PERSONNEL

PC Robertson (138)	PC Wright (2903)	PC Mountjoy (4744)
PC Rogers (2058)	PC Dean (3460)	PC Mawson (7272)
PC Gerard (6785)	PC Green (253)	PC Roberts (3423)
PC Thomas (1865)	PC McKeown (2351)	PC Rowbotham (6057)
PC Matier (3467)	PC Derbyshire (6585)	PC McAleer (5755)
PC Gill (48)	PC Crimp (4592)	PC Cassidy (4812)
PC Spearen (2437)	PC Scribner (3529)	PC Parks (6994)
PC Feather (2327)	PC Lloyd (5736)	

MUSICAL RIDES WERE NOT PERFORMED IN 1985, 1986, 1987, 1988 OR 1989.

THE 1990 MUSICAL RIDE

MUSICAL RIDE PERFORMANCES IN 1990

The Canadian National Exhibition Horse Show
The Police Amateur Athletic Association Field Day
The Royal Winter Fair

1990 MUSICAL RIDE PERSONNEL

Officer-in-Charge: Staff Sgt Pat Woulfe (168)

1st Black Section
PC Fred Lloyd (5736)
Sgt Howie Peers (7040)
PC Paul Greenaway (3647)
PC Jim Bradford (1752)
PC Graham Acott (2897)
PC Steve Noble (7315)
PC Rick Vandusen (2322)

1st Bay Section
PC Nick Spearen (2437)
PC Rick Mamak (6440)
PC Jon Vanhetveld (7165)
PC John Feather (2327)
PC Steve Hitch (3890)
PC Michael Anderson (791)

2nd Black Section
PC Michael Brooks (1538
PC Dennis Rowbotham (6057)
PC Greg Vanderhart (4761)
PC Rick VanDusen (2322)
Spare: PC Michael Roberts (3423)

2nd Bay Section
PC Don Mawson (7272)
PC Michael Chilton (6601)
PC Barbara Hammond (5510)
PC Ken Cassidy (4812)

The following officers rode in one or more performances during the year;

PC Gord Graffman
PC Graham Acott (2897)
PC James McAleer (5755)

Left and right: The Pipes and Drums followed by the Mounted Unit march onto the field at the Fergus Highland Games, 1993. Photographs, Toronto Police Mounted Unit.

The Musical Ride at Fort York, Toronto, 1990. Photograph, Toronto Police Mounted Unit.

The 1990 Musical Ride with the Metropolitan Toronto Police Pipes and Drums. Outside the Coliseum at the Canadian National Exhibition.

The 1991 Musical Ride at Fort York. Photograph, Toronto Police Mounted Unit.

THE 1991 MUSICAL RIDE

MUSICAL RIDE PERFORMANCES IN 1991

The Canadian National Exhibition
Horse Show
The Police Amateur Athletic
Association Field Day
The Royal Winter Fair

1991 MUSICAL RIDE PERSONNEL

Officer-in-Charge: Sgt Howie Peers (7040)

1st Black Section
PC Don Mawson (7272)
PC Graham Acott (2897)
PC Steve Noble (7315)
PC Rick Vandusen (2322)

1st Bay Section
PC Jim Bradford (1752)
PC Steve Hitch (3890)
PC Michael Anderson (791)
PC Barbara Hammond (5510)
PC Greg Woods (7011)

2nd Black Section
PC Dennis Rowbotham (6057)
PC Michael Chilton (6601)
PC Bill Robertson (6793)
PC Michael Brooks (1538)

2nd Bay Section
PC Rick Mamak (6440)
PC Steve Derbyshire (6585)
PC Steve Niemirowski (5895)
PC Jon Vanhetveld (7165)

Spare: PC Bill Wardle (2785)

The following officers rode in one or more performances;
PC Tom Matier (3467)
PC Ken Cassidy (4812)
PC Lenny Kotsopoulos (6669)

THE 1992 MUSICAL RIDE

MUSICAL RIDE PERFORMANCES IN 1992

The Canadian National Exhibition
Horse Show
The Police Amateur Athletic
Association Field Day
The Fergus Highland Games
The Royal Winter Fair

1992 MUSICAL RIDE PERSONNEL

Officer-in-Charge: Sgt Howie Peers (7040)

1st Black Section
PC Don Mawson (7272)
PC Michael Brooks (1538)
PC Michael Anderson (791)
PC Michael Chilton (6601)

1st Bay Section
PC Dennis Rowbotham (6057)
PC Jim Bradford (1752)
PC Greg Woods (7011)
PC Jon Vanhetveld (7165)

2nd Black Section
PC Graham Acott (2897)
PC Steve Noble (7315)
PC Bob Bowen (7350)
PC Steve Derbyshire (6585)

2nd Bay Section
PC Barbara Hammond (5510)
PC Rick Mamak (6440)
PC Bill Wardle (2785)
PC Greg Vanderhart (4761)

Spare: PC Steve Niemirowski(5895)

The Pipes and Drums of the Toronto Police

Pipe Major Thomas Ross organized the Pipes and Drums of the Toronto Police Force in 1912. They gave their first performance at the Police Athletic Games at Hanlan's Point. Many of its members enlisted for service in the army during the First World War. Those that remained in Toronto continued to play together and traveled around Ontario, at their own expense, to help with military recruiting drives.

When the Prince of Wales visited Toronto in 1919 he requested that the band perform at his reception at Allendale Station (near Barrie). The band was later placed under the administrative control of the Police Amateur Athletic Association. In 1927 it played in front of 80,000 people at the police games in Baltimore, Maryland.

The Band performed at many functions through the 1930s. Their ranks were depleted during World War II as many of its members took military leave to serve overseas. The depletion of its personnel forced the Band to disband.

In 1960, Inspector Alexander (Sandy) Johnson re-established the Pipes and Drums. It took five years to recruit members and to prepare the band for public performances. In honour of Thomas Ross, the founder of the original band, the Ross tartan was chosen for the kilts of the band members.

The Pipes and Drums of the Metropolitan Toronto Police made its debut on November 11, 1965. In 1966 the Band became part of the mounted unit's Musical Ride by providing music for the public performances.

In 1973, the Pipe Band was requested to play at the reception held at City Hall for Her Royal Highness, Queen Elizabeth the Second.

Approximately forty-five active members give an average of one-hundred-and-thirty public performances yearly and have been very successful in band competitions all over the world. They continually receive invitations to perform at venues across North America. They make regular appearances at the Edinburgh Military Tattoo in Scotland where they have won the coveted world championships.

In recent years, the Pipes and Drums have assisted the Mounted Unit by accompanying the Drill Ride in its public-order management displays.

The Musical Ride with the Metropolitan Toronto Police Pipes and Drums at Fort York, 1991.
Photograph, TorontoPolice Mounted Unit.

The 1992 Musical Ride outside the Princes' Gate at the Canadian National Exhibition. Note the white "Canada 125" Pennants. Photograph, Toronto Police Mounted Unit.

A casual photograph of the 1993 Musical Ride at the Fergus Highland Games. Front row, Left to right: PC Steve Hitch, PC Don Mawson, PC Jim Bradford, PC Deb Poulson, PC Jon Vanhetveld, PC Greg Vanderhart, PC Greg Woods, PC Ken Cassidy, PC Rick Mamak. Standing: Sgt Bill Wardle, PC Fred Lloyd, PC Brent Dilaine, PC Steve Noble, PC Mike Chilton, PC Graham Acott, PC Mike Anderson, PC Bob Bowen, PC Dennis Rowbotham, PC John Feather. Photograph, Toronto Police Mounted Unit.

THE 1993 MUSICAL RIDE

During one of the final performances of the Musical Ride at the 1993 Canadian National Exhibition, an officer suffered a broken arm when police mount "Bruce" tripped and fell to the ground. The officer immediately remounted his horse and completed the ride, despite the broken arm. You never let "the ride" down. Later in the week police mount "Harry" also tripped and fell to the ground. The ride continued on and the officer remounted and regained his position to the cheers of the crowd. These two events in a one week period were the only times that police officers were dismounted during performances of the Metropolitan Toronto Police Musical Rides.

At another C.N.E. performance, Constable Jim Davis was asked to ride the Inspector's position and lead the Musical Ride into the ring. This was the first time a constable was given this honour. It was in recognition of his devoted service to the mounted Unit. It was a well-deserved public tribute prior to his impending retirement from the police service.

MUSICAL RIDE PERFORMANCES IN 1993

93 - 08 - 12: Canadian National Exhibition Presentation Night.
93 - 08 - 15: The Fergus Scottish Games.
93 - 08 - 18: C.N.E. Horse Show
93 - 08 - 21: C.N.E. Horse Show
93 - 08 - 22: C.N.E. Horse Show
93 - 08 - 28: C.N.E. Horse Show
93 - 08 - 29: C.N.E. Horse Show
93 - 08 - 31: C.N.E. Horse Show
93 - 09 - 04: C.N.E. Horse Show
93 - 09 - 05: C.N.E. Horse Show
93 - 11- 12: The Royal Winter Fair
93 - 11 -13: The Royal Winter Fair
93 - 11 -14: The Royal Winter Fair

1993 MUSICAL RIDE PERSONNEL

Officer-in-Charge: Sgt William Wardle (2785)

1st Black Section	1st Bay Section
PC Fred Lloyd (5736)	PC Donald Mawson (7272)
PC Brent Dilaine (3296)	PC Jim Bradford (1752)
PC Steve Noble (7315)	PC Deborah Poulson (4890)
PC Michael Chilton (6601)	PC Jon Vanhetveld (7165)

2nd Black Section	2nd Bay Section
PC Graham Acott (2897)	PC Greg Vanderhart (4761)
PC Michael Anderson (791)	PC Greg Woods (7011)
PC Bob Bowen (7350)	PC John Feather (2327)
PC Dennis Rowbotham (6057)	PC Rick Mamak (6040)

Officers who rode in one or more Musical Rides
PC Ken Cassidy (4812)
PC Rick Vandusen (2322)
PC Tom Matier (3467)

The 1993 Musical Ride at Fort York.

The administrative section of the 1993 Musical Ride. PC Rick Vandusen, Staff Inspector Jim Jones, Sgt Bill Wardle, Training Constable Jim Davis.

The 1st Black Section of the 1993 Musical Ride. Left to right: PC Mike Chilton, PC Steve Noble, PC Brent Dilaine, PC Fred Lloyd.

The 2nd Black Section of the 1993 Musical Ride. Left to right: PC Dennis Rowbotham, PC Bob Bowen, PC Mike Anderson, PC Graham Acott. Photographs, Toronto Police Mounted Unit.

The 1st Bay Section of the 1993 Musical Ride. Left to right: PC Jon Vanhetveld, PC Deb Poulson, PC Jim Bradford, PC Don Mawson.

The 2nd Bay Section of the 1993 Musical Ride. PC Rick Mamak, PC John Feather, PC Greg Woods, PC Greg Vanderhart. Photographs, Toronto Police Mounted Unit.

The Mounted Unit Drill Team

1996 To help celebrate the Mounted Unit's 110th anniversary, a nine-member drill team was organised and trained. The officers presented mounted public-order movements to the music of the Metropolitan Toronto Police Pipes and Drums. This was a very traditional idea that was implemented for the same reasons as the first military musical rides.

The purpose of the first musical rides was to practice tactical military movements in a way that was interesting to the riders and also entertaining to an audience. The drill team seemed to be an excellent way of providing the police riders and horses with additional training. At the same time it gave the unit a way of demonstrating its abilities to an audience. The drill team performed at the 110th Anniversary Horse Show on August 20, and was very well received by all in attendance.

The drill ride is very different from the musical ride that the unit performed previously. It is not a traditional musical ride and does not pretend to be. Intricate movements used by most musical rides around the world are not included. It does, however, enhance the skills of the riders and the horses, encourages teamwork and provides the unit with a forum to demonstrate how it does its job. The goal of the drill ride is therefore very similar to that of the training given during the original musical rides of a century ago. A fitting way to celebrate the Mounted Unit's 110th anniversary.

1996 MOUNTED UNIT DRILL TEAM

Officer-in-Charge: Sgt Bill Wardle

PC Graham Acott, Ride Leader

PC Greg Woods	PC Derrick Speirs
PC Pat Penny	PC Ted Gallipeau
PC Laura Lowson	PC Bob Bowen
PC Peter Spurling	PC Arlene Fritz

The Pipes and Drums march past the troop during the first performance of the Drill team at the 110th Anniversary Horse Show. Photograph, Toronto Police Mounted Unit.

The Metropolitan Toronto Police Pipes and Drums with the Drill Team in Port Perry, 1997. PC Speirs, Sgt Wardle, PC Matier, PC Spurling, PC Rowbotham, PC Acott, PC Bowen, PC Woods, PC Penney. Photograph, PC Terri Douglas.

 **1997** On July 25, 1997 the Drill Team performed at the Port Perry Tattoo which was part of the Highlands of Durham Scottish Games. The Drill Ride was well received and the highlight of the show. Mounted officers provided a ceremonial escort for the honorary Clan Chieftain and other honoured guests.

1997 MOUNTED UNIT DRILL TEAM	
Officer-in-Charge: Sgt Bill Wardle	PC Graham Acott, Ride Leader
PC Greg Woods	PC Derrick Speirs
PC Pat Penny	PC Dennis Rowbotham
PC Tom Matier	PC Bob Bowen
PC Peter Spurling	PC Greg Ladner

'The March Past' during the opening ceremony at the Port Perry performance. Photograph, PC Terri Douglas.

 **1998** The Royal Canadian Mounted Police celebrated their 125th Anniversary in 1998. The Drill team was requested to represent the Toronto Police in three tattoos being sponsored in Ontario as part of their celebrations. The Drill Team performed at these tattoos in Toronto, London and Collingwood. The Halton Regional Police also requested that the Drill Team take part in their 25th Anniversary Tattoo in Burlington.

1998 MOUNTED UNIT DRILL TEAM	
Officer-in-Charge: Sgt Bill Wardle	PC Graham Acott, Ride Leader
Sgt Peter Spurling	PC Derrick Speirs
PC Pat Penny	PC Dennis Rowbotham
PC Tom Matier	PC Bob Bowen
PC Greg Woods	PC Gino Sonsini
PC Greg Vanderhart	

Left to right: PC Speirs, PC Bowen, PC Matier, PC Sonsini, Sgt Spurling, PC Vanderhart, PC Penney, PC Rowbotham, Sgt Acott, Sgt Wardle.

The Drill Team in Collingwood

In September 1998, the Drill Team was invited to represent the Toronto Police Service at the Royal Canadian Mounted Police 125th Anniversary Tattoo in Collingwood, Ontario.

The Unit participated in the opening and closing ceremonies as well as giving one crowd management demonstration accompanied by the Pipes and Drums of the Ontario Provincial Police.

The "March Out" after the crowd management demonstration. Photographs, Carol Robbins.

The "March In" for the closing ceremony with the Pipes and Drums of the Ontario Provincial Police.

The Pick Up

The following series of pictures were taken of the "pick up" at the Drill Team performance in Collingwood. The "pick up" simulates an officer becoming dismounted in a crowd management situation. His fellow officers perform a rescue drill and extract the officer from the crowd on the back of a horse. PC Greg Vanderhart is the officer on the ground, PC Pat Penney is on the left and Sgt Spurling is on the right.

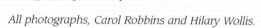

The officer signals his position.

All photographs, Carol Robbins and Hilary Wollis.

PC Vanderhart and Sgt Spurling link arms. The horses slow from a canter to a trot.

PC Vanderhart grabs the saddle of Sgt Spurling's horse.

PC Vanderhart vaults onto the horse's back as PC Penney ensures he does not fall backwards.

PC Vanderhart holds onto Sgt Spurling as they canter back to the troop.

Right. The officers have reformed in a troop and PC Vanderhart leaps off the back of the horse on the right.

435

**2000** The Drill Team was reorganised and expanded to give more officers an opportunity to participate in performances. They previewed with a public dress rehearsal in April at the graduation ceremony at the Sunnybrook Riding Academy. The first official performances were at the Canadian Olympic Trial at Hendervale Equestrian Centre in Milton. After the two Hendervale performance the team followed up with three at the Canadian National Exhibition and two more at the Royal Winter Fair.

The Drill Team at the Canadian Olympic trials.
Photograph, courtesy of the Hendervale Equestrian Centre, Vavuz Photography.

2000 MOUNTED UNIT DRILL TEAM

Officer-in-Charge: Sgt Bill Wardle	Sgt Graham Acott, Ride Leader
Sgt Peter Spurling	Sgt Dale Guest
PC Pat Penny	PC Dennis Rowbotham
PC Vicki Montgomery	PC Bob Bowen
PC Greg Woods	PC Gino Sonsini
PC Mark DeCosta	PC Derrick Speirs
PC Rod Jones	PC Moreen Smith
PC Rick Mamak	PC Ron Gilbert
PC Jim Bradford	

Hendervale Equestrian Centre

A series of photographs from the Drill Team performance at the Hendervale Equestrian Centre in July of 2000.

The Saturday performance took place in a sand ring while the Sunday performance took place on the grass equestrian course.

Performing in different location and on different surfaces forces riders to adapt to the new environment. All of the landmarks change and the movements are harder to anticipate. Changes in venue enhances the training value of the drill team.

Photographs, courtesy of the Hendervale Equestrian Centre and Vavuz Photography.

Bridles on, Mounted Headquarters, Sunnybrook Park, April 2000.

Sunnybrook Park, April 2000.

Above photos: The Drill Team performance at the grand opening of the new Mounted Headquarters, December 4, 2000.

The Drill Team at the Halton Regional Police 25th Anniversary Tattoo.
Back row: PC's Penny, Matier, Speirs, Woods Sonsimi.
Front row: Sgt's Spurling, Wardle, Acott, PC's Rowbotham, Vanderhart.

Photographs, Toronto Police Mounted Unit

Chapter 9

Equestrian Competitions

Horse shows have always been popular events in Toronto. The Canadian National Exhibition and Royal Winter Fair Horse Shows continue to draw large crowds of spectators. When the cavalry regiments were still "mounted" they routinely participated in the city's horse shows and hosted their own mounted field days. Until the 1940s, the Olympic competitors in equestrian events were almost always cavalry officers.

It was natural for the members of the Toronto Police Mounted Unit to want to compete in the city's horse shows. Police riders probably competed in the Canadian National Exhibition horse shows before the turn of the century

Some horse shows had police classes where members of the Mounted Unit competed against one another in closed competition. Other horse shows classed the police officers the same as military riders and permitted them to compete against the soldiers in open competition.

Mounted officers leaving the Canadian National Exhibition Grandstand c.1910. The officers would have just finished taking part in a police class at the horse show or participated in a mounted escort for a visiting dignitary. The fifth officer in line is wearing a medal which indicates that he served in the Boer War in South Africa. Photograph, Canadian National Exhibition Archives, William James.

There were three main types of classes for the police at the horse shows. The uniform class was where the officers were judged on the turn out of themselves and their horses. In the equitation class the rider would be judged on his walk, trot, canter and what ever other movements the show judge requested. The hunt classes were the most exciting as they required a rider to do a circuit of jumps.

The modern police equestrian competitions still have uniform and equitation classes. The hunt courses have been replaced with obstacle courses. The obstacles are based on situations that a police horse might face on a regular patrol in the city. The purpose of the course is to demonstrate the effectiveness of the horse and rider in a police patrol simulation.

The obstacle courses have evolved over the years to contain "fleeing felon" segments. These courses are timed and the rider is judged on how well they negotiates the obstacles as well as the time that they complete it in. Other classes have appeared in recent years such as the "Ride and Shoot" where the officer fires a paint gun at four targets from a cantering horse. Another variation is the "Skill at Arms" course where the rider is judged on his use of the weapons of the cavalry trooper, the lance, sword and gun.

The evolving police classes serve a very important purpose in mounted policing. They encourage officers to work with their horses and enhance their training. It builds pride and morale in the unit as officers work together as teams in the various events. It also allows the officers to meet mounted police officers from other jurisdictions and to observe and learn from them.

The following story appeared in a Toronto newspaper around 1924 that describes the success that the Toronto Mounted Police had in open competitions. It is worth repeating word for word. "No other city in Canada has a mounted police unit to be considered anywhere near the equal of Toronto in any respect. Some of the big cities across the international boarder go in on a larger scale for mounted squads in their police departments but while the numerical

Inspector Crosbie with "Shamrock" (Billy) just prior to his being sold after 16 years of service as a Toronto police horse. Billy was the top show horse and won many trophies in his day including the championship at the Bennett School and horse show in New York City in 1917. Photograph, Toronto Star, *May 17, 1930.*

strength may be greater this city cannot suffer by comparison when all round merit is concerned. As an instance of this a sergeant of the mounted force in a large American city visited Toronto, last, year in regard to an invitation to that force to enter horses in competition at a show here. After inspecting the local squad and its animals, the American admitted quite frankly that it would be futile for his force to come with any hope of success.

"There is a glass case in Chief Dickson's office which holds a dozen handsome silver cups and a tray won by horses in competition at the Eglinton Hunt Club Show, The Dominion Day Horse Parade and the Royal Winter Fair, where there was competition from the Royal Canadian Dragoons and the United States Cavalry. The police horse won the first prize for manners at this latter show. Sergeant Crosbie has a large array of Rosettes (ribbons) of various hues and colours in a frame in his office. All of the ribbons were won by horses from the squad."[1]

Some of the trophies won by the No. 5 Station Troop of the Toronto Mounted Police. Photograph, Toronto Star, *May 17, 1930.*

The following is an annual synopsis of police competitions. It was complied from a number of sources. Unfortunately no information was found for some years.

🏆 **1910** The Military and Canadian Horse Show was held at the Toronto Armouries in April 1910. The show had not been held for three years prior. Newspapers were full of reports about the show and its participants who came from all over Canada and the United States.

The *Toronto Telegram* reported that a new class had been established at the show and a silver cup would be presented to the "best turned out and appointed mounted constable." It felt that this would be "a novel and interesting competition."

🏆 **1923** The Toronto Open Air Horse Show was held on July 2 and PC George Smith riding "Prudence" was the first place mounted police officer. His trophy is on display at the Ontario Police College in Aylmer, Ontario. The Royal Winter Fair Police Class was won by PC Dedlow (177) riding "Patience." His trophy is on display at Mounted Headquarters.[56]

PC Dedlow (177) who won first place in 1923 Royal Winter Fair. Photograph, Toronto Star, May 17, 1930

PC Percy Johnson (375) at Queen's Park after winning a trophy at the Toronto Open Air Horse Show, c.1924. Photograph, Toronto Police Museum.

 **1924** Constable James McMaster won the first place ribbon in his class riding "Fidelity" a 15 year old bay mare at the Toronto Hunt Club Horse Show during the summer.

Constable Walker riding "Colleen" won the first place ribbon in his class at the Royal Winter Fair Horse Show. Constable Walker formerly served in the premier British cavalry corps, The First Life Guards.

 **1925** The Canadian National Exhibition Police Class was won by Patrol Sergeant Masters riding "Sunshine."

Ten horses were entered and exhibited in two classes at the Royal Winter Fair in November. There were twenty-one open entries in the classes. Police horses took the 1st, 2nd and 3rd prizes. The chief constable felt that "the achievement reflects great credit on the officers and men concerned."[2]

The Toronto Police Commission received a letter on December 17th from the Toronto City Council. It read in part "That this city Council congratulates the Board of Police Commissioners, Chief of Police Dickson, Sergeant Crosbie, his officers and men on the splendid showing of police horses and general appearance of the mounted police force at the Royal Winter Fair; and also congratulates the officer commanding Stanley Barracks, his officers and men for their splendid showing at the Royal Winter Fair."[3]

The trophies won by the unit during the year at both the Canadian National Exhibition Horse show and the Royal Winter Fair were put on display at the Police Commissioners meeting on January 7th, 1926. The Commissioners were "proud of the achievement of the Mounted Squad."[4]

A Toronto Newspaper reported that American visitors were so impressed with the Toronto mounted constables in the hurdling contests that, on December 2nd, Chief Dickson got offers to purchase three of the police horses. A Chicago man offered $1,000.00 for "Golden," a New York man offered $800.00 for "Sunshine" and a New England man offered $500.00 for "Connaught." The horses were not for sale even at these extraordinary prices as the Toronto police were averaging between $50.00 and $75.00 for the horses they sold around this time.[5]

 **1926** The Toronto Mounted Police entered the open competition at the Royal Winter Fair and won the 1st, 2nd and 3rd place ribbons for the second year in a row.

Constable Charles Whitford (594) won ribbons for jumping on "Mayflower" at the Eglinton Hunt Club Horse Show.

The Toronto Open Air Horse Parade was won by Constable McVeigh riding "Selkirk." His trophy is on display at Mounted Headquarters.

 **1928** The 1928 Canadian National Exhibition Police Class was won by Constable Hamilton Hutchinson. His trophy is on display at Mounted Headquarters.

 **1929** The Police team at the Royal Winter Fair included Patrol Sgt Masters, PC Chalkin, PC Hainer, PC Harvey and PC Hill.

The presentation of cups at Toronto City Hall to the winners and participants of the Toronto Mounted Police classes at the Canadian National Exhibition. Left to right: Front row: PC Mosher, PC Dedlow, PC Hill, Inspector Crosbie, H.H. Kent, R.H. Jenkinson, T. Bartrem (Exhibition representative), PC Johnson. Back row: PC Keen, PC Master, PC Cooper, PC Lytle, PC Smuck, PC Smith and PC Mitchell. This clipping is from a Toronto Newspaper, c.1925.

Patrol Sgt Masters at the 1929 Royal Winter Fair. Photograph, City of Toronto Archives, Globe and Mail *Collection. SC 266 – 18755.*

The Toronto police team at the 1929 Royal Winter Fair. Left to right: PC Hill, PC Harvey, PC Hainer, PC Chalkin and Patrol Sgt Masters. Photograph, City of Toronto Archives, Globe and Mail Collection. *SC 266 – 18753.*

 **1930** The *Toronto Telegram* reported that there were a number of good jumpers on the Toronto Police Mounted Unit. The smallest horse that the police force purchased was just under sixteen hands. This black horse could jump over the ordinary touring car with its roof down. "Several cups grace the office of Inspector Crosbie, won for show, running and jumping."[6]

The Toronto police team at the 1930 Toronto Open Air Horse Show at Queen's Park. Left to right: Patrol Sgt Andrew Cooper, PC Phillips, PC Lepper, PC Coathup, PC Gallagher. Photograph, City of Toronto Archives, Globe and Mail Collection. SC 266 - 20932.

1931 Mounted officers entered a number of open competitions during the year. Several trophies were won at the Canadian National Exhibition, the Royal Winter Fair, the Eglinton Hunt Club and The Toronto Open Air Horse Show.

The Saturday August 31, *Toronto Telegram* published this story on the Canadian National Exhibition Police Class:

"Blue Coats" Looked Well

The mounted police made a brave showing in their class which was judged by Major-General J.H. McBrien, former Chief of Staff. As customary, the horses went through their paces in splendid fashion and displayed excellent manners. First prize was won by Sergeant Rogerson with the reliable "Norval," who has earned many similar decorations at local shows. PC Hill mounted on "Selkirk," was second and PC Hainer, on "Dan," third.[7]

Constable John Dedlow won the Toronto Open Air Horse Show riding "Dungannon." His trophy is still on display at Mounted Headquarters.

Patrol Sgt Andrew Cooper and "Jean McNeil" at the Toronto Open Air Horse Show, Queen's Park, July 4th, 1931. Photograph, City of Toronto Archives, Globe and Mail Collection SC 266 – 30462.

 **1932** Mounted officers competed at the Canadian National Exhibition, the Royal Winter Fair, the Eglinton Hunt Club, and the Toronto Open Air Horse Show. It was another successful year with several trophies being won at the different shows.

1934 Prize winners from the Police Horse Class at the Toronto Open Air Horse Show, on July 3rd, were:

First Prize Police Horse: Constable Edward Gallagher (180) of No, 8 stable riding "Silver."

Second Prize Police Horse: Constable James McMaster (153) of No. 5 stable.

The other competitors were, Constables Russell, Walker and Murray.

1935 Mounted Unit officers were active in competitions throughout the year. They competed at the Toronto Open Air Horse Show, The Eglinton Hunt Club, The Canadian National Exhibition and the Royal Winter Fair Horse Shows. The showing by the officers was reported as "a credit to the Toronto Police Department and the City of Toronto."[8] The officers were allowed to compete at the shows in uniform with their mounts, but did so on their own time.

1936 Policemen and their mounts competed at the Eglinton Hunt Club, the Canadian National Exhibition and the Royal Winter Fair Horse Shows. They were required to compete on their own time.

PC Andrew Cooper at the Toronto Open Air Equestrian Horse Show, Queen's Park, c.1932. Photograph, Toronto Police Museum.

PC Andrew Cooper and "Snookie," 2nd place police horse. PC John Dedlow and "Dungannon." 1st place police horse. Toronto Open Air Horse Show, June 1, 1931. Photograph, City of Toronto Archives, Globe and Mail Collection, SC 266 – 24532.

 **1937** The mounted men excelled in competition again this year. The officers competed on their own time at the Toronto Horse Show, The Eglinton Hunt Club, The Canadian National Exhibition and the Royal Winter Fair Horse Shows. The officers racked up an impressive 5 first place ribbons; 3 second place ribbons, 5 third place ribbons, and one fourth place ribbon.

POLICE TEAM AT THE HORSE SHOW

The police team at the Toronto Open Air Horse Show, July 2, 1934. PC Gallagher "Silver," PC McMaster, PC Russell "June," PC Walker "Lucknow," PC Murray "Royal York." Photograph, Toronto Telegram.

THE TORONTO MOUNTED POLICE vs. THE CANADIAN CAVALRY

The following article appeared in the *Toronto Telegram* on September 12th, 1936. The story gives an idea of the friendly rivalry that existed in the local horse shows between the police and the military.

POLICE RIDERS OPPOSE THE ARMY

Old Time Rivals meet To-night in Feature at Exhibition

Judging of class 203 in the Horse Show at the C.N.E. tonight for military or police mounts open to N.C.O.'s or mounted police takes place in the coliseum. The riders will be in uniform with regulation saddle and bridle and this event brings together the old time rivals, the Toronto police and the men of Stanley Barracks.

Twelve members of Toronto's mounted squad are entered against five representatives of the Dragoons and one member of the Mississauga Horse.

Members of the Toronto Police who will compete are; P.S. Cooper, on Jim McNeil; PC Banks (631), on Bob; PC Watt (57) on Peggy McNeil; PC Russell (737), on an unnamed 9-year-old mare; PC Frazer (823), on Mack; PC McMater (153); PC Anketell (272), on Royal York; PC Murray (287), on Dungannon; PC Morrison (19), on Lady Bird; P.S. Chalkin, on Golden Rod; PC Gallagher (180), on Silver.

In several cases the Toronto horses are twelve years of age or over and are competing against youthful show ring mounts from the military."[1]

1 *Toronto Telegram*, Saturday September 12, 1936.

Left and right: Awards won by Mounted Officers at the Toronto Open Air Horse Show.

1939 Members competed with their mounts at the Canadian National Exhibition Horse Show winning two firsts, two seconds, two thirds and two fourth-place prizes, in open competition.

1940 Members of the Unit competed with their mounts on their own time at the Canadian National Exhibition Horse Show winning one first, one second, one third and one fourth prize in open competition.

1941 Mounted officers competed at the Canadian National Exhibition horse show winning one first, one second, one third. and one fourth - place prize in open competition.

1954 The members of the unit exhibited horses at The Canadian National Exhibition and the Royal Winter Fair. "They were highly commended on these occasions."9

1955 The Mounted Unit exhibited horses at both the Canadian National Exhibition and the Royal Winter Fair. The officers were complemented on their performance at these shows.

1965 Twelve officers and their mounts entered competitions at the Canadian National Exhibition Horse Show and the Royal Winter Fair. They competed in the new ceremonial dress uniform.

1978 The Royal Winter Fair Police class No. 68 was held on Sunday November 12, 1978, 1:30 p.m. Twelve Officers competed in the equestrian event. Top three riders were:

1st place: PC Thomas McClintock (6158) on "Beauty"
2nd Place: PC Robert Wright (2903) riding "Buck" (Buccaneer)
3rd Place: PC Martin Zakrajsek (3623) Riding "Trooper."

The Toronto Open Air Horse Show July 2nd 1934. It is being held at Stanley Barracks at the C.N.E. grounds. The Royal Canadian Dragoon's officer's mess can be seen in the background. PC Ed Gallagher, 1st place. PC James McMaster, 2nd place. Photograph, City of Toronto Archives, Globe and Mail Collection.
SC -266 –33933.

 **1979** The Canadian National Exhibition Horse Show was held on Tuesday August 21, 1979 at 6:30 p.m. Twelve riders competed in the equitation event. The top three riders were:

1st place: PC Tom Kirkley "Beauty"
2nd place: PC Neil MacKenzie (2011) "Stormy"
3rd Place: PC Michael Brewer "Anne."

The Royal Winter Fair Police class No. 68 took place on Sunday November 11, 1979, at 1:30 p.m. Twelve officers competed in the equestrian event. The top three riders were:

1st Place: PC Al Mackevicius (614) "Trooper"
2nd Place: PC Tom Kirkley "Sandy"
3rd Place: PC Clarence Sauve "Anne."

 **1980** The Canadian National Exhibition Horse Show was held on Saturday August 16 at 6:30 p.m. Class No. 990. Twelve officers were entered in the class and the top three riders and mounts were:

1st Place: PC Richard Barnett (3718) "Royal"
2nd Place: PC Eric Lucas (4753) "Daisy"
3rd Place: PC John Machnik (6026) "Dick."

The Royal Winter Fair police class was held on Sunday November 16, 1980. The top riders were:

1st Place: PC Jeff Rogers (2058) "Prince"
2nd Place: PC Michael Roberts (3423) "General"
3rd Place: PC Barry Gerard (6785) "Queen."

 **1981** The Canadian National Exhibition Horse Show was held on Saturday August 22, at 6:30 p.m. Class No. 990. Twelve officers were entered in the class and the top three riders and mounts were:

1st Place: PC Fred Lloyd # 5736 "Regal"
2nd Place: PC Paul Dean #3460 "Caesar"
3rd Place: PC Gary Mountjoy (4744) "Lady."

Standings of the "Troop Drill Exercise" for the Royal Winter Fair Horse Show:

1st Place: PC Tom Thomas (1865) "Dandy"
2nd Place   PC Michael Roberts (3423) "Colonel"
3rd Place: PC Steven Kemley (2831) "Black Beauty."

The 1981 Royal Winter Fair Police Class

The police class at the Royal Winter Fair had become a standard equitation class. In order to make the class more interesting the Mounted Unit implemented a Troop Drill Exercise for the 1981 Fair. Constable Jim Davis choreographed the following program for the police class.

Royal Winter Fair Troop Drill and Police Class:

- Enter the ring, single file, at the walk, on the right rein.
- Trot, rising or posting trot. Single file.
- From the front, number.
- Tell off by sections.
- Form half sections. Sitting trot.
- Down the centre. Form sections.
- Change the rein.
- Form half sections. Form single file.
- At the halt – to the left, form line. Halt at the centre.

Note: When the ride halts at the centre of the ring, the dressing will be to the right and eight feet knee to knee.

- Prepare to dismount. Dismount. Stand to attention for inspection by the judge.
- Prepare to mount. Mount.
- Four paces side passage - left and right. Four riders at a time.
- Four paces rein back.
- Ribbon presentation. Rider called will ride to the Ringmaster and salute the Royal Box.
- Right turn. Walk march. Left rein. Trot for the victory circuit of the ring and exit.

The above movements added a lot to the previous walk, trot and canter classes. It brought back a little more of the military traditions and encompassed more of what the officers actually did during training.

 **1982** The 1982 Canadian National Exhibition Police Class was held on August 21, 1981. Twelve officers entered into the competition. The standings were:

1st Place: PC Tom Thomas (1865) riding "Dan"
2nd Place: PC Don Vincent (2708) riding "Lancer"
3rd Place: PC Bill Lyons (2730) riding "Sandy."

The Royal Winter Fair Police Class was held on Saturday November 13, 1982. The standings were:

1st Place: PC Malcolm Lyons (2750) riding "Lancer"
2nd Place: PC Bill Lyons (2730) riding "Sandy"
3rd Place: PC Dave Hadlow (1772) riding "Sally."

 **1983** The Canadian National Exhibition Police Class was held on Tuesday August 23, at 6:30 p.m. The final standings of the class were:

1st Place: PC Richard Crimp (4592) riding "Prince"
2nd Place: PC Nick Spearen (2437) riding "Royal"
3rd Place: PC Bill Lyons (2730) riding "Sally."

The Royal Winter Fair Police Class was held during the afternoon of November 13. The exact standings of the officers is not known. The first three ribbons went to:
PC Gary Harrison (2868) riding "Bruce"
PC Allen Parks (6994) riding "Dan"
PC Bob Wright (2903) riding "Princess."

1984 The Canadian National Exhibition Police Class was held on Saturday August 18, at 7:00 p.m. The top three riders were:

1st Place: PC Stephen Niemirowski (5895) riding "Casey"
2nd Place: PC Barry Gerard (6785) riding "Colonel"
3rd Place: PC Donald Mawson (7272) riding "Robin."

The 1984 Royal Winter Fair Police Class was held on Saturday November 10, at 7:00 p.m. The Mounted Unit entered twelve riders in the class and the results were:

1st Place: PC Michael Roberts (3423) riding "Harry"
2nd Place: PC Bill Mathers (2941) riding "Sally"
3rd Place: PC Charlie Gleed (228) riding "Anne."

PC Don Mawson and "Sutherland" negotiate an obstacle course demonstration during the Loblaws Classic horse show at Sunnybrook Park, 1986. Photograph, Toronto Police Mounted Unit.

449

 **1985** The Canadian National Exhibition Police Class was held on August 17, at 7:30 p.m. The first three places were awarded to:

1st Place: PC Fred Lloyd (5736) riding "Regal"
2nd Place: PC Allen Parks (6994) riding "Billy"
3rd Place: PC Thomas Thomas (1865) riding "Nancy."

1986 In the spring of 1986 the Mounted Unit received an invitation to attend the annual Mounted Police Equestrian Competition in Philadelphia, Pennsylvania. The competition was advertised as being an equitation and obstacle course designed to demonstrate the abilities of police horses.

Inspector Heenan felt that the Mounted Unit should add an obstacle course to the police class. It would help to promote the unit's 100th Anniversary and provide a more entertaining display for the audience. It would be a more realistic display of the capabilities of the police horse.

The Police Class at the Canadian National Exhibition Horse Show was restructured accordingly. The class would consist of a "hack class" where the officers would be judged on the walk, trot and canter. After this class the officers would undertake a series of obstacles to demonstrate their riding skill and the prowess of the quiet and well-mannered police horse.

The obstacles were based on situations that the officer and mount might face on the street. The riders were judged on how well they controlled their horse and received a score based on their performance at each individual obstacle. The score from the hack class was added to the score for the obstacle course to determine the winner. The first obstacle course was very well received by members of the Mounted Unit and the audience. All agreed it was a major improvement over the old equitation class. Results of the first new format police class were:

1st Place: PC Mike Best (1778) riding "Rob Roy"
2nd Place: PC Bill Lyons (2730) riding "Barney"
3rd Place: PC Jim Bradford (1752) mount unknown.

In September 1986 Constables Jim Davis and Bill Wardle travelled to Philadelphia to watch the Third Annual Mounted Police Equestrian Competition. The event was held at the Devon Horse Show Grounds, on September 24. The co-ordinator of the event was Patrolman Jeff Miller of the Philadelphia Police Mounted Unit.

Fifty-five competitors came from twelve police forces. The first class was an equitation class similar to what the Toronto Mounted Unit was doing at the Royal Winter Fair and Canadian National Exhibition Horse Shows. The second class was an obstacle course designed to test both horse and rider. Riders were judged on how well they guided their horse through each obstacle and accomplished the task set out for them.

PC Don Mawson and "Sutherland" clear a jump at a police obstacle course demonstration during the Loblaws Classic horse show at Sunnybrook Park, 1986. Photograph, Toronto Police Mounted Unit.

Fresh from the experience of seeing the Mounted Police Competition in Philadelphia, Constable Davis prepared an improved obstacle course for the Royal Winter Fair. Patrolman Miller travelled from Philadelphia to judge the event. The show was very well received by the crowd and the Royal Winter Fair administration. The obstacle course provided a very effective way of celebrating the Mounted Unit's centennial year. The horses were presented to the public in a new and positive way.

It would be 1989, before Toronto officers began their yearly trips to the National Police Mounted Competitions. The training value of the obstacle courses was evident to all concerned. Officers were encouraged to "work" on their horses to prepare them for any obstacle they might face in the show ring. This improved the horses' ability to cope with events that took place on regular patrol.

PC Fred Lloyd preparing to enter a corridor of flares at the 1986 Royal Winter Fair Police Class. Photograph, Toronto Police Mounted Unit.

🏆 **1987**   The Canadian National Exhibition Horse Show results were:

1st Place: PC Graham Acott (2897) riding "Casey"
2nd Place: PC Robert Bagshaw (824) riding "Barney"
3rd Place: PC Mike Brooks (1538) riding "Chummy."

Right: During one of the nights of the 1987 Royal Winter Fair officers from the R.C.M.P. and Rochester, NY Police Mounted Unit were invited to participate in an obstacle course competition.

Left to right: Police Chief Jack Marks, Inspector Heenan, Royal Winter Fair representative, R.C.M.P. officer.

Far right: PC Bill Lyons, Metro Police and Police Officer Charlie Horst of the Rochester police.

Photographs, Toronto Police Mounted Unit.

 **1988** The Canadian National Exhibition Horse Show Police Class was divided into two segments. The hack class and the obstacle course. Separate awards were given for the top positions in each component. It was felt that this would better recognise diverse skills of individual horses. Some horses were better equitation horses than obstacle course horses, and vice versa. The standings for the classes were:

HACK CLASS
1st Place: PC Bob Green (253) riding "Sally"
2nd Place: PC Tony Pietrantonio (3815) riding "Ivan"
3rd Place: PC Don Mawson (7272) riding "Sutherland."

OBSTACLE COURSE
1st Place: PC Bill Lyons (2730) riding "Barney"
2nd Place: PC John Feather (2327) riding "Maureen"
3rd Place: PC Don Mawson (7272) riding "Sutherland."

 **1989** The results of the Canadian National Exhibition Horse Show Police Class:

HACK
1st Place: PC Paul Greenaway (3467) riding "Red"
2nd Place: PC Bob Bagshaw (824) riding "Barney"
3rd Place: PC Roy Smith (3236) riding"Billy."

OBSTACLE COURSE
1st Place: PC Greg Vanderhart (4761) riding "Sutherland"
2nd Place: PC Bob Bagshaw (824) riding "Barney"
3rd Place: PC Ken Cassidy (4812) riding "Caesar."

The National Mounted competition was held in St. Georges County, Maryland. The top two obstacle riders from the C.N.E. competition, Constable Greg Vanderhart riding "Sutherland" and Constable Bob Bagshaw riding "Barney," were allowed to compete there. The officers were the first mounted officers to represent Toronto outside of Canada. Constable Greg Vanderhart won a ribbon from the equitation class.

 **1990** The equitation hack class was dropped from the horse show this year. The obstacle course had grown to where there was no longer time to run both classes. Winners of the 1990 Canadian National Exhibition Horse Show were:

1st Place: PC Bob Bagshaw (824) riding "Barney"
2nd Place: PC Tony Pietrantonio (3815) riding "Sutherland"
3rd Place: PC Jim McAleer (5755) riding "Paddy."

 **1991** The winners of the 1991 Canadian National Exhibition Horse Show were:

1st Place: PC Tony Pietrantonio (3815) riding "Sutherland"
2nd Place: PC Bob Bagshaw (824) riding "Barney"
3rd Place: PC Jim McAleer (5755) riding "Paddy."

The National Mounted Police Competition was held in Virginia Beach, Virginia, on Sunday September 29. Constable Bob Bagshaw won first place in the uniform competition and was awarded a first place ribbon, a silver plate and a dress bridle and reins.

Constable Tony Pietrantonio placed sixth in the obstacle course. Constable Bagshaw was tied for ninth place and after a special runoff finished tenth in the obstacle course.

Constables Bagshaw, McAleer and Pietrantonio also won the award ribbons and a silver plate for being the third place team. The competitors were invited to take part in the Virginia Beach Neptune Festival Parade and the three officers represented Metropolitan Toronto and Canada in their formal dress uniforms.

The Mounted Contingent at the Virginia Beach Neptune Festival Parade, 1991. Photograph, Toronto Police Mounted Unit.

 **1992** The winners of the 1992 Canadian National Exhibition horse show were:

1st Place: PC Peter Scribner (3529) riding "Colonel"
2nd Place: PC Jon Vanhetveld (7165) riding "Rusty"
3rd Place: PC Jim McAleer (5755) riding "Paddy."

The annual Police Equestrian Competition was held in Baltimore, Maryland. Constables Vanhetveld, Scribner and McAleer won the first place team award.

The Columbus Day parade in Baltimore, Maryland. The Baltimore Police Department invited all of the visiting mounted officers to ride in their city's Columbus Day Parade. Left to right: PC Jon Vanhetveld, PC Jim McAleer, PC Peter Scribner. Photograph, Toronto Police Mounted Unit.

🏆 1993

Police officers from other Mounted Units were invited to compete in an obstacle course during the Canadian National Exhibition Presentation night which took place on August 12th. The top three riders in the competition were:

1. PC Peter Febel (2182) Metro Toronto Police Force.
2. Police Officer Frank Marcin, New York City Police.
3. Police Officer Bob McGee, Detroit Police Department.

The winners of the 1994 Canadian National Exhibition horse show were:

1st Place: PC Peter Febel (2182) riding "Barney"
2nd Place: PC Laura Lowson (5593) riding "Sutherland"
3rd Place: PC Jon Vanhetveld (7165) riding "Toby."

The National Mounted Police Competition was held in Virginia Beach, Virginia. A large contingent of Metropolitan Toronto Police officers made the trip down to cheer the team on, at the event. Constables Febel, Lowson, and Vanhetveld won the third place team award.

 **1994** In May, Sgt Bill Wardle (2785) riding "Duke" and PC Graham Acott (2897) riding "Chief" attended the New York City Parks Police Mounted Competition at Coney Island, New York. Constable Cassidy (4812), the unit quartermaster assisted the officers as "coach." The Toronto team had an exceptionally successful trip winning five trophies, six medals, thirteen ribbons. The two Toronto police horses were awarded with cooler blankets for being the "champion horses" at the competition.

In June, Constable Laura Lowson (5593) riding "Chief" and Constable Vicki Montgomery (7114) riding "Duke" took part in the New York State Police Olympics in Syracuse, New York. They came home with a medal for the "Team Ride" competition. PC Ken Cassidy again acted as coach.

The winners of the 1995 Canadian National Exhibition horse show were:

1st Place: Sgt Bill Wardle (2785) riding "Sutherland"
2nd Place: PC Bob Bowen (7350) riding "Chief"
3rd Place: PC Peter Febel (2182) riding "Billy."

The National Mounted Competition was hosted by the United States Park Police. The team sent to compete included PC Peter Febel on "Billy," PC Bob Bowen on "Chief" and PC Jim Bradford on "Bruce." They had an excellent showing and Peter Febel placed first in the obstacle course winning the McCarthy trophy. This was an excellent showing in a field of over ninety riders. PC Bowen placed fourth overall in the obstacle course and Constables Bowen, Febel and Bradford won the third place team award.

Constables Bob Bowen (7350), Paul Greenaway (3647), and Ken Cassidy (4812) went to Providence Rhode Island in October, for the New England Mounted Police competition. Constable Bowen won the top rider award for the obstacle course and the Toronto officers also won the first place team award.

PC Graham Acott and Sgt Bill Wardle at the New York City Parks Police equestrian competition on Coney Island. Photograph, Author's Collection.

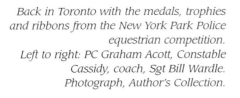

*Back in Toronto with the medals, trophies and ribbons from the New York Park Police equestrian competition.
Left to right: PC Graham Acott, Constable Cassidy, coach, Sgt Bill Wardle. Photograph, Author's Collection.*

The McCarthy Trophy

On Tuesday September 22, 1987, 31 year old patrolman William (Bill) McCarthy was assigned to crowd control duties at a "Grateful Dead" rock concert at the Philadelphia Spectrum. When the concert ended Bill and four other mounted officers started to ride back to their stable. The officers were crossing Broad Street at about 10:30 p.m. when a speeding pickup truck came out of nowhere heading right for them.

"We looked up Broad Street and there was no traffic—none at all," recalled Officer Gene Moore. "Suddenly it was there. Two of us held our hands out to try to get it to stop, and then three of us yelled, 'He's not stopping!' and that quick, he hit Bill."[1]

The two officers in front spurred their horses forward and away from the truck, though it brushed both their tails.

The two officers behind reined back and escaped. Bill was riding in the middle position; there was nothing he could do. The truck slammed into "Skipper" throwing Bill into the windshield, fatally injuring him. "Skipper" was critically injured and had to be shot at the scene by a mounted officer.

Elizabeth, his wife of nine years, and their four children survived Bill. Eight-year-old Elizabeth, five-year-old twins Lauren and Nicole, and month old son, William Jr. Bill had joined the Philadelphia Police Department in 1977 and transferred to the mounted unit in 1985. He was the first Philadelphia mounted police officer killed while on duty.

A 39-year-old off-duty Philadelphia policeman was driving the truck that killed Patrolman McCarthy and "Skipper." He was charged with Drunken Driving and Homicide as a result of the accident. This was a senseless tragedy that never should have occurred.

To help perpetrate the name of the fallen officer, the McCarthy family and the 1st Troop, Philadelphia City Cavalry, (the official name of the mounted unit), donated the McCarthy Trophy to the National Mounted Police Competition. This coveted trophy is presented to the winner of the Obstacle Course each fall. Members of the McCarthy family attend the competition to present the trophy to the winning officer and mount.

In 1995 and 1999 the Toronto Mounted Unit was proud to have the McCarthy Trophy grace the foyer of mounted headquarters at Sunnybrook Park. A tribute to the officers and horses who have won it. PC Peter Febel riding "Billy" and PC Greg Vanderhart riding "Lincoln." The unit was honoured to be able to display this lasting tribute to the memory of Officer William McCarthy, the McCarthy family, and "Skipper."

1 *Philadelphia Daily News*. Thursday, September 24, 1987.

Peter Febel, and "Billy," was the first Toronto Police Officer to win the McCarthy trophy in 1994. Photograph, Toronto Police Service.

 **1995** PC Vicki Montgomery riding "Duke" and PC Karl Seidel riding "Sarge" attended the Livingston County New York Mounted Police Competition. The officers brought home a trophy from the team event and "Sarge" won an award for being the biggest horse at the event.

In 1995, the Mounted Unit changed the format of the competitions. There would now be a "skill at arms" contest immediately followed by the "fleeing felon" obstacle course. The courses were scored separately with awards given for each category. The winners of the obstacle course would be permitted to go to the National Competition in Montgomery County, Maryland.

Sixteen officers applied to take part in the competition. The Canadian National Exhibition requested that the competitions be spread over three different nights of the fair, as it was becoming one of the more popular events at the C.N.E. Horse Show. Eight officers competed in each of the first two nights of competition.

The final night of the series took place on August 26 and was open to all of the contenders. Fifteen officers took part in the competition and the final standings were as follows.

SKILL AT ARMS:
1st Place: PC Bob Bowen (7350) riding "Chief"
2nd Place: PC Graham Acott (2897) riding "Trillium"
3rd Place: PC Laura Lowson (5593) riding "Trooper."

FLEEING FELON COURSE:
1st Place: PC Greg Vanderhart (4761) riding "Duke"
2nd Place: PC Graham Acott (2897) riding "Trillium"
3rd Place: PC Vicki Montgomery (7114) riding "Sutherland."

It takes a lot of people to make a horse show successful. Some of the ring of crew waiting to re set their assigned obstacle. The mounted unit is fortunate to have many people willing to volunteer their time to help with the competition.

Ribbon presentation in the C.N.E. Coliseum after the horse show. Photographs, Toronto Police Mounted Unit.

The next major event was the Twelfth Annual National Mounted Police competition in Montgomery County, Maryland. Sgt Bill Wardle and "Chief" placed fourth overall in the obstacle course and second in the "Ride and Shoot" competition. PC Greg Vanderhart placed fourth in the "Ride and Shoot."

In October PCs Bob Bowen, Graham Acott and Peter Spurling attended the New England Mounted Police Competition in Hartford, Connecticut. The officers placed well and brought home the team trophy and a number of ribbons.

Above: The Toronto Team at the National Police Equestrian competition in Montgomery County, Maryland.
Left to right: Sgt Bill Wardle "Chief," PC Vicki Montgomery "Toby,"
PC Paul Greenaway "Dragoon," PC Greg Vanderhart "Duke."
Standing: PC Ken Cassidy.

Left: A more casual photograph of the Toronto team.
Left to right: Sgt Bill Wardle, PC Vicki Montgomery, PC Greg Vanderhart, PC Paul Greenaway.

Photographs, Author's Collection.

Sgt Bill Wardle and "Chief" riding to a second place finish in the "Ride and Shoot." Photograph, Author's Collection.

 **1996** On June 12, PC Greg Vanderhart and PC Vicki Montgomery attended the New York State Police Olympics in Nassau County, New York. Constable Vanderhart came in fifth in the obstacle course and won the overall high point trophy for the day. The Metro team placed second in the team competition and brought home the silver medal.

In July 1996, PC Greg Vanderhart and Vicki Montgomery attended the Livingston County, New York Police Equestrian Competition. While passing a transport truck on the Interstate 90 Highway in New York a wind shear caused the trailer to become unstable. The trailer started swinging from side to side and the vehicle became impossible to control. Fortunately the vehicle quickly lost speed before the motion of the swinging trailer caused police mounts "Duke" and "Toby" to be ejected from the trailer onto the Interstate Highway.

The trailer was severely damaged, but neither horse was seriously injured. The Rochester New York Police sent a horse trailer to pick up the horses and transported them to the competition site. Despite all the problems the officers still brought home the second place ribbon.

The Canadian National Exhibition Horse Show was held on August 26. The results were as follows:

SKILL AT ARMS:
1. PC Bob Bowen riding "Chief"
2. PC Graham Acott riding "Trillium"
3. PC Greg Vanderhart riding "Duke."

OBSTACLE COURSE:
1. PC Greg Vanderhart riding "Duke"
2. PC Graham Acott riding "Trillium"
3. PC Peter Febel riding "Billy."

The 13th Annual National Mounted Competition was held in Prince George's County, Maryland. A large contingent of the units' officers attended the event. Arrangements had been made for all the officers to meet at the Artillery Ridge Camp Ground at Gettysburg, Pennsylvania, which is also the home of the National Mounted Police School. The competitors from the Rochester Police and Munroe County Police in New York also came to the campgrounds with their horses. All of the officers were taken on a mounted tour of the battlefield using both the police horses and rented camp horses.

Officer Scott Sorenseon of the Reno, Nevada Police riding Toronto police mount "Chummy" in Coronation Park with Sgt Bill Wardle. Scott came to Toronto to compete in the 110th Anniversary Horse Show. Photograph, courtesy of Scott Sorenson.

Staff Inspector Jim Jones presenting police officer Kurt Steinkamp of the New Orleans police mounted unit with an award at the 110th Anniversary Horse Show banquet. Photograph, Toronto Police Mounted Unit.

The out of town competitors at the mounted unit 110th Anniversary Horse Show were taken on a mounted riding tour of Toronto. This group photograph was taken at Fort York, in Toronto. Photograph, Toronto Police Mounted Unit.

The Metro Toronto Police Mounted Unit did very well at the show competing against one hundred competitors from all over the United States. Sgt Bill Wardle was first place in the uniform class. PC Greg Vanderhart placed 11th in the equitation class. In the Obstacle course, PC Peter Febel placed 5th, PC Greg Vanderhart placed 8th, PC Graham Acott placed 9th, and Sgt Wardle placed 18th. The Metro Toronto team won the first place team award.

The Mounted Unit at Gettysburg. Left to right: Sgt Bill Wardle, PC Bob Bowen, PC Peter Febel, PC Vicky Montgomery, PC Greg Ladner, PC Greg Vanderhart, PC Jon Vanhetveld, PC Graham Acott, PC Peter Spurling, Lynda Davis, PC Jim Davis (Ret.). Photograph, Sgt Lorna Kozmik.

No officers were able to attend the New England Police Equestrian Competition on October 25, due to the "Days of Action Protest." All of the horses were needed in Toronto to assist with crowd control duties. PC Bob Bowen and Jon Vanhetveld did attend off duty and assisted with the judging at the competition.

Right: The Toronto team after another successful day of international competition.

Left to right, Top row: Bob Bowen, Peter Spurling, Peter Febel, Vicki Montgomery, Greg Vanderhart, Lynda Davis, Jim Davis. Bottom row: Graham Acott, Bill Wardle, Jon Vanhetveld.

Photographs, Sgt Lorna Kozmik.

Sgt Bill Wardle and "Chief" after winning the uniform competition.

 **1997** The Livingston County Police Equestrian Competition was held on August 6th. Sgt Lorna Kozmik, PC Vicki Montgomery and PC Ken Cassidy attended the event. Sgt Kozmik won the uniform class, while PC Cassidy tied for first place in the obstacle course. The tie was broken by comparing the times of the officers and PC Cassidy ended up in second place. PC Montgomery placed 6th in the obstacle course.

On Tuesday August 20, the Mounted Unit held its annual competition and show at the Canadian National Exhibition Coliseum. A number of different classes were held including a demonstration of the "Bag Game." The honoured guests in the Royal Box were retired Inspectors Geoffrey Rumble, a mounted officer from the 1930s and former Mounted Unit Commanders Ed Johnson and Bob Heenan.

The top three riders were Sgt Dale Guest riding "Trooper," PC Greg Vanderhart riding "Duke" and PC Graham Acott riding "Trillium." The one sad note was that a constable was injured while riding in the show. He was taken to The Toronto Hospital with a broken pelvis and internal injuries.

The 14th annual Police Equestrian Competition was held in Philadelphia on October 12. There were 107 competitors from 34 different mounted units entered into the competitions. Sgt Dale Guest riding "Trooper" won first place in the uniform class and 4th place in the obstacle course. PC Greg Vanderhart riding "Duke" placed sixth in the obstacle course and PC Graham Acott riding "Trillium" was within the top 20 positions. The Toronto officers won the first place team trophy.

On October 25, three Toronto officers attended the 11th annual New England Police Equestrian Competition in Worcester, Massachusetts. PC Bob Low riding "Prince" won the first place award in the equitation class and PC Vicki Montgomery riding "Toby" placed 2nd. PC Peter Spurling riding "Bess" took 6th place.

In the obstacle course PC Low won fourth place while PC Spurling won 10th place and PC Montgomery 11th Place. Toronto won the second place team trophy and PC Bob Low was the High Point reserve champion.

Left: Sgt Dale Guest and "Trooper" ready for the opening ceremonies at the Philadelphia National Mounted Police equestrian competition. Right: A few minutes earlier, Sgt Guest is judged on the turn out of both himself and his mount as part of the uniform class. He was later awarded first place, becoming the third Toronto officer to win this prestigious class. Photograph, Toronto Police Mounted Unit.

PC Vanderhart takes "Duke" through the cans. Photographs, Toronto Police Mounted Unit.

PC Vanderhart holds "Duke" still as he fires the handgun in Philadelphia.

PC Vanderhart and "Duke" negotiate the jump.

Sgt Guest and "Trooper" clear the jump.

The 1st place Toronto team, Philadelphia 1997. PC Greg Vanderhart "Duke," Sgt Dale Guest "Trooper," PC Graham Acott "Trillium."

The 1st place Toronto team, Philadelphia, 1997.
Left to right: Rear row mounted: PC Greg Vanderhart, Sgt Dale Guest, PC Graham Acott. Standing: Sgt Bill Wardle, Carol Robbins, PC Peter Spurling. PC Laura Lowson. Sitting: PC Bob Bowen, Sgt Lorna Kozmik, Hilary Wollis, Helen Curtin.

PC Graham Acott and "Trillium" place a parking tag on the police car. The illegally parked car is used in most obstacle courses. Police officers and horses must be able to work in close proximity to vehicles.

PC Vicki Montgomery and "Toby" get ready to tag the car. Photographs, courtesy of Faye MacLachlan.

 **1998** The standings of the 1998 Canadian National Exhibition obstacle course class were very close. Two officers were tied for 1st place and two officers were tied for second place. The four top riders traveled to the National Police Equestrian Competition in Harrisburg, Pennsylvania where they won the 3rd place team award.

OBSTACLE COURSE:

Tied for 1st: PC Rick Mamak riding "Spencer"

                    PC Greg Vanderhart riding "Duke"

Tied for 2nd: Sgt Bill Wardle riding "Chief"

                    PC Vicki Montgomery riding "Toby"

3rd Place: PC Jim Bradford riding "Bruce."

FLEEING FELON COURSE:

1st   Sgt Dale Guest riding "Trillium"

2nd   Sgt Bill Wardle riding "Chief"

3rd   PC Greg Vanderhart riding "Duke."

VOLUNTEER RIDERS CLASS:

1st   Helen Curtin riding "Trillium"

2nd   Kristen Leaver riding "Bruce"

3rd   Hilary Wollis riding "Billy."

Below: Sgt Bill Wardle "Billy" and Sgt Peter Spurling "General" after competing in the heavy horse equitation class during the Canadian National Exhibition Horse Show. Photograph, Author's Collection.

Skill at Arms Competition at Sunnybrook Park

The "Skill at Arms," or "Mounted Arms" display is a traditional cavalry competition. The officers prove their ability with the sword, lance and revolver in competition with their peers. The mounted unit has developed some very sophisticated courses over the years. The mounted arms competition forces a rider to concentrate on their hand/eye co-ordination. They begin to fully use their instincts to control the mount. It is an excellent way to prepare an officer for violent confrontations in crowd management situations.

Officers use their lance to spear a small ring which is suspended from a stand.

Officers use their swords to knock balls off of the towers.

Officers break balloons as they deposit their swords in a bail of straw. Photographs, Faye MacLachlan, Governor General's Horse Guards.

Other obstacles such as the sponges and trotting poles are placed along the route to slow horses down and to test the riders' skill.

 **1999** During the summer the Mounted Unit sent officers to competitions in Livingston, New York and Buffalo, New York. At the Erie County Fair in Buffalo, PC Greg Vanderhart riding "Lincoln" and PC Moreen Smith riding "Billy" won the first place team award and the uniform award. PC Vanderhart and "Lincoln" placed 1st in the obstacle course. This was "Lincoln's" first competition. He had just come out of training.

The results of the Canadian National Exhibition Police Class were:

OBSTACLE COURSE:
1st PC Greg Vanderhart "Lincoln"
2nd PC Rick Mamak "Spencer"
3rd PC Gino Sonsini "Chief."

SKILL AT ARMS CLASS:
Sgt Peter Spurling "Billy"
PC Bob Bowen "Regal"
PC Greg Vanderhart "Lincoln."

VOLUNTEER CLASS:
Sarah Cutts – Rosen "Trooper"
Kristen Leaver "Teddy"
Hilary Wollis "Sabre."

The Cutts-Rosen family donated a silver plate to the Mounted Unit in honour of the late Commander Cutts of the Royal Canadian Navy. The plate is kept at mounted headquarters and the name of the winner of the volunteer class is engraved on it annually. Volunteer Helen Curtin entered police mount "Regal" in a civilian Flat Class at the C.N.E. Horse Show and finished 2nd in a field of 35 riders.

The C.N.E. Ambassador of the Fair traditionaly hands out the ribbons to the competitors in the police classes.
Left to right: The Fair Ambassador, Staff Inspector Karl Davis, Deputy Chief Steve Reesor, Sgt Bill Wardle.
Photograph, Lynn Cassels-Caldwell.

Volunteer Hilary Wollis and "Sabre" clear a jump at the 1999 Canadian National Exhibition Police Horse Show. Photograph, Lynn Cassels-Caldwell.

The competitors have changed out of their uniforms and into team-coloured tee shirts for the "Bag game" demonstration. The officers are waiting to hear the announcement of the high point winner once all of the evening's scores have been added together.
Left to right: Sgt Peter Spurling "Billy," Sgt Bill Wardle "Trooper," Sgt Dale Guest "Teddy," PC Greg Vanderhart "Lincoln," PC Ron Gilbert "Stuart," PC Derrick Speirs "Regent," PC Greg Ladner "Sabre." Standing horse-show judge, Kenneth Hodges. Photograph, Lynn Cassels-Caldwell.

The National Mounted Police Competition was held in Virginia Beach. Virginia. PC Greg Vanderhart and "Lincoln" finished first in the obstacle course and once again, brought the McCathy Trophy to Toronto. The Toronto team won the first place team trophy. There was very stiff competition with over 100 competitors from the United States. The Toronto officers were given the honour of leading the Neptune Festival Parade.

OBSTACLE COURSE:
1st   PC Greg Vanderhart "Lincoln"
3rd   PC Rick Mamak "Spencer"
8th   Sgt Bill Wardle "Duke"
12th   PC Gino Sonsini "Chief."

UNIFORM CLASS:
3rd PC Greg Vanderhart "Lincoln."

EQUITATION:
PC Greg Vanderhart "Lincoln" and PC Rick Mamak "Spencer" both made it to the final class, but were eliminated prior to the top ten elimination.

TEAM:
1st place: Toronto.

The New England Mounted Police competition was held on October 16. PC Derrick Speirs and "Regent" placed 10th in the Obstacle course while PC Bob Low and "Prince" placed 1st in the Fleeing Felon class. The results of the equitation class were:

1st PC Vicki Montgomery "Toby"
8th PC Bob Low "Prince"
9th PC Derrick Speirs "Regent."

 **2000** The Kingston, Ontario Mounted Unit sponsored its first police equestrian competition on July 8. The two Toronto officers competing at the show did very well in a field of approximately twenty-four competitors. PC Vicki Montgomery and "Toby" finished 3rd in the Equitation Class, in the Obstacle Course she placed 10th, while PC Bob Low and "Prince" finished 2nd.

The first place Toronto Team at the National Mounted police competition at Virginia Beach, Virginia. PC Gino Sonsini is standing at front with the McCarthy Trophy. Left to right: PC Rick Mamak, Sgt Bill Wardle, PC Greg Vanderhart.

The first place Toronto Team at the National Mounted police competition at Virginia Beach, Virginia. Left to right: PC Gino Sonsini "Chief," Sgt Bill Wardle "Duke," PC Greg Vanderhart "Lincoln," PC Rick Mamak "Spencer." Photographs, Author's Collection.

The Canadian National Exhibition competition was changed slightly. The officers would compete in two separate competitions on two nights. Their scores from each night would be added together and averaged. This score would determine who would go on to represent Toronto at the National Police Equestrian Competition in Morris County, New Jersey.

The top riders were:
1st   PC Rick Mamak "Spencer"
2nd   PC Bob Low "Prince"
3rd   PC Gino Sonsini "Chief."

At the end of August, three officers were sent to Lexington, Kentucky, for the National Mounted Police colloquium. The final day of this training session is a competition where the 100 competitors can demonstrate their skills. Sgt Dale Guest and "Trooper" placed 3rd in the uniform class. In the Obstacle Course portion of the event, Sgt Graham Acott and "Chief" placed 7th, while PC Greg Ladner and "Winter Sun" placed 9th.

The National Mounted Police Competition was held in Morris County, New Jersey. Once again Toronto had a great day with three officers in the top ten positions. The only thing that prevented them from winning the first place team award was that the Nassau County, New York team also had three officers place within the top ten positions. This is remarkable when you consider that out of a field of over 100 competitors from almost 30 police departments two of the police services won six off the top ten positions.

The results of the classes were:

EQUITATION:
6th   PC Bob Low "Prince."

OBSTACLE COURSE:
4th   PC Rick Mamak "Spencer"
5th   PC Gino Sonsini "Chief"
7th   PC Bob Low "Prince."

TEAM COMPETITION:
Toronto, 2nd place team.

The New England Mounted Police competition was held in Worcester, Massachusetts, on September 30. PC Vicki Montgomery and "Toby" finished 5th in the Equitation Class. PC Derrick Speirs and "Regent" placed 3rd in the Fleeing Felon Class, while PC Jim Bradford and "Bruce" placed 10th in the same class.

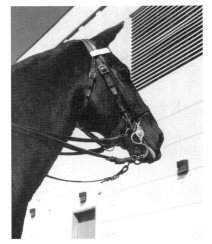

Even the police horses like to win. A Toronto police horse intently watches the other police horses as they negotiate the obstacle course. There is no doubt that the horses know when it is show time. Photograph, Author's Collection.

Police competitors at the Canadian National Exhibition Horse Show. Photograph, Lynn Cassels-Caldwell.

Top left: The Virgina Beach Neptune Festival Parade, 1991.
Left to right: PC Bob Bagshaw, PC Tony Pietrantonio, PC Jim McAleer.
Photograph, Toronto Police Mounted Unit.

Above and below: The Drill Team, Hendervale Equestrian Centre,
Photographs, Vavuz Photography.

Above: Mr. Carl Benn, of Heritage Toronto gives a brief lecture of the
History of Fort York to visiting mounted officers, 1996. Photograph Sgt
Lorna Kozmik.

A Rocherster New York Mounted Officer allows two young Toronto
girls to try out their horses. The Hitching Ring, C.N.E., 1993.
Photograph, Howard Rosenberg.

Canadian and American Mounted officers at Coronation Park, 1996.
Photograph Sgt Lorna Kozmik.

Getting ready for the show ...

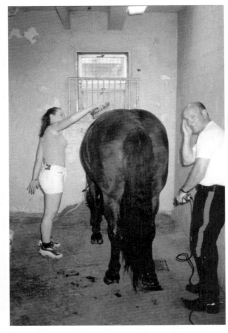

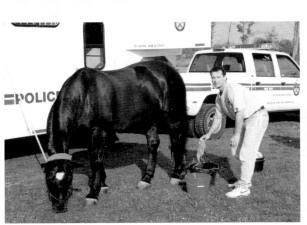

At the show …

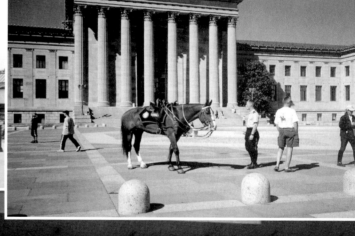

All dressed up …

Nominal Roll of the Mounted Unit

The following Nominal Roll was compiled from newspaper articles, police routine orders, and other documentation that showed the names of officers assigned to the Mounted Unit. There has never been any master record kept showing the names of mounted officers.

Many officers who would have served with the Toronto Police Force Mounted Unit between 1886 and 1956 will have been omitted from the roll. Unfortunately, more complete records are not available. The records, since the formation of the Metropolitan Toronto Police Service, are fairly complete but some officers may have been omitted unknowingly.

The Royal Canadian Mounted Police Landau crew salute as the Queen and Prince leave the carriage after the escort from the Grandstand after the horse race. The Toronto Mounted Unit stands at attention in the background. Photographs, Carol Robbins.

Queen Elizabeth and Prince Phillip at the 1997 Queen's Plate Race. The Mounted Unit has just escorted them to the drop off point at the front of the Grandstand.

OFFICER	RANK	BADGE	JOINED FORCE	SERVED AT MTD	STATUS
Abrames, Lee	PC	6848		S. 1982	Transferred
Acott, Graham	PC	2897	1982	1986- To Date	
Aitken, Susan	PC	6036		1995 - To Date	
Alexander, ?	Cdt.	2202		S. 1966	
Alexander, Anthony	PC	3847	1972	1974 - 1975	Transferred
Allen, ?	PC	5786		1970's	
Allen, Frank	PC	40		1937-1941	
Anderson, Michael	PC	791	1968	1988 - 1993	Transferred
Anketell, ?	PC	272		S. 1936	
Annan, Robert	PC	2990	1967	1975 - 197?	Resigned
Armit, Adam	PC	2451	1967	1959 - 197?	Transferred
Armstrong, William	PC	284	1970	1974 - 197?	
Atkinson, Dave	PC	6879		197? - 1983	Transferred
Atlay, Peter	PC	916	1957	1958 - ?	
Attwood, ?	Cdt.	2095		S. 1966	
Badnall, Hugh	PC	2958	1973	1975-1983	Transferred
Bagshaw, Robert	PC	824	1978	1985 - 1993	Transferred
Baldock, Peter	PC	1730	1960	1962-?	
Balsdon, Larry	Cdt.	2120		S. 1965	
Bamlett, Robert	PC	2468	1969	1970- 1972	Transferred
Bang, ? (Cdt or PC)		2942		S. 1968	
Bangma, J.S.	Cdt.	750	1978	1978	To College
Banks, Hugh	PC	57		1930's, - left for service in WW11.	
Barbour , ? (Cdt. or PC)		2269		S. 1965	
Barger, James	PC	5743	1974	1977 - 198?	Transferred
Barkey, ?	Cdt	2965		S. 1967	
Barless, Michael	Cdt.	2956	1971	1971	
Barnett, Rick	PC	3718		1977 - 1981	Resigned
Bartley,Peter	PC	141		S. 1914	
Bathgate, Daniel	PC	320	1963	1963 - 1966	Resigned
Baugh, Phillip	Cdt.	2942	1967	S. 1967	
Bayley, Ralph	Cdt.	2165	1969	1969 -1971	To College
Beaudoin, Jean	Cdt.	5708	1974	1974	Transferred
Beaudry, Michael	Cdt.	3463	1973	1973	Transferred
Bell, Amos	PC	324	1908	S. 1914-1920	
Bell, David	Cdt.	6915	1976	1976	Resigned
Bent, Maurice	PC	1776	1962	1965	
Best, Michael	PC	1778	1968	1968 - 1993	Transferred
Blackbourn, John	PC	2703	1969	1970	Transferred
Blackbourn, Steven	Cdt.	6223	1975	1975 - 1976	Transferred
Blackmore, Sean	PC	1743	1971	1973 - 197?	Transferred
Blair, James	PC	5887		S. 1982	Transferred
Blake, ?	PC			S. 1960's	
Bland, Edward	PC	1918	1965	1967 - 1968	Transferred
Bland, Ted (Cdt. or PC)		1911		S. 1966	
Blaser, Beth	PC	5038	1995	2000 to Date	
Bloodworth, Thomas	PC	131	1883	1886 - 18??	
Boardman, Albert	P/Sgt	161	1955	1955-1966	Resigned
Boardman, Bert	PC	161		1958 - 1966	Promoted
Bolongo, B.M.	PC	1478		1977 - 197?	
Bond, Ronald	PC	1353	1963	1965 - 1967	Transferred
Bowen, Robert	PC	7350	1976	1991 - To Date	
Bowman, Al	PC	1136	1974	S. 1980's	Transferred
Bradford, James	PC	1752	1973	1978 - To Date	
Brewer, Michael	PC	4669	1973	1974 - 197?	
Brooks, John	Cdt	3254	1968	1968 - 1970	To College
Brooks, Michael	PC	1538	1981	1986 - 1998	Transferred
Brown, Craig	Cdt.	3559	1973	1973 - 1974	Transferred
Brown, George	PC	9	1908	S. 1914	
Brown, Michael	PC	3071	1971	1973 - 1975	Transferred
Brown, Reggie	PC			S. 1940's	
Buffett, George	PC	190	1965	1966 - 1968	Transferred
Buller, Graham	PC	1899	1965	1966-1969	Resigned
Bullock, Larry	PC		1978	1993 - To date	
Bullock, lawrence	PC	864		1994 - To Date	

OFFICER	RANK	BADGE	JOINED FORCE	SERVED AT MTD	STATUS
Burgess, John	PC	3033		1984 - 1985	Transferred
Burgess, Thomas	PC			S. 1930's	
Busch, Cecil	PC	1511	1952	1959 - 1964	Resigned
Butler, Roy	PC	6960	1976	1980 - 1993	Transferred
Byrne, Kevin	PC	490	1965	1966 - 196?	
Cairns, Paul	PC	824	1964	1966-Died 1972/3	
Calderwood, Al	PC	3177		1978 - 1983	Transferred
Camm, ?	Cdt.	4217		1978	To College
Canavan, Leslie	PC	298	1969	1972-?	
Cardy, Roy	PC	410	1949	1951- 1979	Retired
Carew	PC	746		198? - 1982	Resigned
Carr, William	PC	296	1915	1915 - 193?	
Carson, Robert	Cdt.	4587	1949	1973	Resigned
Cass, ?(Cdt. or PC)		1164		S. 1966	
Cassels, ?	PC	1512		S. 1960	
Cassidy, Ken	PC	4812	1974	1975 - To date	
Chalkin, Charles	PC	28	1911	1912 - 1924	Promoted
Chalkin, Charles	P/Sgt	28	1911	1924-1939	Retired
Chilton, Michael	PC	6601		1989 - 1993	Transferred
Clarke, Maurice	PC	1801	1964	1966 - 197?	Resigned
Claus, Halbe (Al)	PC	80	1962	1965-197?	Resigned
Clydesdale, Daniel	Cdt.	1620	1971	1971 - 1974	To College
Coathup, Harvey C.	PC	434	1924	S. 1930	
Cole, Ralph	PC	2925	1967	1972 - 1976	Resigned
Collinson, Gordon	PC	502	1946	1949 - 1976	Retired
Connor, ? (Cdt. or PC)		2975		S. 1968	
Connor, William	PC	239	1912	1912-1914	K.I.A. WW1
Cook, George	PC	256	1902	S. 1908	
Cooke (Cdt. or PC)		1705		S. 1966	
Cooper, Andrew	PC	198	1923	S. 1920's -30's	Promoted
Cooper, Andrew	PS		1923	S. 1930s	
Correia, Susan	PC	2255	1991	1999 to Date	
Cottrell, J.	PC	6628	1975	1988 - 198?	Transferred
Cousens, Peter	PC	3550	1971	1980's	Transferred
Cowan, Allen	Cdt.	6007	1975	1975 - 1976	Transferred
Cowdell, Stanley	PC	937	1957	1962-?	
Crease, ?	Cdt	2795		S. 1967	
Creighton				S. 1930	
Crimp, Richard	PC	4592	1973	1974- 197?	Transferred
Crimp, Richard (Returned)	PC	4592	1973	1982 - 198?	Resigned
Crosbie, Thomas	PC	401	1910	1912 - 1919	
Crosbie, Thomas	P/Sgt		1910	1919 - 1924	
Crosbie, Thomas	Sgt		1910	1924 - 1927	
Crosbie, Thomas	Insp.	13	1910	1927 - 1951	
Croutch, James	PC	947	1965	1967 - 197?	
Cullerton, John	PC	104		1973 - 1974	
Cullum, ?	PC	2444		S. 1980	
Currie, ?	PC	327		S. 1960	
Currie, Andrew	PC	1872	1965	1967 - 199?	Retired
Currie, William	PC	327	1954	1956 - ?	
Curtis, David	PC	3119	1970	1984 - 1993	Transferred
Dainard, Leslie	Civ.	87443	1988	1990 - 1994	
Dalziel, David	PC	7356	1976	198? - 1990	Promoted
Damijonaitis, Maistutis	PC	1700	1970	1972- 1980	Transferred
Danson, ?				S. 1930	
D'Arcy, Harry	PC	2070	1966	1967 - 197?	Promoted
D'Arcy, Harry	Sgt	2070	1966	197? - 1978	Transferred
Dasilva, Jose	PC	489	1982	2000 to Date	
Davis (Cdt. or PC)		73		S. 1966	
Davis, Albert (Jim)	PC	1713	1960	1960 - 1994	Retired
Davis, Karl	S/Insp.	3908	1972	1999 to Date	
Dean, Paul	PC	3460	1970	1971 - 1995	Retired
Deboer, Arend	PC	1038	1961	1967 - 1969	Resigned
Decosta, Mark	PC	2130	1982	1999 to Date	
Dedlow, John	PC	177	1910	S. 191? - 1941	Retired

Nominal Roll

OFFICER	RANK	BADGE	JOINED FORCE	SERVED AT MTD	STATUS
Derbyshire, Steven	PC	6585	1975	1977 - To date	
Devost, Joseph	PC	7069	1976	198? - 1989	Resigned
Dilaine, Brent	PC	3296	1983	1990 - 1995	Transferred
Dillon, Bradley	Cdt.	2088	1966	1969 - 1970	Transferred
Dobson, Alexander	PC	31	1958	1961-1966	
Douglas, ?	Cdt.	2188		S. 1965	
Douglas, Terri	PC	4767	1984	1995 - 1999	Transferred
Dower, John	PC	2706	1973	S. 1980's	Transferred
Draper, Dennis	Chief			1928 - 1946	
Drysdale, Reid	Cdt.	3895	1972	1973	Transferred
Duckworth, Lawrence	Cdt.	5870	1974	1974 - 1975	Transferred
Dulmage, Michael	Cdt.	6917	1976	1976	Transferred
Dundas, Thomas Hugh	PC	448	1912	S. 1914 - 192?	Transferred
Duriancik, Stephen	PC	3205	1973	1974-197?	Transferred
Durling, Bruce	PC	2975	1973	1976 - 198?	
Earle, Rickey	Cdt.	6813	1976	1976	
Earnshaw, Ronald	PC	3051	1971	1975	Resigned
Edmiston, Alexander	PC	3387	1969	1973	
Egan, ? (Cdt. or PC)		2021		S. 1965	
Eisenschmid, ?	PC	7189		198? - 1981	
Evans, Daniel	Cdt.	2527	1971	1973 - 1974	To College
Evans, Michael	PC	924	1963	1963 - 1964	
Evans, Robert	Cdt.	5776	1974	1976	Transferred
Faciol, ? (Cdt. or PC)		906		S. 1966	
Fallis, Samual	PC	39	1886	1886	
Fanning, John	PC	1912	1965	1966-1967	Transferred
Farrell, Kathryn	PC	5590	1975	1986 - 1994	Transferred
Feather, John	PC	2327	1973	1978 - To Date	
Febel, Peter	PC	2182	1973	1991 - To Date	
Fluke, Brian	Cdt.	5676	1974	1974-1975	To College
Flynn	Cdt.	2097		S. 1966	
Flynn, Chris	Civ.	86967		1990-1993	Transferred
Folz, Phil	Cdt.	3676	1974	1974-1976	To College
Fontaine, Nigel	PC	6089		1977 - 198?	Transferred
Foote, Brian	PC	5907		S. 1977	
Forde, James	PC	1795	1970	1971 - 1972	Transferred
Fordham, William	PC	1061	1960	1960-1965	Transferred
Fordham, William	PC	1121	1970	1974-197?	Promoted
Foster, Gary	PC	2328	1966	1970 - 197?	
Fowler, William	PC	212	1902	S. 1908	
Fraser, Kenneth	PC	2236	1971	1974 - 197?	
Fraser, Laurence	PC	5685	1974	1988 -199?	Resigned
Frazer, Thomas	PC	823		S. 1930's - 1950's	
Fritz, Arlene	PC	5539	1981	1991 - 1997	Transferred
Fullerton, Wm. E.	PC	95		S. 1930	
Fulton, John	Cdt.	7093	1976	1976	To College
Fynes, Shaun	PC	1833	1971	1973-197?	Resigned
Galer, Brian	Cdt.	6480	1975	1975 - 1976	To College
Gallagher, Edward	PC	180		S. 1930's	Promoted
Gallagher, Edward	P/Sgt	180		S. 1940's	
Gallipeau, Edward	PC	2035		1990 - To Date	
Ganson, William	PC	592	1920	S. 1920's	
Gatti, Douglas	Cdt.	3067	1973	1973	Resigned
Gelli, Mario	PC	6018	1980	1990 - 1993	Transferred
George, Graham	PC			S. 1962	
George, Matthew	Cdt.	2633	1967	1967	Transferred
Gerard, Barry	PC	6785	1975	1980 - 1985	Promoted
Gerard, Barry	Sgt	6785	1975	1985 - 1994	Resigned
German	PC	915		S. 1965	
Gibbs, Niel	PC	1526	1959	1960 - ?	
Giel, Peter	Cdt.	2099	1966	1966-1967	Transferred
Gilbert, Ron	PC	6384	1975	1979 - To Date	
Gilks, Henry H.	P/Sgt		1887	1906 -	Promoted
Gilks, Henry H.	Sgt		1887	1912	Promoted
Gilks, Henry H.	Insp.		1887	1912 -	Promoted

OFFICER	RANK	BADGE	JOINED FORCE	SERVED AT MTD	STATUS
Gill, John	PC	48	1973	1975-1984	Resigned
Gillmore, Trevor	PC	4377	1973	1975 - 197?	Resigned
Gleed, Charles	PC	228	1960	1962-1992	Retired
Gorrie, Bruce	PC	710	1968	1972 - 197?	Transferred
Gosselin, Roger (Goose)	PC	1243	1955	1963-1986	Retired
Goulding, George	PC	27	1977	1886 - 1887	Promoted
Goulding, George	P/Sgt	27	1877	1887 - 19?	Promoted
Goulding, George	Sgt	27	1877	1886 - 19?	Promoted
Goulding, George	Insp.	27	1877		Retired
Graffman, Gordon	PC	786		1989 -1990	Promoted out of Unit
Green, Joseph	PC	1707	1960	1964 - 1968	
Green, Robert	PC	253	1964	1970 - 199?	Retired
Greenaway, Paul	PC	3647	1971	1984 - 2000	Retired
Grice, David	PC	2446	1967	1968	Resigned
Griffith, Thomas	PC	317	1907	S. 1919	
Grills, Murray	PC	3855	1972	1974 - 197?	Transferred
Grist, Ronald	PC	1495	1963	1965 - 1967	Resigned
Grummett, Dennis	Sgt	84	1970	1998 to Date	
Guest, Dale	Sgt	1975	1979	1996 - To date	
Guthrie, George	PC	105	1898	S. 1908	
Hadlow, David	PC	1772	1961	1973 - 1984	Transferred
Hainer, Charles	PC			S. 1920's	Transferred
Hall, ? (Cdt. or PC)		2054		S. 1965	
Hall, ?				S. 1930	
Hamilton, William	PC	6344		1976 - 1980	
Hammond, Barbara	PC	5510	1977	1987 - 1993	Transferred
Hannaford, David (Returned)	PC	5892	1974	1977 - 1979	Transferred
Hannaford, David (Returned)	PC	5892	1974	1983 - 1986	Promoted
Hannaford, David	Sgt	5892	1974	1987 - 1991	Transferred
Harden, David	Cdt.	7025	1976	1976 - 1978	Transferred
Harder, George	PC	418	1961	1961 - ?	
Hare, Norman	PC	911	1964	1966 - ?	
Harper, ? (Cdt. or PC)		2659		S. 1966	
Harrison, Gary	PC	2868	1971	1983 - 1985	Transferred
Hartsgom, Mark	Cdt.	4359	1973	1973 - 1975	Transferred
Harvey				S. 1930	
Hawley, Simon	PC	1411	1955	1962 - 198?	Retired
Haynes, William	PC	1868	1963	1966 - 1972	
Haywood, Gerald	PC	2732	1967	1968-197?	Resigned
Heard, Chris	PC	90	1990	1998 to Date	
Heath, George	PC	1162	1969	1971 - 197?	Transferred
Heenan, Robert	PC	2118	1966	1968- 1974	Promoted
Heenan, Robert	Sgt	2118	1966	1974 - 1980	Promoted
Heenan, Robert	S/Sgt	2118	1966	1980 - 1985	Promoted
Heenan, Robert	Insp.	2118	1966	1985 - 1990	Promoted
Heenan, Robert	S/Insp.	2118	1966	1990 - 1991	Retired
Hegenauer, Mark	Cdt.	7015	1976	1976 - 1978	To College
Hewson, ?	Cdt.	3851		1978	To College
Hicks, James	Cdt.	6535	1975	1975 - 1976	Transferred
Highet, Henry	P/Sgt	4406		19?? - 1974	Retired
Hill, ?	PC	167		S. 1936	
Hill, Ernest	PC	1921	1970	1970	Transferred
Hill, Joseph W.	PC	617	1920	S. 1926	
Hitch, Stephen	PC	3890		19?? - 1995	Transferred
Hobson, Ernest	PC	223	1903	S. 1908 - 1920's	
Hogg, ?	Cdt.	5669	1978	1978	To College
Hollingshead, David	PC	1746	1960	1964 - 1967	Transferred
Holtorf, Patrick	PC	1512	1969	1974 - 197?	Transferred
Hotton, Kevin	Cdt.	7024	1976	1976 - 1977	To College
Houston, C, McA. (Archie)	PC	461		S. 1930	
Hubbard, ?	Cdt.	3905		1978	To College
Huddleston, Wayne	PC	3382	1966	1974-197?	Transferred
Humphrey	Cdt.	4424	1978	1978	To College
Hunermund, Mark	Cdt.	5665	1974	1974	To College

Nominal Roll

OFFICER	RANK	BADGE	JOINED FORCE	SERVED AT MTD	STATUS
Hunt, ?	PC			S. 1930	
Huszarik, ?	Cdt.	7297		1976	To College
Hutchison, Hamilton	PC			S. 1930	
Ingwersen, Rick	PC	7134	1976	1981 - 1984	Transferred
Ingwersen, Rick	Sgt	7134	1976	1990 - 1998	Transferred
Irwin, ?	Cdt/PC	2529		S. 1969	
Jackson, Wayne	PC	1903	1968	1968	Resigned
James, David A.	PC	1363	1960	1962 - 1966	Resigned
James, David A. (Rejoined)	PC	3026	1967	1968 - 1973	Resigned
Jarvis, James	PC	213	1900	S. 1908	
Johnson, Edwin	PC	368	1945	1949 - 1955	Promoted
Johnson, Edwin	P/Sgt	4958	1945	1955 - 1960	Promoted
Johnson, Edwin	Sgt	4958	1945	1960 - 1963	Promoted
Johnson, Edwin	S/Insp.	4958	1945	1963 - 1985	Retired
Johnson, Morrison	PC	85	1946	1946 - 194?	
Johnston, ?	Cdt	2348		S. 1967	
Johnston, Percy	PC	375	1911	S191? - 194?	Retired
Johnston, Robert	PC	3510		1973	Transferred
Jones, James	S/Sgt	2421		1988 - 1991	Promoted
Jones, James	S/Insp.	2421		1991 - 1999	Retired
Jones, Robin	PC	3509		1988 - 1993	Transferred
Jones, Rod	PC	6349	1975	1999 to Date	
Keleher, ?	PC	6690		1977 - 1981	Transferred
Kellock, James	PC	85	1958	1963 - 1966	Transferred
Kelly, Patrick	PC	1595	1972	1975 - 197?	Transferred
Kemley, Steve	PC	2831		197? - 198?	Transferred
Keper, ?	Cdt	2276		S. 1965	
Kerr, Peter	PC			1800's - 1900's	
Kieman, ?	Cdt	2945		S. 1968	
Kirkley, George	PC	3024	1971	1973 - 197?	Transferred
Kirkpatrick, Andrew	PC	910	1968	1973 - 197?	Transferred
Klous, Steven	Cdt.	6548	1975	1975 - 1976	Transferred
Knight, P.	PC	6698		S. 1983	
Kondo, Gale	Civ.	89359		1994 - To Date	
Kotsopoulos, Leonard	PC	6669	1975	1981 - To Date	
Kozmick, Lorna	Sgt	5629	1980	1995 - 1990	Transferred
Ladner, Greg	PC	4051	1973	1984 - To date	
Lafreniere, Robert	Cdt.	3281	1971	1971 - 1972	To College
Lain, ?	PC			S. 1930	
Laird, James M.	PC	40		1920's	
Lamb, Bruce	Cdt.	3664	1971	1971 - 1973	Transferred
Lance, John	PC	2627	1971	1974 - 197?	Transferred
Lawlor, James	PC	53	1902	S. 1908	
Leary, Chris	PC	587	1914	S. 1926 - 1930's	
Leary, Chris	PC	587	1914	S 1920 - 1930	
Lees, Gerald	PC	1682	1965	1966 - 1968	Transferred
Leeson, Gary	PC	754	1963	1964 - 1968	Resigned
Lefebure, Joseph	Cdt.	5817	1974	1974 - 1976	To College
Leggatt. ?	PC				
Lepper, Frank	PC	276	1927	1928 - 1967	Retired
LeRoy, ?	PC	2213		S. 1965	
Lestor, Neil	PC	1007	1961	1963 - ?	
Lewis, James	PC	132	1950	1951 - 1961	Promoted
Lewis, James	Sgt	132	1950	1961 - 1970	Promoted
Lewis, James	S/Sgt	4432	1950	1970 - 1980	Retired
Lipsett, Ronald	PCV	2620	1971	1974	Transferred
Little ? (Cdt. or PC)		2672		S. 1966	
Little, Herbert	Sgt			S. 1916	Promoted
Little, Herbert	Insp.			S. 1920's	Transferred
Lloyd, Edward	PC	968	1951	1953 - 1983	Retired
Lloyd, Fred	PC	5736	1974	1975 - 1995	Transferred
Loram-Martin, Graham	Cdt.	2569	1971	1971 - 1974	To College
Losier, Yvonne	PC	4118	1991	1995 - 1996	Transferred
Loughlin, John	Cdt.	3275	1973	1973 - 1975	To College
Low, Robert	PC	2339	1969	1976 - 1982	Transferred

Nominal Roll

OFFICER	RANK	BADGE	JOINED FORCE	SERVED AT MTD	STATUS
Low, Robert (Returned)	PC	2339	1969	1989 - 2001	Transferred
Lowe	PC	4988		S. 1982	Transferred
Lowe, Roger	PC	184	1959	1965 - 1973	
Lowson, Laura	PC	5593		1993 - 1998	Transferred
Lucas, Eric	PC	4753		S. 1980	
Lunn, John	PC	2498	1967	1969 - 197?	Transferred
Lunn, John (Returned)	PC	2498	1967	1988 - 1990	Retired
Lynn, Douglas	PC	1690	1967	1972 - 197?	Transferred
Lyons, Malcolm	PC	2750	1967	1968 - 198?	Promoted
Lyons, Malcolm	Sgt	2750	1967	198? - 199?	Transferred
Lyons, William	PC	2730	1977	1981 - 1990	Transferred
Mac Donald, ?(Cdt. or PC)		594			
MacDonald, Stan	PC	6017		S. 1982	Transferred
MacDonald, William	PC	2621	1967	1967 - 1968	Transferred
Macey, William	PC	53	1961	1965 - 1976	Promoted
Macey, William	Sgt	53	1961	1976 - 1988	Transferred
Machnik, John	PC	6026	1975	1978 - 1988	Transferred
MacKenzie, Neil	PC	2611	1969	1973 - 197?	Transferred
Mackevicius, Vitautas	PC	614	1969	1973 - 197?	
MacKinnon, Alexander	PC	3364	1969	1974 - 1976	Transferred
Magee, Edward	Cdt.	717	1973	1973 - 1976	To College
Mahoney, ?	Cdt.	92		S. 1966	
Mamak, Rick	PC	6440	1975	1978 - To Date	
Mann, Christopher	PC	2928	1977	1981 - 1982	Resigned
Mann, Robert	PC	2759	1971	1974 - 197?	
Mapstone, Anthony	PC	1508	1972	1974	Transferred
Martin, George	PC			S. 1930's - 1940's	
Masters, Ernest J.	PC	434	1911	S. 1914 - 1922	Promoted
Masters, Ernest J.	P/Sgt		1911	1922 - 1941	Retired
Mater, ? (Cdt. or PC))		2328		S. 1971	
Mathers, William	PC	2941	1967	1969 - 1992	Died
Matier, Thomas	PC	3467	1970	1972 - 1999	Retired
Mauro, Mario	Cadet			S. 1970	
Mawson, Donald	PC	7272	1976	1979 - 1993	Transferred
Mawson, Donald	PC	7272	1976	1997 - 2000	Retired
Mc Cauley, ?	PC			S. 1930	
McAleer, James	PC	5755	1974	1975 - 1993	Transferred
McAnsh, Ivan	PC	1065	1951	1956-1967	Promoted
McAnsh, Ivan (Returned)	P/Sgt	1065	1951	1975 - 1985	Retired
McAuley, ?	PC			S. 1939	
McCarthy, Kristopher	PC	7519	1997	2000 to Date	
McClintock, ?	PC	6158		1978 - 197?	
McConachie, Scott	PC	2374	1970	1974 - 1976	Transferred
McConachie, Scott (Returned)	Sgt	2374	1970	1987 - 1993	Transferred
McConnell, Hugh	PC	1738	1960	1963 - 197?	Transferred
McConnell, Peter	PC	2374	1959	1960 - 1964	Resigned
McConnell, Peter (Returned)	PC	1338	1959	196? - 1969	Resigned
McCoppen, Kelly	PC	5553		1990 - 1993	Transferred
McCormick, Stephen	Cdt.	5	1974	1974 - 1975	To College
McDermid, James	PC	857	1965	1974 - 197?	
McDernott, Walter	PC	90	1898	S 1908	
McGregor, ?	Cdt.	7295		1976	To College
McIntosh, Rick	PC	6237		198? - 1983	Transferred
McKechnie, Alisteir	PC	2305	1966	1967-1992	Retired
McKenzie, Doug	PC	3560	1980	1981 - 198?	Transferred
McKeown, Albert	PC	2351		1969 - 1992	Retired
McKirdy, Hugh	PC	2899	1967	1969 - 1973	Resigned
McLane, Gregory	Cdt.	6811	1976	1976	To College
McLean, ? (Cdt. or PC)		765		S. 1965	
McLean, James	Cdt.	3583	1973	1973 - 1976	To College
McLearron, ?	PC			1886	
McLelland, ?					
McLush, ?	PC			S. 1930	
McMaster, ? (Cdt or PC)		3112		S. 1968	
McMasters, James M.	PC	153		S. 1923 -1930's+	

Nominal Roll

OFFICER	RANK	BADGE	JOINED FORCE	SERVED AT MTD	STATUS
McMerty, Paul	Cdt.	6782	1975	1976 - 1977	To College
McRae, ?	PC			S. 1930	
McVeygt., ?	PC			S.1926	
Millar, Glen	Cdt.	2736	1970	1970 - 1971	Resigned
Miller, David	PC	6318		1986 - To Date	
Miller, Donald	Cdt.	1817	1974	1974 - 1975	Transferred
Miller, Douglas	PC	6666	1975	1982 - 2000	Retired
Miller, William	PC	2102	1966	1968 - 1970	Resigned
Mills, John	PC	2360	1968	1971 - 1975	Resigned
Milne, ? (Cdt. or PC)		2267		S. 1968	
Milner, ?	PC	3805		1978 - 1982	Transferred
Mitchell, Austin	PC	146	1899	S. 1908	
Mitchell, Thos.	PC	44	1913	S. 1914-1924+	
Moncur, William	PC	3019	1967	1968 - 19??	
Montague, John	PC	824	1959	1960 - 196?	Resigned
Montgomery, Vicki	PC	7114		1993 - To Date	
Moore, Francis	PC	1739	1962	196? - 1966	Resigned
Moore, Francis	PC	1739	1962	1963 - 1966	Resigned
Moore, Robt.	PC	661	1923	S. 1926 - 193?	
Moore, Robt. W.	PC	661	1923	S. 1930	
Morrison, Alvin	PC	19		S. 1930's	
Mottram, ? (Cdt. or PC)		1692		S. 1967	
Mountjoy, Gary	PC	4744		1977 - 1986	Transferred
Mousley, Lorne	PC	3806	1972	1973 - 197?	
Moyes, Roderick	PC	5764	1974	1976 - 19??	
Mulhall, John	PC	116	1882	1886	
Mulqueen, Terance	PC	2380	1966	1967 - 1970	Transferred
Murphy, Paul	PC	3328	1969	1971 - 197?	Transferred
Murray	PC	287		S. 1930's	
Neagle (Cdt. or PC)		2177		S. 1966	
Neath, Alan	PC	1511	1963	1965 - 196?	
Nelson, ?	PC			1886	
Nicholas, ?	PC	1308		S. 1960	
Nicholas, Phillip	PC	1308	1956	1959 - 1963	Resigned
Niemirowski, Stephen	PC	5895	1974	1983 - 1994	Transferred
Nisavic, Nick	PC	4555	1981	1986 - 1993	Transferred
Noble, Stephen	PC	7315		1988 To Date	
Norman, Carey	Cdt.	6554	1975	1975 - 1976	To College
Norris, Robert	PC	139	1968	1969 - 1973	Resigned
Ogle, Jack	PC			S. 1930's	Military Leave
Parkin (Cdt. or PC)		2987		S. 1968	
Parks, Al	PC	6994	1976	1982 - 1986	Transferred
Patrick, Edward	Cdt.	2410		S. 1966	
Patrick, Edward (Returned)	PC	2410	1967	1968	Transferred
Patterson, James	PC	4470	1977	1987 - 1990	Promoted
Patterson, James	Sgt	4470	1977	1994 - To Date	
Patton, David	PC	41	1879	1886	
Pedlar, James	PC	4677	1946	1947 - 1960	Promoted
Pedlar, James	P/Sgt	4677	1946	1960 - 1963	Promoted
Pedlar, James	Sgt	4677	1946	1963 -197?	Retired
Peers, Howie	PC	7040	1976	1982 - 1986	Transferred
Peers, Howie (Returned)	Sgt	7040	1976	1989 - To Date	
Penney, Patrick	PC	2538		1992 - To Date	
Percy	Cdt	2349		S. 1967	
Peterson, ? (Cdt or PC)		1728		S. 1968	
Pheby, Terry	PC	6136	1989	2000 to Date	
Phillips, ?	PC			S. 1930	
Pickering, Edward	PC	430	1954	1965 - 196?	Transferred
Pietrantonio, Tony	PC	3415	1965	1986 - 1993	Retired
Pogue, Tom	PC			S. 1930's	
Pollard, Warren	PC	635	1962	1965 - 1973	Promoted
Pollard, Warren (Returned)	Sgt	635	1962	1978 - 1993	Retired
Potter, ?	Cdt.	2109		S. 1966	
Poulson, Deborah	PC	4890		1991 - 1996	Resigned
Prior, ?	Cdt.	176		S. 1966	

Nominal Roll

OFFICER	RANK	BADGE	JOINED FORCE	SERVED AT MTD	STATUS
Quinn, Robert	PC	163	1951	1958- 1962	Promoted
Quinn, Robert	Sgt	163	1951	1962 - 1966	Resigned
Raney, ?	PC				
Read, Alan	PC	2342	1966	1974 - 1977	Transferred
Read, Alan (Returned)	Sgt	2342	1966	1984 - 1997	Retired
Renny, Chris	PC	3804		1976 - 1980	Transferred
Reynolds, ? (Cdt. or PC)		2997		S. 1968	
Roberts, Michael	PC	3423	1969	1972 - 1996	Retired
Robertson, Greg	PC	138	1970	1979 - 1987	Transferred
Robertson, Ivan	Cdt,	6009	1975	1975	To College
Robertson, William	PC	6793		1990 - To Date	
Robinson, ?	Cdt.	4874	1978	1978	To College
Rogers, Jeff	PC	2058	1968	1977 - To Date	
Rogerson, Robert	PC	3	1908	S. 1917	Promoted
Rogerson, Robert	Sgt		1908	S. 1930's	
Ross, Steven	PC	773	1972	1973 - 1974	Resigned
Roushias, Ray	PC	460	1972	1985 - 1992	Transferred
Rowbotham, Dennis	PC	6057	1975	1982 - To Date 1902 - 19	
Ruddock, David	Cdt.	1057	1970	1970 - 1971	To College
Ruddock, David (Returned)	PC	1057	1970	1972 - 1974	Resigned
Ruddock, Thomas	PC				
Rumble, Geoffrey	PC	465	193?	1935 - 1940	Military Leave
Russell, Andy	PC			S. 1930's	
Russell, James	PC	737		S. 1936	
Sadler, Scott	PC			197? - 1982	transferred
Sandwell, Ernest	PC	1481	1953	1959-1967	Promoted
Sandwell, Ernest	P/Sgt	1481	1953	1967 - 1987	Retired
Sauve, Clarence	PC	2890	1967	1973 - 1986	Died
Sawlor, David	Cdt.	82	1971	1972 - 1973	Resigned
Schewk, David (Gordon)	PC	1286	1962	1964 - 1974	Resigned
Scribner, Peter	PC	3529	1970	1977 - 1993	Transferred
Seeley, Donald	Cdt.	3251	1971	1971 - 1973	To College
Seidel, Karl	PC	6689		1989 - 1999	Retired
Sellar, George	PC	67	1938	1938 - 194?	
Seymour, Charles	Sgt		1870	1886	
Shadwell, Michael	Cdt.	3661	1971	1971 - 1973	To College
Shaw, Brian	Cdt.	3252	1968	1968 - 1970	To College
Shaw, Brian (Returned)	PC	3252	1968	1973 - 197?	Transferred
Shearer, ?	PC	1830		1976 - ?	
Shepherd, Larry	PC	1762	1963	1966 - 1970	Transferred
Sheridan, Robert	PC	1490	1963	1964 -1969	Resigned
Sheridan, Ronald	PC	731	1957	1959 - 1966	Resigned
Shields, Terrance	PC	1668		197? - 198?	Transferred
Short, Doug	PC			S. 1957	
Sinclair, Larry	Cdt.	88	1968	1968	Transferred
Skanes, Tyronne	PC	6890		S. 1982	Transferred
Skrenewski, Steven	Cdt.	1207	1973	1973 - 1974	To College
Smith, ?	PC	6768		1978 - 197?	
Smith, ?	Cdt.	2657	1978	1978	To College
Smith, Anthony	PC	507	1964	1967 - 1981	Promoted
Smith, Anthony	Sgt	507	1964	1981 - 198?	Transferred
Smith, David	Cdt.	6006	1975	1975 - 1976	To College
Smith, George	PC	56	1914	S. 1923	
Smith, Merle	PC	1072	1952	1953 - 197?	Resigned
Smith, Moreen	PC	1608	1989	1998 to Date	
Smith, Paul	PC			S. 1962	
Smith, Roy	PC	2326	1973	1987 - 1993	Transferred
Smith, Stephen	Cdt.	1106	1971	1971 - 1972	To College
Smith, William	PC	1627	1956	1959 - 1967	Resigned
Snelgrove, John	PC	3323	197?	1981 - 1986	Transferred
Sonsini, Gino	PC	4616	1987	1995 - 1996	Transferred
Sonsini, Gino	PC	4616	1987	1997 - To date	
Spearen, Nick	PC	2437	1974	1976 - 1993	Transferred
Spearen. Connie	PC	5615	1976	1989 - 1993	Transferred
Speirs, Derrick	PC	354		1991 - To Date	

OFFICER	RANK	BADGE	JOINED FORCE	SERVED AT MTD	STATUS
Spencer, ?	Cdt.	7370	1976	1976 - 1978	To College
Spurling, Peter	PC	6341	1975	1996 - 1998	Promoted
Spurling, Peter	Sgt	6341	1975	1998 to Date	
Stafford, James	PC	1614	1956	1963 - 1969	Promoted
Stafford, James (Returned)	S/Sgt	1614	1956	1976 - 1988	Retired
Stewart, ? (Cdt. or PC)		3422		S. 1975	
Stewart, Gordon	PC	2991	1964	1968 - 1969	Resigned
Stewart, John	PC	3922	1972	1975 - 1980	Transferred
Strachey, D.E. (Cdt. or PC)		2234		S. 1965	
Strzelecki, Roman	Cdt.	3920	1972	1972 - 1973	To College
Sugden, James	S/Sgt	1434		19?? - 1977	Retired
Sutherland, Ronald	Civ.	65094		1994 - To date	
Sutton, Robert	PC	1345	1954	1961 - 1986	Retired
Switzer, Robert	PC	307	1971	1975 - 197?	
Tapley, Ron	Sgt		1980	2001 to Date	
Thomas, Thomas	PC	1865	1972	1973 - 1986	Resigned
Thompson, George	PC	43	1902	S. 1908	
Thompson, Michael	PC	3313	1969	1973 - 197?	
Thompson, Peter	PC	1846	1977	1989 - 1998	Transferred
Thompson, Robert	PC	66	1907	S. 1924	
Thompson, Robert H.	PC	66	1907	s. 1924	
Thorpe, Timothy	PC	2874	1967	1969 - 19??	Transferred
Timmins, Malcolm	PC	1262	1959	196? - ?	
Tinsley, James	PC	48	1898	S. 1902-1914	Promoted
Tinsley, James	P/Sgt		1898	S. 1914 - ?	Transferred
Tomenson, Henry	PC	456	1913	S. 1915	
Torrance, William	PC			S. 1962	
Trotter, Gordon	PC	3235	1968	1970 - 197?	Transferred
Trubridge, Brian	PC	532	1961	1967 - 1983	Retired
Tucker, Thomas	Cdt.	763	1974	1974	Transferred
Tufts, George	PC	335	1909	S. 1916	
Tull, George	PC	1645	1958	1962 - ?	
Vanderhart, Greg	Cdt.	4761	1981	1981	To College
Vanderhart, Greg (Returned)	PC	4761	1981	1988 - 2000	Transferred
Vandusen, Richard	PC	2322	1968	1974 - To Date	
Vanhetveld, Jon	PC	7165	1976	1982 - 1994	Transferred
Vincent, Charles	PC	221	1957	1962 - 1975	Transferred
Vincent, Donald	PC	2708	1966	1969 - 1992	Retired
Vuyk, Martinus	PC	6611		1989	
Walker, ?				S. 1930	
Walker, Douglas	PC	244	1953	1956 - ?	
Wardle, William	PC	2785	1977	1981 - 1993	Promoted
Wardle, William	Sgt	2785	1977	1993 - 2001	Promoted
Wareing, Terrance	PC	3643	1971	1974	Resigned
Wark, ?	Cdt.	7432	1978	1978	To College
Watson, George	A/Sgt		1882	1886 - 188?	
Watt, John	PC	257	1924	1928 - 1945	Promoted
Watt, John	P/Sgt	257	1924	1945 - 1948	Promoted
Watt, John	Sgt	257	1924	1948 - 1951	Promoted
Watt, John	Insp.	257	1924	1951 - 1963	Retired
Wear, John	PC	170	1949	1954 - 1963	Promoted
Wear, John	P/Sgt	170	1949	1963 - 1966	Retired
Weatherup, George	PC	337	1910	S -19?? - 1941	Retired
Weaver, Roger	S/Sgt	6515	1975	1998 to Date	
Webber, Michael	Cdt.	7338	1973	1973	To College
Webber, Michael (Returned)	PC	7338	1973	1973 - 1974	Resigned
Webber, Michael (Returned)	PC	4738		1976 - 1980	Resigned
Westcott, James	PC	2631	1968	1972 - 197?	Transferred
Weston, George	PC	132	1884	S.1886	
Whalley, Ken	PC	7020	1976	1979 - 1990	Transferred
Whitaker, James	Cdt.	709	1960	1964	
Whitaker, James (Returned)	PC	709	1960	1964 - 1969	Transferred
Whitfield, Tod	PC	7421	1978	1988 - 1990	Promoted
Whitfield, Tod (Returned)	Sgt	7421	1978	1993 - 1995	Transferred
Whitford, Charles	PC	594	1920	S. 1927	

OFFICER	RANK	BADGE	JOINED FORCE	SERVED AT MTD	STATUS
Williams (Cdt. or PC)		16		S. 1965	
Williams, Barry	PC	311	1960	1962	Resigned
Williams, Barry (Returned)	PC	16	1965	1965 - 1966	Transferred
Williams, Derek	PC	1834	1965	1967 - 197?	Transferred
Williams, William	PC	4746		S. 1982	Transferred
Williamson, Bud	PC	303		193?- 194?	WW11 Military Service
Williamson, Charles	PC	2409	1967	1968 - 19??	Transferred
Williamson, Harold	PC	732	1981	2001 to Date	
Williamson, John	PC	1033	1969	1972 - 197?	
Williamson, Thomas	PC	144/551	1914	S. 1914	
Willis, David	PC	3927	1972	1974 - 1979	Transferred
Wilson, Robert	PC	720	1961	1964 - 1966	Resigned
Wilson, Robert (Returned)	PC	1803	1968	1968 - 1973	Transferred
Wilson, Robert (Returned)	PC	1803	1968	1974 - 197?	
Wilvert, Michael	PC	3983	1972	1973 - 197?	Transferred
Wirsta, Paul	Cdt.	6798	1976	1976	To College
Wojnicz, ?	PC	6665		1978 - 197?	
Woods, Greg	PC	7011	1976	1986 - To Date	
Worm, Michael	Cdt.	3590	1971	1976 - 1979	To College
Woulfe, Patrick	PC	168	1957	1957 - 1968	Promoted
Woulfe, Patrick	Sgt	168	1957	1968 - 1985	Promoted
Woulfe, Patrick	S/Sgt	168	1957	1985 - 1993	Retired
Wretham, Ron	Cdt.	6888	1976	1976 - 1979	To College
Wright, George	PC	397	1913	S. 1914	
Wright, Robert	PC	2903	1967	1970 - 1990	Died
Yost, Gary	PC	4707	1973	1973 - 1974	To College
Yule, Kenneth	Cdt.	5904	1975	1974 - 1976	Transferred
Zador, Walter	PC			S. 1962	
Zakrajsek, Martin	PC	3623	1971	1976 - 197?	Transferred
Zayack,Tim	PC	2944	1974	1983- 1985	Transferred
Zwarych, Wayne	PC	Cdt.	1971	1971	To College

The Rank Structure of the Mounted Unit

Year	Insp.	Sgt	P/SGT	PC 1	PC 2	PC 3	Total
1886			1	2	2		5
1887			1	2	4		7
1888 N/A							
1889			1	2	4		7
1890			1	2	3	1	7
1891			1	3	3	1	8
1892			1	3	3		7
1893			1	5	1		7
1894			1	5	2		8
1895			1	3	4		8
1896			1	4	3		8
1897 N/A							
1898			1	6	1		8
1899			1	7			8
1900			1	4	1	2	8
1901		1			4	3	8
1902		1			7		8
1903		1			7		8
1904		1			7		8
1905		1		4	5		10
1906		1	1	1	8		11
1907		1	1	3	4	1	10
1908		1	1	3	8		13
1909	1		1	5	8	1	15
1910		1	1	4	11		17
1911		1	2	3	13		19
1912	1		2	6	15		24
1913	1		2	10	10		23
1914	1		1	10	6		18
1915	1		2	11	6		20
1916			3	12	3		18
1917		1	2	12	3		18
1918		1	2	12			15
1919		1	2	18			21
1920	1		2	17	2		22
1921	1		3	14	8	2	28
1922	1		3	13	12		29
1923	1		3	20	5		29
1924		1	3	24	2		30
1925		1	3	24	3		31
1928	1		3	29	2		35
1929	1	1	2	31	6		41
1930	1	1	2	33	10		47
1931	1	1	2	40	3		47
1932	1	1	2	42	1		47
1933	1	1	2	43			47
1934	1	1	2	43			47
1935	1	1	2	42		1	47
1936	1	1	3	37	2	2	46
1937	1	1	2	38	3		45
1938	1	1	2	38	3		45
1939	1	1	2	33	6	2	45
1940	1	1	2	35	5		44
1941	1	1	2	36	3		43
1942	1	1	2	34	1		39
1943	1	1	2	31			34
1944	1	1	2	27			31
1945	1	1	2	31		1	36
1946	1	1	2	23			27
1947	1	1	2	22	1		27
1948	1	1	2	19	5		28
1949	1	1	2	21	3		28
1950	1	1	1	22	1		26
1951	1	1		22	2		26
1952	1	1		?	?		27
1953	1	1		25	1		28
1954	1			25	1		27
1955	1		1	23	2		27
1956	1		1	23	2		27
1957							

The Rank Structure of the Mounted Unit

Year	Insp.	Sgt	P/SGT	PC 1	Civilian	Total	Year	Insp.	Sgt	P/SGT	PC 1	Civilian	Total
1958							1990	1	2	6	66	2	75
1959	1		1	27		27	1991	1	2	6	66	1	75
1960	1	1	1	28		28	1992	1	2	6	62	1	71
1961	1	1	2	30		34	1993	1	2	6	59	1	68
1962	1	1	3	38		43	1994	1	1	5	37	1	44
1963	1	1	3	39		44	1995	1	1	6	37	1	44
1964	1	1	3	40		45	1996	1	1	6	37	1	44
1965	1	1	2	45	1 Cadet	50	1997	1	1	6	37	1	44
1966	1	1	3	48	1 Cadet	54	1998	1	1	6	37	1	44
1967	1	1	3	48	1 Cadet	54	1999	1	1	6	36	1	44
1968	1	1	4	48	1 Cadet	55	2000	1	1	6	35	1	44
1969	1	1	4	48	1 Cadet	54							
1970	1	1	4	54	1 Cadet	61							
1971	1	1	4	54	5 Cadets	65							
1972	1	2	4	54	5 Cadets	66							
1973	1	2	5	61	6 Cadets	75							
1974	1	2		69		77							
1975	1	2	6	69		90							
1976	1	2	6	69	7 Cadets	85							
1977	1	2	6	72	10 Cadets	98							
1978	1	2	6	80	10 Cadets	99							
1979	1	2	6	75	2 Cadets	86							
1980	1	2	6	71	1 Cadet	81							
1981	1	2	6	70		79							
1982	1	2	6	70		79							
1983	1	2	6	58		67							
1984	1	2	6	57		66							
1985	1	2	6	55		64							
1986	1	2	6	55		64							
1987	1	2	6	56		65							
1988	1	2	6	56		65							
1989	1	2	6	60		69							

The Mounted Unit Budget

Year	Estimate	Actual	Year	Estimate	Actual
1891	1925	1374.08	1919	6000	5818.56
1892	1883	1174.1	1920	9939	8631.35
1893	2098	1626.56	1921	11766	10642.71
1894		1100	1922	9905	7611.83
1895	1560	1347.89	1923	9432.5	8168.14
1896	1485	1260.13	1924	8460	7,233.45
1897	1400	922	1925	9207.5	7847.37
1898	1300	1201.75	1926	9257.5	7846.41
1899	1340	1014.76	1927	9682.5	9010.57
1900	1200	939	1928	10553	8951.05
1901	1550.75	1579.57	1929	12094	11821.56
1902	1635	1384.65	1930	13150	11849.33
1903	1920	2039.92	1931	13150	10981.8
1904	1997.5	1585.37	1932	11000	10576.02
1905	1749	2018.34	1933	5790	5691.38
1906	2150	2047.49	1934	7192	7298.7
1907	2444.5	2354.87	1935	7400	7401.95
1908	3300	3174.79	1936	8011	7794.74
1909	4120	4367.41	1937	7861	7650.53
1910	4253	4205.35	1938	7952	7684.75
1911	4461	3927.63	1939	7777	7412.11
1912	5195	5348.18	1940	7800	7550.38
1913	5765	4674.86	1941		
1914	5197.2	4603.12	1980	124000	
1915	5190	4085.88	1981	124000	
1916	4652.75	3196.18	1982	3,500,000 (includes salaries)	
1917	4000	4541.76	1984	3,264,215 (includes salaries)	
1918	5266	4905.8	1995	3,116,700 (includes salaries)	

Bill Wardle – Author

Bill Wardle was born in Toronto. He joined the Metropolitan Toronto Police Force in 1977. He worked in downtown Toronto's 52 Division until 1981 when he transferred to the Mounted Unit. After training, he was assigned police mount "Susan," a partnership that would last for the next eight years. Shortly after his arrival at the Mounted Unit he was placed into the staff development program and transferred to different police functions each winter in order to gain the experience necessary for promotion.

In 1993, he was promoted to the rank of sergeant and in 2001, to the rank of staff sergeant. During his career he has worked at 52 Division, the Communications Bureau, the Intelligence Bureau, 41 Division Detective Office, the Fraud and Forgery Squad, 52 Division Community Response Unit, 21 Division Community Response Unit and 33 Division.

During his 19 year career as a mounted officer he participated in numerous musical rides as both a rider and the officer in charge. He created the Mounted Unit Drill Team and has participated in and directed numerous mounted escorts including the Royal escort at the 2000 Queen's Plate. He has competed annually in mounted police competitions and was a member of the first place Toronto Team at the 1999 North American Police Equestrian Competition in Virginia Beach, Virginia. He has organized and directed a number of Police Horse Shows and International Competitions here in Toronto.

After joining the police force he continued his education by completing the Police Science and Investigative Studies certificate program at Seneca College. He also studied business at Seneca completing both their Business Studies Certificate and the Ontario Management Development Certificate. He has completed both the Level I and Level II Police Management Certificate programs at Dalhousie University and is completing his History Degree at York University.

Bill continues to work to preserve the history of the Mounted Unit and to promote the use of police horses through historical lectures and the creation of a small museum in the lobby of the new Mounted Unit Headquarters. He lives in Toronto and is currently assigned to Toronto's 33 Division in the former City of North York.

William White – Artist and Illustrator

A native of Ontario, William White studied Fine Art at York University in Toronto. His paintings and drawings are in private collections in Canada, the United States, Britain and Africa. His work as an illustrator and graphic artist has benefited companies both in Canada and overseas. Currently Mr. White resides with his wife and two children in Scarborough, Ontario.

Colour Plate Index

Notes

CHAPTER ONE – Forebears

(1) Critchley, T.A. *A History of Police in England and Wales.* Constable and Company, London, 1967. Page 34.

CHAPTER TWO – The Toronto Police Department, 1834-1956

(1) Jackson, Basil. *To Serve and Protect, The History of the Metropolitan Toronto Police Force, 1834 - 1970.* Unpublished, 1970. Page 2.
(2) Toronto Police Department. *Chief Constables Reports.* Annual Report 1875.
(3) Toronto Police Department. *Chief Constables Reports.* Annual Report 1875.
(4) Jackson, Basil. *To Serve and Protect, The History of the Metropolitan Toronto Police Force, 1834 - 1970.* Unpublished, 1970. Page 55.
(5) Jackson, Basil. *To Serve and Protect, The History of the Metropolitan Toronto Police Force, 1834 - 1970.* Unpublished, 1970. Page 56.
(6) Unknown Toronto Newspaper, probably the *Toronto Telegram*, 1924.
(7) Toronto Police Force. *A Brief Account of the Force since its re-organization in 1859 up to the present date.* E.F. Clarke, Toronto, 1886.
(8) Toronto Police Force. *A Brief Account of the Force since its re-organization in 1859 up to the present date.* E.F. Clarke, Toronto, 1886.
(9) The *Toronto Globe*, Tuesday July 12, 1886
(10) Toronto Police Department. *Chief Constables Reports.* Annual Report 1886.
(11) Toronto Police Department. *Chief Constables Reports.* Annual Report 1886.
(12) Toronto Police Department. *Chief Constables Reports.* Annual Report 1887.
(13) Jackson, Basil. *To Serve and Protect, The History of the Metropolitan Toronto Police Force, 1834 - 1970.* Unpublished, 1970. Page 55.
(14) Toronto Police Department. *Chief Constables Reports.* Annual Report 1887.
(15) Toronto Police Department. *Chief Constables Reports.* Annual Report 1888.
(16) The *Toronto Globe*, April 12, 1889.
(17) Toronto Police Department. *Chief Constables Reports.* Annual Report 1889.
(18) Toronto Police Department. *Chief Constables Reports.* Annual Report 1891.
(19) Toronto Police Department. *Chief Constables Reports.* Annual Report 1891.
(20) Toronto Police Department. *Chief Constables Reports.* Annual Report 1894.
(21) Toronto Police Department. *Chief Constables Reports.* Annual Report 1895.
(22) Toronto Police Department. *Chief Constables Reports.* Annual Report 1896.
(23) Toronto Police Department. *Chief Constables Reports.* Annual Report 1889.
(24) Toronto Police Department. *Chief Constables Reports.* Annual Report 1897.
(25) Toronto Police Department. *Chief Constables Reports.* Annual Report 1898.
(26) Toronto Police Department. *Chief Constables Reports.* Annual Report 1899.
(27) The *Toronto Star*, October 6, 1900.
(28) Toronto Police Department. *Chief Constables Reports.* Annual Report 1901.
(29) The *Toronto Telegram*, June 22, 1902.
(30) The *Toronto Telegram*, June 22, 1902.
(31) Toronto Police Department. *Chief Constables Reports.* Annual Report 1902.
(32) The *Toronto Telegram*, November 1, 1902.
(33) Pieri, Michael, ed. *A Voyage Across the Years, (1894 - 1960).* Toronto Star Newspapers Limited, Toronto. Page 26.
(34) Toronto Police Department. *Chief Constables Reports.* Annual Report 1905.
(35) Toronto Police Department. *Chief Constables Reports.* Annual Report 1908.
(36) Toronto Police Department. *Chief Constables Reports.* Annual Report 1909.
(37) Toronto Police Department. *Chief Constables Reports.* Annual Report 1913.
(38) The *Toronto Telegram*, March 23, 1914.
(38a) *Toronto Telegram*, August 4, 1914.
(38b) *Toronto Telegram*, September 30, 1914.
(38c) *Toronto Telegram*, November 3, 1915.
(39) Filey, Mike & Russell, Victor. *From Horse Power To Horse Power*, Dundurn Press, Toronto and Oxford 1993. Page 75.
(40) Toronto Police Department. *Chief Constables Reports.* Annual Report 1916.
(41) Toronto Police Department. *Chief Constables Reports.* Annual Report 1917.
(41a) Toronto Police Department. *Police Commission Minutes.* November 12, 1918.
(41b) Toronto Police Department. *Police Commission Minutes.* March 4, 1919.
(41c) Toronto Police Department. *Police Commission Minutes.* April 15, 1919.
(42) Goodspeed, Lt. Col. D.J. *Battle Royal.* The Royal Regiment of Canada Association. Brampton, Ontario, Second edition 1979. Page 275.
(42a) Toronto Police Department. *Police Commission Minutes.* July 15, 1919.
(43) Unknown Toronto Newspaper, probably the *Toronto Telegram*, 1924.
(44) *Toronto Star*, August 26, 1919.
(45) Toronto Police Department. *Chief Constables Reports.* Annual Report 1920.
(46) Unknown Toronto Newspaper, probably the *Toronto Telegram*, 1924.
(47) Toronto Police Department. *Chief Constables Reports.* Annual Report 1922.
(48) Unknown Toronto Newspaper, probably the *Toronto Telegram*, 1924.
(49) Toronto Police Department. *Chief Constables Reports.* Annual Report 1922.
(49a) Toronto Police Department. *Police Commission Minutes.* January 11,1922.
(49b) Toronto Police Department. *Police Commission Minutes.* May 25,1922.

Notes

(49c) Toronto Police Department. *Police Commission Minutes*. November 22, 1922.

(49d) Toronto Police Department. *Police Commission Minutes*. May 25,1922.

(50) Unknown Toronto Newspaper, probably the *Toronto Telegram*, 1924.

(51) Unknown Toronto Newspaper, probably the *Toronto Telegram*, 1924.

(52) Unknown Toronto Newspaper, probably the *Toronto Telegram*, 1924.

(53) Unknown Toronto Newspaper, probably the *Toronto Telegram*, 1924.

(53a) Toronto Police Department. *Police Commission Minutes*. October 30, 1924.

(54) *Toronto Telegram*, December 15, 1924.

(55) Unknown Toronto Newspaper, probably the *Toronto Telegram*, 1924.

(56) *Toronto Telegram*, December 15, 1924.

(57) Unknown Toronto Newspaper, probably the *Toronto Telegram*, 1924.

(58) Unknown Toronto Newspaper, probably the *Toronto Telegram*, 1924.

(58a) Toronto Police Department. *Police Commission Minutes*. June 19, 1925.

(59) Toronto Police Department. *Chief Constables Reports*. Annual Report 1925.

(59a) Toronto Police Department. *Police Commission Minutes*. December 17, 1925.

(60) *Toronto Telegram*, December 13, 1925.

(60a) Toronto Police Department. *Police Commission Minutes*. January 7, 1926.

(61) Toronto Police Department. *Chief Constables Reports*. Annual Report 1926.

(62) Filey, Mike & Russell, Victor. *From Horse Power To Horse Power*, Dundurn Press, Toronto and Oxford 1993. Page 59.

(63) No (63) in book, probably in error. Filey, Mike & Russell, Victor. *From Horse Power To Horse Power*, Dundurn Press Toronto and Oxford 1993.

(64) Berton, Pierre. *The Great Depression 1929 - 1939*. McClelland and Stewart Inc. Toronto, Ontario, 1990. Page 19.

(65) The *Toronto Telegram*, May 5, 1930.

(66) The *Toronto Telegram*, May 5, 1930.

(67) Berton, Pierre. *The Great Depression 1929 - 1939*. McClelland and Stewart Inc. Toronto, Ontario, 1990. Page 69.

(68) Toronto Police Department. *Chief Constables Reports*. Annual Report 1931.

(69) The *Toronto Telegram*, February 25, 1931.

(70) The *Globe*, February 27, 1931.

(71) Filey, Mike & Russell, Victor. *From Horse Power To Horse Power*, Dundurn Press,Toronto and Oxford 1993. Page 56.

(72) Toronto Police Department. *Chief Constables Reports*. Annual Report 1932.

(73) Toronto Police Department. *Chief Constables Reports*. Annual Report 1933.

(74) Levitt, Cyril and Shaffir, William. *The Riot At Christie Pits*. Lester and Orpen Dennys, Toronto, 1987. Page 27.

(75) Donegan, Rosemary. *Spadina Avenue*, Douglas and McIntyre, Vancouver, Toronto, 1985. Page 19.

(76) Pieri, Michael, ed. *A Voyage Across the Years, (1894 - 1960)*. *Toronto Star* Newspapers Limited, Toronto. Page 85.

(77) Levitt, Cyril and Shaffir, William. *The Riot At Christie Pits*. Lester and Orpen Dennys, Toronto, 1987. Page 177.

(78) The Daily Mail and Empire, September 28, 1934.

(79) Berton, Pierre. *The Great Depression 1929 - 1939*. McClelland and Stewart Inc. Toronto, Ontario, 1990. Page 23.

(80) Toronto Police Department. *Chief Constables Reports*. Annual Report 1934.

(81) The *Globe*, Monday September 24, 1934.

(82) The *Toronto Star*, March 7, 1934.

(83) Toronto Police Department. *Chief Constables Reports*. Annual Report 1935.

(84) Daily Mail and Empire, January 4, 1935.

(85) The *Globe*, January 26, 1935.

(86) The *Globe*, January 26, 1935.

(87) The *Toronto Telegram*, January 26, 1935.

(88) The *Globe*, May 22, 1935.

(89) Toronto Police Department. *Chief Constables Reports*. Annual Report 1936.

(90) Daily Mail and Empire, October 5, 1936.

(91) Filey, Mike & Russell, Victor. *From Horse Power To Horse Power*, Dundurn Press,Toronto and Oxford, 1993. Page 42.

(92) Pieri, Michael, ed. *A Voyage Across the Years, (1894 - 1960)*. *Toronto Star* Newspapers Limited, Toronto. Page 94.

(93) The *Globe*, August 20, 1938.

(94) Berton, Pierre. *The Great Depression 1929 - 1939*. McClelland and Stewart Inc. Toronto, Ontario, 1990. Page 460.

(95) *Toronto Telegram*, July 5, 1938.

(96) Berton, Pierre. *The Great Depression 1929 - 1939*. McClelland and Stewart Inc. Toronto, Ontario, 1990. Page 461.

(97) Filey, Mike & Russell, Victor. *From Horse Power To Horse Power*, Dundurn Press, Toronto and Oxford 1993. Page 42.

(98) Filey, Mike & Russell, Victor. *From Horse Power To Horse Power*, Dundurn Press,Toronto and Oxford 1993. Page 59.

(99) Toronto Police Department. *Chief Constables Reports*. Annual Report 1948.

(100) Toronto Calling. 1949 Tourist Brochure for the City of Toronto.

(101) Toronto Police Department. *Chief Constables Reports*. Annual Report 1955.

(102) Toronto Police Department. *Chief Constables Reports*. Annual Report 1956.

CHAPTER THREE – The Metropolitan Toronto Police Service, 1957-1997

(1) Unit Commanders Annual Report, 1959.

(2) Unit Commanders Annual Report, *1961*.

(3) Metropolitan Toronto Police Force, Annual Report 1962.

(4) Mackey, James. *I Policed Toronto*. Self Published, Toronto. 1985. Page 139.

(5) Metropolitan Toronto Police Force, Annual Report 1963.

(6) Unit Commanders Annual Report, 1963.

(7) Unit Commanders Annual Report, 1964.

(8) Unit Commanders Annual Report, 1964.

(9) Unit Commanders Annual Report, 1964.

(10) The Scarborough Mirror, March 6, 1964.

(11) Mackey, James. *I Policed Toronto*. Self Published, Toronto. 1985. Page 129.

(12) Unit Commanders Annual Report, 1966.

Notes

(13) MacLean's Magazine, November 6, 1995.
(14) *Globe and Mail*, October 22, 1983.
(15) The Scarborough Mirror, March 6, 1974.
(16) The Quarterly Junior Farmers Magazine, Fall 1968.
(16a) Unit Commanders Annual Report, 1971.
(17) The Scarborough Mirror, March 6, 1974.
(18) Unit Commanders Annual Report, 1974.
(19) Unit Commanders Annual Report, 1976.
(20) *Toronto Star*, April 1977.
(21) Unit Commanders Annual Report, 1978.
(21a) Unit Commanders Annual Report, 1978.
(21b) Unit Commanders Annual Report, 1979.
(22) Unit Commanders Annual Report, 1979.
(23) Unit Commanders Annual Report, 1979.
(24) *Globe and Mail*, Saturday October 22, 1983.
(25) Unit Commanders Annual Report, 1980.
(26) Unit Commanders Annual Report, 1980.
(27) Unit Commanders Annual Report, 1981.
(28) Unit Commanders Annual Report, 1981.
(29) *Globe and Mail*, Saturday October 22, 1983.
(30) *Toronto Star*, July 21, July 27, 1982.
(31) Unit Commanders Annual Report, 1982.
(32) *Toronto Star*, January 28, 1983.
(33) Unit Commanders Annual Report, 1983.
(34) *Globe and Mail*, October 22, 1983.
(35) Unit Commanders Annual Report, 1983.
(36) Unit Commanders Annual Report, 1983.
(37) Unit Commanders Annual Report, 1986.
(38) *Toronto Star*, Sunday January 2, 1988.
(39) *Toronto Star*
(40) *Toronto Sun*, Saturday November 14, 1992, Page 7.
(41) *Toronto Star*, Monday December 7th 1992.
(42) *Toronto Sun*, Saturday June 11, 1994, Page Comment 13.
(43) *Toronto Sun*, Saturday June 11, 1994, Page Comment 13.
(44) *Toronto Sun*, Monday July 18, 1994, Page 5.
(45) *Toronto Star*, Sunday August 14, Page A6.
(46) *Toronto Star*, Friday April,18, 1997, Page A6.
(47) *Toronto Sun*, Sunday April 21, 1997.

CHAPTER SIX – The Horses of the TorontoMounted Police

(1) Unknown Toronto Newspaper, probably the *Toronto Telegram*, 1924.
(2) Evening Telegram, Monday May 5, 1930.
(3) Unknown Toronto Newspaper, probably the *Toronto Telegram*, 1924.
(4) Unknown Toronto Newspaper, probably the *Toronto Telegram*, 1924.
(5) Telegram, December 15, 1924.
(6) *Globe and Mail*, August 20, 1938.
(7) Unknown Toronto Newspaper, probably the *Toronto Telegram*, 1924.
(8) Unknown Toronto Newspaper, probably the *Toronto Telegram*, 1924.
(9) Telegram, December 15, 1924.
(10) *Globe and Mail*, August 20, 1938.
(11) Evening Telegram, May 4th, 1930.
(12) Unknown Toronto Newspaper, probably the *Toronto Telegram*, 1924.
(13) Telegram, December 15, 1924.
(14) Unknown Toronto Newspaper, probably the *Toronto Telegram*, 1924.
(15) Unknown Toronto Newspaper, probably the *Toronto Telegram*, 1924.
(16) Unit Commanders Annual Report, 1961.

CHAPTER EIGHT – The Musical Ride and Drill Team

(1) Greenhous, Brereton. *Dragoon, The Centennial History of The Royal Canadian Dragoons, 1883 - 1983.* The Guild of the Royal Canadian Dragoons, Belleville, Ontario, 1983.
(2) The *Toronto Telegram*, August 26, 1940.
(3) The Chronicle of the Horse, Friday December 16, 1966.
(4) The Chronicle of the Horse, Friday December 16, 1966.
(5) Unit Commanders Annual Report, 1967.
(6) Unit Commanders Annual Report, 1972.

CHAPTER NINE – Equestrian Competitions

(1) Unknown Toronto Paper, (Probably the Telegram, 1924).
(2) Toronto Police Department. *Chief Constables Reports*. Annual Report, 1925.
(3) Toronto Police Department. *Police Commission Minutes*. December 17, 1925.
(4) Toronto Police Department. *Police Commission Minutes*. January 7, 1926.
(5) Unknown Toronto Paper, (Probably the Telegram, 1924).
(6) *Toronto Telegram*, Monday May 5, 1930.
(7) *Toronto Telegram*, Saturday August 31, 1931.
(8) Toronto Police Department. *Chief Constable's Reports*. Annual Report, 1935.
(9) Toronto Police Department. Unit Commander's Annual Report,1955.

Bibliography

1. Books

Berton, Pierre. *The Great Depression 1929 - 1939*. McClelland and Stewart Inc. Toronto, Ontario, 1990.

Brock, David ed. *Metropolitan Toronto Police, To Serve and Protect: Vol 1 and 11*. John E. Wright Studios Limited, Strathroy & The Metropolitan Toronto Police Force. 1978.

Critchley, T.A. *A History of Police in England and Wales*. Constable and Company, London, 1967.

Donegan, Rosemary. *Spadina Avenue*, Douglas and McIntyre, Vancouver, Toronto, 1985.

Filey, Mike. *Reflections of the Past*, Nelson, Foster & Scott ltd., Toronto, 1972.

Filey, Mike & Russell, Victor. *From Horse Power To Horse Power*, Dundurn Press, Toronto and Oxford 1993.

Fortune, Len. *25 Years of Being There*, *Toronto Sun* publishing, Toronto, 1996.

Goodspeed, Lt. Col. D.J. *Battle Royal*. The Royal Regiment of Canada Association. Brampton, Ontario, Second edition 1979.

Greenhous, Brereton. *Dragoon, The Centennial History of The Royal Canadian Dragoons, 1883 - 1983*, The Guild of the Royal Canadian Dragoons, Belleville, Ontario, 1983.

Horrall, S.W. *The Pictorial History of the Royal Canadian Mounted Police*. McGraw - Hill Ryerson Limited, Toronto, 1973.

Jackson, Basil. *To Serve and Protect, The History of the Metropolitan Toronto Police Force, 1834 - 1970*. Unpublished, 1970.

Johnson, Mark. *No Tears to the Gallows*, McClelland & Stewart Inc. Toronto, 2000.

Kelly, William and Kelly, Nora. *The Horses of the Royal Canadian Mounted Police, A Pictorial History*. Double Day Canada Limited, Toronto, 1984.

Kendall, Brian. *Our Hearts Went Boom*, Penguin Canada, Toronto, 1997.

Levitt, Cyril and Shaffir, William. *The Riot At Christie Pits*. Lester and Orpen Dennys, Toronto, 1987.

Mackey, James. *I Policed Toronto*. Self Published, Toronto. 1985.

McWilliams, James and Steel, R. James. *Gas! The Battle for Ypres, 1915*. Vanwell Publishing Limited, St. Catharines, Ontario, 1985.

Metropolitan Toronto Police Amateur Athletic Association. *Centennial Book*. Self Published, 1983.

Muscat, Inspector Patrick. *The Detroit Mounted Police 1893 - 1993*. Self Published. Detroit. 1993.

Obodiac, Stan. *Maple Leaf Gardens, Fifty Years of History*. Kendall / Hunt Publishing Company, Toronto, 1981.

Pieri, Michael, ed. *A Voyage Across the Years, (1894 - 1960)*. *Toronto Star* Newspapers Limited, Toronto.

Riddle, David K. & Mitchell, Donald G. *The Distinguished Conduct Medal Awarded to Members of The Canadian Expeditionary Force 1914 - 1920* The Kirkby - Marlton Press, Winnipeg, Manitoba, 1991.

Riddle, David K. & Mitchell, Donald G.. *The Distinguished Service Order Awarded to Members of The Canadian Expeditionary Force and Canadians in the Royal Naval Air Service, The Royal Flying Corps and the Royal Air Force, 1915 - 1920*. The Kirkby - Marlton Press, Winnipeg, Manitoba, 1991.

Robinson, C. Blackett, *History of Toronto and County of York, Ontario* . Toronto, 1885.

Scott. F.G. Colonel ed., *The Story of the Canadian Corps 1914 - 1934*. Canadian Veteran Associates. Toronto. 1934

Van de Water, Frederic. *Grey Riders*. G.P. Putnam's Sons, New York, 1917. Reprinted by the Trooper Foundation, State of New York, 1992.

Wood, S.T. Commissioner, Royal Canadian Mounted Police. *Law and Order in Canadian Democracy*. Kings Printer., Ottawa, 1949.

Thomas, Jocko. *From Police Headquarters*. Stoddart Publishing Company Limited, Toronto,1990.

Walace, A. *The York County Constabulary*. Unpublished, 1946.

Webster, Jack. *Copper Jack.* Dundurn Press, Toronto and Oxford. 1991

Withrow, John ed. *Once Upon A Century. 100 Year History of the 'Ex'*. J.H. Robinson Publishing Limited, Toronto, 1978.

2. Newspapers

Hamilton Spectator
Philadelphia Daily News
Scarborough Mirror
The Printer
Toronto Globe and Mail
Toronto Mail and Empire
Toronto Star
Toronto Sun
Toronto Telegram

3. Police Department Documents

Johnson, Staff Inspector E.S. *An Outline of the Mounted Unit*, 1984.

Metropolitan Toronto Police Force. *Annual Reports*, 1957 - 1994.

Metropolitan Toronto Police Force. 1*986 Inspection Unit Audit Team report on the Mounted Unit*.

Metropolitan Toronto Police Force. *Mounted Unit Annual Reports*, 1957 - 1989.

Metropolitan Toronto Police Force. *Routine Orders*.

Toronto Police Department. *Chief Constable's Reports*. Annual Reports, 1875 - 1956.

Toronto Police Department. *Mounted Unit Annual Reports*, 1954 - 1956.

Toronto Police Department. *Toronto Police Commission Minutes*.

Toronto Police Force. *A Brief Account of the Force since its re-organisation in 1859 up to the present date*. E.F. Clarke, Toronto, 1886.

Bibliography

4. Research Papers

Blacklock, W.J. *Chief Constables Annual Reports as a Source for Historical Research*. Report submitted to Professor Arthur Silver, 1986.

Leibaers, Jan K. *The Toronto Police Strike of 1918*. Major research paper submitted to Professor N. Rogers, September 1990.

Marquis, Greg. *Early 20th Century Toronto Police Institution*. P.H.D. Thesis submitted to the Department of History, Queen's University, Kingston, Ontario, November 1986.

5. Periodicals

Chronicle of the Horse
International Police Association, Toronto Newsletter
Junior Farmers Magazine, The Quarterly
MacLean's Magazine
Metropolitan Toronto Police Association, News and Views
Police News, Police Association of Ontario
R.C.M.P. Quarterly
Toronto Life Magazine

6. Brochures

Toronto Calling. 1949 Tourist Brochure for the City of Toronto.

Index

Index

Index

Index

Index

Index

Index